The Economy of Odisha

The Economy of Odisha

A Profile

Edited by

Pulin B. Nayak
Santosh C. Panda
Prasanta K. Pattanaik

OXFORD
UNIVERSITY PRESS

OXFORD
UNIVERSITY PRESS

Oxford University Press is a department of the University of Oxford. It furthers the University's objective of excellence in research, scholarship, and education by publishing worldwide. Oxford is a registered trademark of Oxford University Press in the UK and in certain other countries

Published in India by
Oxford University Press
YMCA Library Building, 1 Jai Singh Road, New Delhi 110 001, India

First Edition published in 2016

ISBN-13: 978-0-19-946478-4
ISBN-10: 0-19-946478-2

Typeset in Adobe Garamond Pro 11/13
by Tranistics Data Technologies, New Delhi 110 044
Printed in India by Rakmo Press, New Delhi 110 020

Note: In this volume, 1 lakh is equal to 0.1 million and 1 crore is equal to 10 million.

With deep respect, we dedicate this book to the memory of Maa Ramadevi Choudhury, who devoted her life to serving the poor and whom millions in Odisha affectionately called 'maa' ('mother').

Contents

PART V STATE FINANCES AND THE PLANNING STRATEGY OF THE STATE GOVERNMENT

Tables, Figures, and Boxes

Tables

Figures

Boxes

Preface

This book would not have been possible without the help, advice, and encouragement that we have received from many of our colleagues and several organizations. We are deeply grateful to all of them.

Our greatest debt is, of course, to the authors who have contributed to this book. Despite their numerous other commitments, they readily agreed to contribute to this volume and have been exceptionally patient with the many subsequent queries relating to their chapters.

The idea of compiling such a volume on the economy of Odisha was suggested to us by Professor Adwait Mohanty. We are grateful to him and to Professor Baidyanath Misra for their valuable help and advice at every stage of our work as editors.

In December 2012, Nabakrushna Choudhury Centre for Development Studies, Bhubaneswar, Odisha, hosted a conference where preliminary versions of the chapters of this book were presented by the authors. Professor Raj Kishore Panda, who was then the Director of Nabakrushna Choudhury Centre for Development Studies, was kind enough to put in an enormous amount of time and effort to organize the conference despite his numerous other administrative responsibilities. The Government of Odisha generously provided the funding required for the conference. The organization of the conference was also facilitated with the help that we received from Professor Tapas K. Sen and Mr Jugal Kishore Mohapatra. We take this opportunity to express our gratitude to all these individuals and organizations for making this conference possible; we believe that the discussion in the conference made a significant contribution to the quality of this volume.

The chapters of the book went through peer review. For their help with the review process, we thank Aditya Bhattacharjea, Saudamini

Das, Padmaja Mishra, Srijit Mishra, Manoranjan Mohanty, Narayan Chandra Nayak, Manoj Panda, Sudhanshu Sekhar Rath, Himanshu Sekhar Rout, Partha P. Sahu, Kailash Sarap, Tapas K. Sen, and Damodar Tripathy.

Finally, we would like to thank the editorial team of Oxford University Press India for their help and encouragement.

Abbreviations and Acronyms

AB	aerial bunched
ACHI	area covered under one health institution
AIDS	acquired immunodeficiency syndrome
AMCS	agency marketing co-operative society
ANM	auxiliary nurse midwives
ASA	area specific approach
ASFR	age-specific fertility rates
ASHA	accredited social health activist
AT&C	aggregate technical and commercial
AWW	anganwadi workers
AYUSH	ayurveda, yoga and naturopathy, unani, siddha, and homeopathy
BALCO	Bharat Aluminium Company Limited
BCG	Bacillus Calmette–Guérin
BCM	billion cubic metre
BJKK	Bharatiya Jana Kalyan Kendra
BJPP	Budhikhamari Joint Protection Party
BMI	body mass index
BOJBP	Brukshya O' Jeevara Bandhu Parishad
BPL	below poverty line
BPR	beds available per lakh population
BRGF	backward regions grant fund
CAGR	compound annual growth rate
CAPEX	capital expenditure
CBGA	Centre for Budget and Governance Accountability
CBR	crude birth rate
CCEA	Cabinet Committee on Economic Affairs
CCSP	central and centrally sponsored schemes
CD	community development

CDMO	chief of district medical officer
CDPO	child development project officer
CDR	crude death rate
CDS	current daily status
CEA	Central Electricity Authority
CESCO	Central Electricity Supply Company of Orissa Limited
CFC	common facility centre
CHC	community health centre
CIND	climate-induced natural disaster
CPIAL	consumer price index of agricultural labour
CPP	captive power plant
CPR	common property resources
CPS	central plan schemes
Cr(VI)	hexavalent chromium
CSS	centrally sponsored schemes
CV	coefficient of variation
CWS	current weekly status
DFID	Department for International Development
DHP	district health plans
DISTCOs	distribution companies
DOTS	directly observed treatment short course chemotherapy
DRM	disaster risk management
EDC	Eco Development Committee
EDI	educational development index
EKC	Environmental Kuznets' Curve
EmOC	emergency obstetric care
FAO	Food and Agriculture Organization
FCI	Food Corporation of India
FDI	foreign direct investment
FGT	Foster, Greer, and Thorbecke
FRA	Forest Dwellers (Recognition of Forest Rights) Act
FSI	Forest Survey of India
FSW	female sex workers
FYP	five year plan
GDI	gender development index
GDMO	general duty medical officers
GDP	gross domestic product

GENCOs	generation companies
GER	gross enrolment ratio
GFR	general fertility rate
GMC	government marginal cost
GoI	Government of India
GoO	Government of Odisha
GPI	gender parity index
GRIDCO	Grid Corporation of Orissa Limited
GRR	gross reproduction rate
GSDP	gross state domestic product
GSEB	Gujarat State Electricity Board
HCR	head count ratio
HDI	human development index
HDR	*Human Development Report*
HILP	high-impact, low-probability
HIV	human immunodeficiency virus
HSR	health sector reform
HVDS	high voltage distribution system
HYV	high yielding variety
IBM	Indian Bureau of Mines
ICDS	Integrated Child Development Services
ICHA	international classification of health accounts
ICMR	Indian Council of Medical Research
IDCO	Industrial Development Corporation of Odisha
IDU	injecting drug users
IEC	information, education, and communication
IFAD	International Fund for Agricultural Development
IFPRI	International Food Policy Research Institute
IMR	infant mortality rate
IPC	Indian Penal Court
IPCC	Intergovernmental Panel on Climate Change
IPHS	Indian Public Health Standards
IPICOL	Industrial Promotion and Investment Corporation of Odisha Limited
IPP	independent power producers (plants)
IRDP	Integrated Rural Development Programme
ISHI	India state hunger index
IT	information technology

ITES	information technology enabled service
IUCN	International Union for Conservation of Nature
IUD	intrauterine device
JFM	joint forest management
JRY	Jawahar Rozgar Yojana
JSY	Janani Suraksha Yojana
KBK	Koraput, Bolangir, and Kalahandi
kWh	kilowatt-hour
LAMPS	large size agricultural multi-purpose cooperative societies
LEWE	large scale extreme weather event
LHV	lady health visitors
LTAP	long-term action plan
M&Q	mining and quarrying
MB	marginal benefit
MC	marginal cost
MCDR	Mineral Conservation and Development Rules
MCH	medical college and hospital
MDGs	Millennium Development Goals
MFP	minor forest products
MGNREGA	Mahatma Gandhi National Rural Employment Guarantee Act
MH	maternity home
MHU	mobile health unit
MMR	maternal mortality ratio
MNC	multinational companies
MoEF	Ministry of Environment and Forests
MoU	memorandum of understanding
MPCE	monthly per capita total consumption expenditure
MRP	mixed recall period
MSM	men having sex with men
MSME	micro, small, and medium enterprise
MSP	minimum support price
MTPA	million tonnes per annum
NABARD	National Bank for Agriculture and Rural Development
NACO	National AIDS Control Organization
NALCO	National Aluminium Company

NBMMP	National Biogas and Manure Management Programme
NCDS	Nabakrushna Choudhury Centre for Development Studies
NDP	net domestic product
NEDyM	non-equilibrium dynamic model
NEEPCO	North-Eastern Electric Power Corporation
NER	net enrolment ratio
NESCO	North-Eastern Electricity Supply Company of Orissa Limited
NEUPA	National University of Educational Planning and Administration
NFHS	National Family Health Survey
NFMMI	non-ferrous mining and metallurgical industries
NGO	non-governmental organization
NH	nursing home
NHDP	National Highway Development Project
NHPC	National Hydroelectric Power Corporation
NIN	National Institute of Nutrition
NINL	Neelachal Ispat Nigam Limited
NMR	neonatal mortality rate
NNP	net national product
NOAP	national old age pension
NREP	National Rural Employment Programme
NRHM	National Rural Health Mission
NSDP	net state domestic product
NSS	National Sample Survey
NSSO	National Sample Survey Organisation/Office
NTFP	non-timber forest products
NTP	National Tuberculosis Control Programme
NTPC	National Thermal Power Corporation
NUEPA	National University of Educational Planning and Administration
O&G	obstetrics and gynaecology
O&M	operations and management
OBC	other backward class
ODRAF	Orissa Disaster Rapid Action Force
OERC	Orissa Electricity Regulatory Commission

OFDC	Odisha Forest Development Corporation Limited
OHPC	Orissa Hydro Power Corporation
OHSDP	Odisha Health System Development Project
OLR	Orissa Land Reforms (Act)
OMC	Odisha Mining Corporation
OMDC	Orissa Minerals Development Company
OPCB	Orissa Pollution Control Board
OPEPA	Primary Education Programme Authority
OPGC	Orissa Power Generation Corporation
OPTCL	Orissa Power Transmission Corporation Limited
OREDA	Odisha Renewable Energy Development Agency
ORMAS	Odisha Rural Development Marketing Society
OSDMA	Orissa State Disaster Management Authority
OSEB	Orissa State Electricity Board
OSFC	Odisha State Financial Corporation
OSIC	Odisha Small Industries Corporation
OSPCB	Odisha State Pollution Control Board
OSRTC	Odisha State Road Transport Corporation
OTDP	Odisha Tribal Development Project
OTELP	Odisha Tribal Empowerment and Livelihood Programmes
PCCF	Principal Chief Conservator of Forests
PCHE	per capita health expenditure
PCPIR	petroleum, chemicals, and petro-chemicals investment region
PDS	public distribution system
PEM	protein-energy malnutrition
PESA	Panchayats (Extension to Scheduled Areas) Act
PGCIL	Power Grid Corporation of India Limited
PGE	platinum group of elements
PHC	primary health centre
PLB	poverty line basket
PLF	plant load factor
PMC	private marginal cost
PMI	private medical institutions
PMR	perinatal mortality rate
POL	petroleum, oil, and lubricant
POSCO	Pohang Steel Company

PPL	Paradeep Phosphates Limited
PPP	public–private partnership
PRI	panchayati raj institutions
PSPU	Policy and Strategic Planning Unit
PTGs	primitive tribal groups
PTR	pupil-teacher ratio
PVTGs	particularly vulnerable tribal groups
RCDC	Regional Centre for Development Cooperation
RCH	reproductive and child health
RDE	rural development expenditure
REC	Rural Electrification Corporation
RGGVY	Rajiv Gandhi Grameen Vidyutikaran Yojana
RIDF	Rural Infrastructure Development Fund
RKS	Rogi Kalyan Samiti
RLTAP	revised long term action plan
ROR	record of rights
RRB	regional rural bank
RSPM	Respirable Suspended Particulate Matter
RTE	Right of Children to Free and Compulsory Education Act
RVEP	Remote Village Electrification Programme
SAB	skill attendance at birth
SAII	Supreme Audit Institution of India
SAIL	Steel Authority of India Limited
SC	scheduled caste
SCA	special central assistance
SCR	student-class room ratio
SEB	state electricity board
SEEA	system of integrated economic and environmental accounting
SESCO	Southern Electricity Supply Company of Orissa Limited
SEZ	special economic zone
SF	short fall
SGRY	Sampoorna Gramin Rozgar Yojana
SGSY	Swarnajayanti Gram Swarozgar Yojana
SHG	self-help group
SME	small and medium enterprises

SNA	system of national accounts
SOUTHCO	Southern Electricity Supply Company of Orissa Limited
SPM	suspended particulate matter
SPUs	state power utilities
SRC	special relief commissioner
SRS	sample registration system
SRTUs	state road transport undertakings
SSA	Sarva Shiksha Abhiyan
SSI	small scale industries
ST	scheduled tribe
T&D	transmission and distribution
TAC	tribes advisory council
TB	tuberculosis
TDCC	Tribal Development Cooperative Corporation Limited
TFR	total fertility rate
TH&FEW	total health and family welfare
TMFR	total marital fertility rate
TMI	total medical institutions
TPR	total patients registered
TRADECOs	trading companies
TRANSCOs	transmission companies
TRIFED	Tribal Cooperative Marketing Federation in India Limited
TSP	tribal sub-plan
TSTPS	Talcher Super Thermal Power Plant
U5MR	under-five mortality rates
UEE	universalization of elementary education
UFPL	Utkal Forest Produce Limited
UN	United Nations
UNDP	United National Development Programme
UPS	usual principal status
URP	uniform recall period
US	usual status
VAL	Vedanta Aluminium Limited
VAT	value-added tax
VHSC	village health and sanitation committee

VSS	Vana Samrankhyan Samiti
WDC	Watershed Development Committee
WESCO	Western Electricity Supply Company of Orissa Limited
WFP	World Food Programme
WHO	World Health Organization
WORLP	Western Odisha Rural Livelihoods Project
WUA	Water User Association
WUE	water use efficiency
ZSS	Zilla Swasthya Samities

Introduction*

Pulin B. Nayak, Santosh C. Panda, and
Prasanta K. Pattanaik

This volume brings together 15 contributions (chapters 1 through 15), by different scholars, on the economy of Odisha, which happens to be one of the poorest states of India. Each contribution deals with a specific sector (for example, industries, mining, and transport and power) of the economy or a specific issue (for example, poverty, malnutrition, and the livelihood of the tribal population) relating to the economy. In a large and diverse country such as India, it is important to study in detail the different regional economies. The levels of economic development in different states and the structures of state economies in India often differ widely; there are also significant differences between the historical experiences of different states of India. In view of this, we felt that there was a need for a volume that would give a reasonably detailed picture of the economy of Odisha and would provide insight into the many economic issues faced by the state. This volume aims to fill this gap. There are two points that we would like to clarify here. First, the chapters that follow, written by 26 authors and dealing with

* We are grateful to Lokendra Kumawat, Yi Lu, and Sanjeev Sharma for their generous assistance with the research for this chapter. We are also grateful to Satya P. Das, Anil Deolalikar, and Partha P. Sahu for their comments and suggestions.

different sectors of the economy and very different economic issues, have only one obvious common theme: the economy of Odisha. Each of them deals with some important aspect of the state's economy and, collectively, the chapters give the reader a comprehensive account of the state's economy and the problems confronting it. Besides this, we do not have in mind any other 'unifying theme' for these chapters; in fact, attempts to impose any other unifying theme would have been somewhat contrary to our basic objective in putting together this volume. Second, though all the authors are academic researchers and many of them have behind them decades of research on various facets of Odisha's economy and though we believe that this volume will be useful for academics and students working on specific issues relating to Odisha's economy, the volume is not exclusively for these groups. Administrators, policymakers, and general readers with a serious interest in the economy of Odisha will also find this volume useful. We specifically requested our authors to keep this broader objective in mind, and we believe that, in general, the exposition in the subsequent chapters is accessible to a wide group of readers.

This introductory chapter has two purposes. First, it presents some basic facts about the development of Odisha's economy over the last 30 years or so. Since most other chapters of this volume discuss in detail either specific sectors or specific features of the state's economy,[1] we felt that it might be useful, at least for readers who might not be very familiar with the economy of Odisha, to start with a short review of the state economy. This chapter looks at how Odisha's economy had performed at the macro level during the last few decades and how the structure of the economy had changed over the same period. Second, it also provides an overview of the subsequent chapters.

This chapter is organized as follows. In the section 'Growth of Odisha's GSDP and per capita NSDP, and the structure of Odisha's economy', we discuss: (a) the growth of the gross state domestic product (GSDP) and per capita net state domestic product (NSDP) of Odisha over time; and (b) changes in the shares of the primary,

[1] One exception is Chapter 15 by Prabhat Patnaik, which deals with certain broad issues relating to the development strategy adopted by the Government of Odisha in recent years.

secondary, and tertiary sectors in Odisha's GSDP. In the section 'Structure and organization of the book', we comment on the different chapters in this volume. We end this chapter with concluding remarks.

Growth of Odisha's GSDP and per capita NSDP, and the structure of Odisha's economy

Growth in the 1950s, 1960s, and 1970s

The state of Odisha, which was formed in 1936, has an area of 1,55,707 km^2 and a population of 41.97 million (*Census of India* 2011); among the states of India, it occupies the 9th position in terms of area and the 11th position in terms of population. For much of the time since its formation as a state, Odisha has suffered from slow economic development. At 1999–2000 prices, the average GSDP of Odisha during the three years, 1950–51, 1951–52, and 1952–53, was Rs 98,332.4 million; and the average GSDP during the three years, 1980–81, 1981–82, and 1982–83, was Rs 223,540.7 million (GoO 2012: 27–28, Annexure 2.1). This gives us the notional constant rate of growth of 2.77 per cent over these 30 years, the notional constant rate of growth being the counterfactual constant rate of growth that would have increased Odisha's GSDP by the same magnitude over the same period of time.[2]

At 1999–2000 prices again, the average per capita NSDP for the years 1950–51, 1951–52, and 1952–53 was Rs 5,419; the corresponding average for the years 1980–81, 1981–82, and 1982–83, was Rs 7,557 (GoO 2012: 27–28, Annexure 2.1). Thus, the notional constant annual growth rate of the per capita NSDP was 1.11 per cent over the 30 years. Clearly, the performance of the economy of Odisha was quite poor during the period under consideration. The picture does not improve much when we compare it with the growth of the Indian economy over the same period, which itself was less than impressive. The notional constant rate of growth of

[2] More precisely, if y_t and y_{t+m} are the GSDPs in years t and $t + m$, respectively, then the notional constant rate of growth over the m years following year t is defined to be r, where $y_t(1 + r)^m = y_{t+m}$.

India's gross domestic product (GDP) at 1993–94 prices over the same period was 3.64 per cent,[3] about 31 per cent higher than the notional constant rate of growth (2.77 per cent) of Odisha's GSDP. Similarly, the notional constant rate of growth of India's per capita net domestic product (NDP) at 1993–94 prices over the period was 1.30 per cent,[4] about 17 per cent higher than the notional constant rate of growth of Odisha's per capita NSDP.

Growth of Odisha's GSDP since 1980–81

The growth of Odisha's GSDP after 1980 and how it compares with the growth of India's GDP can be seen in figures I.1(a) and I.1(b).

Figure I.1(a) shows the growth rates of Odisha and India over the period from 1983–84 to 1994–95 and Figure I.1(b) shows the corresponding growth rates from 1996–97 to 2011–12. Before commenting on these growth rates, we would like to note two aspects of the calculations underlying figures I.1(a) and I.1(b).

First, the growth rates for both Odisha and India are calculated on the basis of three-year moving averages to smoothen out large year-to-year fluctuations, especially in the case of Odisha's GSDP.[5] Second, the percentage rates of growth, based on three-year moving averages, of India's

[3] The calculation is based on information in EPW Research Foundation (2004: 29, Table 1A). As in the case of Odisha, we take the average of India's GDP over 1950–51, 1951–52, and 1952–53, and the average of India's GDP over 1980–81, 1981–82, and 1982–83, and then calculate the notional constant rate of growth over the period of 30 years.

[4] The calculation is based on information in EPW Research Foundation (2004: 30, Table 1A). The method of calculation is similar to that described in fn. 3.

[5] On several occasions in this chapter, we use three-year moving averages of variables. In such cases, if x_{t-2}, x_{t-1}, and x_t denote the values of a variable in years $t-2$, $t-1$, and t, respectively, then we assign the average $a_t \equiv [x_{t-2} + x_{t-1} + x_t]/3$ to year t. When calculating the percentage rates of change in three-year moving averages, we take the percentage rate of change in year $t+1$ to be $100(a_{t+1} - a_t)/a_t$. We are aware that while the use of three-year moving averages helps us to smoothen out some year-to-year fluctuations, it is a rather rough tool and has limitations.

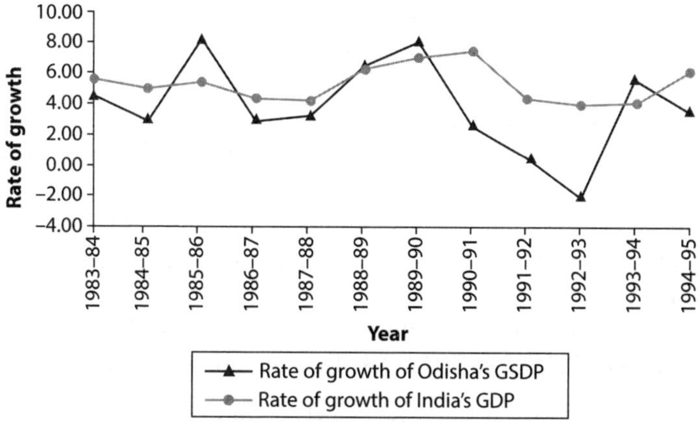

Figure I.1(a) The rates of growth of Odisha's GSDP at constant (1980–81) prices and the rates of growth of India's GDP at constant (1993–94) prices (all rates calculated on the basis of three-year moving averages), 1983–84 to 1994–95

Source of data: For Odisha: EPW Research Foundation (2009: Annexure IV, p. 18); for India: EPW Research Foundation (2004: Table 1A).

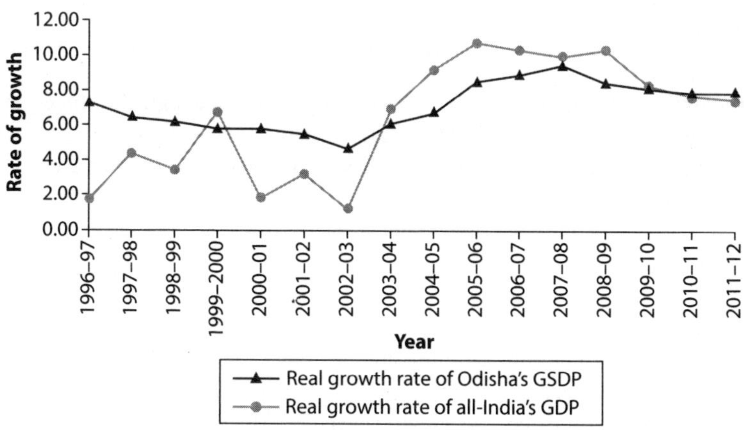

Figure I.1(b) The rates of growth of Odisha's GSDP at constant (2004–05) prices and India's GDP at constant (2004–05) prices (all rates calculated on the basis of three-year moving averages), 1996–97 to 2011–12

Source of data: Planning Commission of India (2012: 103).

GDP and Odisha's GSDP, which have been shown in Figure I.1(b), have been calculated from corresponding percentage annual growth rates given in Planning Commission of India (2012: 103).[6]

Note that Odisha's GSDP has grown at the rate of 4 per cent or more in every year since 1996–97, and at a rate of 6 per cent or more in every year since 2003–04. An inspection of figures I.1(a) and I.1(b) suggests that there was a long-term upward shift in the growth rate around 2003–04. We checked the statistical significance of this shift.[7]

To check the statistical significance, we used GSDP data at 2004–05 prices from 1981–82 to 2012–13. The equation estimated was:

$$\log y_t = \alpha_0 + \alpha_1 D_t + \beta_0 t + \beta_1 t * D_t,$$

where t is the trend variable, D_t is the dummy variable taking the value 0 till 2002–03 and the value 1 2003–04 onwards. Table I.1 summarizes the results. The changes in the rate of growth are significant at 5 per cent, using Newey-West standard errors.

[6] The calculation has been done as follows. Let the absolute level of India's GDP (at constant prices) in year t be denoted by Y_t, and let g_t denote the rate of growth of the GDP (at constant prices) in year t, defined as $\frac{Y_t - Y_{t-1}}{Y_{t-1}}$. In calculating the rate of growth of India's GDP on the basis of three-year moving averages, for any given year t, we assign the three-year average $z_t \equiv [Y_{t-2} + Y_{t-1} + Y_t]/3$ to year t. Then the rate of growth of India's GDP (at constant prices) for year t, based on three-year moving averages, is given by

$$h_t \equiv \frac{z_t - z_{t-1}}{z_{t-1}} = \frac{Y_t - Y_{t-3}}{Y_{t-3} + Y_{t-2} + Y_{t-1}} = \frac{(1+g_t)(1+g_{t-1})(1+g_{t-2})-1}{1+(1+g_{t-2})+(1+g_{t-1})(1+g_{t-2})}$$

Given the information about percentage rates of growth, $100g_t$, $100g_{t-1}$, and $100g_{t-2}$, in Planning Commission of India (2012: 103), we have calculated $100h_t$, the percentage rate of growth of India's GDP, at constant prices, in year t, based on three-year moving averages. The calculation is similar in the case of the rate of growth of Odisha's GSDP, at constant prices, based on three-year moving averages.

[7] For a similar exercise covering the period from 1985–86 to 2006–07, see Panda (2008).

Table I.1 Summary of results: Growth rates of GSDP

	Break point: 2003–04		
Dependent variable (in log form)	Growth rate: 1981–82 to 2002–03 (β_0)	Growth rate: 2003–04 to 2012–13 ($\beta_0 + \beta_1$)	Change in rate of growth after break point (β_1)
GSDP	3.4	7.88	4.48
GSDP: three-year moving average	3.38	8.14	4.76

Source: Authors' calculations based on data in Government of Odisha (2013: Annexure 2.1).
Note: All the coefficients are highly significant (p-values are 0.000).

To understand what might have triggered this upsurge in the rate of growth, it may be helpful to keep in mind several factors. First, the country followed a policy of economic liberalization since 1991. Industrial licensing was mostly abolished and new enterprises were encouraged. In Odisha, these provisions were implemented rather late and around this time, many industrial houses were invited to establish manufacturing units in steel, ferro-alloys, aluminium, and so on. This would have contributed to the growth rate. Second, following the advice of the Finance Commission, the State followed a path of fiscal discipline and Odisha turned into a revenue surplus state. The year 2003–04 turned out to be a pivotal point in this respect (see Chapter 14 by Sen and Rout). This would have created a congenial atmosphere for growth. Third, the state government has taken some innovative disaster management initiatives against cyclone and flood since 2003 (on this see Chapter 8 by Saudamini Das). These initiatives seem to have mitigated the negative impact of natural disasters on the GSDP. This could also have contributed to the increase in the growth rate of GSDP.

Growth of Odisha's per capita NSDP since 2000–01

Figure I.2(a) shows the per capita NSDP of Odisha for each year from 2000–01 to 2011–12.

The per capita NSDP of Odisha at constant (2004–05) prices increased from Rs 10,211 in 2000–01 to Rs 26,900 (Planning

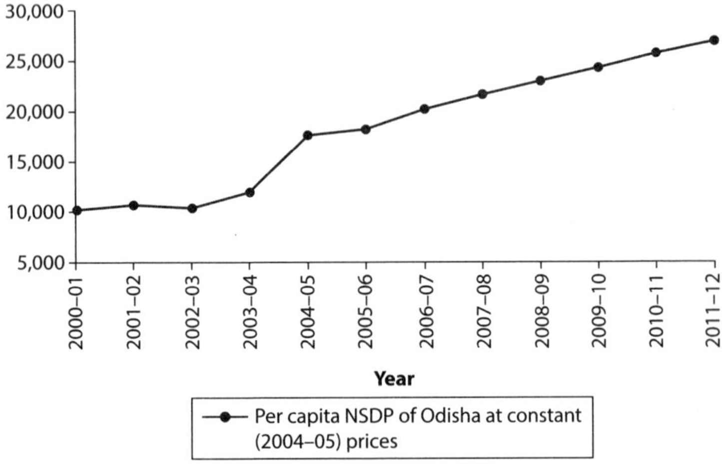

Figure I.2(a) Per capita net state domestic product (NSDP) of Odisha at constant (2004–05) prices, 2000–01 to 2011–12 (Rs)
Source of data: Planning Commission of India (2012: 109).

Commission 2012: 109) in 2011–12. This is an increase of about 163.44 per cent and amounts to a notional constant rate of growth of 9.2 per cent. Despite the impressive growth of Odisha's per capita NSDP over the last 11 years, Odisha's per capita NSDP remains much lower than the per capita net national product (NNP) of India and the per capita NSDPs of several of Odisha's neighbouring states. First, consider the difference between the per capita NSDP of Odisha and the per capita NNP of India in Figure I.2(b).

Figure I.2(b) shows Odisha's NSDP as a percentage of India's per capita NNP over the period from 2000–01 to 2011–12.[8] The per capita NSDP of Odisha in 2000–01 and 2001–02 constitutes

[8] Strictly speaking, we should consider Odisha's per capita NSDP as a percentage of India's per capita NDP. But we have not been able to find the data for India's per capita NDP. We feel that this does not affect our comparisons significantly since the difference between India's per capita NDP and per capita NNP is likely to be quite small.

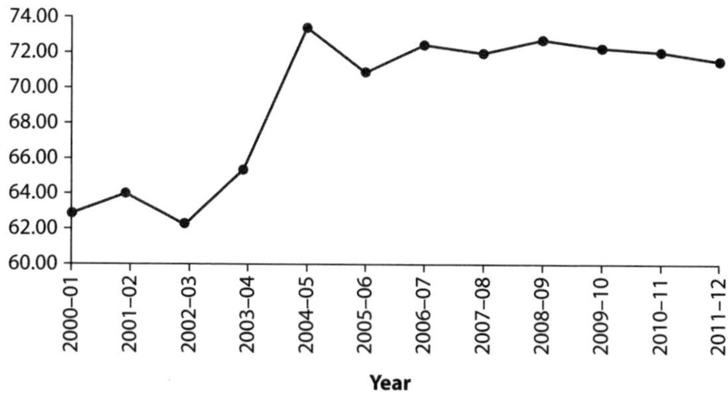

Figure I.2(b) Per capita NSDP of Odisha, expressed as a percentage of the per capita net national product (NNP) of India, 2000–01 to 2011–12
Source of data: Planning Commission of India (2012: 109).

63.14 per cent and 63.83 per cent, respectively, of India's per capita NNP. The figures for 2010–11 and 2011–12 are 71.42 per cent and 70.78 per cent respectively. While this is a significant improvement in Odisha's per capita NSDP in relation to India's per capita NNP, Odisha still has a long way to go to catch up with the per capita NNP of the country. We now compare Odisha and two of its neighbouring states—West Bengal and Andhra Pradesh—in terms of per capita NSDP. The per capita NSDP of both these states was higher than that of Odisha in every year during the period under consideration. Figure I.2(c) shows the per capita NSDP of Odisha as a percentage of the per capita NSDP of West Bengal and as a percentage of that of Andhra Pradesh.

Note that during the period 2000–01 to 2011–12, the gap between Odisha and West Bengal narrowed significantly, but Odisha's per capita NSDP still stood at only 80 per cent or less of the per capita NSDP of West Bengal in each of the years 2009–10, 2010–11, and 2011–12. It is clear that the recent gap between the per capita NSDP of Odisha and that of Andhra Pradesh is much higher than the corresponding gap between the per capita NSDP of Odisha and the per capita NSDP of West Bengal.

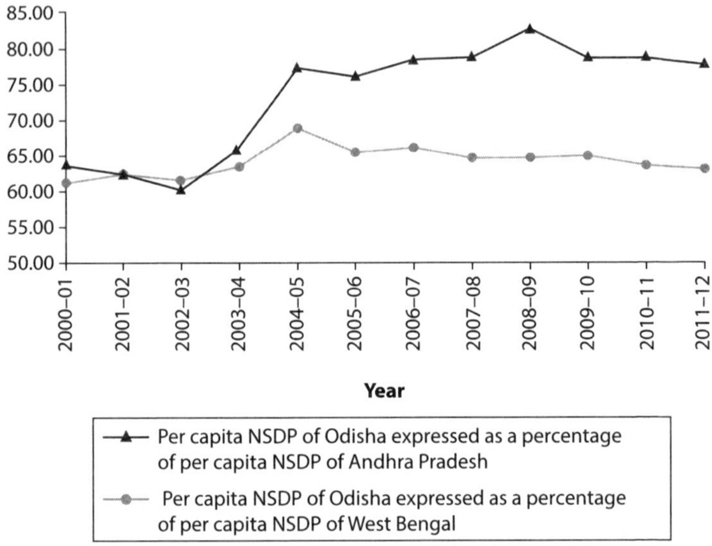

Figure I.2(c) Per capita NSDP of Odisha, expressed as percentages of per capita NSDPs of Andhra Pradesh and West Bengal, 2000–01 to 2011–12
Source of data: Planning Commission of India (2012: 109).

The structure of Odisha's economy

We now briefly consider how the composition of Odisha's economy has changed over the last three decades. Between 1982–83 and 2009–10, the shares of the primary sector (agriculture and animal husbandry, forestry and logging, fishing, and mining and quarrying), the secondary sector (manufacturing [registered and unregistered], electricity, gas, and water supply, and construction), and the tertiary sector (trade, hotels and restaurants, railways and transport by other means, storage, communication, banking and insurance, real estate and ownership of dwelling business services, public administration, and other services) in Odisha' GSDP have changed much.[9]

[9] Note that though our classification of different types of economic activities into primary, secondary, and tertiary sectors conforms to the classification used widely, it differs somewhat from the classificatory scheme adopted by the GoO (2012: 10). GoO (2012) classifies economic activities

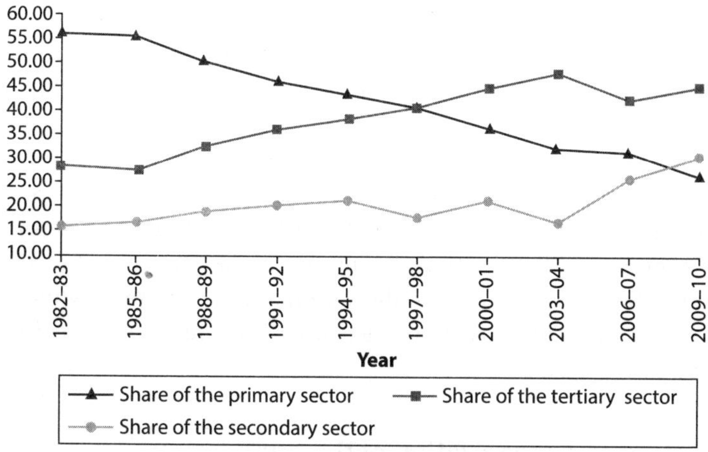

Figure I.3 The shares of primary, secondary, and tertiary sectors in the GSDP of Odisha (calculated on the basis of three-year moving averages), 1982–83 to 2009–10

Source: GoO (2012: Annexure 2.3).

Let x_t be the GSDP of Odisha in year t and let z_t be the absolute level of contribution of a sector to Odisha's GSDP in year t. Then the share of that sector in Odisha's GSDP in year t, calculated on the basis of three-year moving averages, is given by $(z_{t-2} + z_{t-1} + z_t) / (x_{t-2} + x_{t-1} + x_t)$.

The shares of primary, secondary, and tertiary sectors in the GSDP, calculated on the basis of three-year moving averages, over the period from 1982–83 to 2009–10 are shown with three-year intervals in Figure I.3.

As can be seen from Figure I.3, the share of the primary sector in Odisha's GSDP has declined steadily over this period, starting

into: (a) the agricultural sector consisting of agriculture, animal husbandry, forestry, and fisheries; (b) the industry sector consisting of mining and quarrying, manufacturing, electricity, gas and water supply; and (c) the service sector consisting of construction, trade, hotels and restaurants, transport, storage, communication, banking and insurance, real estate, public administration, and other services. While the classificatory scheme used by the Government of Odisha has merits, we have chosen to adopt the more conventional scheme.

at 55.70 per cent in 1982–83 and ending at 26.67 per cent in 2009–10. The share of the secondary sector has increased (though there was a dip in 2003–04): it started at 15.25 per cent in 1982–83 and reached the level of 28.80 per cent in 2009–10. The share of the tertiary sector in the GSDP has recorded a steady increase (except for the year 2006–07): starting at 29.05 per cent in 1982–83, the share of the tertiary sector in the GSDP of Odisha stood at 44.53 per cent in 2009–10. Thus, in terms of the share in the state's GSDP, the tertiary sector is the dominant sector now, while the once-dominant primary sector accounts for a relatively small part of the state's GSDP.

Structure and organization of the book

The chapters that follow provide detailed studies of specific sectors and aspects of Odisha's economy. Chapters 1, 2, and 3, which constitute Part I of this volume, are devoted to issues relating to agriculture. It may seem a little surprising that we have devoted as many as three out of 16 chapters to agriculture, when agriculture and 'allied' activities accounted for only 17.3 per cent of the GSDP of Odisha in 2009–10. It is, however, important to note that though the share of agriculture and allied activities in Odisha's GSDP declined sharply from 54.6 per cent in 1980–81 to 17.3 per cent in 2009–10 (see the introductory section of Chapter 1 by Sarap and Sahu), the share of agriculture and allied activities in the total employment in the state has registered a much smaller decline from 73.3 per cent in 1983 to 59.3 per cent in 2009–10 (National Sample Survey Office [NSSO] 2011). Given that nearly three-fifths of the total workforce continues to depend on agriculture and allied sectors, the importance of studying in detail the condition of agriculture in Odisha and the problems it faces can hardly be exaggerated, especially when poverty eradication is generally accepted to be one of the most important objectives of economic policies. In Chapter 1, Kailas Sarap and Partha P. Sahu provide a detailed analysis of cropping pattern and growth of productivity in agriculture in Odisha. They draw attention to two prominent features of agriculture in Odisha. First, the cropping pattern in the state has changed at a slow pace, though a more diversified cropping pattern can potentially increase the income of peasants and contribute to the fertility of the soil. Second, though productivity varies considerably across crops and over different time periods, productivity has been low for some of the most important crops such as the winter rice crop and pulses. Sarap and Sahu give a careful analysis of the factors that have hindered crop diversification and growth in productivity.

Odisha being primarily an agrarian economy, the issues of land ownership and tenurial rights are of critical importance to its overall performance. Sarthak Gaurav and Srijit Mishra address these issues in Chapter 2. The first point to note is that the distribution of land ownership in Odisha is quite skewed: 5 per cent of households own 12 per cent of the land and 86 per cent of marginal holding households own 42 per cent of the land. The distribution, however, is marginally equitable in Odisha as compared to the country at large. The Gini coefficient of land ownership is 0.69 for Odisha, whereas it is 0.76 for India. The state has a diverse history of land ownership and tenancy. While the zamindari system was the dominant system of tenancy under the Bengal Presidency and was prevalent in the coastal districts of Balasore, Cuttack, and Puri, the peasant–proprietor or the ryotwari system was prevalent in Ganjam and Koraput. Other peasant–proprietor systems like *malguzari* and *gountia* were prevalent in the western regions such as Sambalpur and Phulbani, which were part of the Central Provinces.

A number of proactive land reforms were promulgated in Odisha, an important one being the Orissa Tenancy Protection Act, 1948. This was subsequently replaced by the Orissa Tenants Relief Act, 1955, which conferred occupancy rights in the entire state including the erstwhile princely states where tenants did not have such rights. In the mid-1950s, tenancy practice was widespread and tenants would typically offer 50 per cent of the produce as rent under sharecropping. Under the Fifth Schedule of the Indian Constitution, in scheduled areas, land belonging to a tribal cannot be transferred to a non-tribal without permission from the appropriate authority.

A key problem that needs to be considered is that the average size of operational holdings has registered a secular decline, and pari passu, there has been a growth of marginal holdings, which stand at nearly 72 per cent of all holdings. This unquestionably is the principal cause of agrarian distress and poverty in the rural countryside in Odisha. Two further aspects are worth noting: (a) the proportion of the landless among the scheduled castes (SCs) and scheduled tribes (STs) is relatively higher, and (b) even though the Hindu Succession Act, 1956, stipulated that daughters and sons would have equal rights to inheritance of land, in actual practice that is not the case, and Odisha fares much worse vis-à-vis the all-India picture. For 2010–11, whereas for India, 12.8 per cent of the operational holdings belonged to females, the Odisha figure was much lower at 3.3 per cent.

In Chapter 3, Raj Kishore Panda examines the relationship between rural unemployment and agricultural wages and looks at the trend in the wages of field workers and other rural workers. Since rural unemployment and rural poverty go hand in hand, one would expect that a high level of rural unemployment would result in high level of rural poverty. However, there is a reverse causation also. What Panda finds is that the regions of the state where incidence of poverty is less, the unemployment rate is high. For the regions where incidence of poverty is higher, the unemployment rate is low. In regions that are well off, rural workers can afford to wait for a job (as a result, unemployment is higher) whereas in poor regions of the state, the rural workers cannot afford to remain unemployed and get engaged in low-paid manual work to earn their livelihood. Though the nominal wage in the state has registered a substantial increase between 1994–95 and 2010–11, the growth in real wage has been low, and what is more surprising is that the gap between male wage rate and female wage rate during this period has been widening.

Part II of the volume, comprising chapters 4, 5, and 6, deals with industry, mining, transportation, and power. In Chapter 4, Adwait Mohanty presents an account of the evolution, policy, and performance of the industrial sector in Odisha. It is well known that the process of industrialization in the state has been very slow during the twentieth century. A number of important factors such as inadequate infrastructure, lack of entrepreneurship amongst the local populace, and bureaucratic apathy have undoubtedly contributed to this. The Industrial Policy document of 2001 made a case for aggressive industrialization. In order to attract investment, the state was willing to provide a number of concessions, namely, land at concessional rate, interest subsidy, exemption of new industrial units from electricity duty, tax concessions and rationalization of labour laws, and so on. A further elaboration was made in the Industrial Policy document of 2007, where the objective of government policy was to transform Odisha into a vibrant industrialized state as well as to promote the state as a major manufacturing hub. It was also explicitly stated as a matter of government policy that industrial growth ought to be environmentally sustainable. In addition, a policy statement concerning micro, small, and medium enterprises (MSMEs) was adumbrated in the MSME Development Policy document of 2009. The purpose of this initiative by the state government was to encourage value addition and employment generation. An examination of data shows that while the share of industry in Odisha's NSDP declined somewhat from 22.2 per cent in the 1970s to 20.2 per cent in the 1980s, it increased slowly in the post-reform period to a level of 28.4 per cent at present. The share of manufacturing seems to have followed a similar pattern, with the latest share standing at 8.6 per cent of NSDP, which is much lower as compared to the all-India figure of about 14 per cent. Manufacturing is generally regarded as the most dynamic part of the broader industrial sector; in addition, it offers the best possibilities for employment generation. While growth of employment in registered manufacturing was high in the 1950s and 1960s, industrial employment declined in the 1990s due to low growth in registered factories. However, there has been some recovery during the first decade of the 2000s.

With its vast reserves of natural resources such as coal, iron ore, bauxite, and others, Odisha has great potential to develop large-scale industry, but this, unfortunately, has not been realized as yet. There is also much scope to develop further the traditional industry sector including handicraft and cottage industries. The state is famed for its high-quality handloom and cotton textiles. Being labour-intensive, these industries offer the potential of employment generation, which is much needed in a primarily agrarian state with large reserves of farm labour. Finally, it needs to be recognized that much of the industrialization that the state has experienced in recent times has been mineral-based and mostly concentrated in forest areas. There has already been an alarming degree of deforestation, which has resulted in disturbing the natural drainage system and the groundwater table, destruction of biodiversity, and environmental degradation.

Industrial policy formulation in the coming decades needs to be particularly cognizant of these ecological danger signals.

The mining sector in Odisha has been at the centre of many economic and political debates in recent years. In terms of known mineral reserves, Odisha leads most other states. It is, therefore, not surprising that the Government of Odisha, in its quest for economic growth of the state, has been vigorously pursuing a policy of mining-led growth and industrialization. Also, it is not entirely surprising that mining and mining-based industrialization have often led to deforestation, pollution, erosion of the sources of livelihood of the tribal population in the state, and diversion of agricultural land to non-agricultural uses. All this has sparked off an intense debate and controversy in the state, which has occasionally taken a violent turn. Chapter 5 by Amarendra Das and Satyananda Acharya presents a very balanced assessment of both positive and negative roles of the mining sector in Odisha. The careful factual account of the different aspects of mining in Odisha given by Das and Acharya will be of much help to anybody who wishes to understand the tensions and conflicts that continue to swirl around the policy of mining-led growth pursued by the Government of Odisha in recent times.

There can be no gainsaying that transport and power constitute the most critical infrastructure needed for sustained economic development. They have strong forward and backward linkages in both production and consumption activities. Inadequate development in the extent as well as the quality of road, rail, and waterways networks can often be a severe bottleneck to an otherwise well-structured process of economic development. Likewise, adequate and sustained availability of power is today regarded as the sine qua non of all conceivable modern economic activities. Satya P. Das addresses both these critical aspects in Chapter 6. The first thing to note is that in a 2012 ranking of states in terms of basic infrastructure, Odisha ranks at 13 in a group of 20 major states of India. Much more, therefore, needs to be done to provide the appropriate environment for major industries to locate in Odisha.

National highways constitute less than 1.5 per cent of the total road length in the state. In terms of overall road density, Odisha's position is better than the national average. However, if we are to confine attention to surfaced roads, the state has consistently lagged behind the national average. Likewise, when we consider the railways network, Odisha has consistently remained in the bottom rung amongst the major Indian states. Satya P. Das rightly takes a serious note of the relative absence of railways in the undivided Koraput, Bolangir, and Kalahandi (KBK) districts and tribal areas of Mayurbhanj and Sundargarh. As regards waterways, the state has one major port, Paradip, and two minor ones, Gopalpur and Dhamara. Most of the work at Paradip involves export of iron ore and other minerals. This is decidedly not a picture of ports importing raw materials and exporting finished industrial goods as one would expect in the case of ports with a vibrant industrial hinterland.

As regards power, Odisha has the distinction of being the first state that undertook fundamental restructuring of the power sector soon after economic reforms were introduced at the Centre in 1991. The state introduced the Power Sector Reform Act in 1995, which came into effect in 1996. The erstwhile Orissa State Electricity Board (OSEB) was unbundled into three sectors that looked into generation, transmission, and distribution activities. The distribution sector was also partly privatized. It should be recognized that the reason behind the losses of the erstwhile state electricity boards used to be the large transmission and distribution losses, as well as subsidization to powerful groups owing to political compulsions.

Providing electricity to all the households in a regular, uninterrupted way is still a distant goal in Odisha. By 2001, for which comparable data is available, barely 19 per cent of rural households in Odisha had electricity. For Himachal Pradesh the percentage was as high as 94 per cent. While there were 11 states, including Andhra Pradesh and Mizoram, which had achieved 100 per cent electrification of all villages by the end of 1995–96, Odisha was one of the laggard states with a low electrification rate of 73 per cent, which means that more than a quarter of the villages still had to be electrified. Overall, in the sphere of infrastructure, Odisha has a long way to go.

Part III, comprising chapters 7 and 8, deals with forests and water as well as natural disasters in Odisha. Chapter 7 by Padmaja Mishra studies the important natural resources of water and forests in Odisha and their alternative uses. As Mishra points out, though the per capita availability of surface and groundwater in Odisha is much higher than the all-India per capita availability of water, there is much seasonal and regional variation in the availability of water. In addition, with the recent rapid growth of Odisha's economy, there is an emerging conflict between the demands for water for alternative uses. Given this background, Mishra emphasizes the need for more efficient management of water resources of the state. Mishra also discusses the role of forests in the economy of Odisha and looks at how diversion of land for other uses, such as mining, irrigation, and construction of roads and railway lines, has often caused deforestation.

In Chapter 8, Saudamini Das discusses the economic consequences of natural disasters in Odisha. We specifically decided to have a chapter on natural disasters since, in the case of Odisha, natural disasters such as droughts, floods, and cyclones are not exceptional and rare events. They are recurring phenomena which need to be taken into account and prepared for in a systematic fashion in policy formulation. Das's analysis reveals that natural disasters, particularly drought and flood, have been recurring in Odisha almost every year since 1965 with increased intensity. If the disaster is huge in scale and destruction (such as the super cyclone of October 1999), the state gets international attention followed by substantial aid flow, which helps the state to rebuild the infrastructure. However, outside agencies hardly notice disasters which are moderate in impact but which frequently batter the state's economy, contributing to incidence of poverty in the state. One positive aspect is that since 2003, the state government has taken some innovative disaster management steps against cyclone and flood, which have yielded positive results in terms of lowering the impact on GSDP. However, Chapter 8 shows that a more systematic effort is still required to counter the evil that has plagued the state's economy for decades.

Part IV, which comprises chapters 9, 10, 11, 12, and 13, deals with education, health, and poverty in Odisha. In Chapter 9, Narayan Chandra Nayak, Sharmita Dhar, and Pratap Kumar Mahakur discuss some aspects of the state of education. Given the male literacy rate of 82.45 per cent, the female literacy rate of 64.30 per cent, and the overall literacy rate of 73.45 per cent in Odisha in 2011, basic literacy of the population is still a major concern. However, there are also many other aspects of education in Odisha which deserve serious study. Nayak, Dhar, and Mahakur have provided detailed analysis of:

(a) literacy and enrolment in primary schools; (b) rate of transition from one level of education to another; and (c) dropout rates at different stages of education in Odisha. Their district-level analysis of educational outcomes is particularly valuable insofar it provides a clear idea of regional disparities in education within Odisha. The overall picture that one gets is mixed in nature. While there has been some progress, much needs to be done to improve the enrolment rate, transition rate, and dropout rate, especially in relatively more backward districts of the state. Finally, though the quality of school education in Odisha has not been studied in detail so far, there seem to be reasons for serious concern about it. Nayak, Dhar, and Mahakur cite the following alarming information from a study of the non-government organization Pratham: 'in Odisha, almost 44% of children in class-V could not read text that a child in class-II is expected to have mastered. Similarly, 70% of children in class-V could not solve simple arithmetic problems that a child of class-II could have solved.'

How has the state performed in providing healthcare to its population? Since the state has been growing at a higher rate since 2003–04, it will be of interest to know whether this high growth has resulted in better healthcare in the state. In Chapter 10, Himanshu Sekhar Rout and Abhash Kumar Hota assess the status of healthcare in the state. Like education, here also we get a mixed answer. All health indicators have improved in Odisha over the six-year period of 2005–11. Infant mortality rate (IMR) has declined from 75 in 2005 to 57 in 2011; crude death rate (CDR) (per 1,000) fell from 9.5 to 8.5; crude birth rate (CBR) (per 1,000) fell from 22.3 to 20.1; life expectancy at birth (female) 2006–10 was 64.9 as against 59.6 (2002–06); and life expectancy at birth (male) 2006–10 was 62.3 as against 59.5 (2002–06) (GoO 2013). However, each indicator was lower than the all-India figure; most indicators were also lower than corresponding figures for the neighbouring state of West Bengal. The deficiency in health infrastructure, particularly workforce (doctors, nurses, pharmacists, and others), is huge. The government expenditure on health as a percentage of GSDP has varied from 0.56 per cent to 0.88 per cent during the last decade, which is abysmally low. For India, this figure was 1.2 per cent in 2010. The authors argue that one way to improve the health infrastructure and level of healthcare in the state is to step up public expenditure on health.

In Chapter 11, Baidyanath Misra focuses on income poverty as measured by the head count ratio (HCR), though he also discusses a composite index of development for different blocks[10] in Odisha. The analysis in the chapter confirms that while the level of poverty in Odisha, as measured by HCR, depends on which specific poverty line one uses, it continues to be much higher than the all-India poverty level as well as the poverty level in many other states of India. The chapter also highlights large disparities with respect to poverty between different regions (northern, southern, and coastal regions) of Odisha, and between different social groups. In contrast to Chapter 11, which is mainly devoted to the study of income poverty in Odisha, Chapter 12 by Manoj Panda studies the twin phenomena of malnutrition and food insecurity, which constitute an important 'real' indicator of deprivation. Panda draws attention to two major aspects of malnutrition. First, though per capita calorie consumption in Odisha has been close to or higher than the all-India per capita calorie consumption, the per capita fat and protein consumption in Odisha have been lower than the national average, the difference being particularly large in the case of fat. Second, while malnutrition of children, as measured in terms of the standard anthropometric measures (height for age, weight for age, and weight for height), has declined in Odisha, it is still widespread, and so is malnutrition of the adult population measured in terms of the body mass index. Chapter 12 also studies food insecurity in Odisha and its causes, and suggests possible policy measures that the government may adopt to combat the persistent problems of malnutrition and food insecurity in the state.

Even in Odisha, where deprivations of all types are so widespread, the deprivation of one particular social group, namely the STs, stands out. The STs constitute about 22.1 per cent of the total population of Odisha (GoO 2010), but it seems fair to say that given the structure of political power in the state, the needs of this large segment of the population received, until recently, inadequate attention from the rest of the society, especially from the administrative and political decision-making authorities. Chapter 13 by Sakti Padhi and Nilakantha Panigrahi discusses factors such as deforestation caused

[10] In case the reader is not familiar with the term, a block is an administrative unit covering a specific rural area.

by large irrigation and mining projects, construction of roads and railways, and industrialization, which have contributed to the economic plight of the STs of Odisha. The chapter also discusses the recent movements of tribal people in Odisha against the erosion of their rights and livelihood, and reviews some of the measures taken by the state to promote their welfare.

Part V consists of two chapters—one by Tapas K. Sen and Sarit Kumar Rout on the financial reforms undertaken by the state government and another by Prabhat Patnaik on the overall development strategy of the state government. The state government plays a major role in the less developed economy of Odisha. Therefore, the amount of resources at the disposal of the state government, the way such resources are utilized, and the overall development strategy of the state government are of crucial importance.

For any developmental programme to have a successful run, it is imperative that it be fiscally sustainable, which, inter alia, means that resources ought to be mobilized in an efficient and equitable manner and that the entire process also be non-inflationary. This is invariably a tall requirement for all poor economies and Odisha has been no exception. Due to its low per capita income and high incidence of both rural and urban poverty, Odisha has typically had to contend with the twin problems of low revenue potential and large public expenditure responsibilities. Oftentimes compulsions of electoral politics lead state-level leaders to spend well in excess of their legitimate sources of revenue, resulting in high levels of debt. Unless moderated carefully, this may lead to large fractions of current revenue being earmarked for debt repayment with very limited funds being left over for genuine developmental purposes. In Chapter 14, Sen and Rout address the very important issue of the impact of fiscal adjustment in Odisha.

The vicious circle of repeated borrowing and high interest burden was sought to be broken by instituting purposive fiscal reforms in Odisha sometime around 2003–04 and 2004–05. The main plank of this fiscal consolidation has been fiscal compression. One of the explicit objectives of reform in the fiscal sector has been to severely limit and ultimately eliminate fiscal deficit. Often this objective has unfortunately been fulfilled by curbing revenue expenditure on education and health, the two areas that are often regarded from the bureaucratic standpoint as dispensable. In addition, the standard head on which the axe falls is capital expenditure on essential items like rural infrastructure. There appears to have been an unmistakable withdrawal of the state from the two key areas of education and health and the direction of public policy seems to have been towards greater privatization. The possible deleterious effects of this in the medium to long run can hardly be overemphasized.

In Chapter 15, Patnaik provides a searching critique of the economic strategy ('mining-led growth') which the Government of Odisha has followed over the last decade or so. He starts by pointing out that while Odisha is one of the poorest states of India, in general, the per capita daily calorie intake of Odisha in rural as well as urban areas has been often higher than per capita daily calorie intake for India as a whole. Patnaik explains this in terms of the fact that per capita foodgrain production in Odisha is higher than per capita foodgrain for the whole of India if we calculate the figure for India including Odisha but excluding Punjab and Haryana. Patnaik argues that in a poor country with a traditional agricultural sector, there is a strong link between foodgrain output and employment and, hence, between foodgrain output and foodgrain consumption. He believes that the decline in Odisha's per capita calorie intake between 1993–94 and 2009–10 has been due to the decline in per capita foodgrain output in Odisha. Patnaik attributes the decline in per capita foodgrain output to a combination of two factors: (a) diversion of agricultural land to non-agricultural uses, and (b) the continuing low agricultural productivity in Odisha. Patnaik's carefully reasoned analysis deserves serious attention and study even if one may disagree with him on some points.

The last chapter presents some concluding observations and indicates some pressing problems that deserve urgent attention of the Government of Odisha.

* * *

As editors, we have aimed to put together a collection of essays which will provide readers an insight into, as well as factual information about, various aspects of the economy of Odisha. We hope that readers of this volume will find the subsequent chapters as informative and stimulating as we have found them.

References

Census of India. 2011. Government of India.

EPW Research Foundation. 2004. *National Accounts Statistics of India 1950–51 to 2002–03*, 5th edition. Mumbai.

———. 2009. *Domestic Product of States of India: 1960–61 to 2006–07*, 2nd edition. Mumbai.

Government of Odisha (GoO). 2010. 'Orissa Data Highlights: The Scheduled Tribes, Census of India 2001', *Orissa Review* (*Census Special*). Available at http://orissa.gov.in/e-magazine/Orissareview/2010/December/engpdf/207-210.pdf (last accessed on 16 November 2015).

———. 2012. *Economic Survey 2011–12*. Bhubaneswar: Planning and Coordination Department.

———. 2013. *Economic Survey 2012–13*. Bhubaneswar: Planning and Coordination Department.

National Sample Survey Office (NSSO). 2011. *Employment and Unemployment Situation in India: 2009–10*. New Delhi: GoI.

Panda, M. 2008. 'Economic Development in Orissa: Growth without Inclusion?', working paper 2008-025, Indira Gandhi Institute of Development Research, Mumbai. Available at http://www.igidr.ac.in/pdf/publication/WP-2008-025.pdf (last accessed on 16 November 2015).

Planning Commission of India. 2012. *Databook for DCH 10 April 2012*. Government of India. Available at http://planningcommission.nic.in/data/datatable/index.php?data=datatab (last accessed on 16 November 2015).

PART I

AGRICULTURE

1

Emerging Trends in Cropping Pattern, Crop Diversification, and Agricultural Productivity

Kailas Sarap and *Partha P. Sahu*

For the nearly three decades under review (1980–2010), agriculture in Odisha has been reeling under the subsistence nature of operation, relatively small size of landholdings, high incidence of indebtedness, inadequate and poor irrigation infrastructure, limited access to credit and other crucial agricultural inputs, weak market linkages, recurrence of flood and drought, and concentration of tribal population, although a preponderant majority of the state's population still relies on it for income and livelihood. Agriculture has shrunk from 54.6 per cent in 1980–81 to only 17.3 per cent per cent in 2009–10 of the total state gross domestic product (GDP) in the last three decades. The level and growth of agricultural productivity have also suffered due to various factors; the figures for Odisha are much lower in comparison with that of the many developed states and those at the all-India level. It is in this context that agriculture in Odisha must be elevated from its subsistence nature to being more market-oriented in order to face the challenges of poverty reduction, food security, and an economically viable agriculture sector.

To begin with, Odisha's economy has witnessed several structural changes during the last three decades or so, many of which seem unusual and undesirable. Consistent with the overall pattern of structural changes associated with the process of economic development, the contribution of agriculture to the state GDP declined continuously from 56 per cent in 1983 to 30 per cent 1999–2000, and further to just 17.3 per cent in 2009–10. On the other hand, the increase in the share of the industrial sector in state GDP was, at best, modest, even as the increase in the share of the services sector in GDP was substantial; while the share of secondary sector increased from 17.5 per cent in 1983–84 to 35.8 per cent in 2009–10, that of tertiary sector increased from 26.5 per cent to 46.9 per cent during the same period.

However, during the period from 1983 to 2009–10, the share of agriculture in total employment declined by only about 14 percentage points. On the other hand, the share of the industrial and services sectors in total employment increased by about 8 and 6 percentage points respectively. While this indicates that the workforce has shifted more towards industry than towards services, this pattern is not commensurate with the case of total output. It implies that during the last three decades, the productivity of services has risen relative to industry and agriculture. This inter-sectoral productivity difference is not only likely to affect the nature of employment being created in the sector in terms of wage and non-wage attributes, but it also has serious implication for poverty and inequality.

The Odisha economy, inter alia, is characterized by high incidence of income and other types of poverty. The income poverty has increased in the late 1990s, especially in rural areas. In view of this, there is a need to devise both short- and long-term strategies. While the nature and composition of growth is crucial for reduction of poverty, a vibrant rural non-farm sector and increase in public spending on basic health and education can play a vital role in poverty reduction efforts. The study by Dutt and Ravallion (1996) on India has revealed that poverty measures have responded far more to rural economic growth than to urban economic growth. The geographic composition of growth also affects poverty in India. Their analysis reveals that there is need for synergies between agriculture and rural development and proper non-farm economic growth. However, non-farm economic growth was less effective in reducing poverty in states with poor initial conditions in terms of rural development and human resources (Dutt and Ravallion 1996). Their result also confirms the importance of human resource development. The analysis suggests that fostering the conditions for rural economic growth, especially in agriculture and rural development, is crucial to an effective strategy for poverty reduction in the state. Unless the poor succeed in rising above the poverty line and improve their income further in a sustained manner, growth will only bring them some relief but in effect perpetuate their poverty. The outcome of the poor would depend on the characteristics of the growth process and even more on the policy regime providing support to the poor.

However, in a situation of high inequality in asset holding, it is difficult for many small and marginal farmers to invest in productive investment due to credit constraint. Credit market failure means that the poor are unable to exploit growth-promoting opportunities for investment (physical and human capital). Given high inequality, even the same rate of growth might be less effective in reducing poverty in one situation than another. Asset distribution is likely to influence the extent to which poor people participate in economic growth. The asset-poor are most locked out of growth prospects. Greater initial asset poverty means that the growth that does occur is less (income) poverty reducing. Land is an important asset in this context. One expects greater landlessness to entail that the poor share less in the gains from economic growth.

Similarly, access to improved healthcare and education is equally important for the poor to gain from growth. Low basic educational attainments are often identified as a source of income inequality. Education will influence how much the poor are equipped to participate (relative to farming) in skill-demanding non-farm growth. Another factor influencing the impact on poverty of non-farm economic growth is the productivity of the main competing sector for workers, namely, farming. For example, increasing multiple cropping, irrigation, and spread of high yielding varieties (HYVs) can increase the aggregate demand for agricultural employment. This will help in increasing wage rates in non-farm sectors.

Lastly, in comparison to the non-poor, the poor will be more constrained in their access to markets and infrastructure. The transaction costs of selling of the products as well as availing benefits from the government-sponsored welfare schemes will be high for the poor. In such a situation, the net surplus available to them will be marginal. Clearly, the development of infrastructure will benefit the poor. This analysis suggests that in a state like Odisha, creating conditions for agriculture and rural development, human capital development, and infrastructure are crucial to reduce poverty on a sustainable basis.

In this context, high growth of agriculture could be a crucial route to achieve faster and inclusive growth. What measures are necessary for attaining high agricultural growth in the state? We briefly discuss the performance of agriculture in the state and highlight the factors contributing to it. The growth rate of state GDP in agriculture and allied activities, during 1989 to 1993–94 was –0.5 per cent, while it grew at a rate of 2–2.5 per cent per annum during 1999–2000 to 2009–10. However, the growth of this sector was much less in comparison with that of other two broad sectors, that is, industries and service sectors. Clearly, the growth of this sector has been very slow during the 1980s and it has shown some degree of revival in the 1990s and beyond but the constraints to agricultural growth continue to exist.

This chapter attempts to address following questions: (a) What is the extent and nature of cropping pattern changes in the state? (b) What are the main drivers/factors responsible for changes in cropping pattern and crop diversification? (c) What are the constraints and challenges for an optimal cropping pattern in the state economy? The structure of the chapter is as follows. The following section titled 'Data Sources and Methods' describes the data sources. The section titled 'Changing Cropping Pattern in Odisha: Evidence from State-Level Data' discusses changing cropping pattern in the state in terms of area, production, and yield. The section titled 'Analysing Factors of Slow Pace of Cropping Pattern and Low Levels of Crop Productivity' describes the possible and plausible factors explaining slow pace in cropping pattern, low levels of yield, and temporal productivity differences across crops. The section on 'Strategies towards Improving Crop Diversification, Agricultural Growth, and Productivity' highlights the main conclusions and lists strategies to improve agricultural growth and productivity in the state.

Data sources and methods

The chapter is primarily based on secondary data. It draws data from Odisha Agricultural Statistics published by the Directorate of Economic and Statistics and other publications of the state government. The study is based on the analysis of data at the state level for the period 1980–81 to a recent period for which comparable data are available, that is, 2009–10. The study analyses 30 crops grown in Odisha, which accounts for more than 98 per cent of gross cropped area in the state. This chapter compiles district-level data to generate state-level aggregates. However, district totals often do not add up to state totals. This is so because while state-level estimates are regularly revised and made available by the Ministry of Agriculture, district-level revised estimates of area and production are not published regularly. Therefore, earlier studies have raised doubt on the statistical reliability of the area and production estimates at the district level, since these estimates are taken from different sources and are based on different methods of estimation. For a detailed discussion on limitations of the district-level data, see Bhalla and Singh (2012). To improve the statistical reliability of the data, we have estimated three-year moving average and all our analysis is based on those estimates. To analyse growth of various variables, the study period has been divided into three periods, that is, 1980–81 to 1989–90, 1990–91 to 1998–99, and 2000–01 to 2009–10. The year 1999–2000 has not been included in our analysis because of the event of super cyclone that occurred during the year. However, the above limitations may be noted while interpreting the results and analysis presented in the chapter.

Changing cropping pattern in Odisha: Evidence from state-level data

One of the important channels through which agricultural production and productivity can be raised is cropping pattern. A well-diversified cropping pattern, in addition to raising peasant income, also improves soil quality/fertility. In a state like Odisha where agriculture is so closely associated with the livelihood of a significant proportion of population, it is important to analyse the possibility, desirability, and feasibility of changes in cropping pattern. But unfortunately, as we have discussed in our subsequent analysis, agriculture in Odisha has not witnessed any significant change or shift in its cropping pattern. Recently we have come across a large number of studies analysing the pace, pattern, and determinants of cropping pattern both at the state and district levels, based on standard indicators and indices (Bhalla and Singh 2012; Gupta et al. 2012; Kumar, Kumar, and Sharma 2012; Nayak 2012; Pattnayak and Nayak 2008; Satapathy 2012; Sharma 2011). Most of these studies have used a variety of statistical measures and indices such as Herfindahl index, entropy index, crop yield index, crop concentration ratios based on location quotient method, and so on. Some of these studies have also attempted to analyse the determinants of cropping pattern with the help of household and individual attributes such as age, gender, education, and caste of the farmer, farm size, family size, access to credit, power, irrigation and other crucial agricultural inputs, and availability of infrastructural facilities such as road, market, and so on. As a departure from earlier studies, the present chapter, after analysing long-term trend and pattern in cropping pattern, attempts to highlight the causes of slow or insignificant shift in cropping pattern and their implications on overall growth in agriculture and its productivity. Our exercise also attempts to seek solutions to improve agricultural productivity through changing cropping pattern.

Various factors come into play in determining an optimal cropping pattern. Thematically, all these factors can broadly be categorized under technology, institutions, marketing, agro-climatic, government support structure, and so on. The first question that needs to be addressed is that of scope and possibility of a shift in existing cropping pattern, given the nature and extent of structural constraints such as non-economic and unfavourable landholding size, dominance of small and marginal farmers, increased cost of cultivation, and subsistence nature of agricultural practices in Odisha. In addition, over the years, there has been increasing diversion of agricultural land for non-agricultural purposes and marked decline in public investment on crucial agricultural inputs such as credit, fertilizers, irrigation, power, and so on. Declining water table and lack of access to water also inhibit the use of other inputs such as HYV seeds and fertilizers, causing increasing gap between actual and potential yields. The dominance of low value crops such as coarse cereals restricts the income-generating potential of farmers, especially the small and marginal farmers. Low resource base of farmers further discourage them to undertake any risk in investing on improved technologies or land improvements. Low levels of education and skill and risk-averse attitude of Odisha farmers also hold them back to opt for any alternative cropping pattern. In addition, lack of incentives and inadequate price supporting mechanisms also play a crucial role in dissuading farmers to undertake any change in cropping pattern. To attempt an empirical econometric analysis taking all the above variables is beyond the scope of this chapter. Multiple data sources with different reference period and huge asymmetry in the coverage and concept of different indicators makes it even difficult to undertake any econometric analysis with reasonable degree of specification. However, this chapter makes a comprehensive analytical narration of all these variables in the following sections.

This section is primarily devoted to an analysis of changes in cropping pattern in Odisha's agriculture during 1980–81 to 2009–10, in terms of area, production, and yield.

Temporal changes in cropping pattern: Area

The temporal changes in allocation of area to different crops are presented in Table 1.1. It is interesting to note that during the period under review, there is very little change in the area allocation across broad groups like foodgrains, oil seeds, vegetables, and other crops at the state level for Odisha. Only specific crops within these groups have witnessed significant changes in their area allocation over time. The share of area allocated to total foodgrains was 78.97 per cent during 1980–83. However, within the foodgrains category, rice, which accounted for 48.12 per cent during 1980–83, increased its share to 56.60 per cent in 2001–03, but declined to 50.90 per cent during 2007–10. Other crops within this category, such as wheat, ragi, jowar, bajra, and small millets, witnessed varying degree of decline in their areas. The proportion of area allocated to total pulses has remained more or less stagnant at around 21 per cent. Similarly, the share of area under vegetables has also remained stagnant at around 7–8 per cent. It is evident that hardly any change has taken place in the proportion of area allocated at the broad category level of crops. Area allocated to commercial and cash crops has been very low, say less than even 1 per cent and it has not changed over the years.

Table 1.1 Percentage share of major crops in total cropped area and their growth, 1980–81 to 2009–10

S. No.	Major crop	Triennium average share during the period				Trend growth rate (%)		
		1980–83	1990–93	2000–03	2007–10	1980–81/ 1989–90	1990–91/ 1998–99	2000–01/ 2009–10
1	2	3	4	5	6	7	8	9
1	Rice	48.12	47.06	56.60	50.90	0.41	0.07	–0.17
2	Wheat	0.76	0.31	0.21	0.23	–7.70	–8.64	1.31
3	Ragi	3.49	2.54	2.45	2.13	–2.98	–3.42	–0.76
4	Maize	1.88	2.11	2.14	2.56	0.50	–2.75	3.25
5	Jowar	0.42	0.25	0.16	0.10	–2.09	–5.49	–4.36
6	Bajra	0.11	0.08	0.05	0.03	–3.01	–10.60	–4.41
7	Small millets	2.62	0.74	0.48	0.21	–12.41	–6.11	–9.42
I (1–7)	Total cereals	57.40	53.09	62.10	56.16	–0.37	–0.34	–0.13
8a	Kharif pulses	5.96	7.04	6.64	8.47	3.40	–3.57	4.62
8b	Rabi pulses	15.60	14.86	12.33	14.83	–0.06	–4.37	3.30
8	Total pulses	21.57	21.90	18.97	23.30	0.94	–4.11	3.73
II (1–8)	Total foodgrains	78.97	74.99	81.06	79.46	–0.01	–1.36	0.87
9	Groundnuts	2.59	3.85	2.70	2.88	8.49	–4.25	1.14
10	Til	2.43	4.61	2.75	3.41	5.83	–7.31	3.18
11	Castor	0.51	0.30	0.22	0.20	–4.06	–2.71	–1.35
12	Mustard	1.61	1.70	1.29	1.28	0.36	–5.77	0.31
13	Linseed	0.37	0.35	0.26	0.30	0.08	–2.10	2.01
14	Niger	1.79	2.04	1.82	1.19	2.00	–3.98	–3.91
15	Sunflower	0.01	0.05	0.06	0.20	16.42	2.13	NE

16	Safflower	0.06	0.02	0.03	0.01	-6.16	-2.40	-8.78
III (9–16)	Total oilseeds	9.37	12.92	9.11	9.46	4.20	-5.47	0.97
17	Potato	0.10	0.11	0.10	0.11	2.32	-3.48	2.12
18	Sweet potato	0.62	0.53	0.53	0.56	0.58	0.48	2.21
19	Onion	0.47	0.47	0.26	0.35	1.24	0.54	2.81
IV (17–19)	Total vegetables*	7.98	8.76	6.61	7.77	-0.36	-8.00	6.11
20	Sugarcane	0.58	0.46	0.23	0.43	-1.46	1.13	NE
21	Jute	0.55	0.44	0.18	0.12	-5.94	-12.92	-3.25
22	Mesta	0.49	0.33	0.32	0.23	-2.58	-1.02	-3.85
23	Sunhemp	0.11	0.14	0.14	0.15	3.96	-2.11	-0.91
24	Cotton	0.05	0.07	0.56	0.64	4.67	24.69	4.25
25	Chilies	0.98	0.98	0.92	0.87	0.94	-2.53	-0.85
26	Coriander	0.19	0.22	0.19	0.22	2.39	-0.42	1.41
27	Garlic	0.17	0.20	0.12	0.13	4.15	-3.13	-0.71
28	Ginger	0.06	0.10	0.18	0.19	5.85	4.72	2.94
29	Turmeric	0.28	0.25	0.33	0.29	0.10	0.64	-0.64
V (25–29)	Total C&S	1.68	1.75	1.74	1.69	1.56	-1.33	-0.22
30	Tobacco	0.22	0.15	0.05	0.04	-3.45	-8.07	-4.12
	Total	100	100	100	100	0.35	-2.38	1.17

Source: Authors' own estimates based on Directorate of Agriculture and Food Production, GoO (various years).

Note: NE: Not estimated due to non-availability of data.

Trend growth rates have been estimated using semi-log regression model.

* Total vegetables also include other items, which are not listed here.

Table 1.1 also presents decadal growth rates of area allocated to various crops. Total gross cropped area grew at the rate of 0.35 per cent during 1980–81 to 1989–90, but it declined significantly during the next period, that is, during 1990–91 to 1998–99. However, it further witnessed a growth rate of 1.17 per cent per annum during 2000–01 to 2009–10. During each sub-period, we witness varying degrees of decline and slowdown in the growth rates of area allocated to various crops. For instance, growth of area under foodgrains, accounting for nearly 80 per cent of the total gross cropped area, declined at the rates of 0.01 per cent and 1.36 per cent during 1980–81 to 1989–90 and 1990–91 to 1998–99 respectively. Within foodgrains, the area allocated to rice experienced marginal positive growth during the first two sub-periods, while during 2000–01 to 2009–10, it declined by 0.17 per cent.

Temporal changes in cropping pattern: Production

It is also of our interest to analyse the changes in the share of various crops in the total production, which is presented in Table 1.2. The levels and growth of agricultural output is primarily determined by a multitude of factors, such as fertility of soils, rainfall, weather, technology in use, and level and quality of inputs. The proportion of foodgrains in total agricultural production declined from 47.58 per cent during 1980–83 to 41.18 per cent during 2007–10. The share of total cereals production also declined during this period. However, the production share of total vegetables increased significantly from 37.75 per cent during 1980–83 to 47.93 per cent 2000–03 and further declined to 40.06 per cent during 2007–10. Unlike distribution of area across crops, we observed some degree of reshuffling in the shares of different crops in total agricultural production.

The growth rate of total production was estimated at 2.49 per cent during 1980–81 to 1989–90, which suffered serious setback during the subsequent two sub-periods. It witnessed negative growth rates of 3.44 per cent and 0.87 per cent during 1990–91 to 1998–99 and 2000–01 to 2009–10 respectively. Total production of foodgrains grew at the rate of 2.25 per cent during 1980–81 to 1989–90 and 4.63 per cent during 2000–01 to 2009–10, contributed by both cereals and pulses. Production of total vegetables grew at a rate of 3.15 per cent during 1980–81 to 1989–90, but it slowed down to a rate of 0.67 per cent during 2000–01 to 2009–10.

Table 1.2 Percentage share of major crops in total production and their growth, 1980–81 to 2009–10

S. No.	Major crop	Triennium average share during the period				Trend growth rate (%)		
		1980–83	1990–93	2000–03	2007–10	1980–81/ 1989–90	1990–91/ 1998–99	2000–01/ 2009–10
1	2	3	4	5	6	7	8	9
1	Rice	31.42	34.78	19.97	33.90	3.96	–0.95	4.48
2	Wheat	1.07	0.31	0.09	0.14	-8.62	-12.06	3.25
3	Ragi	4.07	1.28	0.52	0.79	-6.99	-7.83	1.40
4	Maize	1.53	1.12	0.70	2.35	0.08	0.84	11.48
5	Jowar	0.25	0.11	0.03	0.03	-3.28	-10.70	-3.20
6	Bajra	0.07	0.04	0.01	0.01	-3.20	-15.73	-4.02
7	Small millets	1.09	0.22	0.05	0.04	-12.48	-8.39	-0.92
I (1–7)	Total cereals	39.50	37.85	21.36	37.25	2.30	-1.25	4.69
8a	Kharif pulses	1.89	2.39	0.80	1.78	8.12	-8.40	7.16
8b	Rabi pulses	6.20	4.40	1.49	2.72	-0.34	-8.23	4.28
8	Total pulses	8.09	6.79	2.29	4.50	1.91	-8.28	5.33
II (1–8)	Total foodgrains	47.58	44.64	23.66	41.18	2.25	-2.15	4.63
9	Groundnuts	2.40	3.03	1.03	2.02	7.87	-8.55	4.83
10	Til	0.91	0.90	0.28	0.57	7.32	-7.08	6.21
11	Castor	0.20	0.09	0.03	0.05	-3.58	-6.29	1.74
12	Mustard	0.59	0.52	0.12	0.20	2.33	-10.90	3.12
13	Linseed	0.11	0.09	0.03	0.05	1.56	-4.73	4.36
14	Niger	0.54	0.53	0.12	0.17	3.52	-8.09	-0.36
15	Sunflower	0.00	0.02	0.02	0.05	11.97	4.26	-2.12
16	Safflower	0.02	0.01	0.01	0.03	-9.50	-4.58	10.05
III (9–16)	Total oilseeds	4.78	5.18	1.63	3.14	6.07	-8.25	4.64

(*Cont'd.*)

Table 1.2 *(Cont'd.)*

S. No.	Major crop	Triennium average share during the period				Trend growth rate (%)		
		1980–83	1990–93	2000–03	2007–10	1980–81/ 1989–90	1990–91/ 1998–99	2000–01/ 2009–10
1	2	3	4	5	6	7	8	9
17	Potato	0.53	0.62	0.48	0.54	6.70	-1.07	-1.35
18	Sweet potato	3.33	2.42	1.31	1.97	0.29	0.61	2.13
19	Onion	2.63	2.05	0.76	1.31	-0.12	-3.38	1.17
IV (17–19)	Total vegetable*	37.75	42.86	47.93	40.06	3.15	-7.53	0.67
20	Sugarcane	3.20	1.81	6.73	12.49	-2.40	17.66	5.00
21	Jute	3.18	2.27	8.82	0.53	-3.14	-14.31	-14.04
22	Mesta	1.69	1.35	9.74	0.44	0.60	-9.37	-18.70
23	Sunhemp	0.36	0.51	0.15	0.19	5.51	-12.24	0.41
24	Cotton	0.04	0.04	0.20	0.68	9.62	36.98	12.25
25	Chilies	0.56	0.45	0.06	0.30	0.82	-1.94	9.21
26	Coriander	0.07	0.06	0.11	0.04	1.82	-0.08	-9.55
27	Garlic	0.41	0.36	0.12	0.17	1.77	-3.15	0.02
28	Ginger	0.07	0.09	0.23	0.29	8.54	6.20	1.74
29	Turmeric	0.24	0.31	0.61	0.48	4.28	1.33	0.14
V (25–29)	Total C&S	1.34	1.27	1.13	1.28	2.17	-0.61	-4.27
30	Tobacco	0.08	0.06	0.00	0.01	-3.83	-10.82	NE
	Total	100	100	100	100	2.49	-3.44	-0.87

Source: Authors' own estimates based on Directorate of Agriculture and Food Production, GoO (various years).

Note: NE: Not estimated due to non-availability of data.

Trend growth rates have been estimated using semi-log regression model.

* Total vegetables also include other items, which are not listed here.

Variations in agricultural productivity

Table 1.3 gives details about the yield rate, that is, productivity per hectare, for the 30 selected crops during 1980–81 to 2009–10 along with growth rates in productivity.

It is clear from the table that for the state as a whole the production per hectare for the 30 crops which was 1,368 kg/hectare during 1980–83 rose to 1,744 kg/hectare during 1990–93 and to 4,135 kg/hectare during 2000–03 and declined to 2,444 kg/hectare during 2007–10. There exist large variations in the yield rate across various crops within and across various periods. The growth performance of yield rate exhibits a mixed pattern. The growth of aggregate productivity of 30 crops was recorded 2.14 per cent during 1980–81 to 1989–90, but during the next two sub-periods it recorded negative growth of 1.08 and 5.91 per cent respectively. During 2001–01 to 2009–10, in general, the highest increase in productivity was recorded by rice, maize, groundnuts, cotton, chillies, and items under oilseeds. Growth in yield rate, however, suffered various degrees of setbacks in vegetables, jute, mesta, coriander, ginger, turmeric, and so on. However, it is worth noting that these crops constitute a very small share, both in area and production. The temporal variations in yield rate across crops need further incisive analysis.

The important point to note is that growth remained confined to limited crops. Even within a single crop, there are variations across seasons and regions. Rice is produced in three seasons namely, autumn, winter, and summer. The average productivity of winter rice has been 10 to 13 quintals/hectare whereas that of summer rice was 19–22 quintals/hectare. Thus, the productivity of winter rice is nearly half of that of summer rice. However, winter rice covers 75 per cent of area under rice. Thus, rice is the dominant crop and winter rice covers three-fourths of the area under rice but productivity is low during the last two decades. It is noteworthy that the average productivity of autumn rice has declined in the last decade. However, in case of summer rice it has increased substantially during the 1990s in comparison with the 1980s, even though it is relatively lower in comparison with the national level. Similarly, the productivity of pulses as well as those oilseeds is relatively lower in the state in comparison with the national level. The area under oilseeds has been falling in recent years in the state.

Table 1.3 Levels and growth of yield of major crops, 1980–81 to 2009–10

S. No.	Major crop	Triennium average value during the period (kg/hectare)				Trend growth rate (%)		
		1980–83	1990–93	2000–03	2007–10	1980–81/ 1989–90	1990–91/ 1998–99	2000–01/ 2009–10
1	2	3	4	5	6	7	8	9
1	Rice	893	1,291	1,132	1,627	3.53	–1.03	4.80
2	Wheat	1,913	1,732	1,317	1,521	-1.00	-3.74	2.33
3	Ragi	1,755	871	741	906	-4.13	-4.57	2.57
4	Maize	1,115	947	1,162	2,242	-0.41	3.70	9.47
5	Jowar	827	729	558	630	-1.21	-5.51	1.86
6	Bajra	856	804	579	601	-0.19	-5.74	0.84
7	Small millets	554	522	313	508	-0.08	-2.42	14.05
I (1–7)	Total cereals	943	1,245	1,110	1,621	2.68	-0.91	5.02
8a	Kharif pulses	435	592	409	513	4.57	-5.01	3.14
8b	Rabi pulses	545	514	421	448	-0.28	-4.04	0.81
8	Total pulses	515	539	414	472	0.96	-4.35	1.70
II (1–8)	Total Foodgrains	824	1,038	942	1,266	2.25	-0.80	3.80
9	Groundnuts	1,288	1,364	1,226	1,712	-0.57	-4.50	4.75
10	Til	512	360	312	408	1.41	0.24	3.97
11	Castor	550	542	486	630	0.50	-3.68	3.56
12	Mustard	502	530	296	376	1.97	-5.45	3.73
13	Linseed	403	444	356	442	1.47	-2.68	2.56
14	Niger	410	458	225	343	1.49	–4.28	6.07

15	Sunflower	518	562	NE	644	–3.83	2.08	NE
16	Safflower	484	410	505	7,608	–3.57	–2.23	24.56
III (9–16)	Total oilseeds	696	703	573	809	1.79	–2.94	4.86
17	Potato	7,288	9,459	21,839	11,670	4.28	2.50	-6.08
18	Sweet potato	7,281	7,832	8,848	8,612	–0.29	0.13	–0.39
19	Onion	7,716	7,570	13,527	9,064	–1.34	–3.90	–3.59
IV (17–19)	Total vegetables*	6,900	8,534	31,151	12,606	3.52	0.51	–9.63
20	Sugarcane	7,650	6,762	NE	70,488	–0.96	16.35	NE
21	Jute	7,939	9,438	3,09,575	10,412	2.97	–1.61	–18.38
22	Mesta	4,704	7,082	1,97,845	4,604	3.26	–8.44	–22.60
23	Sunhemp	4,290	6,510	3,668	3,831	1.49	–10.35	1.23
24	Cotton	982	951	1,405	2,617	4.73	9.86	8.98
25	Chillies	779	795	351	851	–0.12	0.60	20.97
26	Coriander	515	487	2,094	483	–0.56	0.34	–19.20
27	Garlic	3,187	3,114	3,362	3,226	–2.29	–0.01	0.79
28	Ginger	1,510	1,572	4,461	3,665	2.55	1.41	–4.78
29	Turmeric	1,152	2,147	5,743	4,120	4.18	0.69	–3.82
V (25–29)	Total C&S	1,092	1,263	2,160	1,860	0.60	0.73	–5.11
30	Tobacco	508	709	0	744	–0.40	–3.00	NE
	Total	1,368	1,744	4,135	2,444	2.14	–1.08	–5.91

Source: Authors' own estimates based on Odisha Agricultural Statistics, Directorate of Economic and Statistics, Government of Odisha, various issues.

Note: NE: Not estimated due to non-availability of data.

Trend growth rates have been estimated using semi-log regression model.

* Total vegetables also include other items, which are not listed here.

There is wide regional variation in the productivity of rice between the irrigated and dry regions of the state. For instance, out of 30 districts in the state, about one-third of the districts have average productivity that is below the state average. Moreover, among these districts, there are some for which average productivity figures are significantly lower than the state average. Clearly, the productivity of rice is below the state average in majority of districts (GoO various issues).

Analysing factors of slow pace of cropping pattern and low level of crop productivity

A number of factors may have contributed to slow pace in cropping pattern, low level of agricultural productivity, and productivity differences across crops. These factors may be categorized under agrarian structure, technology, and infrastructure facilities. We briefly discuss these factors below.

Agrarian structure

The agriculture sector of the state is characterized by the following situation. There is declining land–man ratio, increasing marginalization of holding, low dosages of inputs, and low expansion of irrigation and HYV of seeds. According to Agricultural Census 1995–96, there were 39.66 lakh operational holdings. Out of this, small and marginal holdings accounted for 81.97 per cent and operated 50.27 per cent of total operated area with some variation across different districts. By contrast, the semi-medium, medium, and large holdings constituted 18.03 per cent of holdings but operated 49.37 per cent of area. There has been increase in marginal holdings. Marginal holdings, both in terms of operational as well as ownership status, have increased in recent years. For instance, of the total holdings, marginal holdings formed 43.3 per cent during the year 1970–71. It has increased to 54 per cent during the year 1995–96. This trend is also true in case of ownership holdings. Thus, the inequality in the distribution of operational holdings has increased in recent years and the percentage of marginal holdings has increased.

Declining land–man ratio and uncertain property rights on land

Scarcity of land and declining land–man ratio has made operational holdings smaller and uneconomic. The per capita availability of cultivated land, which was 0.39 hectare in 1950–51, has declined to 0.14 hectare in 2004–05. The average operated area per holding has declined from 1.47 hectare in 1985–86 to 1.34 hectare during 1995–96.

The prevalence of tenancy in the state is high in comparison with the national level. As per 50th round of National Sample Survey (NSS) 1992, 22 per cent of cultivators were tenant farmers constituting 11.3 per cent area under them. The average area leased-in per reporting household was 0.38 hectare Sharecropping is the dominant form of tenancy followed by fixed rent. Most of the tenant cultivators have no clear property rights on land and the contracts are short term and oral in nature. In such a situation, there is no incentive for hard work on the tenanted land. Further, tenants have no access to formal credit market as formal credit is given based on collateral, mainly ownership of land. A majority of tenants are marginal and small tenants. They have to depend on the landlord or creditor/trader to arrange working capital requirement. Moreover, the land records are not up to date and there are joint holdings. As a result, many farmers, even if cultivating land for many years, have no clear-cut property rights on the land. This has implications for credit market, which we discuss later.

Preponderance of agricultural labourers and landless population is another serious constraint to agricultural growth in the state. As per 2001 census, out of the total workers of 142.76 lakh, 67.2 per cent were main and the rest 32.8 per cent were marginal workers. Of the total 95.89 lakh main workers, 26.0 per cent were cultivators, 14.7 per cent were agricultural labourers, 28.4 per cent were household industrial workers, and the remaining 30.9 per cent were other workers. It is noteworthy that the proportion of agricultural workers in the total workforce declined from 25.1 per cent in 1991 to 14.7 per cent in 2001. The proportion of cultivators has also decreased from 38.7 per cent to 24.1 per cent during the same period. Clearly, the percentage of landless and near landless population has increased in the recent decade in comparison with the previous decade.

Irrigation facility

Development of irrigation facilities is crucial for agriculture development in the state. Even today, the nature of irrigation in the state is of protective type. It is mainly utilized to protect the kharif crops due to delayed and irregular rainfall. Irrigation intensity in the state was only 31 per cent in 2006–07 in comparison to the all-India average of 44 per cent. As per latest available estimates, only 36.7 per cent of net sown area has been under irrigation facilities during 2007–08. Out of 30.16 lakh hectare net irrigation potential created by the end of 2010–11, 13.50 lakh hectare (44.8 per cent) has been created through major and medium, 5.62 lakh hectare (18.6 per cent) through minor (flow), and 5.08 lakh hectare (16.8 per cent) through minor (lift) irrigation projects. However, it is to be noted that significant proportions of these are very uncertain and dependent on good rainfall, supply of electricity, and other factors. There is uneven distribution of development of irrigation in the state and inefficient use of the created potential. About half of irrigation potential created in the case of flow and 37 per cent in case of groundwater has not been utilized in the state. The efficiency of water use is also low in the case of canal irrigation.

Fertilizer use

Use of chemical fertilizer in the state is far below the national level. Consumption of fertilizer in the state during recent years has increased from 41 kg/hectare in 2001–02 to 62.8 kg/hectare in 2010–11, but these are lower as compared to national level, that is, 128.6 kg in 2008–09. The fertilizer consumption in the state has been lower than the national level for the last several years. Further, there is imbalance in the use of different types of chemical fertilizer. For instance, the proportion of use of nitrogen is relatively higher in comparison with that of phosphates. Continuous use of chemical fertilizer without use of organic manure affects the nutrient status, and the physical and chemical properties of the soil. There is evidence that soils in certain parts of the state, especially in irrigated belt, have become alkaline. One of the reasons may be due to disproportionate use of chemical fertilizer. Increased use of organic manure not only raises the productivity of soil but it can be increased with less cost.

There is regional imbalance in the use of chemical fertilizers. The use of it in eastern ghat and northern plateau is less than half of the state average, which is itself low in comparison with all-India level. A number of factors including lack of irrigation facilities, access to credit, and availability of fertilizer have contributed to the low use of fertilizer. However, irrigation facilities are crucial for the use of chemical fertilizer because the fertilizer's effectiveness is lowered in the absence of irrigation.

HYV seeds

While the use of HYVs of seeds is moderate, there is unevenness in their use across different regions of the state. The use of HYVs of seeds is negligible in southern districts and in some districts of the eastern ghat. It is to be noted that given the irrigation facilities, the use of it could have been much higher. It appears that lack of extension services may have contributed partly the low spread of HYVs, especially in backward districts.

Agricultural credit

Lack of timely and inadequate availability of credit is an important constraint for not only low use of inputs, but also lack of investment in tube well irrigation by individual farmers. The formal credit situation in the state is as follows.

Cooperatives, commercial banks, and regional rural banks (RRBs) provide formal credit. These institutions provided both short-term (working capital) and long-term credit to farmers. Besides, they provide loan under various anti-poverty programmes. For instance, the formal credit institutions (commercial banks, regional rural banks (RRBs), and cooperatives) have advanced loan of Rs 6,751.81 crore during 2010–11. Of the total loan, 57.1 per cent has comes from cooperative institutions and the rest 42.9 per cent from commercial banks and RRBs. However, the amount of credit financed by these institutions is low in the state in comparison with that at the all-India level. For instance, the per capita loan financed by different banks in agriculture was only Rs 227 in the state in comparison with that of Rs 408 at the all-India level during 1999–2000. Further, out of the total loan financed by these institutions, more than three-fourth of it is for working capital arrangement. As a result, hardly one-fourth of it is utilized for investment purposes meant for buying durable assets and land improvement. Moreover, the amount of credit advanced by these institutions to agriculture sector and other rural development activities is meagre. The credit advanced per hectare of gross cropped area is also meagre. Credit per hectare of area in many districts is much below the state average, which itself is also very low.

A number of factors have been cited by formal credit institutions for the low amount of loan advanced by them. These factors include insufficient number of viable proposals, poor recovery of formal loan and high rate of default, inadequate infrastructure facilities, low credit absorption capacity, and inadequate workforce in the financial institutions. The transaction cost of providing credit to poor borrowers situated in dispersed locations is high. Similarly, the risk associated with lending to large number of small borrowers is high due to risk and uncertainty associated with crop production, which, in turn, contributes to defaults in the repayment of loans.

The rate of defaults in the repayment of formal loans in the state is very high. Similarly, the outstanding loan as a percentage of loan advanced is also very high. In such a situation, the defaulters are unable to approach the cooperatives further for any kind of loan. As a result, they are unable to buy inputs in the market in the absence of own funds. The high rate of default of loan repayment weakens the financial position of the institutions. It prevents the defaulters from obtaining any fresh loan from these institutions. Risk and uncertainty in agriculture production, which arise due to frequent drought and flood situation in the state, lead to crop failure. This contributes to high rate of default of loan. Further, there is also wilful default, especially among the large borrowers and borrowers with political and social networks.

The poor borrowers have to incur high transaction cost of loan due to bureaucratic procedures followed by the formal lenders, lack of infrastructure, illiteracy among the borrowers, and rent-seeking behaviour among the personnel associated with providing loan. The formal lenders have to incur high transaction costs, as they have to advance as well as recover the loan to borrowers situated in dispersed and remote areas. As a result, the lending of formal credit institutions to poor borrowers becomes unprofitable. It also discourages the potential borrower from approaching these institutions.

The low absorption of credit in the state may be due to lack of commercialization of agriculture, inadequate irrigation facilities, lack of access to credit, and uncertain property rights on land. It is to be noted that a significant proportion of farmers have no perfect property rights on their land, even though they have user's right. Lack of updating of land records and partition among the co-sharers of the land have contributed to such a situation. Further, many tenants have only user's right but no ownership rights. As formal credit institutions provide loan based on ownership of collateral (land), these farmers have no access to formal credit (Sarap 1991).

Clearly a number of factors including lack of access to property rights on land, default of loan, bureaucratic procedures followed by credit institutions, and high transaction cost of borrowing and lending have contributed towards the lack of adequate access to formal credit by majority of poor farmers. As a result, they have to depend on informal loan for production and consumption purposes. However, the terms and conditions of informal credit are unfair to the poor borrowers. As a result, a substantial proportion of their income is transferred to the lenders. Further, interlinkage of credit, input, and output markets are widespread in backward districts. In such a situation, the borrowers not only have to pay high interest charges but also sell their output at very low prices. Clearly, credit market failure is an important reason for no adoption of new technology by the poor farmers.

Strategies towards improving crop diversification, agricultural growth, and productivity

The main points that emerge from the foregoing analysis are that there has been very insignificant change in cropping pattern in Odisha agriculture. Foodgrains continue to account for about 80 per cent of total area with very little variations during the period under study. Within foodgrains, rice constitutes a significant share in total area and production. Crop-wise distribution of area and production did not witness any marked reshuffle during the last 30 years. However, during each sub-period we witness varying degrees of decline and slowdown in the growth rates of area allocated to various crops, production, and agricultural productivity.

In order to achieve high agricultural growth and productivity improvement through changing cropping pattern, efforts have to be made in the following aspects:

Increase in public investment

Investible resources with the government have to be raised. This has to be achieved through increased central assistance, local resource mobilization, as well as through better cost recovery for the input services provided. Further, the efficiency of the current investment has to be increased through reforms and governance. Investment in infrastructure development including water management, rural roads, electrification and cold chains, and marketing and processing has to be stepped up. The efficiency of public investment in this sector can be increased if farmers have access to irrigation, technology, and resources to adopt the technology especially in the districts where these facilities are low. Further, access to land of farmers and efficiency in the public investment carried out by state, local bodies, or non-governmental organizations (NGOs) has also to be promoted.

Efficient use of agricultural inputs

Better variety seeds are necessary. However, these by themselves cannot produce sustained growth of yield and production. The realization of their yield potential depends on the availability of resources and proper soil and water management. The two key elements among non-price factors that would affect growth and output are: (a) the sustained improvement of yield-augmenting technology and (b) creating conditions for the effective diffusion and widespread application of that technology by farmers. Evidence from western and southern Odisha reveals that the adoption of even the existing technology is very low. Realization of these conditions depends on the land, credit, access to extension services, and spread of irrigation. Further, clear property rights on land are crucial because in the absence of it farmers have no incentive for hard work on land. The access to credit market is also dependent on it.

However, the impact of better varieties of seeds is critically dependent on improving the soil and moisture environment in which crops are cultivated. Here, more public investment, especially in soil and moisture conservation on rained land, land development, expansion and improvement of irrigation, and information for marketing and processing, are necessary.

High risk and uncertainty characterize the rained agriculture in many parts of state, especially in western and southern Odisha. In such a situation, agriculture production needs to be diversified. Measures have to be taken to facilitate the growth of other crops and animal husbandry. The growth of animal husbandry should receive adequate attention in these areas. Expansion of water and direct marketing facilities are necessary for diversification of crops. In the case of animal husbandry credit, extension, veterinary services, and infrastructure facilities are also crucial.

Effectiveness of investment

The effectiveness of investment in agriculture and rural development in the state is low due to a number of reasons. These include fragmented planning, poor design, over capitalization, inordinate delay in completion of work, and large-scale corruption. Delay in completion of work increases the capital–output ratio. Investment is locked in the absence of production, unless the work is complete and has become operational. For instance, a large number of irrigation and other projects started in the state earlier are yet to be completed. Several measures are necessary to raise the effectiveness of investment in this sector. It is discussed in the next few sections.

Rationalization of agricultural development programmes

There is a need to rationalize several programmes carried out under the agriculture sector. The bulk of investment in this sector is towards irrigation, soil, and moisture conservation. For instance, during the Eighth Five Year Plan (FYP) period, about 28 per cent of total investment was allocated to agriculture and irrigation activities in the state as compared to 24 per cent at the all-India level (Kurien 2000). However, the outcome is unsatisfactory. There is too much fragmentation in these programmes. For instance, the programmes of different categories of irrigation in a given area, such as major, medium, minor, surface lift, and ground water are conceived and implemented separately. Some of these are being taken up under different schemes. Some of these programmes can be grouped into one or two entities. There should be integration of land and water development within the watershed (in one or many villages) as the unit of planning. This would improve effectiveness in functioning of these programmes considerably.

Programmes such as rural roads, markets and storage, and others that are local development work should be planned and executed by local authorities like at district, block, or panchayat levels. The monitoring and execution of work by local authorities will be effective. The state/regional authority should coordinate the local efforts.

Reorganization of rural development programmes

A considerable amount of money is spent for rural development activities under antipoverty programmes including the Swarnajayanti Gram Swarozgar Yojana (SGSY), special area development programmes, and others. These programmes have problems as follows.

1. There is considerable overlapping of different schemes and duplication of activities between schemes. There have been some efforts recently to reduce duplication.
2. Insufficient concern for creating durable assets.
3. Poor maintenance and management of such assets compound the above deficiencies.
4. Near total absence of any public accountability for these lapses.
5. Many of these programmes/schemes should be converged under one/two organizations. Area specific approach (ASA) could facilitate integration of these programmes. In such an approach, investment in land, water, and infrastructure (including minor irrigation, rural road), combined with extension and financial support for crops or other activities, are to be encouraged in each region on the basis of its potential as proper alternative.
6. The beneficiary-oriented schemes should be reorganized on the basis of potentiality of the crop and other activities, which can

be sustained in the area. Loan should be given to group of beneficiaries in order to ensure repayment of loan and utilization of assets. The recent approach of the SGSY programme can be effective provided credit and marketing facilities are available to the beneficiaries.

Improving monitoring mechanism in agriculture and rural development

There is near absence of monitoring of activities carried out in rural areas. There is an urgent need for strengthening monitoring and evaluation of the activities carried out under different schemes and policies.

Public sector, including state/local government bodies or NGOs, and autonomous quasi-public entities such as universities and research institutions, has to play a leading role in improving the development and management of common property resources (CPR) like water and, to some extent, land, such as gochar and other public land. These resources cannot be privatized completely. This should be managed on the basis of collective action framework. These institutions can play important role as monitors

There are other areas such as well irrigation, transport, marketing, and processing where private sector is dominant. Of late, NGOs have mobilized considerable amount of resources and are involved in a variety of rural development activities. There is need to monitor and regulate the activities carried out by private sector, as well as by NGOs. It is essential to have well-defined rules and regulations to check monopoly (as, for example, connivance among the traders may lead to distress sale of commodities), ensure fair trading practices, and define fair principle of sharing of common pool resource and sharing of cost and benefits of exploiting them.

There is need for periodic independent social audit of these institutions for ensuring accountability. Participatory processes such as Water Users Association, Watershed Development Committee (WDC), self-help groups (SHGs), and Joint Forest Management (JFM), already underway in the state, need to be stepped up.

There is need for joint liability provision in the construction of infrastructures, such as roads, school buildings, and other such structures, wherein contractors and government officials are involved. For instance, the contractor and the officials should be jointly responsible for maintaining the quality of work of the structure for certain prescribed years. In case of damage, the reserved funds meant for the project should be utilized.

Watchdog/social monitoring committees consisting of both government and independent personnel should be constituted at the block, tehsil, and district levels. These committees should monitor as well as receive information from the public as well grassroots institutions regarding the sub-standard work of the projects under construction or distribution in the areas assigned to them. The present practice of monitoring should be decentralized and information regarding the findings of the monitoring authorities should be widely publicized locally.

To sum up our discussion, there is a need to (a) promote public investment in infrastructure development; (b) increase adoptions of better and cost-reducing technology in those areas where its adoption is very low; (c) improve the efficiency of institutions associated with agriculture and rural development; and (d) bring major reforms in governance and institutions, particularly at the state and sub-regional levels.

References

Bhalla, G.S. and G. Singh. 2012. *Economic Liberalization and Indian Agriculture: A District-Level Study*. New Delhi: Sage Publication.

Dutt, G. and M. Ravallion. 1996. 'Why Have Some Indian States Done Better than Others at Reducing Rural Poverty?', World Bank Policy Research Paper, Policy Research Department, Poverty and Human Resources Division, World Bank, April.

Directorate of Agriculture and Food Production. Various years. *Odisha Agricultural Statistics*. Bhubaneswar, Odisha: Government of Odisha.

GoO. Various years. *Economic Survey 2011–12*. Bhubaneswar, Odisha: Planning and Coordination Department.

Gupta, H.S., S. Pal, A. Singh, and I. Sekar. 2012. 'Agricultural Growth and Diversification for Food Security', in S. Pal (ed.), *Agriculture for Inclusive Growth*, pp. 20–36. New Delhi: Indian Agricultural Research Institute.

Kumar, Anjani, Kumar Pramod, and A.N. Sharma. 2012. 'Crop Diversification in Eastern India: Status and Determinants', *Indian Journal of Agricultural Economics*, 67(4, October–December): 600–17.

Kurien, N.J. 2000. 'Widening Regional Disparities in India', *Economic and Political Weekly*, 35(7): 538–50.

Nayak, D. 2012. 'Changing Cropping Pattern, Diversification and Productivity: A Case of Orissa Agriculture', unpublished MPhil dissertation submitted to Centre for the Study of Regional Development, School of Social Sciences, Jawaharlal Nehru University, New Delhi.

Panda, M. 2009. 'Economic Development in Orissa: Growth without Inclusion', in R.K. Panda (ed.), *Orissa's Economic Development: Experiences and Expectations*, New Delhi: Serials Publications.

Pattnayak, M. and B.P. Nayak. 2008. 'Crop Diversification in Orissa: A Spatio-temporal Analysis', *Agricultural Situation in India*, November: 529–36.

Planning Commission. 2002. *Orissa Development Report*. New Delhi: Government of India.

Sarap, K. 1991. *Interlinked Agrarian Markets in Rural India*. New Delhi: Sage Publications.

Satapathy, S. 2012. 'Crop Diversification in Odisha: An Inter-district Analysis', *Insight*, 1(2): 10–26.

Sharma, H.R. 2011. 'Crop Diversification in Himachal Pradesh: Patterns, Determinants and Challenges', *Indian Journal of Agricultural Economics*, 66(1, January–March): 97–114.

2

Land Ownership and Tenancy in Odisha

Sarthak Gaurav and *Srijit Mishra**

Land is an important factor of production, a non-renewable resource, and a valuable asset. It has been at the centre of many economic thinking for centuries. For instance, the Physiocrats considered agriculture or the returns from land to be the only source of wealth and the Ricardian theory proposed the existence of an economic rent or surplus arising from differences in quality of land. Due to its inelastic supply, the allocation and valuation of a scarce and productive resource such as land becomes intrinsically dependent on its availability and quality. Entitlement of individuals to land and its distribution in a society is critical for society's growth and development; it is also the source of ubiquitous disputes over ownership and rights.

* The authors thank the (anonymous) peer reviewer, Baidyanath Misra, G.N. Rao, and V.M. Rao for their comments; the editors for giving them this opportunity; and to the participants of the symposium at Nabakrushna Choudhury Centre for Development Studies, Bhubaneswar, on 6–8 December 2012.

The distribution of landownership in India continues to be skewed and unequal. For instance, at the time of Independence, more than half of the land was owned by 7 per cent of the landowners, whereas 28 per cent of the marginal and sub-marginal landowners—who were the predominant landholding group in the country—owned only 6 per cent of the land (United National Development Programme; hereafter, UNDP 2008). In 2003, after 55 years of Independence, the inequalities in land distribution persist: nearly 35 per cent of land is owned by 4 per cent of the landowning households; marginal landowners constituting 80 per cent of the households own 23 per cent of the land; and independent of the landowning households, 10 per cent of the total households were landless (National Sample Survey Organisation; hereafter, NSSO 2006b).

Compared to the all-India average, the status of landownership is relatively better in Odisha for 2003: 5 per cent of households own 12 per cent of the land and 86 per cent of marginal holding households own 42 per cent of the land, and from all households, 10 per cent are landless. Consequently, inequality of landownership distribution or Gini coefficient is 0.76 for India and 0.69 for Odisha (Rawal 2008). Moreover, there is a trend of increasing marginalization of landholdings in the country, resulting in the proliferation of fragmented landholdings, which are economically unviable (Deshpande 2003).

To address the problem of inequitable distribution, there have been several land reform legislations in India, comprising four broad interventions: abolition of intermediaries; tenancy regulation to confer security of tenure; ceiling on landholdings to redistribute surplus land to the landless; and consolidation of landholdings for attaining economically viable parcels of land (Appu 1996; Behuria 1997; Sinha and Pushpendra 2000). These measures were driven by the states' obligation to have an equitable distribution of ownership and control over material resources in society, and to prevent the concentration of wealth and means of production in the hands of few (Hanstad and Nielsen 2009).[1]

[1] Keeping these equity concerns, we invoke the ideas of two major thinkers—Gandhi's talisman and Rawls' difference principle. Both identify with the well-being of the most vulnerable person for a just outcome.

One economic argument in favour of land reforms revolves around mitigating the frictions in land allocation, which could be due to either agency costs or imperfect property rights (see review in Ghatak and Roy 2007). From an efficiency perspective, the empirical observations of small farms tending to be more productive than the large farms, that is, the inverse farm-size productivity relationship (see review in Gaurav and Mishra 2015), and that owner-cultivated plots could be more productive than sharecroppers or the 'Marshallian inefficiency' of share contracts in general (for example, Shaban 1987) have been put forth as arguments for redistributing land to small holders and tenancy reforms respectively.

The evidence on the impact of land reforms in India is mixed. Ghatak (2007) and Ghatak and Roy (2007) observe that land and tenancy reforms show considerable variation across states in their impact on agricultural productivity. Besley and Burgess (2000) find land reforms, particularly the abolition of intermediaries and tenancy reforms, to have had significant impact on reducing poverty. With regard to agricultural productivity, they observe that land consolidation has had a positive impact whereas tenancy reforms had a negative impact. On the contrary, Banerjee, Gertler, and Ghatak (2002) find that tenancy reforms have had a positive effect on agricultural productivity in West Bengal. Banerjee and Iyer (2005) show that differences in property rights because of the varied revenue systems instituted by the British resulted in different economic outcomes much later: areas where property rights vested with property owners have significantly lower agricultural investments and productivity than where property rights were vested with cultivators.

In spite of the myriad legislations, there has been limited success in reforming the land tenure and revenue assessment systems. Lack of political will, absence of proper land records, weak revenue administration, and the inveterate diversity of revenue systems are formidable barriers to proper implementation of the legislation (Appu 1975, 1996; Government of India 2009; Mearns and Sinha 1999). In this backdrop, we discuss three aspects of land administration and land policy in Odisha. First, it inherits a diverse system of land administration and tenancy from the British that makes the implementation of land policy cumbersome. Second, like other states, it has brought in legislations to abolish tenancy (land leasing) and promulgated progressive land reforms. A ceiling on individual landholdings is in vogue: the current limit being 10 'standard acres': that is, 10 acres for irrigated land with two crops, 15 acres for irrigated land with one crop, and 30 to 45 acres in rain-fed areas. In addition, three major Acts govern land administration in the state and provide the basis for land survey and settlement, land consolidation/prevention of land fragmentation, and prevention of encroachment on government land respectively (Mearns and Sinha 1999). However, implementation has been weak and tenancy remains widespread (UNDP 2008). Third, in recent years, there has been a radical transformation of land use patterns in the state, with growth in the mining sector and real estate expansion brings in the trade-off between agricultural and non-agricultural land use. As indicated in Ambagudia (2010) and Government of India (2009), these have serious ramifications on land alienation. Further, such a development trajectory has adverse implications on livelihood concerns in contexts such as Kalinga Nagar (Mishra 2006; Mohanty 2012; Padhi and Panigrahi 2011), Niyamgiri hills (Government of India 2010; Sahu 2008), or Jagatsinghpur—POSCO (Mishra and Nayak 2011). Besides, land ownership for tribals is complicated and they face the threat of eviction in land that they have been tilling for ages (Landesa 2011; UNDP 2008).

The chapter is structured as follows. The section titled 'History of Land Ownership and Tenancy in Odisha' briefly discusses the history of landownership and tenancy in Odisha. The section that follows it, 'Trends in Ownership and Operational Holdings of Land by Size-class', discusses the patterns of landownership and operational holdings by size-class. The next section, 'Distribution of Landholdings across Caste and Gender', discusses changes in landownership and operational holdings by size-class of landholding among relevant social groups. The section 'Distribution and Characteristics of Landholdings across Districts' looks at the contemporary spatial pattern of operational holdings and tenancy across the districts of Odisha. The penultimate section titled 'Some Aspects of Tenancy' discusses some other aspects of tenancy at the aggregate level while the last section provides a conclusion.

History of land ownership and tenancy in Odisha

Pre-Independence period

Odisha has had a diverse history of landownership and tenancy. The Mughal conquest in 1576 and the subsequent secession to the Marathas in 1751 had implications for land administration during the British rule. Further, when Odisha (Orissa) was formed in 1936, it got areas from three presidencies. The Permanent Zamindari System (hereafter, zamindari) was the dominant system of tenancy under the Bengal Presidency (later with Bihar in 1912), constituting about 80 per cent of the total privately owned land prevalent in the coastal areas of Balasore, Cuttack, and Puri and also Anugul (Mearns and Sinha 1999; UNDP 2008).[2] The peasant-proprietor system of ryotwari was prevalent in southern regions such as Ganjam and Koraput that were under Madras Presidency (UNDP 2008),[3] whereas other peasant-proprietor systems like malguzari and gountia were prevalent in western regions such as Nuapada, Phulbani, and Sambalpur that were part of Central Provinces (Jena 1957). Besides, the gadjat areas comprising 24 former princely states exacted land revenue from the cultivators and as per the 'subsidiary alliances' with the British, they had freedom in their internal administration so long as they paid regular tributes (Government of Orissa 2004; Jena 1957; Pathy 1981). Although the princely states had separate land settlements and revenue regulations under the Government of India Act, 1935, there was no law to protect the interest of tenants (Pathy 1981).

To visualize the differences emerging from the diverse histories, a comparison of Cuttack and Sambalpur is illustrative (Padhi 1999).

[2] In zamindari, land was held as an independent property and revenue was assessed on the zamindars who organized their own collection, often involving many more layers of intermediaries. There was no tenurial security for the actual tiller (Mearns and Sinha 1999: 12). Fakir Mohan Senapati's classic novel *Cha Mana Atha Guntha* (Six Acres and a Third) is an apt depiction of this system.

[3] Koraput had a dual system of administration; magisterial powers were in the hands of the British, as part of Madras Presidency whereas revenue matters were under the Jeypore Raja (Mishra 1993, based on Bal 1880).

During the precolonial period, Cuttack under the Marathas had a centralized rent collection system, with the collector receiving a portion of the rent as remuneration whereas in Sambalpur, it was the village-chief, also a cultivator with rent-free land, who facilitated collection from other cultivators. Moreover, there also existed in Sambalpur the customary practice leading to periodic redistribution of land. In Cuttack, under zamindari, emerged a class of absentee property owners and agricultural production was more or less stagnant, whereas in Sambalpur, under ryotwari, the cultivating village-chiefs were enterprising who invested in agriculture. Concurrently, Cuttack also witnessed peasant stratification, pauperization, and distress sale of land while a land market was absent in Sambalpur. The similarities that one could identify were an increasing demographic pressure (greater in Cuttack), a common legal system, and an expanding market (non-land).

Post-Independence period

In contemporary Odisha, this history becomes relevant on two grounds (UNDP 2008). First, the diversity makes land revenue administration complex. For example, land records tend to be more complete and accurate in former ryotwari areas and are important documents in resolving land disputes even today. Second, it required legislations to reform the inequitable and diverse system of land revenue assessment that existed earlier. To confer security of tenure, there was abolition of intermediaries and ownership rights were given to tenants. Regulation of rent and de-concentration of landholdings through the fixation of land ceilings were some measures used to push forward the reforms.

Odisha, like other states, promulgated proactive land reforms legislations. Some important ones are Orissa Tenancy Protection Act, 1948, subsequently replaced by the Orissa Tenants Relief Act, 1955, which conferred occupancy rights to the entire state including the erstwhile princely states where tenants did not have such rights (Behuria 1997). A survey carried out by Misra and Jena (1957) in three villages of Balasore just after the Act was passed finds that the tenancy practice was substantial and tenants continued to offer 50 per cent of the produce as rent under sharecropping.

There was the abolition of the zamindari system vide The Orissa Estates Abolition Act of 1951, which aimed at abolishing all forms of intermediaries. The legislation vested all land rights with the state while allowing agrarian land below 33 acres to remain with the intermediaries for their own cultivation (Pathy 1981). Its implementation was completed by 1974 and a total of 4,25,687 estates and 9,301 village offices were abolished (Sahoo and Dharmalingam 2006).

Subsequently, the Orissa Land Reforms (OLR) Act of 1960, with further amendments aimed at granting permanent, heritable, and transferable rights in land to the tiller and ban on leasing-out except under special conditions. It also brought in certain tenancy reforms measures. According to the Act, the title to the land would be transferred to the cultivator if the cultivator operated the land continuously for 12 years or more and the cultivator is someone other than the owner. There was in place a ceiling on the rent at one-fourth of the gross produce and the ceiling on individual holdings was reduced to 20 standard acres in 1965 and 10 standard acres in 1972.

Also, worth mentioning is the Bhoodan-Gramdan Movement of voluntary land gifts by the landowners initiated in the early 1950s under the leadership of Acharya Vinoba Bhave, which is an important aspect of land distribution. The state passed the Orissa Bhoodan Yagna Act, 1953. Subsequently, Shri Nabakrushna Chaudhury, after resigning from the Chief Ministership, also joined the movement. As in the rest of the country, most land received were either not suitable for cultivation or were under disputed possession and the movement had fizzled out by 1975. However, the movement should not be remembered by the material achievement, rather by its intent and the response of voluntary action through peaceful means to address an important question around ownership and distribution of land (Parida 2010). From 1950–51 to 1990–91, under various schemes of land distribution, 16,30,984 acres (or 10.6 per cent of the total cultivated area) were distributed of which 56 per cent is wasteland; 36 per cent is Bhoodan-Gramdan land; and the remaining 8 per cent is ceiling surplus land (Sahoo and Dharmalingam 2006).

Further, The Orissa Prevention of Land Encroachment Act, 1972, with an amendment in 1982, aimed at prohibiting unauthorized encroachment of government land. However, the law allows for settlement of a standard acre of unobjectionable land with the landless and one-tenth of an acre for those without a homestead. During the same period, The Orissa Consolidation of Holding and Prevention of Fragmentation of Land Act, 1972 was promulgated to facilitate economies of scale, reduce transaction costs, and help enhance agricultural productivity. Though it was not meant to alter distribution, its implementation resulted in some discrimination against the vulnerable. The number of parcels per holding declined from an average of 6.4 in 1960–61 to 5 in 1981–82 indicating that some of it had started before the Act by individuals through the voluntary exchange of land in the market (Mohanty 1994).

Additionally, under the Fifth Schedule of the Indian Constitution, in scheduled areas, land belonging to a tribal cannot be transferred to a non-tribal without permission from the appropriate authority. Commensurate to this is the Orissa Scheduled Area Transfer of Immovable Property (by Scheduled Tribes) Regulation, 1956. As per this regulation, until 1999–2000, from the 86,999 cases of land alienation instituted, 84,721 had been disposed of and this benefited 46,439 tribal households through restoration and distribution of 42,497 acres of land (Panigrahi 2007). This law also allows for *suo moto* action by the collector of the district for restitution of alienated tribal lands. Section 22/23 of OLR Act also forbids land alienation from tribals in non-scheduled areas. The Orissa Prohibition of Alienation of Land Act, 1972 prohibits alienation of land by certain persons (companies or corporate bodies). The central government legislated Panchayats (Extension to Scheduled Areas) Act (or PESA) of 1996 will protect vulnerable communities like tribals from exploitation and preserve their land endowment for their economic empowerment by extending the provisions of the 73rd and 74th Constitutional Amendment to scheduled areas. Following PESA, the *gram sabha* (village council) was entrusted with wide-ranging powers starting from consultation on land acquisition to that of ownership over minor forest products and leasing of minor minerals (Vasundahara 2002). Despite these protections, there has been widespread land alienation in these areas under conditions of economic and social duress (Patnaik and Patnaik 2011).

The Scheduled Tribes and Other Traditional Forest Dwellers (Recognition of Forest Rights) Act (FRA), 2006, provides tenurial and access rights to tribals dependent on forests for their livelihood.

Under this, till August 2011 there were 4,78,990 individual claims received by gram sabhas, of which 84 per cent of the cases were approved, but after subsequent scrutiny at the sub-division and district levels, about 59 per cent of original claimants (2,83,029 cases) had been of distributed land; the community claims have more stringent procedures and have not met with much success (Panigrahi and Balabantaray 2012).

Despite several legislations, implementation has been tardy and formidable obstacles continue (Ambagudia 2010; Mearns and Sinha 1999; Padhi and Panigrahi 2011; Sahoo and Daharmalingam 2006; UNDP 2008). What is much more worrying is the connivance of the revenue officials with property owners to delete entries in the record of rights (ROR) that dispossess the assignees their right over the ceiling surplus land that they have been cultivating for decades indicating a reversal of the earlier successes (Sinha 2012). Having discussed the history of the tenurial arrangements and land administration in the state, we now discuss the trends in distribution of land ownership and operational landholdings by size-class based on an analysis of secondary data from various published sources.

Trends in ownership and operational holdings of land by size-class

Using data from National Sample Surveys (NSS), Sharma (1994) shows that between 1953–54 and 1961–62, there was a general decline in the top concentration of area owned associated with an increase in concentration at the middle 30 per cent and 40 per cent levels in most Indian states including Odisha. Further, the share of area owned by the bottom half of the land ownership hierarchy remained practically unchanged in a majority of the states and Odisha was not an exception. However, between 1961–62 and 1971–72, only three states, namely, Jammu and Kashmir, Rajasthan, and Odisha recorded decline in the top concentration at various levels along with concomitant increase in the bottom and middle levels. During 1953–54 to 1971–72, there was a secular decline in the inequality in land ownership in the state, with the Gini coefficient including landless households falling from 0.68 to 0.61 while the Gini coefficient excluding the landless declining from 0.64 to 0.57. This could have been because of the policies and their implementation during those years, or under reporting by owners fearing action by the government or because of land partitioning due to increase in population.

The trends in ownership identified by size-class for rural Odisha from 1970s are indicated in Table 2.1. It shows that the proportion of landless from 1971–72 to 2003 have remained around 10 per cent. The average area owned has been declining over the years and in 2003 for Odisha, it was 0.48 hectare (with inclusion of the landless) and 0.53 hectare (excluding the landless); for India, the figures are 0.73 hectare and 0.81 hectare respectively. The continuing landlessness of one-tenth of the households continues to be a matter of concern and raises eyebrows on the success of land distribution programmes.

One also observes a marginalization of ownership with the proportion of marginal and smallholdings increasing and that of semi-medium, medium, and large holdings declining. For the preponderant marginal owners, there has been an increase in number as well as area owned, and this has been much faster in Odisha than the all-India average. The share of the marginal owners in area owned has more than doubled while their share in numbers has increased by a quarter. For this group, there has been an increase both in absolute as well as relative terms. However, they are the only group that has registered an increase in numeracy.

Small owners share in number of households declined by more than two-fifths but their share of area remained more or less the same. For the semi-medium group, their share in numbers fell by half while the share of area fell by less than one-fourth. In the medium group, the share of numbers has fallen by one-third while share in area owned has fallen by half during the period. With regard to large owners, the share of number fell by three-fourths while the share of area owned has also fallen by two-thirds during the same period. In addition to increasing marginalization, one also observes a reduction in inequality, as measured through Gini coefficient (also see the Lorenz curves in Figure 2.1).

The distribution of operational holdings, Table 2.2, based on the same NSS rounds (as that of Table 2.1) as also for agricultural censuses conducted independently the trend towards marginalization is reiterated. This is somewhat different from the 1980s because then one did observe a shift from large to semi-medium and medium

Table 2.1 Distribution of ownership of holdings by size-class in rural areas of Odisha and India, 1971–72 to 2003

Year	Proportion of households (%)							Proportion of area (%)							Avg. area	Gini
	LL	MA	SL	SM	ME	LA	AL	LL	MA	SL	SM	ME	LA	AL		
Odisha																
1971–72	10.6	61.6	16.2	8.1	3.1	0.4	100.0	0.0	20.5	27.0	25.9	20.7	6.0	100.0	NA	0.61
1982	7.7	61.0	19.2	8.6	3.2	0.3	100.0	0.0	19.9	29.7	25.0	19.5	5.8	100.0	NA	0.58
1992	13.8	64.8	12.4	6.3	2.1	0.1	100.0	0.0	26.4	27.2	26.0	18.1	2.4	100.0	0.97	0.61
2003	9.6	77.3	8.8	3.3	0.8	0.1	100.0	0.0	41.5	27.1	19.7	10.0	1.8	100.0	0.48	0.51
India																
1971–72	9.6	56.6	14.0	10.8	7.1	1.9	100.0	0.0	9.8	14.7	21.9	30.7	22.9	100.0	NA	0.70
1982	11.3	59.1	13.0	9.6	5.7	1.3	100.0	0.0	12.2	16.5	23.6	29.8	18.1	100.0	NA	0.70
1992	11.3	63.8	11.9	8.2	4.0	0.8	100.0	0.0	16.9	18.6	24.6	26.1	13.8	100.0	1.19	0.68
2003	10.0	71.6	9.7	5.4	2.7	0.5	100.0	0.0	23.1	20.4	22.0	23.1	11.6	100.0	0.73	0.66

Source: NSSO (2006b: Statements 4 and 5).

Note: LL, MA, SL, SM, LA, and AL denote landless (up to 0.002 hectare), marginal (0.002–1 hectare), small (1–2 hectare), semi-medium (2–4 hectare), medium (4–10 hectare), large (>10 hectare), and all households, respectively. Avg. area denotes the average area in hectares and has been computed after including the landless. For 2003, the average area owned after excluding the landless is 0.534 hectare for Odisha and 0.806 hectare for India. NA denotes not available. For Gini calculation, we use the method suggested by Nagar and Das (1983).

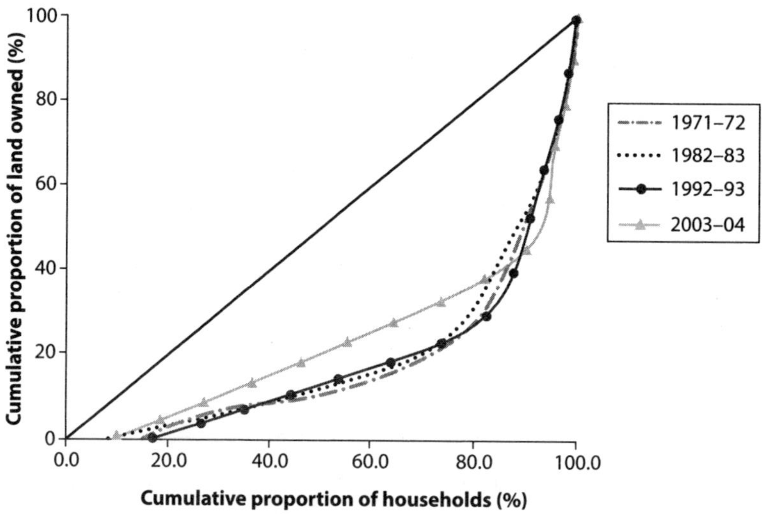

Figure 2.1 Lorenz curve of land ownership distribution (including landless) in Odisha, 1971–72 to 2003.

Source: Authors' representation using data in Table 2.1.

holdings who had a large share of area under them (see also Mohanty 1994; Sharma 1994).

The average size of operational holdings has registered a secular decline (Government of India 2012). In Odisha, from 2004–05 to 2010–11, the total number of holdings increased by 7.14 per cent from 43.56 lakh to 46.67 lakh whereas the total area decreased by 3.14 per cent from 50.19 lakh hectare to 48.62 lakh hectare. Consequently, the average area per holding has reduced from 1.15 hectare to 1.04 hectare, which is lower than the all-India average area per holding figures of 1.23 hectare and 1.16 hectare for 2004–05 and 2010–11 respectively. Further, in Odisha 72 per cent are marginal holdings, which is an increase of more than 12 percentage points from the previous census; this shift is not only higher than India but across all states/union territories (hereafter, states). In fact, the states with the maximum shift after Odisha are Puducherry and Mizoram, where the increase in marginal holdings was less than seven percentage points; in most other states, this change was in the range of two percentage points. These marginal holders operate only 40 per cent of the area. One out of five holdings is operated by smallholders who

Table 2.2 Distribution of operational holdings by size-class in rural Odisha, 1970–71 to 2010–11

State	Year	Proportion of holdings (%)						Proportion of area (%)						Avg Area	Gini
		MA	SL	SM	ME	LA	AL	MA	SL	SM	ME	LA	AL		
NSS Odisha															
	1970–71	68.9	18.1	9.0	3.5	0.4	100.0	20.5	27.0	25.9	20.7	6.0	100.0	NA	0.56
	1981–82	66.1	20.8	9.3	3.4	0.4	100.0	19.9	29.7	25.0	19.5	5.8	100.0	NA	0.54
	1991–92	75.2	14.4	7.3	2.4	0.1	100.0	26.4	27.2	26.0	18.1	2.4	100.0	1.13	0.54
	2002–03	85.5	9.7	3.7	1.0	0.1	100.0	41.5	27.1	19.7	10.0	1.8	100.0	0.72	0.56
Odisha Agricultural census															
	1970–71	40.5	30.9	18.7	8.5	1.1	100.0	10.7	23.8	29.3	25.0	11.3	100.0	1.98	0.70
	1980–81	46.8	26.7	18.3	7.2	0.9	100.0	15.2	22.5	29.9	25.0	7.4	100.0	1.59	0.46
	1990–91	53.6	26.3	15.1	4.7	0.4	100.0	19.7	27.0	29.6	19.1	4.6	100.0	1.34	0.45
	2000–01	56.4	27.4	12.3	3.6	0.3	100.0	23.0	30.0	26.0	16.0	4.0	100.0	1.25	0.43
	2005–06	59.6	26.5	10.8	2.7	0.3	100.0	26.7	31.6	24.9	13.1	3.6	100.0	1.15	0.41
	2010–11	72.2	19.7	6.7	1.4	0.1	100.0	39.5	30.8	18.9	7.8	2.9	100.0	1.04	0.36
India															
	1970–71	51.0	18.9	15.0	11.2	3.9	100.0	8.9	11.9	18.5	29.8	39.0	100.0	2.28	0.62
	2005–06	64.8	18.5	10.9	4.9	0.9	100.0	20.2	20.9	23.9	23.1	11.8	100.0	1.23	0.55
	2010–11	67.0	17.9	10.1	4.3	0.7	100.0	22.2	22.1	23.6	21.2	10.9	100.0	1.16	0.54

Sources: Government of India (2012), Mohanty (1994), NSSO (1993, 2006a), http://agcensus.dacnet.nic.in/ and http://www.indiastat.com/.

Note: See the note appended to Table 2.1. For MA, the range is (0–1 hectare).

operate three-tenths of the area. One out of fifteen is semi-medium holders who operate nearly two-fifths of the area. The remaining are medium and large holders, operating a little over a tenth of the area. This reiterates the preponderance of marginal and smallholdings.

Marginalization assumes significance in the face of the growing empirical evidence on the crisis in Indian agriculture and agrarian distress (Mishra 2009; Mishra and Reddy 2011; Reddy and Mishra 2009). The Situation Assessment Survey of farmers also canvassed in the 59th round NSS of 2003 shows that income for marginal, small, and semi-medium households was lower than their expenditure. There is a paradox here because productivity for these households is higher (Gaurav and Mishra 2015) while absolute returns and overall income are not enough for livelihood sustenance. Given the dominance of agriculture in the state's economy and society, these could pose serious challenges for policymakers in the near future.[4]

One reason for the decline in the size of holdings and an increase in the number of holdings is attributed to the increasing population pressure and the resulting partitioning land. Another reason is the public policy interventions through the distribution of ceiling surplus land to the landless. This would have also contributed to the decline of medium and large holdings at least at the ownership level and perhaps at the operational holding level. Till 2007, the area declared as ceiling surplus land was 1,89,900 acres, of which 1,67,549 acres were taken possession by the state and 1,59,384 acres were distributed among 1,42,616 persons (of which 34.2 per cent were scheduled castes, 37.1 per cent were scheduled tribes, and the remaining were others). Note that distribution through ceiling surplus land is less than 10 per cent of the total land distribution (Sahoo and Dharmalingam 2006). Also, there could be instances where households have partitioned the land legally to retain larger land sizes within the family or reported some *benami* transactions (also see Mohanty 1994). In addition, there have

[4] This may explain low reductions in incidence of poverty for rural Odisha from 63 per cent in 1993–94 to 60.8 per cent in 2004–05. But, the substantially higher reduction to 39.2 per cent in 2009–10 throws up issues of lag effect, other interventions by the government, and that the poverty line does not include health and education requirements among others, which are beyond the scope of the current study.

been some reversals in recent years and the recipients are not in de facto possession of these (Sinha 2012). The deviations and reversals indicate adverse implication on the poor and vulnerable groups. Now, we take up an analysis of land distribution across caste and gender.

Distribution of landholdings across caste and gender

Social group patterns

To analyse the distribution of landholdings across caste, we rely on the latest available data on ownership holdings of 2003 (Table 2.3) from NSS (NSSO 2006b) and operational holdings of 2010–11 (Table 2.4) from the agricultural census (Government of India 2012). Table 2.3 shows that the proportion of landless among the scheduled castes (SCs) and scheduled tribes (STs) is relatively higher. Moreover, the SCs also have a relatively higher proportion of marginal households (82 per cent), a relatively lower proportion of small owner households, and an average area (0.26 hectare) that is the lowest; the quality of their land owned is also likely to be lower. At the same time, medium and large holders not only seem to be doing better among SCs vis-a-vis STs, their average area is also higher.

Compared with other groups, the STs have a relatively lower proportion of marginal holding owners (68 per cent) and an average land size that is equal to that of the other backward classes (OBCs) and others. However, note that the STs primarily reside in scheduled areas that are less densely populated and with relatively lower quality land when it comes to returns from cultivation. The OBCs have a relatively higher proportion of large owners (0.2 per cent among all OBC households and almost all large owners are OBCs) and the lowest incidence of landlessness when compared with other groups. In terms of inequality calculated using Gini, one observes a social gradient with the SCs having the lowest inequality, followed by the STs, OBCs, and others.

The distribution of operational landholdings given in Table 2.4 also shows similar patterns across caste. The SCs continue to have the highest proportion of marginal holdings, while STs had a relatively lower incidence of marginal holdings and higher incidence of small as also semi-medium holdings. Others (which include OBCs, as they cannot be a separate category for agricultural census data) have a relatively higher incidence among marginal holdings.

Table 2.3 Distribution of ownership of holdings by size-class in rural Odisha across social groups, 2003

Sub-group	Proportion of households (%)							Proportion of area (%)							Avg. area	Gini
	LL	MA	SL	SM	ME	LA	AL	LL	MA	SL	SM	ME	LA	AL		
SC	13.2	81.7	3.6	1.1	0.3	<0.1	100.0	0.1	62.6	17.7	10.7	7.1	1.8	100.0	0.26	0.41
ST	13.6	68.2	13.3	4.5	0.4	0.0	100.0	0.0	41.1	33.3	21.7	3.8	0.0	100.0	0.54	0.48
OBC	5.7	79.0	10.3	3.4	1.4	0.2	100.0	0.0	39.9	25.9	15.9	13.8	4.5	100.0	0.54	0.50
Others	7.0	75.8	9.4	6.5	1.3	0.0	100.0	0.0	31.7	23.3	31.0	14.0	0.0	100.0	0.54	0.56
Total	9.5	76.1	9.7	3.7	0.9	0.1	100.0	0.0	41.3	26.8	19.5	9.8	2.5	100.0	0.48	0.50

Source: NSSO (2006b: Table 1R).

Note: See Table 2.1. SC, ST, and OBC denote scheduled caste, scheduled tribe, and other backward classes respectively.

Table 2.4 Distribution of operational holdings by size-class in rural Odisha across social groups, 2010–11

Sub-group	Proportion of holdings (%)						Proportion of area (%)						Avg. area	Gini
	MA	SL	SM	ME	LA	AL	MA	SL	SM	ME	LA	AL		
SC	80.4	15.4	3.8	0.5	0.0	100.0	51.5	29.9	13.3	3.3	2.1	100.0	0.82	0.31
ST	66.6	23.6	8.3	1.5	0.1	100.0	36.2	33.7	21.4	7.6	1.2	100.0	1.14	0.35
Others	73.0	18.7	6.6	1.6	0.0	100.0	39.0	29.3	18.6	9.0	4.2	100.0	1.05	0.38
Total	72.2	19.7	6.7	1.4	0.1	100.0	39.5	30.8	18.9	7.8	3.2	100.0	1.16	0.36

Source: Government of India (2012).

Note: See tables 2.1, 2.2 (for MA range), and 2.3. Others in this table includes OBCs and 'others' of Table 2.3 because such bifurcation is not possible with agricultural census data.

With regard to STs, a matter of concern raised earlier is the increasing pace of land alienation and land acquisition in the name of development (Mohanty 2012; Padhi and Panigrahi 2011; UNDP 2008). Identifying the complexity of land administration in the state, particularly in tribal areas, a report by UNDP (2008: 14) observes:

> Tribals living in forest areas are yet to receive legal entitlement over land in many areas they have been cultivating for decades. They face the constant threat of eviction and dispossession ... In tribal areas, concentration of land in a few hands, illegal possession of land by the elite, passing off irrigated land as unirrigated in land records and use of agricultural land for commercial purposes are some of the stumbling blocks in the individual's rightful access to land.

Gender-wise scenario

Given the patrilineal structure of Indian society in general, increasing women's access to land was legislated in the Amendment (Act) of 2005 to revise the Hindu Succession Act, 1956 which provides for daughters, widow, and mother of a Hindu man dying intestate to inherit property equally with his sons. In practice, however, there are significant gaps between women's legal rights and their actual ownership of land, and between the limited ownership enjoyed by women and their effective control of land (Agarwal 1994).

It is noteworthy that the OLR Act of 1960 is silent on whether the devolution of tenancy land should be based on personal law or other order of devolution (Mearns and Sinha 1999). Further, gender inequalities also relate to the fixing of land ceilings because the definition of the family implicitly excludes women and recognizing only men's independent land rights explicitly excludes women. In some respects, the Act is progressive, as it allows land gifted to a daughter on her marriage to be excluded from the ceiling area of the father. Ostensibly, this is to encourage land transfers to daughters, but it rarely happens in practice. Generally, women do not have *patta* or record of rights (ROR) in their own names, and it is recorded in the name of the husband; even when the patta is in their names, their husbands are the de facto owners. Field evidences indicate that women were willing to have joint pattas with their husbands to prevent indiscriminate sale without their consultation and to claim a share in the eventuality of divorce.

In 2010–11, for India as a whole, 12.8 per cent of the operational holdings and 10.4 per cent of the operated area were operated by females while for Odisha the figures are much lower at 3.3 per cent of the operational holdings and 3 per cent of the operated area. The distribution of operational holdings by gender (Table 2.5) indicates that there is not much difference across them except relatively slightly greater marginalization and relatively higher inequality among females.

The inveterate social arrangements that prevent women from asserting their rights over land can be best understood by the comment by Mearns and Sinha (1999: 16):

> While women would like to have an equal share in their parental land, they are aware of the cultural constraints that are difficult to overcome. For instance, if a woman demands a share of her deceased father's land, she often has to sever all relations with her brothers. There is usually a strong disincentive for many women not to press claims on parental property. This is because culturally a woman is not expected to claim any property from her parents/brothers. If she is unmarried and/or is in a financially difficult situation, she might get some land if the brothers are sympathetic and willing to share. Thus, there are strong pressures on women to cede their legal rights to their brothers, reinforced by social stigma, seclusion practices, and other sanctions. Given the lack of alternatives, women tend to be dependent on their brothers for economic and social support in the event of widowhood or marital break-up.

Next, we take up a district-wise analysis of landholding patterns in Odisha.

Distribution and characteristics of landholdings across districts

District-wise landholdings

In our district-wise analysis, we make use of agricultural census data and the latest available data for this purpose is that for 2005–06 (Table 2.6). The districts where marginal holdings are less than half of the total holdings (in ascending order) are Malkangiri, Kalahandi, Sambalpur, Nuapada, Baragarh, Koraput, Dhenkanal, and Deogarh. These are largely districts from western Odisha in and around Sambalpur; including some predominantly tribal districts of southern Odisha and Dhenkanal, which is centrally located.

Table 2.5 Distribution of operational holdings by size-class in rural Odisha across gender, 2010–11

Sub-group	Proportion of holdings (%)						Proportion of area (%)						Avg. area	Gini
	MA	SL	SM	ME	LA	AL	MA	SL	SM	ME	LA	AL		
Male	72.1	19.7	6.7	1.4	0.1	100.0	39.9	31.2	19.1	7.9	1.9	100.0	1.18	0.36
Female	74.7	17.5	5.8	1.3	0.3	100.0	41.2	29.7	18.2	8.1	2.0	100.0	0.94	0.37
Total	72.2	19.7	6.7	1.4	0.1	100.0	39.5	30.8	18.9	7.8	3.2	100.0	1.16	0.36

Source: Government of India (2012).

Note: See Table 2.1, and Table 2.2 (for MA range).

Table 2.6 Distribution of operational holdings by size-class in rural Odisha across districts, 2005–06

District	Proportion of holdings (%)						Proportion of area (%)						Avg. area	Gini
	MA	SL	SM	ME	LA	AL	MA	SL	SM	ME	LA	AL		
Anugul	59.8	28.9	9.0	2.1	0.2	100.0	28.2	34.9	22.0	12.6	2.3	100.0	1.08	0.39
Balasore	74.9	18.5	5.6	0.9	0.1	100.0	42.6	31.5	18.0	6.2	1.6	100.0	0.84	0.35
Baragarh	45.4	32.0	16.9	4.9	0.7	100.0	14.8	27.5	29.3	22.3	6.2	100.0	1.50	0.46
Boudh	55.7	28.3	13.2	2.6	0.3	100.0	24.9	31.4	27.4	13.3	3.1	100.0	1.26	0.39
Bhadrak	69.2	21.3	8.1	1.4	0.1	100.0	35.7	32.1	22.7	8.4	1.1	100.0	0.89	0.38
Bolangir	58.8	24.5	12.2	3.9	0.5	100.0	24.3	26.2	24.6	19.1	5.8	100.0	1.36	0.44
Cuttack	65.2	25.5	8.2	1.0	0.1	100.0	32.8	36.4	22.5	6.2	2.0	100.0	0.92	0.37
Deogarh	49.2	33.3	14.7	2.6	0.2	100.0	20.9	34.5	30.9	11.5	2.1	100.0	1.34	0.38
Dhenkanal	48.5	36.4	12.8	2.1	0.1	100.0	22.1	40.2	26.1	9.9	1.8	100.0	1.34	0.35
Gajapati	67.5	24.0	7.4	1.0	0.1	100.0	37.7	34.8	20.4	6.4	0.9	100.0	0.96	0.34
Ganjam	65.4	22.6	9.7	2.1	0.3	100.0	28.9	29.5	25.1	12.4	4.0	100.0	0.97	0.43
Jagatsingpur	66.9	25.4	7.0	0.7	0.0	100.0	37.0	38.1	20.3	4.2	0.3	100.0	0.88	0.33
Jajpur	63.4	25.6	9.2	1.7	0.1	100.0	32.8	33.7	22.5	9.0	2.0	100.0	1.12	0.36
Jharsuguda	54.5	29.3	12.2	3.3	0.7	100.0	20.8	29.7	25.0	16.4	8.1	100.0	1.36	0.45
Kalahandi	43.2	32.7	17.8	5.6	0.8	100.0	14.2	26.9	29.8	22.7	6.4	100.0	1.52	0.45
Kendrapada	68.3	22.3	8.2	1.3	0.0	100.0	36.8	32.6	22.5	7.8	0.3	100.0	0.91	0.36
Keonjhar	61.2	29.4	7.7	1.5	0.1	100.0	31.2	38.2	19.6	8.8	2.3	100.0	1.04	0.36
Khurda	67.1	23.1	8.1	1.6	0.2	100.0	32.4	31.4	21.4	8.9	5.8	100.0	0.98	0.41
Koraput	46.8	32.5	16.0	4.2	0.5	100.0	18.7	29.9	28.0	17.3	6.2	100.0	1.53	0.41

(*Cont'd.*)

Table 2.6 *(Cont'd.)*

District	Proportion of holdings (%)						Proportion of area (%)						Avg. area	Gini
	MA	SL	SM	ME	LA	AL	MA	SL	SM	ME	LA	AL		
Malkangiri	43.1	37.7	17.3	1.8	0.1	100.0	20.2	38.9	32.4	7.5	0.9	100.0	1.31	0.32
Mayurbhanj	61.0	27.1	9.7	2.0	0.1	100.0	28.2	34.4	24.3	11.3	1.7	100.0	1.08	0.40
Nabrangpur	61.0	24.6	11.9	2.4	0.2	100.0	30.3	29.2	26.6	11.7	2.1	100.0	1.25	0.37
Nayagarh	66.2	23.2	8.8	1.6	0.2	100.0	32.1	31.9	23.0	9.8	3.3	100.0	1.06	0.40
Nuapada	45.4	34.8	15.9	3.6	0.3	100.0	17.4	32.9	30.8	16.0	3.0	100.0	1.37	0.41
Phulbani	60.7	26.3	10.8	2.1	0.1	100.0	28.9	33.1	25.7	10.8	1.5	100.0	1.10	0.38
Puri	76.4	17.4	5.3	0.9	0.1	100.0	44.6	29.8	17.2	6.5	1.9	100.0	0.78	0.35
Rayagada	53.6	28.4	14.0	3.5	0.5	100.0	23.4	28.7	26.2	16.8	4.8	100.0	1.41	0.41
Sambalpur	44.5	30.3	17.5	6.2	1.4	100.0	13.6	23.6	26.1	24.1	12.6	100.0	1.90	0.55
Sonepur	62.4	23.8	10.7	2.9	0.3	100.0	27.0	29.0	25.0	15.8	3.2	100.0	1.11	0.43
Sundargarh	52.6	31.0	13.4	2.8	0.2	100.0	23.7	33.4	27.1	12.5	3.2	100.0	1.32	0.38
Total	59.6	26.5	10.8	2.7	0.3	100.0	26.7	31.6	24.9	13.1	3.6	100.0	1.15	0.41

Source: Available at http://agcensus.dacnet.nic.in/ (last accessed on 22 January 2016).

Note: See Tables 2.1, and Table 2.2 (for range of MA).

The districts where marginal holdings are more than 65 per cent of the total holdings (in ascending order) are Cuttack, Ganjam, Nayagarh, Jagatsingpur, Khurda, Gajapati, Kendrapada, Bhadrak, Balasore, and Puri. This set of districts are largely coastal and those that are not (particularly, Nayagarh and Khurda) were part of the undivided coastal district of Puri. In line with our earlier discussion on differences in land administration between the cases of Sambalpur and Cuttack, we will refer to this distinction as that between Sambalpur and Cuttack, broadly speaking. The districts that are between these two broad groupings are all non-coastal, spread across from the north to the south.

It follows that the Sambalpur areas have higher proportion of small and higher size holdings and their average size of area operated is also higher. Within this region, the agriculturally prosperous districts of Bargarh, Kalahandi, and Sambalpur have higher inequality of landholdings.[5]

In the coastal districts, the inequalities are relatively lower except for Ganjam, Nayagarh, and Khurda. The higher inequalities in both the groups are because of higher proportion of households with relatively higher proportion of area in the medium and large holdings. While comparing the lower average area and lower inequality of the coastal regions with the tribal and hilly regions, we should be cautious because the quality of land as well as the returns to cultivation is lower in tribal areas. Nevertheless, they are agriculturally disadvantaged when compared with the better-off regions of Sambalpur. Now, we propose to analyse the district-wise characteristics of holdings.

Tenancy characteristics of landholdings across districts

The tenancy characteristics of holdings implies whether they are wholly owned by the cultivator or are wholly leased-in or are wholly otherwise operated (they are neither owned nor leased-in like cultivation in lands without ROR) or are partly owned/leased/otherwise operated (hereafter, partly). The latter is a combination of any of the two from the earlier three categories.

Table 2.7 shows that Cuttack is with the least proportion of wholly owned holdings (less than 65 per cent) and just above Phulbani. This

[5] The popular image of Kalahandi being poor was largely on account of what is now Nuapada; of course, relatively speaking.

Table 2.7 Distribution of operational holdings by their tenancy characteristics in rural Odisha across districts, 2005–06

District	Proportion of holdings (%)					Proportion of area (%)				
	WO	LI	OO	PO	All	WO	LI	OO	PO	All
Anugul	86.9	0.7	0.2	12.2	100.0	86.2	0.6	0.1	13.1	100.0
Balasore	75.3	6.5	0.1	18.2	100.0	75.4	4.1	0.0	20.5	100.0
Baragarh	94.2	0.6	0.6	4.6	100.0	93.4	0.3	0.3	6.0	100.0
Boudh	91.5	1.8	0.7	6.0	100.0	91.3	1.1	0.3	7.3	100.0
Bhadrak	83.4	3.5	0.1	13.0	100.0	80.3	2.8	0.1	16.9	100.0
Bolangir	98.7	0.2	0.1	1.0	100.0	98.0	0.1	0.1	1.8	100.0
Cuttack	64.9	10.3	0.3	24.6	100.0	62.7	8.0	0.2	29.0	100.0
Deogarh	74.1	0.1	2.0	23.8	100.0	76.3	0.0	1.3	22.3	100.0
Dhenkanal	77.1	2.9	0.4	19.6	100.0	77.5	2.6	0.3	19.6	100.0
Gajapati	74.8	0.7	2.1	22.4	100.0	71.2	0.6	1.7	26.4	100.0
Ganjam	94.6	1.5	0.2	3.7	100.0	92.7	1.3	0.1	5.9	100.0
Jagatsingpur	79.4	6.3	0.1	14.3	100.0	77.6	5.5	0.1	16.9	100.0
Jajpur	73.9	4.5	0.0	21.6	100.0	73.3	3.2	0.0	23.5	100.0
Jharsuguda	84.8	2.2	0.7	12.3	100.0	85.6	1.0	0.3	13.2	100.0
Kalahandi	95.2	0.2	0.9	3.7	100.0	93.8	0.2	0.5	5.5	100.0
Kendrapada	83.2	5.5	0.0	11.3	100.0	80.9	4.2	0.0	14.9	100.0
Keonjhar	74.4	1.3	1.7	22.6	100.0	74.5	0.7	0.8	24.0	100.0
Khurda	84.5	6.3	0.1	9.1	100.0	84.3	4.8	0.1	10.8	100.0
Koraput	83.1	0.3	2.5	14.0	100.0	82.9	0.2	1.6	15.3	100.0

Malkangiri	81.0	0.3	3.5	15.2	100.0	79.2	0.2	2.0	18.6	100.0
Mayurbhanj	83.1	2.0	0.3	14.7	100.0	83.0	1.0	0.1	15.9	100.0
Nabrangpur	75.1	0.3	7.8	16.8	100.0	70.3	0.4	7.2	22.2	100.0
Nayagarh	87.4	2.4	0.2	10.0	100.0	87.5	1.6	0.1	10.8	100.0
Nuapada	99.5	0.0	0.2	0.3	100.0	99.4	0.0	0.2	0.3	100.0
Phulbani	61.1	0.3	3.7	34.9	100.0	58.2	0.1	2.0	39.8	100.0
Puri	86.3	3.1	0.0	10.6	100.0	85.0	2.1	0.0	12.8	100.0
Rayagada	89.7	0.4	2.4	7.4	100.0	90.0	0.3	1.3	8.4	100.0
Sambalpur	79.0	1.7	1.8	17.4	100.0	78.6	0.9	0.9	19.6	100.0
Sonepur	98.2	0.1	0.2	1.5	100.0	98.1	0.1	0.1	1.7	100.0
Sundargarh	90.1	0.3	0.6	9.0	100.0	89.1	0.2	0.3	10.5	100.0
Total	84.2	2.3	1.0	12.5	100.0	83.9	1.4	0.7	14.0	100.0

Source: Available at http://agcensus.dacnet.nic.in/.

Note: WO, LI, OO, and PO denote wholly owned, leased-in, otherwise operated, and partly owned.

is also the district with the highest proportion of holdings that are wholly leased-in and the second highest in the proportion where part of the holding is likely to be leased-in. The district of Cuttack is also the one with the highest proportion of holdings that are wholly leased-in (more than one-tenth) and the second highest in the proportion where part of the holding is likely to be leased-in. In fact, all the coastal districts are the one with relatively higher proportion of holdings that are leased-in (these, arranged in ascending order, are Puri, Bhadrak, Jajpur, Kendrapada, Jagatsingpur, Khurda, Balasore, and Cuttack).

Even for the partly owned/leased-in/otherwise operated, one observes that the coastal districts (including Ganjam) have more than 50 per cent of the area under this category as leased-in. In the coastal districts, the share of holdings under the otherwise operated category as also its share of area either independently or under the partly category is negligible. Some of the non-coastal districts, particularly tribal districts, have a relatively higher proportion of holdings under otherwise operated category and a higher share of area (in the range of 20 to 50 per cent) under the partly category. This could reflect a scenario of poor ROR in scheduled areas, as indicated earlier. We will now elaborate on some broad aspects of tenancy in Odisha in recent years.

Some aspects of tenancy

The agricultural census of 2005–06 indicates that more than four-fifths of the number of holdings and area operated are fully owned and from the partly operated category, more than half of the area is owned. This gives the impression that extent of tenancy is miniscule. However, one should keep in mind that tenancy could be underreported or could have taken a different form because of the legislations that have made tenancy illegal. Notwithstanding its underreporting, some recent aspects of tenancy are collected in the 59th round of NSS in 2003 for the agricultural year of 2002–03.

Over time, from 1981–82 to 2002–03 the proportion of number as also area of operational holdings under tenancy has increased in Odisha while it has reduced for all-India (Table 2.8). Across 15 major states, Odisha is among the few where there has been an increase, the

Table 2.8 Proportion of tenant holdings and operated area leased-in for Odisha and India, 1981–82 to 2002–03

Year	Proportion of tenant holdings (%)		Proportion of leased-in area (%)	
	Odisha	India	Odisha	India
1981–82	18.2	15.2	9.9	7.2
1991–92	16.9	11.0	9.5	8.3
2002–03	19.4	9.9	13.0	6.5

Source: NSSO (2006a).
Note: Data for 2002–03 pertains to the Kharif season.

others being Gujarat (for both number and area) and Kerala (for area only). Further, Odisha has the highest incidence in the number of operational holdings under tenancy and the third highest incidence (after Punjab and Haryana where most of it is reverse tenancy) in terms of the area of operational holdings under tenancy.

One also observes that the households reporting leasing-out is much lower than those reporting leasing-in (Table 2.9). This could be because those who lease-out do not reside in rural areas and are not likely to be surveyed or because they underreport, as such activities do not have a legal sanction. Tenants may also not report because this may lead to their eviction (recall Misra and Jena 1957).

The dominant mode of tenancy continues to be sharecropping, which was reported in more than 70 per cent of the cases (Table 2.10). Furthermore, the incidence of sharecropping is also much higher in Odisha compared to all-India. In fact, it is highest for Odisha across 15 major states (as available for leased-in), and if smaller states are also taken into account, and Bihar is bifurcated (as is the case for leased-out), then only Mizoram and Jharkhand have higher incidences of sharecropping than Odisha.[6]

[6] See Eswaran and Kotwal (1985) and Singh (1989) for an excellent discussion on the coexistence of multiple sources of tenancy and the dynamics of the dominance of some agricultural contracts relative to others.

Table 2.9 Incidence of leased-out and leased-in, average area leased-in, and area under leased-in as a proportion of owned area in Odisha and India, 2002–03

Indicators	Odisha	India
Households reporting leased-out (%)	4.84	2.80
Households reporting leased-in (%)	15.70	11.52
Average area leased-in per reporting household (ha)	0.45	0.44
Leased-in area as proportion of total area owned (%)	14.59	7.05

Source: NSSO (2006b).
Note: See Table 2.1.

In the context of tenancy in the state, going back in time, one is reminded of the seminal work of Bharadwaj and Das (1975a; 1975b), which did indicate the persistence of sharecropping under unirrigated and tribal conditions, but observed a transition towards fixed rent in irrigated areas, and for high yielding varieties (HYVs) of paddy even in unirrigated areas. Further, a shift to fixed rent tenancy reduced the uncertainty for the landowner while making it possible to negotiate the tenant as also the amount, which increased the insecurity of the tenant. In some irrigated areas of Sambalpur region, many outsiders, namely migrant tenant farmers from Andhra Pradesh, were also

Table 2.10 Proportion of area leased-out/leased-in by type of tenancy for Odisha and India, 2002–03

Year	Proportion of area leased-out (%)		Proportion of area leased-in (%)	
	Odisha	India	Odisha	India
Sharecropping	71.1	39.6	73.0	40.3
Fixed money	11.5	31.0	11.1	29.5
Fixed produce	10.7	15.3	7.8	20.3
Relatives: no terms	NA	NA	3.5	4.0
Others	6.7	14.1	4.6	5.9
Total	100.0	100.0	100.0	100.0

Source: NSSO (2006a, 2006b).
Note: Data for 2002–03 pertains to the Kharif season.

willing to pay a higher fixed rent and this had adverse implications on the existing tenants in the region.

The instances of increasing insecurity of tenure reminds us of Boserup (1965: 82), who writing in the African context, anticipated that '... the road to private property in land may well create less and not more security of tenure, and a vast amount of litigation is the obvious result'. On similar lines, Bardhan and Udry (1999: 61) argue that while the process of individualization of tenure and transferability of rights enforced on the basis of public records and cadastral surveys can reduce uncertainties and encourage investment and allow for a more efficient allocation of land, in reality, the process is fraught with problems that may harm both equity and efficiency.

* * *

The question of landownership and tenurial conditions has had important implications in economic thinking. In the twentieth century, some major academic debates on agriculture, such as on the mode of production and exploitation from a Marxian perspective or on the efficiency of sharecropping from a neo-classical perspective, veered around these. A brief review of history suggests that at the time of Independence Odisha had different types of land tenure systems—zamindari in the coastal areas, ryotwari in some of the southern districts, malguzari and the gountia system in some of the western districts, and subsidiary alliance in the 24 princely states that had their independent administration.

In the post-Independence period they all got amalgamated under a common set of land reforms laws that included abolition of intermediaries/estates, security of tenure for the cultivator, distribution of ceiling surplus and other available land to the landless, and consolidation of landholdings. Despite good intentions, there have been many hindrances in implementing these reforms and one even observes some reversals in recent years.

The trends in ownership and operational holdings point out the process of marginalization and with a crisis in Indian agriculture including that for Odisha, the vulnerable from an operational holding perspective turn out to be dalits and tribals, who for different reasons also own or operate poor quality land. Across districts, those in and around the western district of Sambalpur seem to be doing relatively better, but they have higher inequalities; the coastal districts have a higher incidence of marginalization as also tenancy. Further, compared to the all-India average, the state has a relatively higher incidence of tenancy indicating that the matter needs a policy revisit. The coexistence of multiple forms of tenancy contracts and the dominance of sharecropping even after five decades since the Green Revolution and the relative causes and productivity differentials also demands a thorough examination, which is beyond the scope of this chapter. Further, who are the participants in the land lease markets becomes an important question from the perspective of equity given the boom in the mining and real estate sectors of the state. In addition, sustainability of agricultural households, the issue of livelihoods, absence of de facto property rights for women and other vulnerable groups such as tribals, and insecurity of tenure are all matters of concern.

References

Agarwal, B. 1994. *A Field of One's Own: Gender and Land Rights in South Asia*. Cambridge: Cambridge University Press.

Ambagudia, J. 2010. 'Tribal Rights, Dispossession and the State in Orissa', *Economic and Political Weekly*, 45(33): 60–67.

Appu, P.S. 1975. 'Tenancy Reform in India', *Economic and Political Weekly*, 10(33–35): 1339–75.

———. 1996. *Land Reform in India: A Survey of Policy, Legislation, and Implementation*. New Delhi: Vikas Publishing House.

Bal, V. 1880. Tribal and Peasant Life in 19th Century India. Calcutta: Geographical Survey of India.

Banerjee, A.V. and L. Iyer. 2005. 'History, Institutions and Economic Performance: The Legacy of Colonial Land Tenure Systems in India', *American Economic Review*, 95(4): 1190–213.

Banerjee, A.V., P.J. Gertler, and M. Ghatak. 2002. 'Empowerment and Efficiency: Tenancy Reform in West Bengal', *Journal of Political Economy*, 110(2): 239–80.

Bardhan, P. and C. Udry. 1999. *Development Microeconomics*. Oxford: Oxford University Press.

Behuria, N.C. 1997. *Land Reforms Legislation in India: A Comparative Study*. New Delhi: Vikas Publishing House.

Besley, T. and R. Burgess. 2000. 'Land Reform, Poverty Reduction, and Growth: Evidence from India', *Quarterly Journal of Economics*, 115(2): 389–430.

Bharadwaj, K. and P.K. Das. 1975a. 'Tenurial Conditions and Mode of Exploitation: A Study of Some Villages in Orissa', *Economic and Political Weekly*, 10(5–7): 221–40.

———. 1975b. 'Tenurial Conditions and Mode of Exploitation: Study of Some Villages in Orissa: Further Notes', *Economic and Political Weekly*, 10(25–26): A49–A55.

Boserup, E. 1965. *The Conditions of Agricultural Growth: The Economics of Agrarian Change under Population Pressure*. London: Allen and Unwin.

Deshpande, R.S. 2003. 'Current Land Policy Issues in India', *Land Reform—Land Settlement and Cooperatives*. Rome: Food and Agricultural Organization. Available at http://www.fao.org/docrep/006/y5026e/y5026e0b.htm (last accessed on 26 November 2015).

Eswaran, M. and A. Kotwal. 1985. 'A Theory of Contractual Structure in Agriculture', *American Economic Review*, 75(3): 352–67.

Gaurav, S. and S. Mishra. 2015. 'Farm Size and Returns to Cultivation in India: Revisiting an Old Debate', *Oxford Development Studies*, 43(2): 165–93

Ghatak, M. 2010. 'Land Reform', in Kaushik Basu and A. Maertens (eds), *The Concise Oxford Companion to Economics in India*, New Delhi: Oxford University Press.

Ghatak, M. and S. Roy. 2007. 'Land Reform and Agricultural Productivity in India: A Review of the Evidence', *Oxford Review of Economic Policy*, 23(2): 251–69.

Government of India (GoI). 2009. 'Committee on State Agrarian Relations and Unfinished Task of Land Reforms', Vol. 1, draft report, Ministry of Rural Development, New Delhi.

———. 2012. *Agriculture Census 2010–11: All India Report on Number and Area of Operational Holdings*. New Delhi: Ministry of Agriculture.

Government of Orissa (GoO). 2004. *Human Development Report 2004, Orissa*, Bhubaneswar: Planning and Coordination Department.

Hanstad, T. and R. Nielsen. 2009. 'Land Tenure Reform in India', in R.L. Prosterman, R. Mitchell, and T. Hanstad (eds), *One Billion Rising: Law, Land and the Alleviation of Global Poverty*, Leiden: Leiden University Press.

Jena, D.D. 1957. 'Effectiveness of Provision in the Tenancy Legislation in Orissa for (i) Security of Tenure and (ii) Improvement in the Tenurial

Status of Tenants', *Indian Journal of Agricultural Economics*, 12(2): 135–41.

Landesa. 2011. 'The Land Rush: A Fact Sheet on Commercial Land Acquisition in Developing Countries', issue brief, Landesa, Rural Development Institute. Available at https://www.landesa.org/wp-content/uploads/Land-Rush-Issue-Brief.pdf (last accessed on 26 November 2015).

Mearns, R. and S. Sinha. 1999. 'Social Exclusion and Land Administration in Orissa, India', World Bank Policy Research Working Paper 2124, World Bank, Washington, DC.

Mishra, S. 1993. 'Exchange Relations in an Agrarian Set-up: Case Study of a Tribal Village from Orissa', unpublished MPhil dissertation, Centre for Development Studies, Trivandrum.

Mishra, B. 2006. 'People's Movement at Kalinga Nagar', *Economic and Political Weekly*, 41(7): 551–54.

Mishra, S. 2009. Poverty and Agrarian Distress in Orissa, working paper, 92nd Annual Conference, The Indian Economic Association, New Delhi.

Misra, B. and B. Jena. 1957. 'Working of Two Recent Tenancy Laws in Orissa', *Indian Journal of Agricultural Economics*, 12(2): 117–20.

Mishra, B. and B.K. Nayak. 2011, 'Paan or POSCO?', *Economic and Political Weekly*, 46(26–27): 12–13.

Mishra, S. and D.N. Reddy. 2011. 'Persistence of Crisis in Indian Agriculture: Need for Technological and Institutional Alternatives', in D.M. Nachane (ed.), *India Development Report 2011*, pp. 48–58. New Delhi: Oxford University Press.

Mohanty, B. 1994, 'Land Reform Measures in Orissa: An Analysis', in A.K. Mitra and B. Sahoo (eds), *Agricultural Planning and Technology in Rural Development*, pp. 81–89. New Delhi: MD Publications.

Mohanty, M. 2012. 'Two Faces of the Indian State: Kalahandi to Kalinganagar and Operation Barga to Lalgarh', in K.B. Saxena, M. Mohanty, and S. Chakravartty (eds), *A Fistful of Dry Rice: Land Equity and Democracy (Essays in Honour of D. Bandyopadhyay)*. New Delhi: Aakar Books.

Nagar, A.L. and R.K. Das. 1983. *Basic Statistics*. Delhi: Oxford University Press.

NSSO. 1993. 'Operational Land Holdings in India, 1991–92: Salient Features, Land and Livestock Holding Survey', NSS 48th round (January–December 1992), Report No. 407, Ministry of Planning and Programme Implementation, Government of India, New Delhi.

———. 2006a. 'Some Aspects of Operational Land Holdings in India, 2002–03', NSS 59th round (January–December 2003),

Report No. 492(59/18.1/3), Ministry of Statistics and Programme Implementation, Government of India, New Delhi.

NSSO. 2006b. 'Household Ownership Holdings in India, 2003', NSS 59th round (January–December 2003), Report No. 491(59/18.1/4), Ministry of Statistics and Programme Implementation, Government of India, New Delhi.

Padhi, S. 1999. *Land Relations and Agrarian Development in India: A Comparative Historical Study of Regional Variations*. New Delhi: Oxford and IBH.

Padhi, S. and N. Panigrahi. 2011. 'Tribal Movements and Livelihoods: Recent Developments in Orissa', Working Paper No. 51, CPRC-IIPA.

Panigrahi, N. 2007. 'Fifth Schedule of the Constitution of India and the Tribals of Orissa: A Retrospective Look', *Journal of the Anthropological Survey of India*, 56(1 and 2): 45–72.

Panigrahi, N. and R. Balabantaray. 2012. 'Implementation of Forest Rights Act in Odisha: An Anthropological Understanding to Upgrade the Livelihood of Tribal People', *Journal of the Anthropological Survey of India*, 61(1): 283–303.

Parida, S. 2010, 'Twenty-Five Years of Bhoodan Movement in Orissa (1951–76)—A Review', *Orissa Review*, May–June: 70–72. Available at http://odisha.gov.in/e-magazine/Orissareview/2010/May-June/May-Junereview.htm (last accessed on 26 November 2015).

Pathy, J. 1981. 'Land Reforms and the Problem of Agricultural Development in Orissa: A Discursive Review', *Indian Journal of Regional Science*, 13(2): 140–50.

Patnaik, K. and P.P. Patnaik. 2011. *Land Alienation and Its Dimensions*. New Delhi: Concept.

Rawal, V. 2008. 'Ownership Holdings of Land in Rural India: Putting the Record Straight', *Economic and Political Weekly*, 43(10): 43–47.

Reddy, D.N. and S. Mishra. 2009. *Agrarian Crisis in India*. New Delhi: Oxford University Press.

Sahoo, B. and G. Dharmalingam. 2006. *Land Reform and Management*. Bhubaneswar: Mayur.

Sahu, G. 2008. 'Mining in the Niyamgiri Hills and Tribal Rights', *Economic and Political Weekly*, 43(15): 19–21.

Shaban, R.A. 1987. 'Testing between Competing Models of Sharecropping', *Journal of Political Economy*, 95(5): 893–920.

Sharma, H.R. 1994. 'Distribution of Landholdings in Rural India, 1953–54 to 1981–81: Implications for Land Reforms', *Economic and Political Weekly*, 29(13): A12–A25.

Singh, N. 1989. 'Theories of Sharecropping', in Pranab Bardhan (ed.), *The Economic Theory of Agrarian Institutions*, pp. 33–72, Oxford: Clarendon Press.

Sinha, B.K. 2012. 'Land Reforms: Evidences of Reversal in Orissa', in K.B. Saxena, M. Mohanty, and S. Chakravartty (eds), *A Fistful of Dry Rice: Land Equity and Democracy (Essays in Honour of D. Bandyopadhyay)*. New Delhi: Aakar Books.

Sinha, B.K. and Pushpendra. 2000. *Land Reforms in India: An Unfinished Agenda*, New Delhi: Sage Publications.

UNDP. 2008. *Status Report: Land Rights and Ownership in Orissa*. New Delhi; Ministry of Rural Development, Government of India, and UNDP.

3

Rural Unemployment and Agricultural Wages in Odisha

Analysis of Major Trends and Policy Options

Raj Kishore Panda

Agriculture continues to be the major source of employment for the rural workforce in India. In recent years there has been slowdown in agricultural growth in almost all states in the country. Moreover, this low growth in agriculture has not been accompanied by employment gains (Jha 2006; Papola 2006; Kiran 2012). In fact, in some of the states there is a negative growth in employment. The burden of this slowdown in agricultural growth and growth not matched by employment is reflected in higher incidence of poverty concentrated in rural areas and among the agricultural labour households.

In Odisha, the rural workforce is predominantly employed in the agriculture sector. More than 60 per cent of the rural households are directly or indirectly engaged in agriculture. Over the years, due to increasing demographic pressure on agriculture, there has been rapid rise in small holdings (less than 1 hectare of holding) in the state. Agricultural Census 2005–06 records the share of small holders in the total holders as more than 86 per cent. Landlessness has remained quite high in the state. The Census data show that the percentage of agricultural labourers constituting the main workers show a marginal decline to 22 per cent in 2001 as against 28.68 per cent in 1991. Thus, with the increase in the size of small holders whose dependency on wage employment for sustenance is quite high and the agricultural labourers constituting nearly a quarter of the total workforce, the percentage of people under the vulnerable category becomes high. About 29.06 per cent of the total rural people during 2009–10 are found below the poverty line (tentative estimates; GoO 2012). Since poverty and unemployment are intertwined, this chapter examines the different dimensions of rural unemployment estimated by the National Sample Surveys (NSSs) and the association of rural poverty with rural unemployment, and measures trends in wage rates of agricultural field labourers vis-à-vis other rural wages and also disparity in wage rates of agricultural labourers across genders and districts. The plan of the chapter is as follows. The section titled 'Materials and Methods' examines the trends in the incidence and intensity of unemployment in rural Odisha. The section on 'Incidence of Unemployment in Rural Odisha' discusses the association of poverty with unemployment over time and across space. The section 'Trends in Agricultural Money and Real Wage Rates and Consumer Price Index' measures the trends in the growth rate in wages of field labourers via-à-vis other rural workers along with inter-district variation in the field labour wage rates in the state. The penultimate section 'Policy Options for Improving the Conditions of Agricultural Labour' discusses options in public intervention for improving conditions of agricultural labour while the last section provides the conclusions of this study.

Materials and methods

The study is based on secondary data obtained from different rounds of National Sample Survey Organisation (NSSO) surveys, Census Reports, Economic Surveys, Government of Odisha, and other Government publications. Unemployment refers to persons without work in a given reference period even though they are available for work. In the NSSO survey, persons remaining unemployed for 365 days preceding the date of survey are taken under as chronically unemployed under usual status (US) criteria and persons remaining unemployed for a weeklong as unemployed for a weeklong. Unemployment under Current Daily Status refers to as underemployment of persons who may be working but their work is inadequate either with reference to a full employment time norm or to a given minimum level of income. In estimating agricultural real wage rate, data on average daily nominal wages of farm field workers are obtained from various issues of the Statistical Abstract of Odisha, Government of Odisha. The real wage rates are worked out by using the consumer price index of agricultural labour (CPIAL) as the deflator. The year 1986–87 is taken as the base year for calculating the prices.

Incidence of unemployment in rural Odisha

Table 3.1 presents the incidence of unemployment (as a percentage of rural population and rural labour force) in rural Odisha based upon the NSS quinquennial 55th (1999–2000), 61st (2004–05), and 66th (2009–10) rounds data. Observation reveals that for males the unemployment rate as a proportion to rural population does not show any trend—it has increased between 55th and 61st rounds and declined between 61st and 66th rounds. The 66th round estimate of unemployment rate is however higher than the 55th round but lower than the 61st round. For females there is a decline in unemployment between 55th and 61st rounds, after which it has increased steadily. Unemployment rate as a percentage to labour force also shows inconsistent trend for males although the incidence of unemployment in the 66th round is higher over the base 55th round. Unemployment rate as a proportion to labour force in case of females reveals less inconsistency than noticed in case of males. Between 55th and 61st rounds the female unemployment as a proportion to its labour force has declined, after which it has increased between 61st and 66th rounds. However, irrespective of the trend in the rates, the absolute number of unemployed, both male and female, are seen increasing over time.

Table 3.1 Incidence of unemployment in rural Odisha: 55th to 66th rounds of the NSS

NSS round	Year	Total rural population (in lakh)		Total rural labour force (in lakh)		No. of unemployed (in lakh)		Unemployed			
								As %age of rural population		As %age of rural labour force	
		Male	Female	Male	Female	Male	Female	Male	Female	Male	Female
55th round	1999–2000	143.17	146.05	80.75	44.11	1.94	0.49	1.35	0.33	2.40	1.11
61st round	2004–05	156.77	159.80	94.69	56.09	2.94	0.47	1.87	0.29	3.10	0.84
66th round	2009–10	168.32	166.30	100.32	41.41	3.03	1.00	1.80	0.60	3.02	2.41

Source: Data sourced from NSSO (various issues).

Table 3.2 shows rates of unemployment and underemployment (the Current Daily Status [CDS] category) under different activities status based on 55th, 61st, and 66th rounds of NSS data. For the 55th round (1999–2000) the rate of US (chronic) unemployment for both males and females is the lowest followed by current weekly status (CWS) (marginal unemployment) and current daily status (underemployment) for both categories. For 2004–05 the rate of US unemployment for males and females is also the lowest followed by current weekly status and current daily status.

Table 3.2 Incidence of unemployment in rural Odisha according to activity status, 1999–2000, 2004–05, and 2009–10 (%)

Sex	Usual status	Current weekly status	Current daily status
1999–2000			
Persons	1.9	3.8	*7.1*
Male	2.4	3.8	*7.6*
Female	1.1	3.8	*5.6*
2004–05			
Persons	5.0	7.4	*10.2*
Male	3.1	6.1	*9.3*
Female	8.3	10.2	*12.6*
2009–10			
Persons	3.00	5.4	*8.1*
Male	3.02	5.4	*8.2*
Female	2.41	5.3	*7.8*
%age point changes in unemployment rates in 2004–05 over 1999–2000			
Persons	3.1	3.6	*3.1*
Male	0.7	2.3	*1.7*
Female	7.2	6.4	*7.0*
%age point changes in unemployment rates in 2009–10 over 2004–05			
Persons	-2.00	-2.0	*-2.1*
Male	-0.08	-0.7	*-1.1*
Female	-5.89	-4.9	*-4.8*
%age point changes in unemployment rates in 2009–10 over 1999–2000			
Persons	1.1	1.6	*1.0*
Male	0.62	1.6	*0.6*
Female	1.31	1.5	*2.2*

Source: Data sourced from NSSO (various rounds).

In 2009–10 the US unemployment rates for male and female is also found the lowest as compared to that of current weekly status and current daily status. Thus, over the time period (1999–2000 to 2009–10) the rates of unemployment under CDS measure are quite high irrespective of the category (male and female). The incidence of chronic unemployment under US is quite low and that of short-term unemployment under current weekly status is relatively modest. Between males and females the rates of unemployment as well as underemployment for males are higher than those of females in 1999–2000 and 2009–10. In 2004–05, however, the female unemployment and underemployment rates are found higher over that of the males. Over the period 1999–2000 to 2009–10 the rate of unemployment shows some uneven trend. While between 1999–2000 to 2004–05, the unemployment rates with respect to all the three measures have increased between 2004–05 to 2009–10 all of them have shown declining trend. However, as regards the changes in 2009–10 over the base period 1999–2000, we find the unemployment rates have increased for both males and females. And the increase in rates are higher for females than for males. This shows that employment opportunities for females have worsened over time.

Table 3.3 presents data on unemployment rates under different age-groups with gender aspects based on 55th (1999–2000), 61st (2004–05), and 66th (2009–10) rounds data. The age-groups are classified under two broad heads: (a) all age-groups (five years and above) and (b) between 15–29 years (youths). The data reveal that the unemployment and underemployment rates are higher among 15–29 age-group as compared to those between age-group of five years and above (persons of all age-groups) in all the three time periods under study. Particularly, unemployment under CDS measure (otherwise called underemployment) is found very high among the youths (15–29 age-group).

A comparative estimate of rates of rural unemployment in Odisha vis-à-vis the all-India average over the period 1999–2000 to 2009–10 is given in Table 3.4. Observation reveals that the unemployment rate is recorded to be higher in Odisha over the all-India average on all three measures—the US, weekly status, and CDS over the time period under study. However, while with respect to US and weekly

Table 3.3 Unemployment rate (%) in rural Odisha for different age groups, 1999–2000, 2004–05, and 2009–10

Status	Male		Female		Persons	
	All age groups	15–29 years	All age groups	15–29 years	All age groups	15–29 years
1999–2000 (55th round)						
PS+SS	2.4	6.6	1.1	3.0	1.9	5.2
CWS	3.8	8.9	3.8	6.2	3.8	8.1
CDS	7.6	12.6	5.6	8.4	7.1	11.3
2004–05 (61st round)						
PS+SS	3.1	7.5	8.3	14.3	5.0	10.2
CWS	6.1	12.7	10.2	18.0	7.4	14.4
CDS	9.3	17.0	12.6	21.7	10.2	18.4
2009–10 (66th round)						
PS+SS	3.1	10.4	2.7	8.2	3.0	9.7
CWS	5.4	14.6	5.3	14.0	5.4	14.4
CDS	8.2	18.4	7.8	18.0	8.1	18.2

Source: NSS 55th (1999–2000), 61st (2004–05), and 66th (2009–10) rounds.
Note: 55th, 61st, and 66th rounds are quinquennial rounds.

Table 3.4 Unemployment rate (%) for all persons according to different status approaches in rural Odisha and India, 1999–2000, 2004–05, and 2009–10

S. No.	Status	Odisha			India		
		Male	Female	Persons	Male	Female	Persons
1999–2000 (55th round)							
1	US	2.4	1.1	1.9	1.7	1.0	1.5
2	CWS	3.8	3.8	3.8	3.9	3.7	3.8
3	CDS	7.6	5.6	7.1	7.2	7.0	7.1
2004–05 (61st round)							
1	US	3.1	8.3	5.0	1.6	1.8	1.7
2	CWS	6.1	10.2	7.4	3.8	4.2	3.9
3	CDS	9.3	12.6	10.2	8.0	8.7	8.2
2009–10 (66th round)							
1	US	3.1	2.7	3.0	1.6	1.6	1.6
2	CWS	5.4	5.3	5.4	3.2	3.7	3.3
3	CDS	8.2	7.8	8.1	6.4	8.0	6.8

Source: NSS 55th (1999–2000), 61st (2004–05), and 66th (2009–10) rounds.
Note: 55th, 61st, and 66th NSS quinquennial rounds.

status unemployment rates there is smaller gap between Odisha and the all-India average, for CDS the gap is larger. For females larger gap is noticed between the all-India average and Odisha with respect to US and CWS measures of unemployment. However, the CDS measure reveals higher unemployment rate for females at the all-India level than that in Odisha. The lower unemployment noticed under CDS in case of females in Odisha might be due to under-reporting. Since incidence of poverty in the state is higher as compared to the all-India average, there is obvious reason that rural women in the state are supposed to work as supplementary breadwinner for the family. From all these the inference is that rural unemployment is a matter of greater concern for Odisha than that at the all-India level.

Unemployment and poverty relationship

As important as the size of unemployment/underemployment is the question of relationship between unemployment and poverty and this has attracted the attention of many scholars. The tendency to associate unemployment with poverty or low productivity work has evoked considerable discussion among economists and a few pioneering works at the all-India level are that of Dandekar and Rath (1971), Raj Krishna (1976), Raj (1976), Visaria (1981), among others. While there lies considerable overlapping between the unemployed and people below the poverty line, yet it seems incorrect to treat them as identical. The relationship between the two varies depending upon the concepts followed, time frame used in measuring employment and poverty, and the unit of analysis adopted in determining the status of each of them (Saunders 2002). Based on the concepts we can see four possible combinations of employment and poverty status: (a) poor and unemployed, (b) employed but poor, (c) unemployed but not poor, and (d) employed and poor. In measuring poverty while we use income on annual basis for unemployment we record labour force status at a point of time. While for determining employment/unemployment an individual in a family is taken as a unit, the household/family is considered a unit for getting income. Besides, low household earnings may be due to several factors other than labour absorption. The poor may not be able to afford to remain unemployed. In other cases, workers with larger number of days of employment may have lower per capita income/consumption. Low asset base may be associated with low per capita income but not with unemployment. Studies by Raj Krishna (1976) and Visaria (1981) have shown negative correlation between person-day of unemployment rate and per capita consumption. Paul (1988) reveals that unemployment rates among poor are higher than the average level in majority of states. In the light of the arguments raised by scholars on the conceptual difficulty in measuring the relationship between unemployment and poverty, empirical findings showing divergent results on the association between the two, and studies showing poverty and unemployment co-existing in rural Odisha (Padhy 2009; Sahu and Tripathy 2009), we have here tried to examine the relationship between the two over time and across space. Tables 3.5 and 3.6 discuss the relevant data in this respect. Poverty estimates taken from 55th, 61st, and 66th rounds of NSS are compared with unemployment rates measured under usual principal status (UPS) and CDS in the respective years (Table 3.5). Observation reveals that between 55th and 61st rounds, poverty incidence in rural Odisha has fallen from 48.01 per cent to 39.80 per cent, while unemployment rates under usual principal status as well as CDS measures have increased, thus showing an inverse relationship between poverty incidence and unemployment/underemployment rates. Between 61st and 66th rounds, however, the incidence of rural poverty has declined from 39.8 per cent to 29.06 per cent and the unemployment rates under usual principal status and CDS measure have also declined from 6.4 per cent to 3.5 per cent and 10.2 per cent to 8.1 per cent respectively. The relationship between poverty and unemployment under UPS and CDS status based on R^2 value is found statistically insignificant (Figure 3.1). Poverty seems to be a bigger challenge in rural Odisha than unemployment. As per the latest available data, among the 16 major states in India, Odisha occupies the 12th rank in the concentration of people below the poverty line (66th round NSS data, 2009–10). Accordingly, overwhelmingly majority of the poor are thus not apparently unemployed but are engaged in some activities at a very low level of productivity and earnings. This is supposed to be the reason for the weak relationship found between unemployment rate and poverty ratio.

Table 3.5 Relationship between unemployment rates and incidence of poverty in rural Odisha (%)

	Usual principal status	CDS	Incidence of rural poverty (% of people below poverty line)
55th round (July 1999–June 2000)	2.7	7.1	48.01
61st round July 2004–June 2005)	6.4	10.2	39.80
66th round (2009–10)	3.5	8.1	29.06*

Source: Data sourced from NSSO (various issues) and GoO (various issues).
Note: *Based on MRP consumption. For 2009–10, tentative poverty estimates from Planning and Coordination Department, GoO (2011–12: 252).

Table 3.6 Interregional differences in the relationship between poverty and unemployment rates in the state (%)

Regions	Incidence of poverty*, 2009–10 (%)	Usual status			Weekly status		
		Male	Female	Persons	Male	Female	Persons
Central	16.42	2.44	0.95	1.73	2.58	0.94	1.79
Northern	32.56	1.00	0.28	0.65	2.54	0.29	1.43
Southern	39.95	1.23	0.99	1.12	1.71	1.20	1.43

Source: Data sourced from NSSO (various rounds).
Note: *Tentative analysis of NSSO 66th round data using MRP method.

Data examining the relationship between poverty ratio and the unemployment rate across three different regions of the state are presented in Table 3.6. Observation reveals a varying relation between the two across region. The central region, which is relatively better-off, shows lower poverty incidence with higher unemployment rates under both US and CWS measures. In contrast, the southern and northern regions, which are relatively worse-off regions, show higher incidence of poverty with lower rates of unemployment under US and CWS measures. Observation reveals that the relation between unemployment and poverty across regions can be explained in terms of the fact that the central region

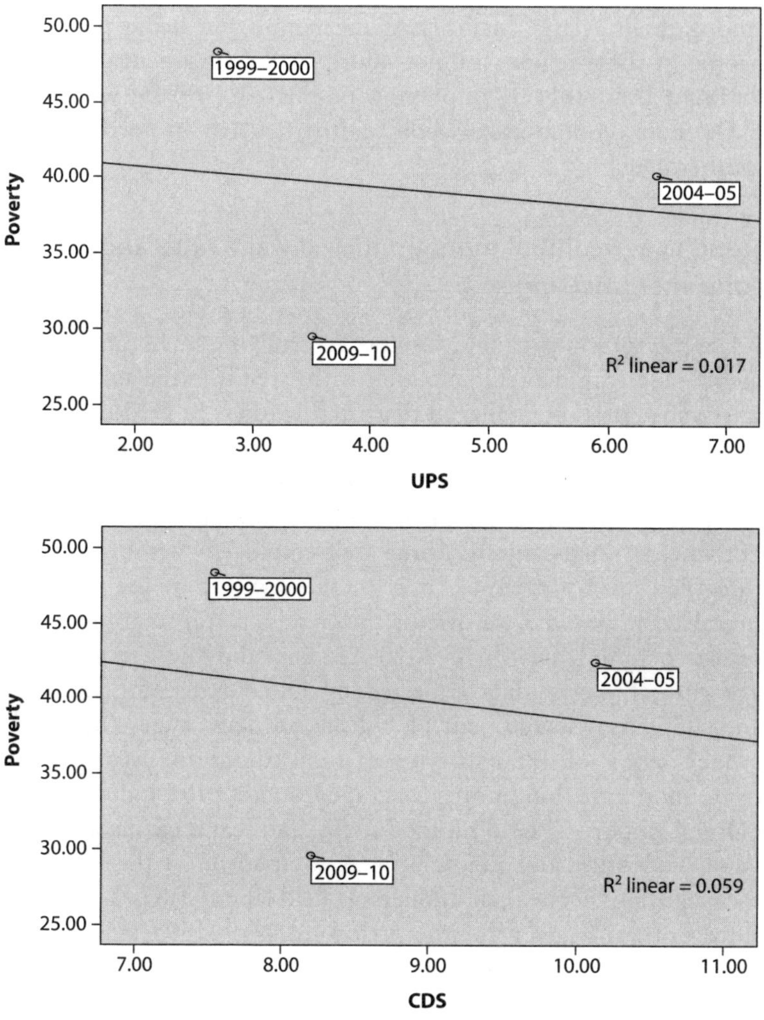

Figure 3.1 Relationship between poverty and unemployment under UPS and CDS
Source: NSSO (various rounds).

being relatively a better-off region in terms of socio-economic standard, the people in this region can afford to remain idle in search of better jobs. In contrast, the other two regions being relatively backward with higher concentration of tribal population and among them a large majority of the population being poor, the people in these regions cannot afford to remain unengaged. The findings, thus, suggest improving productivity of the workforce in the state economy as a whole and particularly in northern and southern regions.

Trend in agricultural money and real wage rates and consumer price index

An aspect of considerable interest in studying rural unemployment/underemployment is to look at the trends in the agricultural wage rates. It is often alleged that rural workers in predominantly agricultural economies are engaged in low productive work, receive low wages, and thus suffer from acute poverty. Unemployment, however measured, is far greater among the agricultural labour households than among those self-employed within agriculture (Parthasarathy 1996). It is in this context of the need for improved wages that we discuss the trends in real wages focusing on the period 1994–95 to 2010–11. For studying the trends in agricultural wages, data collected by Directorate of Economics and Statistics, Government of Odisha on daily wages (nominal/money wages) of different types of rural labour are used. Annual compound growth of money wages, consumer price index of agricultural labour (CPIAL) on food items, and real wage rates of field labour is worked out (Table 3.7). A comparison of the trends in the wage rates of the male and female field labourers vis-à-vis other rural workers is given for the period from 1994–95 to 2010–11 (Table 3.8). The real wages are obtained by dividing money wages with the CPIAL for the respective years, the base year for CPIAL being 1986–87.

The trends in nominal/money wage rate and real wage rate of agricultural field labourers over the period 1994–95 to 2010–11 are shown in Figure 3.2. As noticed, there has been appreciable growth in money wage rates of both male and female field labourers over the period. But the growth in their real wage rates has been found very slow, resulting in widening of the gap between money and real wage rates. This is irrespective of gender. The slow growth in real wages thus speaks of poor economic living of wage labourers

Table 3.7 Annual CPIAL, nominal and real wages of men and women field labourers in Odisha, 1994–95 to 2010–11

S. No.	Year	Index	Men		Women	
			Nominal	Real	Nominal	Real
1	1994–95	204	22.79	11.17	18.70	9.17
2	1995–96	235	24.83	10.57	20.57	8.75
3	1996–97	247	26.87	10.88	22.44	9.09
4	1997–98	256	29.17	11.39	24.31	9.50
5	1998–99	283	31.52	11.14	26.60	9.40
6	1999–2000	309	34.93	11.30	29.52	9.55
7	2000–01	295	38.62	13.09	32.20	10.92
8	2001–02	286	40.59	14.19	33.31	11.65
9	2002–03	280	42.16	15.06	34.42	12.29
10	2003–04	296	43.73	14.77	35.05	11.84
11	2004–05	301	44.81	14.89	36.74	12.51
12	2005–06	317	51.54	16.26	45.01	14.20
13	2006–07	340	58.11	17.09	50.11	14.74
14	2007–08	379	64.68	17.07	55.21	14.57
15	2008–09	420	71.25	16.96	60.32	14.36
16	2009–10	490	71.25	14.54	60.32	12.31
17	2010–11	528	92.00	17.42	74.30	14.07
Annual compound growth rate (%)		4.71	8.25	3.38	8.35	3.48

Source: GoO (2012).

in rural Odisha. Tabular data analysis explaining the trends in money and real wages and consumer price index of agricultural labourers is presented in Table 3.7. Observation reveals that the male money wage rate had increased from Rs 22.79 in 1994–95 to Rs 92 in 2010–11, while their real wage rate had increased merely from Rs 11.17 to Rs 17.42 during the same period. In case of females, the money wage rate had increased from Rs 18.70 in 1994–95 to Rs 74.30 in 2010–11, while their real wage rate had gone up only from Rs 9.17 to Rs 14.07 during the same period. The annual compound growth rate of CPIAL, money wage rates, and the real wage rates for male and female field workers for the period 1994–95 to 2010–11 are worked out to 4.71, 8.25, 3.38,

Table 3.8 Average daily real wages (Rs) for agricultural field labourers, other semi-skilled, and unskilled rural workers in Odisha (base=1986–87)

Years	Agricultural field labourers		Other agricultural labourers		Carpenter	Cobbler	Blacksmith
	Men	Women	Men	Women			
1994–95	11.17	9.17	11.84	9.56	23.34	19.72	21.18
1995–96	10.57	8.75	11.31	9.07	22.18	18.39	19.53
1996–97	10.88	9.09	11.75	9.36	22.93	18.70	19.67
1997–98	11.39	9.50	12.14	9.89	23.65	19.21	20.11
1998–99	11.14	9.40	11.89	9.78	23.63	19.55	19.54
1999–2000	11.30	9.55	12.08	10.10	23.92	18.77	20.69
2000–01	13.09	10.92	13.71	11.22	27.39	21.67	23.40
2001–02	14.19	11.65	15.53	11.86	30.01	23.23	24.89
2002–03	15.06	12.29	15.86	12.44	31.91	24.94	26.14
2003–04	14.77	11.84	15.52	15.58	31.31	25.25	24.73
2004–05	14.89	12.51	15.78	12.68	34.15	29.07	26.62
2005–06	16.26	14.20	17.99	15.23	37.11	30.68	26.29
2006–07	17.09	14.74	17.19	14.49	37.14	30.10	29.83
2007–08	17.07	14.57	17.25	14.12	35.59	28.34	28.44
2008–09	16.96	14.36	17.21	13.76	34.16	26.79	27.18
2009–10	14.54	12.31	16.16	12.66	29.14	22.96	23.97
2010–11	17.42	14.07	18.36	14.62	29.91	24.29	25.64
Annual compound growth rate	3.38	3.49	3.24	3.27	2.97	2.78	2.31

Source: GoO (2012).

8.35, and 3.48 respectively. This indicates that a higher percentage of growth in money wage rate brought in effect through wage revisions is absorbed by rise in prices of different consumer articles consumed by the agricultural labourers. Between male and female wage rates, we find the average money and real wage rates of male field labour is higher than the female field labour and over the period 1994–95 to 2010–11, the gap in the wage rates between the two categories has increased.

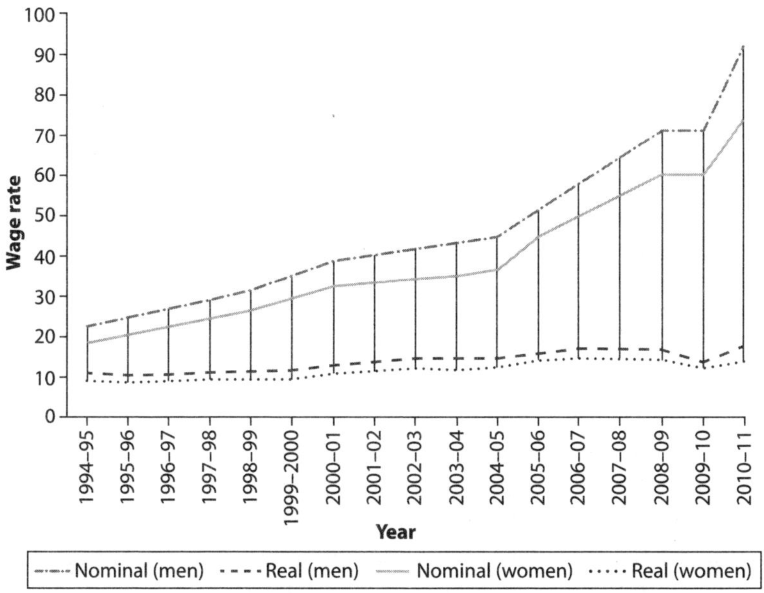

Figure 3.2 Average daily nominal and real wages for agricultural field labourers in Odisha (base=1986–87)
Source: GoO (various issues).

Comparison between wage rates of farm field labourers with other rural workers

A comparison of the real wage rates (based on CPIAL deflator) between field labour and other rural workers (semi-skilled and unskilled) over the period 1994–95 to 2010–11 reveals that farm field labourers were paid less than the rural semi-skilled workers like carpenters, cobblers, blacksmiths, and other unskilled agricultural workers (Table 3.8). Over the period 1994–95 to 2010–11, the real wage rates of farm field labourers had increased from Rs 11.17 to Rs 17.42 in case of males and Rs 9.17 to Rs 14.07 in case of females, while the same for other agricultural workers had increased from Rs 11.84 to Rs 18.36 for males and Rs 9.56 to Rs 14.62 for females.

The compound annual growth rate (CAGR) of real wages for agricultural field labourers during 1995–2011 is works out to 3.38 per cent for men and 3.48 per cent for women. For other rural labourers the CAGR works out to 3.24 for men and 3.27 for women. The CAGR for wage rates of carpenters, cobblers, and blacksmiths works out to 2.97, 2.78, and 2.31 respectively. The higher growth rate in the real wages of agricultural field labourers as observed might be due to the implementation of the Mahatma Gandhi National Rural Employment Guarantee Act 2005, after which the state government has made upward revision of minimum wage rates of rural workers frequently.

Variation in real wage rates of field labourers across districts

Data on the real wage rates of male and female field labourers across districts in Odisha for the four reference years 1994–95, 1999–2000, 2003–04, and 2010–11 are shown in Table 3.9. The real wage rates of field labourers show large variation across districts and genders in 1994–95—the male wage rates from Rs 8.18 in Sundergarh to Rs 14.22 in Bargarh and the female wage rates from Rs 6.54 in Nuapada to Rs 12.08 in Bargarh. Over the years the wage rates of both male and female field labourers at the district level have increased. But inter-district disparity in the wage rates as worked out in terms of value of coefficient of variation (CV) has increased between 1994–95, 1999–2000, and 2003–04 and then declined marginally between 2003–04 and 2010–11. The CV values for the male wage rates across districts work out to 11.97 in 1994–95, 17.40 in 1999–2000, 19.90 in 2003–04, and 12.60 in 2010–11, while for the females the same comes to 13.05, 20.15, 17.56, and 15.76 respectively. The large-scale inter-district variation in wage rates thus amply demonstrates poorer living conditions of field labourers in some districts in the state. Particularly, the field labourers in tribal districts are worse affected in this respect as compared to the coastal districts. Since the wage rates reflect labour productivity and the tribal districts have low level of agricultural development and bottlenecks in developing of non-farm activities, there is need for proactive government intervention to ameliorate the woeful underemployment situation and poverty among agricultural labour in those districts.

Table 3.9 Variation in the real wages (Rs) of farm labourers in different districts of Odisha

Districts	1994–95		1999–2000		2003–04		2010–11	
	Male	Female	Male	Female	Male	Female	Male	Female
Bhadrak	11.55	9.24	14.05	12.39	17.05	14.35	21.23	17.80
Mayurbhanj	9.75	8.27	9.50	7.28	10.56	9.97	16.32	12.65
Jagatsinghpur	12.40	11.13	15.17	14.55	18.63	15.10	17.52	17.00
Nuapada	8.42	6.54	7.42	6.72	10.56	8.05	14.14	11.36
Kalahandi	11.10	9.04	10.15	8.74	13.59	10.14	18.56	14.76
Khurda	12.34	9.91	13.99	12.70	18.59	15.34	20.20	16.12
Ganjam	13.29	10.19	12.84	11.33	18.49	11.86	18.63	11.78
Jharsuguda	11.98	10.04	11.52	10.86	13.51	12.69	15.84	11.93
Cuttack	11.65	9.00	11.91	10.00	17.57	13.42	20.41	16.73
Bolangir	11.08	9.57	8.53	6.90	11.04	10.78	14.61	11.95
Boudh	9.71	8.25	9.71	9.17	14.44	11.88	17.85	12.44
Gajapati	10.45	7.60	11.34	9.75	12.50	10.86	20.00	11.39
Kandhamal	11.55	8.82	10.15	8.74	14.23	11.00	14.05	12.38
Sonepur	11.07	9.56	8.05	6.45	11.05	9.19	15.89	11.15
Bargarh	14.22	12.08	9.71	8.09	10.99	8.45	16.71	13.08
Deogarh	11.05	9.00	11.13	9.55	11.05	9.00	15.64	12.78
Balasore	11.58	9.98	12.84	11.33	16.73	14.53	16.89	16.79
Sambalpur	13.14	9.99	9.29	6.82	15.27	11.57	18.26	14.22
Dhenkanal	12.42	9.00	9.95	8.70	18.62	15.23	15.59	14.09
Malkangiri	10.63	7.73	9.89	9.92	13.26	11.84	14.13	12.49
Angul	10.49	8.89	9.92	8.10	13.72	10.85	18.57	14.75
Keonjhar	10.50	8.90	11.37	10.36	12.11	10.90	17.10	14.59
Rayagada	10.83	7.98	10.79	9.01	15.61	12.00	18.01	15.81
Kendrapara	12.73	9.43	14.49	10.88	18.77	15.42	19.53	17.99
Puri	11.03	10.48	13.05	11.23	20.21	14.91	20.99	18.37
Koraput	9.33	8.17	9.95	7.79	16.31	12.64	15.80	12.81
Jajpur	11.60	9.19	10.83	9.38	14.19	12.16	20.02	13.48
Sundergarh	8.18	6.55	9.47	8.14	12.57	10.84	13.77	11.71
Nayagarh	11.23	9.01	12.16	10.18	17.29	13.58	18.94	15.66
Nawarangpur	11.96	8.92	10.74	9.62	13.01	12.16	17.47	12.57
S.D.	1.35	1.18	1.91	1.91	2.93	2.11	2.19	2.21
Mean	11.24	9.08	11.00	9.49	14.72	12.02	17.42	14.02
CV (%)	11.97	13.05	17.40	20.15	19.90	17.56	12.60	15.76

Source: GoO (2012).

Policy options for improving the conditions of agricultural labour

The foregoing analysis shows that the incidence of unemployment and underemployment in rural Odisha, and particularly among the youths, is quite high. The agricultural labourers in unirrigated and tribal districts in the state are in a more disadvantageous position as these households suffer from higher incidence of unemployment/underemployment with lower wage rates due to low labour and agricultural productivity. In the above context, a major policy intervention should be to influence the productivity of agriculture through development of infrastructure, cropping intensity, diversion towards high value but labour-intensive crops like fruits and vegetables, and use of productivity-raising appropriate technology. However, there is a problem here. A rise in wage rate induced by productivity results in a decrease in demand for labour, and thus leads to greater unemployment. The introduction of productivity-raising technology will also have a similar effect. But overall, an increase in the rate of agricultural growth is necessary. In this context, measures towards diffusion of benefits of agricultural growth are required. Land reforms assume importance since there is high degree of inequality in land distribution in the state (Panda and Tripathy 2009). On different intervention programmes such as Integrated Rural Development Programme (IRDP), National Rural Employment Programme (NREP), Jawahar Rozgar Yojana (JRY), Sampoorna Gramin Rozgar Yojana (SGRY), and the latest Mahatma Gandhi National Rural Employment Guarantee Programme (MGNREGP) for raising rural employment studies at the Odisha level and in other states have shown widespread leakages in these programmes. More so, the rural works approach of employment planning can only be a sub-strategy of temporary relief. As aptly remarked by Dantwala (1978) 'the public works approach to unemployment would make sense if it is so organized that there will be progressively less and less reliance on it'. Since poverty is far more widespread than unemployment, it follows that full employment will not be a solution for rural poverty unless it is accompanied by higher earnings.

Fixation of minimum wages for agricultural labour

Studies conducted on the fixation of minimum wages, their periodical revisions, and effective implementation does not show encouraging results. Agriculture, unlike the organized manufacturing sector, suffers from frequent ups and downs due to its seasonal character. During peak season, the demand for labour increases and so also employment and wages for agricultural labourers. While in lean season, since agricultural activities are at a very low level, employment and wages fall significantly. Under these circumstances it is difficult to implement minimum wages particularly during slack season. The public works programme needs to be so designed to meet the deficiencies in private demand for agricultural labour. However, this requires area planning to identify the infrastructural needs in an integrated perspective of providing the needs of agricultural development as well as development of industrial and non-agricultural activities.

Meeting the basic needs

Apart from lack of employment and low wages, majority of agricultural labour households in the state suffer from illiteracy, poor health, lack of access to good housing, safe drinking water, and others. Hence, these households need to be covered under different programmes for the fulfilment of these basic needs. A significant percentage of child labour is seen in rural areas and among the agricultural labour households in the state. But shifting those children from labour to school entails cost for the household. Provision of schooling facilities during evening hours by the government may work as an incentive. Access to safe drinking water supply and improved shelter are important components of minimum needs programme. It is seen that majority of scheduled caste (SC) and scheduled tribe (ST) households in the state suffer from lack of access to clean water supply and provision of improved habitat. So the various employment programmes in operation, including MGNREGP, should make provision for good shelter and drinking water facility in the workplaces and in rural areas.

* * *

The main findings that emerge from the analysis of the study may be stated as follows: (a) the incidence of rural unemployment has increased in the state over the period (1999–2000 to 2009–10) both for males and females and between different measures of unemployment, intensity under CDS measure, otherwise called underemployment, happens to be more predominant as compared to unemployment under US (chronic unemployment) and CWS (marginal unemployment). (b) Between two different age-groups, unemployment rate in the age-group 15–29 is higher for both males and females. (c) Compared to all-India averages, rural Odisha exhibits higher incidence as well as intensity of unemployment. (d) Inter-temporally the relationship between unemployment and poverty is found negative but statistically insignificant. (e) At the regional level the better-off region (central region) show higher rate of unemployment with lower incidence of poverty while the worse-off regions (northern and southern) exhibit lower unemployment rate with higher poverty incidence. This finding is thus in line with the most common hypothesis that the poor cannot afford to remain unemployed. The central region, being relatively a better-off region and incidence of poverty here being less, the rural workers can afford to wait for getting a job of their choice. In contrast, other two regions being less developed and the higher concentration of tribal communities with greater incidence of poverty (GoO 2012), the rural workers get engaged in petty and low-paid works to eke out their living. (f) The trends in real wages of agricultural field labourers based on CPIAL—deflator have shown a positive but slow growth over the period 1994–95 to 2010–11. Yet, as noticed, the field labourers get less wages as compared to other rural workers. Besides, there lies high degree of disparity in the wage rates across districts and it has widened over the years. The gap in the average wages of male and female agricultural field labourers has widened over time. Since agricultural development in terms of cropping pattern, technology use, and productivity in the state is at a lower level (GoI 2009), need for improving productivity in agriculture through development of infrastructure, diversion towards high-value crops like fruits and vegetables, and introduction of productivity-raising technology is suggested. Besides, as the agricultural field labourers constitute the most vulnerable sections of the rural community, certain basic minimum needs in the shape of access to safe drinking water, good housing, education, among others, need to be provided through government initiatives to improve their conditions of living. Particularly, in tribal districts the vulnerability of agricultural labourers being higher in terms of employment, wages, and availability of basic amenities, there is need for an integrated action programme through government intervention for providing them with certain basic needs and training for developing skill for getting gainful employment.

References

Ahuja, K. 1986. 'Agricultural Labour and Rural Employment', in M.L. Dantwala, *Indian Agricultural Development since Independence: A Collection of Essays*, Delhi: Oxford and IBH Publishing Co. Pvt. Ltd.

Census of India. 1991, 2001. Government of India.

Dandekar, V.M. and N. Rath. 1971. *Poverty in India*. Pune: Indian School of Political Economy.

Dantwala, M.L. 1978. 'Some Neglected Issues in Employment Planning', *Economic and Political Weekly*, 13(6 and 7): 291–95.

Faizi, A.A.A. 2009. 'Rural Unemployment Future Strategy', in A. Vachhani and N.K. Kumaresan Raja (eds), *Poverty, Unemployment and Rural Development Programmes*, Mussoorie: Centre for Rural Studies, L.B.S. National Academy of Administration.

GoI. 2002, 2006, 2020, 2012. *Report on Employment and Unemployment Situation Among Social Groups in India*, NSS 55th, 61st, 64th and 66th rounds. Ministry of Statistics and Programme Implementation.

———. 2009. *Agricultural Statistics at a Glance, 2009*. New Delhi: Directorate of Economics and Statistics, Department of Agriculture and Cooperation, Ministry of Agriculture.

Government of Odisha (GoO). 2012. *Economic Survey 2011–12*. Bhubaneswar, Odisha: Planning and Coordination Department.

———. 2006. *Agricultural Census of Odisha 2005–06*. Cuttack: Board of Revenue.

———. Various issues. *Statistical Abstract*. Directorate of Economics and Statistics.

Jha, B. 2006. 'Employment, Wages and Productivity in Indian Agriculture', Institute of Economic Growth Working Paper Series No. E/266/2006. Available at http://www.iegindia.org/workpap/wp266.pdf (last accessed on 24 November 2015).

Kiran, K. 2012. 'Agricultural Unemployment in India', *International Journal of Multidisciplinary Educational Research*, 1(3): 263–65.

Kumar, Anjani, Sant Kumar, Dhiraj K. Singh, and Shivjee. 2011. 'Rural Employment Diversification in India: Trends, Determinants and Implications on Poverty', *Agricultural Economics Research Review*, 22(1): 47–60.

Padhy, Sakti. 2009. 'Agricultural Growth, Employment and Poverty in Rural Orissa: Some Observations on Recent Trends', in R.K. Panda (ed.), *Orissa's Economic Development—Experiences and Expectations*. New Delhi: Serials Publications.

Panda, R.K and S. Tripathy. 2009. 'Land Distribution and Tenancy in Orissa', in D. Narasimha Reddy (ed.), *Agrarian Reforms, Land Markets and Rural Poor*. Mussoorie: Centre for Rural Studies, L.B.S National Academy of Administration.

Papola, T.S. 2006. *Economic Growth and Employment Linkages: The Indian Experience*. New Delhi: Institute for Studies in Industrial Development (occasional paper).

Parthasarathy, G. 1996. 'Recent Trends in Wages and Employment of Agricultural Labour', *Indian Journal of Agricultural Economics*, 51(1 and 2): 145–67.

Paul, S. 1988. 'Unemployment and Under-employment in Rural India', *Economic and Political Weekly*, 23(29, 16 July): 31–38.

Raj, K.N. 1976. 'Trends in Rural Unemployment in India—An Analysis with Reference to Conceptual and Measurement Problems', *Economic and Political Weekly*, 11(31/33, special issue, August): 41–50.

Raj Krishna. 1976. *Rural Unemployment—A Survey of Concepts and Estimates for India*. Washington, DC: World Bank.

Sahu B.K. and K.K. Tripathy. 2009. 'Agriculture and Poverty in Orissa: Some Observations during Post-Liberalization Period', in R.K. Panda (ed.), *Orissa Economic Development—Experiences and Expectations*. New Delhi: Serials Publications.

Saunders, P. 2002. 'Direct and Indirect Effects of Unemployment on Poverty and Inequality', SPRC Discussion Paper No. 118, December, Social Policy Research Centre, University of New South Wales, Sydney, Australia. Available at https://www.sprc.unsw.edu.au/media/SPRCFile/DP118.pdf (last accessed on 24 November 2015).

Visaria, P. 1981. 'Poverty and Unemployment in India: An Analysis of Recent Evidence', *World Development*, 9(3, March): 277–300.

PART II

INDUSTRIES, MINING, TRANSPORTATION, AND POWER

4

Industry in Odisha

Evolution, Policy, and Performance

Adwait Mohanty

Experience of nations the world over shows that in the process of economic development, the transformation of an agrarian economy takes place first into an industrialized economy and thereafter into a service-dominated one. However, in the case of India, one of the anomalies in the growth process has been the relatively stagnant share of industrial output in gross domestic product (GDP), though rapid industrialization was one of the avowed objectives of planned development since Independence. Notwithstanding the attempts at rapid industrialization, industrial growth of the country was slow. The share of agriculture in GDP fell significantly from around 50 per cent in 1950–51 to around 15 per cent in 2011–12. The share of manufacturing has been around 16 per cent for quite some time. Taking cognizance of the acute need of the country to find employment opportunities for the growing population and relieve agriculture of the pressure, the government has prepared a road map to increase the share of industry in the country's GDP from the present 16 per cent to 25 per cent by the year 2021.

The experience of Odisha has been no different from that of India when it comes to structural changes in output. The share of industry sector in Odisha's net state domestic product (NSDP) has been 28.4 per cent and that of manufacturing a dismal 8.6 per cent during 2001–12. Dependence on agriculture for employment in the state continues at a very high level of around 60 per cent. The state's development process seems to have bypassed the industrial sector. The employment opportunities created by industry have been far from satisfactory. What accounts for this state of affairs is a matter of inquiry.

The present chapter provides a broad overview of the industrial scenario in Odisha. The chapter is schematized as follows. The state's industrial performance vis-à-vis that of India in select attributes is provided in section titled 'Odisha in India's industrial landscape'. The section 'Phases in Odisha's industrialization' chronicles important phases in the state's industrialization process. To trace the correlation between industrialization and government initiatives, the section 'State industrial policies' discusses important industrial policy resolutions. Performance of the major industrial segments in the state is discussed in the section titled 'Industrial scenario of Odisha'. The concluding observations are made in the last section.

Odisha in India's industrial landscape

Odisha is a poor performer in the industry sector and continued being so with a low rate of industrialization until very recently. The share of Odisha's manufacturing industries in the total manufacture output of the country for selected years is given in Table 4.1.

The state's share in total manufacture output of the country has been less than 2 per cent in all the selected years. It declined from 1.83 per cent in 1980–81 to 1.43 per cent in 2000–01, but increased, of course, to a lower level of 1.76 per cent, in 2009–10. The increase in 2009–10 can be attributed to the operation of some power, aluminium, and steel plants in the state during the decade.

Net value added by manufacturing exhibits a slightly different trend with the state's share increasing from 1.76 per cent in 1981 to 2.24 per cent in 1991. The thrust given to labour-intensive village and cottage industries during the 1980s added higher value to locally available cheap raw materials. The industries set up in the decade 2001–10 were engaged in transforming low value minerals into

Table 4.1 Odisha's share in India's total manufacture

S. No.	Characteristics	Year			
		1980–81	1990–91	2000–01	2009–10
1	Number of factories	219 (1.14)	1,465 (1.33)	1,665 (1.27)	2,052 (1.29)
2	Invested capital (Rs lakh)	1,17,412 (2.70)	6,20,949 (3.19)	14,80,891 (2.59)	1,05,62,767 (5.46)
4	Total persons engaged	1,17,316 (1.88)	1,54,532 (1.87)	1,28,662 (1.61)	2,27,525 (1.93)
5	Value of output (Rs lakh)	92,031 (1.83)	4,87,019 (1.80)	13,24,267 (1.43)	65,66,234 (1.76)
6	Net value added (Rs lakh)	18,492 (1.76)	1,15,271 (2.24)	2,35,168 (1.64)	14,79,974 (2.50)

Source: GoI (2002, 2012).

Notes: Annual growth rate refers to annual compound growth rate.

Value figures in Rs lakh, others in number; percentages in parentheses; Odisha's share in total for India is in parentheses.

output with high value, and hence, proportionately high net value addition in 2010.

Capital investment in Odisha's manufacturing sector hovered around 3 per cent of the total for the country in all the selected years of the last century, but increased to 5.46 per cent in 2009–10. Favourable climate for industrialization in recent years attracted large-scale private capital into the state for investment in capital-intensive mineral-based industries.

But Odisha's share in total persons engaged in the manufacturing sector of the country was proportionately less (less than 2 per cent) in all the years considered. It speaks of higher capital intensity per worker in the state compared to that in the country as a whole. In other words, the state has not benefitted much by way of employment generation from industrial investment.

Phases in Odisha's industrialization

Early years

From its very inception in 1936, the state economy of Odisha was predominantly agrarian. Industries of the neighbouring states like

Jharkhand as well as of distant states of Maharashtra, Gujarat, and Tamil Nadu sourced raw materials from Odisha for their industries. At the time of Independence, the main planks of the industrial sector were handlooms and handicraft industries; modern industries were virtually non-existent. The state's share in the total industrial production of the country was only 0.26 per cent in 1950–51.

During the 1950s, concerted attempts were made to lay the foundation for the establishment of industries by creating infrastructure facilities. It was planned to set up ferromanganese plants at Joda and Rayagada, cement factory at Rajgangpur, tube factory and paper mill at Chowdwar, and aluminium and cable factory at Hirakud. Hirakud and Machkund hydroelectric projects were commissioned for transmission of power. The state highways were expanded and the national highways were developed. Establishment of one of the largest steel plants of the country in the public sector at Rourkela by the Government of India was a landmark in the industrial history of Odisha. The state's contribution to India's industrial production increased to 2 per cent in 1960–61.

During the 1960s, the projects planned for in the preceding decade were completed and efforts were intensified for the development of infrastructure facilities. The Industrial Development Corporation of Odisha was set up in 1962 with the objective of promoting industries in the private as well as public sector. The Corporation was expected to play the role of a pacesetter and pathfinder for industrialization in the state. A beginning was made with 800 registered factories with total capital investment of around Rs 290 crore. The small-scale and cottage industries in the state were assured regular supply of raw materials and marketing of finished goods. The state's share in India's industrial output marginally rose to 2.5 per cent in 1965–66.

A few schemes were operated during this period to speed up rural industrialization. One such project was the Pilot Project, which intended to attract and encourage private entrepreneurs to start small-scale industrial units. The state government contributed 90 per cent of share capital of the company floated for the purpose. The management of the unit was entrusted to private entrepreneurs with the option to take it over in due course. These units produced various types of goods, namely, concrete products, timber products, medicine and chemicals, boat-building, fruit processing and canning, foundry and engineering, and others. Unfortunately, most of these projects ended in failure due to bad management, misappropriation of funds, and poor business tradition. Of these, there were only six profit-making units by the end of 1967–68.

Another novel scheme, Panchayat Industries were introduced by the Government of Odisha in 1962–63. The scheme aimed at setting up Panchayat level industries by floating industrial cooperative societies to diversify the occupational pattern of the rural people. These industries included agro-processing, light engineering, and foundry and fabrication industries. Most of the units could not thrive because of difficulties faced in the marketing of products, and due to lack of infrastructure and entrepreneurship. During the latter part of the 1960s, the state along with the country faced recession and the earlier schemes for rural industrialization failed miserably. As a result, the state's share in the country's industrial production fell to 1.9 per cent in 1969–70.

By the end of 1960s, certain features of industrialization in Odisha stand out. First, mining, metallurgical, and metal-based industries predominated. Iron and steel constituted a little more than half the total (52 per cent) industrial output of the state. These heavy industries such as iron and steel, chemical fertilizers, electric light and power, and paper and paper products were very capital-intensive. The total productive capital shared by these few industries accounted for about 89 per cent of the total capital invested in the industrial sector of the state. Value added per unit of productive capital in these industries was very small. Secondly, capital intensity per industrial employment in Odisha was very high compared to that in other states. Thirdly, there was predominance of the public sector industries in the state. The public sector, which contributed about 50 per cent of total value added by the organized factory sector in 1964–65, raised its share to 68 per cent in 1969–70.

During the 1970s, the industrial scenario of the state remained virtually unchanged. Its share in the country's total industrial production remained less than 2 per cent, although the state accounted for more than 3.5 per cent of the population. In terms of gross per capita output as well as per capita value added by manufacture, Odisha lagged behind almost all major states. Gross per capita industrial output in Odisha was Rs 323 as against Rs 679 for all-India during 1978–79. In the same year, per capita net value added by manufacture in Odisha was Rs 73 as against Rs 146 for the country as a whole. Due to political instability, not much effort was made towards industrialization during this decade.

The 1980s and after

The 1980s are a watershed in the history of industrialization in Odisha. By 1980, there were a few small-scale industries in the state. These limited number of small-scale industries included rice mills, oil mills, and a few sick Panchayat industries. Some districts went without an industry. The government's strategy towards industrialization was captured in the slogan to set up 'thousand industries in thousand days investing thousand crore rupees'. Educated unemployed youth, both local and from outside, came forward to set up industries in the state. Hundreds of medium- and small-scale industries came up in industrial estates around Cuttack and Bhubaneswar, the state capital. There was a boom in fish trawling business with funding by Odisha State Financial Corporation; however, most of these loans were defaulted later. Establishment of National Aluminium Company (NALCO), Neelachal Ispat Nigam Limited (NINL), and Paradeep Phosphates Limited (PPL) were other remarkable achievements during the decade.

With the adoption of a policy of liberalization, privatization, and globalization at the national level in the 1990s, the state government formulated policies with the basic objectives of encouraging flow of investment, promoting entrepreneurship, and accelerating industrialization. During the decade, Odisha became a hub for steel industries with the establishment of a number of projects like MESCO Steel, Jindal Steel Limited, Tata Steel, Visa, and others. The state started emerging as a destination for investment in information technology (IT) sector. Major players in this sector like Infosys and Satyam Computer opened their units at Bhubaneswar.

The liberalization process initiated during the 1990s gathered momentum in the first decade of the present century. Various opportunities opened up to attract investment for industrialization of the state, which the government seized. With the boom in the global metal market and rising demand for resources, investors from different parts of the world headed for the state's mineral resources. However, the government insisted upon granting mining lease to companies that were prepared to set up value addition projects.

A number of companies in steel, aluminium/alumina, oil refineries, and fertilizer sectors are keen to set up their units in the state. In view of the expected industrial expansion, the government has shown interest for private capital to take up infrastructure upgradation and development in sectors like road and port. The state envisions emerging as a major IT hub for export. By the end of 2012-13, more than 93 companies had signed Memorandum of Understanding (MoU) with the state for an investment of Rs 5,32,085.91 crore. The estimated annual production of these companies worked out at 77.16 million tonne. Out of this, 30 partially commissioned projects have made an investment of Rs 50,32,577 crore and have a production capacity of 7.79 million tonne per annum (MTPA) of steel and 6.24 MTPA of sponge iron. These plants provided both direct and indirect employment to 74,163 persons.

State industrial policies

The national industrial policy applies equally to all the states. However, its effect differs across states depending upon their level of industrialization. In their zeal for rapid industrialization, the states formulate their own industrial policies to create a suitable investment climate and Odisha has followed suit.

Early years

Four industrial policies were announced by the state government prior to 1980 (February 1968, August 1971, April 1977, and July 1979). None of these policies was comprehensive and focused. These policies were ad hoc measures to promote small scale, village, and khadi industries. They were designed to give concessions to the industrial units in procuring licence and inputs, preparing project report, availing technical and financial assistance, and marketing of products. The policies did not make any dent in industrializing the state due to bureaucratic callousness and lack of political will.

The Industrial Policy Resolution, 1980 aimed at accelerating industrialization in the state. The thrust of the policy lay in encouraging educated youth to set up small-scale and medium industries. The potential entrepreneurs were offered subsidies, concessions, and procedural relaxations.

The policy was followed by the Industrial Policy, 1986 with a 'new deal' emphasizing on development of the modern industries. Its main features were technology upgradation, modernization of the existing units, and establishment of sophisticated industries. New industrial units were exempted from sales tax for five years. Further, districts of the state were divided into three zones depending on their levels of industrialization. Incentives were given on graded basis—maximum to the industries in the least industrialized districts and minimum to those in the most industrialized ones. This provision helped the process of industrialization in the backward districts.

The Industrial Policy, 1989 came up with a lot more concessions to boost the tempo of industrial growth in the state. Along with a novel provision of differentiated fixed capital subsidy to reduce regional inequality, many more tax incentives were given. Special concessions were provided to the units giving more employment to the disadvantaged sections of the society and of special importance for the state. The policy further liberalized many provisions under the earlier policies and offered new incentives and concessions. These provisions were meant for dispersal of industries to rural areas, promotional support to non-conventional energy equipment and devices, adoption of the latest technology, and thrust to exports.

The 1990s

The Industrial Policy, 1991 was announced by the state government when the national economy adopted the liberalization policy with economic reforms and ushered into an era of freedom from government control. The new policy was formulated to create an industry-friendly environment through a selective process of liberalization and privatization. The private investors were provided attractive incentives, concessions, diverse institutional support, and infrastructural facilities. The state government extended special care and financial support to 12 categories of industries identified as thrust areas. The policy devised an attractive and easily administered system of incentives for small-scale industries. It also encouraged equity participation in industries of significance for the state.

In order to improve investment climate and promote opportunities for industrial growth, the state government reformulated the industrial policy in 1996 by offering a package of incentives to the investors. The policy aimed at harnessing the natural resources and industrial potential of the state. The other objectives of the policy were establishing appropriate linkage between agriculture and industry through agro-based industries, strengthening rural economy, generating large-scale employment opportunities in industrial and commercial activities, development of backward regions, and skill and entrepreneurial development.

The twenty-first century

The Industrial Policy, 2001

To attract private capital and foreign direct investment (FDI) into the state, the government formulated the Industrial Policy, 2001. The policy intended to make the state industrially vibrant through aggressive industrialization. It aimed at creating a congenial investment climate by winning the trust of the industrialists through image building of the state as an attractive destination for investment. The specific objectives of the policy were to

- create a business climate conducive for accelerated investment in industry and infrastructure projects;
- raise income, employment, and economic growth;
- reduce regional disparities in economic development; and
- ensure balanced utilization of natural resources for sustainable development in the state.

Inflow of private capital, both domestic and foreign, was encouraged in sectors where the state had comparative advantage. These sectors included minerals, agro and marine based industries, industries based on medicinal herbs and minor forest produce, craft based products, tourism, electronics, information technology, and biotechnology. The policy promised fabulous benefits to the private investors by way of (a) land at concessional rate, (b) exemption of new industrial units from electricity duty, (c) interest subsidy, (d) tax concessions, (e) rationalization of inspection, (f) rationalization of labour laws, and (g) simplification of rules and procedures for speedy and hassle-free government clearance.

Rationalization of inspection stipulated in the policy was intended to enable industries to operate in a free environment and grow fully. The relationship between government and industry was to be based on mutual trust and belief. A system of self-certification as regards social and legal responsibility of an industry was introduced.

For speedy project clearance, single window system was operationalized. The system ensures faster clearance of project proposals and dissemination of project-related information at a single point to enable the potential entrepreneurs to take quick investment decisions. A composite application form system was introduced in place of several applications for clearance from different government departments. It is a three-tier clearance mechanism. Investment proposals are considered for clearance at different levels depending upon the size of investment.

The Industrial Policy, 2007

The achievements of the preceding policy encouraged the government to come up with a more proactive industrial policy in 2007. The objective of the policy was to reinforce and accelerate the process of industrialization in the state. The policy mandated a multipronged approach to provide infrastructure and institutional support as well as pre- and post-production incentives.

The main objectives of the policy include:

- transforming Odisha into a vibrant industrialized state;
- promotion of orderly and environmentally sustainable industrial growth;
- promoting Odisha as a major manufacturing hub;
- maximizing opportunities for both direct and indirect employment generation through development of traditional labour-intensive sectors;

- strengthening linkage between micro, small, medium, and large industries, and making concerted efforts for development of ancillary and downstream industries;
- specially promoting IT/ITES (information technology enabled service), biotechnology, agro, marine, and food processing, tourism, textiles and apparels, and automotive industries with maximum linkages for employment generation and export;
- arresting industrial sickness by reviving and rehabilitating potentially viable sick industries in the micro, small, and medium enterprise (MSME) sector; and
- facilitating industry and institution linkages in workforce planning, research and development, and so on.

In order to achieve these objectives, the state government has adopted a strategy for promoting international-level industrial and social infrastructure by creating competitive, scientific, as well as technical manpower and entrepreneurs. The policy also stipulates to promote ancillary and downstream industrial parks. Five zones have been identified for the development of specific ancillary and downstream industries. Angul-Dhenkanal and Jharsuguda-Sundergarh-Sambalpur zones have been dedicated for the development of both steel and aluminium industries; Cuttack-Paradeep and Kalinga Nagar zones have been earmarked for the promotion of only steel industries; and Rayagada–Kalahandi zone has been kept aside for aluminium sector.

Besides supporting industrialization in general, the policy has directed efforts to incentivize investments in the thrust and priority sectors. It also intends to operationalize and strengthen industrial facilitation and effective grievance redressal mechanism.

Finance is a big constraint for micro enterprises. Therefore, the policy focuses on establishing linkages between micro enterprises and microfinance institutions for product development through design improvement and technology upgradation. Odisha Small Industries Corporation (OSIC) is mandated to set up raw material banks to smoothen raw material supply and distribution. Common Facility Centres (CFCs) are being promoted on community-based public–private partnership (PPP) mode to intensify cluster developments.

The policy provides for modernization of small and medium enterprises (SMEs) through greater flow of institutional finance by reviving the Odisha State Financial Corporation (OSFC). It also tries to ensure marketing of products through government purchase programmes and development of special industrial parks.

The policy contemplates completing construction of three new ports namely, Dhamara, Kirtania, and Gopalpur to provide coastline advantage to port-based large-scale industries like ship-building, chemical and petro chemical complexes, leather, and others. By leveraging concentration of metal industries, the policy will help promote manufacturing industries in the state. Proposed supply chain linkages will bring about faster growth of SMEs.

The policy provides for the formation of Team Odisha with the Chief Minister as its captain for industrial facilitation and investment promotion in all key areas of industrial and economic growth. The Team is intended to synergize all government efforts for investment in the state. Industrial Promotion and Investment Corporation of Odisha Limited (IPICOL) has been mandated to act as a nodal agency to monitor the state's industrial activities. An industrial information service unit would be set up to provide exclusively investment-related information.

The MSME Development Policy, 2009

The contribution of MSMEs to value addition and employment generation is significant. However, development of MSMEs in the state lags behind the national level scenario. These industries need to be leveraged to realize their full potential for broad-based industrial development and export promotion. However, the problems of MSMEs are typical and their needs are specific. To facilitate growth of MSMEs in a focused manner, the government announced the Odisha MSME Development Policy, 2009, to address the impediments in the way of their revival and development.

The policy aims at enhancing the contribution of MSMEs in all potential sectors, particularly in manufacturing and services, and achieving balanced regional development by encouraging local entrepreneurs. In order to achieve this, some specific objectives of the policy were promoting new units, maximizing growth of the existing units, arresting sickness, and reviving sick units in the MSME sector. The strategy adopted towards this end included:

- clustering of MSMEs for enhanced competitiveness;
- promoting ancillary and downstream units in specialized/focused industrial areas/parks with adequate infrastructure facilities; and
- facilitating credit flow, marketing of products, and technological upgradation by encouraging use of cutting-edge technology in MSME sector.

Industrial scenario of Odisha

Manufacturing sector

The share of industry in net state domestic product (NSDP) declined from 22.2 per cent in the 1970s to 20.2 per cent in the 1980s, but increased in the post-reforms period (Table 4.2). The share of manufacturing exhibited a similar pattern—declining in the pre-reforms period (prior to 1991) and increasing thereafter. Large investments explain the increase in the share of industry and manufacturing in NSDP during the post-reforms period.

Table 4.2 Decadal share and growth of industry and manufacturing in Odisha, 1971–2012 (%)

Sector	Share				Growth rate			
	1971–80	1981–90	1991–2000	2001–12	1971–80	1981–90	1991–2000	2001–12
Industry	22.2	20.2	25.1	28.4	6.3	7.26	4.01	9.71
Manufacturing	6.4	5.6	5.8	8.6	7.06	8.65	2.36	15.91
Registered manufacturing	2.8	2.7	3.3	6.3	9.09	15.16	2.03	19.78
Unregistered manufacturing	5.1	4.3	3.6	2.6	3.12	2.56	1.92	5.01
Share of registered manufacturing in total manufacturing	35.2	37.9	47.6	68.8				
NSDP					2.41	4.79	4.02	8.36

Source: Author's calculations based on data obtained from GoO (2012).

Note: Sectoral shares and growth rates correspond to NSDP at constant prices (2004–05).

It is worth noting that the shares of industry and manufacturing, which were relatively low at 4.01 and 2.36 per cent respectively, increased during the 1990s. Due to shrinkage of other sectors and low growth rate of NSDP, shares of these two sectors emerged proportionately high. Contraction in the traditional handicraft and cottage industries and handlooms and textiles, and time lag in the operation of large-scale manufacturing industries accounted for slow industrial growth during this decade. In the following decade, with the commissioning of large industries, which had signed memoranda of understanding (MOUs) with the state government, both industry and manufacturing sectors grew respectively at higher rates of 9.71 per cent and 15.91 per cent.

It is estimated that manufacturing has a higher volatility than industry and the gap between the volatility of these two sectors widened across decades from 1970s till 2012. The coefficient of variation (CV) of output during 1971–80 was 20.1 per cent for industry and 24.2 per cent for manufacturing; the corresponding estimates for 2001–12 were 15.7 per cent and 21.7 per cent respectively. Since industry with other sub-sectors is a broader category than manufacturing, higher variability in the latter is dampened by lower variability in other sub-sectors within industry.

The manufacturing sector comprises two sub-sectors: registered and unregistered. Compared to the registered sector, the unregistered factories dominated the manufacturing sector with higher contribution to the state's NSDP until the end of the last century. In course of time, with the entry of basic metal industries like iron and steel, and aluminium and ferroalloys, output of the registered factory sector went up. As a result, its share (6.3 per cent) exceeded that of the unregistered factories (2.6 per cent) between 2001 and 2012. In the total manufacture production of the state, the registered factories accounted for 35.2 per cent in the 1970s, which systematically went up to 37.9 per cent in the 1980s, 47.6 per cent in the 1990s, and 68.8 per cent in the first decade of the present century.

Decadal growth rate of output of the registered manufacturing sector since 1971 has been consistently higher than that of the unregistered sector. Though the unregistered sector's output grew at a higher rate (5.01 per cent) between 2001 and 2012, the increase was almost one-fourth of the increase experienced in the registered factory sector. This resulted in the dominance of registered factories in the manufacturing sector of the state. The share of registered segment has almost doubled in the past four decades; that of the unregistered ones more than halved. As far as variability in output is concerned, both the segments exhibited marginal decline. The CV of output of the registered manufacturing industries declined from 31.5 per cent in 1971–80 to 30.6 per cent in 2001–12. The decline in unregistered manufacturing sector was from 10.2 per cent to 8.7 per cent over the corresponding period. However, variability of the registered segment continued at very high level.

Registered manufacturing sector

The registered manufacturing sector witnessed phenomenal growth in number of factories, employment generation, value of output, and value addition between 1951 and 2010 (Table 4.3). Increase was high in value of output and net value added, but low in number of units and employment. It implies that workers in this sector are adding more value to output over time (columns 8 and 9). Compared to 2001, output per worker increased 2.8 times while net value added rose by 3.6 times in 2009–10. More value addition to the state's raw materials by the mineral and mineral-based industries explains this phenomenon.

Growth rates in select features of the registered factories in each decade since 1951 have been recorded in Table 4.4. Growth rate in net value added has been consistently high in all the decades under reference. Value of output also registered high growth rate excepting 1960s with a negative value.

As regards employment generation in the sector, growth rates were high in the 1950s and 1960s, but started declining thereafter. In fact, industrial employment declined in the 1990s due to low growth in registered factories, but increased at a faster rate (6.5 per cent) between 2001 and 2010. The number of factories, which was consistently growing at a low rate in the last century, grew at a faster rate (3.7 per cent) during this decade due to favourable industrial climate.

Table 4.3 Organized manufacturing sector in Odisha, 1951–2010

S. No.	Period	Total no. of registered factories	Reporting factories	Total employment (no.)	Value of output (Rs lakh)	Value added (Rs lakh)	Output per employee (Rs)	Value added per employee (Rs)
(1)	(2)	(3)	(4)	(5)	(6)	(7)	(8)	(9)
1	1950–51	136	128	12,239	220	5,621	5,621	1,798
2	1960–61	525	322	30,210	1,283	1,55,823	1,55,823	4,247
3	1970–71	1,253	910	90,281	6,241	25,982	25,982	6,913
4	1980–81	1,660	1,129	1,34,011	21,139	77,076	77,076	15,774
5	1990–91	2,130	1,353	1,55,018	93,446	2,96,070	2,96,070	60,281
6	2000–01	2,253	1,665	1,28,662	2,35,168	10,29,260	10,29,260	1,82,780
7	2008–09	3,243	1,930	2,13,534	16,67,406	32,56,293	32,56,293	7,80,862
8	2009–10	NA	2,052	2,27,525	14,79,974	28,85,940	28,85,940	6,50,467

Source: Select issues of *Economic Survey*, Government of Odisha.

Table 4.4 Growth rates (%) of organized manufacturing sector in Odisha, 1951–2010

Year	Total no. of regd. factories	Reporting factories	Total employment (no.)	Value of output	Net value added (Rs lakh)
1951–61	14.5	9.7	9.5	52.6	19.3
1961–71	9.1	10.9	11.6	–6.7	17.1
1971–81	2.9	2.2	4.0	16.0	13.0
1981–91	2.5	1.8	1.5	16.1	16.0
1991–01	0.6	2.1	–1.8	11.2	9.7
2001–10	3.7	2.3	6.5	19.5	22.7

Source: Calculations are based on data from select issues of *Economic Survey* (GoO various years).
Note: In case of number of regd. (registered) factories, growth rate for 2001–10 corresponds to 2001–09.

Large-scale industry

The state with its vast natural resources has a great potential for the development of large-scale industries. There is heavy concentration of coal, bauxite, iron ore, manganese ore, chromites, limestone, china clay, quartz, precious and semi-precious stones, copper, and vanadium. Notwithstanding this, the state lagged behind many other states in the country as regards large-scale industry. To start with, there were a countable number of large-scale industries like Rourkela Steel Plant, NINL, Hindustan Aeronautics Limited, and NALCO in the public sector. Private capital was not forthcoming. Local capitalists with their feudal background were conservative, not enterprising. Poor infrastructure and inadequate local demand discouraged outside capital inflow into the state.

With the announcement of successive liberalized industrial policies by the state government, a congenial environment for industrial development was created. This led to massive inflow of private capital and rapid growth of investment in large-scale industries. By the end of 2011–12, 207 large-scale industries invested Rs 91,56,719 lakh and employed 1,09,163 persons (Table 4.5).

Table 4.5 District-wise large-scale industries in Odisha, 2012

S. No.	District	No. of units	Investment (Rs lakh)	Employment generated
1	Bargarh	1	14,235.85	156
2	Jharsuguda	18	6,30,222	7,905
3	Sambalpur	15	17,02,290.92	7,011
4	Sundargarh	62	10,48,711.96	47,990
5	Keonjhar	27	8,34,958	7,408
6	Mayurbhanj	2	2,622.66	279
7	Balasore	8	1,75,501.66	4,858
8	Bhadrak	1	6,572	452
9	Jagatsinghpur	6	2,87,974	2,435
10	Cuttack	11	5,63,887	2,449
11	Jajpur	14	11,91,197.66	7,910
12	Dhenkanal	10	6,71,799.21	2,253
13	Anugul	8	6,58,339.84	638
14	Khordha	10	16,796.5	1,046
15	Ganjam	2	24,852	1,978
16	Bolangir	3	63,932	551
17	Kalahandi	1	4,00,000	3,510
18	Rayagada	3	8,207.57	2,026
19	Nawarangpur	1	6,369	552
20	Koraput	4	8,48,249	7,756
	Total	207	91,56,718.83	1,09,163

Source: Directorate of Industries, GoO.

Of the 30 districts in the state, one-third goes without a large-scale industry. The districts close to the source of raw materials, namely, Sambalpur, Sundargarh, Jajpur, Keonjhar, and Koraput have attracted large investment. Though the number of large-scale industrial units is the highest in Sundargarh district (62), Jajpur with fewer industrial units (14) bagged the maximum investment. The newly established steel plants in Kalinga Nagar of Jajpur district are very capital-intensive.

Decadal addition to large-scale industries set up in Odisha since 1973 is given in Table 4.6. The state experienced a spurt in this sector in terms of number of units, investment, and employment in the first decade of the present century. This decade only accounts

Table 4.6 Large-scale industries in Odisha, 1973–2012

S. No.	Period	No. of units	Investment (Rs lakh)	Employment generated (No. of persons)
1	1973–80	2	1,520	833
2	1980–90	20	6,15,147	9,483
3	1991–2000	29	2,77,237	9,134
4	2000–12	91	34,71,775	32,696
	Total	142	43,65,679	52,146

Source: Directorate of Industries, GoO.

for 64 per cent of number of units, 75 per cent of investment, and 59 per cent of employment between 1973 and 2012. Compared to the earlier years, industries set up in the last 12 years were relatively more capital-intensive.

Considering category-wise large-scale industries, engineering and metal-based industries accounted for 70.4 per cent of units, 82.8 per cent of investment, and 75.03 per cent of employment (Table 4.7). In terms of number of units, this sector was followed by glass and ceramics (9.15 per cent) and chemicals and allied (8.45 per cent). However, in terms of investment, the share of chemical and allied industries (8.22 per cent) was higher than that of glass and ceramics (4.89 per cent). Shares of these three sectors taken together accounted for about 90 per cent of number of units and employment, and 95 per cent of total investment.

Shares of different sectors in invested capital did not correspond to their shares in employment generation. Chemical, aluminium, and steel industries had invested proportionately more capital than labour as these were capital-intensive. In all other sectors, the situation was the opposite.

The Government of Odisha has initiated many proactive investment promotion measures to reach out private capital for investment in sectors like minerals, power, cement, agro-processing, IT/ITES, and others. These measures included simplification of documentation procedures, rules and laws for 'doing business in Odisha'. Odisha has emerged as an investment hub in the recent years. Investment in the

Table 4.7 Category-wise growth of large-scale industries in Odisha, 1973–2012

S. No.	Category of industry	No. of units	Investment (Rs lakh)	Employment generated
1	Chemical and allied	12 (8.45)	3,58,695 (8.22)	2,409 (4.62)
2	Electrical and electronics	3 (2.11)	3,378.41 (0.08)	266 (0.51)
3	Engineering and metal-based	100 (70.42)	36,14,679.9 (82.80)	39,124 (75.03)
4	Food and allied	6 (4.23)	28,263 (0.65)	706 (1.35)
5	Forest and wood-based	1 (0.70)	6,369 (0.15)	552 (1.06)
6	Glass and ceramics	13 (9.15)	2,13,342.94 (4.89)	4,454 (8.54)
7	Paper and paper products	2 (1.41)	44,880 (1.03)	975 (1.87)
8	Rubber and plastics	3 (2.11)	44,358.35 (1.02)	2,727 (5.23)
9	Textiles	2 (1.41)	51,712 (1.18)	933 (1.79)
	Total	142 (100)	43,65,678.6 (100)	52,146 (100)

Source: Directorate of Industries, GoO.

Note: Figures in parentheses indicate percentages.

industry sector has increased substantially since 2003. There is an upturn in the number of applications for MoUs as well as MoUs signed, though the latter lagged behind vis-à-vis the former. Implementation of projects is still lower because of difficulties in land acquisition, obtaining environmental clearance, and displacement-related matters.

By 2011–12, the state government has signed 94 MoUs in different industry sub-sectors. Of the estimated investment of Rs 4,63,133.74 crore by companies signing MoUs, the steel sector accounts for half, followed by the power sector with one-third of the total investment. The other sectors with relatively high proportions of total estimated investment are alumina/aluminium (6.5 per cent) and crude oil processing (5.5 per cent) (Table 4.8).

A number of these projects have already been commissioned. In the steel sector, 30 projects have started partial production with

Table 4.8 Sector-wise MoUs signed till 2010–11

S. No.	Category of industry	No. of units	Project cost (Rs crore)	%age of project cost
1	Steel	49	2,30,421.82	49.75
2	Alumina/ aluminium	3	29,925.50	6.46
3	Cement project	4	2,982.00	0.64
4	Power project	30	1,55,672.42	33.61
5	Auto ancillary project	1	365.00	0.08
6	Steel and auto project	1	16,185.00	3.49
7	Titanium complex	1	1,150.00	0.25
8	Crude oil processing unit	1	25,646.00	5.54
9	MoU for downstream park	4	786.00	0.17
	Total	94	4,63,133.74	100.00

Source: Directorate of Industries, GoO.

an investment of Rs 50,326 crore and generating employment for 80,561 persons. Work is under progress in 46 projects, which include 20 steel, two cement, two aluminium, one titanium, and one oil refinery projects.

In view of anticipated entry of mega projects, the state is now poised on creating a strong base for ancillary and downstream industries by declaring them thrust industries. Iron and steel and aluminium industries dominate the downstream sector because of abundant availability of raw materials. Of late, investment in auto-component and petrochemical sectors is rapidly increasing and more are in the pipeline to set up industrial parks and special economic zones (SEZ) in these sectors.

Micro, small, and medium enterprises

The other important segments in the industry sector of Odisha are MSMEs and employment-oriented traditional sectors, which include handicraft and cottage industries, handlooms, sericulture, salt, and coir. The government has put emphasis on the development of small-scale industries since the beginning of the Planning era. These industries play a pivotal role in employment generation and production of consumer goods.

The sector has expanded over time and new units are being added each year. Number of units, investment, and employment in the sector in selected years beginning with 1984–85 up to 2010–11 are indicated in Table 4.9. Over the entire period of about three decades, growth rates in the number of units, investment, and employment were 1.7 per cent, 9.7 per cent, and 0.07 per cent respectively, implying a gradual increase in the capital intensity in these industries.

The sector did not grow smoothly; its rate of growth varied across decades (Table 4.10). Though investment increased consistently in all the decades, number of units and employment witnessed a decline in the later part of the 1980s.

Contraction in the sector had started much earlier. A substantial proportion of enterprises closed down their units. Calculations based on data of the Directorate of Industries, Government of Odisha showed that the proportion of closed units was as high as 69 per cent of the registered MSMEs during the 1970s. There was a gradual decline in this proportion to around 60 per cent in the 1980s, 32 per cent in 1990s, and only 0.4 per cent in the first 11 years of the present century. By the year 2009–10, there were 1,690 sick MSMEs with no addition to the list thereafter.

Table 4.9 Growth of SSIs/MSMEs in Odisha

Year	SSI/MSME units set up (cumulative)	SSI/MSME units set up during the year	Investment made (Rs crore)	Employment generated (No. of persons)
1984–85	23,415	3,202	35.72	24,003
1990–91	38,094	2,249	61.85	15,657
2000–01	66,206	3,676	153.18	18,115
2010–11	1,11,856	5,016	395.02	24,451

Source: Select issues of *Economic Survey* (GoO various years).

Note: SSI: small scale industries; MSME: micro, small, and medium enterprises.

Table 4.10 Growth rate (%) of SSIs/MSMEs in Odisha

Period	SSI/MSME units set up during the years	Investment made (Rs crore)	Employment generated (no. of persons)
1985–90	-8.6	7.6	-10.1
1991–2000	4.9	11.4	1.9
2001–11	5.4	3.2	9.9
1985–11	1.7	9.7	0.07

Source: Calculations are based on select issues of *Economic Survey* (GoO various years).

Many factors, both internal and external, were responsible for large-scale closure of small-scale units in the second half of the last century. The external factors included faulty government policy, widely fluctuating demand, irregular supply of raw materials and power, and continuous rise in cost. The internal factors were inexperienced entrepreneurs, faulty project proposal and appraisal, and diversion of funds. Over time, the local entrepreneurs gained experience and business environment improved, because of which there was no further closure of units. By the end of 2010–11, there were 1,11,856 MSMEs, investing Rs 4,036 crore.

The MSME sector in the state is grouped into 12 categories, as indicated in Table 4.11. Repairing and servicing activities dominate the sector with 32 per cent of the total number of units. These industries are followed by food and allied industries with a share of 22 per cent. These two sectors together constitute 54 per cent of the total number of units in the MSME sector. The other important categories of industry are engineering and metals, textiles, and glass and ceramics.

There is wide disparity in the development of the MSME sector across districts. Most of these industries are concentrated in Cuttack, Sundargarh, Ganjam, Balasore, Mayurbhanj, and Khordha districts where about half of the state's MSMEs are located. Likewise, half of the investment in this sector has been made in Sundergarh, Khordha, Cuttack, Keonjhar, Ganjam, and Jajpur districts.

These industries are mostly based on locally available resources and have not dispersed to other areas in the state due to lack of diversification. Demand constraint is another factor behind this disparity.

Table 4.11 Number of units and investment in MSMEs across sectors in Odisha, 2010–11

Sector	Total no. of MSMEs	Cumulative investment (Rs lakh)	Top five districts with MSME industries
Repairing and servicing	35,973 (32.16)	74,078 (18.35)	Sundargarh, Cuttack, Ganjam, Khordha, and Jajpur
Food and allied	24,798 (22.17)	1,10,532 (27.39)	Ganjam, Balasore, Cuttack, Sundargarh, and Sambalpur
Chemical and allied	12,469 (11.15)	82,718 (20.50)	Sundargarh, Cuttack, Ganjam, Khordha, and Sambalpur
Electrical and electronics	8,331 (7.45)	12,153 (3.01)	Cuttack, Ganjam, Puri, Jajpur, and Mayurbhanj
Engineering and metal-based	8,182 (7.31)	48,922 (12.12)	Ganjam, Cuttack, Dhenkanal, Balasore, and Mayurbhanj
Forest and wood-based	6,799 (6.08)	7,177 (1.78)	Cuttack, Balasore, Mayurbhanj, Puri, and Ganjam
Glass and ceramics	2,876 (2.57)	987 (2.45)	Cuttack, Sundargarh, Khordha, Balasore, and Ganjam
Livestock and leather	2,856 (2.55)	20,622 (5.11)	Cuttack, Ganjam, Sundargarh, Khordha, and Puri
Paper and paper products	1,760 (1.57)	14,605 (3.62)	Cuttack, Sundargarh, Khordha, Balasore, and Ganjam
Rubber and plastics	1,128 (1.01)	4,862 (1.20)	Khordha, Cuttack, Sundargarh, Ganjam, and Balasore
Textiles	443 (0.40)	732 (0.18)	Cuttack, Sundargarh, Ganjam, Sambalpur, and Puri
Miscellaneous manufacturing	6,241 (5.58)	17,324 (4.29)	
	1,11,856 (100)	4,03,595 (100)	

Source: Ernst and Young, India (2012).

Note: Figures in parantheses indicate percentages.

Industries are discouraged to move to less developed districts due to the presence of relatively larger number of poor, inadequate local demand, and underdeveloped infrastructure.

The traditional industries

The traditional industries like handloom and textiles and handicraft and cottage industries are at the lower end of industrialization spectrum of the state; however, they have an important place in its cultural heritage map. Being labour-intensive, these industries hold out gainful employment opportunities for the less trained people in rural areas with less capital investment.

Handicraft and cottage industries

The state has a long tradition of handlooms and handicrafts. Handicraft is considered an integral part of Odisha's cultural tradition. As many as 52 crafts are practised in the state. There are 21 popular crafts, of which brass and bell metal items, filigree works, appliqué works, and stone carving have good market potential. As many as 1.20 lakh artisan families dispersed throughout the state are engaged in handicraft production. The sector is shrinking in terms of number of units, investment, and employment potential. Between 1987–88 and 2011–12, the number of units declined from 1,77,966 to 7,293, investment also registered a fall from Rs 3,774.6 lakh to Rs 3,031.4 lakh and employment from 3,06,960 persons to only 9,187 persons.

Growth rates of the sector were consistently negative as regards number of units and employment generation across decades under reference (Table 4.12). Investment declined in the 1980s, but picked

Table 4.12 Growth rates (%) of handicraft and cottage industries in Odisha, 1988–2012

Period	Units	Investment	Persons employed
1987–90	-26.9	-16.4	-23.6
1991–2000	-15.2	4.6	-15.7
2001–12	-9.1	3.9	-10.0

Source: Calculations are based on data of Directorate of Handicraft and Cottage Industries, GoO.

up in the next two decades implying more use of capital per unit of worker. Use of power-driven equipment due to rising labour cost possibly explains the trend towards higher capital intensity.

Handloom and textiles

Though Odisha is not a cotton producing state, it has a large weaver population. The handloom products of the state are highly acclaimed in the country as well as abroad for their excellent artistic design, super artisanship, and long durability.

But the sector is on a downswing since long. According to Handloom Census of 1987–88, the state had 1.19 lakh looms, out of which 92,000 were active. The number of active looms decreased to 76,600 in 1995–96 Handloom Census and 49,000 in the latest Handloom Census of 2009–10. Likewise, employment in the sector declined from 2.44 lakh persons in 1987–88 to 2.08 lakh in 1995–96 and 49,000 in 2009–10. There were only 38,700 working looms employing 77,500 persons in 2010–11. These numbers further declined to 32,980 working looms, which provided employment to 66,000 persons in 2011–12. Table 4.13 indicates contraction of the sector over time.

Sericulture

Exquisite tassar and sericulture fabrics of Odisha are well known. It is an agro-based industry and provides employment to the scheduled castes (SCs), scheduled tribes (STs), and other backward castes (OBCs) in the rural areas. Sericulture involves rearing of silkworms,

Table 4.13 Growth rates (%) of handloom industry in Odisha, 1985–2012

Period	No. of looms	Production	Employment
1985–90	3.9	-4.8	3.9
1991–2000	-4.5	-14.8	-4.5
2001–12	-6.3	-1.5	-6.3

Source: Calculations are based on data of Directorate of Textiles and State Handloom Development Corporation, GoO.

Table 4.14 Production of tassar, mulberry, and eri cocoons in Odisha, 2007–11

Category	Year				
	2006–07	2007–08	2008–09	2009–10	2010–11
Tassar reeling cocoons (lakh)	465.23	661.00	729.20	915.00	922.96
Mulberry reeling cocoons (lakh)	20.15	20.30	25.50	30.00	17.99
Eri cut cocoons (MT)	4.40	6.53	8.80	9.40	4.40

Source: Planning and Coordination Department, GoO (2012).

extraction of silk fibre yarn, and processing and weaving of the same. It is practised mainly in Mayurbhanj, Keonjhar, and Sundargarh districts. Income from sericulture activities is not very encouraging, for which production in the sector did not improve much, rather declined in the year 2010–11 (Table 4.14).

Salt and coir industries

Salt and coir are traditional industries providing employment in the state's coastal districts like Ganjam, Puri, and Balasore. Productivity in salt industry is low in Odisha, per acre production being 10 MT compared to 70 MT in other salt-producing coastal states. Coir industry provides employment mostly to women in rural areas. Though contribution of these sectors to NSDP is very low, yet they are significant from the point of view of rural employment generation, particularly among the disadvantaged groups.

* * *

The process of industrialization in Odisha was very slow during the twentieth century. Many factors like inadequate infrastructure, lack of entrepreneurship, bureaucratic apathy, and, above all, lack of focus on the part of government were responsible for this. The recent policy changes made by the government, however, have reinforced the industrialization process in the state. At the present juncture, the state appears to be in an enviable position with regard to its prospect for rapid industrialization. This is because of an enabling policy framework coupled with the necessary institutional arrangements. Liberalized policy, single window system, and institutions such as IPICOL, IDCO, and so on are some constituents of this framework. If pursued with the right spirit, these will facilitate massive private capital inflow from within the country as well as from abroad. Such a pattern is already discernible from the increasing number of MoUs signed between the government and potential investors. The task before the government is to ensure that the MoUs are translated into real projects.

Promotion of large and medium industries will accelerate the pace of industrialization in the state. However, heedless industrialization is a mixed blessing. Mineral-based industrialization calls for intensified large-scale mining activities. Mining activities for industries are mostly carried out in forest areas and cause deforestation. Excavation of land for mines lead to degradation of surface area and loss of valued top soil. This disturbs the natural drainage system and groundwater table. Industries along with mining activities add to air and water pollution, thereby causing health hazards, environmental degradation, destruction of biodiversity, and threat to ecology. Out of 17 industry categories identified as most polluting by the Central Pollution Control Board, Odisha has 12. Because of hazardous chemicals present in their effluents, 18 industries in the state have been adjudged grossly polluting. Most of these industries are in the large- and medium-scale categories. For instance, the air and water pollution load is maximum in Talcher-Angul and Rourkela industrial belts. The state cannot afford to stop industrialization for environmental reasons, nor can it go ahead with adding to the present level of environmental pollution. Intensification of industrialization calls for adoption of rigorous pollution abatement measures.

Another critical issue that has assumed significance in recent times is industry-induced displacement, which might constrain state's industrialization in the coming years. Industrialization in conjunction with mining has caused displacement of people from their traditional habitations and destruction of their sources of livelihood, for which stiff resistance is put up by local public, social organizations, and political parties. The displaced have not been rehabilitated long after commissioning of the projects. The issue of rehabilitation has not been settled for SAIL's Rourkela plant, an issue pending for more than six decades. The displaced lose their permanent sources of livelihood. The possible employment opportunities bypass them as in the cases of steel plants in Kalinga Nagar. The worst sufferers are the tribal people as they are uprooted from their ancestral lands and fail to adjust to the estranged environment of resettlement colonies thoughtlessly planned with no regard to their sociocultural needs.

People's movements around rehabilitation and resettlement issues are being organized against the establishment of POSCO, a mega steel plant in the coastal parts of the state. For speedy implementation of the industrialization programmes, the state government needs to come up with an appropriate resettlement and rehabilitation package by consulting all the stakeholders.

References

Aliveler, G., A. Samal, D. Chakravarty, and K. Sen. 2011. 'A Thousand Industries in a Thousand Days: State Business Relations and the Puzzle of Orissa's Industrial Performance', Working Paper No. 97, Centre for Economic and Social Studies, Hyderabad.

Directorate of Handicraft Handicraft and Cottage Industries, Government of Odisha. Available online at http://as.ori.nic.in/dhorissa/ (last accessed on 22 January 2016).

Directorate of Industries, Government of Odisha. Available online at http://as.ori.nic.in/diorissa/ (last accessed on 22 January 2016).

Directorate of Textiles and State Handloom Development Corporation, GoO. Available online at http://odisha.gov.in/textiles/index.htm (last accessed on 22 January 2016).

Ernst and Young, India. 2012. 'Doing Business in Odisha', draft submitted to Industrial Promotion and Investment Corporation of Orissa Ltd (IPICOL), Bhubaneswar.

Government of India (GoI). 2002. *Orissa Development Report*. New Delhi: Planning Commission.

———. 2012. *Annual Survey of Industries*. New Delhi: Ministry of Statistics and Programme Implementation.

GoO. 2012. *Economic Survey 2011–12*. Bhubaneswar, Odisha: Planning and Coordination Department.

———. Various years. *Economic Survey*. Bhubaneswar, Odisha: Planning and Coordination Department.

GoO. 1978. *Annual Survey of Industries in Orissa*. Bhubaneswar: Bureau of Statistics and Economics.

India Brand Equity Foundation. 2011. *Report on Indian States: Economy and Business, Orissa*. Gurgaon, Delhi.

Patnaik, K.M. 1978. 'Industrial Development of Orissa', *Orissa Economic Journal*, 11(2): 43–55.

United Nations Industrial Development Organisation. 2011. *The Findings of the UNIDO Survey of Recent Investors' Experience of the Process of Establishing or Expanding Operations in Odisha*, Report to Government of Odisha. Available at http:/www.unido.org (accessed on 22 January 2016).

5

Mining and Odisha's Economy

Amarendra Das and *Satyananda Acharya*

The mining sector draws the attention of academicians, policy-makers, and common people for several reasons. On the one side, mining is seen as a source of economic growth, industrialization, employment, and revenue generation; on the other, it is seen as a source of social and environmental curse. Mining operations often causes displacement of local communities, which are mostly adivasis (indigenous community) and are vulnerable economically and socially. Mining activities, if not undertaken scientifically, pollute air, water, and soil, and degrade forests. In this context, this chapter provides a systematic account of the positive and negative impacts of the mining sector on the state economy. The chapter is organized as follows: the second section titled 'Reserves and production of minerals in Odisha' presents the major mineral reserves and production of Odisha and its share in the total minerals reserves and production at all-India level. The third section discusses the contribution of mining to the state economy in terms of output, revenue, and employment. The fourth section describes the negative consequences of mining in terms of deforestation, air pollution, water pollution, displacement, and loss of biodiversity. The fifth section points out the nature and causes of regulatory failure in the mining industry. The last section provides some policy suggestions for better management of mineral resources.

Reserves and production of minerals in Odisha

The mineral deposits of Odisha can be divided into three main petrological rock-divisions based on genesis and chemical characters. They are north Odisha, central Odisha, and south Odisha.

The north Odisha rocks are intricately folded and metamorphosed. They contain much iron- ore-bearing minerals. They also contain magmatic rocks, which embody iron ore, manganese ore, chrome ore, nickel, platinum, vanadium and titanium ores, and many secondarily altered deposits (Acharya 2008).

The central Odisha sector has the distribution of essentially coal, shale (including fire clay), and other clays.

The southern Odisha, having a hilly terrain of only two types of rocks, namely, khondalite and charnockite, has deposits of bauxite (aluminum ore) widespread on the hill-tops in many districts, manganese ore, sillimanite, zircon, tin ore minerals (in granites), and the like (Acharya 2000).

Abundant reserves of high grade iron ore, coal, bauxite, chromite along with other minerals such as limestone, dolomite tin, nickel, granite, gemstone, and graphite occur in the state. All the important minerals that occur in the state in different districts are listed in Table 5.1.

Table 5.2 presents the total reserves (which includes proved, indicated, and inferred reserves) of mineral in Odisha and India. Odisha possesses 99.52 per cent of chromite, 92.59 per cent of nickel, 54.97 per cent of bauxite, 44.20 per cent of manganese ore, 33.16 per cent of iron ore, and 23.95 per cent of coal reserves of the country.

Evolution of mining in Odisha

Odisha saw the first mining activities in 1904 in the then feudatory state of Mayurbhanj at Gorumahisani; this was extended later to

Table 5.1 Mineral occurrence and geographical location

S. No.	Mineral	Districts
1.	Bauxite	Balangir, Kalahandi, Kandhamal, Keonjhar, Koraput, Malkangiri, Rayagada, and Sundergarh
2.	China clay	Bargarh, Boudh, Balangir, Keonjhar, Koraput, Mayurbhanj, Sambalpur, and Sundergarh
3.	Chromite	Balasore, Cuttack, Dhenkanal, Jajpur, and Keonjhar
4.	Coal	Ib river valley coalfield, Sambalpur district, and Talcher coalfield, Dhenkanal
5.	Dolomite	Bargarh, Keonjhar, Koraput, Sambalpur, and Sundergarh
6.	Dunite/Pyroxenite	Keonjhar and Sundergarh
7.	Fireclay	Angul, Cuttack, Dhenkanal, Jharsuguda, Khurda, Puri, Sambalpur, and Sundergarh
8.	Garnet	Ganjam, Kalahandi, and Sambalpur
9.	Graphite	Bargarh, Boudh, Balangir, Kalahandi, Koraput, Nuapada, and Rayagada
10.	Iron ore (Hematite)	Dhenkanal, Jajpur, Keonjhar, Koraput, Mayurbhanj, Sambalpur, and Sundergarh
11.	Iron ore (Magnetite)	Mayurbhanj
12.	Limestone	Bargarh, Koraput, Malkangiri, Nuapada, Sambalpur, and Sundergarh
13.	Manganese ore	Balangir, Keonjhar, Koraput, Rayagada, Sambalpur, and Sundergarh
14.	Pyrophyllite	Keonjhar
15.	Quartz/Silica sand	Boudh, Balangir, Kalahandi, Sambalpur, and Sundergarh
16.	Quartzite	Balangir, Dhenkanal, Jajpur, Jharsugada, Keonjhar, Mayurbhanj, Sambalpur, and Sundergarh
17.	Sillimanite	Ganjam and Sambalpur
18.	Talc/Steatite/ Soapstone	Mayurbhanj, Sundergarh, and Sambalpur
19.	Titanium minerals	Dhenkanal, Ganjam, Jajpur, and Mayurbhanj
20.	Zircon	Ganjam
21.	Asbestos	Keonjhar
22.	Cobalt	Cuttack and Jajpur
23.	Copper	Mayurbhanj and Sambalpur

(*Cont'd.*)

Table 5.1 (*Cont'd.*)

S. No.	Mineral	Districts
24.	Granite	Angul, Boudh, Balangir, Cuttack, Deogarh, Dhenkanal, Ganjam, Keonjhar, Khurda, Koraput, Mayurbhanj, Nuapada, Rayagada, and Sambalpur
25.	Lead	Sargipalli area, Sundergarh
26.	Nickel	Cuttack, Keonjhar, and Mayurbhanj
27.	Ruby	Balangir
28.	Emerald	Kalahandi
29.	Platinum group of metals	Keonjhar
30.	Silver	Sundergarh
31.	Tin	Koraput and Malkangiri
32.	Vanadiferous magnetite	Balasore and Mayurbhanj

Source: Indian Bureau of Mines (IBM 2011).

Sulaipat and Badampahar. Iron ore from here was taken by a railway line to Jamshedpur. P.N. Bose was the first to locate and work on these deposits. Almost by that time, local production of manganese ore also started at Rajabasa, off-Koira in Sundergarh district. Mining of iron-rich rocks in Odisha and iron smelting by local process was commonplace around the ore-occurring regions. Gold and copper in their metallic forms used to be collected in the localities of Telkoi in Keonjhar, Subarnarekha River in Mayurbhanj, and Balasore where panning used to be the method for collecting the micro-nuggets. Evidences of export of these metals have been traced through Tamralipta port in eastern part of India. In the second decade of the past century, new iron mines around Noamundi (actual name Luhamundi) were discovered by the early pioneer-geologists and mining people. Modern mining started from the 1940s in this region of iron ore. Since then mineral production in Odisha has grown rapidly.

State-wise analysis reveals that Odisha occupies the top position in mineral production for the year 2009–10 by contributing 34 per cent of the total minerals, enlisted under Mineral Conservation

Table 5.2 Odisha's share in the mineral reserves of India

Mineral	Total reserve in India (Rs)	Reserve in Odisha (Rs)	Odisha's share as %age of India's total reserve	Date of estimation (Time)
Bauxite (thousand tonnes)	32,89,817	18,08,271	54.97	1 April 2005
Chromite (tonnes)	19,45,200	19,35,925	99.52	1 April 2005
Coal (million tonnes)	2,76,810.41	66,307.25	23.95	1 April 2010
Iron ore (thousand tonnes)	178,82,097	59,30,233	33.16	1 April 2010
Limestone (thousand tonnes)	17,53,44,901	17,38,360	0.99	1 April 2005
Manganese ore (thousand tonnes)	4,29,982	1,90,047	44.20	1 April 2010
Nickel (million tonnes)	189	175	92.59	1 April 2010

Source: IBM (2011).

and Development Rules (MCDR) 1988, produced in India. It is followed by Goa 18 per cent, Karnataka 15 per cent, Chhattisgarh 14 per cent, Rajasthan 7 per cent, Andhra Pradesh 5 per cent, Madhya Pradesh 3 per cent, Maharashtra 2 per cent, and Tamil Nadu and Gujarat 1 per cent each (Table 5.3). Share of other states to the gross domestic product (GDP) from mining sector was negligible during the year.

In terms of total quantity of production of minerals, coal sector dominates the other sectors by contributing more than 50 per cent (Table 5.4). The share of coal sector in the total quantity of mineral production of Odisha has gone down from around 65 per cent during 1996–97 to 51.71 per cent during 2008–09. Mining of iron ore has grown rapidly from the early 2000s. Thus, the share of iron ore in the total mineral production has gone up from

Table 5.3 State-wise contribution to the total minerals# produced in India at current prices, 2007–08 to 2009–10

State/union territory	2007–08 (R) (Rs '000)	2008–09 (R) (Rs '000)	2009–10 (P) (Rs '000)	% share of the state in GDP of MCDR in 2009–10
Total MCDR minerals produced in India	27,27,88,836	32,98,34,194	30,30,78,314	19.65
Andhra Pradesh	1,38,08,976	1,78,71,146	1,40,77,030	4.65
Assam	81,922	74,330	78,869	0.03
Bihar	93,308	1,00,036	1,29,262	0.04
Chhattisgarh	4,56,76,796	5,78,95,703	4,29,79,193	14.18
Goa	2,86,08,360	4,43,93,548	5,36,97,959	17.72
Gujarat	41,46,259	30,22,854	29,48,533	0.97
Himachal Pradesh	4,66,921	5,18,696	5,17,260	0.17
Jammu and Kashmir	57,656	25,079	40,353	0.01
Jharkhand	79,50,021	14,01,766	15,86,439	0.53
Karnataka	5,36,10,095	5,26,28,355	4,51,06,402	14.88
Kerala	4,82,411	4,87,846	4,60,898	0.15
Madhya Pradesh	84,66,754	1,06,93,275	89,87,504	2.97
Maharashtra	60,25,409	85,36,484	55,47,179	1.83
Meghalaya	1,99,252	3,33,773	3,68,425	0.12
Odisha	8,53,21,285	11,22,50,070	10,30,27,583	33.99
Rajasthan	1,49,57,177	1,64,99,279	1,99,87,616	6.6
Tamil Nadu	25,68,924	28,54,153	32,56,504	1.07
Uttar Pradesh	40,155	47,027	91,437	0.03
Uttarakhand	1,75,587	1,64,290	1,50,750	0.05
West Bengal	51,568	36,484	39,118	0.01

Source: IBM (2011).

Notes: #Minerals listed under MCDR, 1988.

R: revised estimate; P: provisional

around 20 per cent during 1996–97 to around 41 per cent during 2008–09. The major jump in the production is observed at two

Table 5.4 Share of different minerals in the total mineral production

Year	Bauxite		Chromite		Coal		Iron ore		Limestone		Total mineral (tonne)
	Production (tonne)	Share (%)	Production (tonne)	Share (%)	Production (tonne)	Share (%)	Production (tonne)	Share (%)	Production (tonne)	Share (%)	
1996–97	25,65,936	4.51	13,56,053	2.38	3,71,49,893	65.28	1,13,16,014	19.89	19,01,504	3.34	5,69,06,433
1997–98	26,68,237	4.26	14,39,790	2.30	4,23,36,860	67.53	1,21,56,673	19.39	19,27,775	3.08	6,26,89,398
1998–99	28,17,552	4.44	14,02,054	2.21	4,34,73,279	68.43	1,16,68,181	18.37	18,21,280	2.87	6,35,27,548
1999–2000	28,78,314	4.46	17,52,748	2.72	4,35,43,443	67.46	1,20,52,171	18.67	18,54,702	2.87	6,45,48,019
2000–01	29,06,533	4.22	19,31,526	2.80	4,48,12,840	65.02	1,43,49,730	20.82	21,15,148	3.07	6,89,24,174
2001–02	36,04,703	4.81	17,60,435	2.35	4,78,03,020	63.75	1,67,91,248	22.39	21,52,283	2.87	7,49,82,397
2002–03	49,32,447	5.65	32,87,001	3.76	5,20,30,709	59.57	2,22,56,592	25.48	23,03,170	2.64	8,73,50,586
2003–04	49,38,071	4.57	28,79,676	2.67	6,02,01,302	55.73	3,48,88,125	32.29	22,41,130	2.07	10,80,30,044
2004–05	49,11,739	3.87	34,23,387	2.69	6,68,14,753	52.59	4,60,63,158	36.26	22,63,247	1.78	12,70,50,389
2005–06	48,70,604	3.36	32,90,519	2.27	7,05,48,315	48.67	4,80,59,791	33.15	26,09,469	1.80	14,49,66,932
2006–07	46,67,508	2.89	37,22,633	2.31	8,12,81,053	50.34	6,58,86,005	40.81	26,87,851	1.66	16,14,51,125
2007–08	46,85,998	2.62	32,84,100	1.84	8,96,86,365	50.22	7,45,04,876	41.72	28,31,460	1.59	17,85,82,004
2008–09	47,34,529	2.50	27,94,392	1.48	9,77,86,646	51.71	7,71,95,160	40.82	30,71,180	1.62	18,90,95,390

Source: GoO (2013a).

points: 2003–04 and 2006–07. The production of minerals given in physical quantity reflects the size of economic activity generated by one sector.

Contribution of mining to the state economy

Output

The contribution of mining and quarrying (M&Q) sector in the gross state domestic product (GSDP) during recent years has gone up substantially as compared to that of during early years of Independence (Table 5.5). The average share of M&Q in the GSDP of Odisha has gone up from 0.76 per cent during the 1950s to around 4 per cent in 1990s and highest (6.5 per cent) during 2000s. The share of M&Q in GSDP of Odisha in 2011–12 is recorded at 5.95 per cent, which shows a moderate fall as compared to the 2000s decade. The M&Q sector witnessed maximum growth during the 2000s, starting from the early 2000s (Figure 5.1). The sector recorded around 11 per cent growth during 1950s. However, the growth rate slowed down in the next two decades. The 1970s experienced the slowest growth rate (3.76 per cent average) which coincides with the intensive nationalization of minerals and mining activities. However, the growth

Table 5.5 Share of mining and quarrying in the GSDP and the annual average growth rate of the same sector (%)

Decade	Average share of mining and quarrying in the GSDP	Average annual growth rates
1950–51 to 1959–60	0.76	10.91
1960–61 to 1969–70	1.09	7.88
1970–71 to 1979–80	1.33	3.76
1980–81 to 1989–90	1.62	9.42
1990–91 to 1999–2000	3.83	11.20
2000–01 to 2009–10	6.50	11.95
2010–11	6.13	-3.99
2011–12	5.96	4.29

Source: Planning and Coordination Department, GoO (2013).

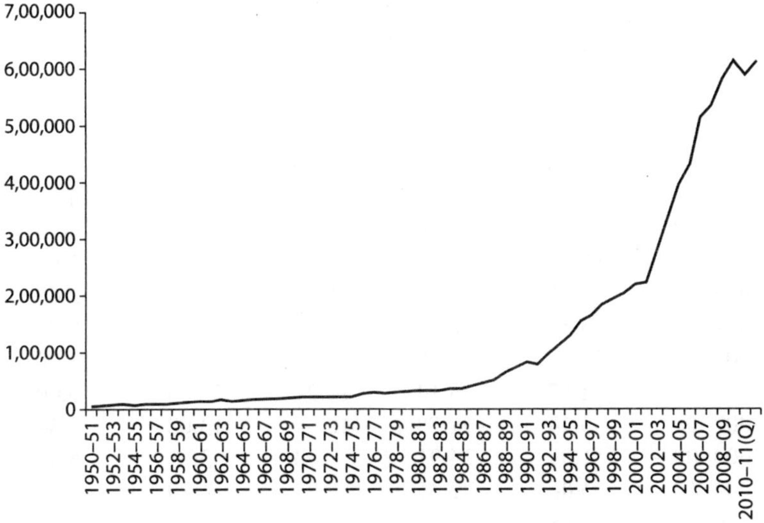

Figure 5.1 Growth trend of mining and quarrying sector in India
Source: Based on CSO data.

rates gradually picked up from 1980s and accelerated further from 2001–02. In Figure 5.1, we see a kink that shows a trend break for the M&Q sector. However, the sector witnessed negative growth in 2010–11 and showed recovery in 2011–12.

Among the major minerals produced in Odisha, which mineral production has pulled the growth of M&Q sector from the early 2000s? Table 5.6 provides the answer to this question. The annual growth rate of iron ore production jumped from 3.29 per cent in 1999–2000 to 19.06 per cent in 2000–01, 32.55 per cent in 2002–03, and highest 56.75 per cent in the year 2003–04. The growth slowed down in the year 2005–06, dipping to 4.33 per cent. Nevertheless, growth of iron ore extraction accelerated during 2006–07 and 2007–08 and then onwards the industry has been witnessing slowdown from 2008–09 that coincides with the global recession and fall of Chinese demand. Finally, in the year 2010–11 the industry recorded shrink in the output by 5.62 per cent. Like the iron ore industry, the coal industry witnessed positive growth from

Table 5.6 Annual growth rates of major mining industries in Odisha (%)

Year	Bauxite	Chromite	Coal	Iron ore	Limestone
1997–98	3.99	6.18	13.96	7.43	1.38
1998–99	5.60	-2.62	2.68	-4.02	-5.52
1999–2000	2.16	25.01	0.16	3.29	1.84
2000–01	0.98	10.20	2.92	19.06	14.04
2001–02	24.02	-8.86	6.67	17.01	1.76
2002–03	36.83	86.72	8.84	32.55	7.01
2003–04	0.11	-12.39	15.70	56.75	-2.69
2004–05	-0.53	18.88	10.99	32.03	0.99
2005–06	-0.84	-3.88	5.59	4.33	15.30
2006–07	-4.17	13.13	15.21	37.09	3.00
2007–08	0.40	-11.78	10.34	13.08	5.34
2008–09	1.04	-14.91	9.03	3.61	8.47
2009–10	3.06	22.35	8.82	4.79	-4.37
2010–11	-0.48	24.41	-3.61	-5.62	27.20
Average growth rate (%)	5	8	8	19	5

Source: Planning and Coordination Department, GoO (2013); data for 2009–10 and 2010–11 from IBM (2011).

early 2000s and negative growth in 2010–11. Bauxite and chromite[1] industries have experienced high fluctuations during 1997–98 and 2010–11. Limestone industry, however, has demonstrated relatively less volatility in output.

Domestic demand vs external demand

Is the growth of Odisha's mining industry driven by the domestic demand or external demand? Table 5.7 presents the share of export

[1] Chromite in Odisha contains PGE (platinum group of elements) and nickel ore that need to be extracted in the state. However, we are not able to do so and lose a huge amount of revenue from this source. Further value addition to these minerals ought to be done to maximize the economic benefits from chromite ore.

Table 5.7 Share of export in total output of selected major minerals

Year	Chromite (% share in total quantity of production)	Iron ore (% share in total quantity of production)	Mineral sand (% share in total quantity of production)	Production value (Rs crore)#	Export value (Rs crore)#	Share of export in total production (%)
1994–95	36.22	12.19	86.97			
1995–96	36.31	7.43	81.01			
1996–97	43.87	6.98	82.68			
1997–98	32.95	2.66	86.96			
1998–99	28.25	2.28	85.00			
1999–00	44.96	4.46	87.26	2,605.05	387.48	14.874
2000–01	41.10	3.98	87.47	2,776.15	453.82	16.35
2001–02	51.86	7.28	62.64	2,910.47	538.79	18.51
2002–03	38.11	4.73	92.48	3,694.17	642.20	17.38
2003–04	37.60	2.65	89.15	3,877.75	1,186.53	30.60
2004–05	29.70	25.26	88.27	6,130.93	NA	NA
2005–06	35.95	28.32	86.20	6,604.41	9,161.20	138.71
2006–07	31.98	27.72	79.80	7,629.63	10,761.20	141.05
2007–08	22.49	28.53	80.47	10,627.05	8,333.00	78.41
2008–09	19.90	23.28	70.75	15,122.90	7,814.64	51.67
2009–10#	13.67	18.66	103.24	15,317.10	4,760.43	31.08
2010–11#	10.09	29.70	86.54	28,286.87	15,894.29	56.19
2011–12#	9.23	19.62	63.93	30,204.38	4,231.79	14.01

Source: GoO (2013b).

Note: # indicates data obtained from Planning and Coordination Department, GoO (2010, 2013).

in the total output of three major exportable minerals of Odisha: chromite, iron ore, and mineral sand. A large part of the mineral sand produced in Odisha is exported to other countries. In most of the years, starting from 1994–95 to 2007–08, the share of export in the total production of mineral sand has remained above 80 per cent. The export share has also touched the peak level of 103 per cent during 2009–10. This implies that some of the inventories have been exported in this year due to high external demand.

Iron ore industry, however, witnessed a major change in the demand composition. During 1994–95, the share of export in total mineral production was around 12 per cent. However, it declined continuously until 2003–04 and export of iron ore constituted only 2.65 per cent in the total iron ore production. The share of export, however, jumped from next year to 25.26 per cent and rose continuously to a high of 29.70 per cent in 2010–11. In the year 2011–12, the share of export has fallen to 19.62 per cent. It is noteworthy to point here that a large part of the iron ore was exported to China to feed the demands of Olympics (held at Beijing in 2008) infrastructure.

The chromite industry witnessed an increasing trend in the external demand in the second half of 1990s and early 2000s. The export share of chromite in the total production increased from 36.22 per cent in 1994–95 to 51.86 per cent in 2001–02. However, then onwards the export share has declined steadily and reached at 9.23 per cent in 2011–12. The growth of chromite industry has fluctuated widely during the entire period of our analysis. Between 2001–02 and 2010–11, the industry recorded negative growth in five years and positive growth in rest five years.

If we analyse the monetary value of all mineral exports and all minerals produced in Odisha, we observe that the share of export in the total value of production increased steadily from 14.87 per cent in 1999–2000 to as high as 141.05 per cent in 2006–07 and then has declined persistently till 2011–12. The share of export in the total production of minerals has gone back to the same position (14 per cent) in the year 2011–12 as it was in 1999–2000. The share of export in total production of minerals has exceeded 100 per cent in two years: 2005–06 and 2007–08. This can be interpreted in two ways. One, due to huge external demand the inventories might have been exported. In this regard, one of the authors of this chapter has field experience that during this period mountain-like heaps of low-grade iron ore fines that were never demanded by anybody vanished because of demand from China. The second reason in this regard could be the difference in the domestic price and export price of minerals. If the production of minerals are valued at domestic price and export of minerals are valued at international price, the latter can show a higher value assuming that domestic price is usually less than the international price.

Table 5.8 presents the growth of internal consumption and export in three major mining industries: chromite, iron ore, and mineral sand. During the entire period from 1995–96 to 2008–09, internal consumption of chromite has increased faster than the export. On the other hand, export of iron ore has grown five times faster than the

Table 5.8 Growth of internal consumption and export of major minerals in Odisha (%)

	Chromite		Iron ore		Mineral sand	
	IC	Export	IC	Export	IC	Export
1995–96	38.86	39.45	5.35	-39.12	67.07	6.79
1996–97	-31.28	-5.80	29.60	21.26	80.66	102.19
1997–98	35.67	-14.70	18.49	-56.88	5.20	46.98
1998–99	0.16	-19.73	-5.55	-19.38	11.41	-5.37
1999–2000	-6.64	93.69	3.38	106.87	9.02	31.78
2000–01	24.59	6.42	6.43	-5.38	-15.99	-14.37
2001–02	-18.15	26.36	31.47	148.91	103.57	-51.11
2002–03	58.72	-9.27	30.76	-17.39	-65.52	152.82
2003–04	19.74	17.19	55.00	-14.86	126.32	51.23
2004–05	29.70	-9.10	-8.21	1,038.50	21.99	11.73
2005–06	-7.74	22.60	22.22	42.81	-0.68	-17.53
2006–07	25.30	4.94	22.97	19.36	26.92	-19.74
2007–08	9.78	-32.25	13.03	17.68	-7.50	-3.54
2008–09	-20.34	-31.79	7.30	-18.46	-5.90	-44.76
Annual average growth rate (%)	11.31	6.29	16.59	87.42	25.47	17.65

Source: GoO (2013b).

Note: IC: internal consumption

internal consumption. In case of mineral sand, internal consumption has increased faster than the export. Therefore, we can conclude that the in case of chromite and mineral sand industry, internal consumption has played a more important role than export. On the other hand, the growth of iron ore industry is largely driven by external demand.

The export profile of iron ore is given in Table 5.9. Traditionally, India's major destination for the export of iron ore was Japan.

Table 5.9 Major destination of iron ore export from India, 1990–91 to 2011–12

Year	Total export of iron ore from India (Rs billion)	People's Republic of China (Rs billion)	Japan (Rs billion)	Share of China in total export (%)	Share of Japan in total export (%)
1990–91	10.49	0.02	6.72	0.20	64.01
1991–92	14.35	0.27	8.81	1.87	61.35
1992–93	11.04	1.17	6.69	10.62	60.62
1993–94	13.74	1.52	7.51	11.07	54.63
1994–95	12.97	1.77	6.86	13.61	52.84
1995–96	17.21	2.32	9.26	13.50	53.82
1996–97	17.06	2.33	8.39	13.63	49.19
1997–98	17.70	3.62	8.58	20.48	48.50
1998–99	16.16	3.69	7.78	22.86	48.16
1999–2000	11.75	3.52	4.16	29.98	35.38
2000–01	16.34	5.94	5.43	36.34	33.23
2001–02	20.34	9.87	5.23	48.51	25.71
2002–03	42.00	19.76	14.92	47.04	35.52
2003–04	51.73	37.84	8.23	73.15	15.90
2004–05	147.26	120.61	11.26	81.90	7.64
2005–06	168.29	144.90	16.34	86.10	9.71
2006–07	176.56	150.83	14.90	85.43	8.44
2007–08	234.00	217.53	10.16	92.96	4.34
2008–09	217.25	199.13	11.76	91.66	5.41
2009–10	283.66	242.64	14.84	85.54	5.23
2010–11	214.16	199.00	5.33	92.92	2.49
2011–12	211.88	191.04	12.64	90.16	5.97

Source: Reserve Bank of India (2013).

However, gradually China has become the major destination for iron ore export. For example, in the year 1990–91 the share of Japan in the total export of iron ore from India was 64 per cent. In the same year share of China was only 0.20 per cent. However, the share of China has continuously increased from 1992–93. The trend break is marked in the year 2000–01 when the share of China (36.34 per cent) in India's total export exceeded that of Japan (33.23 per cent). The share of China has touched around 93 per cent in the year 2007–08 and until 2011–12 it has remained well above 90 per cent.

Mineral prices and output growth

The price of minerals plays a key role in determining its extraction. Therefore, we look into the trend in price of four major minerals: bauxite, chromite, iron ore, and manganese ore from 1991–92 to 2009–10. For this purpose, we take the data published by Indian Bureau of Mines in its *Indian Mineral Year Book* in several volumes starting from 1996 to 2011–12. The price data on minerals, however, remain highly controversial. Many people do not even trust the official price data. From the authors' discussion with the mining officials in the state, we can present some of the major problems with the price data. Most of the times price quoted by mining firms are grossly undervalued to reduce the burden of royalty payments. The price is so much under-reported that one of the mining officials at top position revealed that mining firms some time quote even less than 50 per cent of the original price received by the firm. Similarly, there are varieties of grades of minerals, and price varies widely depending upon the grade and place of production, sold in the domestic market or external market, price at mines and price at destinations. In spite of the awareness of such problems, we use the data published by IBM for the simple reason that there are no better alternatives to this data set. The data set is also incomplete due to unavailability of data for the same grade in different years. In order to maintain consistency, we have selected one particular grade (Table 5.10) for four major minerals: bauxite, chromite, iron ore, and manganese ore.

The price of bauxite has gone up by more than three times between 1991 and 2009. On the other hand, the price of chromite has also gone up a little less than three times during this period. Iron ore

Table 5.10 Price of major minerals of particular grade in India, 1991–92 to 2009–10

Years	Bauxite (Grade AL_2O_3 52–54%) (Rs/tonne)	Chromite (Grade Cr_2O_3, 52% or + 52%) (Rs/tonne)	Iron ore (Grade+ 65% Fe lumps) (Rs/tonne)	Manganese Ore (Grade Mn 82–84%) (Rs/tonne)
1991	125	3,420	210	2,687
1992	125	3,420	183	3,275
1993	125	3,420	191	3,766
1994	125	3,420	153	4,155
1995	–	–	–	–
1996	–	–	189–227	5,049
1997	–	–	189–227	5,554
1998	–	–	189–227	5,833
1999	–	4,780	666.89	5,979
2000	–	4,780	743.74	5,979
2001	–	4,951	801.70	6,015
2002	–	4,951	–	6,015
2003	–	3,756	–	6,015
2004	425–450	3,688	1,020	–
2005	425–450	4,500	2,317	–
2006	425–450	4,363	2,888	10,032
2007	270	8,356	3,730	13,137–25,200
2008	325	16,540	2,619	25,200
2009	400	9,878	5,420	25200
Price rise between 1991 and 2009 (%)	320	289	2,581	938

Source: IBM (1996 to 2010–11).

Note: The price of iron ore given for the years 1999–2000, 2000–01, and 2001–02, which are US$ 15.39, US$ 16.28, and US$ 16.81 respectively, are converted into Rs at the annual average exchange rate of 43.33, 45.68, and 47.69 respectively, published by RBI in its *Handbook of Statistics on Indian Economy* for the year 2011–12 (RBI 2013).

has witnessed a record rise in price during this time. Between 1991 and 2009, price per tonne of iron ore has gone up from Rs 210 to Rs 5,420, which is around 26 times the price of 1991. The price of iron ore in fact declined in the 1990s. For example, the price of iron ore was Rs 210 per tonne in 1991 and it went down to Rs 153 per tonne in 1994; the second half of 1990s showed a moderate rise in price. A major jump in the price of iron ore is observed in 1996 (more than three times rise) and from 2004 onwards the price soared up substantially. Iron ore was priced at Rs 210 per tonne in 1991; the price increased to Rs 1,020 per tonne in 2004 and in the next years, it has increased by more than Rs 1,000 per tonne. As pointed out earlier, the rise in the price of iron ore was due to huge demand from China. Similarly, the price of bauxite has gone up by around nine times between 1991 and 2009. Unlike iron ore, the growth in the manganese industry is driven by the domestic sector. Thus, among four major mineral resources the price of iron ore has risen maximum followed by manganese, bauxite, and chromite.

Employment contribution

Has the growth of mining industry created sufficient employment opportunity in Odisha? If we look at the total number of persons directly employed in the mining sector, it has gone down from 53,209 in the year 1999–2000 to 48,239 in the year 2011–12. However, in two years—2005–06 and 2010–11—employment in the mining sector increased marginally. The simple comparison of total number of employment does not make much sense if we do not compare it with the output growth in the mining sector. Therefore, we have computed the growth rate of employment and output in the mining industry and taking the ratio of the former with the latter, we compute the employment elasticity in the industry. In simple words, employment elasticity implies additional persons employed in the industry for an additional unit of output (here tonne of iron ore). During the 12-year time period, starting from 2000–01 to 2011–12, employment elasticity in the mining industry remained negative for seven years. Negative employment elasticity can be recorded if either the growth of output or employment value is negative. However, we can observe from Table 5.11 that output in the industry has always recorded positive growth except in the year 2011–12. On the other hand, employment in the industry has recorded negative growth in eight years. Therefore, we can conclude that the growth of output

Table 5.11 Year-wise number of workers directly employed in major mineral activities

Year	Persons directly employed	Growth rate of total output (%)	Growth rate of employment (%)	Employment elasticity
1999–2000	53,209	1.61		
2000–01	52,937	6.78	-0.51	-0.08
2001–02	45,135	8.79	-14.74	-1.68
2002–03	44,167	16.49	-2.14	-0.13
2003–04	43,743	23.67	-0.96	-0.04
2004–05	49,837	17.61	13.93	0.79
2005–06	55,764	14.10	11.89	0.84
2006–07	47,376	11.37	-15.04	-1.32
2007–08	49,176	10.61	3.80	0.36
2008–09	44,167	5.89	-10.19	-1.73
2009–10	43,705	5.15	-1.05	-0.20
2010–11	51,877	0.36	18.70	52.66
2011–12	48,239	-7.18	-7.01	0.98

Source: Planning and Coordination Department, GoO (2005, 2012, 2013).

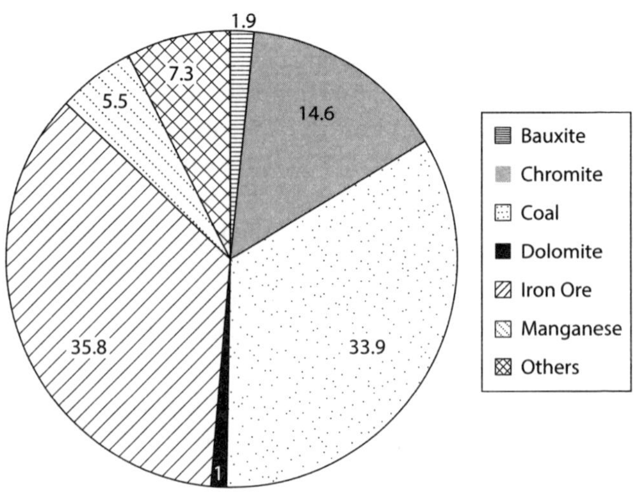

Figure 5.2 Sectoral contribution (%) of employment in the Odisha mining industry

Source: GoO (2013b).

in mining industry has been achieved by cutting down employment except in three years: 2004–05, 2005–06, and 2007–08.

In the total employment of mining sector, iron ore industry contributes the highest percentage (35.8 per cent) followed by coal (33.9 per cent), chromite (14.6 per cent), manganese (5.5 per cent), bauxite (1.9 per cent), dolomite (1 per cent), and rest of the mining industry together generates 7.3 per cent employment opportunity.

Revenue contribution

Apart from contributing a large share to the GSDP and employment, the mining industry also contributes to the state exchequer. The contribution of the mining industry to the state exchequer can be estimated by measuring the share of mineral revenue in the total revenue receipt of the state. Table 5.12 presents the share of revenue generated from Non-ferrous Mining and Metallurgical Industries (NFMMI) as a percentage of Odisha's total own revenue receipts. The share of NFMMI in the total own revenue of the state has gone up from a meager 2.84 per cent in 1987–88 to the highest ever 28.62 per cent in 2010–11. In the next years, however, the revenue share fell by 5 per cent points to 22.57 per cent. The rise in the mining revenue can be explained by the rapid growth of mining industry, huge jump in mineral prices, and implementation of ad valorem based royalty. The Ministry of Mines of government of India in a press release vide No. 3/1/2005-MVI on 17 August 2009 announced the introduction of ad valorem based royalty for eight minerals from 13 August 2009 based on Hoda Committee's recommendation. Similarly, there was a steep increase in the royalty rates of iron ore and chromite and rates of dead rents from second year of mining lease. Such measures yielded higher revenue for the state exchequer from the next year onwards. We can observe a jump in the share of mineral revenue in the total revenue from 2010–11.

Which mining industry contributes more to the state exchequer? Traditionally, the coal industry has remained the largest contributor to the mineral revenue of the state. In the recent years, iron ore has also emerged as the second highest contributor to the mineral revenue. Coal contributed around 71 per cent of the total mineral revenue in the year 1999–2000 and in the same year, iron ore

Table 5.12 Contribution of mining industry to Odisha's total own revenue

Year	Total own revenue (Rs lakh)	Revenue from NFMMI (Rs lakh)	Share of NFMMI in total revenue (%)
1987–88	54,283.68	1,538.98	2.84
1988–89	63,598.88	1,695.91	2.67
1989–90	72,348.07	2,120.21	2.93
1990–91	86,991.37	2,272.37	2.61
1991–92	93,344.78	6,786.51	7.27
1992–93	1,15,004.98	11,593.37	10.08
1993–94	1,27,533.70	13,109.85	10.28
1994–95	1,55,683.73	17,005.34	10.92
1995–96	1,75,542.46	24,173.66	13.77
1996–97	1,82,381.85	26,939.10	14.77
1997–98	1,96,266.38	31,715.38	16.16
1998–99	2,04,461.84	31,405.23	15.36
1999–2000	2,42,056.58	32,008.74	13.22
2000–01	2,86,949.97	36,032.57	12.56
2001–02	3,15,863.29	37,855.66	11.98
2002–03	3,83,301.40	44,357.74	11.57
2003–04	4,39,627.44	55,205.62	12.56
2004–05	5,52,211.64	67,052.42	12.14
2005–06	6,53,418.19	80,502.92	12.32
2006–07	8,65,317.74	93,659.71	10.82
2007–08	9,50,967.00	1,12,606.00	11.84
2008–09	11,17,135.00	1,38,060.00	12.36
2009–10	12,19,454.00	2,02,075.00	16.57
2010–11	15,97,304.00	4,57,157.00	28.62
2011–12	19,88,572.00	4,57,157.00	22.99
2012–13RE	21,81,028.00	5,00,000.00	22.92
2013–14BE	24,43,000.00	5,51,500.00	22.57

Source: Several volumes of Odisha finance accounts and various budget documents.
Notes: NFMMI: non-ferrous mining and metallurgical industries; RE: revised estimates; BE: budget estimates

contributed only 6.12 per cent. The share of iron ore continuously rose and in the year 2009–10, the iron ore industry contributed 33.08 per cent to the total mineral revenue. The substantial jump

Table 5.13 Share of minerals in total mineral revenue

Years	Total revenue (Rs 000)	Chromite	Coal	Iron ore	Other major minerals	Total major minerals	Total minor minerals	Other receipts
1999–2000	32,00,845	11.06	70.84	6.12	11.98	96.04	3.32	0.63
2000–01	36,03,151	11.14	69.39	4.79	14.68	95.05	4.08	0.87
2001–02	37,83,063	8.47	69.03	8.21	14.30	94.29	5.00	0.71
2002–03	44,35,352	4.10	70.06	9.53	16.31	94.10	5.24	0.67
2003–04	55,07,646	4.95	70.09	10.77	14.19	94.34	5.02	0.64
2004–05	67,05,100	6.57	65.91	10.86	16.66	92.33	6.64	1.03
2005–06	80,50,013	10.41	57.16	9.39	23.04	89.04	8.12	2.84
2006–07	93,65,551	11.89	55.10	13.65	19.36	89.35	9.79	0.86
2007–08	1,12,60,936	10.46	56.36	12.96	20.22	86.21	9.94	3.85
2008–09	1,38,05,928	15.02	56.85	10.83	17.30	88.36	10.33	1.31
2009–10	2,02,07,199	6.30	44.55	33.08	16.07	88.82	10.03	1.16

Source: Computed from data available online at http://www.orissaminerals.gov.in/Mines/MineralRevenue.aspx?GL=revenue&PL=3 (last accessed on 10 April 2013).

Note: Data in columns 3–9 is in percentage.

in the share of iron ore can be again owed to the introduction of ad valorem based royalty and rise in the royalty rates. Due to rising share of iron ore, the relative share of coal declined to 44.55 per cent in the year 2009–10. Similarly, the share of other major minerals in the total mineral revenue has risen over years.

It is noteworthy to mention here that the state government has also lost huge amount of revenue due to illegal mining operations and under-reporting of output and prices. Even the Comptroller and Auditor General of India report for the year ended 31 March 2011 has pointed out the unlawful extraction of minerals by both private and public sector mining companies. The resultant total amount of loss incurred by the state exchequer has not been estimated correctly by any agency. Therefore, the media reports have pointed out the revenue loss from a few thousand crores to lakh crores. The inspection report of the special taskforce of the Indian Bureau of Mines, Bhubaneswar branch, available on its website, shows that 78 out of 129 (60.45 per cent) of the inspected mines have been issued a violation-cum-showcause notice. Of these, 37 mining firms were issued the letter of suspension. A commission, with Justice M.B. Shah as the chairperson, is enquiring on the nature and extent of illegal mining in the state.

Value addition for greater economic benefits

For maximizing the economic benefits of natural resource endowments, value addition in the state is essential. However, lack of infrastructure in the state and central government's unfavourable policies like freight equalization undermined the prospects of industrial growth in Odisha. Das (2006) presents the case of utter neglect of vital infrastructure (namely, Paradeep port and the proposed railway line linking the mineral belt to the port) in the state of Odisha by the central government and bureaucracy in connection with harnessing the vast and rich mineral resources of the hinterland, thereby utilizing the immense potential to generate income and employment locally.

In steel production, the state retains 10 per cent of the total capacity of the nation, while it has 25 per cent of total iron ore reserves in the country. However, in recent years, there is a dawn of industrialization in the state. In producing steel, Odisha has been receiving heavy investments in the industrial sector in recent years. There are new potential entrants such as Vedanta, Jindal, and POSCO into this sector in Odisha. If and when these investments fully materialize, the steel producing capacity of the state will improve substantially and Odisha will grow at a much faster rate.

The state government has signed Memoranda of Understanding (MoUs) with 94 reputed investors across sectors covering 50 MoUs for steel, three for aluminium, 30 for power, four for cement, one each for auto components, oil refinery, titanium dioxide, and four for ancillary and downstream industries; the total amount of investment involved in these MoUs amounts to Rs 4,62,768.74 crore. These industries have created employment for more than 89,340 (29,780 direct and 59,560 indirect) persons. Of 94 MoUs, 50 have been signed with various steel promoters with an investment of Rs 2,30,421 crore and an estimated production of 83.66 million tonne per annum (MTPA). Of these 50 MoUs, 30 projects have started partial production with an investment of Rs 80,506.17 crore, achieving a production capacity of 12.66 MTPA of steel, 11.45 MTPA of sponge iron, and 4.23 MTPA of other products. These industries have provided direct employment to 27,690 persons directly and 60,390 persons indirectly so far (GoO 2013).

Odisha occupies the first place in the country in aluminium, both in terms of production capacity and actual output. This has happened after National Aluminium Company (NALCO) and Vedanta Aluminium Limited (VAL) have started to produce aluminium.

Negative consequences of mining

From a study conducted in the Ib valley coalfield, Mishra (2009) shows that the mining of coal, which is a form of physical capital, contributes to the enhancement of financial capital. However, she finds mixed impact on physical and social capital and a negative impact on human and natural capital. She argues that while the benefits seem to be for the short term, the costs are borne over the long run.

Deforestation

Rapid expansion of mining industry has degraded vast patches of forestland, which naturally leads to loss of biodiversity and overall environmental degradation including soil erosion. The estimates from Odisha Economic Survey reports point out that between 1982–83 and 2011–12, 40,008 hectare of forest land has been diverted for various developmental projects which includes mining, irrigation, power, roads, railways, industries, and defence (Table 5.14). Systematic data are not available for the forest diversion for mining purpose during this period. However, we are able to gather data for the forest diversion for mining purpose during 2007–08 and 2011–12. During these five years, 75 projects have diverted 6,583.61 hectare of forestland, out of which 45 mining projects have diverted 4,505.914 hectare, which accounts for 60 per cent in terms of number of projects and 68 per cent in terms of forestland. However, we need to keep in mind that the forestland does not mean that there was forest when the land was cleared. Forest degradation might have taken place well before the beginning of mining projects. If we use the same percentage share for estimating the forestland diverted for mining projects during 1982–83 and 2011–12, it comes at 27,206 hectare of forestland. This would mean that on an average Odisha clears 938 hectare of forestland every year or on daily basis, it clears 2.57 hectare (or 6.35 acres) of forestland for mining purpose.

Most of the mining regions had dense forest cover except the bauxite mining regions. The soil and rocks being somewhat porous used to send down all the rainfall making the top 100–200 feet dry and barren. Thus, we can infer that bauxite mining causes much less deforestation than other mining projects.

Table 5.14 Diversion of forest for non-forest use

Year	Total projects	Non-forest use	Mining projects (hectare)	No. of mining projects
2007–08	20	1,802.58	2,150.681	14
2008–09	14	723.74	280.941	6
2009–10	15	2,310.16	960.785	9
2010–11	13	915.95	571.396	7
2011–12	13	831.18	542.1114	9
Total	75	6,583.61	4,505.914	45

Source: Planning and Coordination Department, GoO (various years).

The forest cover, based on interpretation of satellite data of October 2008 to January 2009, is 48,903 km^2, which is 31.41 per cent of the state's geographical area. In terms of canopy density classes the state has 7,060 km^2 under very dense forest (with a canopy density above 70 per cent), 21,366 km^2 moderately dense forest (with canopy density between 40 per cent and 70 per cent), and 20,477 km^2 area under open forest (Forest Survey of India [FSI] 2011).

As per the report of FSI, for the year 1987, the recorded forest cover in Odisha was 59,555 km^2, which covered 38.2 per cent of the state's geographical area. The forest cover estimated by the FSI was however 53,163 km^2 which covered 34.14 per cent of geographical area of the state. In this year, the state had 28,573 km^2 dense forests (with crown density above 40 per cent[2]) and 24,391 km^2 open forest (crown density between 10 per cent and 40 per cent).

This shows that between 1987 and 2009 Odisha has lost 4,260 km^2 of forest cover if we believe in the FSI data and 10,652 km^2 forest cover if we rely upon the official data. More importantly, the state has lost 147 km^2 of dense forest cover.

Pollution of air and water

Mining activities, if not undertaken scientifically, generate various kinds of pollution in the locality. Fugitive dusts are generated at each stage of mining operation: drilling, blasting, hauling, loading, transporting, unloading, crushing, and beneficiation. The intensity of dust generation depends upon location, wind direction, nature of technology, mode of transportation, level of mechanization, and remedial measures undertaken by the concerned mining firm. In case mining-induced dust exceeds the permissible limit, it may cause diseases such as pneumonoconiosis, silicosis, asbestosis, cataract, corneal ulcers,

[2] The classification of forest has changed in the recent years. Earlier forest used to be classified as dense forest (with canopy density between 40 per cent and 70 per cent) and open forest (with canopy density below 40 per cent). However, in the recent years forests are classified into three categories: very dense forest (with crown density above 70 per cent), moderately dense forest (with crown density between 40 per cent and 70 per cent), and open forest (with crown density below 40 per cent).

glaucoma, and so on. The Centre for Science and Environment in its report *Rich Lands and Poor People* (2008–09) has categorized Angul-Talcher area to be critically air polluted.

In order to assess the impact of mining on the local environment, we need to test the air and water quality near each mine (Table 5.15). During the visit to the mining regions, the authors have witnessed the dusty air, trees, and buildings covered with black dusts in the coal regions (for example, Angul, Talcher) and red dusts in the iron ore mining regions (for example, Joda, Badbil). However, systematic data are

Table 5.15 Status of ambient air quality in residential areas of different mining cities and towns of Odisha, 2009 (μg/m^3)

Location	SPM	RSPM	SO_2	NO_X
NALCO Township, NALCO Nagar, Angul	165 (64–229)	80 (32–112)	8.0 (4.5–11.2)	17.3 (11.8–21.6)
Regional Office Building, Town Planning Office Premises, Sector-5, Rourkela	206 (171–245)	115 (93 –145)	5.5 (4.7–6.1)	10.6 (9.2 –11.5)
Regional Office Building, Baniapat, Keonjhar	157 (74–263)	97 (48–152)	BDL (BDL–BDL)	12.2 (BDL–18.5)
Standard for annual average value in the residential area	140	60	60	60

Source: OSPCB (2013).

Notes: BDL: below detectable limit; SPM: suspended particulate matter; RSPM: respirable suspended particulate matter; SO_2: sulphur dioxide; NO_X: oxides of nitrogen

For SO_2 BDL < 4 μg/m^3

For NO_X, BDL is < 9 μg/m^3

Annual average (24 hourly range) in residential areas parameters* (values expressed in microgram per m^3).

not available for all environmental indicators for each mine. Due to want of systematic firm-level data on the air and water quality, we use the data provided by the Odisha State Pollution Control Board (OSPCB) that are collected from different monitoring stations located in the cities/towns near mining areas. The data on Suspended Particulate Matter (SPM) and Respirable Suspended Particulate Matter (RSPM) shows that the pollution has exceeded too far the National Ambient Air Quality Standard in the residential area of three mining cities: Angul, Rourkela, and Keonjhar. However, the pollution indicators like SO_2 and NO_X have remained below the critically standard.

Mining operations also cause water pollution (both surface and groundwater) in the periphery in four major ways: through acid mine drainage, heavy metal pollution and leaching, pollution from processing chemicals, and through erosion and siltation. Deep mining also pollutes groundwater table. The nature of pollution depends upon the material extracted. For example, coal-mining areas report arsenic contamination, chromite mining regions report the contamination of water with hexavalent chromium Cr(VI). Pollution of surface and groundwater may cause various fatal diseases. The health of mining induced water pollution depends upon the nature of mining and intensity of pollution.

In order to show the impact of mining on the water quality we do not have systematic data for each mine and each pollution indicators. We will present here the findings of a study conducted by the OSPCB. The study by the OSPCB was carried out as a response to the ranking of Sukinda regions (India's largest chromite producing region) by America's Blacksmith Institute as world's fourth most polluted region in the year 2008. The findings of OSPCB, therefore, can be useful for our study.

In Table 5.16 we have presented the quality of water discharged from the Effluent Treatment Plants by the chromite-mining firms in Sukinda valley. The discharged water contains Cr(VI) more than the permissible limit. Cr(VI) beyond a certain concentration, is toxic, inducing such symptoms as skin ulcers, vomiting, diarrhoea, gastrointestinal bleeding leading to cardiovascular shock. It is cytotoxic, mutagenic, and carcinogenic.

Table 5.16 Quality of water discharged by the chromite mining firms from their effluent treatment plants in Sukinda valley

S. No.	Mining firm	Date of sampling	Cr(VI) in mg/l. ETP outlet
1	Kamarda Chromite Mines (B.C. Mohanty and Sons Pvt. Ltd)	19 September 2007	0.220
2	Ostapal Chromite Mines (FACOR)	16 November 2007	1.025
3	Tailangi Chromite Mines (IDCOL)	31 May 2006(I)	0.690
4	Jindal Chromite Mines, Kaliapani	20 September 2007	1.020
5	Chingudipal Chromite Mines (IMFA)	04 February 2005	0.204
6	Saruabil Chromite Mines (Mishrilal Mines Pvt. Ltd)	26 December 2003	0.119
7	South Kaliapani Chromite Mines (OMC)	29 May 2006(I)	0.200
8	Kaliapani Chromite Mines (OMC)	23 August 2005	0.108
9	Sukinda Chromite Mines (TISCO)	20 August 2007	0.169
			0.100

Source: OSPCB (2008).
Note: This shows the mg of Cr.(VI) available per litre of water from ETP outlet.

Displacement, land acquisition, and compensation

Open-cast mining, many times, involves acquisition of private land. Therefore, mining activities have caused the displacement of many adivasi families and taken away their agricultural and non-agricultural lands. Systematic data are not available on the total number of persons displaced, land surrendered, and compensation paid. Mining firms have failed to compensate the economic and social losses resulting from surrendered land and displaced households. A study by Das (2011) points out that the households who surrendered their land to the mining firms were dissatisfied with both public and private sector firms. In such a context, households oppose any kind of land acquisition for mining and non-mining related projects. The growing social unrest in the minerals rich regions of Odisha, Jharkhand, and Chhattisgarh could be explained by the trust deficit between the local communities and the government which has either directly taken the land from the adivasi families or have mediated between the private mining firms and the landowner.

Regulatory failure

The recent outcry in the mining industry reflects the collapse of regulatory mechanism in Odisha and other mineral-rich states. The uncovering of large-scale illegal mining operations, massive deforestation, and deterioration in the environmental quality are evidence in this regard. From various media reports, visit to mining areas, and discussion with the mining officials, we observe several weaknesses in the governance of precious mineral resources of the state and the country. We can list out a few important loopholes in the system.

1. Poor enforcement of environmental laws: Although there are a good deal of laws related to the prudent management of mineral resources, the agencies involved in enforcing the laws have failed to do so. Shortage of staff, vehicles and other advanced technology, and financial resources are the major constraints for efficient enforcement of mining laws pointed out by the officials.
2. Unclear and overlapping jurisdictions: The enforcement responsibilities are vested with multiple agencies like Indian Bureau of Mines, Directorate of Mines, Government of Odisha, Geological Department of the state government, Ministry of Environment and Forest, and State Pollution Control Board. Multiplicity of agencies involved in the enforcement creates confusion and shifting of responsibilities among different enforcing agencies.
3. Lack of systematic data: There is no systematic database on the quantity of mineral extraction and price at which minerals are sold. Due to want of adequate staff, mining officials simply accept the production and price data as reported by the mining lessees. Similarly, due to the political, bureaucratic, and mining lessees' nexus, the state loses enormous amount of revenue.

4. Unusual delay in clearances: For carrying out mining operation, a mining firm has to run from the pillar to post for getting more than a dozen clearances. Due to rent-seeking behaviour of the administrative body, it takes years to obtain a permit to start the mining operation.
5. Non-cooperation of local communities: Local communities perceive the state as a facilitator for the plunderer of the resources available at their disposal. Inadequate payment of compensation to the land surrendering households has created this trust deficit between the local community and the government. Although the state has benefitted from the royalty collected from the mining firms, a negligible part of such resources is transferred to the local communities to compensate their social, economic, and health damages. In such a context, instead of being the informal monitoring agents, local communities play crucial role in facilitating the illegal activities of the mining firms to get the employment and income benefits directly.

Policy suggestions

In the end, we provide the following policy suggestions for improving the mineral governance in the state:

1. The state should improve the mineral governance by tightening monitoring and the enforcement mechanism. Given the fact that the sector contributes enormously to the state exchequer, the state government should fill up all vacant posts and increase the number of staff in the departments responsible for monitoring and enforcement. State-of-the-art technologies should be used for improving the monitoring of the entire mining process. Digitization of the entire process, starting from the mining application to the reporting and monitoring of the mineral production, should be undertaken judiciously.
2. As concluded from the discussions with mining officials, mining firms have often underreported the prices. The state should assign the task of collecting accurate data on mineral production, internal consumption, export, and prices of minerals to a section in the department of Directorate of Mines.

3. To avoid delay in determining and revising royalty rates from time to time, the state should push for getting the rights from the central government for independently determining its royalty rates. Given the fact that different states have different comparative advantage in attracting the mining firms, there is no economic reason why the central government should determine the royalty rates. Das (2009) provides the detailed economic rationales for this policy proposal.
4. The laws related to mineral governance have remained opaque, which causes wrong interpretation and shifting of the responsibilities by the departments from one another. Mining firms take the full advantage of such legal confusions. This is true for any profit-maximizing business entity. Therefore, the legal provisions and jurisdiction of the departments engaged in mineral governance should be clearly described without any confusion and overlapping.
5. Local communities possess better information on the operation of mining firms. Therefore, for improving the monitoring of mineral production further, the state can think of involving the local communities along with Panchayati Raj institutions. This will generate more employment opportunity for the local community and reduce trust deficit between them and the government. Das and Joe (2008) have mooted such proposal earlier.
6. Households who surrender their land should be given a part in the lease of mining. Investing a fixed proportion of the mineral revenue should be made mandatory for all mining firms. This should not be called as corporate social responsibility, rather 'social compliance'. The mining firms failing in the social compliance should be prohibited from mineral extraction and be punished.
7. Government should also transfer a sizeable amount of mineral revenue to the local governments in mining regions to improve the infrastructure, education, health, sanitation, electricity, and drinking water facilities.

References

Acharya, S. 2000. 'Some Observations on Parts of the Banded Iron Ore Formations in Eastern India', Presidential Address, 87th session, Indian Science Congress Association, pp. 1–34.

Acharya, S. 2008. 'Genesis of Banded Iron Ore Formation, Associated Iron and Manganese Ore Deposits of Orissa-Jharkhand Region, India and its role as Exploration Guide', keynote paper presented at the Seminar on Iron Ores-Genesis and Exploration Techniques, Society of Geoscientists and Technologists.

Das, A. 2009. 'Regulatory Authority over Minerals: A Case for Review', *Economic and Political Weekly*, 44(10): 105–09.

———. 2011. 'Does Firm Ownership Differentiate the Social Compliance?: An Enquiry into the Indian Mining Industry', *Indian Economic Journal*, 59(3): 56–70.

Das, A. and W. Joe. 2008. 'Community Participation in Monitoring Coal Production', *Economic and Political Weekly*, 43(06): 77–79.

Das, K. 2006. 'Underdevelopment by Design? Undermining Vital Infrastructure in Orissa', *Economic and Political Weekly*, 41(7): 642–48.

Forest Survey of India. 2011. *State of Forest Report 2011*. Government of India.

Government of Odisha (GoO). 2013a. *Mineral Production*. Directorate of Mines, Government of Odisha. Available at http://www.orissaminerals.gov.in/website/MineralProduction.aspx?GL=resstat&PL=1 (last accessed on 24 February 2013).

———. 2013c. *Mineral Despatch*. Directorate of Mines. Available at http://www.orissaminerals.gov.in/Mines/MineralDespatch.aspx?GL=ming&PL=4 (last accessed on 20 February 2013).

Indian Bureau of Mines (IBM). 2011. *Indian Mineral Year Book-2010*. Nagpur: Ministry of Mines, Government of India. Available at http://ibm.nic.in/imyb2010.htm (last accessed on 10 April 2013).

———. Various years. *Indian Mineral Year Book*. Nagpur: Ministry of Mines, Government of India. Available at http://ibm.nic.in/imyb2010.htm (last accessed on 10 April 2013).

Mishra, P.P. 2009. 'Coal Mining and Rural Livelihoods: Case of the Ib Valley Coalfield, Orissa', *Economic and Political Weekly*, 44(44): 117–23.

Odisha State Pollution Control Board (OSPCB). 2008. *Report on Environmental Issues of Chromite Mining in Sukinda Valley*. Government of Odisha.

———. 2013. 'Ambient Air Quality'. Available at http://ospcboard.org/ambAir_2009.aspx (last accessed on 15 April 2013).

GoO. 2005. *Economic Survey 2004–05*. Bhubaneswar, Odisha: Planning and Coordination Department.

GoO. 2010. *Economic Survey 2009–10*. Bhubaneswar, Odisha: Planning and Coordination Department.

———. 2012. *Economic Survey 2011–12*. Bhubaneswar, Odisha: Planning and Coordination Department.

———. 2013. *Economic Survey 2012–13*. Bhubaneswar, Odisha: Planning and Coordination Department.

Reserve Bank of India. 2013. *Handbook of Statistics on Indian Economy 2011–12*. Available at http://rbi.org.in/scripts/AnnualPublications.aspx?head=Handbook%20of%20Statistics%20on%20Indian%20Economy (last accessed on 12 April 2013).

6

Transportation and Power*

Satya P. Das

As noted in the *World Development Report 1994: Infrastructure for Development* prepared by the World Bank (World Bank 1994), infrastructure is an umbrella term. The scope of this chapter is limited to physical infrastructure and more specifically, to its principal components, namely transport and power (meaning electricity mostly).[1]

Physical infrastructure is a key ingredient for sustained economic growth for any region. India's impressive growth experience starting from the early 1990s has been associated with major improvements

* Comments from a reviewer improved the chapter in several parts. The author would like to thank the participants of the conference held for this volume at Nabakrushna Choudhury Institute Centre for Development Studies, Bhubaneswar, India, in December 2012 for their useful remarks. He would also like to acknowledge Chitta Baral's valuable inputs for the section on railways.

[1] Besides transport and power, indices of physical infrastructure may include measures of banking and telecommunications.

in physical infrastructure. However, it is felt that sustaining such growth would require further and faster infrastructure development; otherwise, the growth process would soon have to be stalled.

In particular, transport provides backward and forward linkages to production in that it enables inputs, both human and non-human, to reach places of production and facilitates outputs to reach their markets. In other words, it helps to 'create' and expand input and output markets.

The power sector powers production and consumption in many ways. The collapse of the national grid of India in late July 2012 bears testimony to the critical importance of power in an economy as well as in our daily lives.

Transport and power are complementary to each other. In a region's growth process, both constitute general purpose technology, which generates various network externalities across sectors and enhances productivity in almost all sectors of an economy in interconnected ways. Of course, the physical presence of physical infrastructure per se does not deliver growth or development. *World Development Report 1994* rightly emphasizes that it is the service generated from the physical infrastructure that is critical.

Against this background, the objective of this chapter is to assess the transport and power situation in the state of Odisha. *Orissa State Development Report 2002*—prepared jointly by the Planning Commission of India and the Nabakrushna Choudhury Institute for Development Studies—gave a rather poor opinion on the state of infrastructure (more generally defined) in Odisha. According to the report, back in 1991, Odisha ranked number 12 among 15 major states.[2] For more recent years, two well-known economists, Bibek Debroy and Laveesh Bhandari, have made rankings of the Indian states on different indices of growth and development, with infrastructure as one of them. Their results have been published in the weekly *India Today*. Among 20 states, Odisha was ranked 16th in three consecutive years, 2006 to 2008; the ranking has improved to 13th in 2012 (*India Today* 2015). That is, relatively to other states, the infrastructure situation in Odisha did not improve significantly until a few years ago.

[2] These are Andhra Pradesh, Assam, Bihar, Gujarat, Haryana, Karnataka, Kerala, Madhya Pradesh, Maharashtra, Odissa, Punjab, Rajasthan, Tamil Nadu, Uttar Pradesh, and West Bengal.

It does not mean that the state of (physical) infrastructure in Odisha has remained stagnant. It is fast improving, as can be observed from casual visits to towns and villages in Odisha. With a view towards becoming a major industrial state, there is a heavy emphasis by the state government on infrastructure development. Transport and power are synonymous with the state's Bijli-Sadak (and Pani) campaign.[3]

Transport

The topography of Odisha is shaped by two distinct landscapes—coastal plains and inland hilly areas—constituting about 25 per cent and 75 per cent of the total area of the state, respectively. Six major rivers, along with their tributaries, flow through the state, namely Subarnarekha, Budhabalanga, Baitarani, Brahmani, Mahanadi, and Rushikulya. For a long time, all-weather transport within the state was limited due to the hills in the interior and the rivers in the plains.

As in other states, roads and railways are the two principal modes of transport within Odisha. Being a coastal state, port facilities are also potentially important for trade in merchandise goods.

Roads

Public roads in India are classified on the basis of ownership or programme, as shown in Figure 6.1.[4] According to the Ministry of Road Transport and Highways (Ministry of Road Transport and Highways 2012), national highway numbers 5, 5A, 6, 23, 42, 43, 60, 75, 200, 201, 203, 203A, 215, 217, and 224 pass through Odisha covering 3,074 km. However, they constitute less than 1.5 per cent of total road length in the state. Figure 6.2 depicts the distribution of roads by the end of 2010–11 according to ownership. We see that most of the roads in the state are of 'rural type'.

[3] It refers to the drive to improve and expand the provision of electricity ('bijli'), roads ('sadak'), and water ('pani').

[4] Ownership refers to the departments or civic bodies which possess the jurisdictions over the respective roads. Programme refers to the fiscal banner under which the road construction is financed.

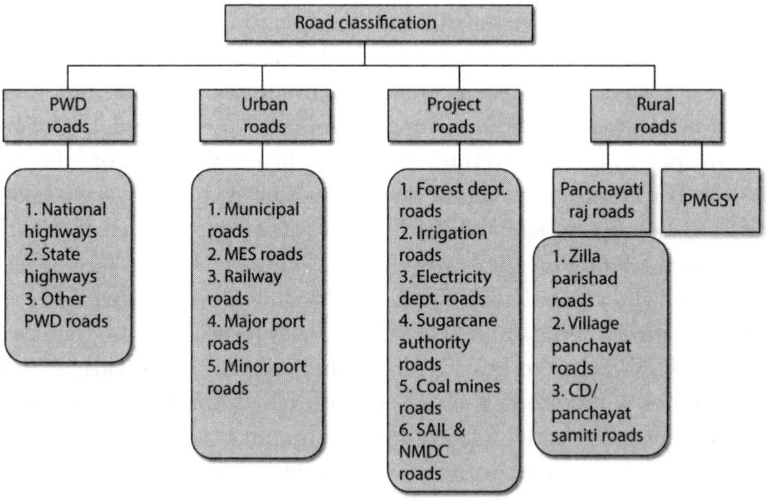

Figure 6.1 Road classification
Source: Ministry of Road Transport and Highways (2012).
Note: PWD: public works department; MES: military engineering service; SAIL: Steel Authority of India Limited; NMDC: National Mineral Development Corporation; CD: community development; PMGSY: Pradhan Mantri Gram Sadak Yojana

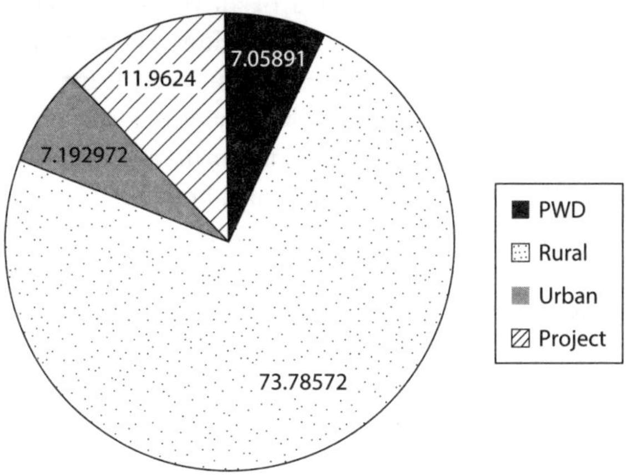

Figure 6.2 Distribution of road types in Odisha, by the end of 2010–11
Source: Ministry of Road Transport and Highways (2012).

Provision of roads rests with central, state, local, and other 'sectors'. In the last 20 years or so, two central schemes have changed the landscape of roads across India, including that in Odisha. National highways have been broadened and revamped through the National Highway Development Project (NHDP), beginning in 1998. Phase I of NHDP, focused on connecting the four metropolises in a better way, was scheduled to be over by January 2012. Rural roads have been created and expanded on a massive scale through the Pradhan Mantri Gram Sadak Yojana (PMGSY) initiated in 2000–01. In 2005–06, it became a part of Bharat Nirman Programme, an overall rural infrastructure programme. The PMGSY's aims to provide all-weather connectivity to villages and habitations with a population of at least 500. While the construction and expansion of roads under this programme are funded by the Centre, the task of maintenance is entrusted with the states.

Some rural road construction projects are funded by Rural Infrastructure Development Fund (RIDF), a national scheme under National Bank for Agriculture and Rural Development (NABARD). There are also central plans such as Backward Regions Grant Fund (BRGF) and Revised Long Term Action Plan (RLTAP), which target backward districts like Koraput, Bolangir, and Kalahandi (KBK) undivided. Some state-level programmes include rural road connectivity as a specific objective, such as the Gopanbandhu Grameen Yojana, Biju KBK plan, and Biju Kandhamal O Gajapati Yojana.

Total road length, the sum total of all types, is a basic measure of the overall presence of roads in a region. Figure 6.3 depicts its progress in the state 1990–91 onwards (except for 1997–98 to 2001–02). The decline in total availability of roads in the late 1990s is partly due to damage caused by severe storms and cyclones afflicting the state during that time. It is important, however, to note that considerable progress has taken place over the last few years. Between 2007–08 and 2010–11, 43,432 km of roadways have been added.

Road density in Odisha has always exceeded the national average. Per 1,000 km^2, it was 1,383 km in 2007–08 (as opposed to the national average of 920 km) and by 2010–11, it jumped to 1,662 km (compared to the national average of 1,153 km).[5]

[5] These figures excludes roads constructed under PMGSY and Jawahar Rozgar Yojana (JRY).

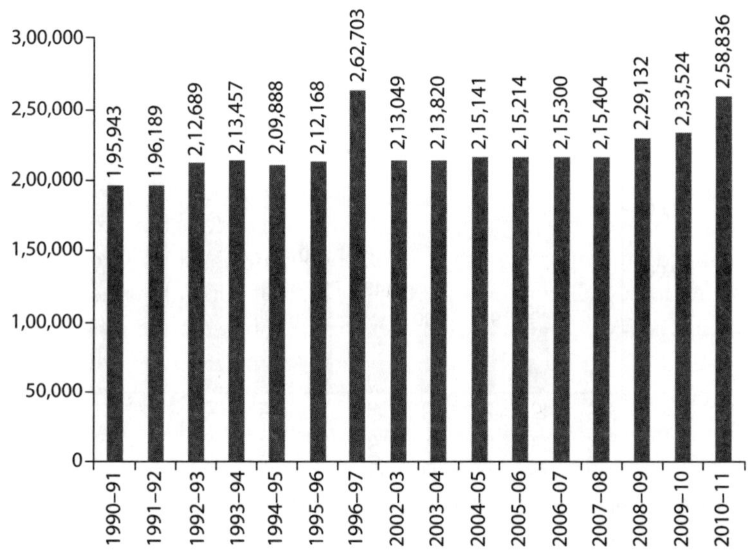

Figure 6.3 Total road length (km) in Odisha, 1990–91 to 2010–11
Sources: Ghosh and De (2005), Ministry of Road Transport and Highways (2012), MOSPI (2010).
Note: These figures do not include roads constructed through PMGSY and JRY.

All roads under PMGSY are surfaced. Progress over time in the state under this programme is illustrated in Figure 6.4. Nearly 5,000 km was completed within a single year, 2010–11.

However, as Figure 6.5 indicates, it is worrisome that the proportion of surfaced-road length to the total in Odisha has lagged behind the national average consistently. Figure 6.6 shows that in terms of this ratio, the state ranks almost at the bottom in comparison to other states by the end of 2010–11. Odisha's *Economic Survey 2011–12* reports that only 62 per cent of villages have all-weather road connectivity. Maintenance of rural roads in particular remains a serious concern across all states. As Planning Commission (2011c) has aptly noted, even though substantial progress has been and is still being made under PMGSY, they will be prone to misuse and disintegration, unless these roads are maintained.

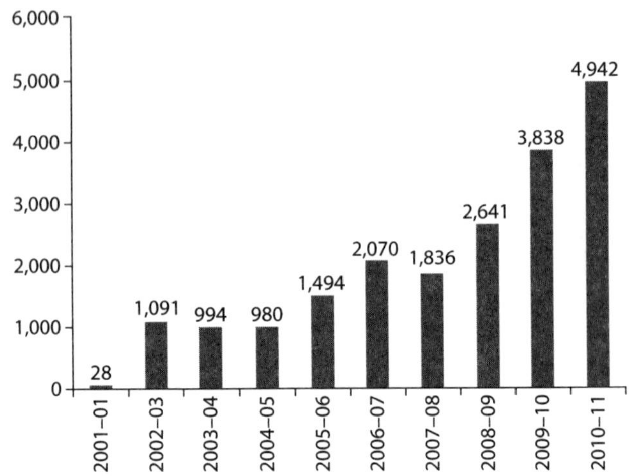

Figure 6.4 Length of roads (km) completed each year in Odisha under PMGSY
Source: GoO (2012).

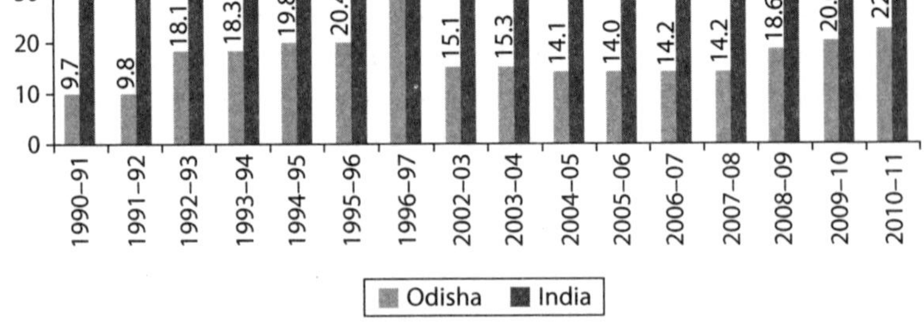

Figure 6.5 Percentage of surfaced roads in Odisha, 1990–91 to 2010–11
Source: Ghosh and De (2005), Ministry of Road Transport and Highways (2012), MOSPI (2010).
Note: These figures do not include roads constructed under PMGSY and JRY.

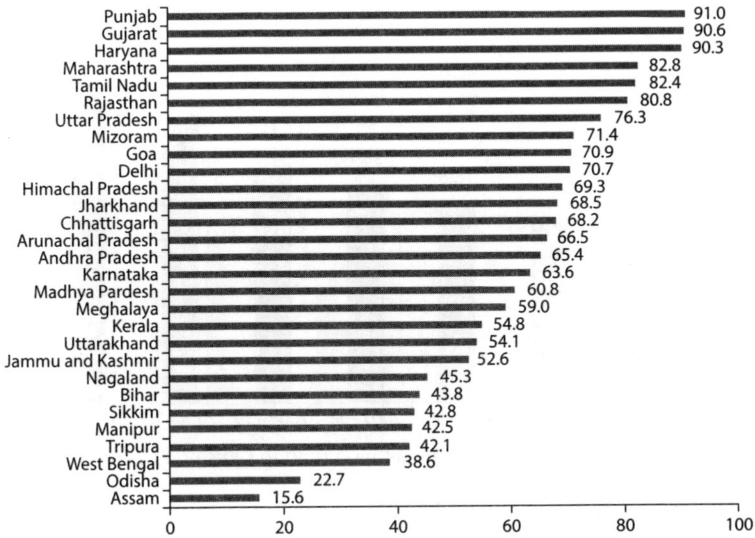

Figure 6.6 Percentage of surfaced-to-total road length across states by the end of 2010–11
Source: Ministry of Road Transport and Highways (2010, 2012).

In a nutshell then, while total road strength in the state appears to be adequate, there are two outstanding problems that limit the total service flow from roads: (a) low proportion of surfaced roads and (b) lack of all-weather connectivity across a large number of villages.

With increases in the number, quality, length, and width of roads, their use has shot up in the state. The total number of vehicles on roads in Odisha has more than doubled since 2004–05. Figure 6.7 graphs its time series since 2004–05. As of 2010–11, about 80 per cent of them are two-wheelers.

For common people, buses provide the principal means of transport. However, the number of public sector buses has increased only marginally over the noughties—from 254 in 2000–01 to 283 in 2010–11—and the total number of passengers travelling in public buses has been declining consistently from 2006–07 (GoO 2012). It implies that the share of private sector in providing bus service has increased markedly.

The Planning Commission provides measures of efficiency of state road transport corporations, namely (a) *vehicle productivity* via revenue generated per bus by kilometre, (b) *staff productivity* in terms

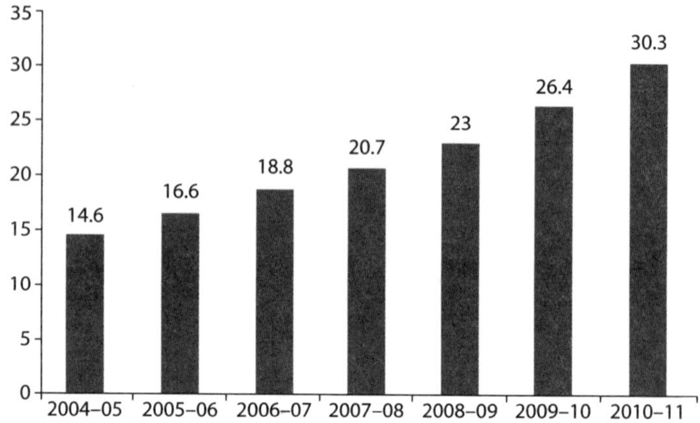

Figure 6.7 Number of vehicles (in lakh) on road in Odisha, 2004–05 to 2010–11

Source: GoO (2012).

of revenue generated per kilometre per worker, (c) *fuel efficiency* by kilometre per litre, and (d) *fleet utilization* in percentage terms. In all these measures, the performance of Odisha State Road Transport Corporation (OSRTC) is about the national average.

In terms of financial health, OSRTC earns a small amount of profit—it was a little above Rs 71.7 million by the end of 2010–11 (Ministry of Road Transport and Highways 2011). This is unlike State Road Transport Undertakings (SRTUs) in other states such as in Andhra Pradesh and Delhi, which incur losses running into hundreds of millions.

Railways

Three railway zones cover the state of Odisha, namely East Coast Railway, South Eastern Railway, and South East Central Railway. Railways are present in 23 districts of the state. The seven excluded districts are Boudh, Deogarh, Kandhamal, Kendrapada, Malkangiri, Nabarangpur, and Nayagarh. Overall, however, railways have remained inadequate in the state. This is particularly relevant in view of the industrial development of the state—since Odisha is rich in mines and transport of mineral products to plants and ports would have been more cost-effective and environment friendly if railway facilities were available more readily.

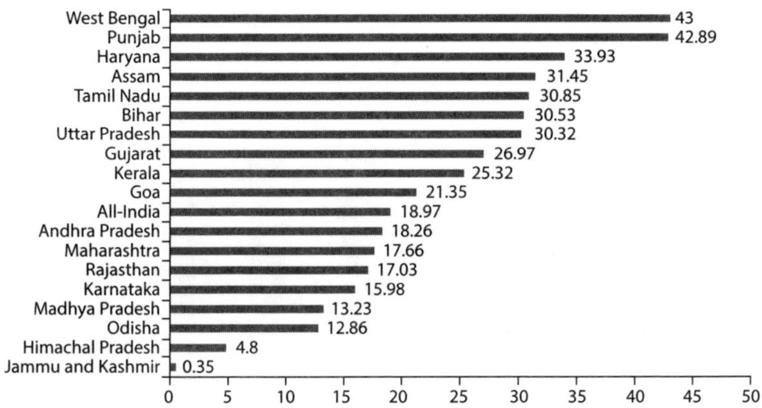

Figure 6.8 Railways density (route length per 1,000 km^2) across states, 1990–91
Source: Ghosh and De (2005).

Railway density measured by route length per 1,000 km^2 was 12.86 km back in 1990–91. It improved to 15.33 km by the end of 2007–08. However, among major states, Odisha until date has remained in the bottom rung in terms of presence of railways. Figures 6.8 and 6.9 show railway density across major states in 1990–91 and 2007–08 respectively. Relatively, little has changed.

It is easy to describe railway paths through the state existing in 1955 when the South Eastern Railway was formed.[6] They consisted of three main lines: Howrah-Madras line, Howrah-Bombay line, and Vijaynagaram-Titlagarh-Raipur line. The first went through all (undivided) coastal districts, the second through (undivided) Sundargarh and Sambalpur districts, and the last cut across KBK districts (undivided). Besides, there were several branch lines. From the Howrah-Madras line within the state the branches were: Khurda road to Puri, Nirgundi to Talcher, Rupsa to Bangriposi, and Naupada to Gunupur. Off the Howrah-Bombay line, the branches were Tata to Onlajori to Badampahar, Onlajori to Gorumahisani, Rajkharswan to Barjamda to Gua, Barjamda to Barbil, Panposh to Biramitrapur,

[6] These were pretty much the same as in 1932. There were no new construction between 1932 and 1960.

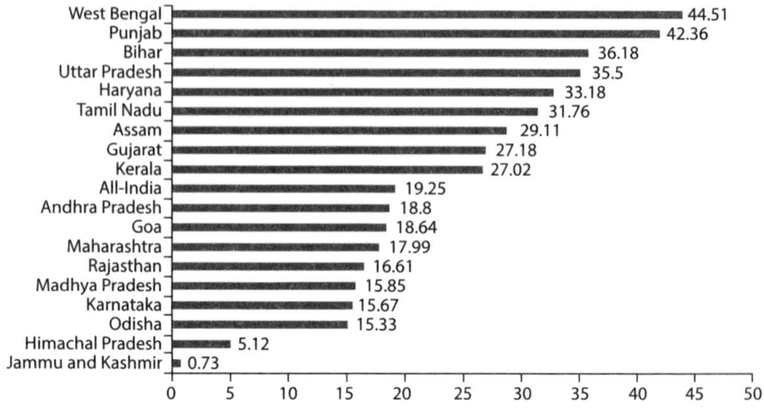

Figure 6.9 Railways density (route length per 1,000 km^2) across states, 2007–08
Source: MOSPI (2010).

and Panposh to Raipura. Box 6.1 lists railways lines or branches that have been created or extended since.

A serious note must be taken of the relative absence of railways in KBK districts and tribal areas in Mayurbhanj and Sundargarh. Ironically, the potential importance of railways in KBK districts was recognized back in 1945 when the first survey was conducted by the Bengal-Nagpur railway authorities. And the approval by the Planning Commission came only almost 50 years later in 1993! Sadly, three proposed railway lines connecting the areas within the region which have been partially constructed—one between Khurdha and Bolangir, one between Lanjigarh and Junagarh, and one between Gunupur and Theruvali—are yet to be opened for passenger traffic (the Lanjigarh-Bhawanipatna segment of the Lanjigarh-Junagarh line has been opened). Apart from improving the economy of this region—considered one of the poorest in the whole nation—better railways in this region would have considerably improved connectivity between the capitals of Odisha (Bhubaneswar) and Chattisgarh (Raipur).

Similarly, there are three proposed railway lines aimed towards bringing connectivity to and within tribal regions in Mayurbhanj and Sundargarh, but they are still unfinished, namely Talcher-Bimlagarh, Badampahar-Keonjhar, and Bangiriposi-Gurumahishsini-Chakulia.

Box 6.1 Railway lines created or extended

Year	Event
1960	Bondamunda-Barsua
1963	Sambalpur-Titlagraph
1963	Bimlagarh-Kiriburu
1965	Barang-Rajathagarh
1965	Bondamunda (near Rourkela)-Hatia (Ranchi)
1966	Kottavalasa-Kirandul (via Koraput and Jeypore)
1970	Barbil-Bolanikhadan
1970	Padapahar-Bansapani
1973	Cuttack-Paradip
1977	Jhakpura-Daitari
1985	Koraput-Damanjodi
1995	Koraput-Raygada
1998	Talcher-Sambalpur
2000	Banspani-Jaroli
2007	Daitari-Bansapani
2007	Rupsa-Baripada (after gauge conversion from narrow to broad)
2010	Nuapada-Parlakhemundi (after gauge conversion from narrow to broad)
2011	Baripada-Bangriposi (after gauge conversion from narrow to broad)
2011	Parlakhemundi-Gunupur (after gauge conversion from narrow to broad)
2011	Bhadrak-Dhamra (private line buit by Dhamra Port Ltd)
2012	Lanjigarh-Bhawanipatna
In progress	Jaleswar-Digha, Khurdha Road-Balangir and Talcher-Bimlagarph
In progress	Haridaspur-Paradip and Sukinda-Angul

Source: Professor Chitta Baral, Arizona State University, Tempe, Arizona, USA.

Ports

Endowed with a coastline of 480 km, being rich in mineral deposits, and aiming rapid growth via industrialization, Odisha must develop

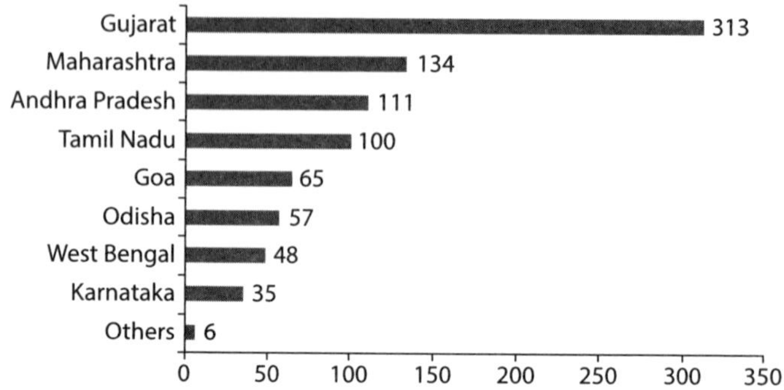

Figure 6.10 Cargo traffic (million tonnes) at ports across maritime states, 2010–11
Source: Ministry of Shipping (2012).

and benefit by port facilities. As Figure 6.10 shows, there are eight major maritime states in India, one of them being Odisha. As of 2010–11, Odisha ranks fifth in terms of total volume of cargo handled.

Till date, the state harbors one major port at Paradip and two non-major ones at Gopalpur and Dhamara. There are smaller potential port sites being explored by the state under public–private partnership at Bahabalpur, Bahuda Muhan, Palur, Baliharichandi, Astaranga, Jatadhar Muhan, Barunei Muhan, Chudamani, Chandipur, and Subarnarekha Mouth (Kirtania). Paradip is the oldest, managed by the Government of India since 1965. It has a handling capacity of 76.5 million tonnes of commodities and is in the process of further mechanization and modernization. Its handling capacity is expected to reach 237 million tonnes by 2020.

Figure 6.11 graphs the time profile of total cargo volume handled at Paradip from 1970–71 to 2010–11. As can be seen readily, it has been growing consistently since the mid-1980s (except for a marginal decline in 2010–11). It has almost tripled during the noughties.[7] While, traditionally, coal and iron ore are the major commodities (exports) passing through Paradip, it is remarkable that in the last few years the movement (mostly imports) of petroleum, oil, and lubricant (POL) has

[7] Breakdown of total cargo volume into exports and imports for years 2000–01 to 2010–11 is given in GoO (2012).

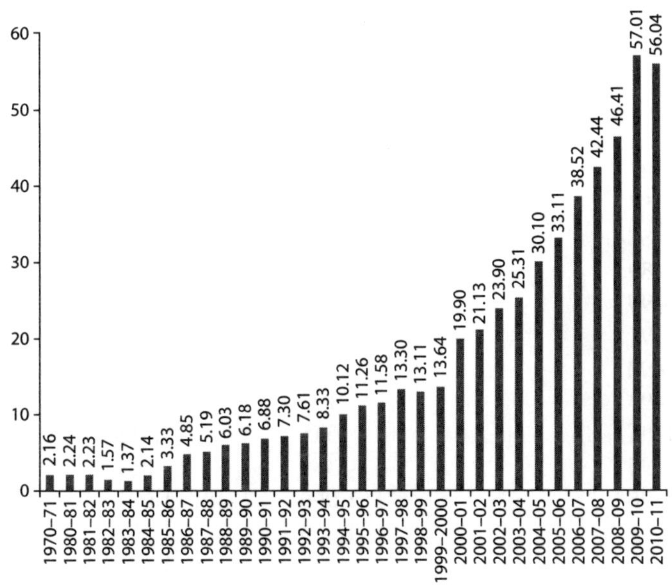

Figure 6.11 Cargo traffic handled at Paradip Port, 1970–71 to 2010–11 (million tonnes)
Sources: MOSPI (2010) and Ministry of Shipping (2012).

surged and by now its volume is close to that of iron ore. A time series of these three commodities are depicted in Table 6.1 and Figure 6.12.

The spurt in POL imports is due to a separate berth allotted to handling petroleum-related products, a large area outside the port given for tanker facility and having a single point mooring (SPM) system.[8] In 2010, the Cabinet Committee on Economic Affairs (CCEA) gave its nod to setting up of the 4th Petroleum Chemicals and Petrochemicals Investment Region (PCPIR) at Paradip.[9] This is likely to boost the traffic of POL through Paradip port further.

Unlike some other ports such as Cochin or Kolkata Dock System, Paradip port has remained profitable. Its net before-tax surplus during the year 2010–11 was Rs 4,159.5 million. The time series of this surplus since 1995–96 is exhibited in Figure 6.13.

[8] SPM system refers to piping under the sea and land so as to directly move oil from ships to tankers.

[9] The earlier three cleared by CCEA are in Andhra Pradesh, Gujarat, and West Bengal.

Table 6.1 POL, iron ore, and coal handled at Paradip Port, 1985–86 to 2010–11 ('000 tonnes)

	POL (crude and products)	Iron ore	Coal
1985–86		1,868	869
1986–87		2,079	1,511
1987–88		1,709	2,305
1988–89		1,678	2,394
1989–90		2,059	2,709
1990–91		1,748	3,614
1991–92	23	1,524	3,954
1992–93	195	1,346	4,542
1993–94	345	1,518	4,845
1994–95	380	1,881	5,830
1995–96	1,066	1,691	5,909
1996–97	1,693	1,381	6,513
1997–98	1,737	1,435	7,852
1998–99	2,007	797	8,198
1999–00	2,219	1,025	7,755
2000–01	2,219	2,992	10,097
2001–02	1,993	3,546	10,722
2002–03	1,923	4,679	11,722
2003–04	1,365	5,934	14,037
2004–05	839	9051	14,209
2005–06	910	10,273	16,287
2006–07	1,376	1,18,801	17,130
2007–08	1,765	12,960	15,932
2008–09	3,240	14,272	20,162
2009–10	11,647	16,159	19,820
2010–11	12,845	13,795	19,340

Source: Ministry of Shipping (2012).

Gopalpur started as a seasonal port in 2007. Within the purview of the state government, it is managed by Gopalpur Port Limited, a private consortium consisting of Orissa Stevedores Limited and Jindal Steel. Dhamara port is operated on a 50:50 joint venture by Larsen & Toubro and Tata Steel. It is envisaged to be developed into a mega port. A major ship-building, repair, and maintenance facility is reported to come up near this port by Bharati Shipyard and

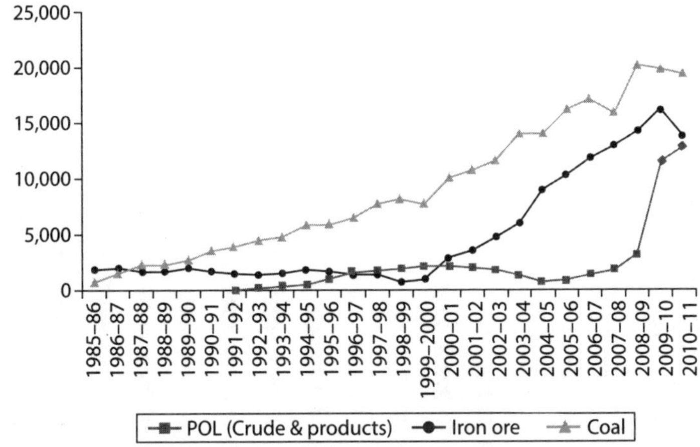

Figure 6.12 Cargo volume of POL (crude and products), iron ore, and coal handled at Paradip Port, 1985–86 to 2010–11 ('000 tonnes)
Source: Ministry of Shipping (2012).
Note: Refer to Table 6.1.

Apeejay Shipping as a 50:50 joint venture. Such a facility (if it comes to fruition) will enhance cargo-handling not only at Dhamara, but also at Paradip and Gopalpur ports.[10]

Power

The evolution of the power sector and power availability in the state are intertwined with that of the institutional framework behind provision of power at the national and state levels.

Evolution of institutional framework and an evaluation of reforms undertaken in the 1990s

At the time of Independence, generation and distribution of power in India were carried out by private utility companies (such as Calcutta Electric Power, Delhi Central Electric Power Authority, Bombay

[10] It is worth mentioning that while there are strong indications that port facilities at Gopalpur and Dhamara will grow, they do face the green hurdle that expansion will destroy mass nesting of ridley turtles.

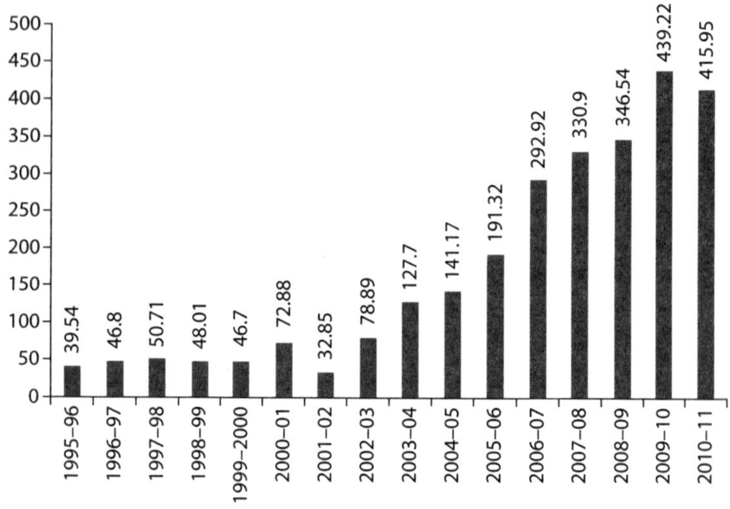

Figure 6.13 Net before-tax surplus of Paradip Port, 1995–96 to 2010–11 (Rs crore)
Source: Ministry of Shipping (2012).

Electric Supply and Tramways Company, and Madras Electric Supply Corporation). Thereafter, the state sector entered the field in a big way because of the Electricity (Supply) Act, 1948. Under the act, State Electricity Boards (SEBs) came into existence in respective states and the Central Electricity Authority (CEA) was constituted at the national level. The CEA was entrusted with national planning with respect to power. By 1950, 37 per cent of total power capacity in the country rested with the public sector. Due to the Industrial Policy Resolution of 1956, power generation, transmission, and distribution came under the purview of the state sector almost exclusively. Orissa State Electricity Board (OSEB) was 'born' in 1961.

It was realized later that state initiatives would not be enough. To accelerate the supply of power, the central sector commenced producing power in the 1970s. The National Thermal Power Corporation (NTPC, now a Maharatna public sector company) and National Hydroelectric Power Corporation (NHPC) were established in 1975.[11] To augment

[11] According to its website, NTPC has now installed capacity to the tune of 39,174 MW of power. It hopes to nearly double its capacity by 2017.

power projects in the North Eastern region, the North-Eastern Electric Power Corporation Limited (NEEPCO) was created in 1976.

Despite the central sector's entry into the power sector in the mid-1970s on a massive scale, by the end of the 1980s, the power sector in the entire nation was plagued by a plethora of problems in technical, managerial, and commercial spheres. In the words of the Planning Commission (2011a): 'The Indian power sector had reached the absolute dead-end by the 1980s.' Lack of proper maintenance, massive transmission and distribution (T&D) losses, rampant slackness in billing due to political interference and corruption, more frequent power cuts than in the previous decades, fluctuating voltage and poor grievance redressal system were routine features. Not surprising, all SEBs were in deep red commercially.

The poor state of Odisha's power sector in the early 1990s in terms of various indicators can be ascertained from the numbers in Box 6.2. At the same time, the state government was in a dire financial situation. The revenue deficit of the state scaled Rs 1,880 million at the end of 1991–92, whereas in 1982–83 the state had enjoyed a revenue surplus of Rs 280 million (Dash 2007).

After the New Economic Policy through a series of policy reforms initiated at the central level in 1991, Odisha was the first state to

Box 6.2 Power sector situation in Odisha in the early 1990s

Installed generation capacity	1,612 MW in 1991–92 ('inadequate')	Against a backdrop of 4.5% increase over the past decade
Peak-period power deficit	23.9%	National average of 18.8%
Average plan load factor	30%	National average of 55.3%
T&D losses	25.3%	National average of 22.8%
Difference between average cost of supply and tariff	18 paise in 1991–92	8 paise in 1989–90
Number of employees per million of units sold	6.2	National average of 4.5

Source: Ramanathan and Hasan (2003).

undertake a fundamental restructuring of the power sector. The World Bank was heavily involved in designing the restructuring programme and the UK government provided the grants through Department for International Development (DFID). The state introduced a Power Sector Reform Act in 1995, which came to effect in 1996. The OSEB was essentially 'unbundled'. Three 'sectors', so-to-speak, emerged: generation, transmission, and distribution. The distribution sector was partly privatized.

Worth noting is that a part of the financial problem facing many state electricity boards in India was due to heavy subsidization offered to the agricultural sector through reduced usage charges. However, in Odisha, the share of agriculture in total electricity sales was less than 1 per cent. This implied less potential political opposition to reforms by farmers as electricity rate hikes were bound to happen once privatization of power distribution was to take place. This is cited as one of the reasons why power sector reforms took place initially in a poor state such as Odisha. The schematic view of the organization of the power sector in Odisha in the new institutional set-up is presented in Figure 6.14.

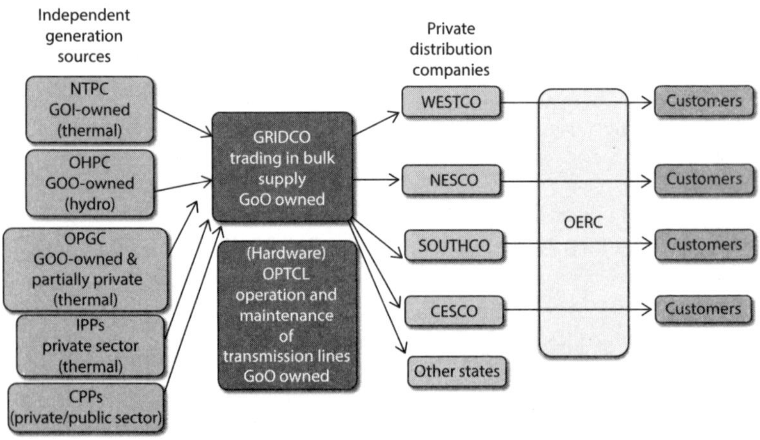

Figure 6.14 Organization of the power sector in Odisha
Source: GoO (2010).

Grid Corporation of Orissa Limited (GRIDCO) purchases power from independent utilities that generate power. Orissa Power Transmission Corporation Limited (OPTCL), which is fully owned by the state, is in charge of operation and maintenance of transmission lines. Power is sold to distribution companies—in short DISTCOs—namely WESTCO (Western Electricity Supply Company of Orissa Limited), NESCO (North-Eastern Electricity Supply Company of Orissa Limited), SOUTHCO (Southern Electricity Supply Company of Orissa Limited), and CESCO (Central Electricity Supply Company of Orissa Limited). In addition, it is sold to other states, who, in turn, sell to final consumers, which comprise industries, households, and public bodies including the government administration.

All DISTCOs became 'privately owned' (having majority shareholding by private companies) by 1999. WESTCO supplies power to nine 'western' districts: Bargarh, Bolangir, Deogarh, Jharsuguda, Kalahandi, Nuapada, Sambalpur, Sonepur, and Sundargarh. NESCO distributes power to five northeastern districts, namely Jajpur, Balasore, Bhadrak, Makyurbhanj, and Keonjhar. 'Sourthern' districts such as Koraput, Ganjam, Gajapati, Kandhamal, Malkangiri, Nawrangpur, Puri (partly), Rayagada, and Phulbani are served by SOUTHCO or SESCO. CESCO supplies power to the central zone consisting of undivided Cuttack, Puri, and Dhenkanal districts.

An important institution created in 1996 because of the Power Sector Reform Act is the Orissa Electric Regulatory Commission (OERC), a regulatory body interfacing between producers and consumers of power. Its main functions are to 'aid and advise' in matters relating to power generation, transmission, and distribution, set tariffs for power generation and transmission, issue and monitor licenses for the same by way of ensuring healthy competition, and settle disputes. There is also a Grievance Redressal Forum as well as an office of Ombudsman.

If designing the restructuring of the power sector is called the first phase, the actual implementation of reforms took place in the second phase (1995–96) and third phase (1996–2001). After Odisha, other states followed the 'Orissa model' and undertook reform and restructuring of their power sectors.

The post-reform story of Odisha's power sector was, however, not exactly that of a thundering success. A committee was appointed by the state to evaluate the power sector soon after the third phase. Its report goes by the name of Kanungo Committee Report (2001). Among many other things, it stated the following:

1. T&D losses did not diminish; in fact, they increased.[12]
2. Power shortage and peak-period shortage continued, perhaps increased.
3. Talcher power plant was a distressing failure. Its plant load factor (PLF) was much below the national average.[13]
4. While 88 per cent investment went to generation and rural electrification, a meager 12 per cent was left for transmission and systems improvement.
5. Tariff structure was still such that the industry was bearing a disproportionately heavy burden of the cost.
6. Government was taking steps to increase revenue collection and reduce theft.
7. For the DISTCOs, neither the private nor the public partner brought any managerial skill. Even working capital was not provided by the private partner.
8. Rural electrification was the worst casualty. Although the state assured 100 per cent capital subsidy, whatever payment was due to the DISTCOs was never paid to them. They had little incentive to expand.
9. Agricultural pumping by use of electricity remained grossly neglected.
10. It explicitly mentioned that the 'power sector in the state is now at the brink of a crisis'. However, the Kanungo report correctly assessed that despite serious and growing problems, rolling back on reforms was not a remedy. Setting up the new institutional framework was an essential step in the right direction, while a lot remained to be done to strengthen the new system. The institutional set-up placed in the 1990s continues till date.

[12] These losses do *not* include those from non-billing, non-collection, or theft.

[13] PLF is defined as gross generation divided by the product of installed capacity and the number of hours operated.

However, the poor condition of the power sector was not something confined to Odisha. In his essay on assessing reforms undertaken in India since 1991, Ahluwalia (2002) notes that the overall power sector performance of the nation was the 'greatest disappointment' given that it was the first sector opened for investment by the private sector.

However, during the decade of noughties, 2000 to 2009, the power sector in India grew in terms of many parameters—more than it did in the previous decade. This held true for Odisha as well. In what follows the dynamics of Odisha's power sector is reviewed in terms of physical and financial attributes.

Capacity, generation, and availability

There are two main technological sources of power in Odisha: thermal power and hydropower. They constitute roughly 63 per cent and 37 per cent, respectively, of total power supplied to the state at present. Power is generated by plants in the central and state sectors, by independent private producers (IPPs), and by captive power plants (CPPs) that mostly serve individual industrial units. A complete list of power plants in central and state sectors that provide power to Odisha is given in Box 6.3.[14]

Installed capacity, a stock concept, is a primary measure of *potential* power supply. At the beginning of the First Five-Year Plan (FYP), 1951, the installed power capacity in the state was 5 MW, all under state sector. Hirakud Dam on Mahanadi River was built in 1957, and it was used for hydro-based power generation as well as regulation of water to avoid floods and irrigation. By the end of the Fourth FYP in 1974, the installed power at Hirakud reached 684 MW.[15]

As a reference point, Figure 6.15 graphs the total installed capacity across states in 1976–77 (before the central sector entered into producing power). Among 16 states, Odisha ranked the 11th.

[14] Talcher houses the second largest thermal plant in the country, next to Vindhachal Super Thermal Power Station in Madhya Pradesh.

[15] There are altogether seven generators at Hirakud. The last one was built during the 1980s.

Box 6.3 Power plants supplying power to Odisha

Name	Source	State's share in %	Capacity in MW
	State sector		
Upper Indrabati HE	Hydro	100.00	600.00
Balimela HE	Hydro	100.00	360.00
Hirakud Power System I and II	Hydro	100.00	349.10
Upper Kolab HE	Hydro	100.00	320.00
Rengali HE	Hydro	100.00	250.00
Macchakunda HE	Hydro	50.00	114.75
Samal SHEP	Hydro	100.00	37.00
Meenakshi SHEP	Hydro	100.00	20.00
Talcher Thermal Power	Thermal	100.00	460.0
Ib I and II	Thermal	100.00	420.00
	Central sector		
Talcher STPS I and II	Thermal	31.80	3,000.00
Kaniha	Thermal	?	?
Farakka STPS, West Bengal	Thermal	13.63	1,600.00
Kahalgaon STPS, Bihar	Thermal	15.24	840.00
Tala HPS, Bhutan	Hydro	4.25	1,020.00
Teesta HPS	Hydro	20.59	510.00
Chhuka Hydro Power, Bhutan	Hydro	15.19	270.00

Source: GoO (2012).

Central sector utilities began to produce power and supply power to Odisha (and other states) in the late 1970s. The private sector's entry into power generation for Odisha is a very recent phenomenon. In 2010–11, Sterlite Energy Limited of Vedanta Resources started to supply power to GRIDCO from its plant in Jharsuguda. Its installed capacity was to the tune of 1,200 MW.

The time trend of total installed capacity in recent years, as a sum of installed capacity in the state sector, percentage of capacity of plants in the central sector allocated to the state, that by independent private producers in the state, and that of captive power plants is

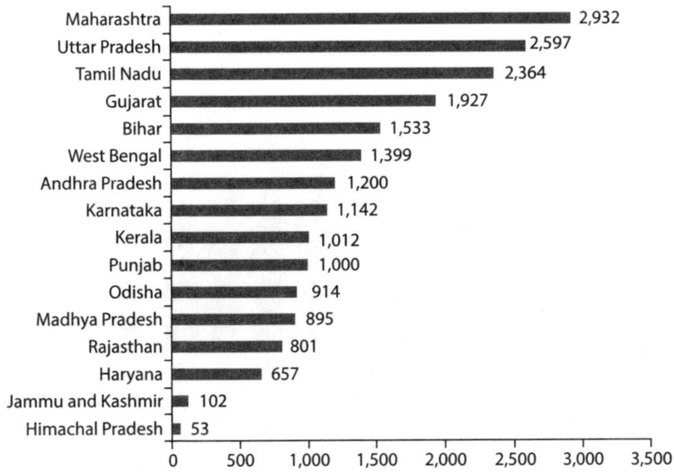

Figure 6.15 Installed capacity across states, 1975–76 (mW)
Source: Wagle and Rao (1978).

shown Figure 6.16.[16] It is heartening to note that it has more than doubled between 1999–2000 and 2010–11. The same figure also graphs installed capacity in the state sector from 1991–92 to 2010–11. As is evident, there was almost zero addition to capacity in the state sector during the 1990s till 1998–99, whereas between 1998–99 and 2011–12 there is an increase in installed capacity over 800 MW.

Captive power plants have also been producing higher quantities of power over time. The time trend of their capacity is depicted in Figure 6.17. While in 1999–2000, the capacity of the plants under the state sector was higher than that of the captive power plants, by 2009–10, the situation had reversed. The current capacity by the latter far exceeds that of the former.

It is clear that capacities by different sub-sectors within the power sector have grown at varying rates. Figure 6.18 shows the average annual growth rates over the period 1999–2000 to 2009–10. The non-state sector has grown more rapidly than the state sector. It is also

[16] The figures exclude capacity of captive power plants that do not supply power to the state.

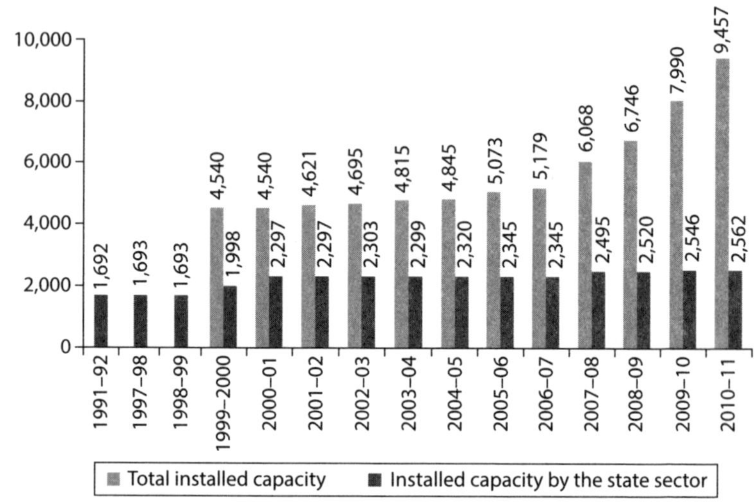

Figure 6.16 Total installed capacity and installed capacity by the state sector in Odisha (mW)

Source: Total installed capacity from, GoO (2005, 2007, 2010, 2012); installed capacity by the state sector from Ministry of Power and Non-Conventional Energy Sources (1992) and Planning Commission (2002, 2012) and Central Electricity Authority (CEA 2012).

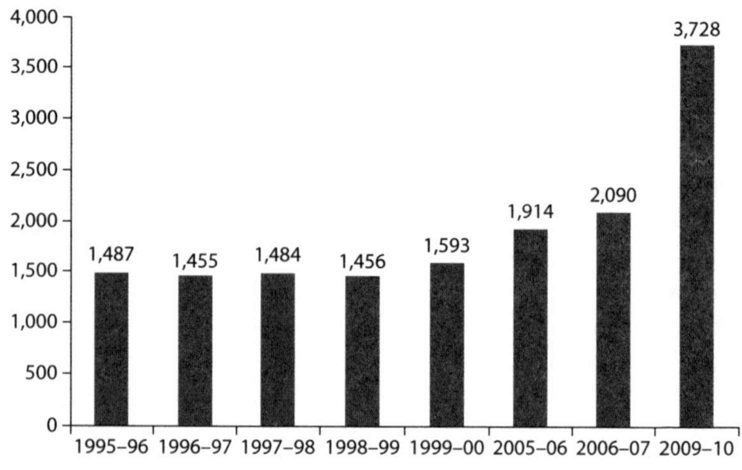

Figure 6.17 Installed capacity by captive power plants in Odisha, 1995–96 to 2009–10 (mW)

Source: CEA (various issues).

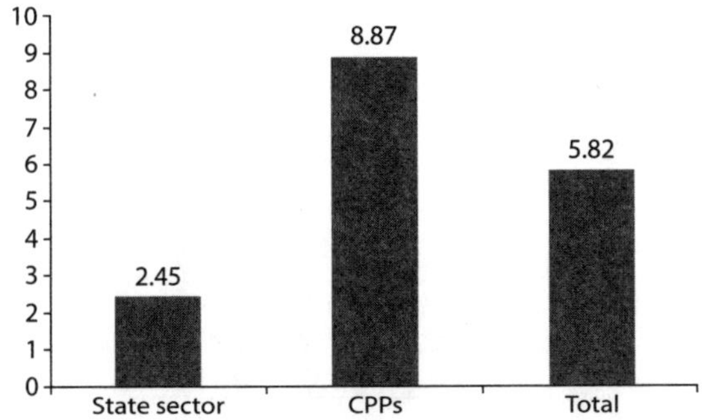

Figure 6.18 Average annual percentage growth rate of capacity: State sector, CPPs, and total, 1999–2000 to 2009–10
Source: CEA General Review various years

very important to note that until 2009–10, the private sector (other than CPPs) had zero or negligible presence in the state. However, from 2010–11, it has come up on a large scale. In 2011–12, the capacity of the private sector reached 72 per cent of the state sector. This has led to a dramatic increase in the potential power supply in the state in the last two-to-three years.

Gross power generation is a flow from the stock of installed capacity over an interval of time, expressed typically in Gwh (gigawatt hours). Some power is consumed while power is generated; this is called 'auxiliary consumption'. Netting it out gives net power generation. 'Availability' refers to the flow of power before it is transmitted and distributed for consumption. It includes 'imports' from national power grids and CPPs.[17] Figure 6.19 depicts the time series of gross power generation from 1995–96 to 2009–10 and power availability from 2002–03 to 2008–09. It is worth noting (but not shown in Figure 6.19) that in 2009–10, CPPs were the largest power-generating sector, ahead of both public sector and the private sector.

T&D losses, AT&C losses, power deficit, and power consumption

Power consumption is less than power availability and the difference is due to T&D losses. In turn, power sales are less than consumption

[17] In other words, it does not include own consumption of power from CPPs.

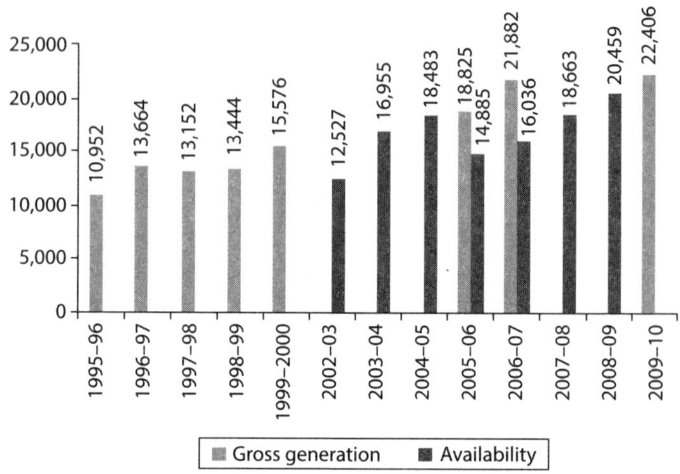

Figure 6.19 Gross power generation, 1995–96 to 2009–10, and power availability in Odisha, 2002–03 to 2008–09 (GWh)

Source: CEA (1998–2002, 2007, 2008, 2011) for power generation data and Planning Commission (2011b) for power availability.

due to non-billing, theft, and so on. To begin with, Figure 6.20 depicts T&D losses in percentage across states in 1991–92. Odisha was a 'high-ranking' state; among major states, it ranked fifth.

Figure 6.21 graphs the T&D losses (as defined earlier) over the period 1991–92 to 2008–09 for the state as well as for India. For earlier years, 1980–81 to 1990–91, data is available on the difference between gross generation, not availability and sales. This is similar but not same as T&D losses. For the sake of clarity, these are termed as T&D-plus losses; these are also depicted in Figure 6.21. It is remarkable that T&D losses are higher in the last decade compared to the previous one, and this reflects that while power generation has vastly improved in the state in recent years, the quality of transmission lines has not kept up. Furthermore, while the national average of T&D loss is declining, it is not so for the state of Odisha.[18]

[18] Even though T&D loss in India is on the decline, it is still pretty high relative to the world average (which, for example, in 2008 was about 9 per cent; see CEA (2011b, Chart 30). The *Economic Times*, 3 June 2010 reports the T&D loss in South Korea to be as low as 4 per cent.

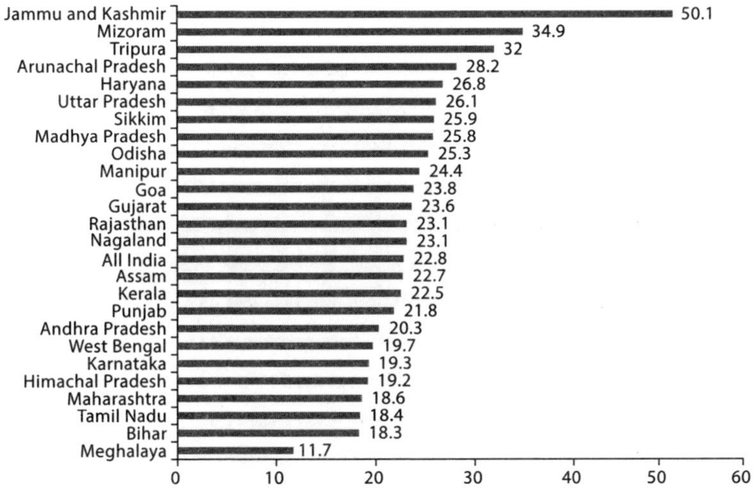

Figure 6.20 T&D losses across states, 1991–92 (%)
Source: Planning Commission (2000).

Technical and commercial losses of power together are captured by Aggregate Technical and Commercial losses or AT&C losses.[19] AT&C losses for the state from 1999–2000 to 2009–10 are shown in Figure 6.22. While it has somewhat come down over time, it remains high in absolute (percentage) terms. In rupee terms, these losses are humungous. *Economic Times* (2010) reported that the state was losing Rs 20 billion per year in the form of AT&C losses, out of which Rs 12 billion of loss occurred due to theft.

How 'regular' is the (available) electricity supply in the state? Peak surplus or deficit measures the gap between estimated requirement

[19] These losses are defined by the formula (Bhattacharya and Patel 2007):

$$1 - \text{AT\&C losses}$$
$$= (1 - \text{T\&DC losses}) \times \text{collection efficiency}$$
$$= \frac{\text{Units bills}}{\text{Units input}} \times \frac{\text{Rupees realized}}{\text{Rupees bills}}$$

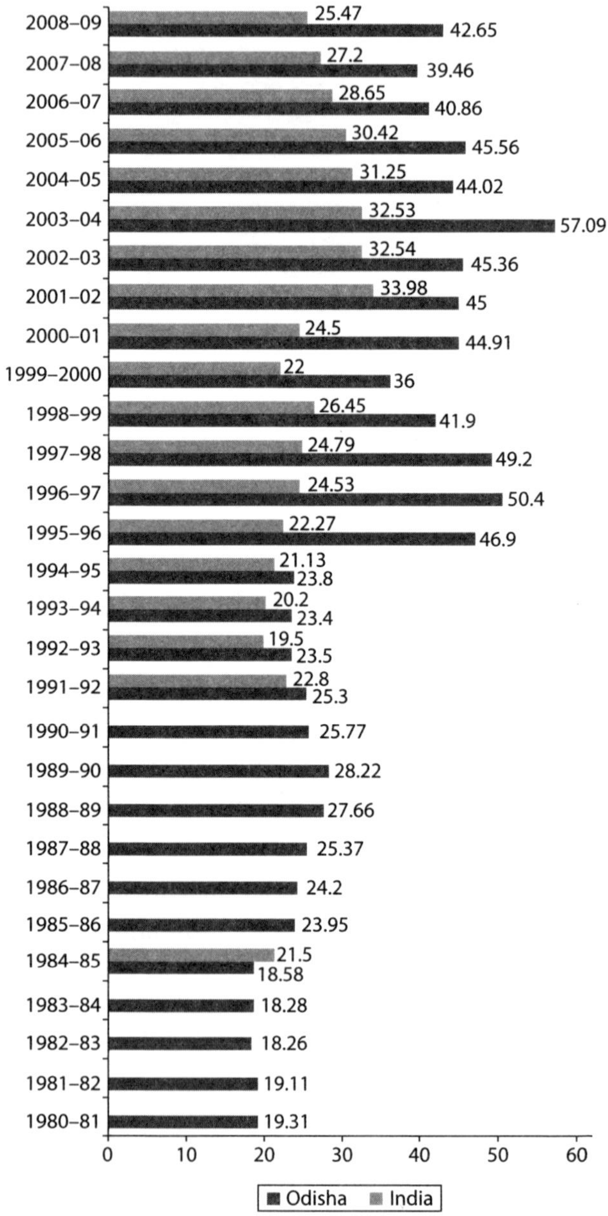

Figure 6.21 T&D-plus losses and T&D losses (%)
Source: Dash (2007) for T&D-plus losses and Planning Commission (2000, 2001, 2002, and 2011b) for T&D losses.

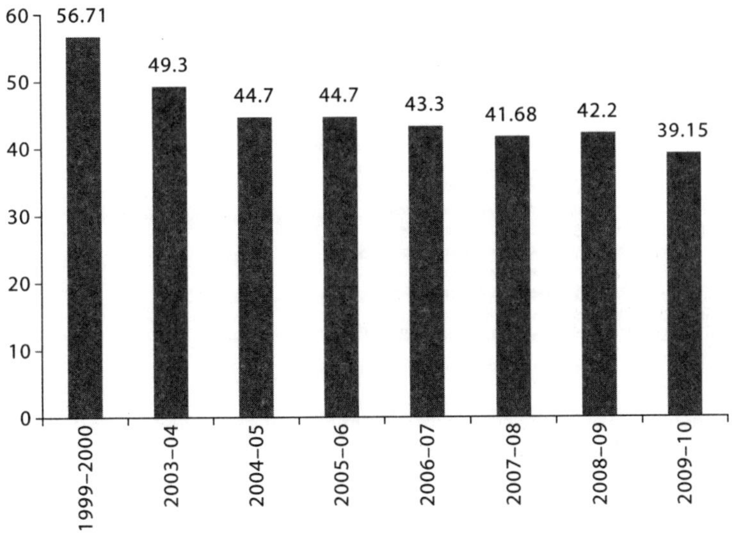

Figure 6.22 AT&C losses in Odisha, 1999–2000 to 2009–10 (%)
Source: OERC (2011) and Planning Commission (2011a).

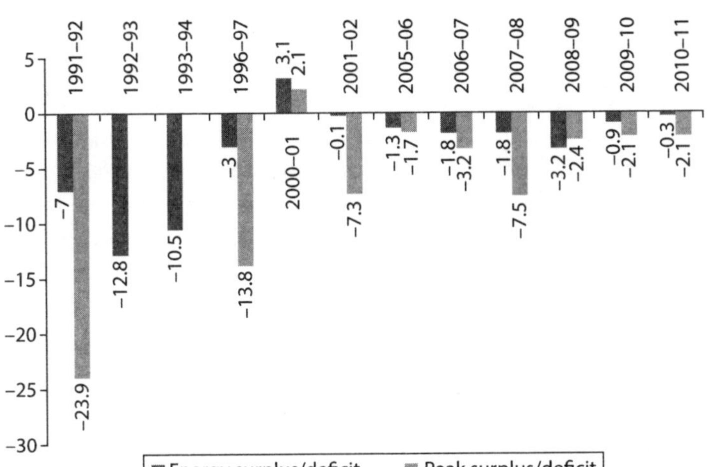

Figure 6.23 Peak and energy surplus/deficit in Odisha, 1991–92 to 2010–11 (%)
Source: Dash (2007) for 1992–93 and 1993–94; Planning Commission (2002) for 1991–92, 1996–97, and 2001–02; Planning Commission (2011a) for 2000–01 and 2006–07; CEA (2006) for 2005–06 and CEA (2008, 2009, 2010, and 2011) for 2007–08, 2008–09, 2009–10, and 2010–11 respectively.

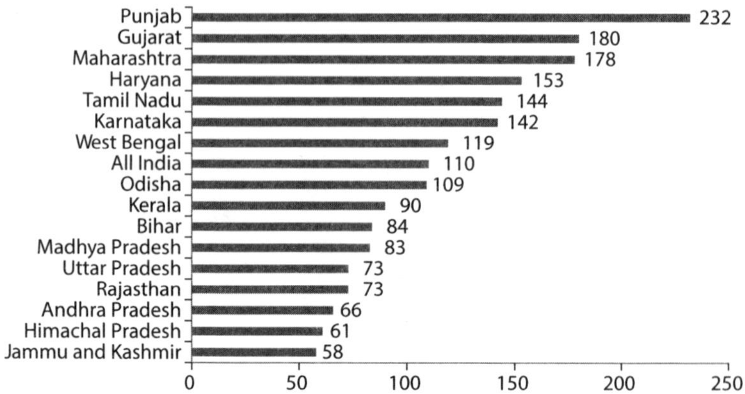

Figure 6.24 Per capita electricity consumption across states, 1975–76 (kW)
Source: Wagle and Rao (1978).

('demand') and availability at peak demand periods.[20] Energy surplus or deficit measures the same over a whole period (a year). Figure 6.23 depicts these measures for the state from 1991–92 to 2010–11. The situation has surely improved over time.

Peak or energy deficit/surplus is, however, not an indicator of the *level* of consumption of power. Modern production methods and consumption are power intensive, both directly and indirectly. Therefore, per capita power consumption (by households and businesses together) is considered as an indicator of material prosperity of a state, region, or country. As a benchmark, interstate ranking in per capita electricity consumption back in 1975–76 can be glimpsed from Figure 6.24.

Figure 6.25 depicts the time series of per capita electricity consumption of the state vis-à-vis that of India. As seen, the per capita electricity consumption of the state has remained slightly higher than that of the average for India. Furthermore, there was little growth in it in the 1990s, but during the last decade, it has grown multifold.

[20] March is typically the peak-requirement month for electricity in Odisha (CEA various years).

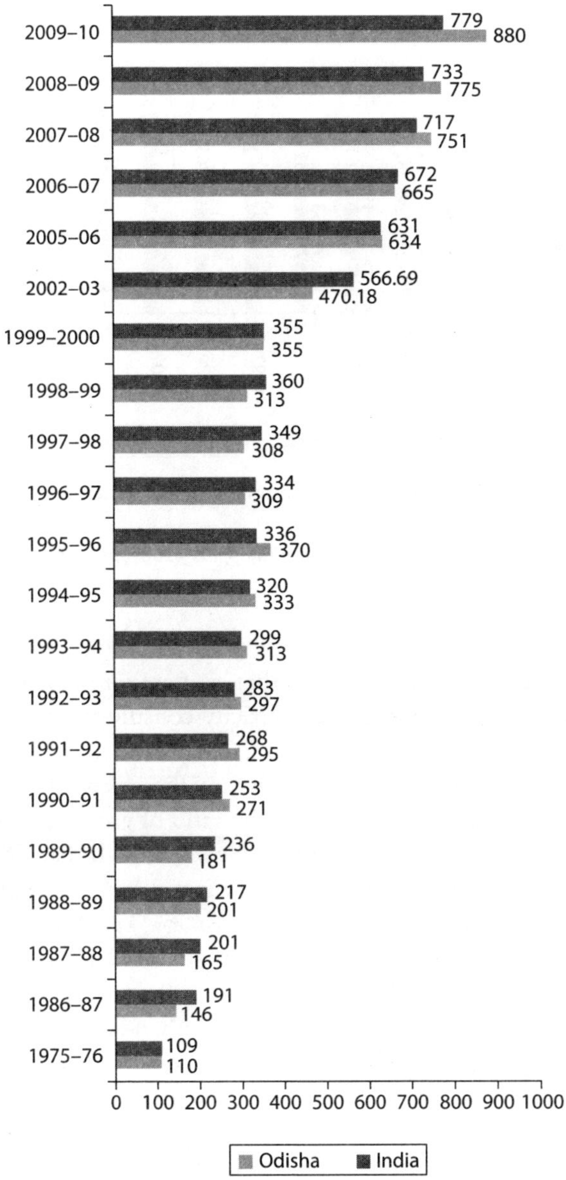

Figure 6.25 Un-adjusted per capita consumption of electricity in Odisha relative to India (kW)

Source: Wagle and Rao (1978), CEA (2007), Planning Commission (2001, 2002, 2011a).

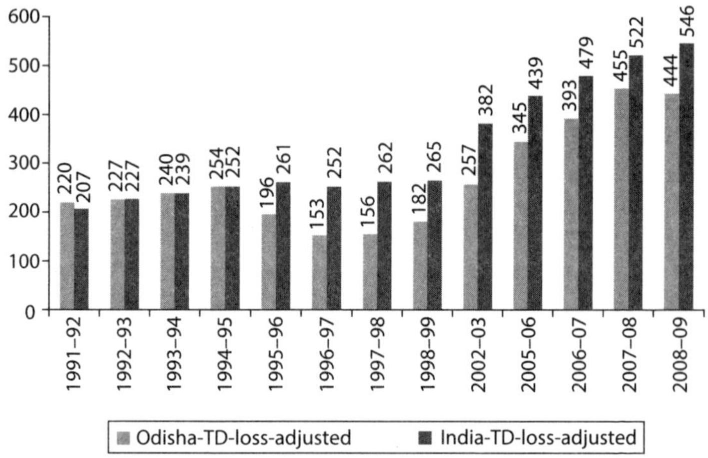

Figure 6.26 Adjusted per capita consumption of electricity in Odisha relative to India (kW)

Source: Dash (2007), Wagle and Rao (1978), CEA (2007), Planning Commission (2000, 2001, 2002, 2011a, 2011b).

However, we should not lose sight that, as a nation, we are far behind the world average of per capita electricity consumption. In 2008 for example, the world average stood at 2,782 kWh (see CEA 2011b).

Figure 6.25 is misleading, however, to the extent that per capita consumption is defined by CEA as the ratio of gross generation plus net imports to mid-year population. However, in India, T&D losses are substantial and they vary among the states. A better indicator would be the per capita consumption, *adjusted* for T&D loss—meaning un-adjusted consumption multiplied by (1–T&D loss). Figure 6.26 depicts the trends of adjusted per capita consumption (correspondingly, the caption of Figure 6.25 mentions 'Un-adjusted' per capital consumption). Thus, the adjusted per capita electricity consumption is less, dictated by the extent of the T&D loss. Its trend over the last two decades is however similar to that of un-adjusted electricity consumption. However, while the state's un-adjusted per capita electricity consumption is higher than the national average, its adjusted per capita electricity consumption is significantly less than the national average.

From the perspective of end users, Figure 6.27 depicts the percentage of households electrified across states as of 2007. Odisha

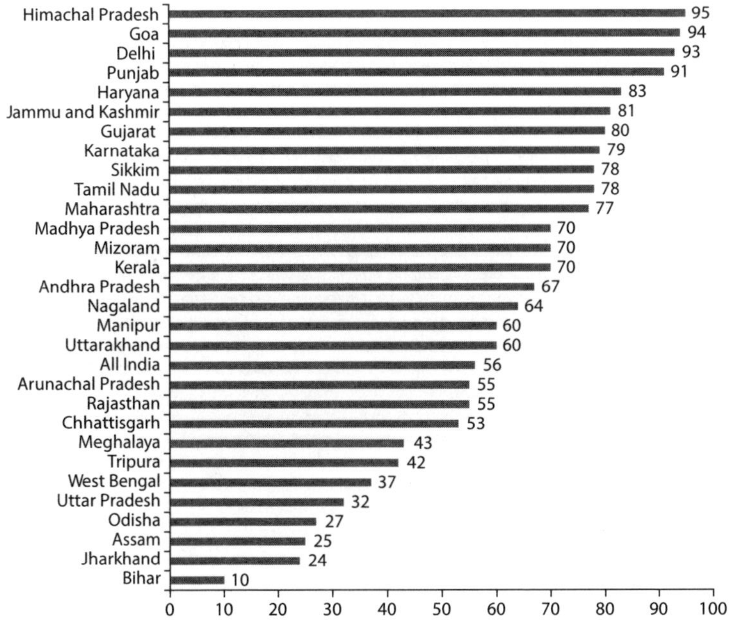

Figure 6.27 Percentage of households—rural and urban combined—electrified across states by 2001 Census
Source: Central Bureau of Health Intelligence (2007).

is near the bottom at 27 per cent, far below the national average of 56 per cent. This implies that the distribution of electricity consumption is much less even than in the whole of India.

Rural electrification

Post Independence, SEBs focused on power generation, and its supply to urban areas. Rural electrification per se was not a major or specific objective in the earlier Five Year Plans.[21]

Villages were electrified gradually as town and cities were to be connected by electricity. In addition, it was accomplished because

[21] There are of course references to it. The second and third Five Year Plans mentioned about electrification of villages and towns having a population of at least 10,000 and 5,000 respectively.

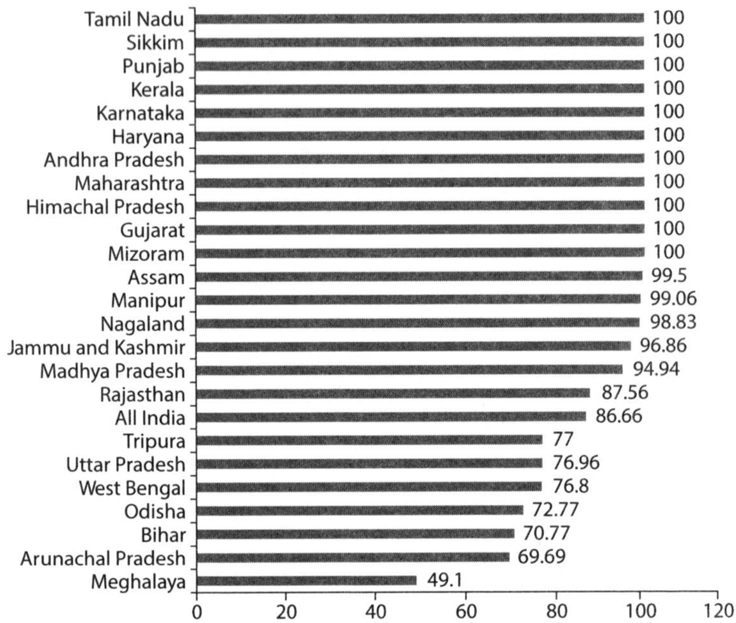

Figure 6.28 Percentage of villages electrified across states by the end of 1995–96
Source: CEA (1998).

of political number game, as the number of villages electrified in a constituency was regarded as a selling point in the political arena (Modi 2005). It is remarkable that Haryana was the first state to have all its villages electrified as early as 1970. Rural Electrification Corporation (REC), now one of the Navratna public enterprises under the Ministry of Power, came into existence in 1969, whose main function is to facilitate financing of rural electrification projects. Rural electrification was incorporated in law for the first time in the Electricity Act of 2003, which talked about formulation of a national policy on the same. Subsequently, the Government of India circulated a draft paper on the issue. It planned for complete village-level electrification by 2007 and household-level electrification by 2012. To accomplish these goals, Rajiv Gandhi Grameen Vidyutikaran Yojana (RGGVY) was launched in 2005. Its objective was to have electricity provided to all villages and households in India having a population of at least 100 by the next five-to-seven years.

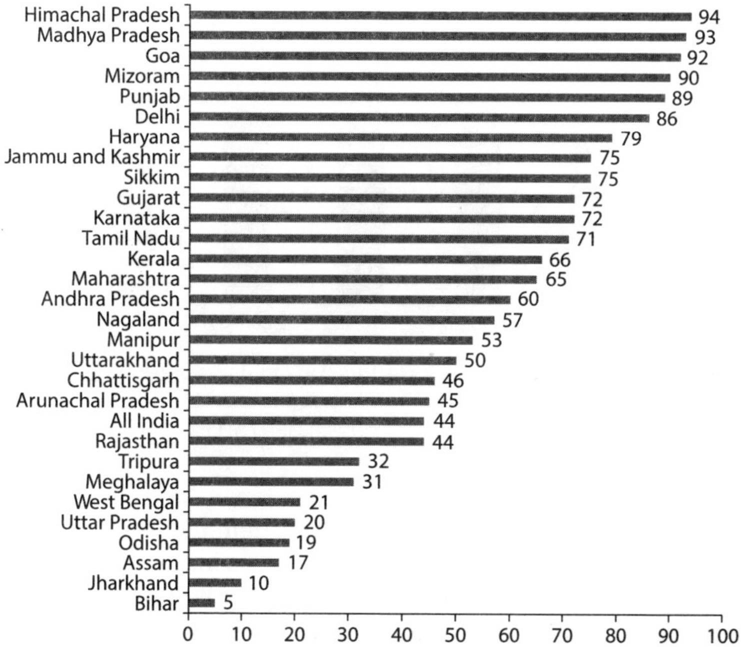

Figure 6.29 Percentage of households in rural areas electrified across states by 2001 Census

Source: Central Bureau of Health Intelligence (2007).

However, progress on rural electrification has been tardy in Odisha compared to most other states. While, as said earlier, 100 per cent electrification was accomplished in Haryana as far back as 1970, in Odisha it reached 43 per cent in 1983 and 67 per cent in 1991 (Kale 2007). Figure 6.28 graphs the extent of village electrification across the states by the end of 1995–96. Odisha's ranking was quite low. In terms of households—rather than the number of villages—having electricity in rural areas in the census year 2001, as Figure 6.29 reflects, the ranking Odisha was as poor. Only 19 per cent of households in rural areas in the state had electricity.

Until 1997, a village was defined to be electrified as long as electricity was used at some spot within the revenue area of the village. This definition was modified slightly after 1997.[22] Since

[22] In 1999, the percentage of villages electrified in Odisha was 73.3 per cent (National Council of Applied Economic Research (2007, Table A1.5).

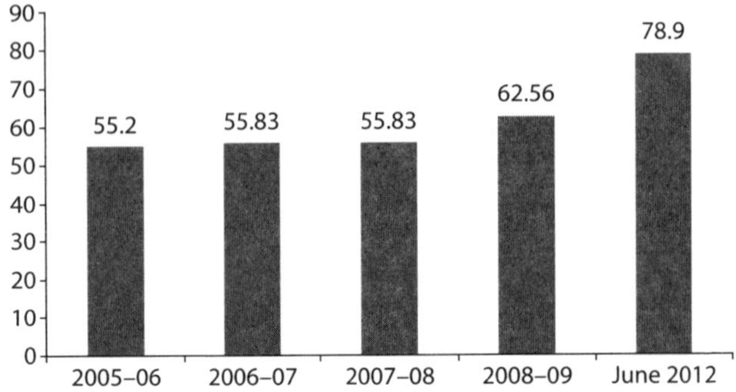

Figure 6.30 Percentage of villages electrified in Odisha as per 2001 Census count of villages, 2005–06 to 2012
Source: CEA (2007, 2012) and Planning Commission (2011a).

2004–05, a more comprehensive definition has been used to measure the extent of electrification in a village. It has three features: (a) basic infrastructure such as distribution lines must be provided to inhabited areas, (b) power must be reaching public places such as schools, health centres, and panchayat offices, and (c) electrification must cover at least 10 per cent of total households in the village.

The progress on rural electrification in Odisha in the recent years based on the new definition is shown in Figure 6.30. It is striking that there was virtually no progress from 2005–06 to 2007–08. However, it is appreciable since. Within Odisha, however, as Figure 6.31 shows, there is a wide variation across districts in the extent of rural electrification, ranging from 23.9 per cent in Malkangiri to 100 per cent in Jarsuguda and Nayagarh.

Agriculture is a rural activity and agricultural productivity is obviously dependent on how much power is used for irrigation and operation of electro-mechanical equipment. However, the share of agriculture in the total power sales has remained very low, around 1 per cent, even until the present time.[23] Figure 6.32 depicts the composition of electricity sales to different types of end users as of 2009–10.

[23] In the neighbouring state of Andhra Pradesh, it is around 30 per cent.

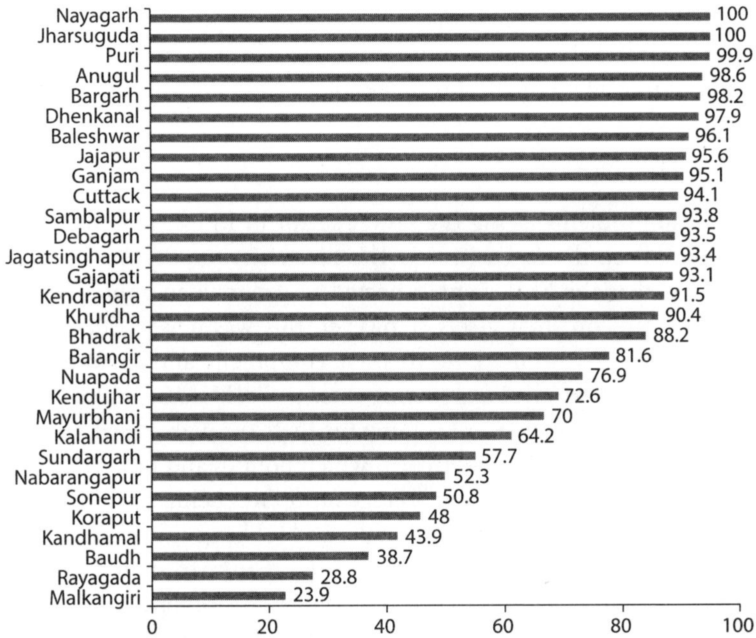

Figure 6.31 Percentage of villages electrified across districts, 2010–11
Source: GoO (2012).

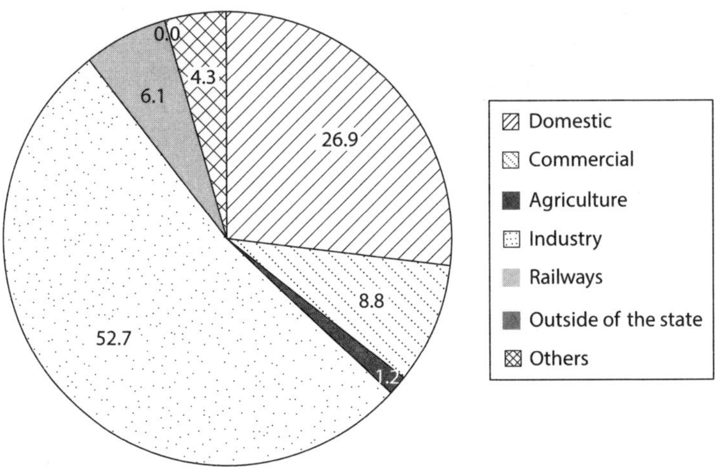

Figure 6.32 Composition of electricity sales in Odisha, 2009–10 (%)
Source: Planning Commission (2011a).

The emerging picture is that while the overall power situation may have considerably improved over time, the gain to rural Odisha in terms of usage by households or agriculture has been small.

Commercial aspects

Financial problems facing the power sector in India are well known and have been discussed earlier. The Electricity Supply Act of 1948 provided that the SEBs were expected to generate an annual return of 3 per cent on their assets. However, this was never realized due to a variety of reasons. Due to poor equipment and maintenance and a lack of professional management, T&D losses were huge. Revenues were low due to (a) rampant theft through illegal tapping of distribution lines and metres, in which politics and bribery played major roles, (b) relatively low average tariff rates being set with much political but little economic rationale, and (c) huge subsidies granted to the agriculture and household sectors (thanks to politics again). Odisha was no exception to this deplorable phenomenon.

A lot of emphasis has been placed on agricultural subsidies as a main source of commercial failure of the power sector in India. Some even argue that this has become a scapegoat for other ills in the sector. What is distinct about commercial losses facing the power sector in Odisha in particular is that (a) agricultural use of electricity is meagre, less than 2 per cent, compared to states like Haryana, Punjab, Rajasthan, Andhra Pradesh, and Madhya Pradesh where the share of agriculture in total sales of power exceeds 30 per cent and (b) the difference between tariffs charged for agricultural use and commercial/industrial use is relatively minor. Figure 6.33 depicts the interstate ranking for 2009–10 of ratio of tariff by state production units charged for agricultural/irrigational use to that charged to commercial users. Odisha ranks fifth, while in Tamil Nadu, Punjab, and Odisha, tariff charged for agricultural/irrigational use is zero.[24] It means that the extent of cross subsidization of electricity in Odisha across industrial/commercial users and agricultural users is less compared to most of

[24] In terms of ratio of tariff charged for agricultural/irrigational use to that for industrial use, Odisha ranked 2nd in 2009–10.

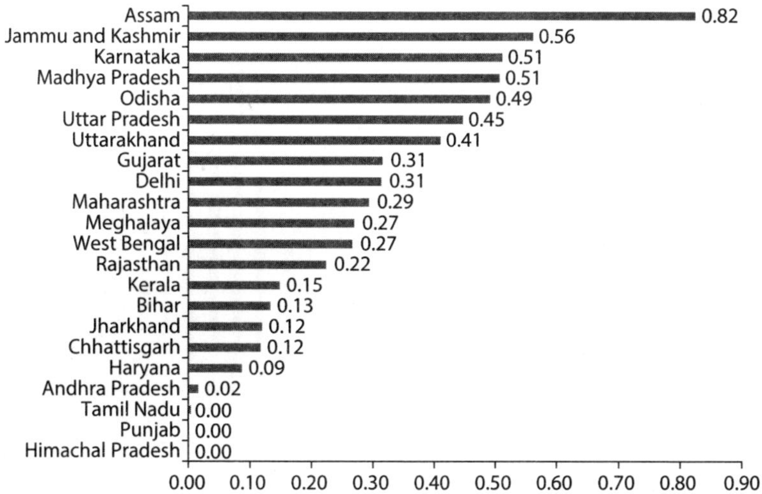

Figure 6.33 Ratio of tariff rates charged for agricultural/irrigational use to that charged for commercial use, 2009–10
Source: Planning Commission (2011a).

the other states, indicating that tariff rates in Odisha are probably more rationalized than in most other states.[25]

Figure 6.34 graphs the loss per unit of kilowatt electricity sold in the state over the period 1974–75 to 2009–10. Not a single year has been a witness to any profits. The *cumulative* effect of losses crystallized into a crisis by the early 1990s. As can be observed from the same figure, losses continued to mount during the 1990s while the reforms were being undertaken. They have somewhat come down in very recent years. Yet, as will be seen further, their absolute levels remain high.

For a distribution utility, revenues are generated from tariffs charged at differential rates to various groups of users such as domestic (households), commercial, agriculture, industrial, railways, and outside state customers. Figure 6.35 depicts average tariff rates charged by State Power Utilities (SPUs) to different groups during 2009–10. Barring tariff for outside state users, commercial users are

[25] Chattopadhyay (2004) finds that for a particular segment of electricity supply in Uttar Pradesh, the cross-subsidy programme was sub-optimal and industrial tariffs were 'too high', compared to the optimum.

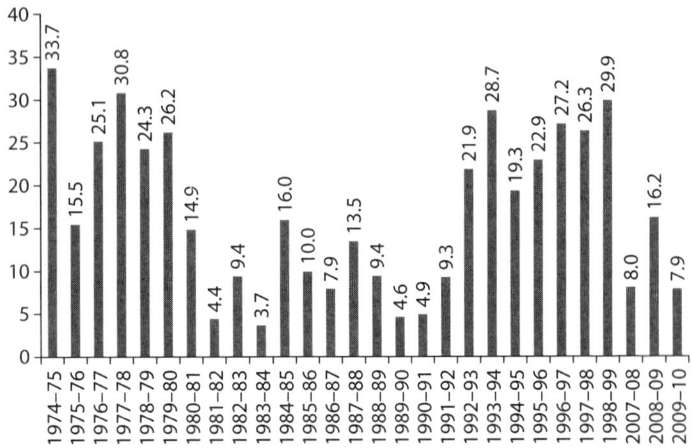

Figure 6.34 Loss per kilowatt electricity sold in Odisha
Source: Planning Commission (2001, 2002, 2011a).

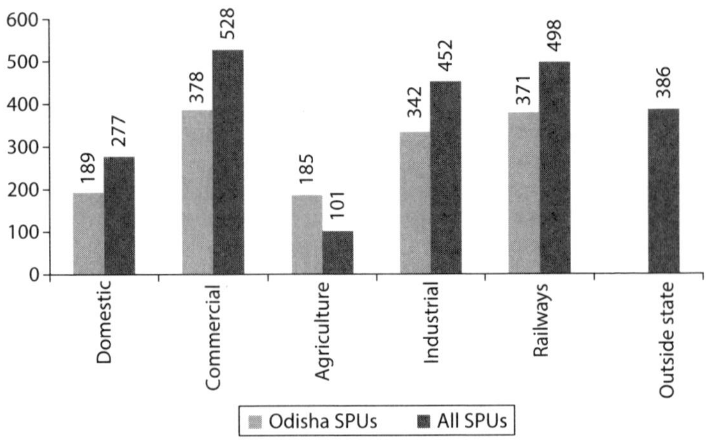

Figure 6.35 Tariff across groups of users in 2009–10: Odisha SPUs versus all SPUs (Paise/kWh)
Source: Planning Commission (2011a).

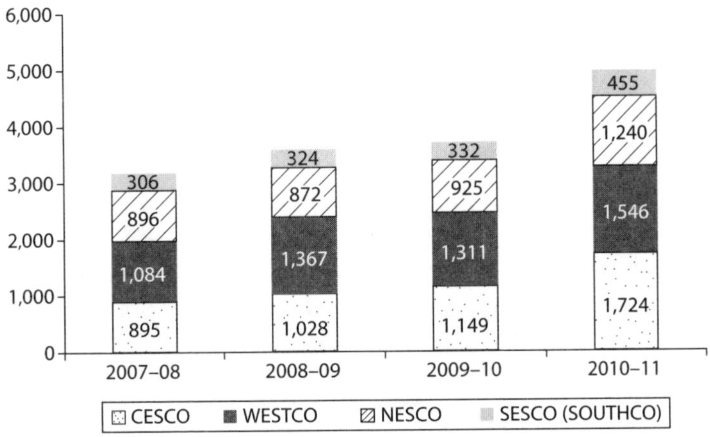

Figure 6.36 Revenues by DISTCOs in Odisha, 2007–08 to 2010–11 (Rs crore)
Source: Power Finance Corporation (2011, 2012).

charged the highest, followed by railways, industrial users, domestic, and agriculture.[26] As noted earlier, in Odisha the difference in tariff charged to domestic users and agriculture is rather small compared to the national average.

Dynamics of revenues earned by the four DISTCOs in Odisha in recent years are depicted in Figure 6.36. CESCO's revenue growth is highest among the four.

Costs facing a distribution company are typically broken into seven categories: fuel cost, power purchase, operation and maintenance (O&M) cost, establishment and administration cost, depreciation, interest, and miscellany. Power purchase is the biggest among the cost components, constituting more than half of the total cost.

There are various measures of profit/loss for firms in the power sector. These are listed in Table 6.2 for reference. Figures 7.37 and 7.38 illustrate profit/loss profile (inclusive of subsidies actually received) of the four DISTCOs in Odisha over the period 2007–08 to 2010–11, respectively.[27] Both measures, even while inclusive of subsidies, exhibit losses, and losses are yet to show any declining trend.

[26] There were no sale to outside state users for Odisha in 2009–10.

[27] These figures correspond to rows N and K in Table 6.2.

Table 6.2 Various profit/loss concepts in the power sector

A	Income or revenues (without subsidy)	
B	Expenditure (without depreciation, writeoffs and tax)	
C	Subsidies booked	
D	Subsidies unpaid	
E	Unrealized revenue	
F	Depreciation and writeoffs	
G	Income tax paid	
H	Deferred tax	
I	Cash profit/loss without depreciation, writeoffs, subsidies and tax	A – B
J	Cash profit/loss without depreciation and writeoffs	I + C – G
K	Cash profit/loss on revenue and subsidy realized basis	J – D – E
L	Book profit/loss	J – F – H
M	Profit/loss without subsidy	L – C
N	Profit/loss on subsidy received basis	L – D

Source: Power Finance Corporation (2012).

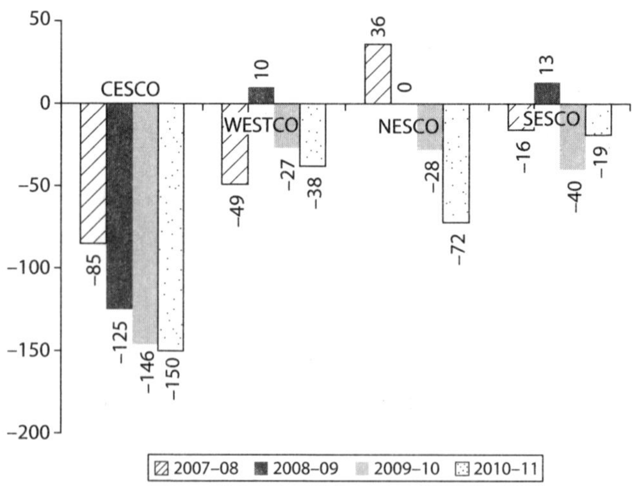

Figure 6.37 (Economic) profits on subsidy received by DISTCOs in Odisha, 2007–08 to 2010–11 (Rs crore)

Source: Power Finance Corporation (2011, 2012).

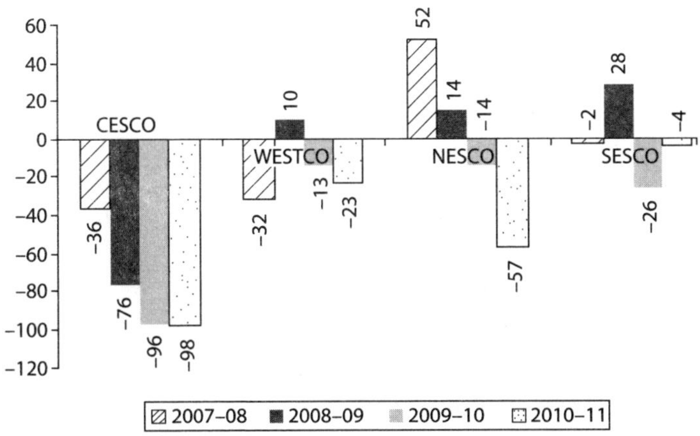

Figure 6.38 Cash profits on subsidy received by DISTCOs in Odisha, 2007–08 to 2010–11 (Rs crore)
Source: Power Finance Corporation (2011, 2012).

It is not surprising that accumulated losses over years or decades would lead to growingly negative net worths. Figure 6.39 confirms this for the DISTCOs. It also graphs the net worth of GRIDCO, a trading company (TRADECO), OHPC and OPGCL, two generation

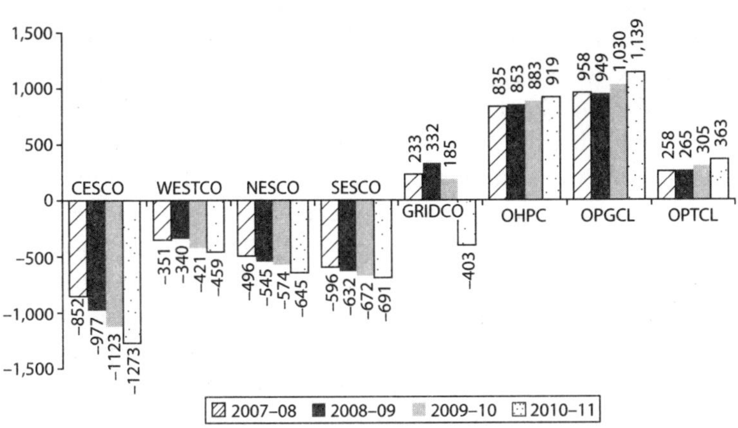

Figure 6.39 Net worth of DISTCOs, GENCOs, TRANSCOs, and 'TRADECOs' in Odisha, 2007–08 to 2010–11 (Rs crore)
Source: Power Finance Corporation (2011, 2012).

companies (GENCOs), and OPTCL, a transmission and maintenance company (TRANSCO). Positive and growing net worth is seen for OHPC, OPGCL, and OPTCL, while GRIDCO's net worth is disturbingly declining and became negative in 2010–11. *Business Standard* of 3 April 2012 reported that during 2010–11, GRIDCO posted losses to a tune of Rs 1.47 billion. *Business Standard,* dated 26 June 2015, reports that GRIDCO's outstanding loan amounted to Rs 48.43 billion by the end of 2014–15.

In sum, while the physical performance of the power sector in the state has improved, its financial woes remain substantial.

Policy initiatives undertaken

Time profiles of some indices of physical and financial performance of the power sector in Odisha have been recorded earlier. Listed further are some of the policy initiatives undertaken by the state government towards this sector.

Apart from the setting up of the organizational structure of the power sector and regular investment to enhance capacity of large hydro and thermal power sectors, the *Economic Survey of Orissa: 2011–12* (GoO 2012) lists various programmes and measures undertaken by the state and the centre.

- In Odisha, the RGGVY scheme has been executed by public sector units such as NTPC, NHPC, and PGCIL. Over 44,000 villages were supposed to be electrified by the target date, 31 March 2012. However, *Business Standard,* 27 February 2012 reported that the progress has been quite slow. By January 2012 the work was completed in about 34,000 villages and, during 2011–12, the work was being executed at the average rate of 765 villages per month, whereas over 10,000 villages needed to be electrified in the next two months if completion was to be achieved by the target date. There is no information available whether work under this scheme has been finished by now.
- Since 2007, a state-funded Biju Gram Jyoti Yojana is in progress, whose objective is to provide electricity to small villages having population below 100, the ones not covered under RGGVY. It is reported that over 8,000 villages have been provided electricity under this programme.

- In 2010, the state launched a CAPEX (capital expenditure) programme of Rs 240 billion towards improving the T&D losses through replacing old transformers and supply wires and buying various equipment. The state government is supposed to put in Rs 120 billion and the remaining half would be invested by the distribution companies. Due to the lingering losses afflicting the discoms, in 2014 the state has proposed to advance an additional loan of Rs 6 billion to target specific areas like aerial bunched (AB) cabling, high voltage distribution system (HVDS) and metering (*Business Standard* 23 September 2014).
- A monitoring committee has been established to ensure that all rural households in the state are provided electricity by the end of 2012.
- The Biju Saharanchala Vidyutikaran Yojana, launched in 2010–11, targets electrification of poor households in urban areas. It is supposed to cover 103 local urban bodies in the whole state.
- The Odisha Renewable Energy Development Agency (OREDA) under the Department of Science and Technology of the Government of Odisha looks after the development of renewable and alternative energy schemes. It sponsors solar powered projects under the Jawaharlal Nehru National Solar Mission. It has commissioned micro hydel projects in Keonjhar and Mayurbhanj districts. The Biju Patnaik Energy Park has been established in Bhubaneswar to spread awareness about renewable energy among the public.
- The Remote Village Electrification Programme (RVEP), funded by the centre and the state, targets electrification of remote villages and areas through non-conventional energy sources. Thus far, 537 villages have been provided power through this scheme.
- Under the National Biogas and Manure Management Programme (NBMMP), a central scheme, 1,969 domestic biogas plants were constructed during 2010–11.
- It is estimated that the state has biomass power potential up to 300 MW. A state technical committee has projects for a cumulative capacity of 138 MW.

Snapshots of relative positions of the state in recent times

It is easy to boast of current achievements compared to own past. However, performance must be judged eventually relative to other states. What is current or recent *relative* position of Odisha vis-à-vis other states in terms of various indicators? Have its *relative* rankings improved over time?

Recent rankings are illustrated by figures 6.40 through 6.46. Box 6.4 summarizes them vis-à-vis rankings in the past. In terms of installed capacity, Odisha's ranking may have improved somewhat from the mid-1970s—thanks to entry by the private sector. Note, however, that Figure 6.40 does not include capacity of CPPs, whereas in Odisha, CPPs constitute a major source of power for the industrial sector.

Odisha continues to rank quite high, that is, *poorly* in terms of T&D losses. Its ranking is also poor on AT&C losses. The relative progress cards on household and rural electrification appear the worst. The only index on which Odisha fares better than all major states (that is with the exclusion Delhi, Goa, and Northeastern states barring Assam) is commercial losses per unit of electricity sold. This, by any means, does *not* imply a financial turnaround since cumulative losses remain substantial and losses are still being incurred.

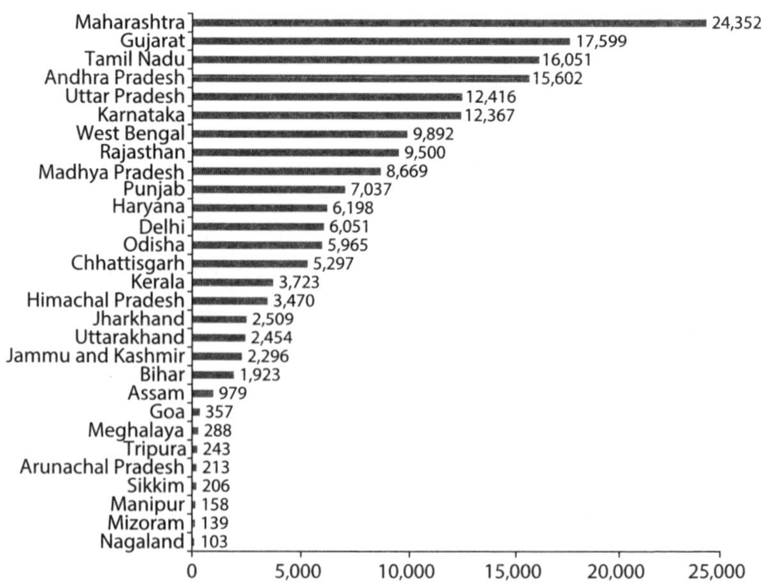

Figure 6.40 Installed capacity across states (except CPPs), 2011 (mW)
Source: CEA (2011).

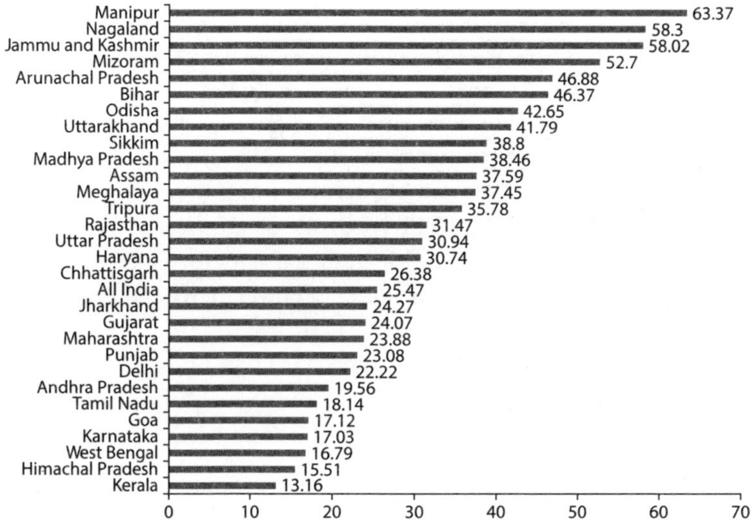

Figure 6.41 T&D loss across states, 2008–09 (%)
Source: CEA (2011).

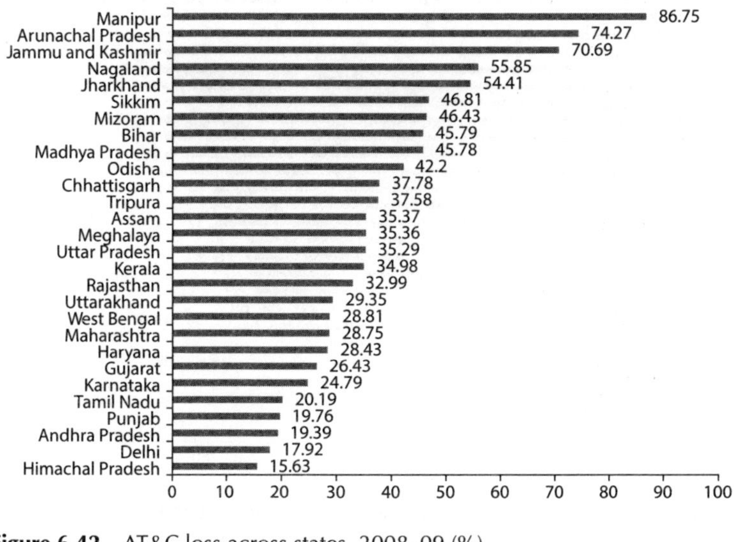

Figure 6.42 AT&C loss across states, 2008–09 (%)
Source: Planning Commission (2011a).

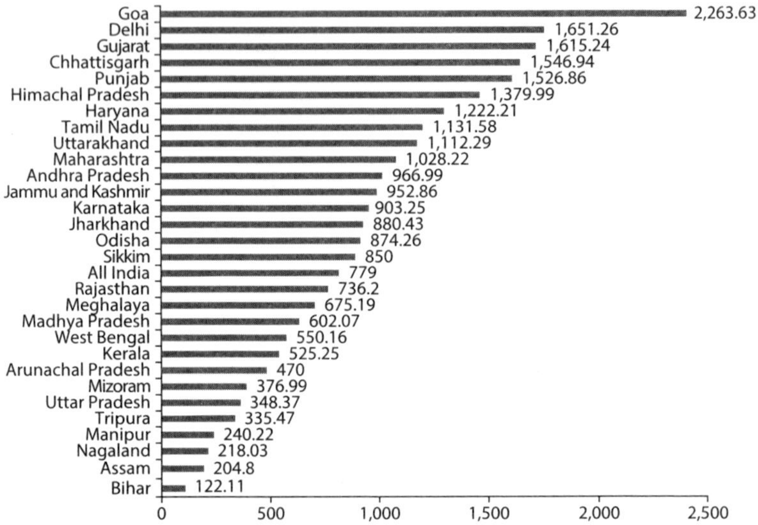

Figure 6.43 Per capita electricity consumption across states, 2009–10 (kW)
Source: CEA (2011).

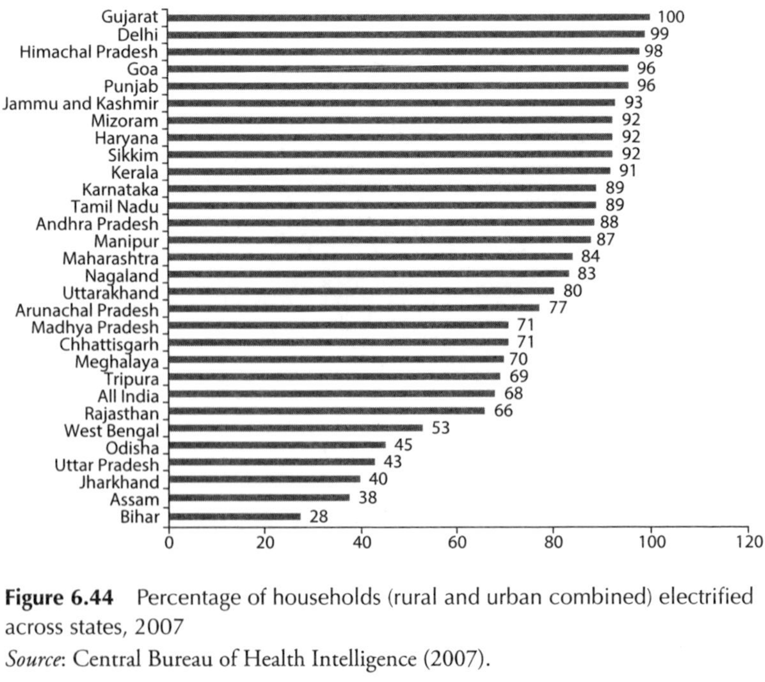

Figure 6.44 Percentage of households (rural and urban combined) electrified across states, 2007
Source: Central Bureau of Health Intelligence (2007).

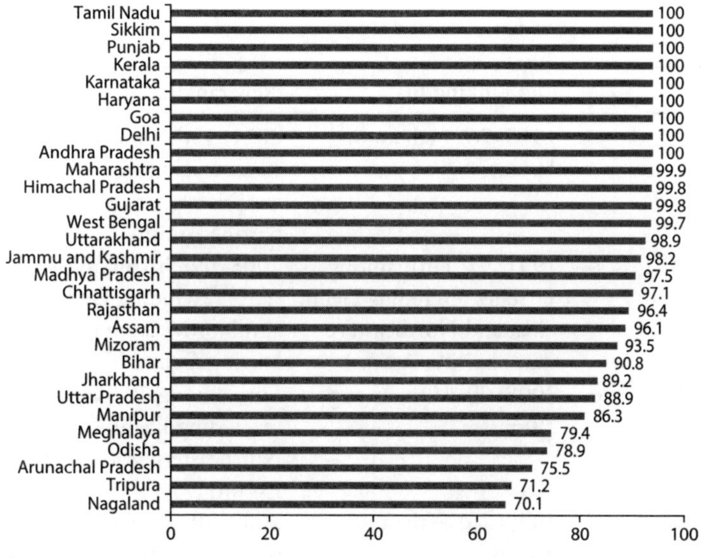

Figure 6.45 Percentage of villages electrified across states, as of June 2012
Source: CEA (2012).

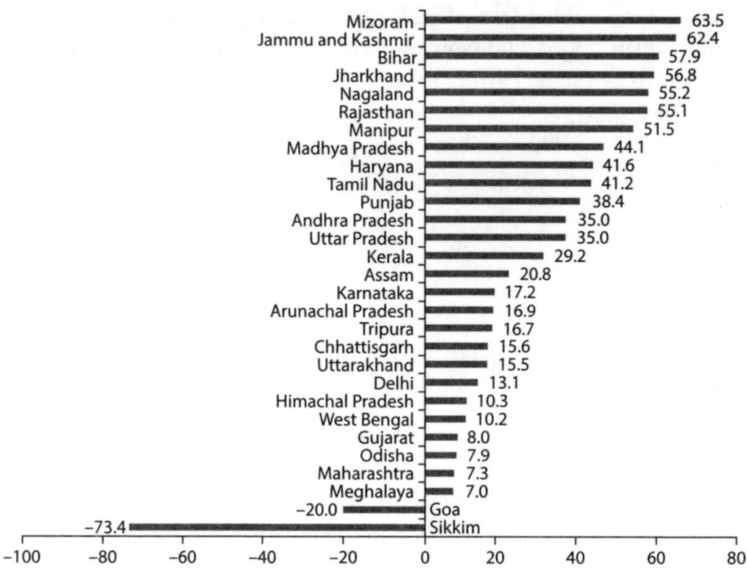

Figure 6.46 Percentage loss per one kilowatt electricity sold, 2009–10
Source: Planning Commission (2011a).

Box 6.4 Past and recent rankings of Odisha

	Old ranking in	New ranking in
Installed capacity	1975–76: 11th among 16 states	2011: 13th among 21 major states (excluding Delhi, Goa, and Northeastern states barring Assam)
T&D losses	1991–92: Fifth among 17 states (excluding Delhi, Goa, and Northeastern states barring Assam)	2008–09: 3rd among 21 states (excluding Delhi, Goa, and Northeastern states barring Assam)
AT&C losses	2008–09: 10th among 28 states	Fifth among 20 states (excluding Delhi, Goa, and Northeastern states barring Assam)
Per capita electricity consumption	1975–76: 11th among 16 states	2009–10: 15th among 22 states (excluding Delhi, Goa, and Northeastern states barring Assam)
Percentage of households (rural–urban combined) electrified	2001: 18th among 21 states (excluding Delhi, Goa, and Northeastern states barring Assam)	2007: 17th among 21 states (excluding Delhi, Goa, and Northeastern states barring Assam)
Percentage of villages electrified	1995–96: 22nd among 25 states	2012: 26th among 29 states
Percentage loss per one kilowatt electricity sold		2009–10: 19th among 20 states (excluding Delhi, Goa, and Northeastern states barring Assam)

Source: Figures 6.15, 6.20, 6.24, 6.27, 6.28, 6.40, 6.41, 6.42, 6.43, 6.44, 6.45, 6.46.

This chapter has not discussed alternative and renewable energy sources in Odisha. It is because these are relatively negligible compared to conventional energy sources. As Figure 6.47 illustrates, recent ranking of availability of renewable energy sources places Odisha nearly at the bottom.

An overall assessment

If one were to pass an overall statement, good progress has taken place on the provision of roadways in Odisha. However, conversion of unsurfaced to surfaced roads needs to be carried out at a more rapid pace. Road maintenance and repair must remain a priority area for the state for *all* time to come on a *routine* basis. It requires a commitment to perpetuity. Inadequate railway network in tribal and most poor areas in the state remains glaring. Integration of these areas into the mainstream economy of the state would require fast and full implementation of proposed or half-finished railways lines in these areas. Major expansion of ports facility is underway, which is conducive to growth of the industrial sector in the state.

The power supply situation in the state has improved substantially in the last decade. However, the power sector has expanded in other states as well and the relative position of Odisha vis-à-vis other states in terms of various indices has not improved much.

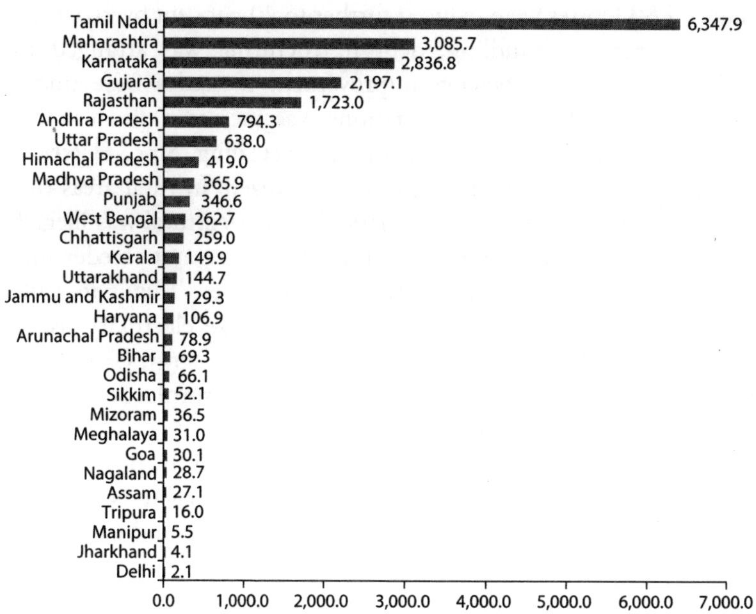

Figure 6.47 Renewable energy sources across states (capacity), 2011 (mW)
Source: Central Electricity Authority (2011a).

There is a visible reduction of power theft through illegal tapping and metre tampering. However, as we have seen, large T&D losses continue to be the order of the day, and hence, remain worrisome. If one were to pick a single index that would measure the performance of the power sector in any region, it is the T&D loss—so argues Subramanian (2012). If so, the power sector's performance in the state is one of the poorest. The state must undertake strong measures to curb T&D losses down.

There is still a long way to go to achieve full rural electrification in the state.

It is ironical that Odisha is the state that pioneered privatization and debundling of the power sector. However, relative to other states, the power situation has not really turned around. Gujarat turns out to be the turn-around state: In 2000–01, the Gujarat State Electricity Board (GSEB) had posted a loss to the tune of Rs 22.46 billion and T&D losses were above 35 per cent. By 2005–06, it was earning profit and the after-tax net profit was Rs 2.03 billion for the same year. T&D losses were down to 28 per cent. In 2008–09, net profits rose to Rs 5.33 billion. T&D losses were reduced further to 20 per cent by 2010–11.

Apart from de-bundling, debt restructuring was arranged for GSEB and various efficiency-improvement measures were undertaken. The number of police stations was increased and criminal proceedings were initiated to arrest power stealing. Since electricity rates for agricultural use are typically subsidized, in rural areas (just as in other states), electricity earmarked for agricultural was illegally used for domestic purposes. To minimize this separate feeder lines were provided for agricultural use and other uses. This is regarded as one of the innovative measures to rationalize electricity use in the state. In addition to conventional sources of energy, Gujarat has invested heavily in solar energy. It is now a power-surplus state, ready to sell power to many other states.

Briefly put, an integrated and sustained focus on the power sector has transformed the power situation in Gujarat. There is much to learn for the state of Odisha from Gujarat's turnaround efforts and positive results.

Whether it is transport or power, until a decade or two ago, the policy and planning view in India towards physical infrastructure was mostly 'reactive', meaning enhancement of supply pressured by an increase in demand. Even today in major cities, roads are widened only when road jams are unbearable. Bypasses along highways are constructed only when traffic through towns becomes choked. Such thinking, planning, and execution are a reflection of shortsightedness and failure to see that Say's Law is particularly relevant to the provision of infrastructure: supply of infrastructure would create its own demand (and create all-around growth [added]). A shift in thinking has fortunately taken place with respect to rural road development programmes (such as PMGSY) and massive development of solar power by some states. A 600 MW solar park was commissioned in April 2012 in Patan district of Gujarat, a jump from 6 MW solar energy capacity in the state in 2011. Rajasthan is the next state moving big on solar energy. A 40 MW solar project was completed in 2012 and a 250 MW project is underway. A *Times of India* editorial dated 20 July 2012 has reported a unique initiative in Bihar towards developing power from rice husks. Apparently, 80 mini plants are up, supplying power to 32,000 households. Although a trickle, it is a significant development, holding considerable promise.

In Odisha, a regime shift, so to speak, has just occurred in terms of large-scale entry of private enterprises into the production of power based on conventional sources. However, there seems to be no serious planning at the state level to develop solar or any other alternative sources of power on a large scale.

References

Ahluwalia, M.S. 2002. 'Economic Reforms in India since 1991: Has Gradualism Worked?', *Journal of Economic Perspectives*, 16(3, Summer): 67–88.

Bhattacharya, S. and U.R. Patel. 2007. 'The Power Sector in India: An Inquiry into the Efficacy of the Reform Process', Brookings Institution–NCAER India Policy Forum, 4th Conference, New Delhi.

Business Standard. 3 April 2012. 'GRIDCO, OPTCOL Post Heavy Losses in 2010–11'.

Business Standard. 26 June 2015. 'Gridco Readies Plan for Turnaround in Finances'.

Business Standard. 23 September 2014. 'Odisha to Modify Capex Scheme, Pump in Additional Rs 600 cr'.

Business Standard. 29 September 2012. 'Odisha to Ask Centre to Include GRIDCO in Debt-Restructuring Scheme'.

Central Bureau of Health Intelligence. 2007. *National Health Profile 2007*. Ministry of Health and Family Welfare.

CEA (Central Electricity Authority). 1998. *All India Electricity Statistics: General Review 1995–96*. Ministry of Power, Government of India.

———. 1999. *All India Electricity Statistics: General Review 1996–97*. Ministry of Power, Government of India.

———. 2000. *All India Electricity Statistics: General Review 1997–98*. Ministry of Power, Government of India.

———. 2001. *All India Electricity Statistics: General Review 1998–99*. Ministry of Power, Government of India.

———. 2002. *All India Electricity Statistics: General Review 1999–2000*, Ministry of Power, Government of India.

———. 2006. *Annual Report 2005–06*. Government of India.

———. 2007. *All India Electricity Statistics: General Review 2007* (Containing Data for the Year 2005–06). Ministry of Power, Government of India.

———. 2008. *All India Electricity Statistics: General Review 2008* (Containing Data for the Year 2006–07). Ministry of Power, Government of India.

———. 2011. *All India Electricity Statistics: General Review 2007* (Containing Data for the Year 2009–10), Ministry of Power, Government of India.

———. 2008. *Load Generation Balance Report 2008–09*, Ministry of Power, Government of India.

———. 2009. *Load Generation Balance Report 2009–10*. Ministry of Power, Government of India.

———. 2010a. *Annual Report 2009–10*, Annexure 10B, Government of India.

———. 2010b. *Load Generation Balance Report 2010–11*. Ministry of Power, Government of India.

———. 2011a. *Monthly Report: December 2011*, Government of India.

———. 2011b. *Growth of Electricity Sector in India from 1947 to 2011*, Government of India.

———. 2011c. *Load Generation Balance Report 2011–12*. Ministry of Power, Government of India.

———. 2012. *Monthly Report: March 2012*. Available at http://cea.nic.in/monthlyarchive.html (accessed on 22 January 2016).

Chattopadhyay, P. 2004. 'Cross-Subsidy in Electricity Tariffs: Evidence from India', *Energy Policy*, 32(5): 673–84.

CSO (Central Statistical Office). 2012. *Energy Statistics 2012*. Government of India.

Dash, B.C. 2007. 'Governance and Service Delivery: A Study of Power Sector Reforms in Orissa', PhD dissertation. Institute for Social and Economic Change, Bangalore.

Economic Times. 31 May 2010. 'Orissa Loses Rs 2000 Crore per Annum on ATC Losses'.

———. 27 June 2011. 'Government Inaction Puts Orissa Power Sector in Doldrums'.

Ghosh, B. and P. De. 2005. *India Infrastructure Database 2005*, Volume II. New Delhi: Bookwell.

India Today. 12 November 2012. 'Best of States'. Available at http://indiatoday.intoday.in/story/best-of-states/1/516291.html (accessed on 22 Janaury 2016).

International Institute of Population Studies. 2007. *National Family Health Survey, 2007*. Maharashtra.

Kale, S. 2007. 'Power Steering: The Politics of Utility Privatization in India', unpublished PhD dissertation, University of Texas-Austin, Austin.

Kanungo Committee Report. 2002. 'Report of the Committee on Power Sector Reform of Orissa', *Journal of Indian School of Political Economy*, 14: 252–330.

Ministry of Road Transport and Highways. 2010. *Basic Road Statistics of India: 2004–05, 2005–06, 2006–07 & 2007–08*. Government of India.

Ministry of Road Transport and Highways. 2011. *Review of the Performance of State Road Transport Undertakings (SRTUs) (Passenger Services for April 2010–March 2011)*. Government of India.

Ministry of Road Transport and Highways. 2012. *Basic Road Statistics of India: 2008–09, 2009–10 and 2010–11*. Government of India.

Ministry of Shipping. 2012. *Basic Port Statistics of India 2010–11*. Government of India, 2012.

Ministry of Statistics and Programme Implementation (MOSPI). 2010. *Infrastructure Statistics 2010*. Government of India.

Modi, V. 2005. 'Improving Electricity Services in Rural India', working paper, The Earth Institute, Columbia University, New York.

National Council of Applied Economic Research. 2007. *India Rural Infrastructure Report, 2007*. New Delhi, Table A1.5.

OERC (Odisha Electricity Regulatory Commission). 2011. *Annual Report 2010–11*. Government of Odisha.

Planning Commission. 2000. *Annual Report on the Working of State Electrical Boards and Electricity Departments*. Power and Energy Division, Government of India, p. 66.

———. 2001. *Annual Report on the Working of State Electrical Boards and Electricity Departments*, Power and Energy Division, Government of India.

———. 2002. *Annual Report (2001–02) on the Working of State Electrical Boards and Electricity Departments*, Power and Energy Division, Government of India.

Planning Commission. 2006. *Uttar Pradesh Development Report.* Government of India.

———. 2011a. *Annual Report (2011–12) on the Working of State Power Utilities and Electricity Departments.* Power and Energy Division, Government of India.

———. 2011b. *Data for Use of Deputy Chairman, Planning Commission.* Government of India.

———. 2011c. *Final Report by Working Group on Rural Roads: In the 12th Five Year Plan.* Submitted to the Ministry of Rural Development, Government of India.

———. 2012. *Data for Use of Deputy Chairman, Planning Commission,* Government of India.

Power Finance Corporation. 2012. *Report on Performance of State Power Utilities for the Years 2008–09 to 2010–11.* Government of India.

Ramanathan, K. and S. Hasan. 2003. *Privatization of Electricity Distribution: The Orissa Experience.* New Delhi: TERI.

Subramanian, A. 2012. 'Can India's Power Problems Be Solved?', *Business Standard,* 5 August.

Wagle, D.M. and N.V. Rao. 1978. *The Power Sector in India.* Bombay: Popular Prakashan.

World Bank. 1994. *World Development Report 1994: Infrastructure for Development.* Washington, DC: World Bank.

PART III

FORESTS, WATER, AND NATURAL DISASTERS

7

Water and Forest Resources in Economic Development of Odisha

Padmaja Mishra

Odisha is endowed with vast natural resources: forests, fisheries, minerals, metals, a long coastline, and water bodies. The state economy, which has been predominantly agricultural and with a slow growth rate for a long period of time, has recently experienced rapid change in its structure and its rate of growth; this necessarily has a significant bearing on the use of resources and the socio-economic fabric of the state.

In this context, this chapter discusses the much-valued and demanded water and forest resources of Odisha. These resources are an integral part of Odisha's economy and are much demanded in the process of economic growth. At the same time, both these resources are of huge ecological and social significance. It needs no emphasis that water, wetlands, and forests are constantly interacting to produce healthy and productive ecosystems. The Millennium Ecosystem Assessment Framework[1] (UN 2000) aptly illustrates how

[1] Millennium Ecological Assessment was called for by United Nations Secretary General Kofi Annan in 2000. The broad objective was

changes caused to the ecosystem by human interventions affect its ecological services that are basic to human life, health, and livelihood security. For example, a global market may lead to regional losses of forest cover which might increase the magnitude of floods, adversely impact food production and catches of fisheries, and cause other losses in several economies at different places and times. Similarly, human wealth and well-being can be adversely affected by water scarcity and pollution. The adverse impacts of degradation of water sources and forests on growth and poverty are experienced worldwide and emphasized in the context of achievement of Millennium Development Goals.

The relationship between economic growth and environmental degradation, such as pollution and deforestation, has been much studied theoretically and empirically examined using the Environmental Kuznets' Curve (EKC) or inverted-U hypothesis in the literature, though the evidences have been mixed. The explanation behind the EKC hypothesis is that during the initial phases of economic growth, pollution or depletion occurs and goes on rising till a very high level of development (that is, a very high level of per capita income) is reached; thereafter, the rate of degradation decreases due to higher demand for better environmental quality and higher motivation and financial ability for its supply.[2] On that logic, a higher rate of resource depletion is expected during the current

to assess the consequences of ecosystem change for human well-being and the scientific basis for actions needed to enhance the conservation and sustainable use of those systems and their contribution to human well-being.

[2] The EKC literature is vast where an empirically inverted U (or inverted V) relationship between economic growth and environmental degradation is hypothesized and tested using reduced form equations with linear or log linear functional relationship estimated with a panel data. The pioneering studies are of Grossman and Krueger (1995, 1996), Selden and Song (1994), Cropper and Griffith (1994), Arrow et al. (1995), and Unruh and Moomaw (1998), to cite a few. Though, the findings have been mixed and inconclusive, the conclusions bear great policy implications.

phase of Odisha's growth story as the states' per capita income is still at a very low level.

It is necessary to understand the role of these resources and the ways of their efficient and optimum utilization for the state's sustained economic development. Moreover, the interdependence between water and forests requires efficient use and integrated management of both.

The following part of this chapter, therefore is arranged in five sections. The second section, which appears after the present one, discusses the water resource scenario in Odisha, its water policy, and the water tariff; it also discusses the developmental conflicts arising over the use of water. The third section discusses issues with regard to forest resources. Thereafter, there is the principle of optimum utilization of resources, followed by the conclusion that includes policy suggestions.

Water resource scenario in Odisha

Water is a natural resource as well as a commodity. It is an economic input and a vital facilitator for economic growth. Numerous studies have examined the relationship between water resource availability and economic growth (Barbier 2004; Barro 1990; Barro and Sal-I-Martin 1992) and have shown that dependable water supply adds to growth and gross domestic product (GDP). Barbier (2004) particularly found a strong support for an inverted-U relationship between economic growth and the rate of water utilization across countries, but cautions that growth may be unsustainable if rate of water utilization is very high.

Odisha has a 480 km long coastline and 11 major river basins. As far as its water resource position is concerned, it is well endowed with 3,300 m^3/year/per capita (m^3/yr/cap) which is well above the United Nations (UN) stress limit of 1,700 cum/year/cap.[3] Per capita water availability in 2001 (both surface and ground) was

[3] Though the UN stress limit is 1,700 cum/yr/cap, the water scarce condition has been defined at 1,000 cum/yr/cap.

3,359 cum/year as compared to the all-India average of 1,820 cum/year. Therefore, it is a water-abundant state in terms of physical measures. However, this average figure neither reflects the actual availability of water at any particular period of time (due to the strong seasonality, 80 per cent of the water is available in the three months of monsoon) nor is it a measure of water availability in a particular area since the eastern coastal areas and the western hilly areas differ with regard to water endowment and availability. While rivers Rishikulya and Budha Balanga entirely and Baitarani mostly flow within the state, all the others are interstate rivers. However, river Mahanadi is the longest river flowing through the state, alone covering 42.15 per cent (65,000 km^2) of the geographical area of the state and providing 43.80 billion cubic metre (BCM) water at 75 per cent dependability.

Notwithstanding the present situation of overall comfort, the state is facing increasing water challenges with a predicted future trend of reduced per capita availability due to population growth, urbanization, and industrialization as well as decreased inflow due to an increase in demand in upstream states (presently 30 per cent of total availability comes from this source). All these will result in 30 per cent reduction in the availability by 2050 (may be 2,200 cum/year/cap). It is forecasted that the Rushikulya basin will experience a scarcity condition and basins like Budhabalanga and Bahuda will be close to a scarcity condition by 2051. An overall erratic supply may be apprehended as intense rain occurring in few days may increase the frequency of floods and simultaneously there can be spatial and temporal droughts due to long dry spells.

Groundwater reserves also constitute an important part of the total water resource. As per the latest (2008–09) estimate by Ground Water Estimation Committee of the Government of India, Odisha has net dynamic groundwater resources of 16.9 BCM, out of which 4.36 BCM has been used. While Koraput, Malkangisri, and Nabrangpur are the low-range utilization districts (5 to 6 per cent utilized), the districts of Bhadrak and Balasore are in the high range (nearly 40 per cent utilized). The state is not free from salinity hazard and waterlogging. A considerable area of about 5,39,000 hectare of the coastal alluvial tract has been affected. The tract ranges from

Balasore district in the north-east to Puri district in the south-west. Waterlogging also occurs due to a steady rise in groundwater table for inadequate drainage of irrigation water. Cuttack and Puri are the highest waterlogged districts.

Water has many uses starting from ecological and basic needs uses to social, commercial, and other developmental purposes. The sectoral dynamics of the state's economic development along with the impending water challenges lead one to think of both the present and the future requirements of water. The existing and predicted demands pattern for water are given in Table 7.1.

Table 7.1 gives the amount of current uses of water in different sectors and forecasts the increasing trend in water demand in all sectors. It will be more than doubled for both agricultural and industrial sector where, as predicted, supply will be reduced and erratic, as mentioned earlier. Table 7.2 shows the per capita water availability by river basins, which also presents a regional picture given the location of the basins.

Table 7.1 Water requirement for different uses for Odisha (BCM)

Uses	2001			2051		
	Surface	Ground	Total	Surface	Ground	Total
Domestic	0.798 (1.97)	1.198	1.996 (3.63)	1.202 (1.87)	1.803	3.006 (3.56)
Agriculture	18.000 (44.4)	4.688	22.688 (41.25)	40.000 (62.4)	9.408	49.408 (58.5)
Industry	0.606 (1.50)	0.100	0.706 (1.28)	1.750 (2.73)	0.200	1.950 (2.31)
Environment	21.000 (51.8)	8.400	29.400 (53.5)	21.000 (32.7)	8.400	29.400 (34.8)
Others	0.100 (0.25)	0.100	0.200 (0.36)	0.200 (0.31)	0.200	0.400 (0.47)
Total	40.504 (100)	14.486	54.990 (100)	64.152 (100) (58.3)*	20.010 (38.1)*	84.463 (100) (53.59)*

Source: GoO (2007a).

Note: *Percentage by which present level of requirement increases by 2051.

Figures in brackets indicate percentage of the total.

Table 7.2 Per capita water availability by river basins, 2001 and 2015

River basin	Basin area (in km^2)	Share (%)	Per capita availability (in m^3)	
			2001	2015
Mahanadi	65,628	42.15	3,651.06	2,434
Brahmani	22,516	14.46	3,634.95	1,928
Baitarani	13,482	8.66	1,976.01	1,348*
Rushikulya	8,963	5.76	1,341.87	1,021*
Indravati	7,400	4.75	4,967.08	3,379
Kolab	10,300	6.61	2,263.65	1,623
Vansadhara	8,960	5.75	8,174.97	5,579
Nagavali	4,500	2.89	4,921.89	3,433
Budhabalanga	6,354	4.08	1,616.61	1,412*
Bahuda	890	0.57	5,194.73	3,758
Subernarekha	2,983	1.92	2,365.24	1,766
Area directly draining to sea	3,731	2.4	–	–
Total/average	1,55,707	100	3,358.17	2,218

Source: Government of Odisha (2007).
Note: (*) implies water-stressed situation.

State water policy and current use scenario

The GoO realized the multiple uses and importance of water resource and gave a much revised State Water Policy in 2007, which said, 'with competing demands for water from the same sources, it is necessary to lay down the priorities in its allocation' and specified the following order of priority in water allocation (GoO 2007: 8):

1. drinking water and domestic use
2. ecology
3. irrigation, agriculture, and other related activities, including fisheries
4. hydropower
5. industries including agro-industries
6. navigation and other uses such as tourism

Drinking water is a basic human right. As far as drinking-water facility is concerned, provision of safe drinking water has always been a concern. As per 2001 Census, percentages of households covered under safe drinking-water facility in both rural and urban areas have been higher in the state compared to respective national averages (GoO 2013: 296). However, the situation has reversed as per the 2011 Census. In both rural and urban areas, such coverages in Odisha are lower than national averages (GoO 2015). However, as per Odisha's *Economic Survey* (GoO 2012), 8 per cent of the rural households are not covered. These figures are of course with wide regional variations and absence of safe drinking water is still a major cause of diarrhoea and other waterborne diseases in the state. Floods and droughts are a regular phenomenon in Odisha and lead to crop loss, rising heat wave and dwindling vegetation, and loss of drinking water for both human beings and animals, and so on.

Poor water quality in the state's rivers (Odisha State Pollution Control Board 2007) and particularly the rivers of Daya, Kathjodi, Mahanadi, Brahmani, and Baitarani is a matter of concern. These rivers are polluted mainly due to wastewater of the cities and other human activities. Industrial water discharges have been considered as the biggest contributor.

Agriculture is the mainstay of Odisha's economy and is the highest consumer of water. Water is the lifeline of agriculture and Odisha's agriculture is mostly rain-fed. Paddy, which is highly water intensive, still contributes 90 per cent of total agricultural production of the state. Erratic rainfall and inadequate irrigation facilities make the agricultural sector highly water insecure. Odisha has only 36.7 per cent of the total area under principal crops (Government of Odisha 2012) as against the corresponding all-India average figure of 44.6 per cent and the highest figure of 97.7 per cent for the state of Punjab. Table 7A.1 in the appendix shows how the state lags behind the all-India average as well as that of the neighbouring states of Bihar, Andhra Pradesh, and West Bengal in terms of irrigated area under principal crops. Surface storage is essential in view of the high variability in availability over time and space. A storage capacity of 17 BCM has so far been created. This scenario within the state is again not free from wide regional disparities. The eight KBK districts[4] have lower irrigation potential with Nuapada at the worst followed by Nawarangpur and Rayagada which are infamous for their abject poverty. Though the non-KBK districts have higher irrigation potential created, there is wide disparity amongst them, with the coastal districts of Cuttack, Puri, Balasore, and Bhadrak having much higher potential than the districts like Jharsuguda and Kandhamal.

Besides agriculture, water also has other uses in economic development. Being one of the eight maritime states of India, Odisha has a considerable scope for ports and water transport as well as inland, brackish, and marine fisheries. With a long coastline and huge mineral reserves, as of 2010–11, Odisha ranks fifth in terms of the total volume of cargo handled by ports, with Paradeep being the major port and Gopalpur and Dhamra being the minor ones. However, inland water transport is not quite developed in the state.

The state also ranks seventh in terms of production of fish in India. Per capita production and consumption of fish have increased over the years. As fish production has increased, export of fish has risen over the years. Particularly, the seafood export sector has shown impressive growth over the last decade. According to the Fishery Survey in India, the fisheries potential of Odisha is 5,13,667 metric tonnes. About 2.95 per cent population (10.84 lakh) depends on inland fisheries and 3.3 lakh on marine fisheries. The fisheries subsector contributed about 6 per cent to the GSDP share of the agricultural sector for the year 2012–13 (advance estimate) (GoO 2013).

Along with all these direct uses of water for economic purposes, ecological significance of Odisha's water resources is vast, given the large number of rivers flowing through the state. The exact quantification of the aquatic ecological services of the existing water resource in Odisha has not been done though the official water policy of the state gives a priority to ecological uses of water after drinking water and domestic uses.[5]

[4] Koraput, Malkangiri, Nawrangpur, Rayagada, Bolangir, Sonepur, Kalahandi, and Nuapada.

[5] Ideally, an environmental flow accounting of water can actually describe the quality, quantity, and timing of water flows required to maintain the components, function, processes, and resilience of aquatic ecosystems which provide goods and services to mankind.

Competing needs and water management issues

Though the state policy clearly lists the priorities, given the trend of increasing demand in all sectors, a situation of conflicting uses and perceived scarcity which may not be purely physical cannot be ruled out. Such a stressed situation over inter-sectoral water allocations, that is, between agriculture and industry in particular, has already been experienced hugely over Mahanadi water. From once being considered as an abundant resource in the state, water is being contested as a scarce resource which is affecting the pace and pattern of economic development.

In Odisha, majority people draw their livelihood support from agriculture. As long as agriculture was the only source of demand, supply of water to agriculture was the sole purpose of water resource planning. Supply management through expansion and diversion from surplus areas to scarce areas through interventions in natural hydrological flows used to be the dominant approach. However, this approach is no longer suitable, as the demand for water uses has been increasing for both agricultural and non-agricultural purposes. The consideration is no longer crop per drop only and there is a plethora of upcoming developmental needs.

However, agriculture is still the largest livelihood provider. Given the current distributional conflicts over water in Odisha's path of progress, efficiency in uses of water should be the main concern. As long as water is not available at the time and place of cropping and Odisha, being one of the lowest amongst the Indian states with less than 40 per cent of the agricultural land being irrigated, agriculture is water scarce and horizontal expansion of irrigation is called for. However, while physical availability and adequate supply to this sector cannot be ignored, what if there is a perpetual non-satiation in demand for water? Water use efficiency in irrigation has been low.[6] Supply augmentation plans have only aggravated inefficiency, not

[6] It is pertinent to observe the remarks made in the Tenth Five Year Plan document which is very apt for Odisha: 'The water use efficiency (WUE) in most Indian Irrigation systems is low in the range of 30 to 40% against an ideal value of 60%. Low WUE leads to lower productivity, inequity in supplies to tail-enders and water logging and salinity. Major reasons attributed

only in Odisha but also in India as a whole. Odisha has a plethora of state-level and nationally sponsored irrigation and water management programmes such as Command Area Development and Water Management, Major and Micro Irrigation Programmes, Watershed Mission, Drought Prone Area Programme, River Valley Projects, and so on. The GoO brought an act named Odisha Pani Panchayat Act, 2002, for strengthening the Water User Association (WUA) meant for better participative management of irrigation water by the farmers. However, these schemes have been neither sufficient nor always efficient in water management. Diversified agriculture is also required. There is a need for shifting to pulses, vegetables, and other cash crop cultivations from water guzzling paddy cultivation depending on the soil quality and water availability. Demand management and an efficient compatible allocation system are required. Pricing can be a useful economic instrument for policy purposes.

Pricing of water

In this context, the importance of rational pricing of water cannot be undermined. It is common knowledge that prices that accurately reflect water's economic and scarcity value give appropriate information to the users to make optimum choices. The growing rationale for treating water as an economic good to be priced is based on relative scarcity and competing uses of water. However, given the social and cultural dimensions of water use, it is not easy and treating water purely as an economic good may not be a viable option here. Pricing can include the objectives of cost recovery, redistribution of income, improvement in allocation, and conservation. Such an optimum pricing should lead towards efficient allocation and conflict resolution, and should reflect the scarcity value of a resource in the true sense. In economics, the issue of scarcity valuation has been dealt

---

for this low WUE are basically due to low water rates, poor O&M, dilapidated conditions of infrastructure in the system and poor participatory irrigation management. All these are interrelated and need to be tackled as a package of measures to improve the WUE' (Government of India [GoI] 2002–07: 879).

with since the classical Ricardian concept of rent and higher price has been taken as an indicator of scarcity for all practical purposes (Barnett and Morse 1963). However, unfortunately for a non-marketed resource like water, it is not possible. Rather the political economy of water has led to an almost zero pricing or negligible price, that is, huge subsidization of irrigation water. Also, pricing of water used for marketed crops or for commercial/industrial uses take precedence over pricing for other uses such as for drinking water.

Water tariff in Odisha

In Odisha, water use is dominated by the canal system of irrigated agriculture. Irrigation water tariff is of two types: (a) basic water rate (kharif crop) and (b) rabi water rate. For the first type, the tariff is determined by the irrigation class, which depends upon the depth of water applied per hectare. For the second type, the rate depends upon the need of crop.

There have been increases in the rates over the years (nearly seven times for agriculture in 2002–03 over 1981–82) and 12 to 15 times for industrial uses. In 2005, revisions and enhancements of water tariff for all kinds of uses were made and thereafter in 2010, Odisha Irrigation Rules of 1961 were amended and the scope for charging was extended to uses for non-irrigation purposes. However, the rates remain low for agriculture and the operations and management (O&M) costs are not recovered. The situation is worse in case of rabi season. Though different charges are levied for different crops, all remain much lower than actual costs.

The political economy of water has always led to almost zero pricing or negligible price , that is, huge subsidization of water for residential and irrigation uses. Constant subsidization and non-recovery of costs have neglected demand side management altogether (Bandyopadhyay and Parveen 2004). Almost everywhere, even in Odisha, the pricing of water for agriculture is less than even O&M cost and much less than the full cost, which should include the opportunity cost if scarcity value is to be taken into account. The allocative role of water pricing requires water rates to capture the scarcity value (or marginal productivity/utility) and to equalize the opportunity costs of the resource across uses (Saleth 2001). Since scarcity is a perceived or related concept, people will be willing to pay for it rather than go without it (Fisher 1995). In Odisha, farmers depending on lift irrigation pay energy costs as high as Rs 5,000 to Rs 10,000 per hectare for high-value crops in the rabi season. People also contribute in Water User Associations (called Pani Panchayats) in Odisha. These facts indicate that there is willingness and ability to pay when the users are convinced. The willingness needs to be assessed for each project and the outcomes of the exercises need be concurred at the river basin levels and the state level. Increasingly, these need to be mutually agreed, leading to reduced conflict possibilities. However, a regulatory authority duly represented by all categories of stakeholders should review the pricing, assess the requirement for O&M, and propose for revision regularly given the fast-changing nature of the economy. In this context, the GoO (2007: 18) states: 'The cost of operation and management will be fully recovered from the beneficiaries. Norms will be established for ensuring water rights commensurate with water rates. The state will explore the possibility of setting up a regulatory authority for fixation of water rates in order to achieve full cost recovery of the O&M charges.'

This is to move towards financial sustainability with cost recovery. However, there remains a question mark on the feasibility and people's acceptability of any changes in allocation system, be it by pricing or by entitlements. Water being a social good as well as a merit good, water utility cannot be priced under strict economic criteria for profitability. Cross-subsidization is justified, and industrial uses with higher ability to pay can pay higher to subsidize water pricing in residential and agricultural uses to cover the overall O&M cost. However, the sources of industrial water supply must be sorted out after a holistic water plan is made. At present, new demands for water are met on a project-by-project basis where the exact criteria are not clear and due to lack of transparency conflict possibilities arise.

While pricing may not be the solution for social allocations such as hospitals, municipal uses, and others, economy and efficiency must be brought about in all categories of water uses. The state water policy declares to have a holistic, participatory, and environmentally sustainable perspective for development of water resource to meet the listed priorities. It also mentions the need for an appropriate institutional and legal framework required to support the activities.

Further, it recognizes that traditional systems of irrigation will be given due importance and development of water resources in tribal and hilly areas would be specially designed to suit the tribal ethos and the agronomic system of the terrain, and should be in tune with the ecology of the area.

For proper use of the water resource with conflict minimization, the state needs

1. a proper valuation of water in each sector, and
2. right pricing for every use.

Existing constraints and some suggestions

The existing key constraints in Odisha's water sector are

1. excessive dominance of canal irrigation as the main water user;
2. a lack of water entitlements and water tariffs which obstructs a balanced equitable allocation;
3. compartmentalized and non-coordinated water planning;
4. a lack of reliable and comprehensive data; and
5. a lack of public awareness and information on the value of water as a resource.

These constrains are the barriers for developing a holistic comprehensive water policy. Along with the removal of these constrains, the following steps can be taken for better use of water.

1. Cost effectiveness and sustainability of water use be taken as the two most important parameters for efficient resource use which will
    - improve resource ability without reduction in water use;
    - reduce water use without reducing the local standard of living;
    - restructure water management in a participatory and equitable manner; and
    - make the users and stakeholders share the actual cost and benefit.
2. Improvement of irrigation efficiency be considered an important component. The way is through correct demand assessment and management.

3. Other sources of irrigation should be given priority over canal irrigation system to reduce inefficiency with wastages and inequitable distribution. Development of a groundwater policy is urgently felt.
4. A clear water policy for industrial uses is required along with new water infrastructures be developed with clear incentives/disincentives for recycling of industrial water uses.
5. Finally, a comprehensive, transparent, and recurring water audit is required to reduce fresh water wastages and increase value addition per unit of water consumed.

In the next section, we move on to discuss the status and role of forests in Odisha's economy, another vital natural resource the state is blessed with.

Forest resources of Odisha

The forest wealth of the state includes 58,136 km^2 of recorded forest area, which constitutes about 37 per cent of the total geographical area. The per capita forest cover in Odisha is 0.15 hectare which is higher than the national average of 0.08 hectare (Forest Survey of India [FSI] 2003). The state lies in the tropical zone and can be divided into four regions—northern plateau, eastern ghats, central tableland, and coastal plains. Within these, the state has 19 different forest types with four major type groups of tropical semi-evergreen (0.68 per cent), tropical moist deciduous (39.88 per cent), litoral and swamp (0.48 per cent), and tropical dry deciduous forests (57.87 per cent). Plantation/trees outside the forests contribute 1.09 per cent. A maximum of all kinds of such forest covers are found within the altitude zone of up to 1,000 m.

Quality of the forests is an important indicator as far as the economic as well as ecological value of the forests is concerned. Based on interpretation of satellite data of October 2008–January 2009 (FSI 2011), the forest cover in the state was 48,903 km^2, out of which very dense forest cover is 7,073 km^2 (4.54 per cent) with 21,394 km^2 (13.74 per cent) of moderately dense forest, and 20,388 km^2 (13.09 per cent) of open forest. Scrubs cover constitutes 3.12 per cent and therefore, non-forests cover is 65.51 per cent. Table 7.3 looks at the status of forest cover change over the past decade.

Table 7.3 Forest cover change matrix, 2001–11 (km^2)

Categories	2001	2011	Net change
Dense forests	27,972	28,290	+ 318
Open forests	20,866	19,789	-1,077
Scrubs	5,782	4,485	-1,207
Total	54,620	52,564	-1,966

Source: FSI (2001, 2011).
Note: Dense forests include both very dense and moderately dense forests.

Table 7.3 shows a negative decadal change taking into account dense, open forests and scrubs together, though there has been an improvement of dense forests, which includes both very dense and moderately dense forests. However, FSI data (FSI 2009, 2011) shows that there has been a decrease of 13 km^2 in very dense forests and 28 km^2 in moderately dense forests over a period of two years only, that is, between the assessment years of 2009 and 2011, with an 89 km^2 addition to open forest and 118 km^2 depletion to scrubs. Though the total forest cover change is negligible due to active plantations and other conservation measures, the reduction in the dense forests is a matter of concern and shows serious depletion and loss in the real resource base.

Again, the forest cover is unevenly distributed over the geographical space of Odisha. While coastal districts have less share, in comparison, the districts located in the eastern ghats, central tableland, and northern plateau are densely forested. Kandhamal district has the highest geographical area covered by forest, that is, 68.37 per cent, followed by Gajapati (57.46 per cent) and Nayagarh (42.83 per cent). The coastal districts of Bhadrak (0.96 per cent), Jagatsingpur (1.32 per cent), and Puri (2.73 per cent) have the lowest coverage. Table 7A.3 in Appendix 7A shows district-wise forest cover for 2001 and 2011.

Odisha forests are considered rich forests due to being well stocked, diverse, multistoried, and dense. These are home to diversified flora and fauna, which are vital resources themselves. The state has 2 national parks, 18 wildlife sanctuaries (7,960 km^2), 1 tiger reserve (2,200 km^2) which is also the great Similipal biosphere reserve.

Odisha is the third largest mangrove zone of India. These coastal tropical forests are found at Balasore coastal zone and in the wetlands of Mahanadi. The wildlife sanctuary of Gahirmatha at Devi mouth and Bhitarkanika is a vast mangrove ecosystem. Similarly, the Chilika Nalabana Wildlife Sanctuary is a world-famous habitat for migratory birds and endangered species. Besides, the Nandankanan Zoological Park is one of the finest parks uniquely set as a natural habitat. All together, they cover 10.37 per cent of the total forest area.

Contribution of forestry sector to state income

Forests, as economic resource, must contribute to the state economy. There are different products, major and minor, harvested from our forests. Odisha is the third largest producer of kendu leaf, next to Madhya Pradesh and Chattisgarh. In 2010–11, 4.44 lakh quintals of kendu leaves were produced and 140 lakh person days of employment was generated. Kendu leaves provide the maximum amount of revenue, followed by timber and fuel wood. Minor products like bamboo also contribute but to a lesser extent. As per the estimates of FSI (2011), the annual production of fuelwood in Odisha is negligible. The state ranks 17th in terms of annual production of wood among all the states and union territories and ranks 12th in terms of potential production of timber and fuelwood. Table 7.4 gives the trend of revenue earned from different products marketed by the government.

If we look at the contribution of the forestry and logging sector in the state domestic product (at 2004–05 base prices) it has increased from Rs 2,263.68 crore in the year 2000–01 to Rs 4,752.51 crore in the year 2012–13. The relative contribution of the sector is 4.67 per cent to 1.83 per cent only (Table 7.5).

Along with this, the recent data shows that the Forest and Environment Department runs into deficit, which is illustrated in Table 7.6.

These facts give an impression that forests have not been very productive as far as their contribution to the state income is concerned. However, at the same time it is known that revenue earned by the government is an imperfect and incomplete indicator of the money values of the forest products in the state GDP. First, state control

Table 7.4 Revenue generated from the forestry sector in Odisha (Rs crore)

Forest products	2001–02	2002–03	2003–04	2004–05	2005–06	2006–07	2007–08	2008–09	2009–10	2010–11
Timber and fuelwood	9.36	9.15	3.70	8.94	6.65	9.84	29.46	32.01	45.13	55.85
Bamboo	2.03	0.07	1.45	1.58	4.21	5.05	17.01	7.07	12.68	5.88
Kendu leaves	69.00	75.00	31.00	24.25	40.14	102.10	261.68	304.76	326.80	364.24
Others	7.42	12.70	13.66	50.23	6.72	8.32	2.96	2.23	7.40	NA
Total	87.81	96.62	49.81	85.00	57.72	125.31	311.00	346.07	392.01	433.72

Source: Author's calculation from various publications of the Department of Forestry and Environment, GoO and Odisha Forest Development Corporation.

Table 7.5 Contribution of forestry and logging in Odisha (Rs lakh)

Year	At 2004–05 base
2000–01	2,26,368 (4.67)
2001–02	2,29,464 (4.43)
2002–03	2,04,880 (3.73)
2003–04	2,78,254 (4.20)
2004–05	2,57,627 (3.31)
2005–06	2,42,120 (2.84)
2006–07	2,74,995 (2.70)
2007–08	3,24,045 (2.50)
2008–09	3,27,073 (2.20)
2009–10	3,56,586 (2.18)
2010–11 (P)*	4,51,007 (2.31)
2011–12 (Q)**	4,26,512 (1.73)
2012–13 (A)***	4,75,251 (1.83)

Source: GoO (2013).
Notes: *P: provisional estimate, ** Q: quick estimate, *** A: advance estimate
Figures in brackets are author's own calculations of percentage contribution of the forestry and logging sector to the GSDP as per the source.

over a majority of Non-timber Forest Products (NTFPs) has been reduced and second, total income and employment generation of the forest-dependent people are not counted here. However, even after that do we really have a correct valuation of all the benefits that the forests are contributing to our economy?

Table 7.6 Revenue and expenditure of Forest and Environment Department, Government of Odisha (Rs crore)

Year	Revenue	Expenditure	Deficit
2006–07	162.10	153.58	+91.48
2007–08	119.71	275.00	-155.29
2008–09	183.37	365.84	-182.47
2009–10	193.54	388.42	-194.88
2010–11	206.02	425.33	-219.31

Source: Department of Forestry and Environment, GoO.

The importance of forests are numerous. Forests provide goods and services, such as timber, fuelwood, fodder and a wide range of non-timber products, are life support systems, provide natural habitat for biodiversity, and act as repository of diversified genetic wealth while serving as means of recreation and eco-tourism also. Besides, forests are life-support systems, help in watershed development, regulate water regime, conserve soil, and above all, act as carbon sink. There are many such direct and indirect benefits of the forests. Therefore, economic and ecological values of the forests are vast and invaluable. Though, conventionally, many economic functions have been accounted for and valued, the flow of benefits from a large number of forest functions such as carbon sequestration, ecotourism, biodiversity, and watershed benefits are not usually counted. The mangrove forests of Odisha are unique having lots of ecological and economic significance (M.S. Swaminathan Research Foundation 2004; Das 2011). As far as the valuation is concerned, a study made by the Indian Institute of Forest Management (Singh et al. 2009) shows that going by the conventional System of National Accounts (SNA) method, forests contribute negatively if the recorded benefits and costs are used. However, factoring in the unrecorded benefits that the local people derive in the form of timber, fuelwood, poles, bamboo, fodder, and other non-wood forest products, the net benefits become hugely positive. If we add the non-tangible benefits too, such as carbon sequestration and other ecological services of the forests, the total benefit would be still much higher![7] For the state of Odisha, the same study by Katar Singh et al. (2009) estimated the net benefit to be Rs 75.58 crore based on Rs 130 per hectare of forest area. While this is certainly not an accurate valuation given the variation in forest types, assets, and benefits, it shows how we tend to grossly undervalue the contribution of forests in our economy. Unfortunately, gross undervaluation of forests very often justifies deforestation for development.

[7] The benefits of forests are numerous, going much beyond what we calculate as per traditional SNA. Using the System of Integrated Economic and Environmental Accounting (SEEA) method, the monetary contribution of our forests will be much more as it consists of stocks and flows of all environmental goods and services of the forests.

Pressures of development have led to destruction of forests. Forest resources have been under great biotic and abiotic pressure. There have been over exploitation, degradation, encroachment, and diversion of forestland to non-forest purposes over the decades. The main purposes have been irrigation and mining followed by diversions for infrastructure projects like transmission lines of railways. However, the exact amount varies from year to year. Then again in single years of 2005–06 and also in 2007–08, a huge 2,207.23 hectare were diverted. During the year 2010–11, an amount of 571.396 hectare of forest land of were diverted for mining and 344.556 hectare for railway transmission lines with no diversion for irrigation purposes whereas during the year 2009–10, a vast area of 3,963 hectare were diverted for irrigation only. In a recent study on underlying causes of forest cover change in Odisha (Basu and Nayak 2011), it has been found that income per capita is a significant factor for deforestation and the EKC hypothesis has been supported. Population density, industrialization, rural poverty, cropping intensity, and forest roads are among the other factors that have caused deforestation according to the study. This shows the impacts of the state's economic growth on the forests.

Non-timber forest products and tribal livelihood

Odisha is a mineral rich state and all the minerals are found concentrated under the forestland. At the same time, the concentration of forests in Odisha is high in scheduled areas inhabited by a substantially large tribal population. This situation has created a complex paradox in the state's development strategy and posed a huge challenge for governance. Tribals and the forest dwellers derive livelihood and food security from the forests. However, chronic poverty and erosion of tribals' livelihood base is a serious matter of concern as the poverty profile of Odisha shows wide regional and social disparities with regard to poverty incidence. There is highest concentration of poverty in the forested areas in southern Odisha and among the tribals at 73 per cent of the scheduled tribe (ST) population below poverty line followed by 52.3 per cent among the scheduled caste (SC) population. This gives a glimpse of the extent of exclusion during the process of economic growth in the state.

Traditionally, the tribals have depended solely on the forests and NTFPs. The NTFPs contribute a lot of meaning to tribal livelihood in Odisha with a substantial tribal population (22.13 per cent of the total as per 2001 Census). Conceptually NTFP (previously known as Minor Forest Produce) refers to all biological materials other than timber extracted for human and animal use. It includes fibre, building material, medicine, edible leaves, roots, flower, fruit, seed, nuts, honey, resin, lac, glue, and others. Therefore, NTFPs provide food security, fodder for livestock, and health-supporting medicinal plants, besides providing employment and income-earning opportunities.

Over a long period, the state had the monopoly over the NTFPs which yielded a good amount of revenue. However, in the year 2000, 68 items of NTFP were decontrolled to ensure better prices and empowerment for the collectors. Local democratic governance institutions—panchayati raj institutions—were authorized to control and manage the procurement and marketing of those NTFPs. However, the system is not functioning much in favour of the local people due to ineffective implementation and continuous confusion and conflict between the forest department and the primary collectors. Moreover, high-value NTFPs such as the kendu leaf, sal seed, timber, and fuelwood are still under the control of the forest department. There is no estimate available for the total volume and value of all major and minor forest products available and traded. Many studies observe that collection of NTFPs now forms nearly 10 per cent of tribal household income, which was previously a substantial part of their household income (Mallick 2000; Mallick and Panigrahi 1998; RCDC 2000). There is no clear mandate for the institutions involved in the process of procurement and trade in NTFPs. The terms of trade has always been determined by the buyers and still a major chunk of non-nationalized NTFPs are traded through complex as well as non-transparent channels and in the process, both the primary collectors and the state lose. Steps such as fixation of floor level prices for local NTFPs, facilitation of value addition, and marketing of those products can take the tribals a long way. The challenge in NTFP management and trade is vast and complex. In spite of various existing policies, gradual decline and uncertainties in the availability of NTFPs to the forest dwellers of Odisha are adding to poverty in tribal areas. Therefore, the NTFP policy must take a center stage in the discussion of the economic contribution of forests for the people.

Lack of clear and enforceable tribal rights over the forests has remained a contentious issue for long. While alternative livelihood options are extremely limited for the people in forest areas, it has been argued by de Haan and Dubey (2005) that the deprivation in tribal districts is not the result of lack of economic growth but rather a case of entitlement failure. Of course, there are various acts for preserving forest dwellers' rights such as Provisions of Panchayat (Extension to Scheduled Areas) (PESA) Act, 1996, Joint Forest Management (JFM), 1988, and Forest Dwellers (Recognition of Forest Rights) Act (FRA), 2006. By all these, the people are entitled to secure a share in usufructs. The ultimate goal is to realize the full value of the growing stock and improve forest conditions and their productivity. However, a number of issues regarding sharing of benefits and responsibilities of management remain unresolved (Mallick 2010).

Forest policy in Odisha

There had always been continuous policy shifts in the forestry sector in India. However, the role of forests in the national economy and in ecology was emphasized in our National Forest Policy of 1988. The GoO also came out with Joint Forest Management Policy in 1988 after the Orissa Forest Act, 1972, to associate people actively in protection, conservation, and management of forests. By the end of 2010–11, 11,915 Vana Samrankhyan Samitis (VSSes) and 398 Eco Development Committees (EDCs) have been formed to ensure the objectives of JFM. The GoO has further revised the JFM resolution in September 2011, which formalized the decision-making role of Palli Sabha in JFM. The forestry sector objective in the Eleventh Five Year Plan in the state of Odisha has been to promote sustainable forest management with the complementary goal of sustaining rural livelihoods. The plan specifically focuses on conservation as well as development of forests along with optimal use of the resources in a sustainable manner. Regeneration, afforestation, eco development, and promotion of ecotourism are in the agenda. For sustainable forest development, a complete understanding and awareness of the contribution of forests is required. Therefore, a holistic approach for valuation of forest resources is also required, which would justify the need for maintenance and expansion of forest cover. The need for conservation and sustainable management of forests are now universally recognized and a complete forest resource accounting is a sine qua non for that.

It needs mention here that 'Forestry Vision', 2020 of the GoO focuses on

1. increased flow of NTFPs and wood;
2. biodiversity conservation; and
3. higher allocations, investment, insurance, and better forest management.

To sum up, two major areas of concern that need immediate attention are

1. proper policy and pricing for NTFPs; and
2. proper (complete) valuation, management, and conservation of forests.

Optimum utilization of resources

Whether it is water or forest, we have discussed that both these resources are vital for the state's further development but are under pressure due to expansion of economic activities. There have emerged many areas of developmental stress over the multiple and conflicting uses of such resources. There is no thumb rule for trade-offs—be it between economy and ecology, agriculture and industry, or tradition and modernity. However, there must be a guiding principle for the best possible allocation with conflict minimization for a smooth developmental process. As environmental and social resources such as water and forests generally are not always traded in markets, scarcity signals for these resources might not be adequate, and therefore, appropriate policy responses for optimum utilization are difficult to emerge in time. A general principle for optimum resource use in case of conflicting demands is discussed in the following part of the section.

Optimal utilization of any resource in any particular use as per the laws of optimality requires that the benefits derived from the last unit used must be equal to the cost of that last unit. In other words, marginal benefits derived from a resource must be equal to the marginal cost for that resource use. For example, when the marginal benefit (MB) of water or forests for any use is equal to the marginal cost (MC) of that use (that is, MB=MC), then optimum use of the resource has taken place for that particular purpose. As long as MB>MC, there is a positive scarcity value of that resource in that use. If resource availability is unlimited and all the uses have positive scarcity value then more resource can be allocated to each purpose until scarcity value is zero (MB=MC) everywhere. The MC must include the opportunity cost forgone when mutually exclusive competing uses are considered. For balanced allocations, the issues of both equity and efficiency can be considered in the aforementioned manner.

Obviously, the critical issue for optimum utilization following the aforementioned principle is the quantification or measurement of the MB and MC of a resource for a particular use. The calculation of all monetary MB and MC can be simple and straightforward. One can calculate the monetary benefits and monetary costs involved in using one extra unit of water in a particular use. However, resources like water and forests have direct and indirect uses having both monetary and non-monetary implications. For example, one additional unit of water use in agriculture creates addition to crop production, generates some employment, reduces absolute poverty for some, or rescues some from suicide or starvation death. At the same time, there might be some loss of employment or livelihood or damage to environment due to diversion from alternative uses or from overuse. Those opportunity costs foregone must be calculated as costs. Therefore, all the positive and negative aspects (both monetary and non-monetary) of an extra unit of water supply to any sector of demand should be considered. Going by direct monetary return criteria, may be the agricultural sector will get less priority than the industrial sector as the money value of industrial output is higher. However, as long as it creates larger livelihood support and food security, and industrial water use involves negative effects such as water pollution and livelihood displacements, the priority may reverse. Resources like water and forests are ecological and social goods besides being economic goods. Therefore, all the costs and benefits need to be considered to achieve all developmental as well as ecological goals.

Another issue is that the valuations of benefits and costs may vary for different stakeholders. The tribals and the miners have different valuations for the same forest. Similarly, the farmers and the industrialists differ over valuation of water. Policies affect valuation also. For example, due to heavy subsidization of irrigation water, there is a vast difference between public or government marginal cost (GMC) and private marginal cost, that is, farmer's marginal cost (PMC). The PMC will always lie below the GMC as the government bears high cost in providing water (in terms of operation and maintenance and in terms of alternative uses foregone). Therefore, a mutually agreed transparent valuation and pricing is to be arrived at to reduce the scarcity perception gap between different stakeholders. That situation will help best possible utilization of the resources in multiple conflicting uses for a smooth process of economic development.

* * *

Resources, underutilized and mis-utilized, have left the Odisha economy backward for a long time in spite of abundance of resources. One question arises: has abundance led to an inefficient and unsustainable path of resource use in Odisha? Does the society realize the importance of demand management? How do abundance and scarcity affect social behaviour towards resource use? The society's ability to cope with changing economic conditions and pressures of economic growth can affect and can be affected by scarcity and competing demands. There have been enough evidences of resource abundance lowering the incentive to innovate leading to lower economic performance (often mentioned 'Dutch disease' and 'Resource curse' in the literature).[8] When a society misuses an easily available natural resource, the resource becomes a limiting rather than an enabling factor in the growth and development process. It seems this has happened to some extent in case of Odisha, for which resource use efficiency has been minimal and has put the state always at the lowest level of per capita income.

Development and livelihood improvements are themselves the basic indicators of efficient resource use. Inclusive growth process with people's participation is the ultimate requirement for conflict minimization and benefit maximization. Therefore, economic development and provision of livelihood alternatives must be Odisha's priorities while using its valuable resources. To curtail misuses and wastages of the valuable resources, demand management is as important as supply management. A paradigm shift in resource management from solely relying on a traditional top-down supply-oriented approach to combining this with a bottom-up demand-management approach requires an extensive and informed user participation. Demand management must analyse modes of uses, issues of access and control, issues of alternative uses and regulation frameworks, and so on. As demand for water and forests are constructed through a complex social process, the whole process has to be understood and unravelled prior to any intervention for change.

May be time has come when policies on water- and forest-related issues in Odisha should be assessed, analysed, reviewed, and resolved within an overall societal and development context with good governance and should be aimed at equity, basic needs fulfilment, and service assurance with fair and logical entitlements to each and all.

[8] 'Dutch disease' is an economic concept that tries to explain the apparent relationship between the exploitation of natural resources and a decline in the manufacturing sector combined with moral fallout. The 'Resource curse' or the paradox of plenty refers to the paradox that countries with an abundance of natural resources tend to have less economic growth than countries without these resources.

Appendix 7A

Table 7A.1 State-wise share of irrigated area under principal crops, 2007–08

State	All crops (% share)
Andhra Pradesh	46.3
Assam	02.4
Bihar	60.6
Chattisgarh	26.5
Gujarat	41.7
Haryana	86.0
Himachal Pradesh	19.2
Jammu and Kashmir	40.8
Karnataka	29.4
Kerala	16.5
Madhya Pradesh	32.2
Maharashtra	19.6
Odisha	*36.7*
Punjab	97.7
Rajasthan	36.4
Tamil Nadu	55.9
Uttar Pradesh	75.5
West Bengal	56.9
All India	*44.6*

Source: GoO (2012: Figure 3.4, p. 85).

Table 7A.2 District-wise irrigation potential created, 2010–11

District	Cultivated area ('000 ha)	Kharif ('000 ha)	Rabi ('000 ha)	As %age of total cultivated area*
Anugul	219.00	78.719	35.5	51.14
Balasore	244.00	157.002	100.013	105.33
Bargarh	345.00	165.125	85.956	72.77
Bhadrak	178.00	145.457	46.286	107.72
Boudh	89.90	59.560	17.147	86.18
Cuttack	177.00	171.967	101.315	154.39
Deogarh	72.00	23.899	14.438	53.24
Dhenkanal	193.00	114.831	66.327	93.86

(*Cont'd.*)

Table 7A.2 *(Cont'd.)*

District	Cultivated area ('000 ha)	Kharif ('000 ha)	Rabi ('000 ha)	As %age of total cultivated area*
Gajpati	80.00	32.303	10.857	53.95
Ganjam	395.00	307.293	66.046	94.51
Jagatsingpur	110.00	75.710	52.277	116.30
Jajpur	166.00	126.183	72.860	119.90
Jharsuguda	86.00	17.141	9.123	30.58
Kandhamal	134.00	32.129	13.059	33.72
Kendrapada	152.00	127.818	77.674	135.19
Keonjhar	302.00	99.609	42.766	47.14
Khurda	140.00	88.603	47.163	96.97
Mayurbhanj	441.00	168.482	81.818	56.75
Nayagarh	134.00	59.293	23.926	62.10
Puri	150.00	152.965	93.035	164
Sambalpur	194.00	74.893	39.900	59.17
Sundergarh	313.00	92.133	38.748	47.81
Non-KBK	*4,314.00*	*2,371.115*	*1,136.233*	*81.30*
Kalahandi	371.00	175.602	111.834	77.47
Koraput	302.00	102.015	67.231	56.04
Malkangiri	141.00	81.414	40.369	86.37
Nawarangpur	216.00	46.590	25.880	33.55
Nuapada	178.00	67.271	18.869	48.39
Sonepur	111.00	92.583	43.053	122.19
Rayagada	194.00	62.583	24.868	48.24
Bolangir	338.00	89.844	33.093	36.37
KBK	*1,851.00*	*718.227*	*365.197*	*58.53*
Odisha	*6,165.00*	*3,089.342*	*1,501.430*	*74.46*

Source: Directorate of Agriculture and Food Production (2010–11).

Note: *Column 5 shows the figures for the total of column 3 and column 4 as percentage of column 2. Multiple cropping and cropping intensity have been taken into account in column 3 and column 4.

Table 7A.3 District-wise forest cover in Odisha, 2001 and 2011 (area in km²)

District	Dense forest		Open forest		Total		Percentage	
	2001	2011	2001	2011	2001	2011	2001	2011
Angul	1,658	(–)1,416	992	(–)951	2,650	(–)2,367	41.57	41.34
Baleswar	147	(+)149	159	(–)155	306	(–)304	08.04	7.99
Bargarh	423	(+)548	481	(–)348	904	(–)896	15.49	15.35
Bhadrak	23	(–)11	8	(+)13	31	(–)24	1.24	0.96
Bolangir	504	(–)293	488	(+)644	992	(–)937	15.09	14.25
Boudh	770	(+)807	510	(–)448	1,280	(–)1,255	41.32	40.51
Cuttack	362	(–)262	294	(+)405	656	(+)677	16.68	16.96
Deogarh	781	(–)775	577	(–)566	1,358	(–)1,341	46.19	45.61
Dhenkanal	660	(–)515	606	(+)827	1,266	(+)1,342	28.44	30.14
Gajapati	1,429	(+)1,608	1,123	(–)879	2,552	(–)2,487	59.01	57.50
Ganjam	1,095	(+)1,193	1,093	(–)800	2,188	(–)1,993	26.66	24.29
Jagatsinghpur	15	(–)7	9	(+)16	24	(–)23	1.44	1.38
Jajpur	122	(–)75	137	(+)180	259	(–)255	8.93	8.80
Jharsuguda	107	(+)148	169	(–)151	276	(+)299	13.26	14.37
Kalahandi	1,161	(–)1,110	978	(+)1,213	2,139	(+)2,331	27.01	29.43
Kendrapada	196	(–)168	21	(+)26	217	(–)194	8.21	7.34
Keonjhar	1,669	(+)1,709	1,709	(–)1,507	3,378	(–)3,216	40.68	38.73
Khandamal	3,063	(+)3,302	2,327	(–)2,167	5,390	(+)5,469	67.20	68.18
Khurda	277	(–)214	157	(+)180	434	(–)394	15.43	14.01

(*Cont'd.*)

Table 7A.3 *(Cont'd.)*

District	Dense forest		Open forest		Total		Percentage	
	2001	2011	2001	2011	2001	2011	2001	2011
Koraput	669	(+)820	815	(+)874	1,484	(+)1,694	16.85	19.23
Malkangiri	1,076	(–)868	1,112	(+)1,318	2,188	(–)2,186	37.78	37.75
Mayurbhanj	2,883	(+)3,051	1,249	(–)941	4,132	(–)3,992	39.66	38.32
Nuapada	588	(–)566	649	(+)663	1,237	(–)1,229	32.11	31.91
Nabrangpur	687	(–)651	463	(+)491	1,150	(–)1,142	21.74	21.58
Nayagarh	1031	(+)1,159	674	(–)506	1,705	(–)1,665	43.83	42.80
Puri	179	(–)56	32	(+)44	211	(–)100	6.06	2.87
Rayagada	1,308	(+)1,349	1,425	(+)1,767	2,733	(+)3,116	38.64	44.05
Sambalpur	2,291	(–)2,268	998	(+)1,041	3,289	(+)3,309	49.41	49.71
Sonepur	173	(+)203	140	(–)121	313	(+)324	13.39	13.86
Sundargarh	2,625	(+)2,817	1,471	(–)1,235	4,096	(–)4,052	42.17	41.72
Total	27,292	(+)28,326	20,886	(+)20,477	48,838	(+)48,903	31.37	(+)31.41

Source: FSI (2001, 2011).

References

Arrow, K., B. Bolin, R. Costanza, P. Dasgupta, C. Folke, C.S. Holling et al. 1995. 'Economic Growth, Carrying Capacity, and the Environment', *Science*, 268 (28 April): 520–21.

Azar, E. 1990. *The Management of Protracted Social Conflict: Theory and Cases*. Dartmouth: Aldershot.

Bandyopadhyay, J. and S. Parveen. 2004. 'Interlinking of Rivers in India: Assessing the Justification', *Economic and Political Weekly*, 39 (50): 5308–16.

Barbier, E.B. 2004. 'Water and Economic Growth', *Economic Record*, 80(248): 1–16.

Barnett, H. and C. Morse. 1963. *Scarcity and Growth: The Economics of Natural Resource Availability*. Washington, DC: REF Press.

Barro, R.J. 1990. 'Government Spending in a Simple Model of Endogenous Growth', *Journal of Political Economy*, 98(5): S103–S124.

Barro R.J. and X. Sala-I-Martin. 1992. 'Public Finance in Models of Economic Growth', *Review of Economic Studies*, 59(4): 645–61.

Basu, A. and N.C. Nayak. 2011. 'Underlying Causes of Forest Cover Change in Odisha, India', *Forest Policy and Economics*, 23(7): 563–69.

Biswas, A.K. 2001. 'Water Policies in the Developing World', *Water Resource Development*, 17(4): 489–99.

Cropper, M. and C. Griffith. 1994. 'The Interaction of Population Growth and Environment Quality', *American Economic Review*, 84(2): 250–54.

Das, S. 2011. 'Examining the Storm Protection Services of Mangroves of Orissa During the 1999 Cyclone', *Economic and Political Weekly*, 46(24): 60–68.

De Haan, A. and A. Dubey. 2005. 'Poverty, Disparities, or the Development of Under Development in Orissa', *Economic and Political Weekly*, XL(22–23, 28 May).

Directorate of Agriculture and Food Production. 2010–11. *Odisha Agricultural Statistics 2010–11*. Bhubaneswar, Odisha: Government of Odisha.

Department of Forestry and Environment. *Various Budget Documents*. Government of Odisha.

Fisher, F.M. 1995. 'The Economics of Water Dispute Resolution, Project Evaluation and Management—An Application to the Middle East', *Water Resource Development*, 11(47): 377–89.

Forest Survey of India. 2001, 2003, 2009 and 2011. *Status of Forest Report*. Government of India.

Freeman, A.M. 1993. *The Measurement of Environment and Resource Values: Theory and Methods*., DC: Resources for the Future.

Government of India. 2001. *Tenth Five Year Plan, 2002–2007, Volume II: Sectoral Policies and Programme*. New Delhi: Planning Commission.

Government of Orissa (GoO). 2007a. *Annual Report 2006–07*, Department of Water Resources.

———. 2007b. *State Water Policy*. Department of Water Resources, Government of Odisha.

Government of Odisha. 2007c. *State Water Policy*. Department of Water Resources, Government of Odisha.

———. 2012. *Economic Survey of Odisha 2011–12*. Bhubaneswar: Planning and Coordination Department.

———. 2013. *Economic Survey 2012–13*. Bhubaneswar: Planning and Coordination Department.

———. 2015. *Economic Survey 2014–15*. Bhubaneswar: Planning and Coordination Department.

Grossman, G.K. and A.B. Krueger. 1995. 'Economic Growth and the Environment', *Quarterly Journal of Economics*, 110 (2, May): 353–77.

———. 1996. 'The Inverted U: What Does it Mean?', *Environment and Development Economics*, 1(1, February): 119–22.

Haripriya, G., P. Sukhdev, P. Kumar, R. Sinha, and S. Sanyal. 2006. *Green accounting for Indian States and Union Territories, Monograph 4*. New Delhi: Green Indian States Trust.

Homer-Dixon, T. 1999. *Environment, Scarcity and Violence*. Princeton, New Jersey: Princeton University Press.

M.S. Swaminathan Research Foundation. 2004. *Atlas of Mangrove Wetland, 3, Orissa*. Chennai, India: General Publication of the Foundation.

Mallick, R.M. 2000. *Impact of NTFP Policies on Sustainable Livelihood of Forest Dependent Communities in Orissa: An Empirical Excercise*. Bhubaneswar: NCDS.

———. 2010. *Food Security: Livelihood and Chronic Poverty in some Forest Regions of Orissa: A Study of Forest Policy and Sustainable Forest Management*. New Delhi: ICSSR.

Mallick, R.M. and N. Panigrahi. 1998. *Non-Timber Forest Produce Collection: Benefits and Management*. Bhubaneswar: NCDS.

Mathur, A. and A.S. Sachdeva. 2003. *Towards an Economic Approach to Sustainable Forest Development*. New Delhi: Planning Commission, Government of India.

Mehta, L. 2003. 'Contexts and Constructions of Water Scarcity', *Economic and Political Weekly*, XXXVIII(48, 29 November 2003).

Ohlson, L. and A.R. Turton. 1999. 'The Turning Point of a Screw: Social Resource Scarcity as a Bottleneck in Adaptation to Water Scarcity', SOAS Occasional Paper No. 19, University of London Press, London.

Pandey, R. and S. Ghosh. 2002. 'Estimating Industrial Pollution in India: Implications for an Effluent Charge', *National Institute of Public Finance and Policy Report*. New Delhi.

Regional Centre for Development Cooperation (RCDC). 2000. 'Social and Institutional Analysis and Livelihood System Study of Tribal Communities in Selected Villages in Kandhamal and Gajapati districts', in IFAD, *Second Orissa Tribal Development Programme Formulation Report*.

Saleth, M.R. 2001. 'Water Pricing Potential and Problems', in R.S. Meinzen-Dick and M.W. Rosegrant (eds), *2020 Focus 9: Overcoming Water Scarcity and Quality Constraints*. Washington, DC: International Food Policy Research Institute. Available at http://www.ifpri.org/publication/overcoming-water-scarcity-and-quality-constraints (last accessed on October 2001).

Selden, T. and D. Song. 1994. 'Environmental Quality and Development; Is There a Kuznets' Curve for Air Pollution Emissions?', *Journal of Environmental Economics and Management*, 27(2): 147–62.

Singh, K. 1994. *Managing Common Pool Resources*. New Delhi: Oxford University Press.

Singh K., P.C. Kotwal, M.P. Omprakash, and P. Mallick. 2011. *Forest Resource Valuation and Accounting: An Exploratory Study in the State of Orissa*. Bhopal: Indian Institute of Forest Management, p. 126.

Ward, F.A. and A. Michelses. 2002. 'The Economic Value of Water in Agriculture: Concepts and Policy Applications', *Water Policy*, 4: 423–46.

8

Economics of Natural Disasters in Odisha*

Saudamini Das

Types of natural disasters

Natural disasters (such as earthquakes, droughts, floods, heat waves, storms) or human-made disasters (such as spillage of hazardous waste, explosion, fire, and others) are shocks to the functioning of the economic system and cause socio-economic vicissitudes depending on the intensity of the shocks and the shock-bearing capacity of the system. The United Nations (UN) defines a disaster as 'a serious disruption of the functioning of a society, causing widespread human, material, or environmental losses which exceed the ability of the affected society to cope using its own resources' (UN-DHA 1992), indicating that a natural shock is a disaster only if its impact exceeds the system's ability to cope. Natural disasters can set an economic

* I sincerely thank Kanchan Chopra and the reviewer of this chapter for their useful comments on the draft of this manuscript.

system back by a few years depending on their impact, and whether they cause more loss, or more displacement, or both—may be categorized as either 'sudden impact' (floods, earthquakes, tropical storms, volcanic eruptions, and so on), 'slow-onset' (drought, famine), or 'epidemic diseases' (cholera, measles, plague, and others).[1] Research shows that sometimes natural disasters also brings in positive externalities to society by stimulating innovation, replacing old capital by new, bringing in traditional knowledge based adaptation to disaster, and flow of aid, flow of technology, and flow of ideas.

The state of Odisha is an intriguing case of regular and multiple disasters and economic backwardness, and may be an example of natural disaster led underdevelopment. This chapter tries to analyse if the state's economic backwardness is partially due to the economic losses from frequent disasters as these limit capital accumulation and investment capacity. First, this chapter discusses the different types of natural disaster impacts on society. Subsequently, it presents a theoretical model that links economic backwardness to the frequency and intensity of disaster and to the resource constraints of the economy. Next, it discusses in detail the natural disasters befalling Odisha—the occurrences, spatial spread, and intensity of the four disasters (flood and heavy rain, drought, storm, and heat wave) that frequent the state, and the other less frequent, less impactful disasters briefly. Finally, it presents a brief econometric analysis of the state's gross domestic product (GDP) and disaster occurrences, thereafter concluding the chapter.

Natural calamities and social interactions

Direct and indirect losses

Disasters affect the economic system in multiple ways, —destroying assets and factors of production; affecting consumption, employment, saving, and investment potential; and imposing both direct and indirect costs, the identification and assessment of which has been the subject of much discussion (Cochrane 2004; Hallegatte and Przyluski 2010; Hallegatte, Hourcade, and Dumas 2007; Lindell and Prater 2003; Pelling, Özerdem, and Barakat 2002; Rose 2004). Direct losses are the

[1] Available at http://bit.ly/P9qkjgbvv, last accessed on 4 October 2012.

consequences of a disaster's physical impact (consequences of high wind, storm surge, and ground shaking); indirect losses or 'higher ordered losses' (Rose 2004) include all losses from the disaster's consequences. These could be future 'output losses' or 'welfare losses' from the long-term consequences of the infrastructure and capital damages wrought by the disaster (Hallegatte and Przyluski 2010). This means that indirect losses are a consequence of direct losses, but the link is mediated by many factors and may not be linear. A disaster-struck economy having high direct losses can face a low indirect loss if endowed with an efficient reconstruction process that repairs direct losses quickly. On the other hand, another economy with the same direct loss may incur massive indirect losses if its reconstruction capacity is low and inefficient and loss repair takes years (Freeman et al. 2002; Mechler et al. 2006).

Developing countries and small economies face much larger output declines than developed countries or big economies following a disaster of similar magnitude (Rasmussen 2004). Countries and economies with good institutions and a high literacy rate, per capita income, degree of openness to trade, and government spending level are able to withstand the initial disaster shock better than those without, and prevent further spill-over into the macroeconomy (Noy 2009). The scale effect affects indirect loss estimates along with reconstruction efficiency. Using economic cost estimates of Hurricane Katrina over Louisiana in the US, Hellagatte and Przyluski (2010) found indirect losses remained negligible (or even negative) for direct losses below US$ 50 billion. However, indirect losses increased non-linearly (exponentially in this case) and reached US$ 200 billion, corresponding to direct losses of US$ 200 billion; and US$ 300 billion corresponding to direct losses of US$ 250 billion, and so on. Two conclusions can be drawn from this. One is that the scale and time effect of the disaster impact are important in indirect loss estimates (Brown-Gaddies et al. 2007; Jonkman et al. 2008). The other is that past catastrophes can provide some insights into the present state of affairs in economies, especially those with poor economic indicators.

Disasters stimulate innovation and productivity

Natural calamities are also claimed to have some positive externalities or impacts on national economies (flow of aid, reconstruction of old capital by new infrastructure, stimulation of innovation, local knowledge base, and so on), which can lead to gains in productivity (the 'productivity effect'). This may happen because of the higher productivities of the new capital and technologies that replace the old capital destroyed by the natural disaster (Albala-Bertrand 1993; Benson and Clay 2004; Okuyama 2003; Stewart and Fitzgerald 2001; Tol and Leek 1999). There are also instances of innovation based on local knowledge that help people to cope after a disaster and improve their economic well-being, although the net impact on the rural poor is mostly ambiguous. Two distinct views are noticed in research on how rural communities in developing countries cope with extreme weather events. One is that the natural resource–reliant poor are acutely vulnerable and need external assistance to prepare for such events. The other is that climate-related shocks can offer windows of opportunity that trigger latent local adaptive capacities and lead to systemic improvement.

Results from the longitudinal study in a Tawahka community in Honduras before and after Hurricane Mitch[2] indicate that residents, especially poor ones, were highly vulnerable to the hurricane that destroyed 80 per cent of rice fields and 95 per cent of cocoa plantations. However, the disaster enabled the poor to get more paid jobs and thus initiated institutional change that led to more equitable land distribution, slowed primary forest conversion, and positioned the community well to cope with the severe flooding that occurred 10 years later (McSweeney and Coomes 2011). This experience has its echo in Japan, where natural disasters have been understood for centuries to redistribute wealth from the wealthy who lose property to the poor who earn wages to rebuild it (Vermeulen 2011). Both benefits (low-regret adaptations) and loss scenarios (adaptations involving high cost) were found when the adaptations following the catastrophic 2010–11 flooding in Victoria, Australia were studied (Wilby and Keenan 2012). Archive-based studies of socio-economic responses to climate variability in colonial Mexico reflect similar findings. Interactions between the environment and society influence the degree to which regional livelihoods may be vulnerable or resilient

[2] The hurricane occurred in 1998. The span of the longitudinal data used to study the impact of the hurricane is 1994–2002.

to disruption, and illustrate that vulnerability to change can lead to improved understanding of risk and increased adaptive capacity. The experience of climate variability, extreme weather events, and crises can challenge societal resilience, but can also increase opportunities for learning and innovation and extend the repertoire of adaptive responses, as found in Mexico (Endfield 2012). This evidence shows that communities seize the opportunity created by climate-induced shocks to generate sustained social-ecological improvement and thus advocate future interventions to foster local capacities for endogenous institutional change to enhance their resilience to climate shocks. Local innovation and flexibility—not top-down intervention—is seen to be the best route to adaptation and resilience to climate-related extreme weather events.

On the question of disasters causing GDP growth by triggering productivity, the arguments given are that households, firms, governments, and public bodies will replace the old destroyed capital by new houses, production plants, infrastructure, and other facilities based on recent—and therefore, more productive and efficient—technology (Albala-Bertrand 1993; Tol and Leek 1999). Some argue that this growth in GDP stems from Keynesian-type aggregate demand push growth because of reconstruction activities rather than the embodiment of new technology (Benson and Clay 2004; Stewart and Fitzgerald 2001). The other, more plausible reason for the spurt in GDP (at least for a low-income country) could be the inflow of development aid and capital inflows in the aftermath of the event that help replace the old dilapidated capital by new ones and increase aggregate demand because of increased spending. As disasters reduce production capacity, GDP growth because of these last two arguments will be visible only if the pre-disaster economy was in a phase of depression—so that resources available in areas not hit by disaster can be used to produce more to meet increased aggregate demand. Otherwise, the effect could be negative, such as diverted resources, hoardings, accelerated inflation, and others.

On scrutiny, the disaster-induced accelerated productivity argument may not be tenable for several reasons (Hallegatte and Dumas 2009). After a disaster, small producers and producers in poor economies where people have no alternative means of survival try to restore production as soon as possible (Tierney 1997). Replacing the destroyed capital by more advanced ones requires time to adjust the production set-up, prepare, or hire more skilled workforce, and so on, and may not be possible when the producers are in a hurry. In such a situation, the destroyed capital is replaced by the same capital to restore production quickly; this may not increase productivity and even decrease it in some cases (Hallegatte and Dumas 2009). Second, if the capital stock is partially destroyed, the existing undestroyed capital may be combined with new capital, or the old capital may be completely repaired to lower replacement cost; such 'technological inheritance' cannot boost productivity.

Even under the most optimistic assumption of a disaster increasing productivity, whether a natural disaster can improve long-term growth is inconclusive. One study found no effect of a disaster on long-term growth (Albala-Bertrand 1993); another found negative effects (Benson 2003; Raddatz 2009); another showed that weather disaster (as opposed to geologic disaster) increased capital accumulation and long-term growth (Skidmore and Toya 2002). These studies are based on different countries' experience of disasters of differing frequency and intensity. The results, though contradictory, confirm that the impact of natural disasters on productivity and growth is country-specific and should not be generalized without enough discussion on the economy's nature and resource base. Despite an increase in productivity after the disaster, the effect on long-term growth will depend on how reconstruction activities are carried out and on the net impact of the disaster that considers direct and indirect losses, which again depend on the intensity and frequency of disasters. Considering all these effects, one is more likely to find instances of natural disasters pushing an economy into a poverty trap rather than having had a positive effect.

Modelling economic impacts of natural disasters[3]

Hallegatte, Hourcade, and Dumas (2007) model economic impacts of natural disasters using a Non-equilibrium Dynamic

[3] This section is based mainly on discussions in Hallegatte, Hourcade, and Dumas (2007).

Model (NEDyM). It is based on the Solow Model (1956), with one modification: the authors introduced short-term dynamics in the NEDyM to bring in delays (such as price and wage rate react with delays to change in demand and employment) in the pathways towards equilibrium. These pathways help to analyse and show the effect of temporary shocks to the economy due to natural disasters before they reach the pre-disaster steady state. A part of the model is presented in Appendix 8A to highlight how recurring and severe disaster events can lead to permanent underdevelopment or poverty trap scenarios.

The other finds were that the future simulation of annual average production loss due to large-scale extreme weather events (LEWEs) using this NEDyM showed the loss to be highly dependent on three parameters: (a) the probability of occurrences of LEWEs; (b) the intensity of LEWEs; and (c) the capability of the economy to mobilise resources (called f_{max} in the model; see Appendix 8A). Expectedly, the loss increased with an increase in the value of the former two and decreased with an increase in the value of the third parameter. Interestingly, all three parameters have some threshold values. For each value of f_{max}, the damage from LEWEs is limited if both the probability and intensity of the disaster are below the threshold values, beyond which the loss increases sharply as the reconstruction investment cannot cope with the amount of damage because of the financial or technical constraints represented by f_{max} value. In this case, the fraction of capital destroyed by the disaster does not return to zero between events, and the economy remains in a perpetual state of reconstruction that prevents any significant increase in potential capital or economic development.[4]

This scenario presents a realistic picture, as recurring disasters can destroy the assets and savings of households at each occurrence and make it impossible for them to rebuild their asset base and, thus,

[4] However, as talked about in the second section titled 'Natural calamities and social interactions', there can be a quick turn around after a natural disaster if the positive externalities overpower the economic losses. High inflow of capital can transform the investment constraint as redundant or stimulation of local knowledge based innovations can shift the production function up.

force them into permanent poverty unless some high external financial flow is ensured. Further, disasters affect human resources too. It has been shown that disasters can have long-lasting consequences on psychological health (Norris 2005); child development, such as fewer schooling years and diminished cognitive abilities (Alderman, Hodditnott, and Kinsey 2006; Cuaresma 2009; Santos 2007) and can perpetuate poverty for poor households (Lindell and Prater 2003). This micro-household level poverty trap can add to a macro regional-level poverty trap, where an entire region is trapped in poverty because of the amplifying feedback effect (Figure 8.1).

This situation can be amplified by other mechanisms, such as the change in risk perception that discourages investment in affected regions or the migration of qualified workers from the region, leaving the affected region permanently deprived of a highly productive resource.

The state of Odisha is being described as the 'disaster capital of India' because of frequent disasters in the state, and probably presents a good example of the 'poverty trap scenario due to repeated occurrences of natural disasters'. The state has low capital base and the pathway to disaster-led poverty trap scenario due to frequent loss of productive capital as described earlier may not be the exact pathway for the state. The state is poor with low productivity of capital (capital output ratio is more than one) and repeated disasters must have overwhelmed the state with high direct and indirect losses.

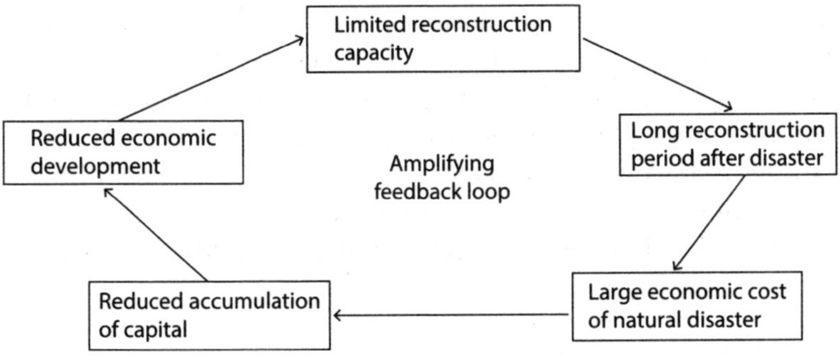

Figure 8.1 Natural disasters lead to macro-level poverty trap
Source: Hallegatte and Przyluski (2010).

Natural disaster scenario in Odisha

Odisha is witness to frequent natural disasters, primarily climate-induced natural disasters (CIND). The state falls under a tropical climatic zone, and the south-west and the retreating north-east monsoons have a preponderant influence on the climatic conditions of the state. Depending on their nature and strength, any perturbation in the monsoon pattern wreaks havoc in the state in the form of CINDs. Odisha is economically one of the most backward states in India—nearly half its population is below the poverty line. Their socio-economic vulnerability, combined with low coping capacity, turns most hazards into disasters. The erratic geo-climatic conditions could also be adding to disasters, as severe floods in major river basins are common. Frequent disasters force the state to focus on repair, reconstruction, and preparedness or on relief and rehabilitation; it has little scope to engage in developmental activities. Between 1900 and 2011, the state had experienced high floods in 59 years; severe cyclones in 24 years; droughts in 42 years; severe heat waves in 14 years; and tornadoes in 7 years. Odisha has experienced 146 calamities in 112 years—1.3 natural calamities a year since the beginning of the nineteenth century (Roy, Mruthyunjaya, and Selvarajan 2002; Special Relief Commissioner (SRC) 2003–04 onwards). However, since 1965, the state has faced two to three disasters almost every year; floods and droughts have occurred regularly (Table 8.1).[5]

The economic damage from natural disasters has increased in Odisha over the years along with their frequency. The value of property lost in the state during the 1970s was estimated at Rs 10.5 billion (nearly 11 per cent of average GDP of the state for the period); it increased nearly seven times in the 1980s and nearly 10 times in the 1990s (*Human Development Report* (HDR) 2004), causing serious fiscal imbalance. This increase is in line with the steady and significant upward trend in economic damage from weather-related natural disasters witnessed worldwide since the

[5] The Government of India does not consider heat waves as natural disasters; the state of Odisha, which does and compensates heat stroke victims, is pressing it to do so (OSDMA 2010).

Table 8.1 Natural disasters in Odisha: A chronology

Year	Natural calamities (flood, drought, cyclone, heat waves)	Year	Natural calamities (flood, drought, cyclone, heat waves)
1951	–	1982	Severe flood, drought, very severe cyclone
1952	–	1983	Heat waves, flood
1953	–	1984	Drought, severe flood, cyclone
1954	–	1985	Severe flood, cyclone
1955	Flood	1986	Drought, cyclone, flood
1956	Flood	1987	Drought, cyclone, flood
1957	–	1988	Drought, severe heat waves
1958	–	1989	Drought, cyclone, heat waves, flood
1959	–	1990	Severe flood
1960	–	1991	Severe flood
1961	Flood	1992	Severe flood, drought
1962	–	1993	Drought
1963	–	1994	Severe flood
1964	–	1995	Severe flood, cyclone, heat waves
1965	Severe drought	1996	Severe drought, heat waves, flood
1966	Drought	1997	Severe flood, drought
1967	Cyclone, flood	1998	Severe drought, severe heat waves, flood
1968	Cyclone, flood	1999	Super cyclone, flood, heat waves
1969	Flood	2000	Severe drought, heat waves
1970	Flood	2001	Severe flood, heat waves
1971	Severe cyclone	2002	Severe drought, heat waves
1972	Flood, drought	2003	Heat waves, flood
1973	Flood	2004	Heat waves, flood
1974	Severe drought, flood	2005	Severe heat waves, flood, drought
1975	Severe flood, heat waves	2006	Heat waves, severe flood
1976	Severe drought, cyclone, flood	2007	Heat waves, drought, flood
1977	Flood, drought	2008	Severe heat waves, drought, severe flood
1978	Flood, heat waves	2009	Severe drought, cyclone, severe heat waves, flood
1979	Severe drought, cyclone, heat waves	2010	Severe heat waves, drought, flash flood
1980	Severe flood, drought	2011	Heat waves, drought, flood
1981	Flood, drought, cyclone, heat waves		

Source: GoO (2004); IMD (2002); SRC (2003–04 and onwards).

1960s (Ikefuji and Horii 2012). The trend is explained partly by the frequency and intensity of disasters in recent decades and partly by the expansion of the economy and capital accumulation—the economy accumulates more capital as it expands and has more to lose from a natural disaster of any given physical intensity. Thus, economic development also makes disasters more expensive. Additionally, there is loss of precious lives, livestock, and migration of skilled labour.

Generally, eight different calamities—floods/heavy rain, cyclones, droughts, heat waves, lightning, hailstorms and whirlwind, fire accidents, and boat accidents—occur in the state. The last two are human-made hazards; the first six are natural. Floods/heavy rain, cyclones, droughts, and heat waves occur regularly, affect larger parts of the state, and impose a heavy economic burden. The last two are localized in occurrence and impact. The next section describes the four main natural disasters between 1975 and 2011 by annual occurrence and districts affected.

Floods/heavy rains

Floods are caused by heavy rains in the upper catchments area of major rivers of the state in combination with the very flat coastal plain, with the average elevation being as low as the sea level at river deltas.[6] The low elevation makes the coastal belt prone to storm surges, which when accompanied by heavy rain makes the estuary region and river basins vulnerable to flooding due to drainage congestion. Almost all the river basins of the state are flood-prone. The main river systems (Mahanadi, Brahmani, Baitarani, and Subarnarekha) cause almost regular floods. Table 8.2 presents flood-affected districts between 1975 and 2011 by year; as observed, the state has suffered floods in 31 of 36 years. Of these 31 years, 9 were minor flood years when less than 40 per cent of the state was flooded; 6 moderate flood years when 40–60 per cent of the state was flooded; and 16 major flood years when over 60 per cent of the state got flooded.

[6] The deltas of major rivers of the state are all mangrove habitats—an indicator of the low elevation and flatness of the area.

Table 8.2 Flood-affected districts, 1975–2011

Year	Number of districts affected*	Districts affected
1975	8 (0.62)	Balasore, Cuttack, Dhenkanal, Keonjhar, Koraput, Mayurbhanj, Puri, Sambalpur
1976	NA	NA
1977	5 (0.38)	Balasore, Cuttack, Koraput, Mayurbhanj, Sundargarh
1978	2 (0.15)	Kalahandi , Koraput
1979	0	–
1980	10 (0.77)	Balasore, Bolangir, Cuttack, Dhenkanal, Ganjam, Kalahandi, Koraput, Phulbani, Puri, Sambalpur
1981	2 (0.15)	Balasore, Ganjam
1982	8 (0.62)	Bolangir, Cuttack, Dhenkanal, Ganjam, Kalahandi, Phulbani, Puri, Sambalpur
1983	3 (0.23)	Cuttack, Koraput, Sambalpur
1984	8 (0.62)	Balasore, Cuttack, Dhenkanal, Ganjam, Keonjhar, Koraput, Phulbani, Puri
1985	9 (0.69)	Balasore, Bolangir, Cuttack, Ganjam, Kalahandi, Keonjhar, Phulbani, Puri, Sambalpur
1986	9 (0.69)	Balasore, Bolangir, Cuttack, Dhenkanal, Koraput, Mayurbhanj, Phulbani, Puri, Sambalpur
1987	2 (0.15)	Balasore, Sambalpur
1988	2 (0.15)	Balasore, Cuttack
1989	5 (0.38)	Balasore, Cuttack, Puri, Keonjhar, Mayurbhanj
1990	8 (0.62)	Balasore, Cuttack, Bolangir, Ganjam, Kalahandi, Koraput, Mayurbhanj, Puri
1991	10 (0.77)	Balasore, Cuttack, Dhenkanal, Ganjam, Kalahandi, Keonjhar, Koraput, Phulbani, Puri, Sambalpur
1992	11 (0.85)	Balasore, Bolangir, Cuttack, Dhenkanal, Ganjam, Koraput, Kalahandi, Phulbani, Puri, Sambalpur, Sundargarh
1993	0	–
1994	20 (0.67)	Anugul, Balasore, Bolangir, Bhadrakh, Boudh, Cuttack, Jagatsinghpur, Jajpur, Jharsuguda, Kalahandi, Kendrapada, Khurda, Koraput, Malkangiri, Nayagarh, Nawarangpur, Puri, Sambalpur, Sonepur, Sundargarh
1995	23 (0.77)	Anugul, Balasore, Bhadrakh, Boudh, Cuttack, Dhenkanal, Ganjam, Gajapati, Jagatsinghpur, Jajpur, Kalahandi, Kandhamal, Kendrapada, Keonjhar, Khurda, Koraput, Malkangiri, Nayagarh, Nawarangpur, Puri, Rayagada, Sambalpur, Sonepur

(*Cont'd.*)

Table 8.2 (*Cont'd.*)

Year	Number of districts affected*	Districts affected
1996	1 (0.03)	Koraput
1997	18 (0.6)	Balasore, Bhadrakh, Cuttack, Dhenkanal, Jagatsinghpur, Jajpur, Kalahandi, Kandhamal, Kendrapada, Keonjhar, Khurda, Mayurbhanj, Nayagarh, Nawarangpur, Nuapada, Puri, Sambalpur, Sundargarh
1998	0	–
1999	7 (0.23)	Balasore, Bhadrakh, Cuttack, Jagatsinghpur, Jajpur, Kendrapada, Mayurbhanj
2000	0	–
2001	24 (0.8)	Anugul, Balasore, Baragarh, Bhadrakh, Bolangir, Boudh, Cuttack, Deogarh, Dhenkanal, Jagatsinghpur, Jajpur, Jharsuguda, Kalahandi, Kendrapada, Khurda, Koraput, Nayagarh, Nawarangpur, Nuapada, Puri, Rayagada, Sambalpur, Sonepur, Sundargarh
2002	0	–
2003	26 (0.87)	Anugul, Balasore, Baragarh, Bhadrakh, Bolangir, Boudh, Cuttack, Deogarh, Ganjam, Gajapati, Jagatsinghpur, Jajpur, Jharsuguda, Kalahandi, Keonjhar, Kendrapada, Khurda, Koraput, Malkangiri, Nayagarh, Nawarangpur, Nuapada, Puri, Rayagada, Sambalpur, Sonepur
2004	5 (0.17)	Balasore, Bhadrakh, Jajpur, Kendrapada, Mayurbhanj
2005	13 (0.43)	Balasore, Bhadrakh, Boudh, Cuttack, Gajapati, Jajpur, Kandhamal, Kendrapara, Malkangiri, Mayurbhanj, Nayagarh, Puri, Rayagada
2006	27 (0.9)	Anugul, Balasore, Baragarh, Bhadrakh, Bolangir, Boudh, Cuttack, Dhenkanal, Ganjam, Gajapati, Jagatsinghpur, Jajpur, Kalahandi, Kandhamal, Keonjhar, Kendrapada, Khurda, Koraput, Malkangiri, Mayurbhanj, Nayagarh, Nawarangpur, Nuapada, Puri, Rayagada, Sambalpur, Sonepur
2007	13 (0.43)	Anugul, Balasore, Bhadrak, Deogarh, Dhenkanal, Ganjam, Jajpur, Keonjhar, Koraput, Kandhamal, Mayurbhanj, Nayagarh, Sundargarh
2008	21 (0.7)	Anugul, Balasore, Baragarh, Bhadrakh, Bolangir, Boudh, Cuttack, Gajapati, Jagatsinghpur, Jajpur, Kalahandi, Keonjhar, Kendrapada, Khurda, Mayurbhanj, Nayagarh, Nuapada, Puri, Rayagada, Sambalpur, Sonepur

(*Cont'd.*)

Table 8.2 (*Cont'd.*)

Year	Number of districts affected*	Districts affected
2009	15 (0.5)	Balasore, Bhadrakh, Cuttack, Ganjam, Jajpur, Kalahandi, Kandhamal, Kendrapada, Keonjhar, Khurda, Koraput, Nayagarh, Puri, Sonepur, Sundargarh
2010**	3 (0.1)	Gajapati, Kalahandi, Nawarangpur
2011	13 (0.43)	Anugul, Baragarh, Bhadrakh, Boudh, Cuttack, Jagatsinghpur, Jajpur, Kendrapada, Keonjhar, Nayagarh, Puri, Sambalpur, Sonepur

Source: Information taken from data available online at http://bit.ly/QIY6jA (last accessed on 4 October 2012); IMD (2002); SRC (2003–04 and onwards).
Note: *Figures in parentheses are ratios of flood-affected areas (number of affected districts to total number of districts). Total number of districts are 13 until 1993 and 30 1994 onwards.
**flash flood.

However, a look at the percentage of districts flooded over the years (Figure 8.2) shows this problem to be as grim in the 2000s as it was in the 1970s and 1980s; the years of developmental planning have not perceptibly reduced the havoc that floods cause. The trend coefficient of percentage of districts affected remains positive but insignificant (0.0018, *t*-value 0.38).

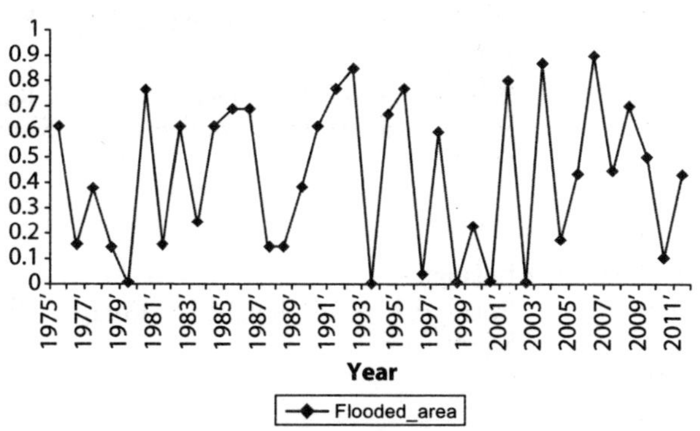

Figure 8.2 Flood-affected districts in Odisha, 1975–2011 (%)

Drought

The next major disaster affecting the state is drought, a very regular disaster that cripples its agricultural sector. Nearly 70 per cent of the agricultural land is drought-prone as rainfall is scanty and irrigation facilities few.

Table 8.3 describes the drought scenario between 1975 and 2011 in Odisha—drought has affected some district or the other in 25 of

Table 8.3 Drought-affected districts, 1975–2011

Year	Number of districts affected*	Districts affected
1975	1 (0.08)	Kalahandi
1976	NA	NA (reported as a very severe drought year)
1977	2 (0.15)	Koraput, Sundargarh
1978	0 (0)	–
1979	11 (0.85)	Balasore, Bolangir, Cuttack, Dhenkanal, Ganjam, Kalahandi, Keonjhar, Koraput, Mayurbhanj, Sambalpur, Sundargarh
1980	NA	NA
1981	NA	NA
1982	3 (0.23)	Keonjhar, Mayurbhanj, Sundargarh
1983	0 (0)	–
1984	NA	NA
1985	1 (0.08)	Kalahandi
1986	NA	NA
1987	13 (1)	Whole state, severely affected (Bolangir, Kalahandi)
1988	NA	NA
1989	13 (1)	Whole state, severely affected (Ganjam, Kalahandi, Kandhamal, Koraput, Phulbani, Puri, Sambalpur, Sundargarh)
1990	0 (0)	–
1991	0 (0)	–
1992	1 (0.08)	Bolangir
1993	6 (0.46)	Bolangir, Ganjam, Kalahandi, Koraput, Phulbani, Sundargarh
1994	0 (0)	–
1995	0 (0)	–

(*Cont'd.*)

Table 8.3 (*Cont'd.*)

Year	Number of districts affected*	Districts affected
1996	28 (0.93)	Whole state (28 districts except Koraput and Malkangiri)
1997	15 (0.5)	Balasore, Bhadrakh, Gajapati, Ganjam, Jagatsinghpur, Kalahandi, Kendrapada, Koraput, Malkangiri, Mayurbhanj, Nawrangpur, Puri, Rayagada, Sambalpur, Sonepur
1998	25 (0.83)	Anugul, Balasore, Bolangir, Baragarh, Bhadrakh, Boudh, Deogarh, Dhenkanal, Ganjam, Jagatsinghpur, Jajpur, Jharsuguda, Kalahandi, Kendrapada, Kandhamal, Keonjhar, Koraput, Mayurbhanj, Nawrangpur, Nayagarh, Nuapada, Puri, Sambalpur, Sonepur, Sundargarh
1999	0 (0)	–
2000	29 (0.97)	Anugul, Balasore, Bolangir, Baragarh, Boudh, Cuttack, Deogarh, Dhenkanal, Ganjam, Gajapati, Jagatsinghpur, Jajpur, Jharsuguda, Kalahandi, Kendrapada, Kandhamal, Keonjhar, Khurdha, Koraput, Mayurbhanj, Malkangiri, Nawrangpur, Nayagarh, Nuapada, Puri, Rayagada, Sambalpur, Sonepur, Sundargarh
2001	0 (0)	–
2002	18 (0.6)	Angul, Balasore, Bargarh, Bolangir, Boudh, Deogarh, Dhenkanal, Gajapati, Ganjam, Jajpur, Jharsuguda, Kalahandi, Maurbhanj, Nawrangpur, Nayagarh, Nuapara, Sundargarh, Kendrapada
2003	0 (0)	–
2004	0 (0)	–
2005	5 (0.17)	Baragarh, Gajapati, Ganjam, Mayurbhanj, Nawarangpur
2006	0 (0)	–
2007	5 (0.17)	Jagatsinghpur, Puri, Deogarh, Kendrapada, Khurda
2008	5 (0.17)	Anugul, Malkangiri, Ganjam, Nawarangpur, Rayagada
2009	18 (0.6)	Angul, Baragarh, Bolangir, Deogarh, Dhenkanal, Gajapati, Ganjam, Jharsuguda, Kalahandi, Kandhamal, Koraput, Malkangiri, Mayurbhanj, Nawrangpur, Nuapada, Sambalpur, Sonepur, Sundargarh

(*Cont'd.*)

Table 8.3 *(Cont'd.)*

Year	Number of districts affected*	Districts affected
2010	15 (0.5)	Angul, Balasore, Bargarh, Boudh, Debagarh, Dhenkanal, Jajpur, Jharsuguda, Mayurbhanj, Kendrapada, Keonjhar, Puri, Sonepur, Sambalpur, Sundargarh
2011	16 (0.53)	Angul, Bargarh, Bolangir, Kalahandi, Deogarh, Koraput, Jharsuguda, Sonepur, Bhadrakh, Boudh, Cuttack, Malkangiri, Nawrangpur, Nayagarh, Nuapada, Ganjam

Source: Author's calculations based on data taken from IMD (2002); SRC (2003–04 and onwards).

Note: *Figures in parentheses are ratios of drought-affected areas (number of affected districts to total number of districts).

the 36 years. Although the list of districts affected is unavailable for some years, almost the entire state suffered crop loss of 50 per cent or more due to the severe drought conditions in 9 of the 25 years.

Figure 8.3 plots the percentage of drought-affected districts over the years and although there seems to have been a marginal improvement, statistically the scenario is as grim as before. The trend coefficient of percentage of drought-affected districts is negative but insignificant (–0.00081, *t*-value 0.14).

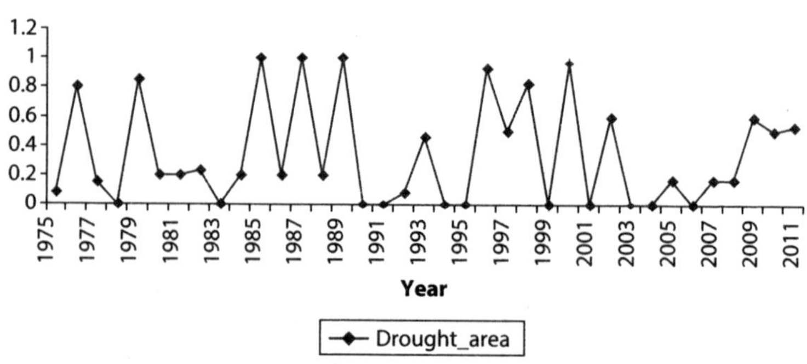

Figure 8.3 Drought-affected districts in Odisha, 1975–2011 (%)

Source: Author's calculations based on data taken from IMD (2002); SRC (2003–04 and onwards).

Cyclones

The entire east coast of Odisha bordering the Bay of Bengal and, specifically, the northern districts of the state are highly vulnerable to cyclones and storm surges. These areas are likely to face increased threats due to climate change, being located on the core area of cyclogenesis (Das 2012).[7] Baleswar, Bhadrakh, Kendrapada, and Jagatsinghpur are the most vulnerable districts by cyclone frequency, population density, and height of storm surge generated. Some studies have ranked Kendrapada as the most vulnerable district in India (Patwardhan et al. 2003; Sharma and Patwardhan 2007) whereas some other studies rank it as the second most vulnerable district (Jayanthi 1998; Kavi Kumar 2003). Depression (wind speed = 31–49 km/h); and Deep Depression (wind speed = 50–61 km/h) do not cause damage. However, cyclones (wind speed = 61–68 km/h), severe cyclones (wind speed = 88–114 km/h), very severe cyclones (wind speed = 114–220 km/h), and super cyclones (wind speed > 220 km/h) cause much loss of lives and properties over landfall. The damage is moderate from cyclones, severe with severe cyclones, and catastrophic or disastrous from very severe cyclones and super cyclones.

Odisha experiences all forms of cyclonic disturbance. The damage from the super cyclone of October 1999 that ravaged 12 of the 30 districts of the state was unprecedented in recent history. Ironically, of all the east Indian states bordering the Bay of Bengal, the state of Odisha experiences the most cyclones,[8] followed by Andhra Pradesh and West Bengal. Between 1975 and 2011, 12 damaging cyclonic storms have battered the state, of which three are cyclones, five severe cyclones, three very severe cyclones, and one is a super cyclone (Table 8.4).

Table 8.4 shows all coastal districts to be cyclone-prone. These districts have suffered havoc from cyclones with different frequency,

[7] Cyclogenesis is the origination of cyclones in the given basin of the sea. The Bay of Bengal, North Pacific Ocean, and South China Sea are the three core areas of Cyclogenesis (Intergovernmental Panel on Climate Change [IPCC] 1997).

[8] Available online at http://bit.ly/QK2GLJ (last accessed on 4 October 2012).

Table 8.4 Cyclone-affected districts, 1975–2011

Year	Type (number)	Districts affected
1975	–	–
1976	Severe cyclone	Balasore
1978	–	–
1979	Severe cyclone	Cuttack, Balasore, Mayurbhanj, Keonjhar, Puri
1980	–	–
1981	Severe cyclone	Puri, Ganjam, Bolangir, Cuttack, Balasore
1982	Very severe cyclone	Balasore, Cuttack, Puri
1983	–	–
1984	Severe cyclone	Balasore, Cuttack
1985	Cyclone (two)	Puri, Balasore, Cuttack, Dhenkanal, Keonjhar, Mayurbhanj
1986	–	–
1987	–	–
1988	–	–
1989	Severe cyclonic	Balasore, Cuttack, Puri
1990	–	–
1991	–	–
1992	–	–
1993	–	–
1994	–	–
1995	Very severe cyclone	Balasore, Cuttack, Ganjam
1996	–	–
1997	–	–
1998	–	–
1999	1. Very severe cyclone 2. Super cyclone	Anugul, Balasore, Bhadrakh, Cuttack, Dhenkanal, Ganjam, Gajapati, Jagatsinghpur, Jajpur, Kandhamal, Kendrapada, Khurdha, Keonjhar, Mayurbhanj, Nayagarh, Puri
2000	–	–
2001	–	–
2002	–	–
2003	–	–
2004	–	–
2005	–	–
2006	–	–

(*Cont'd.*)

Table 8.4 (*Cont'd.*)

Year	Type (number)	Districts affected
2007	–	–
2008	–	–
2009	Cyclone	Cuttack, Jagatsinghpur, Kendrapada, Bhadrkh, Balasore
2010	–	–
2011	–	–

Source: IMD (2002); SRC (2003–04, and onwards).

depending on the landfall point and cyclone track. After the 1999 super cyclone, cyclone preparedness received a strong boost. Many multipurpose cyclone shelters were built by the OSDMA and the Red Cross Society of India. A skilled and dedicated Orissa Disaster Rapid Action Force (ODRAF) was created. It trains volunteers and conducts grassroots capacity building programmes to help and motivate the coastal population to face any such future calamity (OSDMA 2006).

Heat waves

A 'heat wave' is an extended period of abnormally and uncomfortably hot and humid weather. During a heat wave, the evaporation of perspiration, which cools the human body, slows down, and the body has to work extra hard to maintain normal temperature. Humans maintain a core body temperature around 37°C, irrespective of the local climate; the human skin temperature is strongly regulated at 35°C or below under normal conditions (Sherwood and Huber 2010). For metabolic heat to be transmitted to the skin, it must be cooler than the core body. Sustained skin temperature above 35°C due to heat waves elevates the core body temperature and it may attain lethal values (42°C–43°C causing hyperthermia) for skin temperatures of 37°C–38°C even for acclimated and fit individuals (Bynum et al. 1978; Mehnert et al. 2000). Thus, high temperature with humidity can pose serious threats to all individuals depending on their exposure to heat, irrespective of their age and health status. With climate change, heat stress is argued to impose a robust upper limit to human adaptation to global warming by rendering some parts of the world uninhabitable if no strong mitigation measures are undertaken (Sherwood and Huber 2009). In recent years, severe heat waves have caused high mortality and morbidity in many parts of the world (for example, in Chicago in 1995 and 1999 and in most parts of Europe in 2003) including two coastal states of India—Odisha in 1998 and Andhra Pradesh in 2003. Since 1998, a new addition to the list of natural disasters in Odisha has been the casualties from regular heat waves. In 1998, the state witnessed unprecedented heat waves. The administration and people were caught unawares; a calamity ensued. Compared to single digit casualties (1–5) due to heat stroke in some previous years, the death toll rose to 2042 in 1998, alarming the state administration (Table 8.5).

Table 8.5 Heat wave-affected districts, 1975–2011

Year	Districts	Heat wave intensity	Death toll
1975	May: whole state, June: interior Orissa	Moderate	0
1976	–	–	–
1977	–	–	–
1978	Coastal districts	Moderate	0
1979	Whole state	Moderate	0
1980	–	–	–
1981	Districts bordering MP	Moderate	0
1982	–	–	–
1983	Whole state	Moderate	3 (Bolangir)
1984	–	–	–
1985	–	–	–
1986	–	–	–
1987	Dhenkanal	Moderate	1
1988	Cuttack, Bolangir, Balasore, Phulbani, Sundargarh	Severe	22
1989	Bolangir	Severe	1
1990	–	–	–
1991	–	–	–
1992	–	–	–
1993	–	–	–
1994	–	–	–

(Cont'd.)

Table 8.5 *(Cont'd.)*

Year	Districts	Heat wave intensity	Death toll
1995	Interior Orissa	Severe	9
1996	Koraput	Severe	3
1997	–	–	–
1998	Whole state	Severe	2042
1999	Whole state except Nayagarh	Severe	91
2000	20 districts	Moderate	29
2001	20 districts	Moderate	25
2002	29 districts	Severe	41
2003	Whole state	Severe	68
2004	21 districts	Moderate	45
2005	Whole state	Severe	236
2006	19 districts	Moderate	21
2007	22 districts	Severe	47
2008	19 districts	Severe	68
2009	Whole state	Severe	85
2010	Whole state	Severe	100
2011	Whole state	Moderate	22

Source: IMD (2002); SRC (2003–04 and onwards).

The heat wave situation continues to be grim. The entire state is affected almost every year. However, the state administration has adopted some innovative and effective ways of dealing with this calamity. There is evidence that the death toll has been low in districts where the Disaster Risk Management (DRM) Programme of the United Nations Development Program (UNDP) and the Government of India was implemented (Das and Smith 2012).

Other natural calamities

Other than the four major natural calamities discussed in the previous sections, the state witnesses many minor natural calamities from time to time and suffers loss of life and property depending on the intensity of such events. Table 8.6 lists the monthly frequencies of such disasters along with droughts, floods, cyclones, and heat waves between 1975 and 1996.

Table 8.6 Natural disasters in Odisha (monthly frequency), 1975–96

Type of disaster	Jan	Feb	Mar	Apr	May	Jun	Jul	Aug	Sep	Oct	Nov	Dec	Total
Drought	1	2	1	3	2	2	1	4	4	1	1	1	23
Flood/heavy rain	0	0	1	2	3	11	15	28	15	8	5	0	88
Cyclonic storm	0	0	0	0	1	1	1	2	3	2	1	1	12
Heat wave	0	0	0	0	8	5	0	0	0	0	0	0	13
Thunderstorm/ tornado	0	7	6	15	12	8	2	2	2	0	0	0	54
Hailstorm	1	10	17	16	8	1	0	0	0	0	0	2	55
Lightning	0	1	2	5	1	2	10	7	12	3	0	0	43
Gale	0	3	3	8	8	2	0	0	0	0	0	0	24
Squall	0	0	4	1	8	2	0	0	0	0	0	0	15
Dust storm	0	0	0	0	1	0	0	0	0	0	0	0	1
Total	2	23	34	50	52	34	29	43	36	14	7	4	328

Source: IMD (2002).

Table 8.7 Casualties due to lightning in Odisha, 2001–10

Year	Number of deaths due to lightning	Year	Number of deaths due to lightning
2001	183	2006	204
2002	220	2007	351
2003	221	2008	362
2004	277	2009	214
2005	250	2010	227

Source: OSDMA (2006, 2012); SRC (various years).

During 1975–96, the annual frequency of thunderstorms/tornadoes and hailstorms has been 2.5 and nearly 2 and 1 for lightning strikes and gales, respectively. Squalls and dust storms are less frequent. Table 8.6 shows that disaster strikes Odisha every month other than November, December, and January.

Lightning strikes are also a regular and big killer (Table 8.7), but there is no report of any DRM initiative to spread awareness among people, although these deaths are reported from every district and the state government compensates victims' families from the Chief Minister's Relief Fund.

The impact of natural disaster on Odisha's economy

Sections titled 'Natural calamities and social interactions' and 'Modelling economic impacts of natural disasters' of this chapter describe two different hypotheses for how natural disasters affect national and regional economies. One is that natural calamities can trigger local innovations and thereby push up the economy. The other is that recurring disasters put a heavy economic burden on a state and may lead it into a poverty trap if their impact is beyond its reconstructive capacity. Odisha is a predominantly agricultural economy; until 1998–99, over 40 per cent of its gross state domestic product (GSDP) came from agriculture. The share of the agriculture and animal husbandry sectors in its GSDP dropped to a little over 26 per cent at constant prices (1999–2000 prices) by 2009–10, but still exceeds that of the industrial and tertiary sectors. At current price estimates, agriculture's contribution to GSDP is still over 30 per cent (GoO 2010). Floods, droughts, and cyclones are the three major disasters in Odisha and these disasters can lead to crop loss and adversely affect the GSDP in an agriculture-dominated economy unless people develop smart adaptation techniques.

To judge the impact of natural disasters on Odisha's economy, the total GSDP of the state, the GSDP from the agriculture and animal husbandry sectors (both at 1999–2000 prices), and the first differences of these two variables were regressed on

1. time trend (to capture the technological innovations over time);
2. number of floods, droughts, and cyclones in a year; and
3. three dummy variables.[9]

One dummy variable was for severe drought years, when over 60 per cent of the districts lost over half their crop. Another was for severe floods or very severe cyclone years, as cyclones also cause crop loss due to flooding. Yet another was for 1965 and onwards, to capture the structural break in CIND occurrences in the state (Table 8.1).

The data used is for the period between 1951–52 and 2010–11. The coefficient estimates and elasticity of only severe drought and severe flood/cyclone year dummies are shown in Table 8.8.

The first row in Table 8.8 shows the *y* variables. The other rows show the estimated coefficients of the respective explanatory variables. The coefficient estimates in all the four columns show that the severe drought and severe flood/cyclone years significantly and adversely affected the total GSDP and the GSDP from the agriculture and animal husbandry sectors. In addition, these show the adverse effect on the annual changes in both variables. This proves that natural disasters have put a severe economic burden on the state economy. The GSDP is more strongly affected by severe flood/cyclone occurrences than by severe drought occurrences, as a one-year increase in severe flood/cyclone occurrences decreases the GSDP by Rs 96.9 billion, whereas the same one-year increase in severe

[9] The regressions estimated are not based on the Non-Equilibrium Dynamic Model (NEDyM) presented in the section with the heading 'Modelling economic impacts of natural disasters'. The NEDyM, when simulated, can show the trajectory of state's output following each disaster whereas the empirical results presented in Table 8.8 are a simple static analysis showing the marginal impact of severe disaster years on the state's output. With less data available, it was one possible way of showing disaster impact on the state's economy.

Table 8.8 Coefficient estimates of natural disaster impacts on GSDP of Odisha and state's GSDP from agriculture and animal husbandry sectors

Variables/dependant variable	GSDP_state	Δ (GSDP_state)	GSDP_agriculture	Δ (GSDP_ agriculture)
Dummy severe drought	−6.94* (1.83)	−3.48*** (4.47)	−2.28*** (5.95)	−2.49*** (4.66)
Dummy severe flood/cyclone	−9.69*** (3.12)	−1.66** (2.60)	−0.96*** (3.06)	−0.86* (1.96)
Number of disasters (floods+droughts+ cyclones)	1.38 (0.81)	−0.32 (0.90)	0.33* (1.92)	−0.33 (1.35)
Dummy 1965 onwards	−18.20*** (3.12)	−1.26 (1.23)	0.91* (1.81)	0.79 (1.14)
Time trend	1.50*** (14.75)	0.15*** (6.97)	0.13*** (12.97)	0.016 (1.09)
Constants	0.43 (0.16)	−0.59 (1.04)	5.56*** (20.82)	0.12 (0.30)
Elasticity of severe drought year	−0.033*	−0.334*	−0.033***	−2.399
Elasticity of severe flood/ cyclone year	−0.092***	−0.319**	−0.028***	−1.65
Other parameters	R^2 = 0.84, n = 61, F (5, 55) = 58.83, Root MSE = 9.37	R^2 = 0.56, n = 60, R (5, 54) = 13.77, Root MSE = 1.93	R^2 = 0.89, n = 61, F (5, 55) = 91.28, Root MSE = 0.95	R^2 = 0.31, n = 60, F (5, 54) = 4.87, Root MSE = 1.32

Source: Author's own calculation.

Note: ***, **, and *indicate levels of significance to be 1 per cent, 5 per cent, and 10 per cent, respectively.

Values in parentheses next to coefficient estimates are *t*-values.

(Dependent variables: GSDP_state, Δ(GSDP_state), GSDP_agriculture, and Δ(GSDP_Agriculture) in Rs 10 billion).

drought occurrence decreases it by Rs 69.4 billion. Severe flood/cyclones affect sectors other than agriculture and, thus, have a stronger impact on total GSDP. Value added from agriculture, in comparison, has been more adversely affected by severe drought occurrences than by flood/cyclone occurrences; one-year increase in severe drought occurrence reduces agricultural value added by Rs 22.8 billion, whereas the same in severe flood/cyclone occurrence decreases it by Rs 9.6 billion. In terms of percentage change, a 1-percentage-point increase in a severe drought year decreases both total and agricultural GDP by 0.033 per cent whereas a 1 per cent increase in flood/cyclone year decreases the total GDP by 0.092 per cent and agricultural GDP by 0.028 per cent. However, the annual changes in GDP have been strongly affected by increase in severe disaster years as observed from the elasticity measures in the third and fifth columns. The other noticeable features are comparatively small coefficient on time trend indicating slow progress and high and negative coefficient of 1965 onwards dummy in case of total GDP. High frequency of disasters seems to have pulled back the economy of the state largely.

There are positive indications, however. The state government has taken some innovative disaster management initiatives against cyclone and flood from 2003 with the implementation of DRM project of the Government of India and the UNDP in the state. Putting an additional dummy for years 2004 and onwards to the models described in Table 8.8 shows this initiative to have given significant increase in total GDP (not GDP from agriculture) and makes the severe flood/cyclone dummy insignificant. The severe drought dummy, however, remains highly significant with a negative sign in all the four equations.

Other important disaster management initiatives that could have affected the state economy and are worth exploring are renovation and rehabilitation measures after each natural disaster and the flow of disaster-induced external financial aid both from within and outside the country. Though beyond the scope of the chapter, these are potential research areas and can through some insight on the present state of Odisha economy, especially fiscal scenario.

* * *

Climate-induced natural disasters have battered the economy of Odisha in almost every year and with greater frequency and intensity since 1965, as has occurred globally (Ikefuji and Horii 2012).

The intensification of climate change is predicted to intensify the occurrences and severity of CINDs like flood, drought, and cyclone (IPCC 2001). The possible consequences for the state of Odisha can be well imagined. The vulnerable state, which has a sizeable population below the poverty line, may land up with another huge chunk of transient poor, and add to the already overburdened social security sector. Alternatively, it may overwhelm government poverty eradication programmes and fall into a poverty trap. A serious disaster management and mitigation attempt is called for. Unlike the super cyclone of October 1999, a high-impact, low-probability (HILP) mega disaster that attracted international attention and aid for relief and rehabilitation, most disasters choking the state's progress are low-profile (like persistent floods, droughts, cyclones, and so on), and such events can be equally destructive (Lee, Preston, and Green 2012). These events do not evoke flow of aid or other transfers but push the economy backwards as the experience of Odisha demonstrates. Therefore, the usual approaches to poverty alleviation, such as growth-mediated and public support-mediated strategies (Drèze and Sen 1989), need to be reformulated keeping such disaster frequency, intensity, and expected impact on the economy at the background.

Both floods and droughts have crippled agricultural production in Odisha. Droughts are considered the most complex but least understood phenomenon that affects more people than any other hazard (Hangman 1984). Unlike the smart cyclone or heat waves, management strategies initiated by the Government of Odisha or even flood management strategies to some extent that seems to be working well, the drought management is yet to receive the type of urgency that is warranted to push the economy upwards. Research shows erratic rainfall as the major factor causing drought in western Odisha, but these areas are endowed with enough irrigation potential (ground water to micro watersheds) which can be harnessed (Swain and Swain 2011) with some state support. The traditional reactive approach to drought management (relief, crop insurance, and rescue livestock) relies on crisis management and such measures often increase societal vulnerability by reinforcing existing resource management methods. Like other disasters, there should be a paradigm shift in the approach to drought management by making use of drought monitoring tools, early warning systems, emphasis on drought policy, preparedness, mitigation measures, and vulnerability analysis. A systematic approach to disaster management by implementing preparedness and mitigation measures is necessary before the state economy is tracked on economic growth process.

Appendix 8A

Modelling economic impacts of natural disasters using a non-equilibrium dynamic model

A simple Cobb-Douglas production function describes the production scenario before the disaster strikes.

$$Y = f(L, K_0) = AL^{\lambda} K_0^{\mu} \tag{1}$$

In Equation 1, Y is output, A is efficiency, L is labour, and K_0 is capital or the potential productive capacity of the economy. The disaster is assumed to affect production by destroying productive capital and has no effect on the labour market.[10] The disaster causes loss of productive capital irrespective of its productivity, which means there is loss of both productive capacity and productive efficiency as some highly productive capital is destroyed. Thus, after the disaster and depending on the level of efficiency loss, the production function may shift downward. Let ξ_K be the proportion of un-destroyed capital ($\xi_K \leq 1$) so that the effective capital stock present after the natural disaster is $K = \xi_K K_0$ where K_0 is the potential productive capacity of the economy in the absence of natural disaster. The post-disaster production function can be written as[11]

$$Y' = \xi_K f(L, K_0) = \xi_K AL^{\lambda} K_0^{\mu} \tag{2}$$

After a disaster, two types of investment take place (Albala-Bertrand 1993): (a) regular investment (I_n) to increase potential

[10] With new evacuation and warning mechanisms, the loss of lives due to disasters has been drastically controlled. Of course, a big or complete loss of capital stock can cause a massive migration of labour, which can affect the labour market, but this process can be halted if reconstruction activities start immediately after the disaster.

[11] For details see Hallegatte et al. 2007.

production capacity, K_0; and (b) reconstruction investment (I_r) to restore back the productive potential or the value of ξ_K (the reconstruction investment goes on till ξ_K attains the value 1).

$$\therefore I = I_n + I_r \tag{3}$$

$$\frac{\partial K}{\partial t} = I_r + \left(I_n - \frac{K}{\tau_{dep}} \right) \tag{4}$$

In Equation 4, τ_{dep} is the depreciation period. The equation shows the change in productive capital to be the sum of the two types of investment minus the depreciation. Replacing K by $\xi_K K_0$, we also get the following:

$$\frac{\partial K}{\partial t} = \frac{\partial(\xi_K K_0)}{\partial t} = \frac{\partial \xi_K}{\partial t} K_0 + \xi_K \frac{\partial K_0}{\partial t} \tag{5}$$

In Equation 5, the first term on the right hand side (RHS) is reconstruction investment or I_r and the second term is regular investment, which is equalled to $I_n - \dfrac{K}{\tau_{dep}} = I_n - \dfrac{\xi_K K_0}{\tau_{dep}}$.

Equating, we get

$$I_r = \frac{\partial \xi_K}{\partial t} K_0 \;\; or \;\; \frac{\partial \xi_K}{\partial t} = \frac{I_r}{K_0} \tag{6}$$

And
$$\xi_K \frac{\partial K_0}{\partial t} = I_n - \frac{\xi_K K_0}{\tau_{dep}} \;\; or \;\; \frac{\partial K_0}{\partial t} = \frac{I_n}{\xi_K} - \frac{K_0}{\tau_{dep}} \tag{7}$$

Equation 6 shows the change in restoration of potential capital due to reconstruction investment. Equation 7 shows the change in potential capital due to regular investment. Both these equations show ξ_K, the proportion of non-destroyed capital to influence the investment decisions. If $\xi_K = 1$, then reconstruction or replacement investment is zero and $I = I_n$. If $\xi_K < 1$, then replacement investment is the first priority compared to regular investment and is undertaken first. The volume of replacement investment is the following:

$$I_r = \begin{Bmatrix} \min(I,(1-\xi_K)K_0 & if\ \xi_L < 1 \\ 0 & if\ \xi_K = 1 \end{Bmatrix} \tag{8}$$

$$I_n = I - I_r \tag{9}$$

If the destroyed capital is small compared to the annual investment, then the recovery is quick and the economy returns to the pre-disaster state in a few months or years, depending on the disaster severity. This happens if the economy has no resource constraint. If enormous capital is destroyed and the economy has short-term resource mobilization or technology constraints, as developing economies do (Benson and Clay 2004), then recovery can be slow or may not happen and lead to a poverty trap. To capture how resource constraints affect pathways to recovery, Hallegatte et al. (2007) bounded the total investment by a fraction f_{max} that shows the percentage of total investment that can be mobilized as reconstruction investment.

$$\begin{cases} I_n = I - I_r \\ I_r = \begin{cases} \min(f_{max} * I, (1-\xi_K)K_0) & if\ \xi_K < 1 \\ 0 & if\ \xi_K = 1 \end{cases} \end{cases} \tag{10}$$

Using different values for f_{max} (varying between 10 per cent to 1 per cent), this model is calibrated for a steady state economy to see how the economy behaves and for how long the production loss continues if the economy is struck by a disaster that destroys capital stock worth 2.5 per cent of its GDP. Depending on the value of f_{max}, the duration of production loss is found to continue from two-and-a-half years to several years, the longest being under the most restrictive resource constraint of f_{max} = 1 per cent. The total economic loss of the disaster measured in terms of total production loss was much higher than the total direct loss due to the disaster; the ratio was called economic amplification ratio (EAR). Measured this way, the total production loss due to a high-intensity disaster causing direct loss amounting to 5 per cent of GDP came to be around 22 per cent of the GDP with an EAR of 4.4 for an economy capable of mobilising just 1 per cent of its investment as reconstruction investment. If the economy can mobilise 10 per cent of its GDP as reconstruction investment, the production loss for the same disaster is merely 5.98 per cent of the GDP with an EAR of 1.2.

References

Albala-Bertrand, J.M. 1993. *The Political Economy of Large Natural Disasters with Special Reference to Developing Countries*. Oxford: Clarendon Press.

Alderman, H., J. Hodditnott, and B. Kinsey. 2006. 'Long-Term Consequences of Early Childhood Malnutrition', *Oxford Economic Papers*, 58(3): 450–74.

Benson, C. 2003. 'The Economy-wide Impact of Natural Disasters in Developing Countries', doctoral thesis, University of London.

Benson, C. and E. Clay. 2004. 'Understanding the Economic and Financial Impact of Natural Disasters', The International Bank for Reconstruction and Development, Washington, DC, The World Bank.

Brown Gaddis, E., B. Miles, S. Morse, D. Lewis. 2007. 'Full-cost Accounting of Coastal Disasters in the United States: Implications for Planning and Preparedness', *Ecological Economics*, 63(2–3): 307–18.

Bynum, G., K.B. Pandolf, W.H. Schuette, R.F. Goldman, D.E. Lees, J. Whang-Peng, E.R. Atkinson, and J.M. Bull. 1978. 'Induced Hyperthermia in Sedated Humans and the Concept of Critical Thermal Maximum', *American Journal of Physiology—Regulatory, Integrative and Comparative Physiology*, 235: R228–R236.

Cochrane, H. 2004. 'Economic Loss: Myth and Measurement', *Disaster Prevention and Management*, 13: 290–96.

Cuaresma, J.C. 2009. 'Natural Disasters and Human Capital Accumulation', Policy Research Working Paper No. WPS4862, The World Bank Sustainable Development Network Vice Presidency Global Facility for Disaster Reduction and Recovery Unit, March 2009, Washington, DC.

Das, S. 2012. 'The Role of Natural Ecosystems and Socioeconomic Factors in the Vulnerability of Coastal Villages to Cyclone and Storm Surge', *Natural Hazards*, 64(1): 531–46, doi: 10.1007/s11069-012-0255-9

Das, S. and S. Smith. 2012. 'Awareness as an Adaptation Strategy for Reducing Mortality from Heat Waves: Evidence from a Disaster Risk Management Program in India', IIEP-WP-2012-06, Institute for International Economic Policy Working Paper Series, Elliott School of International Affairs, The George Washington University.

Drèze, J. and A. Sen. 1989. *Hunger and Public Action*. New York: Oxford University Press.

Endfield, G.H. 2012. 'The Resilience and Adaptive Capacity of Social-environmental Systems in Colonial Mexico', *Proceedings of the National Academy of Sciences of the United States of America*, 109(10): 3676–81.

Freeman, P.K., L.A. Martin, J. Linnerooth-Bayer, R. Mechler, S. Saldana, K. Warner, and G. Pflug. 2012. *Financing Reconstruction: Phase II Background Study for the Inter-American Development Bank Regional Policy Dialogue on National Systems for Comprehensive Disaster Management*. Washington, DC: Inter-American Development Bank.

Government of Orissa (GoO). 2004. *Human Development Report*. Bhubaneswar.

Government of Odisha. 2010. *Economic Survey 2009–10*. Bhubaneswar: Planning and Coordination Department.

Hallegatte, S. and V. Przyluski. 2010. 'The Economics of Natural Disasters: Concepts and Methods', Policy Research Working Paper No. 5507, Sustainable Development Network, Office of the Chief Economist, The World Bank, Washington, DC.

Hallegatte, S, J.C. Hourcade, and P Dumas. 2007. 'Why Economic Dynamics Matter in Assessing Climate Change Damages: Illustration on Extreme Events', *Ecological Economics*, 62(2): 330–40.

Hallegatte, S. and P. Dumas, 'Can Natural Disasters have Positive Consequences? Investigating the Role of Embodied Technical Change', *Ecological Economics*, 68(3): 777–86.

Hangman, G. 1984. *Prevention Better than Cure: Report on Human and Natural Disasters in the Third World.* Stockholm: Swedish Red Cross.

Ikefuji, M. and R. Horii. 2012. 'Natural Disasters in a Two-Sector Model of Endogenous Growth', *Journal of Public Economics*, 96(9–10, October): 784–96.

IMD (Indian Meteorological Department). 2002. *Climate of Orissa*. New Delhi: Indian Meteorological Department, Government of India.

Intergovernmental Panel on Climate Change [IPCC]. 2001. 'Summary for Policymakers', in J.J. McCarthy, O.F. Canziani, N.A. Leary, D.J. Dokken, and K.S. White (eds), *Climate Change 2001: Impacts, Adaptation and Vulnerability, Contribution of Working Group II to the Third Assessment Report of the Intergovernmental Panel on Climate Change.* Cambridge: Cambridge University Press.

———. 1997. 'The Regional Impacts of Climate Change: An Assessment of Vulnerability', in R.T. Watson, M.C. Zinyowera, R.H. Moss, and D.H. Dokken (eds), *Special Report by Working Group II: Summary for Policy Makers*, p. 517. Cambridge: Cambridge University Press.

Jayanthi, N. 1998. 'Cyclone Hazard, Coastal Vulnerability and Disaster Risk Assessment along the Indian Coasts', *Vayu Mandal*, 28(1–4): 115–19.

Jonkman, S.N., M. Bočkarjova, M. Kok, and P. Bernardini. 2008. 'Integrated Hydrodynamic and Economic Modeling of Flood Damage in the Netherlands', *Ecological Economics*, 66(1): 77–90.

Kumar, K.S. Kavi. 2003. 'Vulnerability and Adaptation of Agriculture and Coastal Resources in India to Climate Change', Environmental Economics Research Committee working paper series, NIP-4, Indira Gandhi Institute of Developmental Research, Mumbai.

Lee, B., F. Preston, and G. Green. 2012. *Preparing for High-impact, Low-probability Events: Lessons from Eyjafjallajökull.* Chatham House. Available at http://www.preventionweb.net/english/professional/publications/v.php?id=24513 (last accessed on 22 January 2016).

Lindell, M. and C. Prater, 'Assessing Community Impacts of Natural Disasters', *Natural Hazards Review*, 4(4): 176–85.
McSweeney, K. and O.T. Coomes. 2011. 'Climate-Related Disaster Opens a Window of Opportunity for Rural Poor in North-eastern Honduras', *Proceedings of the National Academy of Sciences of the United States of America*, 108(13, 29 March): 5203–08.
Mechler, R., J. Linnerooth-Bayer, and D. Peppiatt. 2006. *Microinsurance for Natural Disasters in Developing Countries: Benefits, Limitations and Viability*. Geneva: ProVention Consortium. Available at http://www.proventionconsortium.org/themes/default/pdfs/Microinsurance_study_July06.pdf (last accessed on 22 January 2016).
Mehnert, P., J. Malchaire, B. Kampmann, A. Piette, B. Griefahn, and H. Gebhardt. 2000. 'Prediction of the Average Skin Temperature in Warm and Hot Environments', *European Journal of Applied Physiology*, 82(1–2): 52–60.
Norris, F.H. 2005. *Range, Magnitude, and Duration of the Effects of Disasters on Mental Health: Review Update 2005*. Hanover and Boston: Dartmouth Medical School and National Center for PTSD.
Noy, I. 2009. 'The Macroeconomic Consequences of Disasters', *Journal of Development Economics*, 88: 221–31, doi:10.1016/j.jdeveco.2008.02.005
Okuyama, Y. 2003. 'Economics of Natural Disasters: A Critical Review', Research Paper 2003–12, Regional Research Institute, West Virginia University, USA.
OSDMA, 2006. *The Response*, Newsletter of Orissa State Disaster Management Authority, Government of Odisha, Bhubaneswar.
———. 2012. The Government of Orissa website. Available at http://www.osdma.org/ViewDetails.aspx?vchglinkid=GL002&vchplinkid=PL008 (accessed on 28 September 2012).
Patwardhan A., K. Narayan, D. Parthasarathy, and U. Sharma, 2003. 'Impacts of Climate Change on Coastal Zone', in P.R. Sukla, S.K. Sharma, N.H. Ravindranath, A. Garg, and S. Bhattacharya, *Climate Change and India: Vulnerability Assessment and Adaptation*, pp. 326–59. Hyderabad, India: Universities Press.
Pelling, M., A. Özerdem, and S. Barakat, 'The Macro-economic Impact of Disasters', *Progress in Development Studies*, 2(4): 283–305.
Raddatz C. 2009. 'The Wrath of God: Macroeconomic Costs of Natural Disasters', World Bank Policy Research Working Paper No. 5039, World Bank.
Rasmussen, T.N., 'Macroeconomic Implications of Natural Disasters in the Caribbean', IMF Working Paper No. WP/04/224, Western Hemisphere Department, IMF.
Rose, A. 2004. 'Defining and Measuring Economic Resilience to Disasters', *Disaster Prevention and Management*, 13(4): 307–14.

Roy, B.C., Mruthyunjaya, and S. Selvarajan. 2002. 'Vulnerability to Climate Induced Natural Disasters with Special Emphasis on Coping Strategies of the Rural Poor in Coastal Orissa, India', paper prepared for the UNFCC COP8 Conference organized by the Government of India, United Nations Environment Programmes, and FICCI, New Delhi.

Santos, I. 2007. 'Disentangling the Effects of Natural Disasters on Children: 2001 Earthquakes in El Salvador', doctoral dissertation, Kennedy School of Government, Harvard University.

Sharma, U. and A. Patwardhan. 2008. 'Methodology for Identifying Vulnerable Hotspots to Tropical Cyclone Hazards in India', *Mitigation and Adaptation Strategies for Global Change*, 13: 703–17, doi:10.1007/s11027-007-9123-4

Sherwood, S.C. and M. Huber. 2010. 'An Adaptability Limit to Climate Change Due to Heat Stress', *Proceedings of the National Academy of Sciences*, 107(21): 9552–55, doi:10.1073/pnas.0913352107

Skidmore, M. and H. Toya, 'Do Natural Disasters Promote Long-Run Growth?', *Economic Enquiry*, 40(4): 664–88.

Solow, R.M. 1956. 'A Contribution to the Theory of Economic Growth', *Quarterly Journal of Economics*, 70(1): 65–94.

Special Relief Commissioner (SRC). Various years. *Annual Reports on Natural Calamities, 2003-04 to 2011-12*. Bhubaneswar: Revenue and Disaster Management Department, Government of Orissa.

Stewart, F. and E.V.K. Fitzgerald. 2001. *War and Underdevelopment*. Oxford: Oxford University Press.

Swain, Mrutyunjay and Mamata Swain, 'Vulnerability to Agricultural Drought in Western Orissa: A Case Study of Representative Blocks,' *Agricultural Economics Research Review*, 24(1): 47–56.

Tierney, K. 1997. 'Business Impacts of the Northridge Earthquake', *Journal of Contingencies and Crisis Management*, 5(2): 87–97.

Tol, R. and F. Leek. 1999. 'Economic Analysis of Natural Disasters', in T.E. Downing, A.J. Olsthoorn, and R.S.T. Tol (eds), *Climate, Change and* Risk, pp. 308–27. London: Routledge.

UN-DHA (United Nations Department of Humanitarian Affairs). 1992. *Internationally Agreed Glossary of Basic Terms Related to Disaster Management*. Geneva: UN-DHA, IDNDR.

Vermeulen, S. 2012. *Climate Shocks can Unlock Local Innovations (Blog), Climate Change Agriculture and Food Security, 2011*. Available at http://ccafs.cgiar.org/blog/les-chocs-climatiques-peuvent-d%C3%A9bloquer-linnovation-locale?utm_source=AgClim+Letters+and+Announcements&utm_campaign=1c2f3eaaec-AgClim_Letters_Feb_2012&utm_medium=email (last accessed on 12th July 2012).

Wilby, R.L. and R. Keenam. 2012. 'Adapting to Flood Risk Under Climate Change', *Progress in Physical Geography*, 36(3): 348–78.

PART IV

EDUCATION, HEALTH, AND POVERTY

9

Educational Outcomes in Odisha

Trends and Issues

Narayan Chandra Nayak, Sharmita Dhar, and
Pratap Kumar Mahakur

Education is a critical dimension of human development and it carries enormous significance to a nation's economic well-being. Being educated is a valuable achievement in itself and the opportunity to have it can be of direct importance to a person's effective freedom (Drèze and Sen 2002). This approach to educational attainment has gained momentum since the inception of 'human development' as a new development paradigm (UNDP 1990). Millennium Development Goals have reinforced the same while targeting universalization of primary education by 2015 (UN 2007). In achieving growth with social justice, universal primary education remains a basic prerequisite. Nonetheless, higher levels of education are desirable to sustain the same.

In Odisha, there persist two-way inequalities on the education front. First, even today, a significant proportion of people in the state remain illiterate. The incidence is higher in the backward districts including females, scheduled castes (SCs), and scheduled tribes

(STs). Second, there persist inequalities in enrolment rates at different levels. Since each stage of education plays a crucial role in the development path, there arises a critical need to analyse the scenario with regard to educational outcomes at different levels. The objectives of the study are thus (a) to analyse the trend and the current status of education in Odisha; and (b) to find out the transition rates, retention rates, and dropout rates and other such important indicators of educational performance at various levels of enrolment across the districts of Odisha. The study puts thrust on disparities pertaining to regions, castes, and gender. The primary focus is on access, inclusion, equity, and quality aspects of education in Odisha.

Accordingly, the chapter is organized as follows. The first section outlines the concepts and database. In the second section, the trend of education in Odisha is presented. The next section presents the district-level scenario on education with special emphasis on transition rates, retention rates, and dropout rates at various levels of enrolment. This is followed by discussion and implications of the findings. Thereafter, the chapter presents the concluding comments.

Concepts and database

The formal education system follows a hierarchical pattern with various stages such as primary, upper primary, secondary, and higher secondary. Literacy level is often treated as a key representative of educational performance and consequently, it is considered as a deciding factor for achieving societal goals (Datt and Ravallion 1996; Le Vine et al. 2004; UNESCO 2005). However, distribution of social opportunities and earning differentials do not necessarily depend upon mere literacy. Rather each successive level of education has a bearing, hence reinforcing the importance of aspects like transition rate, dropout rate, and retention rate at each level of such a hierarchy.

In this study, four levels of education—primary, upper primary, secondary, and higher secondary—are considered. The primary objective is to examine the educational outcomes like gross enrolment ratio (GER), net enrolment ratio (NER), transition rates, retention rates, and dropout rates of the students from one level to the other in the educational ladder. Based on the computed values, comparison is made across regions and probable implications are offered. Due to paucity of relevant data, district-level analysis is, however, largely restricted to elementary education only.

The measures used to compute transition rates, retention rates, dropout rates, GER, and NER are as follows (UNESCO 2009: Educational Indicators Technical Guidelines):

Transition Rate:

$$TR_{h,h+1}^{t} = \frac{E_{h+1,1}^{t+1} - R_{h+1,1}^{t+1}}{E_{h,n}^{t}} \times 100$$

where

$TR_{h,h+1}^{t}$ is transition rate (from cycle or level of education h to $h+1$ in school year t)

$E_{h+1,1}^{t+1}$ is number of pupils enrolled in the first grade at level of education $h+1$ in school year $t+1$

$R_{h+1,1}^{t+1}$ is number of pupils repeating the first grade at level of education $h+1$ in school year $t+1$

$E_{h,n}^{t}$ is number of pupils enrolled in final grade n at level of education h in school year

Retention Rate:

$$\frac{\text{Enrolment in Grade IV/V in year `t'- Repeaters in grade IV/V in year `t'}}{\text{Enrolment in Grade I in year `t-3'/`t-4'}} \times 100$$

Dropout Rate: $d_g^t = \dfrac{D_g^t}{E_g^t} \times 100$

where

d_g^t is dropout rate from grade 'g' in year 't'

D_g^t is number of students dropping out from grade 'g' in year 't'

E_g^t is total number of students in grade 'g' in year 't'

$$\text{GER:}\frac{\text{Total enrolment in Grades I} - \text{V}}{\text{Population of age } 6-11 \text{ years}} \times 100$$

$$\text{NER:}\frac{\text{Enrolment, I} - \text{V}/6-11 \text{ age group}}{\text{Population of age } 6-11 \text{ years}} \times 100$$

The data required for the study were collected from the sources like Odisha Primary Education Programme Authority (OPEPA), National University of Educational Planning and Administration (NUEPA), and Odisha's *Economic Survey*.

Trends of education in Odisha

Odisha's progress on the education front is decidedly mixed. According to 2011 Census, in overall literacy, Odisha ranked 10th among 15 major states of the country. Although the literacy rate of the state is improved from 49.09 per cent in 1991 to 73.45 per cent in 2011, it remains far below Kerala's (93.91 per cent). In line with India's continued discrimination against girls, in Odisha, while male literacy stands at 82.40 per cent, a meager 64.30 per cent of females are literate (Table 9.1). It is further disquieting to note that enrolment at the primary and upper primary level has registered a decline in recent years. The fall is visible among both boys and girls. Over the last few years, the number of ST students enrolled at each level of education exhibits a continual rise. Enrolment among SC has receded at the elementary level, while that at the secondary and higher secondary levels has shown some improvement (tables 9.2, 9.3, 9.4, and 9.5).

Table 9.1 Literacy rate of Odisha vis-à-vis 15 major states of India, 2011

S. No.	States	Male literacy rate	Female literacy rate	Total literacy rate
1	Andhra Pradesh	75.56	59.74	67.66
2	Assam	78.81	67.27	73.18
3	Bihar	73.39	53.33	63.82
4	Gujarat	87.23	70.73	79.31
5	Haryana	85.38	66.77	76.64
6	Karnataka	82.85	68.13	75.60
7	Kerala	96.02	91.98	93.91
8	Madhya Pradesh	80.53	60.02	70.63
9	Maharashtra	89.82	75.48	82.91
10	Odisha	82.40	64.36	73.45
11	Punjab	81.48	71.34	76.68
12	Rajasthan	80.51	52.66	67.06
13	Tamil Nadu	86.81	73.86	80.33
14	Uttar Pradesh	79.24	59.26	69.72
15	West Bengal	82.67	71.16	77.08
	India	82.14	65.46	74.04

Source: Census of India (2011).

Table 9.2 Primary enrolment and gender parity index in Odisha (enrolment figures in '000)

Year	All community			SC			ST		
	Boys	Girls	GPI	Boys	Girls	GPI	Boys	Girls	GPI
2002–03	2,244	2,029	0.90	464	424	0.91	606	504	0.83
	(52.53)	(47.47)		(52.29)	(47.71)		(54.60)	(45.40)	
2003–04	2,449	2,245	0.92	506	470	0.93	645	548	0.85
	(52.17)	(47.83)		(51.86)	(48.14)		(54.07)	(45.93)	
2004–05	2,431	2,243	0.92	497	466	0.94	634	548	0.86
	52.02	(47.98)		(51.59)	(48.41)		(53.63)	(46.37)	
2005–06	2,392	2,222	0.93	484	458	0.95	644	569	0.88
	(51.84)	(48.16)		(51.36)	(48.64)		(53.09)	(46.91)	
2006–07	2,266	2,052	0.91	482	440	0.91	623	546	0.88
	(52.48)	(47.52)		(52.29)	(47.71)		(53.29)	(46.71)	
2007–08	2,317	2,196	0.95	456	438	0.96	639	610	0.96
	(51.34)	(48.66)		(50.99)	(49.01)		(51.15)	(48.85)	
2008–09	2,354	2,184	0.95	456	438	0.96	679	649	0.96
	(51.31)	(48.61)		(50.97)	(49.03)		(51.11)	(48.89)	
2009–10	2,309	2,233	0.94	441	424	0.96	678	647	0.95
	(51.39)	(48.48)		(51.00)	(49.00)		(51.15)	(48.85)	
2010–11	2,307	2,182	0.95	437	421	0.96	680	648	0.95
	(51.40)	(48.60)		(50.93)	(49.07)		(51.22)	(48.78)	
2011–12	2,285	2,147	0.94	428	410	0.96	711	674	0.95
	(51.55)	(48.45)		(51.11)	(48.89)		(51.34)	(48.66)	

Source: OPEPA (2011).

Note: Figures in parentheses represent percentages of the total.

Table 9.3 Upper primary enrolment and gender parity index in Odisha (enrolment figures in '000)

Year	All community			SC			ST		
	Boys	Girls	GPI	Boys	Girls	GPI	Boys	Girls	GPI
2002–03	507 (55.31)	409 (44.69)	0.81	92 (56.41)	71 (43.59)	0.77	92 (61.03)	59 (38.97)	0.64
2003–04	563 (54.69)	467 (45.31)	0.83	106 (56.14)	83 (43.86)	0.78	98 (60.50)	64 (39.50)	0.65
2004–05	618 (54.27)	520 (45.73)	0.84	116 (55.25)	94 (44.75)	0.81	111 (59.60)	75 (40.40)	0.68
2005–06	659 (53.83)	565 (46.17)	0.86	126 (54.50)	105 (45.50)	0.83	127 (58.78)	89 (41.22)	0.70
2006–07	851 (53.75)	732 (46.25)	0.86	173 (54.57)	144 (45.43)	0.83	144 (57.85)	105 (42.15)	0.73
2007–08	1047 (52.43)	950 (47.57)	0.91	201 (52.55)	182 (47.45)	0.90	203 (55.45)	163 (44.55)	0.80
2008–09	1106 (51.97)	1022 (48.03)	0.92	214 (51.85)	199 (48.15)	0.93	220 (54.73)	182 (45.27)	0.83
2009–10	1098 (51.64)	1028 (48.36)	0.94	217 (51.34)	205 (48.66)	0.95	229 (53.46)	199 (46.54)	0.87
2010–11	1073 (51.34)	1017 (48.66)	0.95	209 (50.99)	201 (49.01)	0.96	227 (52.91)	202 (47.09)	0.89
2011–12	1068 (51.19)	1019 (48.81)	0.95	205 (50.76)	199 (49.24)	0.97	236 (52.16)	217 (47.84)	0.92

Source: OPEPA (2011).

Note: Figures in parentheses represent percentages of the total.

Table 9.4 Secondary-level enrolment and gender parity index in Odisha (enrolment figures in '000)

Year	All community			SC			ST		
	Boys	Girls	GPI	Boys	Girls	GPI	Boys	Girls	GPI
2001–02	669	465	0.7	99	60	0.61	89	50	0.56
	(58.99)	(41.01)		(14.80)	(12.90)		(13.30)	(10.75)	
2002–03	710	535	0.75	103	72	0.70	92	58	0.63
	(57.03)	(42.97)		(14.51)	(13.46)		(12.96)	(10.84)	
2003–04	727	569	0.78	109	79	0.72	94	62	0.66
	(56.10)	(43.90)		(14.99)	(13.88)		(12.93)	(10.90)	
2004–05	727	598	0.82	117	90	0.77	97	64	0.66
	(54.87)	(45.13)		(16.09)	(15.05)		(13.34)	(10.70)	
2005–06	743	602	0.81	115	86	0.75	98	69	0.7
	(55.24)	(44.76)		(15.48)	(14.29)		(13.19)	(11.46)	
2006–07	745	618	0.83	117	92	0.79	101	73	0.72
	(54.66)	(45.34)		(15.70)	(14.89)		(13.56)	(11.81)	
2007–08	746	633	0.85	118	96	0.81	103	74	0.72
	(54.10)	(45.90)		(15.82)	(15.17)		(13.81)	(11.69)	
2008–09	772	670	0.87	132	109	0.83	116	87	0.75
	(53.54)	(46.46)		(17.10)	(16.27)		(15.03)	(12.99)	
2009–10	774	682	0.88	136	119	0.87	119	95	0.79
	(53.17)	(46.83)		(53.46)	(46.54)		(55.77)	(44.23)	
2010–11	797	712	0.89	141	125	0.88	127	109	0.86
	(52.82)	(47.18)		(53.14)	(46.86)		(53.80)	(46.20)	

Source: GoO (2008, 2011).

Note: Figures in parentheses represent percentages of the total.

Table 9.5 Enrolment at higher secondary level and gender parity index in Odisha (enrolment figures in '000)

Year	All community			SC			ST		
	Boys	Girls	GPI	Boys	Girls	GPI	Boys	Girls	GPI
2006–07	207	161	0.78	22	14	0.64	22	16	0.69
	(56.25)	(43.75)		(60.94)	(39.06)		(59.11)	(40.89)	
2007–08	213	162	0.76	23	15	0.67	24	16	0.68
	(56.86)	(43.14)		(59.91)	(40.09)		(59.44)	(40.56)	
2008–09	212	167	0.79	24	16	0.67	24	17	0.69
	(55.99)	(44.01)		(59.91)	(40.09)		(59.00)	(41.00)	
2009–10	212	167	0.79	28	19	0.67	30	20	0.68
	(56.01)	(43.99)		(59.96)	(40.04)		(59.61)	(40.39)	
2010–11	225	177	0.79	31	21	0.67	32	21	0.68
	(56.00)	(44.00)		(59.95)	(40.05)		(59.60)	(40.40)	

Source: GoO (2011).

Note: Figures in parentheses represent percentages of the total.

Interestingly, gender parity index (GPI)—a measure to find out the extent of parity in enrolment between girls and boys—records consistent rise especially at the primary and upper primary level, hence exhibiting decline in gender disparity. Despite such improvements, ironically, female literacy rate continues to remain low. At the secondary level, despite improvement in enrolment, GPI remains very low. Gender disparities are increasingly felt at the higher secondary level and more so with SC and ST with GPI becoming as low as 0.67 and 0.68, respectively, in 2010–11 (tables 9.2, 9.3, 9.4, and 9.5).

The present study estimates transition rates at three different levels of education until higher secondary education for Odisha vis-à-vis select major states. The purpose of such an estimate is to elicit information on the degrees of access or transition from one cycle or level of education to a higher one. Viewed from the lower level of education, it is considered as an output indicator. Viewed from the higher level, it constitutes an indicator of access. It can also help in assessing the relative selectivity of an education system, which can be due to pedagogical or financial requirements (UNESCO 2009).

In Odisha, transition rate continues to remain very low especially at the elementary level. Largely, similar trend is observed for both boys and girls. Low transition rates indicate a low level of access or transition from one level of education to the other. They may also reflect low intake capacity of the next level (UNESCO 2009). Construed from the aforementioned perspectives, a state, which records lower transition rate from primary to upper primary level may be considered as a poor performer. Low transition rates at lower levels indicate that fewer proportion of people enter into the educational system early, whereas higher values indicate the reverse (Dhar, Nayak, and Chatterjee 2010). The latter follows the stipulations of the Right of Children to Free and Compulsory Education Act (RTE) of 2009, which primarily puts emphasis on universalization of elementary education (UEE) and guarantees free and compulsory education to all in the age group of 6 to 14 (*Gazette of India* 2009). Odisha has to go a long way to achieve this target, as in 2009–10, the transition rate from primary to upper primary stood at a meager 84.54 per cent (Table 9.6).

Table 9.6 Transition rates of enrolment to upper primary and secondary levels in Odisha vis-à-vis select states of the country

State	2005–06						2009–10					
	TrUP			TrS			TrUP			TrS		
	Boys	Girls	Total	Boys	Girls	Total	Boys	Girls	Total	Boys	Girls	Total
Odisha	61.32	58.69	60.07	82.70	79.44	81.20	85.16	83.90	84.54	74.57	75.03	74.79
Andhra Pradesh	92.67	89.66	91.19	88.45	87.83	88.15	96.95	95.96	96.46	66.41	94.02	77.70
Kerala	99.40	98.58	99.00	–	–	–	101.44	102.20	101.82	98.71	100.00	99.97
Tamil Nadu	98.63	97.12	97.91	93.37	94.85	94.08	96.68	96.79	96.73	92.26	92.06	92.16
Maharashtra	90.23	90.44	90.33	–	–	–	99.34	99.16	99.25	99.82	98.95	99.41

Source: NUEPA (2007, 2008, 2012, 2013).

Note: TrUP, TrS: Transition rate to upper primary and secondary level respectively.

Table 9.7 Transition rate to higher secondary level in Odisha vis-à-vis select states of the country

State	TrHS in 2009–10		
	Boys	Girls	Total
Odisha	51.30	45.54	48.60
Andhra Pradesh	37.67	33.89	35.81
Kerala	58.08	67.37	62.75
West Bengal	81.16	68.11	74.64
Maharashtra	63.79	63.33	63.58
Tamil Nadu	73.26	84.20	78.70

Source: NUEPA (2012).
Note: TrHS: transition rate to higher secondary level

Odisha's record on transition to secondary and higher secondary education is equally upsetting. Contrary to the current mandate to universalize secondary education, in Odisha, only about three-quarter of the students enrolled at upper primary in 2009–10 transitioned to secondary level in 2010–11 (Table 9.6). More precarious is its scenario at the higher secondary level as in 2009–10, only about 48.60 per cent of those enrolled at secondary level moved to higher secondary level. In West Bengal, Tamil Nadu, Maharashtra, and Kerala, the said figures stood at 74.64 per cent, 78.70 per cent, 63.58 per cent, and 62.75 per cent, respectively (Table 9.7).

Considering elementary education only, among several other educational outcome indicators, improvement is visible apparently in GER, NER, and dropout rates. Comparing 2011–12 with 2002–03, GER at the primary level has increased from 87.77 per cent to over 101 per cent. Correspondingly, NER has risen from 74.17 per cent to 93.27 per cent (Table 9.8). Despite such improvements, Odisha continues to lag behind many other comparable states. For instance, in 2009–10, the state's GER and NER at primary level were 98.04 per cent and 92.88 per cent compared to 139.40 per cent in Madhya Pradesh and 99.20 per cent in Karnataka, respectively. At upper primary level, the scenario was equally bad with GER and NER registering as low as 104.11 per cent and 85.68 per cent, respectively.

Table 9.8 Odisha state-level GER and NER, 2002–03 to 2011–12

Year	GER			NER		
	Primary	Upper primary	Total	6–14 yrs	6–11 yrs	11–14 yrs
2002–03	101.57	73.96	87.77	74.17	89.69	58.64
2003–04	102.68	79.37	91.03	78.74	91.51	65.96
2004–05	104.26	81.29	92.77	73.65	93.13	69.04
2005–06	92.25	83.3	87.78	78.58	78.58	71.84
2006–07	90.98	100.31	95.65	82.02	82.06	63.11
2007–08	96.66	106.09	99.47	82.03	84.23	76.62
2008–09	96.92	99.06	98.27	90.47	92.28	85.52
2009–10	98.04	104.11	99.79	91.29	92.88	85.68
2010–11	99.06	105.45	101.32	90.78	91.83	83.84
2011–12	99.69	104.93	101.31	93.27	93.3	93.24

Source: OPEPA (2011).

Compared to Odisha, GER and NER of Tamil Nadu at upper primary level stood at 119.60 per cent and 91.30 per cent, respectively (Table 9.9).

Evidently, Odisha has witnessed phenomenal improvement in dropout rates. For both primary and upper primary levels respectively, the dropout rates seem to have decreased quite significantly from 36.02 per cent and 55.36 per cent in 2002–03 to 0.43 per cent and 3.07 per cent in 2011–12. The dropout rate among girls at upper primary level is higher than that at primary level. In 2011–12, it was 0.62 per cent at the primary level, while it was 2.23 per cent at upper primary level. A more disturbing picture is in sight for the secondary level as significant proportions of students drop out at this level. The dropout is higher among SC, ST, and girls at all these levels, hence positing a serious challenge for the state (Table 9.10).

A broad picture on elementary education for the state can be presented based on the estimates of the outcome index as provided by NUEPA. Outcome index encompasses indicators namely GER, SC and ST enrolment, GPI, repetition rate, dropout rate, transition rate, and ratio of exit. During 2010–11, in outcome index, Odisha's rank

Table 9.9 Educational outcome of Odisha vis-à-vis other major states of India, 2009–10

Education indicators	Odisha	Highest value	Lowest value
Overall literacy rate*	73.45	93.91 (Kerala)	63.82 (Bihar)
Male literacy rate*	82.40	96.02 (Kerala)	73.39 (Bihar)
Female literacy rate*	64.36	91.98 (Kerala)	52.66 (Rajasthan)
GPI: Primary grades	0.95	0.99 (Assam)	0.83 (Punjab)
Retention rate (primary)	77.51	96.97 (Punjab)	51.55 (Assam)
Dropout rate (primary(I–V)): All	6.30	16.70 (Uttar Pradesh)	0.10 (Tamil Nadu)
Dropout rate (Elementary): All**	5.51	NA	NA
Dropout rate (Elementary): SC**	6.32	NA	NA
Dropout rate (Elementary): ST**	8.09	NA	NA
Dropout rate (Elementary): Girls**	5.67	NA	NA
GER primary	119.40	139.40 (Madhya Pradesh)	75.60(Kerala)
GER upper primary	69.20	119.60 (Tamil Nadu)	53.60 (Bihar)
NER primary	96.40	99.20 (Karnataka)	63.00 (Punjab)
NER upper primary	47.20	91.30 (Tamil Nadu)	42.40 (Gujarat)

Source: Census of India (2011); NUEPA (2012); OPEPA (2011).

Note: NA stands for 'not available'.

* 2011 Provisional Census; **OPEPA; Remaining data are procured from the State Report Cards 2009–10, NUEPA, New Delhi.

was 14th among all the states and union territories. This may seem satisfactory. However, in terms of values, Odisha's index is 0.809, while for Tamil Nadu it is 0.969 (NUEPA 2012).

These descriptions on Odisha's educational outcomes are primarily based on enrolment figures. It may be pertinent to state here that mere enrolment may at times be misleading. To begin with, enrolment does not mean attendance (De et al. 2011). As per the 64th round National Sample Surveys of 2007–08, only about 85 per cent of 6–14 year olds were attending elementary schools in rural areas

Table 9.10 Odisha state-level dropout rate, 2002–03 to 2011–12

Year	Primary*				Upper primary*				Secondary**			
	All	SC	ST	Girls	All	SC	ST	Girls	All	SC	ST	Girls
2002–03	36.0	38.2	45.9	36.8	55.4	57.5	72.6	56.5	67.2	75.3	77.3	68.5
2003–04	32.4	34.4	41.3	33.1	49.8	51.8	65.9	50.8	64.4	74	75.8	66.7
2004–05	24.5	25.9	31.0	24.9	37.5	38.9	49.4	38.3	63.5	72.5	75.3	66
2005–06	18.5	19.5	23.3	18.9	28.4	29.3	37.1	28.9	62	71.7	74	64
2006–07	10.5	16.9	22.9	10.7	18.1	25.6	32.4	18.5	61	70.9	74	62
2007–08	7.4	12.5	16.9	7.8	13.3	18.8	23.8	13.5	59.6	70.0	72.8	61
2008–09	4.9	7.9	10.7	4.9	8.4	11.9	15.1	8.4	59.3	69.6	71.6	60.6
2009–10	2.8	4.2	6.5	3.1	8.2	8.4	9.7	8.2	54.0	64.4	69.2	NA
2010–11	2.6	3.4	4.9	2.9	7.2	6.2	7.8	7.3	51.0	61	65.4	52.1
2011–12	0.4	2.4	3.1	0.6	3.1	2.7	4.7	2.2	NA	NA	NA	NA

Source: GoO (2012); OPEPA (2011).

Note: * OPEPA; ** Director, Elementary Education, Odisha

of Odisha (NSSO 2010). Further, attendance may not imply learning. It is often alleged that the states while trying to achieve enrolment target end up providing substandard education in the process. Odisha is no exception. The results of a study by Pratham—a non-governmental organization (NGO)—indicate that in Odisha, almost 44 per cent of children in class-V against the national average of 40 per cent could not read text that a child in class-II is expected to have mastered. Similarly, 70 per cent of children in class-V in Odisha, against 57 per cent at the national level, could not solve simple arithmetic problems that a child of class-II is expected to have solved. This clearly reflects the state's deteriorating quality of elementary education (Shiva Kumar and Rustagi 2010).

Educational outcomes at the district level

The preceding section analysed the educational situation of Odisha at the aggregate level. However, Odisha is a land of great diversity. Socio-economic and cultural climates vary widely across regions. To be specific, rural poverty ratios in the southern and northern region are two-and-half times and one-and-half times, respectively, than that of the coastal region. The incidence of poverty among SC and ST population in the southern and northern region is very high. It is in these regions that about 88.56 per cent of the state's ST population and 46.23 per cent of the state's SC population reside. Considerable inter-regional differences are noticed on human development front as well (GoO 2004). Hence, a state-level analysis may not reveal the complete scenario. Considering heterogeneous distribution of education across districts, district-wise analyses may unfold region-specific situations for targeted interventions. The current section, thus, presents the educational outcomes across the districts of Odisha.

Literacy level and enrolment status across districts

If one compares census data of 2011 with 2001, there have been improvements in literacy rates in all the districts (Table 9.11). However, no district has yet achieved literacy rate above 90 per cent. Interestingly, female literacy rate has improved at a faster rate compared to male literacy rate. Despite that, in 2011, female literacy rate in backward districts like Nabarangpur, Koraput, Malkangiri, and Rayagada fell below 37 per cent. There persist striking disparities across districts. The literacy rates of districts like Khurda, Jagatsinghpur, Kendrapara, Puri, and Cuttack exceed 84 per cent each, while that of bottom five districts namely Nabarangpur, Malkangiri, Koraput, Rayagada, and Gajapati remain below 55 per cent. As many as six districts have witnessed a fall in their rank in literacy rate in 2011 compared to their corresponding ranks in 2001. Evidently, these districts have experienced slower growth in literacy rate compared to their counterparts during 2001–11. Nabarangpur's literacy rate was a meager 48 per cent in 2011 followed by Malkangiri's with 49.49 per cent only. Though gender gap in literacy rate is found to have lessened, attainment of parity seems to be a distant reality. In 2011, gender gap was the highest in Nuapada (26.34) with female literacy rate remaining as low as 45 per cent compared to 72 per cent of male literacy followed by female literacy rate of Kalahandi (26.07), Kandhamal (25.95), and Boudh (24.05).

The enrolment data for the primary level exhibit mixed results. Comparing 2011–12 with 2006–07, though the state at large records improvement, many districts have shown a decline in enrolment at the primary level. However, upper primary and secondary enrolments have increased in all the districts (Table 9.12). The decline in enrolment at the primary level may possibly be attributed partly to fall in population in the age group of 6–11 in these districts. The possibility of other factors cannot, however, be ruled out.

Over time, though gender disparity in enrolment has lessened, disparity continues to remain a concern at the secondary level. A cross-district comparison for the year 2010–11 indicates that at the primary level, some of the economically backward districts rank ahead of advanced districts in GPI, while at later levels, the GPI is better with most of the advanced districts (Table 9.13). This may possibly suggest that in backward districts, primary enrolment remains high and more so among girls, thanks to the special initiatives under the current mandate to bring every child to school especially in backward regions. However, in later stages, girls are discriminated. Moreover, as the data on enrolment pertains to enrolment at the primary level, it may be difficult to infer if the girls enrolled in class-I continue

Table 9.11 Literacy rate (%) across the districts of Odisha

District	2001					2011					Decadal difference in literacy rate			
	Male	Female	Total	Rank	Gender gap in literacy rate	Male	Female	Total	Rank	Gender gap in literacy rate	Male	Female	Total	Rank
Angul	81.43	55.37	68.79	12	26.06	87.06	70.44	78.96	11	16.62	5.63	15.07	10.17	1
Balasore	81.69	58.90	70.56	8	22.79	88.06	72.95	80.66	7	15.11	6.37	14.05	10.1	1
Bargarh	77.41	50.26	63.99	15	27.15	84.28	65.84	75.16	14	18.44	6.87	15.58	11.17	1
Bhadrak	84.65	62.85	73.86	6	21.80	89.92	76.49	83.25	6	13.43	5.27	13.64	9.39	0
Bolangir	71.67	39.51	55.70	21	32.16	77.08	53.77	65.50	21	23.31	5.41	14.26	9.8	0
Boudh	76.23	39.02	57.73	20	37.21	84.49	60.44	72.51	18	24.05	8.26	21.42	14.78	2
Cuttack	85.82	66.89	76.66	5	18.93	90.51	77.64	84.20	5	12.87	4.69	10.75	7.54	0
Deogarh	73.33	47.18	60.36	18	26.15	82.62	63.36	73.07	17	19.26	9.29	16.18	12.71	1
Dhenkanal	80.57	57.89	69.42	11	22.68	87.08	71.40	79.41	9	15.68	6.51	13.51	9.99	2
Gajapati	54.71	28.42	41.26	26	26.29	65.58	43.59	54.29	26	21.99	10.87	15.17	13.03	0
Ganjam	75.22	46.44	60.77	17	28.78	81.85	61.84	71.88	19	20.01	6.63	15.4	11.11	–2
Jagatsinghpur	88.55	69.28	79.08	2	19.27	93.20	80.88	87.13	2	12.32	4.65	11.6	8.05	0
Jajpur	81.89	60.76	71.44	7	21.13	87.36	73.37	80.44	8	13.99	5.47	12.61	9	–1
Jharsuguda	82.08	58.36	70.55	9	23.72	86.27	70.05	78.36	12	16.22	4.19	11.69	7.81	–3
Kalahandi	62.66	29.28	45.94	24	33.38	73.34	47.27	60.22	24	26.07	10.68	17.99	14.28	0

(Cont'd.)

Table 9.11 *(Cont'd.)*

District	2001					2011					Decadal difference in literacy rate			
	Male	Female	Total	Rank	Gender gap in literacy rate	Male	Female	Total	Rank	Gender gap in literacy rate	Male	Female	Total	Rank
Kandhamal	69.79	35.86	52.68	22	33.93	78.41	52.46	65.12	22	25.95	8.62	16.6	12.44	0
Kendrapara	87.11	66.76	76.81	4	20.35	92.45	79.51	85.93	3	12.94	5.34	12.75	9.12	1
Keonjhar	71.99	46.22	59.24	19	25.77	79.22	58.70	69.00	20	20.52	7.23	12.48	9.76	–1
Khurda	87.90	70.36	79.59	1	17.54	92.55	82.06	87.51	1	10.49	4.65	11.7	7.92	0
Koraput	47.20	24.26	35.72	28	22.94	61.29	38.92	49.87	28	22.37	14.09	14.66	14.15	0
Malkangiri	40.14	20.91	30.53	30	19.23	60.29	38.95	49.49	29	21.34	20.15	18.04	18.96	1
Mayurbhanj	65.76	37.84	51.91	23	27.92	74.92	53.18	63.98	23	21.74	9.16	15.34	12.07	0
Nabarangpur	47.04	20.67	33.93	29	26.37	59.45	37.22	48.20	30	22.23	12.41	16.55	14.27	–1
Nayagarh	82.66	57.64	70.52	10	25.02	86.63	71.08	79.17	10	15.55	3.97	13.44	8.65	0
Nuapada	58.46	25.79	42.00	25	32.67	71.55	45.21	58.20	25	26.34	13.09	19.42	16.2	0
Puri	88.08	67.57	77.96	3	20.51	91.84	78.67	85.37	4	13.17	3.76	11.1	7.41	–1
Rayagada	48.18	24.56	36.15	27	23.62	62.61	39.87	50.88	27	22.74	14.43	15.31	14.73	0
Sambalpur	79.01	55.21	67.29	13	23.80	85.17	68.47	76.91	13	16.70	6.16	13.26	9.62	0
Sonepur	78.94	46.17	62.84	16	32.77	84.78	63.63	74.42	15	21.15	5.84	17.46	11.58	1
Sundargarh	75.34	53.88	64.86	14	21.46	82.13	65.93	74.13	16	16.20	6.79	12.05	9.27	–2
Odisha	75.35	50.51	63.08		24.84	82.40	64.36	73.45		18.04	7.05	13.85	10.37	

Source: Census of India (2011).

Table 9.12 Enrolment at different levels of education across the districts of Odisha (in '000)

District	Primary: 2006–07			Primary: 2011–12			Upper primary: 2006–07			Upper primary: 2011–12			Secondary: 2006–07			Secondary: 2010–11		
	All	SC	ST	All	SC	ST	All	SC	ST	All	SC	ST	All	SC	ST	All	SC	ST
Angul	127	28	25	122	27	26	56	10	6	68	14	10	45	5	3	51	8	5
Balasore	265	70	43	251	60	45	101	22	7	124	28	14	96	16	4	110	22	7
Bargarh	138	33	32	126	29	27	71	16	14	77	17	16	50	10	8	58	12	10
Bhadrak	178	52	6	165	43	7	71	16	1	88	21	2	63	11	0	80	15	1
Bolangir	155	31	39	179	35	45	53	11	10	85	16	18	49	10	8	58	12	11
Boudh	49	13	7	49	13	7	16	4	1	29	7	4	11	2	1	18	4	1
Cuttack	225	57	14	211	41	13	108	23	3	117	22	5	96	14	1	104	16	2
Deogarh	37	7	15	35	6	16	12	2	3	18	3	7	11	2	3	9	2	2
Dhenkanal	120	28	24	106	23	23	60	11	7	61	13	9	47	6	3	53	9	5
Gajapati	48	6	28	80	5	55	12	2	4	25	2	14	11	2	3	8	2	4
Ganjam	369	87	18	370	86	20	123	21	2	193	38	6	88	10	1	97	15	3
Jagatsinghpur	98	28	1	95	24	3	49	12	0	56	14	1	55	10	0	57	11	0
Jajpur	211	67	24	185	50	27	83	21	4	96	26	7	78	15	2	91	21	4
Jharsuguda	55	11	22	51	10	17	27	5	10	30	6	10	22	4	6	18	3	5
Kalahandi	206	42	66	197	39	66	59	13	14	81	18	21	36	7	5	47	9	7
Kandhamal	86	18	49	109	23	66	23	5	11	42	10	22	20	6	8	26	7	12
Kendrapara	146	39	2	132	32	2	71	16	0	76	18	1	64	8	0	65	8	0

(Cont'd.)

Table 9.12 *(Cont'd.)*

District	Primary: 2006–07			Primary: 2011–12			Upper primary: 2006–07			Upper primary: 2011–12			Secondary: 2006–07			Secondary: 2010–11		
	All	SC	ST	All	SC	ST	All	SC	ST	All	SC	ST	All	SC	ST	All	SC	ST
Keonjhar	185	25	100	215	25	121	61	9	24	83	12	36	77	10	25	70	10	24
Khurda	198	37	15	202	30	21	89	14	4	110	14	9	105	11	4	63	8	3
Koraput	134	22	78	181	32	97	23	5	9	44	10	18	14	2	3	21	5	5
Malkangiri	79	19	51	102	21	68	11	5	3	20	7	9	7	3	2	9	4	3
Mayurbhanj	265	26	168	303	21	210	74	8	36	120	10	71	72	6	33	97	8	51
Nabarangpur	151	25	93	167	25	105	26	6	12	54	11	29	13	4	4	17	5	6
Nayagarh	105	18	9	87	15	7	46	6	2	50	7	3	35	5	1	37	5	2
Nuapada	86	13	34	86	12	36	21	4	6	37	6	13	15	3	2	18	5	3
Puri	168	42	1	144	33	2	82	17	0	84	17	1	62	10	0	79	14	1
Rayagada	110	19	67	127	20	83	23	5	9	38	8	18	12	3	3	15	4	4
Sambalpur	93	18	40	91	18	38	41	8	15	51	10	19	29	5	9	32	6	11
Sonepur	59	17	7	56	16	6	31	9	3	34	9	3	20	5	2	25	6	2
Sundargarh	174	24	90	207	24	127	63	9	28	96	11	54	63	7	31	74	8	43
Total	4,319	922	1,168	4,433	838	1,385	1,583	317	250	2,087	405	453	1,363	210	175	1,510	266	235

Source: OPEPA (2011) for primary and upper primary data; Government of Odisha (2011) for secondary data.

Note:

to join the schools in subsequent primary classes. Besides, as Shiva Kumar and Rustagi (2010) argue in their assessment of the progress of elementary education in the context of India, the enrolment figures lose their credibility for the fact that there exists a large gap between GER and reports on actual attendance. In many instances, enrolment figures are said to be fudged for a variety of reasons including the pressure to report universal enrolment, the opportunity to get additional allocations of foods and other materials, and at times, the need to retain a teacher's post. Such reasons may not be completely ruled out in the districts of Odisha.

It might be of importance to present here the differences in the share of girls, and SC and ST students in elementary education across the districts of Odisha. While there are differences for all, the dispersion is more pronounced in case of SC and ST students. In Mayurbhanj, the share of ST students is 66.45 per cent, whereas in Puri it is a meager 1.20 per cent. Similarly, in Jajpur (27.08 per cent), the share of SC students is much higher than that in Gajapati (6.91 per cent). The distribution according to SC and ST is mainly based upon the share of population from the respective caste or community (Table 9.14).

Transition rates across districts

The estimates of the transition rates provide many interesting findings (Tables 9.15 and 9.16). Considering 2007–08 and 2010–11, the state experiences considerable improvement in transition rates to upper primary and secondary level for all. However, Malkangiri, Koraput, Kalahandi, and Nayagarh have witnessed decline in transition rates from primary to upper primary level in 2010–11. The transition rates for the former two are abysmally low, thus needing serious attention.

The scenario with respect to disadvantaged groups like SC, ST, and girls is not very satisfying. Not only does the state witness decline in transition rates from primary to upper primary level among SC and ST students during 2010–11, but also many of its backward districts have recorded low and declining transition rates at this level. Especially, Malkangiri and Koraput need urgent intervention as a meager 39.9 per cent and 44.77 per cent of ST students, respectively,

Table 9.13 GPI among the districts of Odisha

Educational outcomes		Better performing districts	Poor performing districts	Educational outcomes		Better performing districts	Poor performing districts
GPI at upper primary level (2010–11)	All communities	Cuttack (0.98)	Rayagada (0.81)	GPI at secondary level (2010–11)	All community	Sundargarh (1.06)	Kalahandi (0.57)
		Ganjam (0.98)	Koraput (0.83)			Sonepur (1.03)	Kendrapara (0.58)
		Sundargarh (0.98)	Malkangiri (0.83)			Deogarh (1.00)	Nuapada (0.61)
		Deogarh (0.98)	Nabarangpur (0.86)			Jajpur (0.99)	Rayagada (0.65)
		Bhadrak (0.98)	Kalahandi (0.89)			Puri (0.99)	Koraput (0.67)
	SC	Jajpur (1.01)	Rayagada (0.84)		SC	Sundargarh (1.05)	Nuapada (0.60)
		Sonepur (1.01)	Nuapada (0.88)			Sonepur (1.03)	Kalahandi (0.60)
		Kandhamal (1.01)	Ganjam (0.90)			Puri (1.02)	Rayagada (0.61)
		Jharsuguda (1.00)	Sambalpur (0.91)			Jharsuguda (1.01)	Gajapati (0.65)
		Cuttack (0.99)	Nabarangpur (0.91)			Jajpur (1.01)	Koraput (0.67)
	ST	Puri (1.04)	Bhadrak (0.55)		ST	Sonepur (1.26)	Ganjam (0.47)
		Nayagarh (1.00)	Koraput (0.72)			Sundargarh (1.10)	Rayagada (0.42)
		Nuapada (1.00)	Malkangiri (0.73)			Deogarh (1.08)	Koraput (0.41)
		Jharsuguda (0.99)	Rayagada (0.77)			Jharsuguda (1.02)	Malkangiri (0.38)
		Deogarh (0.99)	Ganjam (0.79)			Sambalpur (1.02)	Kendrapara (0.17)

Source: OPEPA (2011).

Table 9.14 Percentage share of girl students, SC and ST in Odisha in elementary level, 2011–12

Category	District having highest share	District having lowest share	Odisha value
Girls	Boudh (49.37)	Nayagarh (47.04)	48.56
SC	Jajpur (27.08)	Gajapati (6.91)	19.06
ST	Mayurbhanj (66.45)	Puri (1.20)	28.12

Source: OPEPA (2011).

transition to upper primary level. At the secondary level, the districts that have failed to ensure satisfactory transition rates for SC are Koraput, Malkangiri, Keonjhar, Khurda, and Kandhamal, and for ST are Koraput, Jagatsinghpur, Khurda, Balasore, and Angul. The failing costal districts for SC and ST have low or very negligible representation of SC and ST population. Their failure may not carry much significance in absolute number as compared to their counterparts with predominance of such population. With regard to girls, though the state at large has shown improvement in transition rates, upper primary transition rates in Mayurbhanj, Malkangiri, and Kalahandi are low and have declined in 2010–11 compared to that achieved in 2007–08.

The orders of the transition rates are as much important as the values. With regard to transition rates to the upper primary level, the best performing districts in decreasing order are Cuttack, Puri, Bargarh, Sonepur, Sundargarh and Khurda, while the bottom five are Malkangiri, Koraput, Rayagada, Nabarangpur and Gajapati. The order remains more or less same for both boys and girls. In transition among SC and ST students, the aforementioned bottom five districts continue to fail in some form or the other. The estimates of the transition rates to secondary education reveal some changes in the order. In 2010–11, the districts that topped the list were Sundargarh followed by Puri, Boudh, Cuttack and Khurda, while at the bottom end were Malkangiri, Koraput, Deogarh, Kalahandi and Nabarangpur. In girls' transition, Malkangiri, Koraput and Deogarh continued to have been in bottom five with Kalahandi and Kandhamal joining them.

Table 9.15 Transition rates (%) up to secondary education across the districts of Odisha, 2007–08

District	Transition from primary to upper primary								Transition from upper primary to secondary							
	All communities				SC		ST		All communities				SC		ST	
	Boys	Girls	Total	Rank	Total	Rank	Total	Rank	Boys	Girls	Total	Rank	Total	Rank	Total	Rank
Angul	89.60	86.60	88.14	16	82.84	21	77.47	18	73.72	77.60	75.57	19	57.91	28	81.78	7
Balasore	91.03	90.72	90.88	4	85.93	13	87.45	7	82.01	87.73	84.74	10	80.26	11	82.48	6
Bargarh	89.62	89.54	89.59	11	86.54	11	87.40	8	78.86	78.41	78.64	16	72.71	19	95.94	3
Bhadrak	88.70	89.17	88.93	12	85.17	17	75.06	20	89.62	91.31	90.45	3	82.57	9	66.49	22
Bolangir	85.66	82.56	84.16	21	83.31	20	78.46	17	74.51	72.18	73.43	23	73.50	18	44.51	29
Boudh	90.55	88.66	89.63	10	85.42	16	89.65	5	71.55	73.24	72.38	24	63.33	26	69.15	20
Cuttack	88.47	91.77	90.09	7	79.06	24	66.49	24	81.26	87.31	84.19	11	66.21	25	68.18	21
Deogarh	89.53	90.06	89.79	8	89.16	4	85.43	11	87.08	83.45	85.32	9	87.09	3	76.23	10
Dhenkanal	88.47	86.82	87.67	18	84.94	18	76.31	19	70.75	73.72	72.15	25	56.47	29	75.70	11
Gajapati	70.01	65.43	67.87	26	65.26	30	63.92	25	72.55	76.63	74.29	22	70.37	20	131.38	1
Ganjam	77.78	78.29	78.03	24	66.93	29	68.29	22	78.48	77.63	78.06	17	69.30	21	74.29	13
Jagatsinghpur	92.17	91.69	91.93	3	88.14	7	81.31	13	87.04	93.20	90.02	4	83.99	7	73.53	15
Jajpur	89.00	88.24	88.62	14	84.01	19	79.41	16	83.26	88.85	85.93	7	75.04	15	77.43	9
Jharsuguda	87.86	88.84	88.33	15	85.57	15	88.11	6	76.59	78.81	77.64	18	67.66	24	85.52	5
Kalahandi	91.63	87.62	89.72	9	90.13	2	84.92	12	89.78	86.00	88.15	5	96.50	2	51.55	28
Kandhamal	78.51	74.92	76.80	25	78.26	26	70.79	21	79.35	86.82	82.75	13	86.08	4	94.81	4

(*Cont'd.*)

Table 9.15 (*Cont'd.*)

Kendrapara	87.25	88.99	88.11	17	87.02	8	54.54	27	84.30	88.85	86.54	6	80.78	10	24.58	30
Keonjhar	79.56	79.66	79.60	23	89.06	5	67.39	23	83.77	88.32	85.92	8	85.26	5	60.46	25
Khurda	84.64	85.12	84.87	19	81.22	23	94.04	3	83.16	84.32	83.71	12	84.89	6	104.00	2
Koraput	61.81	53.33	57.78	30	69.37	27	46.72	30	69.53	69.39	69.47	27	74.58	17	80.13	8
Malkangiri	62.65	56.98	60.13	29	86.29	12	47.11	29	49.29	46.58	48.12	30	49.99	30	57.31	27
Mayurbhanj	83.21	84.11	83.64	22	86.89	9	79.76	15	74.64	74.16	74.42	20	68.26	22	69.63	19
Nabarangpur	69.79	64.58	67.34	27	78.72	25	62.16	26	66.66	66.78	66.72	28	78.59	12	70.65	18
Nayagarh	95.97	94.60	95.31	1	88.60	6	95.93	2	92.10	93.23	92.63	2	83.80	8	60.63	24
Nuapada	86.67	82.57	84.73	20	85.83	14	81.22	14	94.76	91.16	93.21	1	98.24	1	59.72	26
Puri	90.95	90.22	90.59	6	86.74	10	238.49	1	81.07	83.10	82.05	14	74.79	16	74.88	12
Rayagada	63.22	57.90	60.77	28	68.53	28	51.00	28	73.57	75.17	74.31	21	77.01	13	71.09	17
Sambalpur	92.64	91.52	92.08	2	89.74	3	89.84	4	74.20	68.83	71.56	26	67.89	23	63.24	23
Sonepur	89.37	92.08	90.72	5	90.41	1	85.63	10	65.94	67.46	66.68	29	62.57	27	71.34	16
Sundargarh	89.23	88.03	88.64	13	81.50	22	86.92	9	78.69	81.31	79.96	15	75.73	14	73.85	14
Total	84.33	83.56	83.96		82.16		73.53		79.57	81.54	80.50		74.88		73.21	

Source: Computed by the authors based on pre-published data provided by OPEPA in Microsoft Excel.

Table 9.16 Transition rates (%) up to secondary level across the districts of Odisha, 2010–11

District	Transition from primary to upper primary in 2010–11								Transition from upper primary to secondary in 2010–11							
	All community				SC		ST		All community				SC		ST	
	Boys	Girls	Total	Rank	Total	Rank	Total	Rank	Boys	Girls	Total	Rank	Total	Rank	Total	Rank
Angul	93.51	88.94	91.32	18	84.63	12	78.93	14	95.30	97.23	96.22	19	83.60	12	77.48	22
Balasore	96.90	94.26	95.60	10	84.20	16	80.12	12	91.37	95.36	93.32	24	78.27	24	67.04	27
Bargarh	106.12	99.19	102.76	3	96.09	1	95.32	2	99.12	96.50	97.83	13	85.82	8	85.19	10
Bhadrak	95.68	94.03	94.87	11	85.14	10	93.24	3	98.66	102.17	100.40	10	83.18	15	130.17	1
Bolangir	96.44	88.81	92.67	16	86.14	9	84.44	9	98.74	94.01	96.48	18	85.15	10	80.26	17
Boudh	91.89	87.09	89.53	21	80.16	20	87.45	6	109.63	105.15	107.44	3	97.92	1	102.39	3
Cuttack	106.51	102.78	104.70	1	79.21	21	76.99	18	106.84	106.12	106.48	4	76.03	25	80.22	18
Deogarh	100.33	92.10	96.27	7	89.07	5	85.75	7	92.56	89.18	90.88	28	79.13	23	78.70	21
Dhenkanal	97.07	91.42	94.36	14	89.19	4	78.37	15	96.78	96.85	96.81	16	80.92	21	75.93	23
Gajapati	83.63	74.10	79.07	26	77.64	25	66.09	26	99.13	90.49	95.03	22	81.79	18	85.37	9
Ganjam	88.85	86.58	87.74	23	78.25	23	69.14	23	94.25	92.74	93.50	23	84.93	11	88.58	5
Jagatsinghpur	97.34	92.14	94.86	12	84.44	15	81.79	10	101.28	100.69	101.00	7	83.55	13	44.02	30
Jajpur	97.84	91.67	94.82	13	84.80	11	70.24	21	100.27	101.04	100.65	8	83.13	16	74.22	24
Jharsuguda	98.26	93.87	96.15	8	89.53	3	88.01	4	96.55	93.72	95.17	21	81.33	19	83.92	12
Kalahandi	92.79	84.85	88.88	22	84.55	13	76.17	19	94.75	87.22	91.24	27	81.14	20	73.85	25
Kandhamal	89.50	79.74	84.69	24	80.52	19	73.26	20	93.18	89.87	91.59	25	74.10	26	81.04	14

(Cont'd.)

Table 9.16 *(Cont'd.)*

Kendrapara	97.58	94.04	95.85	9	87.58	7	55.25	28	99.59	101.30	100.43	9	87.50	5	79.89	19
Keonjhar	84.13	81.93	83.06	25	79.00	22	66.24	25	95.86	98.61	97.17	14	72.60	27	80.39	16
Khurda	102.47	94.48	98.59	6	71.33	28	77.09	17	105.71	100.00	102.94	5	72.17	28	70.21	26
Koraput	59.02	51.32	55.25	29	64.65	30	44.77	29	70.39	69.83	70.13	29	71.66	29	58.24	29
Malkangiri	60.16	48.77	54.44	30	69.15	29	39.90	30	73.06	65.36	69.25	30	62.91	30	60.48	28
Mayurbhanj	89.93	90.96	90.43	20	78.04	24	81.39	11	94.12	97.95	95.97	20	82.71	17	81.91	13
Nabarangpur	75.98	73.87	74.94	27	80.59	18	69.02	24	90.90	92.28	91.53	26	87.95	4	86.58	8
Nayagarh	95.26	90.87	93.18	15	82.83	17	70.13	22	103.00	102.62	102.82	6	87.48	6	88.21	6
Nuapada	93.99	87.37	90.75	19	86.49	8	77.60	16	101.41	92.43	97.08	15	92.09	3	80.85	15
Puri	107.43	100.85	104.21	2	89.80	2	115.04	1	109.99	106.68	108.38	2	85.23	9	106.99	2
Rayagada	72.78	70.90	71.87	28	74.26	27	60.39	27	93.81	100.32	96.71	17	83.49	14	86.73	7
Sambalpur	94.57	89.38	92.02	17	84.48	14	80.01	13	100.26	99.42	99.85	12	79.21	22	79.55	20
Sonepur	102.14	95.82	99.01	4	88.17	6	84.92	8	101.35	99.37	100.36	11	86.64	7	84.28	11
Sundargarh	100.26	97.71	99.01	5	75.25	26	87.79	5	108.36	108.90	108.63	1	95.25	2	89.85	4
Total	92.52	87.90	90.27		82.07		72.87		97.89	97.32	97.61		82.02		80.98	

Source: Computed by the authors based on the data taken from GoO (2011).

Other key educational outcomes
A cross-district comparison

Besides enrolment and transition rates, there are many other critical indicators pertaining to educational achievements. Noteworthy among them are GER, NER, dropout rates, and retention rates. Over time, Odisha and most of its districts have shown consistent rise in GER and NER at primary and upper primary levels, indicating thereby that there seems to be improvement in coverage at the corresponding level of education. However, there persist wide cross-district disparities in the achievements. In 2011–12, at primary level, Jharsuguda achieved GER of 113.43 per cent, while GER of Sonepur was a meager 84.38 per cent. At upper primary level, Bolangir achieved GER of 129.66 per cent, while Ganjam's GER was 90.89 per cent only. In NER, Jagatsinghpur and Cuttack respectively attained 99.98 per cent and 99.91 per cent at primary and upper primary level. On the other side, Keonjhar registered a low of 64.32 per cent and 52.07 per cent NER at primary and upper primary level, respectively (Table 9.17).

Although the state has witnessed a significant fall in dropout rates in recent years both at primary and upper primary levels, yet there exist wide disparities across districts. In 2011–12, against the state average of 0.43 per cent primary dropout rate, Jagatsinghpur followed by Kendrapara, Dhenkanal, and Nayagarh have witnessed dropout rates ranging between 9.31 per cent and 6.06 per cent. Girls' dropout rate is higher in Jagatsinghpur (8.68 per cent) followed by Dhenkanal (7.13 per cent) and Kendrapara (6.84 per cent). Similarly, while the average primary level dropout rate among the ST students of the state stands at 3.13 per cent that for Sonepur is a high of 7.56 per cent, for Rayagada 6.80 per cent, for Nayagarh 6.61 per cent, and for Mayurbhanj 6 per cent. The dropout rates at upper primary level are higher than that at primary level and the districts show large variations among themselves in this regard. In 2011–12, against the state average of 3.04 per cent only, the dropout rates for Koraput, Malkangiri, Gajapati, Kalahandi, and Kandhamal were 19.66 per cent, 19.22 per cent, 8.51 per cent, 7.22 per cent, and 6.91 per cent, respectively. Such high dropout rates in these districts may be attributed to high dropout rates among girls at upper primary level. On the average, the dropout rates among girls and the students of SC and ST are higher compared to boys and all (Table 9.17).

Table 9.17 Educational outcomes (%) among the select districts of Odisha

Educational outcomes		Better performing districts	Worse performing districts	Educational outcomes		Better performing districts	Worse performing districts
GER (2011–12)	Primary	Jharsuguda (113.43)	Sonepur (84.38)	NER (2011–12)	Primary	Jagatsinghpur (99.98)	Keonjhar (64.32)
		Sundargarh (109.38)	Nayagarh (87.82)			Cuttack (99.95)	Sambalpur (68.93)
		Koraput (109.20)	Sambalpur (88.64)			Kendrapara (99.95)	Deogarh (74.65)
		Jagatsinghpur (107.15)	Kendrapara (88.96)			Jajpur (99.94)	Bolangir (83.96)
		Jajpur (105.50)	Angul (90.03)			Dhenkanal (99.90)	Sonepur (84.05)
	Upper primary	Bolangir (129.66)	Ganjam (90.89)		Upper primary	Cuttack (99.91)	Keonjhar (52.07)
		Malkangiri (127.61)	Gajapati (98.09)			Angul (99.90)	Bhadrak (68.16)
		Angul (126.00)	Bargarh (98.73)			Ganjam (99.88)	Boudh (68.35)
		Deogarh (124.04)	Keonjhar (99.04)			Jajpur (99.88)	Sonepur (69.60)
		Sundargarh (118.63)	Boudh (99.17)			Khurda (99.85)	Kalahandi (74.67)

(*Cont'd.*)

Table 9.17 *(Cont'd.)*

Educational outcomes		Better performing districts	Worse performing districts	Educational outcomes		Better performing districts	Worse performing districts
Dropout at primary level (2011–12)	All community	Bargarh (0.10)	Jagatsinghpur (9.31)	Dropout at upper primary level (2011–12)	All community	Sonepur (0.05)	Koraput (19.66)
		Bolangir (0.10)	Kendrapara (6.88)			Cuttack (0.26)	Malkangiri (19.22)
		Cuttack (0.10)	Dhenkanal (6.48)			Sundargarh (0.32)	Gajapati (8.51)
		Gajapati (0.20)	Nayagarh (6.06)			Puri (0.36)	Kalahandi (7.22)
		Sundargarh (0.30)	Bhadrak (5.14)			Khurda (0.40)	Deogarh (7.21)
	SC	Gajapati (0.15)	Sundargarh (9.44)		SC	Puri (0.14)	Khurda (8.70)
		Deogarh (0.49)	Cuttack (9.13)			Bhadrak (0.49)	Mayurbhanj (8.61)
		Bolangir (0.45)	Malkangiri (8.15)			Angul (1.01)	Malkangiri (8.60)
		Nuapada (0.95)	Dhenkanal (7.83)			Koraput (1.45)	Sundargarh (8.11)
		Sambalpur (1.02)	Jagatsinghpur (7.72)			Dhenkanal (1.73)	Nuapada (7.54)

(Cont'd.)

Table 9.17 (*Cont'd.*)

ST	Ganjam (0.47)	Sonepur (7.56)	ST	Bargarh (0.46)	Malkangiri (11.60)
	Keonjhar (0.59)	Rayagada 96.80)		Deogarh (0.80)	Rayagada (9.80)
	Deogarh (0.60)	Nayagarh (6.61)		Dhenkanal (0.90)	Nuapada (9.30)
	Jajpur (0.70)	Bhadrak (6.30)		Angul (1.04)	Jharsuguda (9.11)
	Jharsuguda (0.84)	Mayurbhanj (6.00)		Keonjhar (1.60)	Bhadrak (9.10)
Girls	Gajapati (0)	Jagatsinghpur (8.68)	Girls	Nayagarh (0.12)	Malkangiri (18.46)
	Koraput (0)	Dhenkanal (7.13)		Sonepur (0.14)	Koraput (17.97)
	Nuapada (0)	Kendrapara (6.84)		Sundargarh (0.14)	Kalahandi (8.19)
	Nabarangpur (0)	Nayagarh (5.34)		Khurda (0.20)	Gajapati (8.11)
	Bolangir (0)	Angul (5.10)		Cuttack (0.21)	Deogarh (7.68)

(*Cont'd.*)

Table 9.17 *(Cont'd.)*

Educational outcomes		Better performing districts	Worse performing districts
Retention rate (2009–10)	Primary	Sonepur (99.10)	Mayurbhanj (59.90)
		Kendrapara (95.30)	Keonjhar (63.60)
		Nayagarh (94.60)	Kalahandi (64.20)
		Khurda (91.80)	Kandhamal (65.10)
		Sambalpur (88.80)	Nuapada (67.70)

Source: OPEPA (2011).

Note: Dropout rates at primary level for girls is nil for 12 districts. However, names of only five districts are cited.

One of the basic prerequisites of UEE is to retain the students in the education system. There, however, exists wide inter-district disparities on this front as well. In 2009–10, the primary level retention rate in Sonepur stood at 99.10 per cent, while Mayurbhanj had a retention rate as low as 59.90 per cent. The other laggard districts were Keonjhar (63.60 per cent), Kandhamal (65.10 per cent), Kalahandi (64.20 per cent), and Nuapada (67.70 per cent) (Table 9.17).

Discussion and implications

It is clear from the preceding analyses that Odisha's performance on educational outcomes is mixed. Despite the state's visible improvement on literacy front, more than a quarter of the population is still illiterate. Amidst indications of declining gender disparity in enrolment especially at primary and upper primary level, female literacy continues to remain abysmally low. Gender disparities are increasingly felt at higher secondary level and more so among SCs and STs. Though GER and NER exhibit improvement, and dropout rates are, in general, on the decline, girls, SC, and ST continue to experience low GER and NER and high dropouts. The dropout rate at secondary level remains higher. Odisha's record on transition rates at the elementary level is also miserable, hence questioning the ability of the state to accomplish the goals of UEE. The transition to secondary and higher secondary level is still a greater challenge.

The problems for the state are two-fold. On the one hand, the state fails to catch up with better performing states in several important indicators. On the other hand, there are glaring inter-district disparities. The laggard ones on the education front are five southern districts namely Malkangiri, Koraput, Rayagada, Gajapati, and Nabarangpur. Little less than half of the population in these districts is still illiterate. The other poor performing districts, in some form or the other, are Kalahandi and Kandhamal. The SC and ST students, in general, are at a disadvantage. Most of the tribal-dominated districts witness abysmally higher dropout rates at upper primary level.

It might be important to note that a state's achievements on the education front might rest upon the following four critical indicators: access, equity, inclusion, and quality. In the course of time, several measures have been taken up by the government, at the centre, and the states, to address these pertinent aspects especially at the elementary level. Two constitutional amendments (42nd and 86th) are a testimony to such efforts. While the 42nd constitutional amendment has brought education from the state list onto the concurrent list, the 86th constitutional amendment has gone ahead and made elementary education a fundamental right. In a renewed pursuit to universalize elementary education, RTE was passed in 2009, which has created a legal obligation on the central and state governments to ensure elementary education to all children in the age group of 6 to 14 years. This also marks the movement towards adopting a right-based framework in the field of elementary education.

Several schemes have also been instituted in the country towards ensuring universal coverage especially of elementary education. The latest in row is the Sarva Shiksha Abhiyan (SSA), a flagship programme of the central government, which has been effective since 2001–02. Mid-day meal scheme is another widespread scheme. Provision of free textbooks and uniforms, scholarships, and bicycles to girl students are some other schemes that are under implementation in different states including Odisha. In Odisha, in order to improve access to elementary education and achieve full enrolment, the government has relaxed norms for opening primary schools. Till 2010–11, 8,623 new primary schools have been opened. Additionally, 9,005 primary schools have been upgraded to upper primary level and 6,774 upper primary schools have been upgraded to class-VIII. More than 14,000 Sikhya Sahayaks have been regularized as primary school teachers (GoO 2012).

Despite these measures, Odisha has ironically failed to achieve the desired objectives. It might be necessary, in this context, to examine why the state fails. Though the authors of the present study do not intend to identify the factors behind such failures, they attempt to make a critical assessment of Odisha's positions particularly from the input side vis-à-vis other comparable states and offer implications.

It might be argued, in this context, that the performance of a region in educational outcomes depends upon several interrelated factors—both proximate and underlying. Broadly, one can categorize these factors into five different heads namely household characteristics, village characteristics, school characteristics, individual characteristics, and cost of education (Figure 9.1). Among the individual factors,

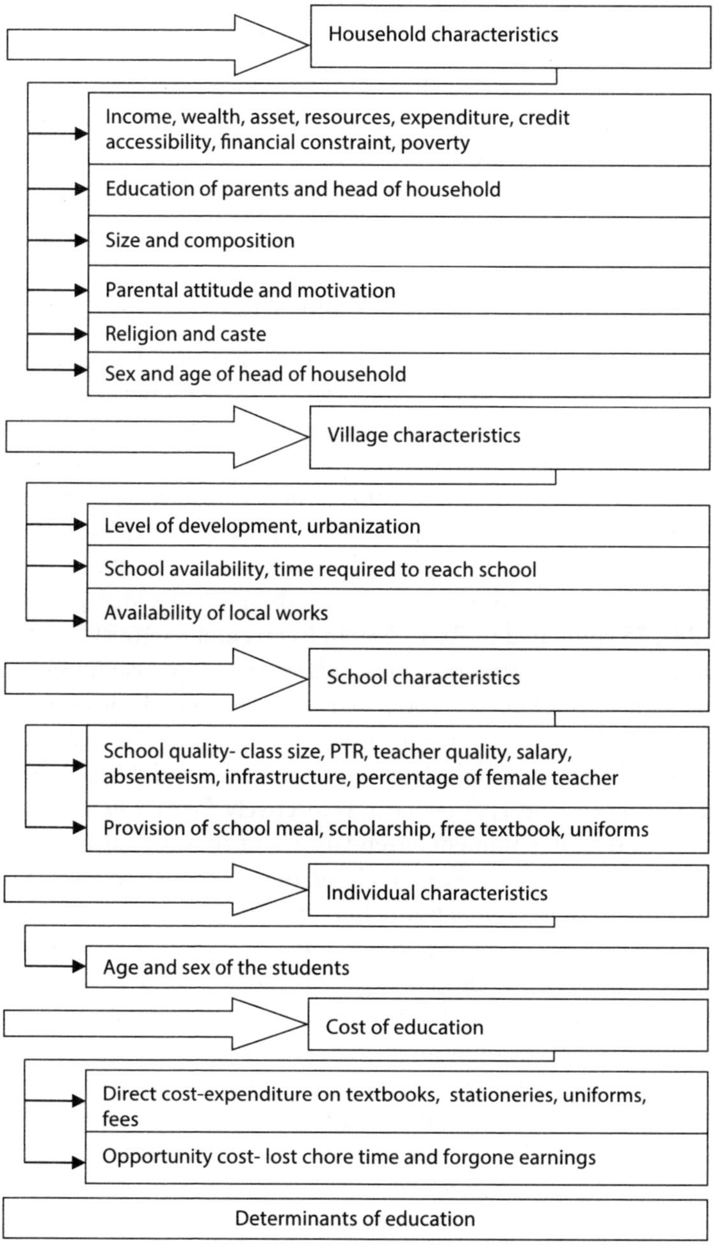

Figure 9.1 Factors determining educational outcomes
Source: Dhar (2013).

the most prominent ones are income level, poverty, school infrastructure, private and public cost of education, and so on. Odisha, in general and its laggard districts in particular, are feared to have failed in almost all such parameters in some form or the other. Due to paucity of relevant data, the authors try to present the scenario with respect to select parameters, which may help one infer possible implications.

Status of Odisha vis-à-vis other major states

To begin with, one might consider household incomes. High parental and family income is proved to exert positive influence on educational attainment (Blanden and Gregg 2004). There is also evidence that increase in household income leads to greater investments in the schooling of girls (Glick and Sahn 2000). Considering income per capita as a proxy, interestingly, Odisha's per capita income is found to be one of the lowest among 15 major states. In 2009–10, the per capita net state domestic product (NSDP) of Odisha stood at Rs 24,275 compared to Rs 43,539 in Kerala and Rs 46,511 in Tamil Nadu. There are seven other major states, whose per capita incomes were higher (GoO 2012). The state is also confronted with very high incidence of poverty. In 2009–10, about 37 per cent of Odisha's population was below poverty line, while in Kerala and Tamil Nadu, it was 12 per cent and 17.1 per cent, respectively. Poverty exerts adverse effects on school enrolment, attendance, and educational attainment (Jayachandran 2002). It keeps children out of school and forces them to join the class of child labour (Blunch 2006, Shafiq 2007). A pilot time-use survey conducted in six states including Odisha reveals that boys and girls spend about 21.46 hours a week on System of National Accounts (SNA) activities, which is about 47 per cent of the time spent by an adult on the same. Girls (in the age group 6–14) in these states participate in extended SNA activities much more than participating men of all ages (Burra 2007). According to 2001 Census, the child labour in Odisha was about 3 per cent as against only 0.2 per cent in Kerala (Census of India 2001).

While the aforementioned factors carry significance for the apparent reason that demand for education may depend upon household's capabilities, the issues from the perspectives of access, equity, and quality, which largely depend on the efforts of the government, are equally and at times, more significant. It may be noted here that the present study, while attempting to measure the quality aspect of education, primarily considers certain important input indicators—PTR, SCR, trained teachers, availability of toilets, water and electricity in schools, and so on. In essence, it focuses on the school and teacher quality rather than the academic achievements of the children in terms of their learning abilities. Due to paucity of requisite data, the latter aspect cannot be captured, which remains a limitation of the study.

In the present context, one may consider the classifications made by NUEPA under educational development index (EDI). As NUEPA suggests, three important indicators crucial for educational achievements are access, infrastructure, and teachers. To illustrate further, access to schools, availability of basic school infrastructure like drinking water, toilets, and electricity, and availability of adequate teachers with requisite qualification and experience are critical factors. Odisha seems to have failed or lagged behind in ranks in all the three indicators. In 2010–11, Odisha ranked 20th in access index and 24th in infrastructure and teacher index (NUEPA 2012).

A further probe into the individual dimensions may provide interesting implications. To be specific, according to prescribed norms, the threshold limits for pupil-teacher ratio (PTR) at primary and middle level are 30 and 35, respectively. Paradoxically, about 46.46 per cent of primary schools and 47.61 per cent of middle schools of Odisha have PTR greater than 30 and 35, respectively. These values are much greater than that in Kerala (16.22 per cent) and Andhra Pradesh (10.46 per cent), respectively. Average number of teachers per school in Odisha stands at 3.2, while it is 11 in Kerala (Table 9.18).

What is far more upsetting is the share of contractual teachers (Shiksha Sahayaks) to total teachers in the state at the elementary level. In 2009–10, about 37.27 per cent of the total teachers were on contract, who are feared to have been poorly trained and less experienced (Table 9.18). In Odisha, while most of the regular teachers are professionally trained, little less than half of the contractual teachers are not trained. It may be noted here that the concept of contractual teachers was initially proposed as an aid to the regular

Table 9.18 Status of Odisha according to education indicators among 15 major states, 2009–10

Education indicators		Odisha	Better performing state	Education indicators		Odisha	Better performing state
Density of schools per 10 km^2	Primary schools/ sections	3.32	8.64 (West Bengal)	Pupil-teacher ratio	Primary	32	24 (Kerala)
	upper primary schools/ sections	1.38	2.63 (Uttar Pradesh)		Upper primary	37	18 (Andhra Pradesh)
Average SCR in all schools		30	23 (Punjab)	% of primary schools with PTR > 30		46.46	16.22 (Kerala)
% schools with SCR > 30 primary level		35.74	23.78 (Karnataka)	% of upper primary schools with PTR > 35		47.61	10.46 (Andhra Pradesh)
% schools with SCR > 35 upper primary level		41.72	14.58 (Punjab)	% schools having electricity connection in all schools		15.75	94.8 (Gujarat)
% single-teacher schools		12.27	0.63 (Kerala)	Average number of teachers per school in all schools		3.2	11 (Kerala)
% enrolment in single-teacher schools in all schools		5.63	0.26 (Kerala)	% distribution of professionally trained regular teachers in all schools		89.07	100 (Punjab)

(*Cont'd.*)

Table 9.18 *(Cont'd.)*

% schools having pupil-teacher ratio > 60 in all schools	7.57	1.55 (Kerala)	% distribution of professionally trained contractual teachers	56.21	100 (Punjab)
% schools with female teachers with teachers greater than equal to 2	66.74	99.45 (Kerala)	% distribution of contractual teachers to total teachers	37.27	0.36 (Madhya Pradesh)
% schools having common toilet in all schools	80.79	88.15 (Karnataka)	% schools having drinking water facility in all schools	89.07	99.87 (Tamil Nadu)
% schools having girls' toilet in all schools	37.85	98.59 (Punjab)	education and training budget as % of GSDP	3.49	4.9 (Assam)
State-budgeted expenditure on education on plan and non-plan account as a % of total plan and non-plan expenditure (2008–09)	17.08	21.23 (Rajasthan)			

Source: NUEPA (2011).

teachers in single teacher schools. It was a strategy under SSA to ensure rapid universal access to school. Contrarily, the current trend of the state is to hire part-time or contractual teachers in place of regular teachers. This clearly signifies de-professionalization of the teaching profession and compromise in quality. It is understood that it is a cost-cutting exercise on the part of the state in the face of resource constraints. It is, however, hard to justify appointment of poorly trained teachers at modest salaries to overcome fiscal crisis if one is serious about universalizing elementary education (Shiva Kumar and Rustagi 2010).

A similar scenario is observed with respect to student-class room ratio (SCR). At the primary level, while the percentage of schools with SCR greater than 30 for Karnataka stands at 23.78, in Odisha it is 35.74. At upper primary level, about 41.72 per cent Odisha's schools have SCR greater than 35. Staggering 12.27 per cent of its elementary schools are provided with single teachers. In the face of continued shortage of teachers, multi-grade teaching at the elementary level is reported to be common, which might exert adverse consequences in terms of attentions children receive. As 'PROBE revisited' ascertains, multi-grade teaching implies at least one grade being ignored (De et al. 2011). Availability of female teachers is also very low in Odisha (66.74 per cent) in comparison with Kerala (99.45 per cent). Shortage of female teachers might be acting as a significant deterrent to girls' enrolment and attendance especially in middle schools (Kumar and Rustagi 2010).

Distance to school is yet another critical dimension. In Odisha, interestingly, average density of primary schools per 10 km^2 is 3.32 compared to West Bengal's density of 8.64 (Table 9.18). While a fall in attendance among all is imminent with increase in distance, in comparison to boys, the probability of girls dropping out is likely to be higher. While there is no denying that proximity to primary schools in the state has risen quite considerably, it remains a concern at middle and secondary levels. Parents' reluctance to send their girls to middle and higher schools due to distance factors eventually becomes a potent reason for the girls dropping out (De et al. 2011). In drinking water, Odisha may be found to be catching up. However, the state fails miserably in provision of separate girls' toilets as a meager 37.85 per cent of elementary schools have such provisions. In

Punjab, as much as 99 per cent of schools have girls' toilets. Absence of a functioning toilet for girls in middle schools and above is a serious discouraging factor for the girls to attend schools (Kumar and Rustagi 2010). A meager 15.75 per cent of the primary and upper primary schools of Odisha have access to electricity, while in Gujarat, it is around 95 per cent (Table 9.18).

In the face of continued failure, partly it may be inadequate expenditure to receive the blame as well. The state's budgeted expenditure on education on plan and non-plan account as a percentage of total plan and non-plan expenditure was a meager 17.08 per cent in 2008–09 compared to 20.28 per cent in Maharashtra and 20.4 per cent in Bihar. In 2010–11, in Odisha, education and training budget as a percentage of its gross state domestic product was mere 3.49 per cent as against 4.90 per cent in Assam and 4.07 per cent in Bihar (Table 9.18). The state must prioritize its spending if it is serious to achieve desired goals on the education front. At the same time, the centre-state transfer mechanisms need to be revisited as a poorer state like Odisha is likely to have a low expenditure on education.

Interestingly, the laggard districts of the state fail to achieve the desired outcomes in almost all the above parameters (tables 9.19 and 9.20). It is observed that at upper primary level, PTR is the least in Malkangiri (15.95) followed by Kandhamal (17.05), Deogarh (17.50), Rayagada (17.51), and Gajapati (17.85). Though at the primary level, PTR of Malkangiri and Koraput is better, very low PTR at the upper primary level may be a possible factor deterring enrolment at and transition to that level. The SCR of the laggard districts is no better.

While trained teachers are in short supply across the state, the situation is far worse in most of the laggard districts. The availability of female teachers in Nuapada, Malkangiri, Kalahandi, Gajapati, and Rayagada falls below 27 per cent as against 64 per cent in Jagatsinghpur and 61 per cent in Khurda. A staggering 44.46 per cent of primary schools in Nabarangpur, 40.87 per cent in Malkangiri, and 38.51 per cent in Keonjhar have SCR greater than 30. At least 13 per cent of the schools in Rayagada, Gajapati, Kandhamal, and Boudh have single classrooms. About three-quarter of schools in Malkangiri, Nuapada, Sundargarh, and Kandhamal

Table 9.19 Status of the districts of Odisha in teacher characteristics

Educational outcomes		Top 5 districts	Bottom 5 districts
PTR	Primary level 2011–12	Nabarangpur (42.05)	Deogarh (20.22)
		Malkangiri (40.59)	Jagatsinghpur (20.66)
		Keonjhar (37.27)	Dhenkanal (22.86)
		Balasore (36.63)	Jharsuguda (22.99)
		Koraput (33.08)	Sambalpur (24.21)
	Upper primary level 2011–12	Ganjam (36.72)	Malkangiri (15.95)
		Kalahandi (36.42)	Kandhamal (17.05)
		Bolangir (30.97)	Deogarh (17.50)
		Khurda (29.99)	Rayagada (17.51)
		Boudh (29.92)	Gajapati (17.85)
	Elementary level 2011–12	Nabarangpur (36.14)	Deogarh (19.33)
		Ganjam (32.97)	Jagatsinghpur (20.22)
		Malkangiri (32.74)	Jharsuguda (21.81)
		Keonjhar (32.74)	Kandhamal (22.18)
		Kalahandi (32.26)	Sundargarh (23.02)
% of schools having adverse SCR (govt. schools): 2011–12	% of primary schools having SCR>30	Nabarangpur (44.46)	Jharsuguda (10.12)
		Malkangiri (40.87)	Sambalpur (10.79)
		Keonjhar (38.51)	Jagatsinghpur (12.99)
		Bolangir (37.32)	Bargarh (14.33)
		Balasore (36.73)	Kandhamal (14.82)
	% of upper primary schools having SCR>35	Ganjam (66.33)	Deogarh (15.79)
		Bolangir (52.27)	Jharsuguda (15.81)
		Boudh (46.37)	Jagatsinghpur (21.08)
		Jajpur (45.98)	Sambalpur (22.16)
		Nabarangpur (44.39)	Sundargarh (23.54)
Single-classroom schools	% of single-classroom school of govt. (S & ME + SC/ST dev.) school	Rayagada (13.07)	Bhadrak (0.91)
		Gajapati (12.95)	Nuapada (1.81)
		Kandhamal (12.54)	Sundargarh (2.03)
		Boudh (12.52)	Jharsuguda (2.04)
		Bolangir (11.89)	Jagatsinghpur (2.07)

(Cont'd.)

Table 9.19 *(Cont'd.)*

Educational outcomes		Top 5 districts	Bottom 5 districts
% of trained teachers (govt. and aided)	Elementary level 2011–12	Khurda (90.12)	Nabarangpur (62.22)
		Cuttack (84.42)	Kalahandi (64.66)
		Jagatsinghpur (87.34)	Nuapada (64.91)
		Puri (86.96)	Gajapati (65.80)
% of govt. female teachers	Primary level 2011–12	Keonjhar (86.40)	Deogarh (69.19)
		Jagatsinghpur (65.71)	Gajapati (21.92)
		Khurda (60.36)	Malkangiri (22.01)
		Dhenkanal (54.96)	Nuapada (22.06)
		Puri (52.70)	Kalahandi (22.49)
		Cuttack (51.36)	Rayagada (23.95)
	Upper primary level 2011–12	Jagatsinghpur (62.51)	Nuapada (27.05)
		Khurda (62.40)	Sonepur (28.40)
		Sundargarh (53.77)	Nabarangpur (28.59)
		Cuttack (53.49)	Boudh (29.25)
		Puri (51.03)	Kalahandi (29.33)
	Elementary level 2011–12	Jagatsinghpur (64.19)	Nuapada (24.76)
		Khurda (61.38)	Malkangiri (25.37)
		Cuttack (52.42)	Kalahandi (25.37)
		Sundargarh (52.26)	Gajapati (26.84)
		Dhenkanal (52.24)	Rayagada (27.03)

Source: OPEPA (2011).

have no girls' toilets and over 90 per cent of schools in Nabarangpur, Kandhamal, Kalahandi, Koraput, and Nuapada have no access to electricity. More than 20 per cent of schools in Malkangiri and Rayagada have no drinking water facilities.

In income per capita, no specific pattern seems to be imminent for the districts. This is possibly because many of the educationally backward districts have of late witnessed trends of industrialization. Conversely, many educationally advanced districts remain poorly industrialized. Districts like Keonjhar, Sundargarh, and Jharsuguda are on the path of industrialization, while Balasore, Bhadrak, and Puri lag behind in this respect. Industrial operation inter alia possibly

Table 9.20 Status of the districts of Odisha in facilities at elementary level in government schools (%)

Educational outcomes		Top 5 districts	Bottom 5 districts
Facilities at elementary level in govt. schools (Dept. of full form S & ME + SC/ST dev. dept.) (2011–12)	Schools without girls toilet	Malkangiri (88.88) Nuapada (81.51) Puri (80.05) Sundargarh (76.23) Kandhamal (75.35)	Khurda (21.94) Boudh (32.34) Angul (39.63) Nayagarh (51.08) Bargarh (51.58)
	Schools without drinking water facility	Rayagada (20.46) Malkangiri (20.39) Puri (15.49) Deogarh (15.40) Kandhamal (10.82)	Sundargarh (0) Bolangir (0) Gajapati (0) Jajpur (0) Ganjam (0)
	Schools without electricity	Nabarangpur (91.75) Kandhamal (91.60) Kalahandi (91.53) Koraput (90.69) Nuapada (90.45)	Balasore (69.85) Ganjam (73.13) Khurda (74.31) Bhadrak (75.06) Jharsuguda (75.47)
	School having no building	Malkangiri (5.17) Puri (3.66) Ganjam (2.72) Khurda (2.43) Nabarangpur (2.28)	Ten districts (Kandhamal, Jharsuguda, Koraput, Bhadrak, Sambalpur, Nuapada, Jagatsinghpur, Keonjhar, Angul, and Gajapati)

Source: OPEPA (2011).

has pushed the per capita income upward in the former districts. In per capita income, educationally laggard districts like Nabarangpur and Malkangiri are still found to be in the list of bottom five. It may, however, be mentioned here that improvement in income does not necessarily mean reduction in the incidence of poverty. This is evident from the fact that the incidence of poverty is the highest among the SC and ST households and they primarily inhabit southern and northern region (GoO 2004). Most of the educationally backward districts belong to these regions.

Amidst glaring failure, decentralization of management is often advanced as a solution. While there is no denying that decentralized management carries profound significance, in practice, its benefits are restricted to financial and administrative decision-making but it is not so effective in improving the quality of education. Decentralization is often found to create excessive bureaucracy and it increases incidents of corruption and elite capture of public resources (Kumar and Rustagi 2010). Village education committees and parent-teacher associations are found to be largely nonfunctional. In a highly unequal power structure of Odishan villages, active and informed community participation requires much more than token committee formations only (De et al. 2011).

The way ahead

It may, thus, be imperative to say that the state, and more so its educationally laggard districts, may perhaps need renewed attention in several aspects. The immediate necessity could be maintaining an ideal PTR and SCR. Mere improvement in PTR may not suffice as the appointment of teachers in the state is mostly contractual, who have no or inadequate experience. It is perhaps necessary to revisit the policy in this regard. Non-availability of classrooms and teachers in schools is a pointer towards compromise in quality of interaction between students and teachers, hence defeating the very purpose of teaching-learning process especially at the elementary level. There is no denying that SSA has brought in enormous changes in the quality and quantity of infrastructure in schools. However, much needs to be done to improve the conditions, especially in the laggard districts. Attainment of mere literacy is not the only requirement. The state has to go a long way in achieving noteworthy progress in enrolment, attendance, retention rates, transition rates, and dropout rates across all including girls, SC, and ST. In the face of continued disparities across gender, caste, and region, more targeted intervention may be required. Greater official commitment supported by active civic cooperation and state initiatives may be useful towards bringing a turnaround in education in the state.

References

Blanden, J. and P. Gregg. 2004. 'Family Income and Educational Attainment: A Review of Approaches and Evidence for Britain', CMPO Working Paper No. 101(04), Centre for Market and Public Organisation, London, April.

Blunch, N.H. 2006. 'Children's Work and School Attendance in Ghana', in Emily Hannum and Bruce Fuller (eds.), *Children's Lives and Schooling across Societies*, Book Series: Research in the Sociology of Education, Vol. 15, pp. 177–205. Bingley, City of Brad Ford: Emerald Group Publishing Limited.

Burra, N. 2007. *Born Unfree: Child Labour, Education and the State in India*. New Delhi: Oxford University Press.

Census of India. 2001. *Primary Census Abstract.* New Delhi: Office of the Registrar General of India.

Census of India. 2011. *Provisional Population Totals Paper 1 of 2011, State of Literacy, Chapter–6*. New Delhi: Office of the Registrar General of India. Available at http://censusindia.gov.in/2011-prov-results/data_files/india/Final_PPT_2011_chapter6.pdf (last accessed on 22 January 2016).

Datt, G. and M. Ravallion. 1996. Why Some Indian States Have Done Better Than Others at Raising Rural Living Standards. Washington, DC: Policy Research Department, The World Bank.

De, A., R. Khera, M. Samson, and A.K. Shiva Kumar. 2011. *PROBE Revisited: A Report on Elementary Education in India*. New Delhi: Oxford University Press.

Dhar, S. 2013. 'Trends and Determinants of Transition Rate of Education in India', unpublished PhD thesis, Indian Institute of Technology, Kharagpur.

Dhar, S., N.C. Nayak, and B. Chatterjee. 2010. 'An Analysis of Hierarchical Distribution of Education in India', *Journal of the Institute of Political Economy*, 22(1–4): 93–126.

Drèze, J. and A. Sen. 2002. *India Development and Participation*. New Delhi: Oxford University Press.

Glick, P. and D.E. Sahn. 2000. 'Schooling of Girls and Boys in a West African Country: The Effects of Parental Education, Income and Household Structure', *Economics of Education Review*, 19(1): 63–87.

Government of India. 2009. 'The Right of Children to Free and Compulsory Education Act, 2009', *Gazette of India*, Act No. 35, 26 August.

Government of Odisha. 2004. *Odisha Human Development Report 2004*. Bhubaneswar, Odisha: Planning and Coordination Department.

———. 2008. *Statistical Abstract of Orissa 2008*. Bhubaneswar: Directorate of Economics and Statistics, Planning and Coordination Department.

GoO. 2011. *Education in Odisha 2010–11*. Bhubaneswar: Directorate of Elementary Education (Statistics Cell).

———. 2012. *Economic Survey 2011–12*. Bhubaneswar: Planning and Coordination Department.

Jayachandran, U. 2002. 'Socio-Economic Determinants of School Attendance in India', Working Paper No. 103, Centre for Development Economics, Delhi School of Economics, New Delhi, June.

Kumar, A., K. Shiva, and P. Rustagi. 2010. 'Elementary Education in India: Progress, Setbacks and Challenges', Oxfam India Working Papers Series, Oxfam India, New Delhi, September.

Le Vine, R.A., S.E. Le Vine, M.L. Rowe, and B. Schnell-Anzola. 2004. 'Maternal Literacy and Health Behaviour: A Nepalese Case Study', *Social Science & Medicine*, 58(4, February): 863–77.

NSSO. 2010. 'Education in India: 2007–08, Participation and Expenditure', NSS 64th round (July 2007–June 2008), Report No. 532, Ministry of Statistics and Programme Implementation, Government of India, May.

NUEPA (National University of Educational Planning and Administration). 2007, 2008, 2011, 2012, 2013. *State Report Cards: Elementary Education in India*. New Delhi. Available on http://www.dise.in/src.htm (accessed on 22 January 2016).

———. 2012. 'Elementary Education in India: Progress towards UEE', Flash Statistics of DISE 2010–11, NUEPA and Department of School Education and Literacy, Government of India, New Delhi.

OPEPA (Odisha Primary Education Programme Authority). 2010, 2011. 'Status of Elementary Education in Odisha', District Information System for Education, Government of Odisha, Bhubaneswar.

Planning and Coordination Department, GoO. 2012. *Economic Survey 2011–12*. Bhubaneswar, Odisha: Planning and Coordination Department.

Shafiq, M.N. 2007. 'Household Schooling and Child Labor Decisions in Rural Bangladesh', *Journal of Asian Economics*, 18(6): 946–66.

United Nations (UN). 2007. *Millennium Declaration*. New York: UN.

United Nations Development Programme. 1990. *Human Development Report*. New York: Oxford University Press.

United Nations Educational Scientific and Cultural Organization (UNESCO). 2005. 'Education for All Global Monitoring Report 2006—Literacy for Life'. Paris: UNESCO Publishing; New York: United Nations, Millennium Declaration, United Nations.

United Nations Educational Scientific and Cultural Organization. 2009. *Education Indicators Technical Guidelines*. Institute for Statistics, November. Available at http://www.uis.unesco.org/Library/Documents/eiguide09-en.pdf (last accessed on 22 January 2016).

10

Health and Healthcare in Odisha

Himanshu Sekhar Rout and *Abhash Kumar Hota*

Health is a state of complete physical, mental, and social well-being and not merely the absence of disease or infirmity (World Health Organization [WHO] 1946). It is an output produced from a set of inputs like genetic factors, diet, water, sound sleep, immunization, income, education, housing, working conditions, environment, livelihood strategies, and healthcare facilities. Healthcare or health services are a subset of the set of inputs. Good health is an asset that enables people to participate in work and socio-economic development. Ill health causes misery and impoverishment. Improved health contributes to economic growth in four ways: (a) it reduces production losses caused by worker illness; (b) it permits the use of natural resources that had been totally or nearly inaccessible because of disease; (c) it increases the enrollment of children in school and makes them better able to learn; and (d) it frees from alternative uses of resources that would otherwise have to be spent on treatment of illness. The economic gains are relatively greater for poor people who are typically handicapped by ill health (World Bank 1993).

The present health status of India and Odisha

India has achieved many positive health outcomes during the last 65 years. Government of India's (GoI's) initiatives in the public health sector has recorded some noteworthy successes over time.[1] These achievements are very impressive and we have every reason to be proud of them, but it is also realized that our failures are even more glaring. In a spirit of optimistic empathy for the health needs of the people, particularly of the poor and underprivileged, the GoI had hoped to provide health for all by the year 2000 AD, through the universal provision of comprehensive primary healthcare services. In retrospect, it is observed that the financial resources, public health administrative capacity, and health infrastructure that were possible to marshal, were far short to achieve such an ambitious and holistic goal (Rout and Panda 2007).

In Odisha, the disease burden is high. Communicable diseases like malaria, tuberculosis, leprosy, diarrhoea and dysentery, worm infection, and typhoid; pregnancy-related problems like anaemia; and childhood ailments are the major diseases of the state. About 45 per cent of children under age five are stunted or too short for their age, which indicates that they have been undernourished for some time. About 20 per cent are wasted, or too thin for their height, which may result from inadequate recent food intake or a recent illness. About 41 per cent are underweight, which takes into account both chronic and acute undernutrition (IIPS and Macro International 2008). The publicly provided health service outlets

[1] Smallpox and guinea worm disease have been eradicated from the country; polio is on the verge of being eradicated; Leprosy, Kala Azar, and Filariasis can be expected to be eliminated in the foreseeable future. There has been a substantial drop in the Total Fertility Rate (TFR) and Infant Mortality Rate (IMR). The successes of the initiatives taken in the public health field are reflected in the progressive improvement of many demographic/epidemiological/infrastructural indicators over time. Life expectancy has gone up from 36.7 years in 1951 to 67.14 in 2011 (CIA 2012). Infant mortality rate is down from 146 in 1951 to 46.7 in 2012 (CIA 2012). Crude birth rate has been reduced from 40.8 in 1951 to 20.6 in 2012 and crude death rate from 25.1 to 7.43 in the same period (CIA 2012).

are available, more or less, in accordance with the all-India norms, but factors such as low population density (269 persons living in per km^2), geographic inaccessibility, cultural barriers, ignorance, poor service quality, and the deep-rooted influence of traditional healers make the overall outcome of service systems unsatisfactory. Frequent droughts, floods, and other natural calamities not only impoverish the people, but also make them morbidly stoic towards the pace of development. Despite some attempts by successive political leadership, fairness in resource distribution has evaded the disadvantaged groups. The inability of these groups to demand their own rights has impeded the improvement of the situation (Gupta 2002). Table 10.1 illustrates that Odisha is not far behind India in demographic and health indicators but definitely far behind in economic parameters.

Interstate comparison of life expectancy

Life expectancy in India has more than doubled in the last 60 years. It has increased from around 30 years at the time of Independence to over 63.5 years in 2002–06 (GoI 2010a). This is due to the decrease in death rate and improvement in the quality of health services. However, there are wide variances in performance across states (Table 10.2) due to low literacy, differential income levels, and socio-economic conditions and beliefs. While in Kerala, a person at the time of birth is expected to live for 74 years, the expectancy of life at birth in states like Assam, Bihar, Madhya Pradesh, Odisha, Rajasthan, and Uttar Pradesh is in the range of 58–62 years, a level Kerala achieved during the period 1970–75. India's life expectancy is lower than the global average of 67.5 years (GoI 2010a).

During 2006–10, except Bihar, in all other states the life expectancy at birth of female was more than male (highest difference in Kerala, that is, 4.8 years). The life expectancy at birth in five states—Andhra Pradesh, Assam, Madhya Pradesh, Odisha, and Uttar Pradesh—were below the national figure. The male and female life expectancies vary by nearly 11 years and 14 years, respectively, among Indian states during 2006–10. The longevity of the people of Odisha (both sexes) continued to increase in the last decade. A women in Odisha lived 2.5 years more than her

Table 10.1 Demographic, economic, and health profile of Odisha as compared to figures for the rest of India

S. no.	Indicator	India	Odisha	Source
01	Total population, 2011	1,21,01,93,422	4,19,47,358	
02	Decadal growth rate of population (%)	17.64	13.97	
03	Sex ratio, 2011	940	978	GoI 2011a
04	Population density, 2011	382	269	
05	Literacy rate, 2011 (%)	74.04	73.45	
06	Life expectancy at birth (female), 2011–15*	69.6	67.3	NCP 2006
07	Life expectancy at birth (male), 2011–15*	67.3	64.3	
08	Crude birth rate (CBR), 2010	22.1	20.5	
09	General fertility rate (GFR), 2010	83.9	75.3	
10	Total fertility rate (TFR), 2010	2.5	2.3	
11	Gross reproduction rate (GRR), 2010	1.2	1.1	
12	Total marital fertility rate (TMFR), 2010	4.4	4.4	
13	CDR, 2010	7.2	8.6	GoI 2012a
14	IMR, 2010	47	61	
15	Neonatal mortality rate (NMR), 2010	33	42	
16	Early NMR, 2010	25	33	
17	Perinatal mortality rate (PMR), 2010	32	41	
18	Under-five mortality rate (U5MR), 2010	59	78	
19	Maternal Mortality Ratio (MMR), 2007–09	212	258	GoI 2011b
20	People below poverty line (BPL)** (%)	16.18	29.69	GoO 2012a
21	PCNSDP at current prices, 2010–11 (Rs)	54,835	36,923	GoI 2012b
22	Per capita health expenditure (Rs)	1,201	902	GoI 2009

Note: *Projected levels of expectation of life at birth (without AIDS) for India and states (excluding Goa): 2001–25.

**Based on MRP consumption for 2009–10, tentative poverty estimates.

PCNSDP: Per capita net state domestic product

Table 10.2 Interstate comparison of life expectancy, 2002–15

State	2002–06		2006–10		2010–15*	
	Male	Female	Male	Female	Male	Female
Andhra Pradesh	62.9	65.5	65.4	69.4	66.9	70.9
Assam	58.6	59.3	61.6	62.8	63.6	64.8
Bihar	62.2	60.4	67.1	66.7	68.6	68.7
Gujarat	62.9	65.2	67.2	71.0	69.2	72.5
Haryana	65.9	66.3	67.9	69.8	68.9	71.3
Karnataka	63.6	67.1	66.5	71.1	68.0	72.3
Kerala	71.4	76.3	72.0	76.8	73.2	77.6
Madhya Pradesh	58.1	57.9	62.5	63.3	64.5	65.3
Maharashtra	66.0	68.4	67.9	71.3	68.9	72.5
Odisha	*59.5*	*59.6*	*62.3*	*64.8*	*64.3*	*67.3*
Punjab	68.4	70.4	68.7	71.6	69.7	72.8
Rajasthan	61.5	62.3	66.1	69.2	67.6	70.7
Tamil Nadu	65.0	67.4	67.6	70.6	68.6	71.8
Uttar Pradesh	60.3	59.5	64.0	64.4	66.0	66.9
West Bengal	64.1	65.8	68.2	70.9	69.2	72.1
India	*62.6*	*64.2*	*65.8*	*68.1*	*67.3*	*69.6*

Source: GoO (2012a).
Note: *projected figures

male counterpart during 2006–10 and the gap is increasing. While a woman lived for 64.8 years, the life expectancy of an Indian man stood at 62.3 years. Table 10.2 illustrates the inter-state life expectancy as measured by SRS and National Commission on Population appointed by the Registrar General of Ministry of Home Affairs, GoI.

Fertility indicators

This section explains the fertility indicators like CBR, GFR, TFR, GRR, and TMFR for Odisha vis-à-vis India. The CBR is defined as the number of live births occurring in a year per 1,000 populations, estimated at midyear. The CBR for India is higher than Odisha in 2010 as depicted in Table 10.1. Among the major states,[2] Kerala and Uttar Pradesh recorded the lowest and highest CBR in 2010, respectively, that is, 14.8 and 28.3. The CBR for urban and rural Odisha has been estimated at 15.2 and 21.4, respectively, against the corresponding national averages of 18.0 and 23.7 (GoI 2012a).

The GFR is defined as the number of live births per thousand women in the reproductive age-group 15–49 years. In 2010, it was 83.9 and 75.3 for India and Odisha, respectively (Table 10.1). At the national level, this number varied from 64 in urban areas to 91.9 in rural areas, and the corresponding figures in Odisha are 52.3 and 79.3.

The TFR is defined as the average number of children expected to be born per woman during her entire span of reproductive period assuming that the age-specific fertility rates (ASFR) to which she is exposed to continue to be the same and that there is no mortality. The TFR for India and Odisha in the year 2010 was 2.5 and 2.3, respectively. It varied from 2.8 in rural areas to 1.9 in urban areas in India; in Odisha, it varied from 2.4 in rural areas to 1.6 in urban areas. Among the major states, it varied from 1.7 in Tamil Nadu to 3.7 in Bihar (GoI 2012a).

The GRR is defined as the average number of female children a woman is expected to give birth during her entire reproductive span conforming to the ASFRs for a given year, if there is no mortality. The estimated value of GRR for India in the year 2010 was 1.2 and varied from 0.9 in urban areas to 1.3 in rural areas. In Odisha, it was 1.1 in the same period and varied from 0.8 in urban areas to 1.1 in rural areas (GoI 2012a). In all the major states the value of rural area's GRR exceeded its corresponding urban area's GRR except Tamil Nadu and Punjab where the rural and urban GRR were same in 2010.

The TMFR is defined as the average number of children expected to be born per married woman during the entire span of her reproductive period, if the age specific married fertility rates continue to be the same and if there is no mortality. The TMFR for India was

[2] Here major states include Andhra Pradesh, Assam, Bihar, Chhattisgarh, Delhi, Gujarat, Haryana, Himachal Pradesh, Jammu and Kashmir, Jharkhand, Karnataka, Kerala, Madhya Pradesh, Maharashtra, Odisha, Punjab, Rajasthan, Tamil Nadu, Uttar Pradesh, and West Bengal.

the same as Odisha in the year 2010. It is found to be 4.4 and varies from 3.8 in urban areas to 4.5 in rural areas. The TMFR is 5 and above in the states of Assam, Bihar, Jharkhand, and Uttar Pradesh (GoI 2012a).

Mortality indicators

The mortality indicators are CDR, PMR, NMR, early NMR, IMR, U5MR, and MMR. For the present analysis, all the mortality figures are brought from SRS published by Registrar General, GoI (2012a). The CDR at national level has declined significantly from 14.9 in 1971 to 7.2 in 2010. The decline has been steeper in rural areas as compared to urban areas. Among the major states, it varied from 4.2 in Delhi to 8.6 in Odisha. The PMR has been estimated to be 32 and 41 for India and Odisha, respectively. At the national level, the PMR ranges from 35 in rural areas to 22 in urban areas and the corresponding figure for Odisha are 42 and 32.

In India, the NMR was 33 and ranged from 19 in urban areas to 36 in rural areas in 2010. In Odisha the NMR was 42, higher than the national level by nine and ranged from 33 in urban areas to 42 in rural areas in 2010. The percentage of neo-natal deaths to total infant deaths in Odisha was 68.9 per cent varied from 68.5 per cent in urban areas to 75.0 per cent in rural areas.

At the national level, the early NMR has been estimated at 25 and ranges from 28 in rural areas to 15 in urban areas in 2010. Among the major states, Kerala (5) and Madhya Pradesh (34) are the two extremes. In Odisha, it is 33 and ranges from 35 in rural areas to 21 in urban areas in the same period. The percentage of early neo-natal deaths to the total infant deaths during the year 2010 at the national level and in Odisha has been 53.9 and 55, respectively.

At the national level, IMR was reported to be 47 and varied from 51 in rural areas to 31 in urban areas in 2010 (Table 10.1). Among the major states, it varied from 13 in Kerala to 62 in Madhya Pradesh. Female infants experienced a higher mortality than male infants in all states. Odisha has made notable achievements in reducing its IMR to 61 in 2010 from 124 in 1991 but it is high as compared to the national average of 58 (Table 10.3). Three factors explain such a high level of IMR in Odisha: (a) poor availability of professional

Table 10.3 Birth rate, death rate, and IMR in India vis-à-vis Odisha as per SRS bulletin

Year	Birth rate		Death rate		IMR	
	Odisha	India	Odisha	India	Odisha	India
1981	33.1	33.9	13.1	12.5	135	110
1991	28.8	29.5	12.8	9.8	124	80
1995	27.8	28.3	10.8	9.0	103	74
2000	24.3	25.8	10.5	8.5	96	68
2001	23.4	25.4	10.2	8.4	90	66
2002	23.2	25.0	09.8	8.1	87	63
2003	23.0	24.8	09.7	8.0	83	60
2004	22.7	24.1	09.6	7.5	77	58
2005	22.3	23.8	09.5	7.6	75	58
2006	21.9	23.5	09.3	7.5	73	57
2007	21.5	23.1	09.2	7.4	71	55
2008	21.4	22.8	09.0	7.4	69	53
2009	21.0	22.5	08.8	7.3	65	50
2010	20.5	22.1	08.6	7.2	61	47

Source: GoO (2012a).

attendants at birth, (b) high percentage of low birth weight babies, and (c) lack of professional pre- and post-natal care (GoO 2012a).

The U5MR in India and Odisha are estimated at 59 and 78, respectively. It varied from 66 in rural areas to 38 in urban areas at the national level. The corresponding U5MR for Odisha were 81 and 46. Among the major states, it varied from 15 in Kerala to 83 in Assam. All the major states have higher U5MR of female than that of male. At the national level, the death rates for persons in the age group 5–14 years, 15–59 years, and 60 and above years were 0.9, 3.6, and 46.2, respectively, in 2010. The corresponding death rates in Odisha were 1.3, 4.2, and 48. In all age groups, the death rates were higher in Odisha than India.

Health infrastructure of Odisha

As per GoI norm, there should be one sub-centre for every 5,000 people (3,000 in hilly areas), one primary health centre for every

30,000 people (20,000 in hilly areas), and one community health centre for every 120,000 people (80,000 in hilly areas). In this connection, Table 10.4 shows that Odisha is far better with respect to the availability of community health centres (CHCs), health worker (female)/auxiliary nurse midwives (ANM) at sub-centres and primary health centres (PHCs), and the actual/in-position is more than the required/sanctioned. However, it cannot tell us about whether the facilities are appropriately located and utilized. It is also clear from the same table that Odisha is worst-off in many of its components of health infrastructure.

There are wide differences between what it *needs* or is *required*, and what is *actually in place/in-position*: it has only 42 radiographers compared to the 377 needed, which is a shortfall of 88.86 per cent; 330 laboratory technicians at PHCs and CHCs compared to the 1,605 needed (a shortfall of 79.44 per cent); 1,046 nurses/midwives at PHCs and CHCs compared to the 3,867 needed (a shortfall of 72.95 per cent); 438 specialist doctors at CHCs compared to the 1,508 needed (a shortfall of 70.95 per cent); and 6,688 sub-centres compared to the 8,136 needed (a shortfall of 17.80 per cent). As compared to India, Odisha has better health infrastructure in PHCs; CHCs; health worker (female); health assistant (female)/LHV at PHCs; and surgeons, obstetricians, gynecologists, and pediatricians at CHCs.

The infrastructure and service status of public health facilities in Odisha was much lower than the average picture of health sector development at the national level (Planning Commission of India 2002). In Odisha, healthcare services are mainly provided by the government. Private hospitals are providing only less than 10 per cent of the total hospital-bed strength in the state. This is at variance with the pattern elsewhere in India. Private medical institutions (PMIs) are, largely, located in urban areas and are unevenly distributed among districts. About 64 per cent of private hospitals, with 71 per cent of the total private hospital beds, are located in urban areas. The uneven distribution of private hospitals among districts is evident from the fact that while the public–private hospital ratio is 77:22 in Cuttack district, the same in Kalahandi (in western Odisha is 95:5. The actual ratio may be slightly higher in favor of private facilities across the districts because many single doctor clinics are not officially registered (Gupta 2002).

Table 10.4 Health infrastructure in Odisha vis-à-vis India, as on March 2011

Par. of HI	Odisha							India						
	Required	Sanctioned	In position	Vacant	SF	% of Vacant	% of SF	Required	Sanctioned	In position	Vacant	SF	% of vacant	% of SF
1	2	3	4	5 (3–4)	6 (2–4)	7	8	9	10	11	12 (10–11)	13 (9–11)	14	15
SCs	8,136	8,136	6,688	1,448	1,448	17.80	17.80	1,78,267	1,78,267	1,48,124	30,143	30,143	16.91	16.91
PHCs	1,308	1,308	1,228	80	80	6.12	6.12	29,213	29,213	23,887	5,326	5,326	18.23	18.23
CHCs	327	327	377	*−50*	*−50*	−15.29	−15.29	7,294	7,294	4,809	2,485	2,485	34.07	34.07
HW(F)/ANM at SCs and PHCs	7,916	7,442	7,934	*−492*	*−18*	−6.61	−0.23	1,72,011	1,77,103	2,07,868	*−30,765*	*−35,857*	−17.37	−20.85
HA(F)/LHV at PHCs	1,228	1,162	920	242	308	20.83	25.08	23,887	23,182	15,908	7,274	7,979	31.38	33.40
HA(M) at PHCs	1,228	NA	0	–	1,228	100	100	23,887	22,964	15,622	7,342	8,265	31.97	34.60
Sur. at CHCs	377	307	172	135	205	43.97	54.38	4,809	2,182	1,018	1,164	3,791	53.35	78.83
Obs. & Gyn. at CHCs	377	227	125	102	252	44.93	66.84	4,809	1,958	1,389	569	3,420	29.06	71.12
Phys. at CHCs	377	108	41	67	336	62.04	89.12	4,809	1,437	819	618	3,990	43.01	82.97
Ped. at CHCs	377	170	100	70	277	41.18	73.47	4,809	1,731	1,041	690	3,768	39.86	78.35
GDMOs All. at CHCs	NA	367	316	51	–	13.90	–	NA	12,631	11,798	833	–	6.59	–
Doc. at PHCs	1,228	725	525	200	703	27.59	57.25	23,887	30,051	26,329	3,722	−2,442	12.39	−10.22

(*Cont'd.*)

Table 10.4 (*Cont'd.*)

Par. of HI	Odisha							India						
	Re-quired	Sanc-tioned	In position	Vacant	SF	% of Vacant	% of SF	Re-quired	Sanc-tioned	In position	Vacant	SF	% of vacant	% of SF
1	2	3	4	5 (3–4)	6 (2–4)	7	8	9	10	11	12 (10–11)	13 (9–11)	14	15
Tot. Sp. at CHCs	1,508	812	438	374	1,070	*46.06*	*70.95*	19,236	9,831	6,935	2,896	12,301	29.46	63.95
NS at PHCs & CHCs	3,867	1,230	1,046	184	2,821	*14.96*	*72.95*	57,550	63,325	65,344	*-2,019*	*-7,794*	-3.19	-13.54
Radiog. at CHCs	377	61	42	19	335	*31.15*	*88.86*	4,809	2,806	2,221	585	2,588	20.85	53.82
Phar. at PHCs & CHCs	1,605	1,720	1,265	455	340	26.45	21.18	28,696	24,460	24,671	*-211*	*4,025*	-0.86	14.03
Lab. Tech. at PHCs & CHCs	1,605	476	330	146	1,275	*30.67*	*79.44*	28,696	16,153	16,208	*-55*	12,488	-0.34	43.52

Source: Compiled by the authors from GoI (2012c).

Note: Abbreviations used in this table (row-wise)– Par. of HI: parameters of health infrastructure; SCs: sub-centres; PHCs: primary health centres; CHCs: community health centres; HW(F)/ANM at SCs and PHCs: health worker (female)/auxiliary nurse midwives at SC and PHC; HA(F)/LHV at PHCs: health assistant (female)/lady health visitor at PHCs; HA(M) at PHCs: health assistant (male) at PHCs; Sur. at CHCs: surgeon at CHCs; Obs. & Gyn. at CHCs: obstetricians and gynecologists at CHCs; Phys. at CHCs: physicians at CHCs; Ped. at CHCs: paediatricians at CHCs; GDMOs All. at CHCs: general duty medical officers allopathic at CHCs; Doc. at PHCs: doctors at PHCs; Tot. Sp. at CHCs: total specialists at CHCs; NS at PHCs & CHCs: nursing staff at PHCs and CHCs; Radiog. at CHCs: radiographers at CHCs; Phar. at PHCs & CHCs: pharmacists at PHCs and CHCs; Lab. Tech. at PHCs & CHCs: laboratory technicians at PHCs and CHCs.

Table 10.5 Total medical institutions and hospital beds in Odisha as per SRS 2009–10, 2003–04, and 2011–12

Year	TMI	Total beds	ACHI	HILP	BPR
2003–04	2,884	14,370	10.84	8	38
2004–05	2,884	14,370	10.84	7	37
2005–06	2,887	14,370	10.84	7	37
2006–07	2,884	14,370	10.84	7	36
2007–08	2,886	14,565	10.69	7	36
2008–09	2,887	16,261	9.58	8	44
2009–10	2,887	16,261	9.58	8	44
2010–11	2,943	16,261	9.58	8	44
2011–12	2,940	16,261	9.58	7	40

Source: GoO (2012a, 2012b).
Note: Abbreviations used–TMI: total medical institutions includes allopathic (hospitals, PHCs, and CHC excluding MHUs and sub-centres), homeopathic (hospitals and dispensaries), ayurvedic (hospitals and dispensaries), and unani dispensaries; ACHI: area covered under one health institution (in km^2); HILP: number of health institutions per lakh population; BPR: number of beds available per lakh population.

Table 10.5 illustrates that the number of total medical institutions in the state has increased from 2,884 in 2003–04 to 2,940 in 2011–12. The total number of hospital beds has increased by only 13.16 per cent in the last 10 years. In 2011–12, one health institution covered around 10 km^2. During the last 10 years, on an average, 7 to 8 health institutions and 38–40 hospitals beds have been available for 1 lakh population. It seems that all the health infrastructure indicators mentioned in Table 10.5 have not shown any significant increase in their number.

Table 10.6 illustrates district-wise government and private allopathic medical institutions in Odisha with number of hospital beds as on 31 March 2011. All the medical institutions can be categorized into three: large, medium, and small for a better analysis. Columns 5, 10, and 16 of the table show the large, medium, and small medical institutions, respectively, and the total of these is shown in column 17. Khurdha district has the highest number of large medical institutions (hospitals), that is, 60 and Boudh district has only one hospital. Cuttack district has the highest number of medium category medical institutions (CHCs, PHCs, new PHCs, nursing homes, and maternity homes), that is, 160 whereas Deogarh district has the minimum, that is, 11. Mayurbhanja district has the highest number of small category medical institutions (MHUs, hospital sub-centres, and private clinics), that is, 610 whereas Deogarh district has the minimum, that is, 43. Mayurbhanj district stands first in total medical institutions including health sub-centers followed by Ganjam, Cuttack, Sundergarh, and Keonjhar districts. Though Cuttack district has the third position in medical institutions including health sub-centers, it stands first in a number of available hospital beds because it has the biggest medical college and hospital (MCH) in the state. The worst sufferer districts of Odisha in terms of medical institutions including health sub-centers and indoor beds availability are Deograh, Subarnapur, and Boudh. The population to bed ratio has been 2,677, that is, one bed per 2,677 people in the state.

Odisha required 4,385 doctors as on 28 February 2011, out of which 3,675 doctors were in position. This indicates that around 16.2 per cent of the posts for doctor were lying vacant. However, it is surprising to note that Gajapati and Mayurbhanj districts had more doctors in-position than their requirement. Anugul district suffered the most where around 36 per cent doctors were not in position followed by Rourkela, Malkangiri, Nawarangpur, Jagatsingpur, Jharsuguda, Jajpur, and Boudh where more than one-fourth of the doctor posts were vacant.

Odisha has three government and four private medical colleges only. The total MBBS (Bachelor of Medicine and Bachelor of Surgery) seats are 650, that is, 450 in government and 200 in private medical colleges. Table 10.4 states that in Odisha there are 88.6 and 72.95 per cent shortfall in radiographers and nurses, respectively, but every year only 50 radiographers and 26 BSc nursing personnel are produced/trained in the state. There are only 50 government BDS (Bachelor of Dental Surgery) seats and 340 postgraduate medical seats in the whole state. Most of the MBBS graduates, after completing their education and training in Odisha, go to serve in different parts of India for better avenues and packages. This creates a serious problem in the healthcare system of Odisha.

Table 10.6 District-wise government and private allopathic medical institutions in Odisha with beds, as on 31 March 2011

S. No.	District	Hospitals			CHC	PHC	NH	MH	Total CHC/PHC/NH/MH	MHU			Clinics	SC	Total MHU/clinics/SC	TMI	Beds
		Govt.	Pvt.	Total	Govt.	Govt.	Pvt.	Pvt.		Govt.	Pvt.	Total	Pvt.	Govt.			Govt
1	2	3	4	5 (=3+4)	6	7	8	9	10 (=6+7+8+9)	11	12	13 (=11+12)	14	15	16 (=13+14+15)	17 (=5+10+16)	18
1	Angul	4	3	7	10	31	15	1	57	1	0	1	6	166	173	237	472
2	Balasore	3	5	8	16	68	13	1	98	2	0	2	5	275	282	388	636
3	Baragarh	2	15	17	14	46	12	2	74	5	0	5	4	204	213	304	249
4	Bhadrak	4	3	7	7	50	10	0	67	1	2	3	2	178	183	257	409
5	Bolangir	5	2	7	15	42	5	2	64	15	0	15	6	226	247	318	444
6	Boudh	1	0	1	5	12	1	0	18	2	0	2	0	67	69	88	167
7	Cuttack	13	43	56	18	57	85	0	160	0	2	2	10	332	344	560	1,962
8	Deogarh	2	0	2	4	7	0	0	11	1	0	1	0	42	43	56	118
9	Dhenkanal	7	3	10	10	32	7	0	49	5	2	7	2	167	176	235	385
10	Gajapati	2	1	3	8	20	4	0	32	8	0	8	0	136	144	179	259
11	Ganjam	5	21	26	30	89	32	2	153	0	0	0	6	460	466	645	1,541
12	Jagatsinghpur	1	3	4	9	37	8	0	54	1	0	1	4	189	194	252	268
13	Jajpur	4	7	11	12	56	6	0	74	1	1	2	1	260	263	348	482
14	Jharsuguda	2	3	5	6	15	3	0	24	1	1	2	0	66	68	97	182
15	Kalahandi	4	6	10	16	43	5	0	64	19	3	22	2	242	266	340	525
16	Kandhamal	6	3	9	14	36	5	0	55	17	0	17	0	172	189	253	494
17	Kendrapara	2	3	5	9	45	5	0	59	0	0	0	0	227	227	291	268

(*Cont'd.*)

Table 10.6 (*Cont'd.*)

S. No.	District	Hospitals			CHC	PHC	NH	MH	Total CHC/ PHC/NH/ MH	MHU			Clinics	SC	Total MHU/ clinics/SC	TMI	Beds
		Govt.	Pvt.	Total	Govt.	Govt.	Pvt.	Pvt.		Govt.	Pvt.	Total	Pvt.	Govt.			Govt
1	2	3	4	5 (=3+4)	6	7	8	9	10 (=6+7+ 8+9)	11	12	13 (=11+12)	14	15	16 (=13+14+15)	17 (=5+10+16)	18
18	Keonjhar	8	3	11	17	61	3	0	81	12	1	13	4	351	368	460	533
19	Khurda	21	39	60	13	46	38	4	101	1	0	1	33	202	236	397	965
20	Koraput	2	3	5	16	48	3	0	67	15	0	15	7	307	329	401	354
21	Malkanagir	4	0	4	8	25	0	0	33	10	1	11	1	158	170	207	286
22	Mayurbhanj	8	4	12	28	82	7	0	117	20	0	20	1	589	610	739	852
23	Nabarangpur	2	1	3	11	39	0	0	50	11	0	11	1	289	301	354	236
24	Nayagarh	1	5	6	12	37	5	1	55	1	0	1	3	166	170	231	489
25	Nuapada	4	1	5	6	17	0	0	23	7	1	8	0	95	103	131	180
26	Puri	6	6	12	16	45	16	0	77	1	2	3	3	241	247	336	684
27	Rayagada	4	4	8	11	36	5	0	52	17	0	17	0	235	252	312	293
28	Sambalpur	4	10	14	11	31	17	3	62	4	0	4	4	167	175	251	1,139
29	Subarnapur	3	0	3	6	18	2	0	26	7	0	7	0	89	96	125	161
30	Sundergarh	8	16	24	20	56	8	2	86	14	0	14	9	390	413	523	635
Odisha		142	213	355	378	1,227	320	18	1,943	199	16	215	114	6,688	7,017	9,315	15,668

Source: Compiled by the authors from GoO (2012a).

Note: Abbreviations used in this table–CHC: community health centre; PHC: primary health centre (it also includes new PHCs); MHU: mobile health unit; NH: nursing homes; MH: maternity homes; SC: health sub-centre.

Table 10.7 System load in government hospitals of Odisha

Year	Inpatient to total population	Outpatient to total population	Bed turnover rate*	Bed occupancy rate
2005–06	6.61	64.20	166.9	091.40
2006–07	6.59	64.01	168.6	092.40
2007–08	6.55	55.00	169.8	093.00
2008–09	7.30	58.04	191.5	104.93
2009–10	8.78	60.62	233.39	127.84

Source: GoO (2012a).
Note:* Number of times there is change of occupant for a bed during a year (total inpatient discharged/number of beds).

Utilization of health services in Odisha

Utilization of healthcare is a complex outcome of several factors including providers' behaviour, severity of the disease, cost of the care, payment systems, facilities, and physical accessibility. The general factors guiding choice of healthcare utilization in Odisha are reputation of the healthcare provider, cost of the care, and the ability to physically access care providers (Ager and Pepper 2005).

In 2010, 2,056 lakh outpatients and 48.9 lakh inpatients were treated in government allopathic medical institutions (Figure 10.1). Figure 10.1 illustrates that in 2010, a smaller number of outpatients and inpaitents were treated than in 2009. The decline in the number of reported patients is probably due to a substantial drop in the number of people suffering from minor diseases. This may also be due to increased participation of the private healthcare sector as well as better public awareness about health and hygiene. Table 10.7 illustrates the system load in government hospitals of Odisha. In 2009–10, the inpatients and outpatients were 8.78 per cent and 60.62 per cent of total population of Odisha, respectively. The bed turnover rate and bed occupant rate were 233.39 and 127.84, respectively, in the same period. Additional 138.7 lakh patients were treated in in the alternative system of medical institutions, that is, ayurvedic, homeopathic, and unani.

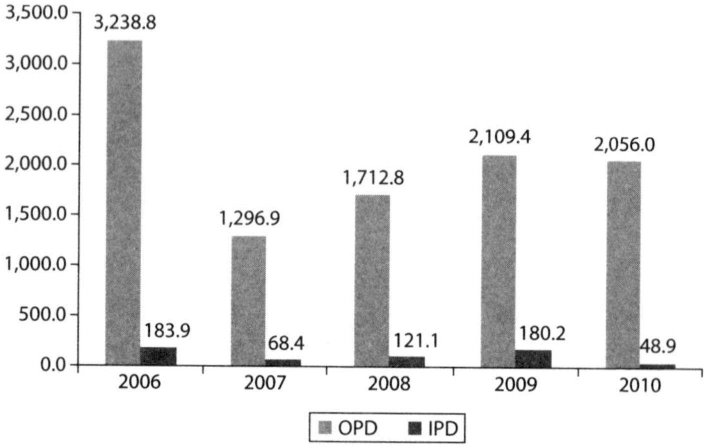

Figure 10.1 Indoor and outdoor patients treated in Odisha, 2006–10 ('000)
Source: GoO (2012).

Around 7.2 lakh polio doses and 7.85 lakh Bacillus Calmette–Guérin BCG doses were administered during 2010–11 in the state. Institutional deliveries have significantly increased from 64.68 per cent in 2008 to 74.67 per cent in 2010 (GoO 2012a). Around 6.81 lakh people used different methods of population control like sterilization, intrauterine device (IUD) insertions, conventional contraceptives, and oral pills. By the end of March 2011, 18 districts have achieved the leprosy elimination goal while in the remaining 12 districts[3] the decrease is significant (GoO 2012a).

Health sector reform in Odisha

Generally, health sector reform (HSR) is defined as a process which brings fundamental changes in health policies and its institutional arrangements, generally done by the governments, to achieve the desired health objectives. Kundu (2010) divided this into two

[3] These districts are Mayurbhanj, Jharsuguda, Koraput, Bargarh, Anugul, Kalahandi, Dhenkanal, Sonepur, Sambalpur, Bolangir, Boudh, and Nuapada. Action Plan has been drawn to achieve the goal by 2015.

categories—HSR and systemic changes. According to him, HSR is defined as 'any initiative by the state since the later part of twentieth century, which tries to reduce the role of government in health sector while creating a space for a larger role for the private sector'. For example, some of the HSR initiatives are introduction of user charges, contracting out health services, public–private partnership (PPP), setting up private medical colleges and hospitals, contractual paramedical staff and doctors at the district level and so on. Systemic changes are 'any initiative by the state to maintain the "efficiency" of the system so that it could produce optimum output' (Kundu 2010). Some of the systemic change initiatives are decentralization, change in the drug system, introduction of mobile health units, and reviewing the performance of all hospitals on a monthly basis.

Odisha experienced HSR in the late 1990s. The HSRs in the state included creation of Policy and Strategic Planning Unit (PSPU),[4] the Odisha Health System Development Project (OHSDP),[5] handing over PHCs to NGOs,[6] introduction of user charges in 1997, recruitment of contractual district level paramedical staff, privatizing cleaning services in government hospitals, multi-skilling of health personnel,[7] allowing private practices by government doctors, and introducing contractual doctors scheme at the block level. Systemic change initiatives in Odisha included establishment of diseases surveillance program,[8] introduction of new drug

[4] PSPU has been started by the initiative of DFID of UK during 2002–03 to help in program design, implementation, monitoring, and revision of health initiatives by department of health, GoO.

[5] OHSDP was wholly funded by the World Bank with a cost of US$ 76.4 million. The project started on 9 August 1998 and closed on 31 March 2006 including two years' extension.

[6] To provide better healthcare in remote and difficult areas, GoO handed over the PHCs/PHCs (new) to NGOs in these areas due to the long absence of the medical officers and supporting staff. However, it could not succeed due to lack of resources and expertise on the part of the NGOs (Kundu 2010).

[7] In 1998, due to the fiscal austerity measures and using the existing resources efficiently and effectively, training programs were imparted to laboratory technicians to make them multi-skilled from single-skilled.

[8] For detail, please refer http://pipnrhm-mohfw.nic.in/index_files/high_focus_non_ne/Orissa/53.A.IDSP.pdf (accessed on 7 October 2012).

policy,[9] Pancha Byadhi Chikitsa scheme,[10] mandatory pre-PG rural services,[11] and creation of ZSS (Zilla Swasthya Samities or District Health Society).[12]

It is important to mention two events which marked the beginning of health sector reforms in the state: (a) the formation of a committee of the Odisha legislature (house committee) to look into the permanent problem of health, and (b) an initiative by the DFID to evaluate the existing system of healthcare for its two projects in the health sector. The house committee suggested for additional resources by introducing user charges in medical colleges and district hospitals, granting autonomy to the hospitals and abolition of private practices by government doctors during 1995–96. The evaluation by DFID suggested that reforms were needed in three main areas: maintenance of buildings, equipment, and mobility. Further, Phase III of the Odisha Health and Family Welfare Reform Project (1997–2001) of DFID, which aimed at improving quality primary healthcare in two selected districts of Odisha, resulted in the introduction of a number of measures. Some of the efforts were in relation to handing over responsibility of maintaining the buildings to medical officers, introduction of waste management in primary health institutions, and making ZSS functional and involving them in the implementation of project activities and repair and maintenance of health institutions.

On the policy front, the state government declared an integrated health policy for the first time in 2002 whose mission was to facilitate

[9] The new drug policy was introduced in 1998 by adopting Tamil Nadu model. This policy led to the purchase of 80 per cent of the total drugs centrally with the remaining 20 per cent of the drug budget being handed over to the chief of district medical officer (CDMO).

[10] It means treatment for five diseases—leprosy, malaria, acute respiratory infections, scabies, and diarrhoea. This scheme was introduced in 1999 to cure these five diseases free of cost at any government institutions including free medicines.

[11] It is mandatory on the part of the PG medical students of any government medical college to serve for one year in rural and remote areas.

[12] In 1999, different district level societies like societies for blindness, leprosy, TB, malaria, and others are amalgamated and formed ZSS for better management where the district collector as the chairman and CDMO as the secretary.

improvement in the health status of the people of Odisha with their participation, and to make available healthcare in a socially equitable, accessible, and affordable manner within a reasonable timeframe, creating partnerships between the public, voluntary, and private health sectors and across other developmental sectors (GoO 2002). Along with this the state government also published the vision document in health sector which covered a wide range of issues such as organizational changes, financing, administrative reforms, involvement of panchayati raj institutions and PPP to improve the health status of the people (GoO 2003). The implementation of National Rural Health Mission (NRHM) has brought about some changes like preparing program implementation plan at the state and district levels, creating partnership between the public and private health sectors, involving the community, and appointing professionals to deal with the challenges of the health sector in the state.

Public health expenditure in Odisha

Total health expenditure of India from all the sources was Rs 1,30,726 crore during 2004–05 constituting 4.25 per cent of gross domestic product (GDP) whereas it was Rs 3,456 crore (2.64 per cent of India) in Odisha during the same period. Of the total health expenditure of India, the share of private sector was maximum with 78.05 per cent, public sector at 19.67 per cent, and the external flows contributed 2.28 per cent (GoI 2009). In the national level, among all the sources, households contributed a significant portion at 71.13 per cent of total health expenditure for availing healthcare services from different healthcare institutions. State governments, central government, and firms contributed 12 per cent, 6.78 per cent, and 5.73 per cent, respectively. As per the international classification of health accounts (ICHA) 77.96 per cent of India's total health expenditure was incurred on curative care, followed by 8.07 per cent on reproductive child health and family welfare, and 1.80 per cent on medical education and research.

The health expenditure of India was 1.3 per cent of its GDP and 4.8 per cent of total expenditure in 2011–12 (GoI 2012b). In Odisha, the total public spending on healthcare was Rs 1,797.67 crore in 2012–13. This constitutes 3.68 per cent of the state budget and 0.69 per cent of gross state domestic product (GSDP). The proportion of GSDP spent on health varies from 0.88 to 0.56 over the last one decade. However, when taken as a share of state expenditure, it varies within a range of 3.18 to 4.7 per cent over the years (Table 10.8). This low public expenditure on health by the state and central governments indicates that investment in health is insufficient. One can draw a conclusion that there is 'a shift from the neo-Keynesian position that stressed the role of the government in the provision of welfare services to the philosophy of Reaganism and Thatcherism that shifted the onus of financing welfare services from the state to the individual' (Baru 1994).

Public health problems

Public health is a method of preventing diseases and promoting good health within groups of people, from small communities to entire countries. Most important public health problems are malnutrition, malaria, leprosy, diarrhea, acute respiratory infections, scabies, tuberculosis (TB), vitamin A deficiency, human immunodeficiency

Table 10.8 Health expenditure of the GoO (Rs crore)

Year	TH& FWE	Outside the state budget	PCHE	THE as % of TE	TH& FWE as % of GSDP
2004–05	630.9	40.85	162.18	4.7	0.88
2005–06	467.02	107.89	118.83	3.18	0.56
2006–07	607.18	110.52	118.83	3.47	0.6
2007–08	746.59	162.55	188.06	3.56	0.58
2008–09	894.57	199.28	225.33	3.52	0.6
2009–10	1,170.86	204.31	225.33	4.03	0.72
2010–11	1,272.35	NA	382.94	3.75	0.65
2011–12	1,549.54	NA	379.76	3.64	0.68
2012–13	1,797.67	NA	428.72	3.68	0.69

Source: GoO (2012b).

Note: TH&FWE: total health and family welfare, PCHE: per capita health expenditure, TE: total expenditure

virus (HIV), acquired immunodeficiency syndrome (AIDS), mortality indicators explained in the Section titled 'Mortality indicators', life style diseases, violence, crime, and so on. The GoO has focused attention on *panchvyadhi*, the five most prevalent diseases: malaria, leprosy, diarrhea, acute respiratory infections, and scabies that contribute about 70 per cent of patient load (GoO 2012a). The Panchvyadhi Chikitsa scheme has been in operation since 2001 to provide free treatment and medicines for these diseases. Some of the major public health problems in Odisha are explained in Table 10.8.

Malnutrition

Malnutrition is a very complex and multidimensional public health problem. According to National Family Health Survey III of 2005–06, under age five years, 48 per cent of the children were stunted and 23.7 per cent were severely stunted; 19.8 per cent were wasted, and 6.4 per cent were severely wasted; 42.5 per cent were underweight and 15.8 per cent were severely underweight in India. Odisha was in a better position than India in all the above indicators of malnutrition. However, anaemia, which is caused due to malnutrition suffered by both pregnant mothers and infants, explains 8.1 per cent of infant deaths. In Odisha, 62 per cent women suffer from anaemia against the national average of 55.3 per cent (GoO 2012a).

The GoO has implemented various welfare programmes for malnourished children, women, infirm, and destitute persons. These include the Integrated Child Development Scheme (ICDS), rehabilitation of cured leprosy patients, emergency feeding programme, mid-day meal scheme, and heavily subsidized rice at the rate of Re 1 per kilogram. Besides, pension schemes like the National Old Age Pension (NOAP), Madhu Babu Pension Yojna, and National Family Benefit Scheme are in operation to provide social security to the poor, old, and destitute.

Malaria

India contributes 77 per cent of the total malaria in Southeast Asia (Kumar et al. 2007). In the Southeast Asia Region of WHO, malaria is clearly declining in the smaller countries but the burden appears persistently high in the major endemic centres—Bangladesh, India,

Indonesia, and Myanmar (WHO 2011). Due to widespread DDT resistance and patches of pyrethroid and OP (malathion) resistance, the decline rate of malaria in India is low. Odisha contributes 24.73 per cent of malaria cases and accounts for the largest share of deaths (24.63 per cent) due to malaria in the country (Table 10.9). More than 60 per cent population of the state is living in the malaria high-risk areas, particularly in the tribal districts (GoO 2003).

HIV/AIDS

National AIDS Control Programme is being implemented in Odisha through National AIDS Control Organization (NACO), New Delhi. Accordingly, State AIDS Control Society has been formed in each state for smooth implementation of the programme. The first case of HIV infection in India was reported in 1986. In Odisha the first case of HIV was identified in 1993 in the Nayagarh district. In the year 2009, there were 23.95 lakh people living with HIV/AIDS in India and 4,020 people in Odisha. The number of HIV deaths was 1.72 lakh persons for India and 297 persons for Odisha. The general population accounts for approximately 95 per cent of total HIV infections at the national level in 2009 whereas the higher risk groups of female sex workers (FSW), men having sex with men (MSM), and injecting drug users (IDU) account for 2.68 per cent, 1.72 per cent, and 0.75 per cent of HIV infections, respectively, in 2009 (GoI 2010b).

Sex disaggregated data for number of people living with HIV is estimated at approximately 61 per cent male and 39 per cent female for India in 2009 (GoI 2010b) and 64.66 per cent male and 35.34 per cent female for Odisha by the end of 2011 (GoO 2012a). The percentage distribution of HIV infection by age is estimated at 4.4 per cent among children below the age of 15 years, 82.4 per cent among adults aged 15 to 49 years, and the remaining 13.2 per cent among people over 50 years of age for India (GoI 2010b). The corresponding figures for Odisha were 10 per cent, 86 per cent, and 4 per cent, respectively. Of the 1.2 lakh estimated new infections in 2009, the six high-prevalence states[13] account for 39 per cent of the

[13] Maharashtra, Tamil Nadu, Karnataka, Andhra Pradesh, Manipur, and Nagaland.

Table 10.9 Malaria cases, deaths, and CF rate, 2000–10

Year	Odisha			India			World		
	Cases	Deaths	CF rate	Cases	Deaths	CF rate	Cases	Deaths	CF rate
1	2	3	4	5	6	7	8	9	10
2000	5,09,497(25.08)	467(50.11)	0.09	20,31,790	932	0.05	22,30,00,000	7,55,000	0.34
2001	4,54,541(21.80)	305(30.35)	0.07	20,85,484	1,005	0.05	22,50,00,000	7,71,000	0.34
2002	4,73,224(25.69)	465(47.79)	0.10	18,42,019	973	0.05	22,60,00,000	7,89,000	0.35
2003	4,21,323(22.54)	333(33.10)	0.08	18,69,403	1,006	0.05	13,30,00,000	8,01,000	0.60
2004	4,16,732(21.76)	283(29.82)	0.07	19,15,363	949	0.05	23,50,00,000	8,10,000	0.34
2005	3,96,573(21.83)	255(26.48)	0.06	18,16,342	963	0.05	23,70,00,000	8,01,000	0.34
2006	3,80,216(21.30)	257(15.06)	0.07	17,85,129	1,707	0.10	23,10,00,000	7,82,000	0.34
2007	3,71,879(24.65)	221(16.86)	0.06	15,08,927	1,311	0.09	22,90,00,000	7,56,000	0.33
2008	3,75,430(24.60)	239(22.65)	0.06	15,26,210	1,055	0.07	22,50,00,000	7,11,000	0.32
2009	3,80,904(24.36)	198(17.31)	0.05	15,63,574	1,144	0.07	22,20,00,000	6,91,000	0.31
2010	3,95,651(24.73)	252(24.63)	0.06	15,99,986	1,023	0.06	21,60,00,000	6,55,000	0.30

Source: Columns 2, 3, 5, and 6: Data taken from http://www.indiastat.com (last accessed on accessed on 24 November 2012).

Columns 4, 7, and 10: calculated by the authors from columns 2, 3, 5, 6, 8, and 9.

Column 8 and 9: WHO (2011).

Note: 1. CF rate is defined as the percentage of cases died.

2. Figures in parenthesis are Odisha as a percentage of India.

cases, while the states of Odisha, Bihar, West Bengal, Uttar Pradesh, Rajasthan, Madhya Pradesh, and Gujarat account for 41 per cent of new infections (GoI 2010b).

Tuberculosis

The National Tuberculosis Control Programme (NTP) has been implemented in Odisha since 1964 to provide free and domiciliary treatment to patients detected through the passive case landing method. The NTP did not achieve the desired success. It was revised as RNTCP in 1997 and implemented DOTS (Directly Observed Treatment Short Course Chemotherapy).[14] It aimed at detecting 70 per cent of infectious new sputum positive TB cases and curing at least 85 per cent of them. It is implemented through 31 implementing units, 106 TB units, and 545 microscopy centres. In addition, there are 33,746 DOTS providers identified and trained under the program to administer DOTS to patients (GoO 2012a).

India is the largest TB prevalent country accounting for one-fifth of the global incidence. In 2009, out of the estimated global annual incidence of 94 lakh TB cases, 20 lakh were estimated to have occurred in India (GoI 2010c). Odisha constitutes 3.28 per cent of total TB patients registered in India and 4.04 per cent of total TB death cases (Table 10.10).

National rural health mission

National rural health mission (NRHM) is a flagship scheme launched by the GoI in 2005 with a synergistic approach relating to determinants of good health namely, segment of nutrition, sanitation, hygiene, and safe drinking water. The main objective of NRHM is to 'provide universal access to equitable, affordable and equality healthcare through target interventions as well as institutional changes such as more decentralization of healthcare' (Centre for Budget

[14] DOTS provides a sure cure for tuberculosis and is available free of cost to the patient. But the entire strategy to combat tuberculosis becomes ineffective if the patient does not have the will and patience to complete the course, which spans to 6–8 months.

Table 10.10 Registered tuberculosis patients and their mortality rate, 2005–10

Year	Odisha			India		
	TPR	Total died	Mortality rate	TPR	Total died	Mortality rate
2005	44,501 (3.44)	2,215 (3.91)	0.050	12,93,083	56,585	0.044
2006	44,790 (3.21)	2,276 (3.64)	0.051	13,97,498	62,545	0.045
2007	49,285 (3.34)	2,529 (3.90)	0.051	14,75,587	64,802	0.044
2008	51,031 (3.36)	2,791 (4.22)	0.055	15,17,333	66,121	0.044
2009	52,145 (3.40)	2,524 (3.81)	0.048	15,33,309	66,241	0.043
2010	49,869 (3.28)	1,347 (4.04)	0.027	15,22,147	33,356	0.022

Source: Data available online at http://www.indiastat.com (last accessed on 23 November 2012).
Note: TPR: total patients registered

and Governance Accountability (CBGA) and UNICEF 2011). The major targets that NRHM has covered so far are reduction of IMR to 30 per 1,000 live births, maternal mortality to 100 per 100 thousand live births, and TFR to 2.1 by the year 2012 through Janani Suraksha Yojana (JSY),[15] appointment of Accredited Social Health Activist (ASHA), mainstreaming AYUSH (ayurveda, yoga and naturopathy, unani, siddha, and homeopathy), upgradation of the public health facilities to Indian Public Health Standards (IPHS), formation of village health and sanitation committee (VHSC), and Rogi Kalyan Samiti (RKS),[16] implementation of inter-sectoral district health plans

[15] JSY is a safe motherhood intervention under the NRHM, being implemented with the objective of reducing maternal and neo-natal mortality by promoting institutional delivery among the poor pregnant women. The yojana launched on 12 April 2005, by the then prime minister of India, is being implemented in all states and union territories with special focus on low-performing states. It is a 100 per cent centrally sponsored scheme and integrates cash assistance with delivery and post-delivery care.

[16] RKS is a registered society, yet effective management structure, acting as a group of trustees for CHC/hospitals/to manage the affairs of the hospitals. It consists of embers from local panchayat raj institutions, NGOs, local elected representatives, and officials from government sector, who are responsible for proper functioning and management of hospitals/CHCs/

(DHPs) prepared by the District Health Mission to educate and mobilize the community.

Under NRHM, Odisha has reduced its IMR to 65 in 2009 from 73 in 2006, that is, only 8 per cent in three years (CBGA and UNICEF 2011). According to GoI (2008), 42,777 ASHA were selected and 17,538 were trained up to IVth Module and 7,94,815 VHND were successfully conducted in Odisha till 2009 as a result of which there has been an increase in ANC registration and immunization. The key achievements of NRHM in Odisha are: (a) 412 district-level doctors, pediatricians, and CDPOs and 1,200 basic health workers (ANMs and AWWs) have been trained on integrated management of neonatal childhood illness; (b) 22 FRUs and 105 PHCs (24×7 health services) have been made functional; (c) 12 doctors (obstetrics and gynaecology (O&G) specialist) have been trained on Emergency Obstetric Care (EmOC) and 23 doctors have been trained in anesthesia to deliver multi-skilling specialized services; (d) 616 paramedics and ayush doctors have undergone skill attendance at birth (SAB) training to promote safe delivery services; (e) 200 sub-centres, 25 block hospitals, 32 district hospitals, and 22 sub-divisional headquarter hospitals have been provided with infrastructure support; (f) 721 additional ANMs, 470 staff nurses, and 27 LTs have been recruited to strengthen healthcare delivery system; (g) 266 block program organizers, 234 block accountants, 23 works consultants, and 25 immunization assistants have been appointed to reinforce programme management of health sector; (h) 18,807 beneficiaries from outreach areas have been covered under Swasthya Mela; (i) 332 RCH camps have been organized catering services to 91,342 beneficiaries; (j) 1,20,057 couples have benefitted from permanent family planning methods; (k) 17 private/public sector institutions have been accredited for disbursing JSY benefits; and (l) over 7 lakh mothers have benefited under JSY where institutional delivery rate has increased from 38 per cent in 2005–06 to 62 per cent in 2007–08 (GoO 2008).

FRUs. The RKS is free to prescribe, generate, and use the funds placed with it, as per its best judgment for smooth functioning and maintaining the quality of services.

Healthcare of tribal people

Odisha is one of the major tribal states in the country. Out of the 30 districts, around 14 districts are tribal districts in the state. Both scheduled castes (SCs) and scheduled tribes (STs) constitute about 38.66 per cent of the state's total population according to the 2001 Census. Out of 635 tribal communities in India, 62 are found in Odisha and 13 are particularly vulnerable tribal groups.

The tribal people are socially and educationally backward. Their exposure to the outer life is very low. The people of the community have strong and deep-rooted faith in their age-old superstitions and myths for which they suffer from health problems. They opt for modern methods of healthcare only after the problem was seriously aggravated and hence the recovery rate is very low. The common belief of primitive tribes of Odisha is that god has sent diseases because the earth was getting overcrowded by human beings. It is the belief of the Didayis tribe that *mapru* (god) sends epidemics to earth with purpose of keeping the population under control. That the hungry god sends diseases to earth to take the offerings from his devotees is another variant of this faith (Pati 1998). This type of social belief is present among the tribal people of Odisha.

The tribal people are generally affected with relatively higher diseases burden because of their backwardness. Communicable, pregnancy-related ailments and childhood ailments account for about 65 per cent of the diseases. The publicly provided health service outlets are available, more or less, in accordance with the national norms, but factors such as low population density, geographical inaccessibility, cultural barriers, ignorance, poor service quality, and the deep-rooted influence of traditional healers constitute an unsatisfactory outcome of the service systems (Gupta 2002). It has also been found that among Kutia Kondha the delivery is conducted by the mother herself in a half squatting position holding a rope tied down from the roof of the house, which helps her in applying pressure to deliver the child. In complicated labour, it might lead to maternal as well as child mortality (Indian Council of Medical Research (ICMR) 2003). This happens either because there is unavailability of institutional delivery system or because they think this conventional method to be safer as they are unaware of proper healthcare during childbirth.

Therefore, both awareness among the tribal people and sufficient health infrastructure are very important for them.

Policy suggestions

Till today our policymakers and political leaders are unable to understand the importance of investment in health and education sector. Before India's independence, in 1946, Bhore Committee suggested spending 15 per cent of the government expenditure on healthcare but even now, it is only 4.8 per cent in India and 3.68 per cent in Odisha. If there is a financial constraint for the government, why it does not implement a specific amount of health tax (an earmarked or so-called hypothecated tax) devoted to healthcare. Again, spending more on health services does not necessarily buy better health. It needs an efficient management and use of resources. The principle of equal opportunity for access to services based on need and equal risk, irrespective of the ability to pay, should be followed.

There is no doubt that the health status of the people of Odisha has improved more or less similar to the people of India. In the demographic and health indicators, Odisha is not far behind India, but it certainly lags behind in economic parameters. The generic twin challenges of Odisha are poverty and illiteracy, which are the roots of all maladies. We hope, if we can tackle these twin problems, many of our ancillary challenges will be solved easily.

It is found that Odisha is lagging behind India in its all mortality indicators, especially in child and reproductive healthcare. This may be due to lack of necessary health infrastructure. In this regard, four suggestions can be made. First, whatever infrastructures are in-position may be equitably distributed among all the districts, executed properly, and responsibility may be fixed for a better health output. Second, the vacant posts of health personnel may be filled up in a war footing manner without further delay. Third, immediate action may be taken to resolve the infrastructural shortfalls as per the population norm. Fourth, initiatives may be taken to open new medical colleges and the intake capacity may be increased in existing medical institutions as Odisha at present can produce only 340 specialist doctors (1.5 per cent of India), 750 MBBS (1.8 per cent of India), 360 BDS, and 50 radiologists every year from both government and private medical institutions.

It is said that prevention is always better than cure and this is truer for the poor than for the rich. When someone becomes sick, one loses workdays and must have to take curative services. So, on both accounts—loss of workdays and curative health expenditures—it is costlier for the poor than for the rich because generally the poor people are not covered by insurance and do not have an employer who would pay them during illness. In this connection, providing health education to them is an appropriate alternative to prevent them from sickness. Of course, there is a need to test the efficacy of health education in improving the health and economic condition of the poor.

References

Ager, A. and K. Pepper. 2005. 'Patterns of Health Service Utilization and Perceptions of Needs and Services in Rural Odisha', *Health Policy and Planning*, 20(3): 176–84.

Baru, R.V. 1994. 'Structure and Utilization of Health Services: An Inter-state Analysis', *Social Scientist*, 22(9/12): 98–111.

CBGA and UNICEF. 2012. *Budgeting for Change Series 2011*. New Delhi: National Rural Health Mission (NRHM), Centre for Budget and Governance Accountability (CBGA), and UNICEF. Available at http://www.cbgaindia.org/files/working_papers/NRHM.pdf (accessed on 23 November 2012).

CIA (Central Intelligence Agency). 2012. *The World Fact Book, 2012*. Available at https://www.cia.gov/library/publications/the-world-fact-book/rankorder/2102rank.html (accessed on 10 September 2012).

Government of India (GoI). 2009. *National Health Accounts India 2004–05*. New Delhi: Ministry of Health and Family Welfare.

———. 2010a. *Annual Report to the People on Health*. New Delhi: Ministry of Health and Family Welfare.

———. 2010b. *Technical Report: India HIV Estimates*, New Delhi: National Institute of Medical Statistics and National AIDS Control Organization, Ministry of Health and Family Welfare.

———. 2010c. *TB India 2011, Revised National TB Control Programme, Annual Status Report*. New Delhi: Central TB Division, Directorate General of Health Services, Ministry of Health and Family Welfare.

———. 2011a. *Provisional Population Totals, Paper 1 of 2011, Odisha Series 22*. Bhubaneswar, Odisha: Directorate of Census Operation.

GoI. 2011b. *Annual Report to the People on Health*. New Delhi: Ministry of Health and Family Welfare.

———. 2012a. *Sample Registration System Statistical Report 2010, Report Number 1 of 2012*. New Delhi: Office of the Registrar General, Ministry of Home Affairs.

———. 2012b. *Economic Survey 2011–12*. New Delhi: Economic Division, Ministry of Finance.

———. 2012c. *Odisha State Report*. Available at http://mohfw.nic.in/NRHM/Documents/High_ Focus_Reports/Orissa_Report.pdf (accessed on 23 November 2012).

Government of Odisha (GoO). 2002. *Odisha State Integrated Health Policy 2002*. Bhubaneswar, Odisha: Department of Health and Family Welfare.

———. 2003. *Odisha Vision 2010—A Health Strategy*. Bhubaneswar, Odisha: Department of Health and Family Welfare.

———. 2012. *Annual Report 2007–08*. Mission Directorate, National Rural Health Mission, Ministry of Health and Family Welfare. Available at http://www.nrhmorissa.gov.in/pdf/Introduction.pdf (accessed on 23 November 2012).

———. 2012a. *Economic Survey 2011–12*. Bhubaneswar, Odisha: Planning and Coordination Department.

———. 2012b. *Odisha Budget 2012–13: At a Glance*. Bhubaneswar, Odisha: Finance Department.

Gupta, M. 2002. 'State Health Systems: Odisha', Working Paper No. 89, Indian Council for Research on International Economic Relations, New Delhi.

ICMR (Indian Council of Medical Research). 2003. 'Health Status of Primitive Tribes in Odisha', *ICMR Bulletin* 33(10): 1–6.

IIPS (International Institute for Population Sciences) and Macro International. 2008. *National Family Health Survey (NFHS-3), India, 2005-06: Orissa*. Mumbai: IIPS.

Kumar, A., N. Valecha, N. Jain, and A.P. Dash. 2007. 'Burden of Malaria in India: Retrospective and Prospective View', *American Journal of Tropical Medicine and Hygiene*, 77(6): 69–78.

Kundu, S. 2010. *Health Sector Reforms in Odisha: Lessons for Developing Countries*. UK: Cambridge Scholars Publishing, 2010.

NCP (National Commission on Population. 2006. *Population Projections for India and States 2001–2026, Report of the Technical Group on Population Projections*. New Delhi: Office of the Registrar General and Census Commissioner, Government of India.

Pati, B. 1998. 'Siting the Body: Perspectives on Health and Medicine in Colonial Odisha', *Social Scientist*, 26(11/12): 3–26.

Planning Commission. 2012. *Odisha Development Report.* New Delhi: Government of India. Available at http://planningcommission.nic.in/plans/stateplan/sdr_orissa/sdr_orich9.pdf (accessed on 20 October 2012).

Rout, H.S. and P.K. Panda. 2007. 'Introduction and Overview', in H.S. Rout and P.K. Panda (eds), *Health Economics in India*, pp. 1–12. New Delhi: New Century Publications.

WHO (World Health Organization). 1946. *Preamble to the Constitution of the WHO as adopted by the International Health Conference.* New York

———. 2011. *World Malaria Report 2011.* Geneva: World Health Organization.

World Bank. 1993. *World Development Report 1993: Investing in Health.* New York: Oxford University Press.

11

Dimensions of Poverty and Prospects of Economic Change in Odisha

Baidyanath Misra

It is really difficult to precisely define poverty since its connotation includes many features and it varies from time to time in the process of development and between different countries according to their level of development. In India also different scholars have defined poverty from different angles of vision. Instead of discussing all these definitions and analysing their scope, we confine our analysis as per the definitions accepted by the Planning Commission of India for determining the poverty of India and of different states because this definition has more or less helped in formulating the economic programme of the country. At the outset, poverty was related, as per the definition of the Planning Commission to a certain minimum consumption standard. If a person is not in a position to secure a certain amount of income to satisfy such consumption standard, he was deemed to be poor. The Planning Commission appointed a study group in July 1962 to examine what is to be considered the nationally desirable minimum level of consumption expenditure. The study group recommended a standard of private consumption expenditure of Rs 20 (at 1960–61 prices) per capita per month as a bare minimum. But the recommendation did not indicate the minimum living standard, nor did it make a distinction between rural and urban living costs. As such there was a lot of criticism against the recommendation by different authors. However, this norm continued to be used by the Planning Commission and other stakeholders during the 1960s and 1970s.

During the period several individual researchers attempted on their own to compute the poverty lines for India for a rural–urban break-up. A more scientific and refined outcome, however, came out in respect of poverty line estimation in the *Report of the Task Force on Projections of Minimum Needs and Effective Consumption Demand.* The Task Force integrated the concepts of 'normative' consumption with 'effective' consumption to work out calorie norms for the determination of poverty lines for rural and urban India separately. Per capita calorie requirements of 2,435 per day in rural areas and 2,095 per day in urban areas were computed to be the minimum levels. The corresponding monetary equivalents being Rs 49.09 and Rs 56.64 at 1973–74 prices and Rs 61.80 and Rs 71.30 at 1976–77 prices set poverty lines for rural and urban parts of India, respectively. The minimum calorie requirements were disputed on the ground that these were simple averages, not minimum. Minimum calorie requirements in a cross-section vary on grounds of age, sex, and occupational structure. To accommodate the observation, a consensus was reached in terms of inflating each of the monetary equivalents of per capita per day calorie requirements defining poverty lines by 75 per cent to determine the appropriate cut-off points which were considered in the Draft Five Year Plan (1978–83) documents.

The Planning Commission again appointed an expert committee under the chairmanship of D.T. Lakdawala which submitted its report in 1993. In the official poverty estimates of the Lakdawala Committee, the methodology was based on food requirements of different individuals. It was estimated that if a person per day could procure food items to the extent of 2,400 calories in rural areas and 2,100 calories in urban areas, he or she is not below the poverty line.

On this basis, poverty estimates were calculated for both 1993–94 and 2004–05. The poverty estimates for both India and Odisha are given in Table 11.1.

Table 11.1 Poverty estimates for Odisha and India

	1993–94			2004–05		
	Rural	Urban	Combined	Rural	Urban	Combined
Odisha	49.7	41.6	48.6	46.8	44.3	46.4
India	37.3	32.4	36.0	28.3	25.7	27.5

Source: GoI (2011).

There does not seem to be much difference in poverty of Odisha between the two years. In case of India, poverty is not only much lower than that of Odisha, there is also a decrease in poverty between 1993–94 and 2004–05.

Though Rath (2011) raised some questions with regard to methodology, the major difficulty of Lakdawala Committee in determining poverty was that it did not take into account the basic needs of the people. As a matter of fact, the concept of poverty is associated with socially perceived deprivation with respect to basic human needs. These basic human needs include food for adequate nourishment, decent clothing, housing for reasonable shelter, healthcare to escape avoidable diseases, some minimum level of education to understand and appreciate social, economic and political responsibilities, and certain other attributes which go on changing with ongoing changes in society. Since the poverty estimates of the Planning Commission as per the recommendation by Lakdawala Committee were criticized on several counts, the former set up another expert group under the chairmanship of Suresh Tendulkar to examine the issue and suggest a new poverty line and make estimates. The expert group submitted its report in 2009. Several changes were made by Tendulkar Committee on poverty lines and estimates (Government of India 2009). Some of the major changes are as follows:

1 While acknowledging the multidimensional nature of poverty, the estimates of poverty will continue to be based on private household consumer expenditure of Indian households as collected by National Sample Survey Organisation (NSSO). But the proposed poverty lines, while moving away from calorie norms, have been validated by checking the adequacy of actual

private expenditure near the poverty lines on food, education, and health by comparing them with normative expenditure consistent with nutritional, educational, and health outcome. The earlier calorie-anchored poverty lines did not explicitly account for private household expenditure on education and health.

2 The quinquennial National Sample Surveys (NSS) of household consumer expenditure surveys carried out by NSSO had shifted from URP (uniform recall period) to MRP (mixed recall period) for all its consumption surveys, namely 365 days for low frequency items (clothing, footwear, durables, education, and institutional health expenditure) and 30 days for all remaining items. This change captures the household consumption expenditure of the poor households on low frequency items of purchase more satisfactorily than the earlier 30 day recall period. The expert group decided to adopt the MRP based estimates of consumption expenditure as the basis for future poverty lines.

3 In regard to PLB (poverty line basket) of household goods and services consumed, according to the expert group, the estimated urban share of population (described as a head count ratio or poverty ratio) in 2004–05, namely 25.7 per cent at the all-India level, is generally accepted as being less controversial than its rural counterpart at 28.3 per cent that has been heavily criticized as being too low. In the interest of continuity as well as in view of the consistency with broad external validity checks with respect to nutritional, educational, and health outcomes, it was decided to recommend a mixed reference period (MRP)—equivalent of urban PLB at the all-India level corresponding to 25.7 per cent urban head count ratio as the new reference PLB to be provided to rural as well as urban population in all the states after adjusting it for within—state urban—relative to rural and rural and urban state-relative—to all-India price differentials.

4 The committee also noted that although those near the poverty line in urban areas continue to afford original calorie norm of 2,100 per capita per day (as recommended by Lakdwala Committee), their actual observed calorie intake from the 61st round of NSS is 1,776 calories per capita per day. This actual intake is very close to the revised calorie intake from 1,770 per capita per day currently recommended for India by the Food and

Agriculture Organization (FAO). Actual observed calorie intake of those near the new poverty line in rural areas (1,999 calories per capita) is higher than the FAO norm.

5 Tendulkar Committee also made a basic corrective departure in price data. The proposed price indices are based on the household-level unit values (approximated price data) obtained from the 61st round (July 2004–05 to June 2005) of NSS household consumer expenditure survey for food, fuel, and light, clothing and footwear at the most detailed level of disaggregation, and hence, much closer to the actual prices paid by the consumers in rural and urban areas. Price indices for health and education were also obtained from unit level data from the related NSSs. The proposed price indices (Fisher ideal indices in technical terms) incorporate both the observed all-India and state-level consumption patterns in the weighting structure of the price indices for rent and convergence, actual expenditure share for these items used to adjust the poverty line for each other.

On the basis of Tendulkar Committee's recommendations, poverty estimates of Odisha and all-India are given in Table 11.2.

We can note three differences. First, poverty head count ratio is much higher in Odisha than in India. Second, poverty head count ratio in rural areas is higher than in urban areas both in Odisha and all-India. Further, Lakdawala Committee recommended that aggregate poverty ratio in 2004–05 was 27.5 per cent while according to Tendulkar Committee, it was 37.20 per cent during the same year. Table 11.3 shows that rural poverty is higher both in 1993–94 and 2004–05 as per the recommendation of Tendulkar Committee than what it was in Lakdawala methodology.

Table 11.2 Poverty lines (Rs) and poverty head count ratio (%), 2004–05

	Poverty lines		Poverty head count ratio		
	Rural	Urban	Rural	Urban	Total
Odisha	407.78	497.31	60.80	37.60	57.20
All India	446.68	578.80	41.80	25.70	37.20

Source: GoI (2011).

Table 11.3 Poverty head count ratio (%) in India, 1993–94 and 2004–05

Year	Lakdawala methodology			Tendulkar methodology		
	Rural	Urban	Combined	Rural	Urban	Combined
1993–94	37.3	32.4	36.0	50.1	31.8	45.3
2004–05	28.3	25.7	27.5	41.8	25.7	37.2

Source: GoI (2011: 4).

It is evident that if the percentage of population below the poverty line in 1993–94 is computed using new technology, the number also goes up because the rural poverty line itself has been raised. Whether we use the new methodology or the old, the decline in percentage of population in poverty turns out to be roughly of the same magnitude. Tendulkar Committee has specifically noted that 'even though the suggested new methodology gives a higher estimate of rural head count ratio at the all-India level for 2004–05, the extent of poverty reduction in comparable percentage point decline between 1993–94 and 2004–05 is not different from that inferred using the old methodology'.

The Planning Commission considered the Tendulkar Committee report, which had based itself on the then recent consumption pattern and uses price data that more closely reflected price differences implicit in the consumption survey used to estimate poverty. While these are clearly improvements, it makes inter-temporal comparisons difficult. Some questions may also be raised about equating rural and urban consumption baskets. Tendulkar Committee has also not addressed the issue of growing divergence between household consumption expenditure as derived from NSS and as derived from National Accounts Statistics.

Before we consider the level of poverty in Odisha, we may examine the question whether economic growth can reduce poverty or not. According to Datt and Ravallion (1996), experience prior to the 1990s suggests that economic growth in India has typically reduced poverty. Using data from 1958 to 1991, Ravallion and Datt find the elasticity of the incidence of poverty with respect to net domestic product per capita was –0.75 and with respect to private consumption per capita it was –0.9, as shown in Table 11.4.

Table 11.4 Elasticities of national poverty measures to economic growth in India, 1958–91

Elasticity with respect to	Head count index[#]	Poverty gap index	Squared poverty gap index
Mean consumption from NSSs	-1.33(15.19)	-1.88(12.83)	-2.26(10.22)
Mean private consumption from national accounts	-0.90(4.23)	-1.36(3.98)	-1.67(3.45)
Mean net domestic product from the national accounts	-0.75(3.68)	-1.15(3.59)	-1.45(3,27)

Source: Datt and Ravallion (2002: 90, Table 1).
Note: #: Head count ratio is the percentage of people below the poverty line. The poverty gap index is the mean distance below the poverty line as a proportion of the poverty line, counting the non-poor as zero poverty gap. The squared poverty gap index is the measure proposed by Foster, Greer, and Thorbecke ([FGT] 1984), in which the proportionate poverty gaps are weighted by themselves to reflect the extent of inequality among the poor. The Gini index illustrates the extent of inequality.

The first column of the table measures poverty with head count index: the percentage of people below the poverty line set by the Indian government. The next two columns of the table show two other measures of poverty which have historically responded to change in consumption and net domestic product—the poverty gap index is the mean distance below the poverty line as a proportion of the poverty line; squaring the individual poverty gaps gives additional weight to observations further below the poverty line. The higher absolute elasticities for measures of the depth and severity of poverty in the second and third columns of the table indicate that those well below the poverty line have benefitted from macroeconomic growth, as well as those near the poverty line. Nor is there any convincing evidence that economic growth in India prior to the 1990s has tended to be associated with rising overall inequality (Bruno, Ravallion, and Squire 1996). These observations clearly refute claims that the pre-1990s growth in India tended to leave the poor behind.

However, the picture for the 1990s is more contentious. Some observers have argued that poverty fell far more rapidly in the 1990s than previously (for example, Bhalla 2000). Others have argued that poverty reduction stalled and that poverty might even have risen (see, for example, Sen 2001).

The major question is whether poverty continued to fall with growth in the 1990s or whether the nature of the growth process changed, so that the poor were not left behind. It turns out that the interpretation of the 1999–2000 NSS data depends heavily on whether one uses 7 day or 30 day recall for food expenditure. If one uses the 30 day recall estimates (uniform recall period [URP]) for food and ignores the other differences in the 1999–2000 data, then the consumption distribution for that year implies a sizeable reduction in poverty. The erstwhile Planning Commission of India (2001) makes its estimates along these lines and indicates that the national poverty rate fell by about 10 percentage points between 1993–94 and 1999–2000, from 36 per cent in 1993–94 to only 26 per cent in 1999–2000. Instead, if one compares the seven-day estimates (MRP) for 1999–2000 without ignoring other differences, that is, if we include non-agricultural output, then one gets an increase in poverty.

However, among the conditions that are found to matter significantly to prospects for pro-poor growth, the role played by initial literacy is particularly notable. If we consider the overall pattern of poverty reduction of some of the major states, our results show that higher farm yields and higher development spending reduce the incidence of poverty and the coefficient are highly significant. Among other things, an increase in non-agricultural output per person and lower inflation also play an important part in reducing poverty.

Dev and Ravi (2007) and Himanshu (2007) have also updated their analysis up to 2004–05. Himanshu (2007) has considered comparable estimates of poverty and inequality for all the major states of India, whereas Dev and Ravi (2007) have analysed the poverty gap, FGT (squared poverty gap) and Gini for rural and urban areas for the country as a whole. We present here only poverty gap, FGT, and Gini for India as a whole as analysed by Dev and Ravi (2007).

In their analysis of poverty and inequality, Dev and Ravi (2007) have given much information regarding the percentage of poor and very poor, absolute number of poor and very poor, and poverty gap, FGT and Gini for rural and urban areas. We present in Table 11.5 only the last one on the basis of uniform reference period, that is, survey of 30 day.

Table 11.5 Poverty gap, FGT, and Gini for rural and urban areas in India

	Poverty and inequality			Changes (percentage points, per annum)		Changes in poverty (per annum changes as percentages of base year)	
Rural	1983	1993–94	2004–05	1983–94	1993–2005	1983–94	1993–05
Poverty gap	13.46	8.58	5.9	-0.46	-0.24	-3.45	-2.84
FGT	5.27	2.55	1.47	-0.26	-0.10	-4.93	-3.92
Gini	30.79	28.55	30.45	-0.21	0.17	-0.68	0.60
Urban							
Poverty gap	11.95	8.37	5.76	-0.34	-0.24	-2.85	-2.87
FGT	4.31	2.61	1.46	-0.16	-0.11	-3.71	-4.21
Gini	34.06	34.31	37.51	0.02	0.29	0.01	0.85

Source: Dev and Ravi (2007: 510, Table 3).

The table estimates poverty gap index, FGT, and Gini coefficient as a measure of inequality for the pre- and the post-reform periods. As we find from the table, the rate of decline in the distribution sensitive measures (poverty gap and FGT) in rural areas was slower in the post reform period as compared to the pre-reform period. In the urban areas also, the percentage point decline was slower in the post-reform period. The decline for FGT when normalized with the lease year seems to be higher in 1993–05 as compared to 1983–94. However, inequality in consumption represented by the Gini coefficient seems to have increased significantly for both rural and urban areas in the post-reform period—the rate of increase being much higher for the urban as compared to rural areas.

With this background we can now analyse the poverty position in Odisha. Odisha's *Economic Survey 2011–12* has also made a detailed estimate of poverty line in Odisha on the basis of such recommendations. While defining poverty, the *Economic Survey* noted that the concept of poverty is no longer associated with material deprivation. It has acquired several dimensions and forms an integral component of human development. In most general terms, it is defined as 'deprivation in well-being and encompasses several dimensions such as material deprivation, social deprivation, political deprivation, intellectual deprivation, deprivation in health and inability to cope with vulnerabilities and risks. Though the definition is broad and wide, the measurement of poverty has been done as per Tendulkar recommendation based on MRP consumption. Table 11.6 presents poverty the head count ratio for Odisha and India, from 1993–94 to 2009–10. Poverty estimates for 2009–10 are tentative.

Table 11.6 shows that rural poverty in Odisha has come down only from 63.0 per cent in 1993–94 to 50.5 per cent in 2009–10. Though there is some decrease, still the poverty is substantial. In case of urban areas, poverty has been reduced from 34.5 per cent to 28.5 per cent during the same period. All that we find here that poverty is higher in rural areas than in urban areas. When we compare with India as a whole, India's poverty both in rural areas and urban areas in all these three years is much lower than that of Odisha. In aggregate, while poverty in Odisha is 47.3 per cent, it is only 32.0 in India during 2009–10.

We have already discussed the methodology adopted by the Tendulkar Committee. The Tendulkar Committee has increased the consumption basket and thus increased the poverty line for which different consumption baskets have been suggested. For example, the poverty line of the Tendulkar Committee for the year 2009–10 would be Rs 567.10 and Rs 736.00 for rural and urban Odisha, respectively. Further, since the Tendulkar Committee recommended MRP methodology over URP methodology for estimation of poverty, poverty head count ratio has been calculated for NSS rounds of 1993–94, 2004–05, and 2009 in Table 11.6.

Table 11.6 Poverty head count ratio (%) for Odisha and India by the Tendulkar Committee methodology

Year	Odisha			India		
	Rural	Urban	Total	Rural	Urban	Total
1993–94	63.00	34.50	59.10	50.10	30.80	45.30
2004–05	60.80	37.60	57.20	41.80	25.70	37.20
2009–10	39.20	25.90	37.00	33.80	20.90	29.80

Source: GoO (2013: 264, Table 7.1).

There are also several criticisms in regard to the methodology followed by the Planning Commission in measuring poverty. We will refer to three major criticisms. Krishnaji (2012) points out that there is no case whatsoever to construct a single poverty line based on a calorie expenditure norm: all such lines are arbitrary and do not take into account the different dimensions of poverty. Manna (2012) points out that the major limitation of the new poverty line is its acceptance of 25.7 urban head count ratio (HCR) based on the earlier methodology as the benchmark of proceeding further to arrive at the estimation of poverty lines. Subramanian (2011) discusses both the methodologies, 1993 and 2009, and points out that the identification of methodologies advanced by successive task forces and expert groups have little by way of logical appeal or outcome plausibility to commend them. All these criticisms do not offer any alternative system which can provide a proper measurement of poverty line for the country as a whole. We, therefore, follow Tendulkar methodology to measure poverty of both rural and urban years till a suitable alternative methodology is evolved.

Hence, we study the incidence of poverty and head count ratio by social groups of rural Odisha as analysed in Odisha's *Economic Survey 2012–13* on the basis of Tendulkar methodology. Table 11.7 presents these figures.

As we see in the table, HCR is highest in case of scheduled tribe (ST) and next comes scheduled caste (SC). In case of others, there is substantial decrease. All this means economic growth has not helped ST and SC to a great extent. Most of the STs stay at far off places and therefore, poverty programmes do not contribute much to their benefit.

Table 11.7 Head count ratio (%) by social classes for rural Odisha as per Tendulkar Committee poverty line

NSS round	ST	SC	OBC	Others	Total
2009–10	66.0	47.1	25.6	24.5	39.2
2004–05	84.4	67.9	52.6	37.1	60.8

Source: GoO (2013: 265, Table 7.2).

Odisha's *Economic Survey 2012–13* has also discussed incidence of poverty by NSS regions of rural Odisha for 2009–10 and 2004–05. Table 11.8 presents such incidence of poverty.

As the data in Table 11.8 shows, the southern region has the highest poverty followed by northern region. In 2009–10, only about 25.3 per cent of the population lived below the poverty line in the coastal region. However, all the three regions have witnessed substantial reduction in poverty between 2004–05 and 2009–10. No reason is given in *Economic Survey* for the disparity in poverty in different regions. We may find some reason for the disparity when the Report of the Regional Disparity Committee which the Government appointed is published.

But there is no doubt that there is considerable disparity between different social groups and different regions. Papola (2012) observes that incidence of poverty in southern Odisha is 2.5 times as high as the incidence of poverty in coastal Odisha and the incidence of poverty in northern Odisha is 1.5 times as high as that in coastal Odisha. He also observes that poverty among ST and SC is much higher compared to other social groups—incidence of poverty among ST is twice that among others, and, of SC, the incidence of poverty is 1.7 times the incidence of poverty among others. If we look at inequality, Odisha has higher inequality compared to all India and less inclusiveness. It is also mentioned in *Economic Survey* that due to several economic, social, and institutional obstacles, all regions in Odisha have not shared the gains of development. Some regions continue to languish in abject poverty. The undivided districts of Koraput, Bolangir, and Kalahandi (popularly known as KBK districts) form one such region where the incidence of poverty is very high. Several other pockets of southern and western Odisha are also socially and

Table 11.8 Incidence of poverty by NSS regions of rural Odisha by the Tendulkar Committee's poverty line HCR (%)

NSS round	Southern	Northern	Coastal	Total
2009–10	52.4	41.7	25.3	39.2
2004–05	73.4	70.5	41.6	60.8

Source: GoO (2013: 265, Table 7.3).

economically depressed. These regions are also frequently visited by natural calamities including severe droughts and floods. Persistence of heavy incidence of poverty in these regions is a cause of concern.

The Planning and Coordination Department of the Government of Odisha also appointed a committee under the chairmanship of Prafulla Chandra Ghadei, the then minister of state to consider the constitution of separate Development Board in Odisha for selected areas in the state of Odisha under the provisions of Article 371 of the Constitution of India. The committee visited different districts of Odisha and even some blocks, reviewed some of the recommendations of different committees in regard to their approach to backwardness, visited some of the states, and decided to use the following 11 indicators for the use of identification of blocks in regard to their level of backwardness or their level of development in individual sectors and to follow Sudarshan and Iyengar method for arriving at the composite index for overall measurement. The report was published in 1994. Even though it is an old report, it is worth considering their recommendation since some of their recommendations are still valid. The following indicators have been mentioned in the report.

1. Density of population per km^2 (1991 Census)
2. Percentage of agricultural workers to total main workers (1991 Census)
3. Net area shown per agricultural worker
4. Percentage of net area irrigated to net area shown
5. Percentage of cropping intensity
6. Percentage of literacy (1991 Census)
7. Number of primary schools per lakh of population
8. Percentage of villages connected with all-weather roads
9. Percentage of villages electrified
10. Percentage of problem villages provided with safe drinking water facilities
11. Number of medical institutions for lakh of population

To fulfil the requirement of the study, data in respect of the selected indicators for all the 314 blocks of Odisha were collected from secondary sources and the entire exercise of the compilation, scrutiny, tabulation, and analysis of data for the committee was done by the

Planning and Coordination Department of the government. The value of the selected 11 indicators for all the 314 blocks in the state relating to 31 March 1992 that exhibit the development scenario of a block in different sectors shows that not a single block exhibits uniform level of development in respect of all the selected indicators. When the performance of a block is very good in one sector, it is not even good in other sectors. Therefore, the overall development of each of the blocks based on the selected 11 indicators had to be calculated in accordance with the aforementioned composite index. It is observed that the value of the composite development index of a block as on 31 March 1992 varies from 0.1809 to 0.6827. Lower the value more is the backwardness and more the value more is the level of development.

As per their analysis of composite index of development, the number of blocks under different categories of development groups is given in Table 11.9.

The committee has given a detailed break-up of blocks of all the 30 districts in the state under different categories of development groups such as A, B, C, D. Out of 314 blocks in the state only 145 seem to be somewhat developed and the rest 169 come under backward categories. To be more specific, not a single one out of 77 blocks of 8 districts, that is, Bolangir, Deogarh, Gajapati, Kalahandi, Koraput, Nawapada, Nowarangpur, and Rayagada come under developed categories. While backward categories of blocks are concentrated in 8 districts, 82 very backward blocks are spread over 18 districts and 87

Table 11.9 Number of blocks under different categories of development groups

Category	Level of development	Range of composite development index		Number of blocks
		From	To	
A	Developed	0.5056	Less than '1'	75
B	Developing	0.4500	0.5055	70
C	Backward	0.3952	0.4499	87
D	Very backward	More than '0'	0.3951	82
	Total			314

Source: GoO (1992: 1, Table 4.1).

backward blocks over 25 districts including the above 8 districts. To generalize, blocks coming under any one category of development do not conform to a continuous area within the state and they are more or less spread throughout the state.

The committee on the basis of above analysis has categorically indicated the names of the blocks in each district belonging to different categories. But since these figures refer to March 1992, probably there are some changes in the pattern of development of different blocks. We, therefore, do not consider it worthwhile to mention district wise number of blocks in different development blocks as given in the report.

The Panchayat Department of the Government of Odisha had made a district-wise information on below poverty line (BPL) families both in 1992 and 1997. One further study was made in 2002 but since the BPL families could not be decided in that study, a further study in different name is still in progress. Since the study report is not yet published, we can only indicate the variation in Survey Reports of 1992 and 1997. The variation shows that except for Debagarh there is decline in poverty between 1992 and 1997, but there is no uniformity in the decline, in some of the developed districts, the decline is much greater and in some of the backward districts the decline of poverty is much less. But since 1997, there has been a great deal of change in development pattern of the districts, the result of the 1997 survey cannot be taken as a true picture of poverty in different districts.

We have another study, 'Levels of Living and Poverty Pattern: A District wise Analysis for India', by Chaudhury and Gupta (2009). The data refers to 2004–05. In the NSSO's Consumer Expenditure survey held in 2004–05, the sample design had taken districts as strata in both the rural and urban sectors, which make it possible to get unbiased estimates of parameters at the district level. The authors with the help of these data present a profile of levels of living, poverty, and inequality for all the districts of 20 major states of India. They have made an attempt to map poverty in the districts to examine their spatial disparity within and across the states. We will extract the findings for Odisha and make some comparison with some other states or of all India wherever necessary. As the authors point out it was only in the 61st round survey of NSS (2004–05) that the sampling design

Table 11.10 Population share of the poorest and the richest states in the all-India percentile classes (rural)

States	Total rural population 2001	Population in the bottom 10 percentile classes (%)	Population in the top 10 percentile classes (%)
Odisha	31,287,422	31.1	3.7
Chhatisgarh	16,648,056	24.1	3.3
Kerala	23,574,449	2.3	37.5
Punjab	16,096,488	0.5	31.9

Source: Chaudhury and Gupta (2009: 95, Table 1R).

defined rural and urban parts of districts as strata for selection of sample villages and urban blocks, respectively, and thus, it paved the way for generating unbiased estimates of socio-economic parameters at the district level adequately supported by the sample design.

In their study they have made a comparison of the population share of poorest and richest states in the all-India percentile classes both for rural and urban areas. Tables 11.10 and 11.11 provide information in respect of poorest and richest 10 per cent both in respect of rural and urban areas.

The figures in Table 11.10 show that Punjab has lowest number of people in rural areas in regard to poorest 10 percentile classes and Kerala has highest number of top 10 percentile classes. Odisha has both highest number of poor and lowest number of top 10 percentile classes. Even Chhatisgarh is better than Odisha. When we come to urban areas Bihar seems to be worse than Odisha, but in respect of population in the top 10 percentile classes, Bihar seems to be better than Odisha, though the difference is not so significant. In Table 11.11 we have also made a comparison between Punjab and Himachal Pradesh. As Table 11.11 shows, Punjab is better than Himachal Pradesh in rural sphere whereas Himachal Pradesh is much better than Punjab in the urban sphere.

When we consider an overview of state-level estimates of major parameters, we find that in rural India, the average MPCE was the lowest in Odisha (Rs 399) and the highest in Kerala (Rs 1,013). All India rural HCR was around 28 per cent. States like Punjab and

Table 11.11 Population share of the poorest and the richest states in the all-India percentile classes (urban)

States	Total urban population 2001	Population in the bottom 10 percentile classes (%)	Population in the top 10 percentile classes (%)
Bihar	86,81,800	28.2	3.4
Odisha	55,17,238	24.6	3.2
Punjab	82,62,511	1.3	13.6
Himachal Pradesh	5,95,581	1.7	19.1

Source: Chaudhury and Gupta (2009: 95, Table 1U).

Jammu and Kashmir had less than 10 per cent poor while Odisha and Jharkhand each had more than 46 per cent of their population below the respective poverty lines. Average urban MPCE again varied from Rs 696 and Rs 757 in Bihar and Odisha respectively, to more than Rs 1,390 in Punjab and Himachal Pradesh. Odisha had the highest urban poverty (45 per cent) while it was less than 4 per cent in Himachal Pradesh and Assam. Inequality was found to be low in states like Assam and Bihar where average level of living was also low. On the other hand, the two best average MPCE states in the rural part of Kerala and Haryana were the two most unequal states. Thus, in rural India there was some indication of a trade-off between prosperity and inequality at state level. The most critical position was that of Chhatisgarh which had the highest inequality coupled with high poverty and low average MPCE. Urban inequality was also high in Kerala and Punjab, the states which were placed at the third and second highest position respectively, in terms of average per capita expenditure. Thus, the high urban inequality in the better-off states as well as in some of the poor states made the issue more complex. Table 11.12 gives the state-level estimate of average MPCE, HCR, and Lorenz ratio in 2004–05.

To get a good understanding of the level of living prevailing in the districts, Chaudhury and Gupta (2009) have studied the average level of living, poverty, and inequality in the 20 major states of India. They find that the number of sample observation was too small in urban Odisha and Chhatisgarh and therefore, there are restrictions

Table 11.12 District-wise population proportion, MPCE, HCR, and LR-S for rural and urban sectors in Odisha

District name	Rural						Urban					
	(1)	(2)	(3)	(4)	(5)	(6)	(7)	(8)	(9)	(10)	(11)	(12)
Baragarh	4.2	159	351	5.95	61.7	0.234	1.2	40	891	33.29	44.7	0.427
Jharsuguda	1.2	40	441	39.52	58.7	0.406	3.9	39	756	33.44	57.5	0.396
Sambalpur	2.3	80	275	6.41	79.5	0.224	4.6	39	652	4.89	46.9	0.320
Deogarh	0.9	40	285	7.25	73.4	0.233	0.3	20	697	4.24	35.3	0.231
Sundargarh	3.6	160	308	7.22	69.9	0.224	13.0	80	768	8.83	28.7	0.296
Keonjhar	4.4	160	430	8.98	46.1	0.304	4.8	40	648	4.65	58.5	0.303
Mayurbhanj	6.6	200	428	5.61	52.5	0.324	3.3	40	915	17.45	30.4	0.346
Baleswar	5.9	200	491	5.30	28.3	0.280	4.4	40	620	13.72	67.0	0.344
Bhadrak	4.1	160	534	8.65	22.9	0.288	3.5	40	993	27.44	27.3	0.332
Kendrapara	3.8	160	404	3.17	31.5	0.193	1.2	40	517	7.11	69.4	0.262
Jagatsinghpur	2.9	120	412	7.92	37.3	0.224	1.3	40	762	14.70	41.6	0.284
Cuttack	5.3	160	578	10.58	14.0	0.281	11.9	70	832	17.07	25.9	0.268
Jajpur	4.8	200	513	5.20	4.9	0.175	1.1	40	1048	8.33	25.2	0.297
Dhenkanal	3.0	119	356	11.27	57.1	0.219	2.3	40	650	11.87	54.5	0.277
Angul	3.2	120	358	6.27	53.0	0.199	3.9	39	647	23.63	49.6	0.300
Nayagarh	2.5	120	364	7.06	47.0	0.208	1.0	20	661	10.67	35.3	0.169
Khurda	3.3	160	470	7.54	27.8	0.235	13.8	80	809	23.94	50.2	0.395

(*Cont'd.*)

Table 11.12 *(Cont'd.)*

District name	Rural						Urban					
	(1)	(2)	(3)	(4)	(5)	(6)	(7)	(8)	(9)	(10)	(11)	(12)
Puri	4.4	160	417	5.82	27.0	0.193	4.9	40	616	18.69	51.3	0.243
Ganjam	7.9	240	435	4.96	33.6	0.233	5.6	80	758	15.20	45.3	0.314
Gajapati	1.5	78	347	16.03	61.4	0.317	1.1	20	503	40.63	91.2	0.285
Phulbani	1.9	80	295	17.45	76.6	0.266	1.0	20	784	50.61	39.0	0.406
Boudh	1.1	40	303	9.70	70.5	0.188	0.5	20	490	0.33	85.6	0.310
Sonepur	1.5	80	350	10.29	51.3	0.233	0.7	20	529	15.06	63.8	0.288
Bolangir	4.0	160	341	6.56	66.3	0.248	2.2	40	704	15.46	48.3	0.320
Nuapara	1.8	80	315	9.96	70.1	0.230	0.7	20	527	30.24	62.3	0.253
Kalahandi	4.0	160	304	6.17	70.5	0.250	1.9	40	741	40.42	60.3	0.536
Rayagada	2.4	80	307	11.30	67.1	0.315	1.9	40	918	15.97	21.8	0.280
Nawarangpur	3.1	120	255	7.73	80.6	0.232	0.8	40	563	29.09	87.7	0.429
Koraput	2.7	120	277	13.34	74.2	0.268	2.6	40	971	55.53	61.0	0.528
Malkangiri	1.5	80	307	22.01	67.9	0.310	0.6	20	593	21.35	70.8	0.355
Odisha	100.0	3836	399	1.68	46.9	0.282	100.0	1187	757	5.60	44.7	0.349

Source: Government of Odisha (n.d.).

Note: (1) Proportional population; (2) No. of sample households; (3) MPCE (Rs); (4) RSE of MPCE; (5) Percentage of poor; (6) Lorenz ratio (S); (7) Proportional population; (8) No. of sample households; (9) MPCE (Rs); (10) RSE of MPCE; (11) Percentage of poor; (12) Lorenz ratio (S).

for making conclusive remarks. Table 11.12 presents district-wise population proportion, MPCE, HCR, and LR-5 for rural and urban sectors within Odisha.

In their analysis, Chaudhury and Gupta (2009) have made a comparison among the different districts in different states. Even though we are not giving the data regarding districts of all the 20 states, we can mention some of the major conclusions of their study which pertain to Odisha, along with some common problems.

1 In both the sectors, there were some districts in almost all the states for which within district inequality (Lorenz ratio) was higher than the inequality at state level.
2 The critically high HCR districts were concentrated in states like Odisha, Chhatisgarh, Jharkhand, Bihar, Madhya Pradesh, and eastern Uttar Pradesh. On the other hand, zero poverty districts were mainly from Himachal Pradesh, Jammu and Kashmir, Gujarat, and Assam.
3 In the rural sector, more than half of about 500 districts had HCR of 30 per cent or less, while in 16 per cent of the districts HCR was 50 per cent or more. Out of 30 districts in Odisha, 18 districts had more than 50 per cent HCR, 7 districts had more than 70 per cent, and 1 Nowrangpur more than 80 per cent.
4 The urban poverty scenario was grimmer. Most abject poverty could be found in Gajapati, Odisha with more than 90 per cent people below the state poverty line.

We can mention here three conclusions of the study:

1 It is felt that the state-level aggregates may often mislead us and draw away our attention from some imminent areas of concern. The district-level estimates are found to be absolutely necessary for a complete understanding of the level of living prevailing in any part of the country.
2 In rural India at the state level, there has been an indication of a trade-off between prosperity and inequality with rich states having high level of inequality as against a low Lorenz ratio in the poor states. But the situation is a lot more complicated in the

urban sector where many of the poor states also suffer from high level of inequality.

3 It is also found that a district with excellent indicators in terms of any of the parameters under study in one sector often failed to perform at the same level in the other sector.

When we compare the poverty position of different districts in Odisha referring to 2004–05 (Table 11.12) we find that even though according to the Tendulkar Committee the ratio of poverty in rural areas in 2004–05 comes to 60.80 per cent, many districts numbering 13 have more than 61 per cent poverty ratio, even some of the districts have more than 70 per cent, and Nowarangpur has 80.6 per cent. In urban areas, though poverty ratio is 37.60, many districts numbering 22 have more than 40 per cent and more than 4 districts have more than 70 per cent. And Gajapati has 91.2 per cent, Boudh has 85.6 per cent, and Nowarangpur has 87.7 per cent. These districts still continue to be poor compared to other districts of Odisha.

While the GoO published figures of human development index (HDI) for 2004, Odisha's *Economic Survey 2011–12*, has updated the figures of HDI for 2007–08. The HDI, which is a summary indicator of human development, brings together the twin objectives of economic progress and social development. The HDI is now widely used as a basic measure of human development. This HDI is a composite index representing three dimensions of human development—economic, education, and health. While the all-India HDI in the year 2007–08 comes to 0.381, Odisha's comes to 0.362. All the other major 15 states for which figures have been given in the survey have higher HDI, the indices for Kerala and Punjab being 0.790 and 0.605 respectively. Odisha's rank is 15 among these 15 states. Instead of presenting the figures of different states, in Table 11.13, we present Odisha's district-wise comparison of HDI, gender development index (GDI), and infrastructure development index (assuming index value of states as 100) for the year 2001.

While HDI for Odisha as a whole comes to 0.579, 16 districts out of 30 have less than Odisha's average, the lowest being in the three districts—Malkangiri, Kendujhar, and Jajpur—having 0.37, 0.53, and 0.54 respectively. It is surprising why Kendujhar and Jajpur have such a low HDI. In many other respects they are comparatively

Table 11.13 District-wise comparison of HDI, GDI, and infrastructure development index, 2001

S. no.	Name of the district	HDI (Range: 0 to 1)		GDI (Range: 0 to 1)		Infrastructure development index (assuming index values of state as 100)	
		Value	Rank	Value	Rank	Value	Rank
1	Angul	0.663	6	0.637	4	90.68	18
2	Balasore	0.559	18	0.519	14	118.46	8
3	Bargarh	0.565	17	0.528	13	114.01	11
4	Bhadrak	0.646	8	0.497	21	119.8	5
5	Bolangir	0.546	21	0.518	16	100.24	15
6	Baudh	0.536	23	0.509	19	86.34	21
7	Cuttack	0.695	3	0.618	7	134.87	4
8	Deogarh	0.669	5	0.647	3	86.55	20
9	Dhenkanal	0.591	12	0.531	12	96.88	16
10	Gajapati	0.431	28	0.401	27	89.45	19
11	Ganjam	0.551	20	0.518	15	119.15	6
12	Jagatsinghpur	0.557	19	0.491	22	140.4	3
13	Jajpur	0.54	22	0.386	28	114.19	10
14	Jharsuguda	0.722	2	0.687	1	109.59	12
15	Kalahandi	0.606	11	0.579	8	79.75	25
16	Kandhamal	0.389	29	0.372	29	73.28	29
17	Kendrapara	0.626	10	0.516	18	105.52	13
18	Kendujhar	0.53	24	0.504	20	82.09	24
19	Khordha	0.736	1	0.632	5	160.04	1
20	Koraput	0.431	27	0.415	26	95.93	17
21	Malkangiri	0.37	30	0.362	30	75.65	27
22	Mayurbhanj	0.639	9	0.621	6	86.31	22
23	Nabrangpur	0.436	26	0.422	25	66.06	30
24	Nayagarh	0.571	15	0.452	23	77.36	26
25	Nuapada	0.581	14	0.561	9	75.39	28
26	Puri	0.657	7	0.516	17	154.04	2
27	Rayagada	0.443	25	0.428	24	84.37	23
28	Sambalpur	0.589	13	0.56	10	119.01	7
29	Sonepur	0.566	16	0.543	11	115.82	9
30	Sundargarh	0.683	4	0.659	2	104.17	14
	Odisha	0.579	–	0.546	–	100	–

Source: GoO (2004).

better than many other districts. Three better districts in terms of HDI are Khordha 0.736 (more developed in respect of education), Jharsuguda 0.722 (industrially more developed), and Cuttack 0.695 (the commercial capital of Odisha). When we come to GDI, we note from Table 11.13 that the aggregate value for Odisha is 0.546 and 20 districts have less value compared to Odisha's aggregate. In particular, we find that Malkangiri, Kandhamal, and Jajpur have very low values standing at 0.362, 0.372, and 0.386 respectively. In many respects, the first two are among the most backward areas of the state, and therefore, it is not surprising that GDI is very low there. The low index for Jajpur is a bit puzzling since it is commercially somewhat developed and is not far from Cuttack, the commercial hub of the state. We also note that Jharsuguda, Sundergarh, and Deogarh are among the best districts of the state in terms of GDI having index figures of 0.687, 0.659, and 0.647 respectively. We know that Jharsuguda has a large number of industries, Sundergarh is close to Rourkela housing the biggest steel factory of the state, and Deogarh probably benefits from being a neighbouring district of Sundergarh, Jharsuguda, and Sambalpur.

When we come to infrastructure development index, we note that infrastructure plays a major part in economic development. Therefore, one would expect that economically backward districts would have a low infrastructure development index and the data confirms this. We find that three districts which have the lowest value are Nabarangpur (66.06), Kandhamal (73.28), and Nuapada (75.39), which are among the most economically backward districts. Nuapada is a relatively new district which is also surrounded by three poor districts—Bolangir, Nabarangpur, and Kalahandi. Three districts which are comparably more developed are Khordha (160.04), which also occupies the first position in terms of HDI index; Puri (154.04), which is a centre of pilgrimage and therefore, has some infrastructure development to attract tourists; and Jagatsinghpur (140.4), which is surrounded by three developed districts namely Khordha, Cuttack, and Puri, and gets the benefit of its location.

As we see from this analysis, economic growth, average per capita income, and poverty aggregate level do not reveal true state of economy of a country or a state. Odisha is making steady progress in recent years. But still there are large communities who are deprived of basic necessities of life. There are also some regions which are much worse off than the others. It is therefore, said that gross domestic product (GDP) or per capita income reveals less and hides many things regarding the extent of deprivation of different sections or regions. It is therefore desirable to find out disaggregated data across different regions and different groups in respect of access to opportunities and also assets so as to find out the level of their development. But unfortunately such data are not available in many of the areas. Particularly the areas where most of the tribal people live, these are not easily accessible to collect accurate data regarding the state of economic or social condition. As such the overall growth does not give a true picture of the state of the economy of each region or social group.

The Government of Odisha has also introduced a large number of poverty reduction programmes to alleviate the economic and social condition of the poor people. The Government of India also provides economic assistance to all states to improve the economic and social condition of depressed regions, marginalized classes including ST, SC, and women, and to substantially reduce regional, social, and gender disparities. But many studies which have been conducted at different places have shown that there are huge leakages in the funds allotted for these purposes. Even in respect of Mahatma Gandhi National Rural Employment Guarantee Act (MGNREGA) programmes which are supposed to provide employment to needy people do not make any provision for employment. Even where some employment is provided, wages prescribed for them are not provided. It is surprising that some higher authorities in districts are involved in such misappropriation. Atul Kohli, who has written a path-breaking book *Poverty Amid Plenty in the New India*, points out in an interview to *Economic Times* (10 September 2012) that India is relatively incompetent and the Indian business is not all that public minded; the inclusive component of inclusive growth tends to get neglected in India. Power also tends to have increasing returns, those who become more powerful, say, Indian business groups, are likely to tilt the future political process in their own favour. If that comes to pass, who will push for inclusive growth? If growth in India is not inclusive, who would like to deal with the social and political consequences? These are the real dangers.

He further adds that besides MGNREGA, there are very few real welfare policies being pursued in India on a significant scale. There are of course two dozen schemes to benefit this or that group on paper. Some of these are helpful but, on the whole, India does very poorly on delivering health, or unemployment benefit, or pensions or poverty relief. While the MGNREGA scheme is impressive and full of promise, implementation has been half-hearted. If the government was really serious about implementing, it would be focused on how to improve capacity of local governments to deliver such programmes. But no such effort has been made. He therefore says efforts towards inclusion have been half-hearted. Another interesting point made by him is that caste, regional, and religious identities often trump class identities in India. But Mayawatis and DMKs of India take the steam out of any cohesive lower class challenge.

All the estimates show that there is not only colossal poverty in Odisha, but there is also great disparity in the field of poverty between different regions and social classes. Due to such high poverty, the level of HDI in Odisha is much lower than many other states of India. These findings do not give us any hope that we can make any significant change in the poverty ratio of Odisha unless there is a substantial change in the direction and content of the economy.

The following general observations are suggested for making an overall change in the economy.

1 Agricultural development is a crucial factor in economic and social change in Odisha. As we observe from Odisha's *Economic Survey*, development of agriculture in Odisha has lagged behind due to several constraints such as traditional methods of cultivation, inadequate capital formation and low investment, inadequate irrigation facilities, and uneconomic size of holdings. Further, the domestic sector of the state's economy has become more often than not a helpless victim of natural calamities like flood, drought, and cyclone. What is therefore necessary is to accelerate the process of agricultural development by increasing both production and productivity, improving cropping pattern and agricultural practices, evolving new varieties of seeds, expanding irrigation facilities, and extending the supply of institutional credit. All these require more investment on agriculture

along with proper use of inputs. For example, if we increase the use of fertilizer in an unbalanced manner, we cannot increase the productivity of fertilizers. The implication is, not only will we have to increase the use of fertilizer, but maintain its proper balance for its effective use. A change in technology is also necessary. It has been observed that in many cases due to lack of adequate knowledge and research constraint, additional application of inputs such as irrigation and fertilizers has not increased total factors productivity. It is said that there is almost a technological fatigue which has not increased productivity. On the other hand it has led to erosion of resource base of agriculture. Since in the Twelfth Five Year Plan, the Planning Commission has made a number of concrete recommendations for improving agricultural growth for an 'inclusive growth', we need not elaborate these recommendations for attaining Millennium Development Goals in Odisha. However, we can only mention that Rural Development Expenditure (RDE) should aim at increasing the income of farmers by increasing the investment in agriculture, improving infrastructure in rural areas for facilitating successful operational mechanism of village and small scale industries, accelerating irrigation facility with greater emphasis on water-harvesting structures and controlling floods, providing a number of special area programmes to assist the small and marginal farmers along with poor artisans and persons below the poverty lines. In addition, steps should be taken to complete the land reform measures, which were initiated in the 1950s and early part of 1960s and abandoned when the new technology of high yielding variety (HYV) developed in the later part of 1960s. In China, for example, much of the extreme poverty was reduced in the first-half of the 1980s mainly as a result of (a) the spurt in agricultural growth following decollectivization (agricultural output grew at 7.1 per cent per year on an average during 1979–84 compared to 2.7 per cent during 1970–78); (b) land reform, which by an egalitarian redistribution, subject only to differences in regional average and demographic size, provided a floor to rural income; and (c) readjustment of farm procurement prices (Bardhan 2007). This shows agricultural development should play a major role in reducing poverty.

2 And what is more, according to Agricultural Census 2000–01 conducted by the Board of Revenue, there were 40.67 lakh operational holdings in Odisha with 50.81 lakh hectare of area. Small and marginal holdings accounted for 83.8 per cent with 53.12 per cent of total area. Remaining 16.2 per cent of holdings belonged to semi-medium, medium, and large categories with 46.88 per cent of total area. Average size of operational holdings, which was 1.30 hectare in the 1995–96 Census declined to 1.25 hectare in the 2000–01 Census. Land resources remaining almost the same, the per capita availability of land in Odisha has considerably gone down from 0.39 hectare in the year 1950–51 to 0.14 hectare in 2005–06 due to increase in population. Heavy pressure on land has resulted in huge unemployment and underemployment in rural areas. It is therefore essential that along with increase in productivity of land, a large number of non-farm occupations should be created in rural areas to reduce the pressure on land and improve the economic status of rural people by increasing their income. Even at present the productivity of non-farm sector in rural areas is greater than that of farm sector. Such non-farm occupations will also provide scope for application of new technology. It may also be mentioned here that agriculture and industry should not be competitive but complementary to sustain rural population with greater scope for employment and livelihood. As it is, a large number of distressed people migrate to urban areas. We cannot prevent this unless we are in a position to absorb them in rural areas. This calls for setting up of large number of food processing and agro-processing units, which can absorb surplus labour from farming, help in value addition in the farm product, and at the same time, will reduce wastage in storage and transit. We can also develop a number of other manufacturing industries to provide adequate productive employment to surplus labour force in agriculture to increase their economic well-being and change the economic structure of rural areas.

3 In this context, we have to point out that many subsidies are given today for water or power or fertilizers which are regressive as well as ecologically damaging even though they may be politically popular. As Desai (2011) has said, redistribution is always bigger

in ambition than in actual transfers and is often appropriated by the not-so-poor who control the transmission channels of aid. In his book, *The Politics of Hunger in India—A Study of Democracy, Governance and Kalahandi's Poverty*, Currie (2000) points out that there exists a widening implementation gap between public expectation and government delivery, and indirectly, an erosion in legitimacy of government authority. Indeed, to borrow words from Parenti (2010), '[e]lections come and go, and the life of poverty goes on pretty much as before'. He concludes by saying: 'In many countries, some groups remain incapable of exercising their rights and obligations. We face a new monster democracies without an effective citizenship for large sections of the political community. In such a case how can we create necessary capacity to improve effectiveness, efficiency and economy (the '3 Es') in welfare administration, and hence to translate public preferences more fully into policy outcomes.'

In such a context we should, therefore, make direct investment in both physical infrastructure like roads, electricity, and irrigation, which will facilitate capital formation and social infrastructure like education, health, sanitation, and drinking water to improve the capability of the people who are engaged in different types of economic and social activities. Amartya Sen in 1982 argued that development economics has been discredited because of its very narrow focus on growth and its relative neglect of development which is not synonymous with growth. He stressed that the purpose of development was not merely to generate a higher income: higher income is not an end but an instrument for achieving a better quality of life. He developed the concept of entitlement and capability and increasingly defined development in terms of capability. Entitlement is the link between production and what a person actually consumes. A person's entitlement may be more or less than what he produces. This explains why the relation between per capita income and development in terms of health, education, and poverty may be very weak. In fact, even though per capita income in India has increased substantially due to higher level of economic growth, there is great short-fall in social development. India is seen as a wounded civilization—a place of pestilence, malnutrition, illiteracy, poverty, and hunger. Capability is the ability of a person to function autonomously.

This may be partly a function of his consumption—what commodities do to the individual or what Sen calls functioning, is also a function of a society's institutional arrangements. Poverty, ill health, and illiteracy are major constraints to a person's level of functioning and capabilities. Enhancing capability means tackling these debilitating factors.

4 It is often argued that adequate price support should be given to farmers, which will place the agricultural sector on a safe-and-sound footing. We will rather argue that instead of higher prices of foodgrains, it would be better to have development of sustainable technology, improvement of infrastructure, and increase of human skill that will provide better scope for agricultural development and quality of life of farmers. For the last several years there have been large increases in the minimum support price (MSP) of rice and wheat due to the pressure of big farmers as a result of which there was a large gap between the cost of production and the MSP. One of the important impacts of this development was the regional segmentation of the market; for example, prices of foodgrains in the primary grain markets remained below MSP in some northern states that substantially reduced private trade from the grain markets and excessive financial cost to the FCI for procurement and storage of foodgrains. Reduction of private trade in wheat and rice in the northern states of Punjab and Haryana also possibly led to crowding out of private investment in agricultural marketing channels. Market prices were often lower than the MSPs and therefore, there was unabated build-up of foodgrain stocks with the FCI. Very often more than three times of the buffer requirement were procured that resulted in extremely high carrying costs and bloated food subsidy. In spite of higher MSP, the pressure on the part of large farmers' organizations is always there for higher support price with the support of many political parties. But the economic analysis shows that the supply response of higher price in Indian agriculture is much less important than the improvement in technology, infrastructure, and human capital. Narain (1976) who has done pioneering work on the supply response of Indian agriculture has pointed

out 'an over simplistic and therefore, excessive preoccupation with price can do more harm than good by distracting attention from the harder but more important tasks which belong in the non-price world of achieving technological breakthroughs and releasing such real constraints as stand in the way of becoming a reality in the farmers' fields'. Krishna (1982) who made a survey of agricultural supply response in several developing countries found that the elasticity of output with respect to major technological shifters such as irrigation was 1.5 to 5.5 times the price elasticity. He therefore, suggested to pay more attention to the development of technology (which can increase productivity), infrastructure particularly in rural areas (which will facilitate the improvement of agro-based industries thus reducing pressure on agriculture), and human capital (which will enable the farmers to improve their skill for operational efficiency). There is also great need to evolve new biotechnologies to save on chemical inputs and increase productivity in irrigated and dry land areas without associated ecological harm. The new research inputs should aim at achieving agricultural revolution in five areas to sustain and expand the gains already achieved and improve the ecological balance which will prevent degradation of land due to depletion of soil fertility and moisture. These five areas are productivity, quality, income and employment, small farm management, and enlarging the food basket along with nutritional dimension (Swaminathan). All this implies that adequate funds would be provided to improve research to evolve new technologies, create favourable institutional set-up which can carry such research programmes with success and design proper incentives for the absorption of new technology for the development and diffusion of adequate new technology (Rao 2005), not only in irrigated areas but also in dry land areas.

5 Since inclusive growth has been emphasized by the Planning Commission , there is need to improve the system of governance which would ensure that the type of investment which are injected are utilized for the people for whom it is meant. But now there is not only a lot of leakage but also delay in the process of distribution. As we all know, the nature of administrative system is insensitive and inflexible. The development administration

instead of confining itself to general and regulatory function needs to be developed, adapted, or expanded to increase the pace of development, which will aim at a sustained and widely diffused improvement in material and social welfare.

All these formidable functions require a different approach. The administrators who will be responsible for development programme must play a new role, a catalytic role, of a carrier of change instead of continuing only stereotyped functions. Further, since they have to work with the people who are poor and illiterate, they have to motivate them, mobilize and build up effective grassroot institutions so that they can get the support and services from these institutions which will ultimately act as agent of change—a difficult task, but absolutely necessary to secure inclusive growth and improve the economic well-being of the poor. This calls for a major institutional change without which there cannot be any improvement in poverty situation in Odisha.

In conclusion, we may point out that in order to maintain sustainable economic development, reduce poverty and improve equity, entitlement, and capability, we have to change the pattern of development and involve the people directly in the process of development. The people should not be passive agents in the process of change. The proponents of development need to urgently produce the micro basis for human development. The development debate is mostly concerned with issues of stabilization, fiscal balance, and GDP growth. But these really do not help in attaining human development. The approach of neoclassical economics may ensure micro approach and involve people in the process of change.

References

Bardhan, P. 2007. 'Poverty and Inequality in China and India: Elusive Link with Globalization', *Economic and Political Weekly*, XLII(38, 22 September): 3849–52.

Bhalla, G.S. 2000. 'Political Economy of Indian Development in the 20th Century: India's Road to Freedom & Growth', Presidential Address in the 83rd Annual Conference of Indian Economic Association, University of Jammu, Jammu, Jammu and Kashmir.

Bruno M., M. Ravallion, and L. Squire. 1996. 'Equity and Growth in Developing Countries: Old and New Perspectives on the Policy Issues', Policy Research Working Paper No. 1563, Poverty and Human Resources Division, World Bank, Washington, DC.

Chaudhury, S. and N. Gupta. 2009. 'Levels of Living and Poverty Patterns: A District-wise Analysis for India', *Economic and Political Weekly*, 44(9, 28 February): 94–110.

Currie, Bob. *The Politics of Hunger in India*. New Delhi: Macmillan India Ltd.

Datt, G. and M. Ravallion. 2002. 'Is India's Economic Growth Leaving the Poor Behind', *Journal of Economic Perspectives*, 16(3): 89–108.

Desai, M. 2011. *The Rediscovery of India*. New York: Penguin.

Dev, S. Mahendra and C. Ravi. 2007. 'Poverty and Inequality—All-India and States, 1983–2005', *Economic and Political Weekly*, 42(6, 10 February): 509–21.

Foster, J., J. Greer, and E. Thorbecke. 1984. 'A Class of Decomposable Poverty Measures', *Econometrica*, 52(3): 761–66.

Government of India. 1993. *Review of Methodology for Fixing of Poverty Line and Estimating the Increase of Poverty*, Report of the D.T. Lakdawala Committee.

———. 1997. *Report of the Task Force on Projections of Minimum Needs and Effective Consumption Demand*, Prospective Planning Division, Planning Commission, January.

———. 2009. *Report of the Expert Group to Review the Methodology for Estimation of Poverty*, Planning Commission, November.

———. 2011. *Press Note on Poverty Estimates*, Planning Commission, January.

Government of Odisha. 1992. *Ghadei Committee Report*. Bhubaneswar: Planning and Coordination Department.

———. 1994. *Report of the Committee on the Constitution of Separate Development Board*. Planning and Coordination Department.

———. 2004. *Human Development Report*. Bhubaneswar: Planning and Coordination Department

———. 2013. 'Human Development and Poverty', *Economic Survey* 2012–13, Planning and Coordination Department Report.

———. n.d. Directorate of Economics and Statistics, Bhubaneswar. Available at http://desorissa.nic.in/ (last accessed on 22 January 2016).

Himanshu. 2007. 'Recent Trend in Poverty and Inequality: Some Preliminary Results', *Economic and Political Weekly*, 42(6, 10 February): 497–508.

Kohli A. 2012. *Poverty amid Plenty in the New India*. New York: Cambridge University Press.

Krishna, Raj. 1982. 'Some Aspects of Agricultural Growth, Price Policy and Equity in Developing Countries', *Food Research Institute Studies*, XVIII(3).

Krishnaji, N. 2012. 'Abolish the Poverty Line', *Economic and Political Weekly*, 47(15, 14 April): 10–11.

Manna, G.C. 2012. 'On Some Contentious Issues of the New Poverty Line', *Economic and Political Weekly*, 47(5, 14 April): 11–14.

Narain, Dharm. 1976. 'Growth of Productivity in Indian Agriculture', in K.N. Raj, Amartya Sen, and C.H. Hanumantha Rao(eds), *Studies in Indian Agriculture*, Delhi: Oxford University Press.

Papola, T.S. 2012. 'Economic Growth, Inclusiveness and Regional Disparities, India's Experience of the Last Two Decades', Nabakrusna Choudhury Memorial Lecture, Nabakrushna Choudhury Centre for Development Studies, Bhubaneswar, 13 July 2012.

Parenti, M. J. 2010. *Democracy for the Few*, 9th Edition, USA: Wadsworth, Cengage Learning.

Rao, C.H. Hanumant. 2005. *Agriculture, Food Security, Poverty and Environment*. New Delhi: Oxford University Press.

Rath, N. 2011. 'Measurement of Poverty: In Retrospect and Prospect', *Economic and Political Weekly* 46(42, 15 October): 40–43.

Sen A. 1982. *Choice, Welfare and Measurement*. Oxford: Basil Blackwell.

———. 2001. *Development as Freedom*. Oxford: Oxford University Press.

Subramanian, S. 2011. 'The Poverty Line: Getting It Wrong Again', *Economic and Political Weekly* 46(48, 26 November): 37–42.

12

Malnutrition and Food Insecurity in Odisha

*Manoj Panda**

Adequate nutrition and food security are important aspects of human well-being. Lack of adequate food consumption by individuals is the primary cause of prevalence of malnutrition. Nutritional security is thus closely related to food security, though it may be distinct from it in some respects. Malnutrition is considered as the greatest single threat to the state of public health in the world. In recent decades, there has been a renewed concern regarding widespread prevalence of malnutrition and food insecurity in the world despite fairly high economic growth in several of the most populated countries. According to Food and Agriculture Organization (FAO)

* The author would like to thank Akhilesh Sharma for help in estimating the NSSO consumption data at regional and social group level and to Ankush Agrawal for helpful discussion. He would also like to thank a referee of this volume and participants at a workshop at the Nabakrushna Choudhury Centre for Development Studies (NCDS), Bhubaneswar for many useful suggestions.

(2012), about 870 million or 12.5 per cent of the world's population suffered from chronic undernutrition during 2010–12. Of them 850 million live in developing countries. Recognizing the seriousness of the problem at the turn of the century, world leaders set reduction in poverty and malnutrition as the first of the Millennium Development Goals (MDGs).

Food security has been part of major policy agenda in India since India's independence. The country then faced the threat of famine and widespread starvation due to insufficient production of foodgrains and absence of a country-wide distribution network. Policy focus in the early decades was on foodgrain production to meet domestic demand and building up of a distribution system. The introduction of the Green Revolution helped India in achieving self-sufficiency by the mid-1970s. However, this success did not translate to household-level food and nutritional security due to lack of purchasing power of a large section of the population. Famine-like situation has been avoided over the last six decades and starvation deaths are few and far between. But malnutrition and food insecurity among a fairly large section of the population persist in the country.

While food production has been by and large in the private sector in India, the government intervenes in the foodgrains market in a significant way through procurement from producers at a minimum support price and distribution to consumers at a subsidized price. This mechanism also helps in influencing price stability in a limited manner. More recently, the Parliament has passed the food security bill that recognizes the right to food by the citizens so that they are free from hunger. Although the right to food is not a fundamental right of the citizens in the Constitution of India, the Supreme Court has created legal entitlements to food through its judgements in recent years by interpreting right to food as an essential element of the fundamental right to live.

Odisha, which is at the bottom end among the Indian states in the ranking of per capita income, has relatively high prevalence of food and nutritional insecurity. Its per capita income, which was low to begin with, diverged away further from the national average for several decades. The growth rate in gross state domestic product (GSDP) has picked up impressively in the last decade, yet its relative position among Indian states on the income scale has not changed much. Productivity of rice, the dominant crop in the state's agriculture, remains way below several other states. In addition, the state also has a large proportion of tribal population, almost three times the all-India average, inhabiting in the western and northern forest belt. Reaching the hitherto unreached is a major challenge for the government machinery and non-governmental organizations (NGOs).

Against this backdrop, this chapter attempts to examine some issues related to malnutrition and food insecurity in Odisha. The section titled 'Incidence of malnutrition' discusses trends in malnutrition in Odisha in a comparative perspective against developments at the national level. The third section titled 'Prevalence of food insecurity' examines issues regarding food security in the state. Thereafter, some major policy interventions related to reduction of malnutrition and of food insecurity are discussed, followed by the concluding remarks.

Incidence of malnutrition

Concept of malnutrition

The human body needs various types of nutrients such as calorie, protein, fat, and several vitamins and minerals in adequate amounts and in the right proportions for proper functioning and growth. Malnutrition is a condition of health disorder that results due to lack of sufficient and proper diet. The food we take must provide all essential nutrients in the required amount. Nutritionists recommend balanced diet baskets that meet the essential nutrients in the required amount. But complexities arise in specifying what adequate nutrient is because of inter- and intra-individual variations in nutritional need. For example, calorie need of a person is not fixed but varies over a large range[1] depending on the age, sex, activity, body weight, and climatic conditions. Further, it varies from one day to another for the same person doing similar kind of work due to adaptation mechanism in the body. Thus, nutritional need of people is better viewed by means of a statistical distribution. Nutritionists recommend

[1] The calorie range for an adult man varies from 2,320 to 3,490 depending on activity status (National Institute of Nutrition (NIN) 2009).

balanced diet baskets separately for various age-sex-activity groups corresponding to the average requirement of the group. Any shortfall of intake from the average recommended level does not imply that nutritional need of a specific person is not met. When studies that treat a person as undernourished are observed, the intake falls short of average requirement considerably, overestimating the incidence of undernourishment.[2] But if the intake of a person falls below the minimum of a desirable range, there will be overwhelming statistical evidence that the nutritional need of the person is not met. Let m denote the mean and sd the standard deviation in calorie intake estimated from a healthy and active population; then under normal distribution of nutrient need, we may state that when a person's nutrient intake falls below $m-2.sd$, there is a high probability that she/he will not be meeting the calorie need and may be called undernourished. Similarly, obesity might be defined for intake above $m+2.sd$.

Malnutrition may then be operationally defined as a condition when certain nutrients are less than or in excess of the required range. In the developing countries, malnutrition is mostly present in the form of undernutrition caused by a diet lacking adequate calorie, protein, and other nutrients, though obesity has emerged as a matter of concern among the wealthy section in these countries due to excess energy and fat intake. In this chapter we shall be dealing with undernutrition or issues related to inadequate nutrients in the diet.

Certain sections of the population such as women, children, and the elderly have high risk of malnutrition in several developing countries. More than half of children's deaths are attributed to

[2] The official income poverty line estimates in India till recently was anchored to 24,00 and 21,00 calories intake per capita per day in rural and urban areas respectively in the base year in 1973–74. These figures correspond to the mean in the distribution of calorie need, while the lower limit $m-2sd$ would be around 20 per cent lower than the mean. While the average calorie figures were used earlier only to obtain a minimum desirable income level for the *base year*, many analysts have used the mean calories as the norm to estimate the proportion of undernourished population, though there is large uncertainty in linking the mean of the distribution to undernutrition. The Tendulkar Committee has rightly delinked the poverty line from the calorie requirement norm (GoI 2009).

malnutrition. Women need additional nutrients during pregnancy and breastfeeding. Children can be at the risk of malnutrition even before birth if mothers do not receive adequate nutrients. The elderly have a larger probability of malnutrition because of changes in appetite, chewing problem, and dependency on others.

Consequences of malnutrition are severe. According to the World Health Organization, malnutrition is present in half of all cases of child mortality and is considered as the single-most factor contributing to child mortality. Certain effects of malnutrition, if it occurs in the first two years of life, are mostly irreversible; hence, child malnutrition needs priority attention. It may result in stunting (less than normal height for age) and wasting (less than normal weight for height). Protein-energy malnutrition (PEM) results from inadequate energy and protein intake on a sustained basis. PEM may be severe, moderate, or mild depending on the extent of stunting and wasting and is often associated with deficiencies of specific vitamins and minerals (micronutrients). Insufficient intake of vitamin A causes blindness and that of iodine leads to goitre. Malnourished persons are more likely to have infectious diseases such as pneumonia and tuberculosis which contribute to high mortality rate in many developing societies. Further, their immunity system is likely to be affected adversely. Nutrition-deficient individuals are less productive at work and low productivity results in low income that traps the poor in a vicious circle of undernutrition. Deficiencies in nutrition thus inflict long-term damages to both individuals and society.[3]

Magnitude of malnutrition

Turning to the issue of estimation of incidence of malnutrition, consumption surveys have been widely used to estimate food and nutritional

[3] Though not considered in this chapter, overnutrition or obesity too has severe consequences. Obesity causes several diseases such as cardiovascular diseases, diabetes, cancers, and chronic respiratory diseases. Some of them are also referred to as diseases of affluence. Estimates indicate incidence of obesity to be roughly about 15 per cent in India with some urban areas having higher rates. Interestingly, Ramachandran (2007) states the possibility of childhood undernutrition as a factor responsible for adulthood obesity.

intake. Consumption data reflect some important aspects of access to food as well as food acquisition and allocation behaviour of household expenditure. Given the conceptual problems in nutritional intake measures indicated earlier, there is now a growing realization to focus on nutritional outcome measures. Anthropometric outcome measures based on relations among height, weight, and age capture nutritional outcome and are likely to be more appropriate than nutrient intake estimates in understanding malnutrition impact. We discuss in the next section both nutrient intake as well as anthropometric measures.

Average nutrient intake

We start with levels of average nutritional intake of Odisha in comparison to other states. Tables 12.1, 12.2, and 12.3 show the intake of calorie, protein, and fat for major states in India as revealed by the National Sample Survey data[4] from its quinquennial rounds which have large sample size. It may be noted that the relation between per capita calorie intake across states and per capita income is not very strong. While developed states such as Punjab and Haryana do have high calorie intake, other developed states like Maharashtra and Gujarat have low energy intake. On the other hand, per capita calorie intake in some of the underdeveloped states is high compared to other states—Rajasthan, Uttarakhand, and Odisha fall in this category.

Per capita calorie intake[5] in rural Odisha has been close to national average during 1993–94 to 1999–2000 and above it in some of the years (Table 12.1). It has been consistently above the national average in urban areas. Per capita intake of calorie per day in Odisha stood at 2,126 in rural areas and 2,096 in urban areas in 2009–10 compared to national average of 2,020 and 1,946 respectively. Odisha's position in interstate comparison belongs to the top one-third among

[4] See Tandon and Landes (2011) for problems in calorie intake estimation from NSSO household survey data for components like purchase of processed food and meals consumed outside the household. Note that the NSSO survey aims at obtaining data on household consumer expenditure and it is not specially designed to serve the needs of a nutrition survey.

[5] The nutrient intake data considered in this section are from NSSO Report No. 540 (GoI 2012). The web version provides state-level detailed tables.

Table 12.1 Estimated per capita calorie intake per day in different years: Major Indian states

State	Rural				Urban			
	1993–94	1999–2000	2004–05	2009–10	1993–94	1999–2000	2004–05	2009–10
	50th round	55th round	61st round	66th round	50th round	55th round	61st round	66th round
Andhra Pradesh	2,052	2,021	1,995	2,047	1,992	2,052	2,000	1,975
Assam	1,983	1,915	2,067	1,974	2,108	2,174	2,143	2,003
Bihar	2,115	2,121	2,049	1,931	2,188	2,171	2,190	2,013
Chhattisgarh	–	–	1,942	1,926	–	–	2,087	1,949
Gujarat	1,994	1,986	1,923	1,982	2,027	2,058	1,991	1,983
Haryana	2,491	2,455	2,226	2,180	2,140	2,172	2,033	1,940
Jharkhand	–	–	1,961	1,900	–	–	2,458	2,046
Karnataka	2,073	2,028	1,845	1,903	2,026	2,046	1,944	1,987
Kerala	1,965	1,982	2,014	1,964	1,966	1,995	1,996	1,941
Madhya Pradesh	2,164	2,062	1,929	1,939	2,082	2,132	1,954	1,854
Maharashtra	1,939	2,012	1,933	2,051	1,989	2,039	1,847	1,901
Odisha	*2,199*	*2,119*	*2,023*	*2,126*	*2,261*	*2,298*	*2,139*	*2,096*
Punjab	2,418	2,381	2,240	2,223	2,089	2,197	2,150	2,062
Rajasthan	2,470	2,425	2,180	2,191	2,184	2,335	2,116	2,014
Tamil Nadu	1,884	1,826	1,842	1,925	1,922	2,030	1,935	1,963
Uttar Pradesh	2,307	2,327	2,200	2,064	2,114	2,131	2,124	1,923
Uttarakhand	–	–	2,160	2,179	–	–	2,205	1,984
West Bengal	2,211	2,095	2,070	1,927	2,131	2,134	2,011	1,851
All India	2,153	2,149	2,047	2,020	2,071	2,156	2,020	1,946

Source: NSSO (2009–10) refers to Schedule 1 which is comparable with most of the past years.

Table 12.2 Per capita protein intake per day in different years: Major states

State	Rural				Urban			
	1993–94	1999–2000	2004–05	2009–10	1993–94	1999–2000	2004–05	2009–10
	50th round	55th round	61st round	66th round	50th round	55th round	61st round	66th round
Andhra Pradesh	50.8	49.4	49.8	50.7	49.6	50.8	50.9	50.8
Assam	49.5	47.7	52.7	48.7	53.5	56.5	55.9	52.6
Bihar	60.2	58.7	57.8	53.6	61.4	61	62.2	56.5
Chhattisgarh	–	–	47.4	44.7	–	–	53.9	49.5
Gujarat	55.6	54.2	53.3	54	54.9	54.7	57.3	53.3
Haryana	78.4	75.3	69.6	67	63.6	62.5	60.5	57.6
Jharkhand	–	–	51.2	48.5	–	–	69.5	56.2
Karnataka	55.1	54.2	48.8	49	53.1	53.5	52.2	51.8
Kerala	50.8	52.4	55.4	52.7	52.4	55.2	56.7	54
Madhya Pradesh	63	58.2	58.8	58.4	59.8	60.6	58.2	54.1
Maharashtra	54.8	56.5	55.7	56.2	55.5	55.9	52.1	52.7
Odisha	*52.7*	*49.9*	*48.3*	*49.7*	*57.2*	*57.8*	*55.2*	*52.5*
Punjab	74.7	71.7	66.7	65.4	61.8	64.8	63.4	60.4
Rajasthan	79.4	76.9	69.6	67.8	66.5	70.4	64	60.5
Tamil Nadu	46.8	44.9	44.9	47.3	48.7	51.7	49.2	50.2
Uttar Pradesh	70.4	69.7	65.9	60	63.2	62	65.1	56.2
Uttarakhand	–	–	61.6	58.6	–	–	62.8	55.5
West Bengal	54.8	51.6	52.0	47.9	56.6	55.5	55.1	49.0
All India	*60.2*	*59.1*	*57*	*55*	*57.2*	*58.5*	*57*	*53.5*

Source: NSSO (2009–10) refers to Schedule 1 which is comparable with most of the past years.

Table 12.3 Per capita fat intake per day in different years: Major states

State	Rural				Urban			
	1993–94	1999–2000	2004–05	2009–10	1993–94	1999–2000	2004–05	2009–10
	50th round	55th round	61st round	66th round	50th round	55th round	61st round	66th round
Andhra Pradesh	27.2	29.5	33.5	37.9	34.9	41.5	43.2	43.2
Assam	21.0	22.3	26.7	25.3	30.8	38.7	36.8	33.5
Bihar	23.0	26.5	28.4	28.3	32.7	34.2	40.4	35.2
Chhattisgarh	–	–	19.9	24.7	–	–	37.2	37.4
Gujarat	47.4	53.8	50.9	56.9	57.9	67.0	63.5	65.9
Haryana	53.6	59.1	55.4	58.7	49.4	56.3	54.4	54.4
Jharkhand	–	–	22.8	27.0	–	–	53.8	41.6
Karnataka	28.6	36.6	33.9	40.0	37.6	45.1	43.3	46.9
Kerala	32.7	38.8	40.8	42.8	37.0	42.9	44.9	45.6
Madhya Pradesh	28.3	31.3	35.1	36.8	40.3	43.5	43.4	46.4
Maharashtra	33.5	39.7	41.5	48.3	47.9	52.6	50.1	54.3
Odisha	*14.8*	*16.3*	*17.8*	*23.2*	*28.1*	*27.4*	*28.3*	*31.3*
Punjab	59.8	58.7	58.7	61.9	53.7	57.9	61.0	61.9
Rajasthan	52.8	53.5	50.9	55.0	51.6	61.5	56.4	55.7
Tamil Nadu	24.7	29.5	29.6	36.8	33.9	43.2	41.1	44.0
Uttar Pradesh	35.5	37.6	37.5	36.6	41.2	45.5	46.1	42.3
Uttarakhand	–	–	41.3	48.9	–	–	48.0	48.4
West Bengal	21.4	24.2	26.5	28.4	34.2	40.2	39.1	38.4
All India	*31.4*	*36.1*	*35.5*	*38.3*	*42.0*	*49.6*	*47.5*	*47.9*

Source: NSSO (2009–10) refers to Schedule 1 which is comparable with most of the past years.

18 major states in 2009–10 with respect to calorie-intake level. These levels are higher than those of all the neighbouring states of West Bengal, Jharkhand, Chhattisgarh, and Andhra Pradesh. The quantum of food consumed on an average basis as indicated by calorie intake in Odisha thus seems to be fairly good by interstate comparison. A note of caution in such a comparison is that work intensity is assumed to be similar across states.

The per capita calorie intake per day has been declining in several states, including Odisha, since 1993–94. The decline could be attributed to several factors such as changing consumption pattern, changes in lifestyle of middle- and high-income groups, reduced physical activity, and fall in proportion of workforce engaged in high-energy intensive work due to mechanization of agriculture and other activities. Rao (2000) observes that reduction in cereal consumption—a dominant source of calorie—need not be an indication of welfare deterioration.

Protein intake in Odisha was 55 grams per capita per day in rural areas and 53.5 grams in urban areas. Both rural and urban areas show a decline by 3–5 grams per capita per day since 1993–94. On this dimension, Odisha's position is consistently below the national average and belongs to the bottom one-third category in interstate comparison in recent years (Table 12.2). In 2009–10, rural Odisha consumed less protein compared to its neighbours except Chhattisgarh, while urban Odisha consumes more protein than its neighbours. This reflects higher urban–rural disparity in protein intake in Odisha than the neighbouring states. In terms of fat intake, Odisha occupies the bottommost position across the major Indian states in both rural and urban areas (Table 12.3). Its average intake is 23 grams in rural areas and 31 grams in urban areas as against all-India average 38 grams and 48 grams respectively.

One might thus conclude that at the macro level, the problem in Odisha lies in the *composition* of food and not so much in the *quantum* of food which often refers to adequacy of calorie intake. The compositional problem is also evident from the fact that cereals supplied as much as 74 per cent and 69 per cent of calorie intake in rural and urban areas of Odisha in 2009–10 compared to 60 per cent and 50 per cent for all India. Cereals also accounted for 71 per cent and 65 per cent of total protein intake in rural and urban Odisha while it was lower by 7–9 percentage points at the all-India level

(Government of India (GoI) 2012). The health concerns associated with micronutrients (vitamins and minerals) are also essentially due to lack of diversification of the food basket.

Nutrient intake distribution

We now turn to distribution issues to understand whether quantity of food is adequate for all sections of the population. Calorie intake differs considerably across households arranged by per capita total consumption expenditure. The per capita per day calorie intake for the lowest two consumption expenditure classes[6] in rural areas is 1,612 and 1,834 calories while it is 2,483 and 2,676 calories for the top two classes (Figure 12.1). Similarly, it varies from 1,752 to 2,504 in urban areas. Notwithstanding the calorie norm debate, the calorie intake at the lower end of income distribution is extremely low to have any chances of meeting the need adequately. It is also worth noting that the calorie need would be higher for poor households than non-poor households because the poor are often engaged in heavy manual work.

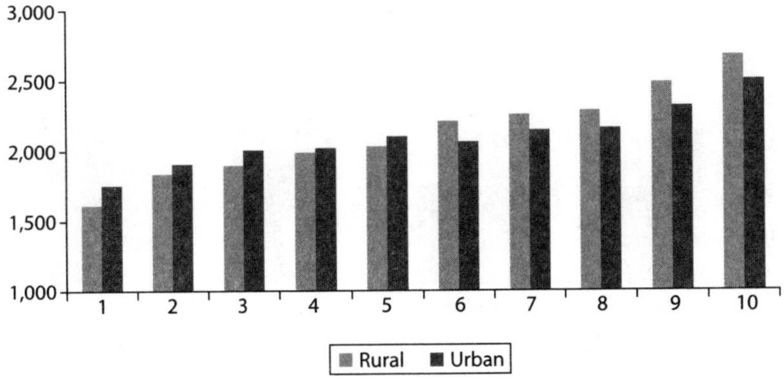

Figure 12.1 Per capita calorie intake by expenditure class (corresponding to all-India deciles) (no. of calories)
Source: GoI (2012).

[6] The expenditure classes in the NSSO publication have been formed in such a manner that they represent the deciles at the all-India rural or urban level (GoI 2012).

Given the earlier discussion on calorie need, we may use 80 per cent of the recommended average of 2,700 calories per consumer unit[7] as a minimum calorie norm. When households are arranged by calorie intake per consumer unit per day basis, 21.4 per cent of the population in rural areas and 22.2 per cent in urban areas of Odisha remain below this norm in 2009–10 compared to 30.8 per cent and 27.2 per cent in 2004–05 (Figure 12.2), indicating that incidence of calorie deficiency has declined in recent years. The decline in calorie deficiency in rural areas of Odisha between 2004–05 and 2009–10 by 9.4 percentage points is particularly commendable. Odisha's position is better compared to corresponding all-India incidence of calorie deficit of 29.9 per cent rural and 34.1 per cent urban in 2009–10. Considering these evidences, a broad conclusion is that the quantum of calorie intake is inadequate for at least 20 per cent of the population in both rural and urban areas even though the per capita calorie intake for the entire population might look satisfactory. On the whole, then, nutritional intake deficiency in Odisha must address two concerns: (a) increase in quantity of food for lower income groups, and (b) better quality of food for an average household by changing the composition of the food basket towards non-cereal items.

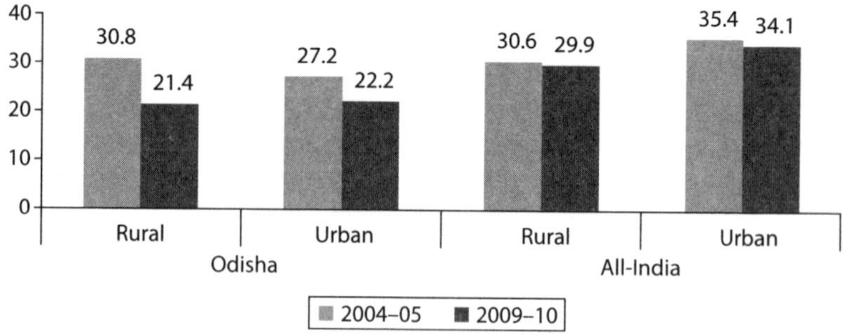

Figure 12.2 Proportion of population below 80 per cent of recommended calorie per consumer unit
Source: GoI (2012).

[7] Consumer unit refers to a standardized person generally corresponding to an adult male engaged in moderate work.

Anthropometric measures

Three standard anthropometric measures of malnutrition are stunting (low height for age), wasting (low weight for height), and underweight (low weight for age) that capture quantitative dimensions of health outcome. The National Family Health Survey (NFHS) data collected over three rounds in 1992–93, 1998–99, and 2005–06 have been widely used for assessing anthropometric-based nutritional status. Undernutrition is defined as a situation where the observed level for a particular individual is lower than two standard deviations below the median level expected in a healthy, well-nourished population with no significant morbidity. Table 12.4 gives the estimates of malnutrition for children under three years of age in Odisha. The first three years of life are critical for physical growth and certain effects of malnutrition in early childhood are irreversible later. Low birth weight, inadequate food, and frequent infection can result in stunted growth among children.

Children's nutritional status in Odisha has improved between 1998–99 and 2005–06 by all the aforementioned three measures. Undernutrition was less widespread by 6–10 percentage points

Table 12.4 Malnutrition among children 0–3 years: Percentage of children under three years

Indicator	Odisha			India		
	NFHS-1 (1992–93)	NFHS-2 (1998–99)	NFHS-3 (2005–2006)	NFHS-1 (1992–93)	NFHS-2 (1998–99)	NFHS-3 (2005–2006)
Stunted (low height for age)	44.9	44	38.3	52	45.5	38.4
Wasted (low weight for height)	23.4	24.3	18.5	17.5	15.5	19.1
Under-weight (low weight for age)	52.4	54.4	44	53.4	47	45.9

Source: GoI (2005–06)

Note: NFHS-1 figures are not strictly comparable with the other two sets due to coverage differences.

during 2005–06 than it was during 1998–99. Yet, the latest numbers are alarming. As many as 38 per cent of children were stunted in 2005–06 or too short for their age reflecting the fact that they were undernourished at least for some time in the first three years. Among children below three years, 18 per cent were wasted, meaning that they were too thin for their height. Another 44 per cent had low weight for their age. Low weight might be due to inadequate food consumption for a long time or for a short time prior to the interview due to illness. In terms of anthropometric measures, prevalence of child undernutrition in Odisha is similar to the all-India level.

Among adult population, the body mass index (BMI) (weight divided by square of height) is a useful measure of undernutrition and obesity. The BMI for more than a third of the population in the age group 15–49 years is below the normal range (Table 12.5). The NFHS data also reveal considerable gender gap in undernourishment as measured by BMI. Proportion of population below the normal BMI among men in Odisha is 32 per cent, while it is larger at 41 per cent among women. Gender gap is higher in Odisha than that prevailing at the all-India level where incidence of undernourished is about 5 percentage points more among women than that among men.

The NFHS data also provide estimates of anaemia which prevails due to iron deficiency (Table 12.6). Anaemic condition prevails among as high as three-fourths of children below three years. It is more widespread among adult women in the 15–49 age group at 63 per cent compared to 37 per cent for men. Children of

Table 12.5 Malnutrition among adults (15–49 years): Percentage below normal BMI

	Odisha		India	
	NFHS-2 (1998–99)	NFHS-3 (2005–06)	NFHS-2 (1998–99)	NFHS-3 (2005–06)
Women	48	40.5	36.2	33
Men	NA	32.1	NA	28.1

Source: GoI (2005–06)

Note: BMI (weight/height^2) of 18.5 to 25 is considered as normal when units are kg/mt^2.

NA: not available

Table 12.6 Prevalence of anaemia (%)

Population group	Odisha		India	
	NFHS-2 (1998–99)	NFHS-3 (2005–06)	NFHS-2 (1998–99)	NFHS-3 (2005–06)
Children (6–35 months)	72.3	74.2	74.2	79.2
Women (15–49 years)	63	62.8	51.8	56.2
Men (15–49 years)	na	37	na	24.3

Source: GoI (2005–06).

anaemic mothers are highly vulnerable to anaemia.[8] There is also large urban–rural disparity in respect of all the aforementioned indicators (Table 12.7). For example, 33 per cent of children are stunted in urban areas as against 39 per cent in rural areas of the

Table 12.7 Rural–urban differentials (%)

Population group/indicator	Odisha		India	
	Urban	Rural	Urban	Rural
Children (0–3 years)				
Stunted	32.9	39.1	31.1	40.7
Wasted	12.6	19.4	16.9	19.8
Underweight	33.3	45.7	36.4	49
Adults (15–49 years): BMI below normal				
Women	24.1	43.7	19.8	38.8
Men	19.4	34.5	17.5	33.1
Anaemia prevalence				
Children (6–35 months)	63.2	75.8	72.7	81.2
Women (15–49 years)	56.4	64	51.5	58.2
Men (15–49 years)	26.7	39	17.2	27.7

Source: GoI (2005–06).

[8] The GoI banned non-iodized salt around the time NFHS-3 survey was getting completed and its effect may be noticed only in the next round of the survey.

state. Similarly, 64 per cent of women are anaemic in rural areas compared to 56 per cent in urban areas.

Prevalence of food insecurity

Like malnutrition, there are several conceptual issues in defining the term 'food security'. It has been used by different people to mean different things. A few decades ago, the term food security was used in India to mean self-sufficiency, that is, producing enough to meet demand without being too much dependent on imports. Food security here implied national food sovereignty. Availability at the national level does not assure access by households. In the current usage, food security is considered from the point of view of household- or individual-level welfare and food security normally refers to enough food being available at the community or household level. But that again begs the question—what is meant by 'enough'. One approach could be that if a society meets its economic demand, we might regard it as food secured. In this case, one related question is: at what price? After all, market demand can be met by a given supply if prices are allowed to clear the market without restrictions and a society could declare itself as food secure. Hence, an acceptable definition must link food security to food need.

A household is considered food secure if it can meet the food needed by its members. Household food security, however, may not translate to food security for all its members due to several reasons. First, the ability of a household to acquire enough food may not necessarily be converted into actual food acquisition because household preferences may be different from normatively prescribed food consumption levels.[9] Second, the intra-household allocation of food may not be based on consideration of adequate nutritional requirements of each member. It is not uncommon, for example, to find households where one member is undernourished while another is obese. Third, individual food security resulting in optimal nutritional

[9] This point is well recognized in models developed by Panda (1986), and Panda and Rath (2004).

outcome depends on several non-food factors such as safe drinking water, good sanitation, and prevalence of diseases. Looked at this way, food security may be viewed as a *necessary but not sufficient* condition for nutritional security.

The World Food Summit organized by the FAO in Rome in 1996 declared: 'Food security exists when all people, at all times, have physical and economic access to sufficient, safe and nutritious food to meet their dietary needs and food preferences for an active and healthy life.'[10] Many analysts have used this as a working definition of food security in recent years. This definition highlights aspects of food safety and nutritional composition and recognizes the need to consider consumer behavioural aspects. Thus, two societies with equal access and affordability to food might have different levels of food security if they have different food preferences. For practical policy purpose, food preferences in this definition may mean food that is culturally acceptable by a community rather than person-specific preferences.

The aforementioned declaration noted that global food supplies had increased substantially, but 'constraints on access to food and continuing inadequacy of household and national incomes to purchase food, instability of supply and demand, as well as natural and man-made disasters, prevent basic food needs from being fulfilled.' It called for urgent and focused action at various levels to achieve the food security goal. Unfortunately, the concern expressed by the World Summit is no less serious today as it was more than one-and-a-half decades ago.

Production and consumption

There are various critical aspects of food security that need to be considered: availability, accessibility, affordability, and absorption. Food production at the national level is a primary determinant of food security at the macro level supplemented by net imports and stock

[10] FAO Corporate Document Repository, Rome Declaration on World Food Security and World Food Summit Plan of Action, available at http://www.fao.org/docrep/003/w3613e/w3613e00.HTM (accessed on 20 January 2016).

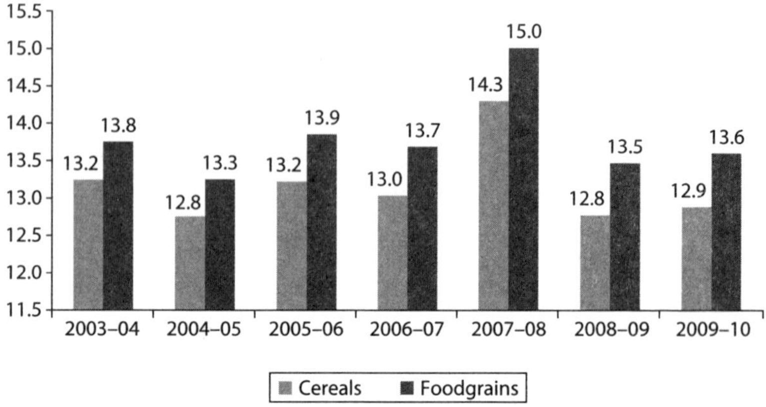

Figure 12.3 Per capita net production of cereals and foodgrains in Odisha (kg per month)
Source: GoO (2012).

changes to augment domestic availability. In the Indian federal set up, the centre operates in a big way to procure rice and wheat from surplus states and distributes them through a public distribution system with a country-wide network. The centre also holds a fairly good amount of buffer stocks to meet production shortfalls in bad years. Foodgrain production and consumption at the state level must be judged against this backdrop.

Figure 12.3 depicts the production of cereals and foodgrains (cereals + pulses) per capita per month in Odisha in recent years. There are large variations in production from one year to another. Odisha is often affected by natural calamities, drought, or flood, and the production gets influenced by such calamities. Average net production of cereals (mostly rice) was 13.3 kg per capita per month during 2007–08 to 2009–10 and of foodgrains 14.0 kg. These correspond closely to per capita monthly consumption of cereals 13.6 kg and foodgrains 14.2 kg in 2009–10 as revealed by the NSSO survey.[11]

[11] The production data used here is the same as the one provided by the central government for computing agricultural production at all-India level using comparable method for all states. The methodology involves estimates

A serious concern, however, arises from the fact that per capita cereals production has reached a stagnant situation as depicted by Figure 12.3. Cereals production recorded an average growth rate at –0.3 per cent per annum on a per capita basis during 2003–04 to 2009–10. It looks like the momentum generated by the spread of Green Revolution has died down and a sort of complacency has set in. According to GoO (2012), the area under cereals has been falling, a phenomenon witnessed in many other parts of the country. Hence, production possibilities would basically depend on increasing yield rate through various measures. Yield of rice in Odisha at 13.9 quintals per hectare is low compared to 14.9 in Assam and 15.7 in Bihar. Two factors that are likely to contribute to higher cereals demand in the future are: (a) increase in demand of the low-income groups as their income rises up to a decent minimum, and (b) increase in population. Macro-level food security in Odisha without too much dependence on production from outside the state in the future thus calls for policy attention to raise yield of rice.

Access and purchasing power

Local access to adequate food by different groups of households is an important aspect in food security. Even when there is no shortage of food at the macro level, households may not have access to adequate food if spatial distribution of aggregate production is not proper. Apart from local availability, affordability or purchasing power is a critical factor in determining household access to adequate food. Provision of a minimum level of income to households is an

---

of area for various crops provided by village- or panchayat-level officials and sample survey estimates on crop cutting for yield. Net production may be different from consumption due to inter-state grain movement and changes in stocks. While movement of rice from Odisha to neighbouring states may not be negligible, this does not affect the consumption data used here which are independently estimated by household sample surveys. On the whole, *net* exports, including movements in and out of the state through the public distribution system, are likely to be small proportion of output given the closeness of the two independent estimates of consumption and net production.

essential condition for food security for all its citizens and it poses a major challenge in a low-income state like Odisha.[12] Since various dimensions of high-incidence income poverty are discussed in detail in another chapter, we do not repeat them here. Instead, we examine as follows the relative consumption levels of various socio-economic groups of the population.

Table 12.8 gives monthly per capita total consumption expenditure (MPCE) levels by quintile group for 2009–10 at that year's prices. The quintiles are formed by arranging the households in ascending order of MPCE; for example, quintile 1 represents the poorest 20 per cent of the population and quintile 5 the richest 20 per cent. The state's average MPCE in 2009–10 is Rs 716 for the rural population and Rs 1,469 for the urban population. The MPCE of the bottom quintile at Rs 367 is about half of overall MPCE in rural areas and at Rs 554 only about a third in urban areas.[13] The very low MPCE levels of bottom quintile did not support purchase of adequate calories-based food. As noted earlier, there is overwhelming evidence that the bottom quintile in both rural and urban is undernourished. Absence of adequate purchasing power is the major constraint in meeting the calorie needs for this group and enhancement of their income must get priority attention in public policy.

The rural and urban population is classified by two other categories in Table 12.9: (a) three geographical regions, and (b) four social groups, namely, scheduled tribes (STs), scheduled castes (SCs), other backward castes (OBCs), and 'others'. The Coastal region has the highest level of living in terms of per capita consumption expenditure and the southern region the lowest in both rural and urban areas. The difference between the two regions is more than 20 per cent on an average. The MPCE in the northern region is very close to the average in the state. Magnitude of MPCE differences across social groups

[12] A simple way to perceive the magnitude of the challenge for Odisha is that while there are 10 per cent of rural population at the all-India level below an MPCE cut-off line of Rs 537, there are more than 20 per cent people in rural Odisha below the same cut-off.

[13] The per capita consumption level of the lowest quintile is only about US$ 8 in rural areas and US$ 12 in urban areas in nominal US$ terms and about US$ 20 and US$ 30 respectively in purchasing power parity terms.

Table 12.8 Estimates of MPCE (Rs) for Odisha by quintiles, 2009–10

Quintiles	Rural	Urban
1	366.81	554.44
2	512.64	782.56
3	632.24	1,062.44
4	786.00	1,536.63
5	1,281.93	3,432.38

Source: Author's own computation based on unit-level data obtained from NSSO.

Table 12.9 Estimates of MPCE (Rs) for Odisha by region and social group, 2009–10

	Rural	Urban
NSS Regions		
Coastal	801.39	1,639.39
Southern	639.79	1,166.67
Northern	694.11	1,439.27
Social groups		
ST	522.16	1,097.03
SC	645.08	971.87
OBC	799.86	1,190.44
Others	856.21	1,952.79
All	*715.58*	*1,468.83*

Source: Author's own computation based on unit level data obtained from NSSO.

are larger than those observed across regions. Within rural areas, the STs have MPCE as much as 27 per cent below the state rural average, while MPCE of the SCs is 9 per cent below. The OBCs and 'others' have MPCE higher than the average. In urban areas, SCs have the lowest MPCE, though STs and OBCs too occupy positions below the state average. The very low MPCE of STs in rural areas again seems to be a major constraint to meet their calorie need.

Consumption pattern

We had noted in the previous section that nutrient intake in Odisha is favourable towards calories and against other nutrients, a typical

Table 12.10 Share of total consumption expenditure (%)

	2009–10				1993–94			
	Rural		Urban		Rural		Urban	
	Odisha	India	Odisha	India	Odisha	India	Odisha	India
Food	61.91	56.98	48.38	44.39	68.1	63.2	57.8	54.7
Non-food	38.09	43.02	51.62	55.61	31.9	36.8	42.8	45.3
Specific food								
Cereals	18.64	13.71	11.85	8.12	38.9	24.2	19.9	14
Pulses	3.57	3.19	2.68	2.37	2.6	3.8	2.9	3
Milk	2.27	7.64	3.5	6.9	2.4	9.5	4.9	9
Meat, egg, and fish	6.2	4.74	5.18	3.36	4.1	3.3	5	3.4

Source: NSSO (1996).

characteristic of low-income level. This gets reflected in the consumption pattern in Odisha compared to all-India (Table 12.10). The commodity composition of the food basket in Odisha is more oriented towards food and, within food, towards cereals in both rural and urban areas. Cereals accounted for 39 per cent and 20 per cent of total consumption expenditure in rural and urban Odisha in 1993–94. This share has reduced substantially over time and stood at 19 and 12 per cent for rural and urban areas respectively in 2009–10 due to changing consumption pattern, a normal feature of a growing economy. Yet, an average person in Odisha spent 3–5 percentages more of total consumption expenditure on cereals compared to an average Indian in 2009–10. Since cereals are a major source of calorie, it explains the high calorie intake in Odisha despite low per capita income. The food basket in Odisha yields much higher calorie per rupee spent on food. Turning to sources of protein, share of expenditure on pulses in Odisha is similar to all-India; but, share of milk consumption is considerably low, though it partly gets compensated by meat, egg, and fish as a source of animal protein.

Per capita quantity of consumption of various food items by different social groups in 2009–10 is given in Table 12.11. In the rural areas, consumption of all items, including cereals, is lower among STs than the rest of the population. Per capita milk consumption by STs in rural areas is negligible at 200 grams per month while the state average is 1 kg in rural areas. But, milk consumption of STs

Table 12.11 Social group-wise average per capita monthly consumption (kg) of food items in Odisha, 2009–10

Social groups	Cereals (kg)	Pulses and pulse products (kg)	Milk (litre)	Sugar (kg)	Edible oil (kg)	Fish and meat (kg)
Rural						
STs	12.88	0.39	0.20	0.30	0.29	0.23
SCs	13.89	0.48	0.63	0.40	0.38	0.31
OBCs	14.16	0.61	1.36	0.49	0.43	0.37
Others	13.90	0.63	1.68	0.46	0.45	0.38
All	*13.75*	*0.54*	*1.01*	*0.42*	*0.39*	*0.32*
Urban						
STs	13.95	0.49	1.51	0.40	0.45	0.35
SCs	12.49	0.60	1.35	0.51	0.45	0.35
OBCs	12.46	0.62	1.77	0.55	0.50	0.40
Others	12.07	0.82	3.51	0.60	0.61	0.56
All	*12.53*	*0.68*	*2.41*	*0.54*	*0.53*	*0.45*

Source: Author's own computation based on unit-level data obtained from NSSO.

residing in urban areas is broadly similar to that of SCs and OBCs. Low income and availability appear to be dominant reasons for low consumption of various items among the tribal community.

It may be noted that cereals consumption has stabilized at about 14 kg a month in rural areas and a little above 12 kg in urban areas among non-ST groups despite large income (MPCE) differences among them. Thus, the perceived need of cereals seems to be 470 grams per day in rural areas and 410 grams in urban areas which supply about 1,600 and 1,400 calories[14] respectively; the balance calorie intake is met from non-cereal sources. Given the expected rise in per capita cereal demand among STs and other low-income groups as well as the population growth rate, an average growth rate in cereal production by 2 per cent per annum will be desirable in the medium term. This reinforces the earlier point that Odisha should not be complacent on cereals production.

[14] Using a coefficient of 3.4 calories per gram of cereals (GoI 2012).

The International Food Policy Research Institute (IFPRI) has constructed India state hunger index (ISHI) comparable to that of their global hunger index which is a composite index of three components: (a) prevalence of calorie based on a cut-off of 1,632 calories per capita per day, (b) proportion of underweight among children below five years, and (c) under-five mortality rate. When arranged in ascending order of the hunger index, Odisha ranks 12 among 17 Indian states with Punjab and Kerala at the top and Jharkhand and Madhya Pradesh at the bottom (Figure 12.4). None of the Indian states get low (<5) or moderate (5–10) score; 4 get serious status (10–20), and 12 other states, including Odisha, get alarming status (20–30). Odisha's hunger score on the ISHI at 23.8 is close to the all-India score of 23.7 and better than that of Gujarat whose per capita income is way above Odisha's. Sub-Saharan countries such as Ghana, Uganda, Nigeria, Kenya, and Sudan have lower (better) hunger index than that of India which is placed 67 among the 80 nations.

This discussion clearly indicates that malnutrition and per capita income across countries or regions need not necessarily move together. No doubt, per capita income of a region is an important determinant of macro-level affordability of a well-nourished food basket, but

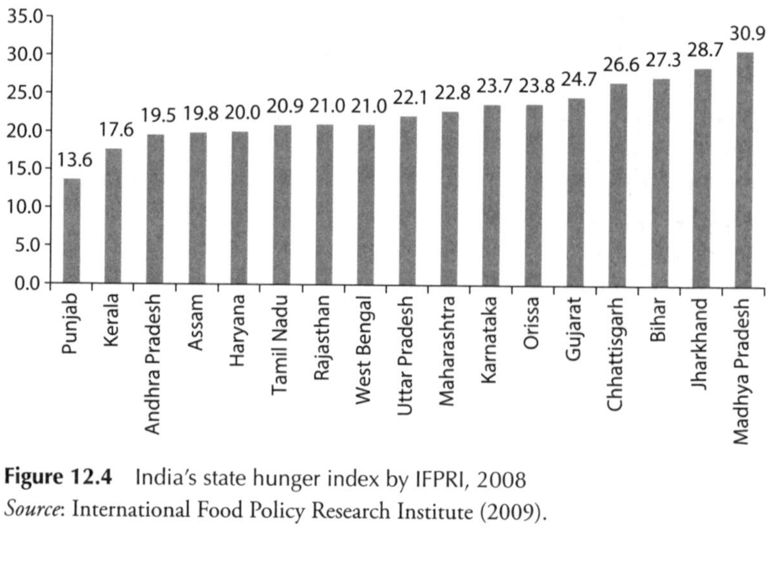

Figure 12.4 India's state hunger index by IFPRI, 2008
Source: International Food Policy Research Institute (2009).

micro-level access, affordability, and absorption are equally critical factors as emphasized earlier. Thus, while per capita net state income in Gujarat at Rs 75,000 is substantially above that of Odisha at Rs 40,000, certain sections of the population in Gujarat are more alienated from the mainstream and do not benefit from economic growth as indicated by the aforementioned index of IFPRI. An inclusive growth process along with nutritional education and communication would be important factors influencing nutritional security.

Livelihood and vulnerability

In a low-income state such as Odisha, the vulnerable groups need to be identified and specially monitored for nutritional and food security. We have discussed earlier special nutritional needs of women and children. But, there are other groups that face high risk of malnutrition and food insecurity or likely to face such risks with small perturbations in their living conditions due to lack of a coping mechanism. A working paper of the FAO (2007)[15] provides a good account of livelihood and food security issues for some vulnerable groups using survey data from four districts of Odisha: Gajapati, Kendrapada, Keonjhar, and Nuapada. The study identified six vulnerable groups of households: marginal and small farmers, landless labourers, mining workers, rural artisans, fishermen, and STs.

Small sizes of the landholdings and low productivity are two major problems for the marginal (less than 1 hectare of land) and small (1–2 hectares of land) farmers. Most of them are vulnerable to the threat of frequent cyclone, drought, and erratic rainfall. They do not produce enough food to last for the whole year and their household members do not get enough food for at least some months in a year. Small farmers harvesting two assured crops are more food-secure and consume a diversified diet (rice along with pulses, seasonal vegetables, and fruits) and sell small surplus to purchase non-food consumption. It is not easy for those with relatively small land size to secure loan and invest on land development or adopt modern farming methods.

[15] The discussion in this subsection is based on section 3 (p. 30–45) of FAO (2007). I thank the referee for drawing my attention to it.

The working class in Odisha is mostly dependent on the agricultural sector due to lack of diversification of the economy and its employment gets affected by natural disasters in agriculture. Decent earnings and food security for these households depend on the number days of employment and wages per day. One major problem faced by them is non-implementation of specified minimum wage rate even in employment schemes funded by government departments. Households with more than one earning members are more food-secure than single earning member households. Many labour households in Central Plate and Eastern Ghats migrate for several months in a year searching for jobs in irrigated or non-agriculture areas within and outside the state.

Mining is an important activity in some districts of Odisha. Mining workers in the Northern Plateau often receive double the agricultural wage rate, but work and live in harsh conditions. However, their wage rate does not get translated in to proportionately higher total wage income since they work for 15–18 days per month due to non-availability of work and health conditions. They incur additional health expenditure and are vulnerable to sudden closure of mines.

The rural artisan households are not able to meet the challenges of modernization and the market for their produce is shrinking due to substitution by mass-produced industrial goods. Their average living conditions are no better than that of agricultural labourers. Shifting to other means of livelihood has not been easy for them in the absence of training, marketing guidance, and financial support.

The fishing community accounts for more than 1 million population and about 3 per cent of the state's income. Large-scale mechanization of marine fishing has led to lower stocks and reduced catch affecting their livelihood. Food insecurity is common due to low earnings and seasonal variations. Lack of ownership of assets is a major reason for their vulnerability and households which own boats of their own are less vulnerable. Loss of boat due to cyclone and death of an earning member add to their vulnerability.

The tribal households constitute 22 per cent of Odisha's population and mostly live in remote forest areas. Their traditional skill base is wide, covering agriculture, horticulture, hunting, gathering, and handicrafts. The productivity of their land is low due to subsistence cultivation practices and a household owning even a medium-sized land may not be food-secure. They supplement their food with wild fruits, roots, and tubers gathered from the forest. Service delivery of many government-sponsored programmes is weak due to remoteness and low population density.

The coping strategy of these groups to meet vulnerability involves reduction in food intake, sale of assets, and use of credit. During distress, they seek additional employment in government programmes or in the informal sector. Access to common property resources such as forests and subsidized food through public distribution systems help in reducing food insecurity. A disturbing point noted in FAO (2012) is that pawning of BPL (below poverty line) ration card. The pawning practice blocks the supply of cheap food for the poor household.

Policy interventions

Breaking the stagnancy in post-Independence era, the last decade has witnessed a decent expansion of the purchasing power of the people in Odisha. The commendable growth performance over the last decade at above 8 per cent per annum has started the process of bridging the per capita income gap from the all-India level in a slow but steady way. Poverty has declined appreciably during 2004–05 to 2009–10 as per the recent estimates of the Planning Commission (GoI 2009). As many as 7 million people have been lifted above the poverty line during this period helping them to cross a minimum desirable income threshold with better access to food through the market.

Even though economic growth is a major driver of developments in the social sectors, the government has not left malnutrition and food security problem to be solved by the growth process alone. Since benefits of the growth do not reach all the sections equally, the poor and the vulnerable groups need social protection measures to assure food and nutritional security at a minimum level. Several social protection programmes have been undertaken by the central government and implemented by the state government to address deprivations in the sphere of malnutrition and food insecurity.

Public distribution system (PDS) has been a major programme in operation aiming at food security for several decades. The government directly distributes to the consumers certain amount of foodgrains to the people through a network of distribution outlets called fair price shops at subsidized price. The PDS was introduced as an important policy instrument for managing food scarcity and for distribution of foodgrains at a subsidized price. It has evolved with several modifications over time to contain the level food subsidy. The centre allocates foodgrains to the states who, in turn, are responsible for distribution to the poor with proper targeting. The success of the PDS has been mixed. The PDS has made significant contribution in 'protecting the poor by smoothening their consumption from shocks' (Radhakrishna 2005). Its major failure lies in its inability to fully reach the targeted group due to large exclusion errors and leakages. Some of the measures suggested for improvement by Dev and Sharma (2010) are: (a) involvement of local-level governments, farmers' cooperatives, and self-help groups in procurement and distribution, (b) digitization of records, and (c) vigilance mechanism for monitoring and enforcement. Introduction of food coupons has helped some states to improve efficiency.

The food security bill passed recently by the Parliament is another major step in so far as it recognizes the right of the citizens to be free from hunger. It has further extended the coverage of the PDS system and made the system accountable to the people if it did not reach out to the deserving section. The act aims at providing 5 kg of cereals per person per month at a very subsidized price to the bottom two-thirds of the country's population. Some authors (see, for example, Himanshu and Sen 2011) have advocated that the PDS should be a universal entitlement to avoid targeting errors that exclude the deserving poor. The rights approach to development is a new angle in the policy framework in creating legally binding obligation for the state. An independent and strong grievance redressal mechanism could be crucial for the success of the rights approach.

Another type of intervention by the government and some non-government agencies is the creation of grain banks in chronically food-scare areas to address acute seasonal food shortages. It helps households borrow grains during agricultural lean season and pay back the grains with interest at the end of the next harvest season. It thus helps small famers to smoothen their food consumption over the agricultural cycle. Unlike the PDS whose operations are centralized, grain banks operate at the local level to provide consumption credit in kind. Examining a sample of surviving and failed grain banks in Koraput district of Odisha, Bhattamishra (2012) finds that grain bank failure is high in drought years, indicating that local-level institutions find it difficult to 'cope well with covariate shocks'. Other interesting findings by her are: (a) grain banks have higher chances of survival in villages which are less developed and (b) social cohesion created through other community-based programmes such as self-help groups support success of grain banks.

A programme aimed at checking malnutrition among the most vulnerable group is the Integrated Child Development Services (ICDS) that covers children up to six years, besides expectant and nursing mothers. The services include: health check-ups, immunization, supplementary feeding, non-formal preschool education, advice on health and nutrition. Despite the existence of the programme for more than three decades, the 'overall impact of ICDS on malnutrition is very limited' (Radhakrishna 2005) as is evident from the fact that child malnutrition continues to be widespread. Gragnolati et al. (2005) observed that the emphasis of ICDS on food supplement was at the cost of other objectives like childcare behaviour. They also noted that the ICDS failed to focus on the more vulnerable groups such as girls, lower caste households, or most backward villages.

Another child-specific nutrition programme is the Mid Day Meal Scheme that provides meals to children in primary and upper primary school during study hour as a supplement to the meals at home. The scheme is managed by the school or local community. It needs several improvements such as sensitizing teachers and others associated in nutrition and hygiene norms, involving experts in planning low-cost nutritious menu from locally grown food basket, universal provision of drinking water in schools, and promoting parental audit.

The introduction of the National Rural Employment Guarantee Act a few years ago providing at least 100 days of employment on demand to any household willing to do manual work is a major step in provisioning income security to the poor labour households, particularly during lean agricultural season. Further, it has ensured implementation of the minimum wage act in a more effective way and provides for compensation for those who do not get work on demand within 15 days. This rights approach is a departure from the past policy framework and could help the poor households acquire the required purchasing power for food security at the household level. Odisha, however, is not able to take full advantage of such programmes funded by the central government and has been performing poorly compared to other states. Some states which have adopted social audit and involved local groups like self-help groups in design and monitoring have performed better. Odisha might adopt similar measures.

So far as vulnerable groups such as children and women are concerned, their diet must be monitored properly and special needs be met by supplementary diet schemes. In spite of sustained government programmes to reduce child malnutrition, there has not been much success in reducing child malnutrition. Low birthweight is a good predictor of infant undernutrition. Malnourished mothers are more likely to give birth to babies with low birthweight and might face constraints on breastfeeding. Efforts are needed to reduce child undernutrition through income as well as non-income measures including information, education, and communication (IEC)[16] on proper infant and child feeding practices such as exclusive breastfeeding of infants up to six months, supplementary semi-solid food during 6–9 months.

* * *

Food security is a useful indicator of individual welfare. We need to look at issues from various angles: food availability, household acquisition, and behavioural decisions on budgetary allocation. Moreover, household food security is of limited value in the absence of proper intra-household food allocation behaviour. Nutritional security goal also requires that access to food should be coupled with access to clean water and sanitation.

Malnutrition and food insecurity is widespread in Odisha. While the average calorie intake in the state is higher than the national average, protein and fat intake are much lower than the national average. At a low level of income, this implies that a person in Odisha typically derives more calories and less protein or fat per rupee of expenditure. The food basket of Odisha is more oriented towards calories due to its more urgent need to perform various daily activities.

[16] The role of IEC is emphasized by Ramachandran (2007).

Disaggregated analysis shows that even calorie intake is not sufficient to meet the needs of a fifth to a quarter of the population of the state. Anthropometric evidences do point towards the prevalence of an even larger incidence of undernourishment due to the deficiency of calories, protein, and other nutrients. Lack of adequate income or purchasing power is the most important reason for such deficiency apart from intra-household distribution and behavioral factors. Children and women particularly belong to the vulnerable malnourished groups apart from low-income socio-economic groups. Policy measures include an inclusive growth process that pays sufficient attention to vulnerability groups along with nutritional education and communication.

Even though food availability meets the current market demand, higher growth rate in food production is needed to make sufficient and diversified food available to the people in the coming decades. The eastern states are likely to enjoy comparative advantage in rice production in the future due to water scarcity and other emerging supply constraints in Punjab and Haryana. Odisha should take advantage of its comparative growth potential in the new scenario and focus on rice productivity growth with the help of introduction of appropriate technology and development of infrastructure for market linkage. Admittedly, agricultural production cost has risen in recent years and most farmers do not find agriculture as profitable an occupation anymore. But this feature has been observed across all states and Odisha could still has a relative advantage in terms of water and labour costs, especially in potential growth centres in backward regions. Higher rice yield could help in the shifting part of the cultivable areas for growing other food such as pulses, edible oil, and fruits and vegetables leading to diversification of the food basket and enhanced income-earning capability of the farmers. Policy focus would also be needed on the institutional aspects such as legalizing fixed period tenancy and contract farming.

Some recent studies have drawn attention to 'double nutrition burden' of undernutrition and overnutrition due to changes in lifestyle and dietary pattern. Awareness and information about the consequences of obesity must be pursued more vigorously among the affluent section for their better health. Or else, there is a risk that the available food supply, particularly of non-cereal items, might be pre-empted by the rich to a large extent.

Last, programme implementation issues obviously need more effective interaction of citizens, government machinery, political party forums, and non-governmental organizations. Odisha is possibly lacking on the social mobilization front and needs the building up of an effective social institutions to empower the people by making them aware of their rights, and providing a democratic platform to voice their demand. The recognition of the rights approach to basic food needs is the first step in this direction.

References

Bhattamishra, R. 2012. 'Grain Bank Survival and Longevity: Evidence from Orissa', *Margin—Journal of Applied Economic Research* 6(3): 311–36.

Dev, S. Mahendra and A.N. Sharma. 2010. 'Food Security in India: Performance, Challenges and Policies', Oxfam India Working Paper Series, OIWPS-VII, Oxfam India, New Delhi.

Food and Agricultural Organization. 2007. 'Understanding the Dynamics of Food Insecurity and Vulnerability in Orissa, India', ESA Working Paper No. 07–28, Agricultural Development Economics Division, Rome.

———. 2012. *The State of Food Insecurity in the World, 2012*. Rome: Food and Agricultural Organization.

Government of India (GoI). 2005–06. *National Family Health Survey—Fact Sheet*. Odisha: Ministry of Health and Family Welfare.

Government of India. 2009. *Report of the Expert Group to Review the Methodology for Estimation of Poverty*. New Delhi: Planning Commission.

———. 2011. 'Level and Pattern of Consumer Expenditure 2009–10', NSS Report no. 538, National Sample Survey Office, New Delhi.

———. 2012. 'Nutritional Intake in India', Report No. 540 (66/1.0/2), National Sample Survey Office, Ministry of Statistics and Programme Implementation, New Delhi. Available at http://mospi.nic.in/mospi_new/upload/nss_rep_540.pdf (last accessed on 22 January 2016).

Gragnolati, M., M. Shekar, M. Das Gupta, C. Bredenkamp, and Y.K. Lee. 2005. 'India's Undernourished Children: A Call for Reform and Action', HNP Discussion Paper, World Bank, Washington, DC.

Himanshu, and A. Sen. 2011. 'Why Not a Universal Food Security Legislation?' *Economic and Political Weekly*, 46(12, 19 March): 38–47.

International Food Policy Research Institute. 2009. *India State Hunger Index: Comparisons of Hunger across States*. Washington, DC.

National Institute of Nutrition. 2009. *Nutrient Requirements and Recommended Dietary Allowances for Indians—A Report of the Expert Group of the Indian Council of Medical Research*. Hyderabad.

National Sample Survey Organisation (NSSO). 1996. *Level and Pattern of Consumer Expenditure*, Report No. 402 and 538. New Delhi: Government of India.

———. 2009–10. *Report No. 540*. New Delhi: Government of India.

Panda, M. 1986. 'Fixing Income and Price Targets for the Poor in India', *Journal of Development Economics*, 20(2): 287–97.

Panda, M. and K. Rath. 2004. 'Price Changes and Some Underlying Aspects of Measurement of Poverty', *Journal of Quantitative Economics*, 2(1): 25–43.

GoO. 2012. *Economic Survey 2011–12*. Bhubaneswar, Odisha: Planning and Coordination Department.

Radhakrishna, R. 2005. 'Food and Nutrition Security of the Poor', *Economic and Political Weekly*, 40(18, 30 April): 1817–21.

Ramachandran, P. 2007. 'Poverty Nutrition Linkages', *Indian Journal of Medical Research*, 126(4): 249–61.

Rao, C.H.H. 2000. 'Declining Demand for Foodgrains in Rural India: Causes and Implications', *Economic and Political Weekly*, 35(4, 22 January): 201–06.

Tandon, S. and R. Landes. 2011. 'The Sensitivity of Food Security in India to Alternative Estimation Methods', *Economic and Political Weekly*, 46(22, 28 May): 92–99.

13

Tribal Movements and Livelihoods*

Recent Developments in Odisha

Sakti Padhi and *Nilakantha Panigrahi*

The traditional livelihood system of tribal people (also known as Adivasis) was sustainable due to the adoption of a highly diversified pattern of production, a pattern of utilization of land and forest resources, which ensured a self-generating capacity. The decline of shifting cultivation from about the second decade of the twentieth century forced some tribal people to adhere to settled agriculture mainly on the uplands, since they were actively adapted to upland conditions by growing a large variety of crops. While the physical yield of these crops was quite low in comparison to that of modern mono-crop agricultural practices, it minimized the risk of a complete crop failure. Such a livelihood system also provided for a nutritionally balanced food consumption basket. All in all, one may say that tribal people were perhaps the earliest 'social ecologists' since their

* An earlier version of the paper was published in 2011 by Indian Institute of Public Administration, New Delhi, as Working Paper 51.

economic conditions of existence were rooted in both subsistence and conservation ethics.

In social terms, the traditional livelihood system was based on customary, usufructuary rights of tribal communities over land and forests. It was also an 'extensive' system of production. The 'common pool' nature of resources supported customary rights and prevented the intensification of production, in the interest of conserving and sustaining the long-term productivity of livelihood resources. The sustainability of tribal people's livelihoods was thus firmly rooted in a system of 'property' rights over land and forests. As a consequence, the livelihood system's 'carrying capacity' was relatively low and it typically supported sparse populations relative to the size of the 'territory'.

The customary rights of tribal people over livelihood resources and their territorial sovereignty (insofar as land was considered as 'territory', not 'property') increasingly came in to conflict with the forces of 'modernization', which were defined by the developmental state and by 'outsiders' (whom we may call the plains people). In this discourse, it was thought that tribal people's traditional livelihood system was characterized by underutilized, wasteful, and 'inefficient' use of productive resources. Thus, the developmental state, mainly using the logic of the market, created a policy and legal framework for gaining control over resources from the 'tribal territory'. The territories of tribal people were thus open. There was widespread resentment and organized protests by tribal communities when this process of territorial intrusion was initiated by the colonial state through its land tenure policies in the uplands of Odisha in the mid-19th century and through forest conservation policies introduced at the end of that century. This indirectly facilitated the entry of Hindus into tribal territory for the commercial exploitation of productive resources. Thus, the space for the penetration of varied forms of commercial capital into the tribal hinterland was created. All this threatened to undermine the viability and sustainability of tribal people's livelihood base as their access to productive resources would be reduced. It is against this background that we can understand the role and effectiveness of developmental interventions by the Indian nation state and international development agencies for the protection and promotion of tribal livelihoods, and how tribal people have played a role in this.

Objectives

- The chapter appraises the sociocultural life and livelihood resources historically enjoyed by the tribal communities of Odisha.
- It reviews the tribal development policies and programmes of Odisha within the broad framework of planned development efforts.
- It examines the state sponsored development interventions and their impact on on the livelihood base of tribal people particularly since 1990.
- It explains the manner in which the tribal people have articulated their collective concerns in the form of protest movements from the point of view of the prospects of their livelihood promotion and protection in Odisha.
- At the end, the chapter recommends how the livelihood question for tribal people needs to be addressed in order to mainstream tribal development processes in an era of rapid macro-economic changes.

Odisha: Its physiography and tribal people

The administrative division of the state comprised of 13 districts and restructured into 30 districts in subsequent periods, which are subdivided into 59 sub-divisions, 314 community development blocks (CD blocks), and 56,887 villages. Despite immense diversity in its agro-climatic conditions, the state can be classified into four distinct agro-climatic zones. They are the coastal plains, the central table land, the northern plateau, and the Eastern Ghats. Odisha has 480 km of coastline. It has an essentially undulating topography, with highlands constituting 64.2 per cent and 50.6 per cent of the cultivated area in the northern plateau and the Eastern Ghats regions respectively.

In the ancient times, this land was known variously as Udra, Kosala, Tosali, Kalinga, and Utkal, representing the different territorial, political, and cultural contexts of the rajas and maharajas. The important dynasties that ruled over Odisha at different periods had their capital in the coastal region. Odisha lost its independence to the Afghan invasion (1568–1578), the Moghul domination (1578–1751), the Maratha control (1751–1803), and the British rule (1803–1947).[1] Towards the end of the 19th century more than half of the land area of present-day Odisha was under the control of 24 feudal chiefs. In 1936 Odisha became the first state (after Sindh) to be formed on the basis of language. These inland regions, which were divided into garjats[2] were more or less independent of the kings of coastal Odisha until the Maratha and Moghul rule. During the British rule most of these garjats were raised to the status of the princely states and maintained their identities until India achieved independence.

In 1956 the President of India declared 62 different tribal communities in Odisha to be 'Scheduled Tribes' (STs), of whom 13 communities are considered as Particularly Vulnerable Tribal Groups (PVTGs), and have been assigned with special treatment. Almost 44.25 per cent of the total land area in Odisha has been declared as a Scheduled Area.[3] The major tribes of Odisha, in terms of their numerical strength, are the Kondh, Gond, Santhal, Saora, Bhuiyan, Paraja, Koya, Oraon, Gadaba, Juanga, and Munda. The smaller tribal

[1] The British annexed Odisha in three different phases: southern Odisha in 1768, coastal Odisha in 1803, and the western hilly tracts, that is, Sambalpur in 1849, which were under the three different provinces of Madras, Bengal, and Central Provinces respectively.

[2] 'Garjats': From thirteenth to mid-sixteenth century, western Orissa was inaccessible and neither the kings of Utkal nor Kalinga ever ruled this area directly. The eastern ghat hill ranges with thick forest running through the entire region was divided into several garjats of different sizes and ruled by chiefs, though sometime some of them owed allegiance to the kings of Odisha.

[3] Fifth Scheduled Area in Odisha includes Mayurbhanj, Sundargarh, Koraput, Rayagada, Nabarangpur and Malkangiri districts in whole, Kuchinda Tehasils of the Sambalpur district, Keonjhar, Telkoi, and Champua. Barbil Tehasil of the Keonjhar district, Kondhamal, Balliguda and G. Udayagiri Tehasils of Kondhamal district, R. Udaygiri tehsil, Gumma and Rayagada block of Parlekhemundi Tehasils in the Parlekhemundi sub-division, and Suruda Tehsil of the Ghumsur sub-division in the Ganjam district, Thuamul Rampur and Lanjigarh blocks of the Kalahandi district and the Nilagiri block of the Balasore district. The total area of the Scheduled Areas of the state contains almost 70 per cent of Odisha's forest areas, even though they form only 44 per cent of the state area.

communities living include Chenchus, Mankiridia Kharia, Baiga, Birhor, and Ghara. The tribal communities can be classified on the basis of geographical regions, ethno-language, and crude techno-economic development. These communities by and large possess certain common characteristics, like the practice of animism, use of crude technology, concentrated habitations, use of dialects, and subsistence economy.

Tribal livelihood resources

Customary land tenure and land-use systems

For historical and ecological reasons, most tribal people inhabit the forests and physically inaccessible regions of the state. These communities practise various customary land tenure systems, which have often been modified by state policies and legislation. The clan-based land tenure system was based on customary rights over land, trees, and forests. For example, the Kondh clans called as Muttas, who may be further sub-divided into their lineage-based territories, as observed in the case of Dongaria Kondhs and Kutia Kondhs. It may be noted that the tribal-dominated regions of Odisha inherited land and forest administration systems from the Madras Presidency (south Odisha), the Central Province (parts of western Odisha), the Bengal Province (coastal Odisha), and many princely states like Mayurbhanj, Keonjhar, Bamara, Bonai, Boudh, Kalahandi, and Rairakhol. During the pre-British period most of the tribal areas were autonomous; therefore, during the British period the inclusion of tribal areas in the state and state administration was often violently contested. This often led to the dispossession of tribal people as zamindars (village headmen) and tribal cultivators with usufructuary rights within the customary land tenure system. This was perhaps the beginning of forced displacement and forced migration of the tribals to the plains.

Immediately after Independence, the land administration in the state moved from an intermediary land system to a rayatwari system following the principle of tillers as owners, accompanied by laws to regulate the concentration of landholding through a process of fixing a land ceiling. The Odisha Estate Abolition Act, 1952, provided for abolition of all intermediary tenure holders and vested all the rights in the state and intermediary tenure holders. The Odisha Land Reforms (OLR) Act, 1960, provided for permanent heritable and alienable land under the principles of land to tillers and the act was amended in 1965 and 1972. Historically the corporate and joint rights of tribal people over land did not allow it to be a saleable commodity. Whatever quantity of the land tribal people would cultivate, only a negligible percentage of it would be recorded against their name. Land above a 9° slope from sea level would normally be declared government land both at individual and community levels. The land patches used for shifting cultivation and terracing would normally be above 9° elevations. The GoO (2000) much lately realized that the non-conferment of entitlement rights to the tribal people for cultivation of land in the hill slopes below 30° represents a major non-performance of the state in the matter of land reforms and a reason for unrest among tribal communities.

Shifting cultivation

Shifting cultivation[4] is a primitive farming technique known by different names in different tribal communities of Odisha. Increased population pressure has not discouraged the shifting cultivators much, mainly because of the non-suitability of 'better' farming and multicropping (mixed cropping of 10 to 20 varieties) which have proved to be more productive and agriculturally viable for tribal people. Estimates of shifting cultivation in Odisha carried out by

[4] *Podu* or shifting cultivation in Odisha is also known as dangar, bagad, toila, rami, dabi, and biringa. This type of cultivation is largely practised by 11 tribal communities living in the districts of Phulbani, Keonjhar, Sundargarh, Rayagada, Gajapati, Koraput, Kalahandi, and Ganjam. The tribal communities practising shifting cultivation are the Bonda, Didayi, Koya, Gadaba, Paraja, Kutia Kondh, Dangaria Kondh, Lanjia Saora, Malua Kondh, Pengo Kondh, Desia Kondh, Juanga, and Pauri Bhuiyan. This cultivation is essentially a mixed cropping where 10 to 20 varieties of cereals, millets, like *ragi* (*Elucive corocema*), *kodo* (*Paspalam scrobiculatum*), *swnua* (*Echinochloa frummeta cea*), bajara (*pennisetum typhoidessno*), jawar (*Sorghum vulgara*), maize (*Zea mays*), pulses, oilseeds, vegetables, and perennial crops.

different agencies and experts suggest that around 11 tribal communities follow this practice, constituting around 30 per cent of the total tribal population of the state (GoO 1960–61, 1971–72). The crop cycle, crop quality, and quantity depends on the cultivation cycle and distance of podu patches. This type of crop diversity ensures conservation of minerals of the soils, checks damage from pests and diseases, ensures foodgrains for a couple of months, conserves soil nutrients, and acts as an insurance against total crop failure, unlike under mono-culture systems (Pathy 1987). There is no doubt that over the decades the growth of population, restricted government forest policies, commercial plantation, deforestation, land alienation, non-availability of suitable hill slopes, and availability of viable livelihood alternatives have substantially reduced the cycle of shifting cultivation and its production (Mohapatra 1968).

Pathy (1987) points out that cash crops are more or less of equal importance to staple crops because in many cases in tribal societies crops are found mortgaged even before they are harvested.[5] In this regard Fernandes, Menon, and Viegas (1984) write: '[I]n this marginalized stage a large section of tribal cultivators instead of living from forest as earlier, now live on forest'.

Forest resources

The relationship of tribal people and forest resources has been symbiotic in nature (Behura 1990; Mallik and Panigrahi 1998). Until the intervention of the British, tribal people believed that they were the owners of the forest and forest resources that surround them. Their attitude towards forest resources as a source of food did not change much until Independence. They were more forest-friendly and were not exploiting forest resources randomly. The customary laws of various tribal communities had become the guiding force for binding them closely with the forest (Behura 1982).

[5] Many times shifting cultivation is interpreted as subsistence economy without any surplus for exchange. As a matter of fact Juanga, Bhuiyan, and Kondhs produce oil seeds, turmeric, mustard, castor, niger and tobacco for the oil seeds for the market. This means cash crops were equally important to staple crops. A large number of such crops were also mortgaged before harvest or sale and thus receiving low returns.

The Odisha Forest Act, 1972, the Forest Conservation Act, 1980, and the Odisha Forest (Grazing of Cattle) Rules, 1980, sections 5 and 6 have all had an immense impact on the livelihood resources of the tribals. The forest rights on ancestral lands and their habitat were not adequately recognized in the consolidation of state forests during the colonial period as well as in independent India, resulting in injustice to the forest-dwelling scheduled tribes. Since they were deprived of entitlements over land, they were not eligible for certain state programmes and welfare measures intended for them.

In the post-Independence era in Odisha, the establishment of development projects like irrigation dams, mines, roads, railways, new townships, refugee settlements and major industries have no doubt have benefitted people and the state, but have also damaged its forest resources. Deforestation carried out for various purposes—irrigation, mining, building roads and houses, building railway lines, for defence and industry. In 1999, there were 190 projects established in Odisha which had acquired 24,124 hectares of land. The 1990 data with respect to the diversion of forest land for various non-forest uses indicates that mining projects have diverted the highest forest land to the extent of 8,228 hectares (32.46 per cent), followed by irrigation projects 5,739 hectares (22.64 per cent) of land, and defence requirements to the extent of 3,865 hectares (15.29 per cent) (Pande 1998). During the period 2000–01 to 2009–10 the state of Odisha established 176 projects which acquired 12,361.12 hectares of forest land. Except 2002–03 and 2008–09, in all other years quite a sizeable forest area is diverted for non-forest use. A sectoral distribution of forest area shows that irrigation and mining has taken the largest share (PCCF 2009–10).

The impact of massive deforestation has been observed in the lifeway processes of the tribal people, and can be categorized as environmental effects, social effects, and economic effects. The social effects of deforestation restricted tribal people's access to the forest and affected their religious activities, lifecycle rituals, customs, practices, and habits. Similarly, the economic effects of deforestation have drastically influenced the traditional livelihood resources of tribal people, which were providing them with food and economic security. Saxena

(1995) has rightly observed that in the Odishan context, studies have shown that tribal people have followed the best practices in managing their land-based resources. In this regard the role of a few regional people's organizations—like 'Brukshya O' Jeevara Bandhu Parishad' (BOJBP) in Kesharpur, Nayagarh district, 'Budhikhamari Joint Protection Party' (BJPP) in Baripada, Mayurbhanja district, and Budatika Anchalik Committee, in Negipalli, Balangir district—is remarkable.

Tribal people largely depend on minor forest products (MFPs) as a source of food security. Since 1970 policymakers, environmentalists, researchers, and the government have been highlighting the significance of MFPs in the life and livelihood of the tribal people. In spite of this, tribal people are denied a fair price of these produces and more often receive a price lower than the prevailing market price (Burman 1982, Mallik and Panigrahi 1998). The Government of Odisha, from time to time, has formulated and implemented a host of policies and enacted laws with regard to the collection, processing, and marketing of non-timber forest produces (NTFPs). Trade in *kendu* leaf, sal seed, and bamboo was nationalized in 1973, 1983, and 1988 respectively. The objectives behind the nationalization were partly to enable the primary collectors to obtain a remunerative price for their produce. Still there exist rampant corrupt practices, exploitation of tribals, state monopoly over forest resources, lack of management skills, and non-responsive attitudes of the government agencies working for the procurement, processing, and marketing of NTFPs. Government organizational networks for the procurement and marketing of NTFPs have largely failed.[6] This is reflected in the

[6] A few of such networks established over the time are: Tikabali Agency Marketing Co-operative Society (AMCS) in 1950s; Odisha Forest Development Corporation Limited (OFDC) in 1962; Tribal Development Co-operative Corporation Limited (TDCC) in 1973; Large Size Agricultural Multi-Purpose Co-operative Societies (LAMPS) in 1977; Tribal Co-operative Marketing Federation in India Limited (TRIFED) in 1989; Utkal Forest Produce Limited (UFPL) in 1989; and Odisha Rural Development Marketing Society (ORMAS) in 1989.The fact remains that many of these agencies are suffering from structural and operational constraints which have affected the larger goals of the organization.

proportion of revenue generated from NTFPs (excluding kendu leaf) to total revenue from the forest (PCCF 2009–10).[7]

Paradigm shift in forest policy

In the post-1990s era, one finds a shift in the approach of the state towards forests, forest resources, and forest dwellers. For the first time under Forest Dwellers Rights Act (FRA), 2009 the nation has recognised the rights and concessions for the forest communities including tribal people living in and around forest. It involved tribal people in the management of forest and to provide gainful employment to the inmates of the forest. On 5 May 2002, the Inspector General of Forests issued an order requiring the eviction of all 'encroachments' from forest areas across India. The ensuing eviction drive also in Odisha was one of the most brutal in the Indian history—millions of families saw their houses and fields destroyed, hundreds of villages were razed to the ground, and dozens killed in police firings. Accordingly, MoEF in the Parliament of India on 16 August 2004 presented the fact that they have cleared 0.15 million hectare of forest land. The erstwhile Planning Commission of India (2006) estimate suggests that 2,13,00,000 people were earlier displaced by development projects from 1951 to 1990, pushing them into a cyclical process of poverty. Large sections of the people in India came together showing their solidarity with the tribal and other forest dwellers, and demanded legislation in favour of the tribals of the country.

[7] The revenue collected from various forest produces in Odisha shows that kendu leaf, timber, bamboo, and sal seeds are the major products. For example, the total sale value of kendu leaf in Odisha was Rs 4,137.7 million in 2011, Rs 3,642.6 million in 2010, Rs 3,266.4 million in 2009, Rs 3,019.6 million in 2008, Rs 2593.2 million in 2007, Rs 2485.5 million in 2006. Similarly, the revenue generated from the sale of timber in Odisha has generated Rs 296.2 million in 2008–09 and Rs 406.8 million in 2009–10 (PCCF 2009–10). The contribution of income from the forestry sector to the National State Domestic Product (NSDP) (current price) in the state of Odisha constituted 1.00 per cent and 1.4 per cent respectively during 1960s and 1970s and 1980s, and 1.9 per cent during 1989–94–95.

In the subsequent period, the Ministry of Tribal Affairs formed a Technical Resource Group consisting of different ministries, civil society, and legal experts to make a draft of the Scheduled Tribes (Recognition of Forest Rights) Bill (2005). The Joint Parliamentary Committee reviewed the draft of the act in December 2005, which was placed in both the houses of the Parliament in May 2006 and finally the act was passed by the Parliament on 18 December 2006 and the Rule of the Act in 2008. Thus, the Parliament of India passed the Scheduled Tribes and Other Traditional Forest Dwellers (Recognition of Forest Rights) Act (the act), 2006, which emerged as a remedial legislative means to undo the historical injustices suffered by tribal communities in India. The major focus of the act includes: (a) recognizing and vesting forest rights and occupancy right to those forest dwellers who have been living in such forest for generations but their rights were not recorded; (b) providing a framework for recording the rights of the people on forests; (c) the responsibilities and authority for sustainable use, conservation of biodiversity, and maintenance of ecological balance so as to strengthen the conservation regime; and finally ensure livelihood food security of the scheduled tribes and other traditional forest dwellers.

Panchayati Raj in scheduled areas of Odisha

It was felt that the introduction of formal panchayats might not be suitable to these areas where community organizations and authority of traditional tribal councils still prevail and play a significant role for various purposes. This laid the Government of India for the appointment of a political committee, Chaired by Dileep Singh Bhuria, to suggest the necessary modifications as may be considered suitable which would be approved by the Parliament. In the subsequent period, the Central Act 40 for the Panchayat Raj in Scheduled Area, which is popularly known as Panchayat (Extension to the Scheduled Area) [PESA] Act, 1996, was formulated in the country. Following the PESA 1996, the State Act in Orissa for the scheduled area was formulated which is popularly known as Gram Panchayat (Amendment) Act, 1997.

While giving a comparative analysis of both the State Act act and the Central Act which have been extended to the scheduled areas, attempts have been made to highlight the major distinctions there in. The new Central Act of Panchayat Raj for the Scheduled Area of 1996 envisages community as the basic unit of self-governing system. Under the new Scheduled Area act the formal recognition of the 'community' and the '*gram sabha*' is the most significant achievement in the history of democratic institutions so far built. This has laid the foundation for participatory democracy in the real sense. The significance of community command over natural resources has been recognized in this new act not in isolation or as merely an economic issue, but in relation to the cultural identity of the people. Since community in the form of gram sabha as a functional unit enjoys the constitutional recognition, its authority shall not be questioned henceforth. *Gram Sabha* shall act as the supreme in matters of decision-making, implementation of the programmes relating to land and NTFPs under the extended Panchayat Act in Scheduled Area, whereas, according to Section 4(iii) in the context of the state of Orissa, *gram sasan* has been conferred with this power to plan and approve the programmes in various matters of socioeconomic development. Here power has been conferred on the gram sasan which comprises of all the voters of a gram consisting of all communities having distinct sociocultural practices, who elect a formal body known as the gram panchayat, practically known as the executive council of the gram sasan.

As regards the traditional rights of the tribal people are concerned, in Section 4(iv) the state provides the right to the gram sasan and makes it competent to safeguard and preserve the traditions and customs of the people, their cultural identity, community resources, and customary mode of dispute resolution in consistency with the relevant laws which are in force (this is not in Central Law) and in harmony with the basic tenets of the constitution. This, in fact, implies that in case of any dispute the rules of CrPC, and IPC will prevail instead of the customary laws of these communities. By this the state practically does not give any right to the tribal people to safeguard, exercise, and preserve their traditional rights. Besides the power of the gram panchayat to frame rules, as has been mentioned in Section 6(ii) it has been observed that the state government has handed over the power to gram panchayats to enforce restrictions for the prohibition or sale and of consumption of any intoxicant, enjoy ownership and to provide licences for the use of minor forest resources, and finally, to control the practice of moneylending by amending the existing regulations like Orissa Bihar Excise Act 1915, Orissa Forest Act 1980 and Money Lenders' Regulation 1967. However, this power has to be vested with Gram Panchayats by amending the Orissa Land Reforms Act 1960, Regulation 2 of 1956 regarding the distribution of wasteland and transfer of Immovable Properties in Scheduled Areas.

The data indicates that the awareness level of tribal PRI members about various policies pertaining to tribal development—such as job and seat reservation, bonded labour eradication, and implementation of various Constitutional provisions—is very low. As a result, the bureaucratic processes control the implementation of tribal welfare programmes (Behura and Panigrahi 2002).

Induced displacement

Establishment of mega-projects in tribal regions has encroached on tribal people's age-old lands and thereby displaced them. These projects have an immense impact on their life and livelihood. They include hydroelectric-cum-irrigation projects like Hirakud (1948), Balimela (1963), Machhkund (1949), Upper Kolab (1978), Indravati (1978), Mandira, Rengali (1973), and Subarnarekha (1995–96); mineral-based industries like Rourkela Steel Plant (1950), National Aluminium Company at Angul (1985), Hindustan Aeronautics Limited (1962); the bauxite mining project at Koraput (1981); and projects on cement, iron, dolomite, and limestone. Estimates of the magnitude of human population displacement in Odisha resulting from the establishment of various mega-projects during 1951–95 show that hydroelectric multi-purpose projects have displaced around 3,25,000 people, of whom only 90,000 (27.69 per cent) have been rehabilitated. Similarly, out of 71,794 people displaced by industrial projects, only 27,300 (38.03 per cent) have been rehabilitated. Mining projects have displaced around 1,00,000 people, of whom almost 60 per cent have been rehabilitated and around 50,000 people have been displaced through declaration of sanctuary, of which only 15,540 (31.08 per cent) have been rehabilitated (Mohapatra 1998). All these projects have had an immense impact on tribal village economies, family life, and village power structures, as has been documented through various empirical studies in the state (Behura and Nayak 1993;

Behura and Panigrahi 2001; Mohapatra 1998; Panda and Panigrahi 1989; Patnaik 2000; Swain and Panigrahi 1999). The study of Pande (1998) on the decadal variations of the families displaced from 1950–51 to 1980–90 shows that the magnitude of displacement has increased in case of industrial and irrigation projects while it has reduced in case of power projects. A state-sponsored standard resettlement and rehabilitation (R&R) policy in Odisha introduced in 2006 seems to be unique in content but unable to meet the multiple demands of the increasing displacement in the state.

Tribal sub-plan policy and tribal livelihood development

The Government of India Act of 1919 and 1935 created a number of partial and fully excluded areas. The founding fathers of the Constitution of India laid a firm policy for development of tribal communities of India. The 'compensatory discrimination' in the form of protective provisions has been made in 20 constitutional articles, clauses, and sub-clauses, two special schedules, and directive principles of state policy (Article 46). In addition to this, there are some central laws which protect the interest of tribal communities, and these are: Protection of Civil Rights Act, 1955; S.C. and S.T. (Prevention of Atrocities) Act, 1989; Bonded Labour System (Abolition) Act, 1976; Child Labour (Prevention and Regulation) Act, 1986; and Forest Conservation Act, 1980, Mahatma Gandhi National Rural Guarantee Act (MGNREGA), 2005, and Forest Dwellers Rights Act, 2009.

Tribal welfare programmes in Odisha

The Nehruvian Panchsheel principle of non-interference also influenced the tribal development policies in the state.[8] To examine the backwardness of the tribal people and tribal regions of Odisha, the Partial Excluded Areas Enquiry Committee, under the chairmanship

[8] The five fundamental principles popularly known as the Nehuru's Panchasheel Principle of tribal development includes: People should develop along the lines of their own genius and we should avoid imposing anything on them; tribal rights on land and forest should be respected; we

of A.V. Thakkar, visited Odisha in 1938. Based on its recommendations, finally, the Government of Odisha formed a separate department in 1948, known as the Backward Class Welfare Department, presently known as the ST and SC Development Department. The Tribes Advisory Council (TAC) formed in Odisha on 24 June 1950 has been advising the state from time to time on matters of the welfare of tribal communities in the state. The Scheduled Areas Order of 1950 first issued in Odisha by the Government of India and revised during 1977 added two full administrative districts as fully scheduled areas, with a few districts as partial scheduled areas. Presently Odisha includes six districts covered under fully Scheduled Areas and five districts covered under partially Scheduled Areas. Considering the recommendations of Elwin Committee regarding the implementation of the structure of Tribal Development Blocks (where more than 50 per cent of the total populations are numerically represented by the tribals) the state of Odisha initially declared 62 blocks as Tribal Development Blocks, which were later on increased to 74 blocks and presently there are 118 CD blocks in the state covered under Tribal Sub-plan Blocks which are covered under 17 micro projects for 13 Particularly Vulnerable Tribal Groups/Primitive Tribal Groups (PTGs) covering 61,240 households in 537 villages distributed over 20 CD blocks in 12 districts.

Fund flow for TSP

The financial support under TSP for tribal development in the state generally comes from three different sources—State Plan, Special Central Assistance (SCA), and Central and Centrally Sponsored Schemes (CCSP). The Tenth Five Year Plan (FYP) adopted a

---

should try to train and build up a team of their own people to do the work of administration and development, and we should avoid introducing too many outsiders into tribal territory; we should not over administer these areas or overwhelm them with multiplicity of schemes, rather we should work with their own social and cultural institutions; and lastly, we should judge result not by statistics or the amount of money spent, but by the quality of human character that is evolved.

multipronged approach for the development of tribal people through educational development and economic empowerment. The Eleventh FYP adopted 'Inclusive Growth of the STs'. A scrutiny of the budgetary resources for the STs during Tenth and Eleventh FYP periods reflects gaps in the budget allocation as per the TSP guidelines and actual allocations. During Eleventh FYP the state plan for TSP increased by 8.70 per cent when compared to the Tenth FYP period. The central plan during this period has reduced, while allotment under Centrally Sponsored Plan was almost double in the Eleventh FYP. Except the Central Plan, allocation for TSP found to have increased in Odisha (GoO 2002–03 to 2011–12). The state plan to TSP in the Eleventh FYP period has increased almost six fold when compared with the Tenth FYP period. This has influenced the quality of the investment in different tribal development programmes (GoO 2002–03 to 2011–12).

Tribal livelihood enhancement programmes

In order to reduce poverty and to minimize regional gaps, the Government of Odisha, from time to time, has implemented special livelihood-enhancement projects with the help of external agencies. A couple of such projects are presented here, highlighting aspects such as the rationale of the projects, pattern of funding, and the execution and socio-economic effects on the people and the area. It also tries to highlight some of the debates raised on development since the 1980s by the people at various levels.

Odisha Tribal Development Project (OTDP) in Kashipur

The project aimed to achieve sustainable economic progress for the tribal population of Kashipur region of Rayagada district through an integrated programme including agricultural production, cash crop introduction, and natural resources development. The project covered around 12,500 tribal households and 4,000 non-tribal households. The total project cost was US$ 24.4 million, of which International Fund for Agricultural Development (IFAD) provided a US$ 12.2 million loan at a highly concessional rate, the World Food Programme (WFP) granted US$ 1.4 million, and the balance was met from domestic contributions (GoI 1998). The Harijan and Tribal Welfare Department of the Government of Odisha was the executing agency. The project continued from May 1988 to December 1997, followed by 21 months of extension. Around 84 per cent of IFAD's loan was disbursed (BJKK 1998).

Tribal people in the Kashipur region observe shifting cultivation as an age-old practice. The project initiated conferring land titles on these shifting patches, promoted sound environmental management practices, and helped tribal people to restore the agro-ecological balance. The coffee plantations promoted by the project as a cash crop have never been traditionally favoured by tribal people for cultural and economic reasons (Industrial Management Consultants of Odisha 1998). From a socio-economic point of view the initiative of providing land titles in the names of both spouses enhanced the social status, security, and confidence of the tribal people and provided opportunities for income generation. However, this manner of privatizing landed property imposed on tribal villages partially upset the existing community-based social security networks. This created mistrust and discontent between the tribal people and the development agencies, which were reflected when the state entered through the corporate sector to explore bauxite minerals in the Kashipur region (Bharatiya Jana Kalyan Kendra (BJKK) 1998). In the later period of the project the state attempted to explore bauxite from the Kashipur region in the name of development by leasing land to outside private/corporate agencies. However, the mining project is strongly protested by the local tribal people.

Revised Long Term Action Plan (LTAP) for KBK districts

The LTAP, popularly known as Koraput-Bolangir-Kalahandi or KBK[9] programme, was launched by the then prime minister on 18 August 1995 for an initial period of seven years, with an objective to

[9] The term 'KBK' refers to the three old districts of Kalahandi, Bolangir, and Koraput, since sub-divided. A seven-year Action Plan, comprising of rural employment and social schemes was announced in 1995; in July 1998 the then prime minister Atal Bihari Vajpayee ordered a revised KBK Plan, including finance for watershed development in 1980 in 800 micro-watersheds.

pool the available resources and integrate them scientifically to affect the speedy development of the extremely backward KBK districts of India. Over time the undivided KBK districts have been divided into eight districts, comprising of 14 sub-divisions, 37 tehsils, 80 CD blocks, 1,437 GPs, and 12,293 revenue villages. The demographic composition of KBK districts includes SCs, STs, and many other caste communities, who, despite their similarities, maintain cultural specificity, distinct practices, values, and customs. Tribal communities like the Bonda, Didayi, Dangaria Kondha, Chuktia, and Bhunjia, as well as the Kutia Kondha, still express their distinct identities in their backwardness and development features.

Looking at the development gaps in the envisaged achievements of the LTAP, the project implemented the revised LTAP (RLTAP) for the period from 1998–99 to 2006–07, consisting of central plans and centrally sponsored schemes in various sectors, such as drought proofing, poverty alleviation, and improved quality of life in the region, through strategies like building a productive rural infrastructure, income generation on a sustainable basis, mobilizing and energizing the rural poor, and restructuring and energizing the social security system. Many studies and review reports have established the fact that the project could not overcome the major challenges affecting life and livelihood of the deprived sections of the region. A few of these problems are non-enrolment of and high dropout in primary education and the primary health service delivery system. That apart, deaths from starvation in Kashipur and Nabarangpur region, occurrence of anthrax in Koraput and Rayagada districts, eating of mango kernels by the tribal people in Kandhamal and Rayagada districts, bonded labour, child labour, selling of children, and distress migration of the poor from this region are still featured in the media and in the reports of various committees and commissions. The programme later on reflected more on the need of political will than development needs of the region and the people.

Western Odisha Rural Livelihoods Project

The Western Odisha Rural Livelihoods Project (WORLP) had the overriding goal of reducing poverty in rain-fed areas of the western districts of Odisha and aims to establish a more effective approach to sustainable rural livelihoods, particularly for the poorest, to be achieved by 2010. The DFID had provided Rs 2.3 billion to be spent over 10 years, while TC funds to support capacity building for government and generation of knowledge by non-governmental organizations (NGOs) accounted for around Rs 9.075 billion. The operational area of the project covers 14 blocks in Balangir and 5 in the Nuapada district, while a mid-period review would consider extending it to 6 blocks in Kalahandi and 4 in the Bargarh district also. The project implemented Watershed Plus activities, that is, capacity building, minor irrigation, drinking water, and livelihood initiatives for the poorest. The project has three major components including livelihood improvement, capacity building for primary and secondary stakeholders, and encouraging an enabling environment. For the implementation, the project largely depended on the normal line departments of the government which were already suffering from structural and operational impediments. This diluted the spirit of the project and made it a normal departmental functioning rather than improving the livelihood base of the region substantially.

Odisha Tribal Empowerment and Livelihood Programmes (OTELP)

On 2 October 2004, the Government of Odisha, with assistance from IFAD-DFID-WFP, implemented a new project popularly known as Odisha Tribal Empowerment and Livelihood Programme (OTELP) in 32 blocks of northern and southern districts. The project has a strategy of long-term development intervention in seven districts—Gajapati, Kalahandi, Kandhamal, Koraput, Malkangiri, Nawarangpur, and Rayagada—in south-west Odisha and in Sundargarh representing northern tribal belts of the state and is being implemented in three phases over a period of 10 years. The programme ensures that the livelihoods and the food security of poor tribal households are sustainably improved by promoting a more efficient, equitable, self-managed, and sustainable exploitation of the natural resources at tribal people's disposal through off-farm and non-farm enterprise development. The total cost of the project over 10 years is estimated at US$ 91 million. The IFAD loan represents 22 per cent (US$ 20 million), the DFID grant tunes to 44 per cent (US$ 40 million), while WFP is contributing US$ 12 million

(14 per cent) in the form of food. The Government of Odisha is contributing US$ 9.7 million (11 per cent of the total).

Under the livelihood enhancement programme the project has implemented land and water management, production system enhancement, farming system approaches, rural financial services, community infrastructure, and participatory forest management. The project has also made certain policy initiatives in respect of settlement of land rights over hill slopes between 10° to 30° land slope above the sea level and ensuring food security for tribal people. The project is trying to establish watershed plus activities, particularly with respect to community empowerment, diversifying livelihood sources, identifying the root causes of vulnerability, strengthening Government of Odisha–NGO partnerships, encouraging convergence programmes, emphasizing on development processes rather than targets, strengthening institutional structures, and improving the mode of delivery of tribal development programmes at the ITDA level (GoO 2012). Also, it has prioritized investment at the ITDA level, based on the village-level development plan to aim to overcome the problems of podu cultivation, moneylending, migration, MFPs, market linkages, and health improvements.

Articulation of tribal rights

During the last three decades, Odisha has witnessed repeated protest by tribal people against state encroachment on their age-old land rights. While protesting, many tribal people have lost their lives. A few of such incidents reported since 1990 are in Maikanch of Raigada district, Mandrabaju of Kandhamal district, and Kalinganagar of Jajpur district. In the past, the tribal people of Odisha had taken part in many movements and revolts. Odisha has a history of tribal uprisings against the unlawful interventions in tribal life and livelihood. A few of them are the uprisings of the Kondhs of Ghumasar (1835–37), the Gonds of Sambalpur (1857–64), and the Bhuiyans of Keonjhar (1867–68). These regional anti-feudal and anti-British agitations and movements gave birth to a class of regional leaders. F.G. Bailey (1963), in his village study among the Kondhs of Odisha, rightly pointed out that land alienation, moneylending, killing of marginalized groups, burning of crop fields and huts of the poor, and imposition of collective fines were some of the major causes of such uprisings. Pathy (1987) opines that this milieu of underdevelopment, destitution, and disunity seems to be reproduced even after more than six decades of the formation of the state and more than six decades after Independence.

Tribal people's struggle against bauxite mining in Odisha

The southern belt of Odisha, that is that stretch consisting of the undivided KBK districts, is endowed with 1,733 million tonnes—70 per cent of the total bauxite resources of the country. In the post-liberalization period, this mineral resource has attracted foreign investment, bringing the state into the international arena. During 1992–97, bauxite resources in Odisha pulled in foreign investment to the tune of Rs 973 billion or US$ 20.5 billion (as per an agreement signed by the state). Since 1986 several attempts have been made in western Odisha to explore bauxite ores. The deposits of bauxite in different regions of the districts include 2.13 million tonnes in Gandhamardan in Balangir and Bargarh region, 195.73 million tonnes in the Baphlimali hill range, 81 million tonnes in Sasubohumali in the Kashipur block of Rayagada district, 86 million tonnes in the Sijumali region, 40 million tonnes in the Kutrumali region of Rayagada district and Kalahandi district, and 91.4 million tonnes in Kodingamali in the Laxmipur block of Koraput district (GoO 2000).

Among the companies which have tried but ultimately failed to explore bauxite mining in Odisha at different times are Bharat Aluminium Company (BALCO) Limited in 1986, Utkal Alumina, Indal, Tata, Hydro (Norway), Alcan (Canada), and Hindalco in subsequent periods. Mining has been projected as the major means to combat famine, flood, starvation, and the consequences of all other forms of natural calamities. The state has pushed the 'globalization mantra' through mining and industrialization to attract the middle and lower middle classes of the Odia people in the hope of providing ample employment opportunities to the young unemployed in the state.

In all these mining-project areas, forest resources, hill slopes, and natural water bodies constitute the major livelihood sources of tribal people. Due to the paucity of suitable land, wet cultivation is not feasible in these regions. Depletion of forest resources has become the biggest threat to tribal people in the wake of the many hydro-electric projects established in the state. In addition, mining projects result in the piling up of solid effluents such as red mud and tons of sodium hydroxide, leaving a high pH level in the soil and loss of vegetation and natural habitats. The establishment of bauxite mining by NALCO (National Aluminium Company Limited) at Damanjodi only 100 km from Kashipur has adversely affected the tribal people and their livelihood. The tribals have been pushed out to the level of wage labour in the informal market. Similar situations have resulted in the tribal-dominated Mayurbhanj, Sundargarh, Keonjhar, and Sambalpur districts in northern and western Odisha, where iron ore mining operations and open cast coal mining operations are underway. It was purposively ignored that any such mining projects will have an adverse impact on the life and livelihood of tribal people. The physical displacement of villagers caused by such projects involves serious consequences, both in the long and short run. The tribal people in Odisha have raised their voice against such mega-development interventions. They have questioned the development process by asking 'development for whom and at whose cost?', noting that it basically affects tribal people and their non-renewable livelihood resources.

Bauxite mining in Sambalpur

BALCO is a Government of India undertaking. It entered the Gandhamardan hills in the district of Sambalpur and Balangir on the basis of a lease of 9.6 km^2 of the hill range, which carries 213 million tonnes of bauxite on 2 May 1983. A delay in the completion of the project increased its cost from Rs 320 million to Rs 560 million. The Paikmal project region comprises of tribal peasants and scheduled castes who together constitute 55 per cent of the population. The Marwaris and Gujaratis, though numerically fewer, control trade and commerce in the region and have often entered the agrarian economy, occupying a sizeable landholding in the region. The landed gentry is popularly known as Gauntias. The average number of landless households ranges from 30 to 50 per cent in each village. They largely depend on forestry and wage labour (Rao et al. 1987).

Gandhamardan hill is considered the mother of all the local people in terms of providing food, firewood, fodder, water (22 streams and 150 perennial springs), and medicines, both for home consumption and sale (Panigrahi 1986). The major NTFPs collected by the people are mahua flowers, sal seed, bamboo shoots, charseed, kendu leaf, mango, *harida*, and *bahada*. Forest produces and paddy are siphoned through credit markets with cheaper rates. Bamboo cutting for orient paper on Gandhamardhan hill continues for five months in a year, which provides wage employment to the local population. The festivals and religious practices of the local people centre on the Gandhamardan hill, which acts as their 'cultural terrain' (Panigrahi 1986).

The state's modernization process showed a lack of trust in the people and their socio-cultural resources linked with the larger ecology of the region. It has ignored the people's strength and their cultural wealth. But the movement has established the fact of people's capacity, including the hidden strength of youth, women, and children. The processes of people's organization helped them to access information on their right to life and livelihood. The people's movement also established the fact that the state's interests, which normally represent the fewer well-to-do sections of society, are not above the interest of the common people, who need sustainable development as their natural right.

Bauxite mining in Kashipur

Kashipur is one of the tribal-dominated blocks of Rayagada district. There are 412 villages distributed over 20 gram panchayats, accommodating a total population of 1,01,995. The Paraja and the Kondhs are the two major tribal communities of the region. The agro-products of the region include ragi, paddy, millet, grams (chickpeas), maize, and niger seed. Hill broom is the most important forest product of the region. The weekly local haat (market), where the barter system still dominates, is the major mode of transaction in the region. Tribals are often forced to make distress sales of their produce, including their own labour. The tribal people maintain a symbiotic relationship with nature and natural resources. They enjoy natural rights over the resources surrounding them.

The systematic exploitation of the forest resources was started in the name of national development by JK Paper Mills of Rayagada, which ruthlessly destroyed the ecological balance of the region and the people, as a result of which food security in the region turned to food scarcity. The development interventions by different agencies have promoted dependence. In this process tribal people received a different image of the state, which they now considered indispensable to their welfare. People were told that welfare measures were not reaching them as a result of dishonesty in the delivery system. This notion became fixed in people's minds following the continuous famine and resultant food crisis of the 1980s, which invited increasing intervention by outside agencies, including the state. Now people are challenging the government over their rights and opposing exploitative elements, reviving community strength, and helping their communities to escape from the clutches of the moneylender network. UAIL (Utkal Alumina International) and other companies have entered the region to mine the bauxite in the guise of developing the area. The local communities understood the latent interest opposed the mining project which continued in various form of protests for quite a long period. Local tribal people died due to police firing, but did not allow the miners to mine the minerals in their region. Local communities irrespective of their ethnic, economic, and political background sacrificed themselves for the larger cause of sustainable development.

Tribal people's protest at Kalinga Nagar

The tragic death of 12 tribal people on 2 January 2006 at Kalinga Nagar, while protesting against the mega-industrial complex encroaching on their age-old rights over the land, added another page in the history of protest by the people of Odisha against mining and industry. The tribal people of this region had migrated from Mayurbhanj and Keonjhar in Odisha and from Ranchi and Singhbhum in Jharkhand at different times in the nineteenth century (Maddox 1897). The last official land record of settlement during 1928 did not give a land entitlement to the people of the region, despite their having lived there for generations. In the post-liberalization period, the dream of creating growth in Odisha through industrialization made the state look to Kalinga Nagar as the steel hub of Odisha. Perhaps this is why 12 industrial complexes have been built in and around Kalinga Nagar and a few new companies are in the pipeline. Of the total land (13,000 acres) acquired by the Industrial Development Corporation of Odisha (IDCO), around 6,900 acres are privately owned. Lack of legal entitlement over the land deprived many tribal people of getting compensation for the loss of their land. In addition, undervaluation of the land paid in the form of compensation to the landholders, and the role of IDCO on behalf of the state in order to make a profit out of the transactions, are the issues to which the people affected are yet to receive an answer from the state. In a situation where the state government claims to have the best R&R act of its own but manages the situation through ad hoc strategies, displacing poor people and expecting people to sacrifice their life and livelihood. The affected/displaced people are still objecting to any form of displacement. They are promoting adoption of a land-for-land strategy and conferring absolute rights in the form of a share for tribal people in companies' profits.

Vedanta Alumina project at Lanjigarh

Vedanta's plan to start bauxite mining on an area of 250 hectare reserved forests of Niyamgiri hills has proposed to displace 120 villages inhabited by Jharania Kondhs and Dongaria Kondhs. These pristine forest-covered hills have rich varieties of wild lives and animals living here have been listed on International Union for Conservation of Nature's (IUCN) red list of endangered species (Hirvela 2008). The Forest Survey of India admits the contiguity of dense forest from Devagiri in Rayagada district to the Niyamgiri and Karalapat forests linking to the Narayanpatna forest of Koraput district (*The Hindu* 8 August 2004).

The Niyamgiri range is located in the district of Kalahandi and Rayagada, a part of the fifth schedule area of the state. Half of the mining site covers the reserve forest, which is declared by law to be preserved. Both Niyamgiri and Karalapat hills are biodiversity hotspots declared as protected area under Section 18 of the Wildlife Protection Act, 1972. The presiding deity of these mountains, the Niyam Raja, means lord of the law or lord of dharma and has a very strong socio-psychological bondage with the local tribal people. Therefore, due to the construction of the Vedanta Alumina project at Lanjigarh, the Dongaria Kondhs living in and around the Niyamgiri hill ranges feel uprooted from their religious base.

Mining development in this area started when, on 5 October 2004, the Odisha government gave the mining rights to Vedanta Alumina for its integrated alumina plant in Niyamgiri hills of Lanjigarh in Kalahandi and Odisha Mining Corporation entered into a memorandum of understanding (MoU) with Vedanta Alumina for the supply of bauxite ore from Lanjigarh and Karalapat. It is commonly alleged that the district collector was physically present in all the gram sabhas and forcefully obtained the consent in favour of Vedanta for the mining. Therefore, the inhabitants of four villages in Lanjigarh have been forcibly evicted and rehabilitated in the colony.[10]

The Dongarias, one of the PVTGs of the state, protested against the mining on the premise that as per the 5th schedule Dongarias have the right over their territory, right to profess religious practices and beliefs. Since 2003, the number of protests by the Dongarias have been organized at local, national, and international levels. This opened up the eyes of foreign investors, international organizations, and social activists, and morally compelled the Church of England to withdraw its share from Vedanta which raised certain ethical questions on the mining and indigenous peoples' right over life and livelihood. Struggle continues till today. As a result, Vedanta is struggling to win over both on the ground and also in the Supreme Court to achieve its goal of mining bauxite either from Niyamgiri or Karlapat hill system.

The Lanjigarh project of Vedanta has been in controversy from the very beginning owing to its inherent contradictions. A couple of committees, from Central Empowered Committee to N.C. Saxena Committee, all formed by the state, have raised their voice against the company and in favour of the local community. The Dongarias are considered illiterate and attached with them are the many negative value judgment by the outsiders. All Dongaria people living in Niyamgiri hills united and strongly opposed the mining project proposed by Vedanta, which would cause environmental destruction

[10] The fully displace villages are Sindhabahali, Barbhatta, Kinari, while the partially affected villages are Basantapada and Bandhaguda.

and unsustainable development. Since the project is not approved in the gram sabha, so the Dongaria people questioned the legal validity of the approval of the project and went to the court of law. Their fight against the mining project has proved that they are the champion of the cause of environment and sustainable development.

* * *

As a concluding remark, certain theoretical and methodological issues relating to the development of the indigenous tribal communities with specific reference to Odisha have been raised here. During the last couple of decades, one finds a plethora of research material on tribal issues. But in spite of this, there is a need for further studies which will refine the concept of development and welfare of the tribal population. Tribal development programmes so far implemented during last six decades have always been state sponsored. As a result, it could not bring much transformation in the life and livelihood structure of the tribal societies. Rather, this has led to the formation of tribal development as a political ideology.

The welfare measures adopted by the state in the post-Independence period seems to be an outcome of both constitutional safeguards and political ideologies which have influenced the fundamental approach to tribal development policies. The special packages for Kalahandi, Balangir and Koraput (KBK) districts cited was started in the year 1995 and renamed as RLATP in the year 1998–99 by the then government ruled by the Congress (the then dominant political party) and the region more so reflect the political intentions rather than designed to bring about structural transformation among the tribal communities and the tribal dominated regions with regards to land-man-resource relation. However, the expressed intention is to upgrade their socio-economic status above the poverty line through various welfare measures. The formation of Western Odisha Development Council in July 1999 by the Government of Odisha is another example of over-politicization of the development processes. The welfare programmes are politicized and seems to be performed as more out of political commitments than of constitutional commitments. In subsequent periods such political packages do not get adequate support by the government if led by other political parties ruled at state and national levels, as observed in case of KBK–RLATP in case of Odisha.

In addition to the government funding, various international agencies and charitable organizations are also engaged in tribal development activities in the state. By doing this, the state, since 1990, has diverted attention from performing its constitutional responsibilities towards the welfare options for the tribal people. The quality of services for a better life support system often has been ignored in the process of globalization. Under the situation of the quality of life of the tribal people could not be revitalized through redistribution of resources, emphasizing more on primary sectors, where the societal payoff is largest in the long run. The Tribal Sub Plan programme in the state could not make a remarkable impact largely because the tribal development approach did not take into account the core culture of these communities, which embodies the totality of knowledge of articulation.

The current discourse on tribal movements and tribal empowerment mainly revolves around securing well-defined rights to land and forests through participatory practices. At a more fundamental level, the question of the abuse of tribal people's human rights and the violation of their right to life and livelihood should be a central concern for the nation. However, it is important to recognize that, by the very nature of the issues involved, tribal people's protest movements, however well organized, have to contend with the powerful interests of a local economic elite and industrial capital—both domestic and foreign—who wield considerable political power. On the other hand, making the state do its job of enhancing capabilities is essential. There is an immediate sense in which pragmatic considerations (for example making tribal people realise that it is their right to have a doctor at primary health centres) play a useful and important role in mobilizing tribal people. This may contribute to strengthen the organized articulation of the fundamental livelihood struggles of tribal people.

References

Bailey, F.G. 1963. *Politics and Social Change: Orissa in 1959*. Bombay: Oxford University Press.

Behura, N. and N. Panigrahi. 2001. *Functioning of the Fifth Schedule of the Constitution of India: The Role of Welfare Agencies in the State of Odisha*, report submitted to ICSSR, New Delhi. Bhubaneswar: NKC Centre for Development Studies.

Behura, N. and N. Panigrahi. 2002. 'Marginalization of the Vulnerable Tribal Communities in the State of Odisha through the Process of Sponsored Development', *Journal of Anthropological Survey of India*, 51: 41–72.

Behura, N.K. 1982. 'Forest and Tribal World View', *Journal of Social Research*, 35(1): 1–8.

———. 1990. 'Socio-economic Problems and Social Change', in V. Sudarshan and M.A. Kalyan (eds), *The Uprooted*, pp. 1–22. New Delhi: Gyan Publishing House.

Behura, N.K. and P.K. Nayak. 1993. 'Involuntary Displacement and the Changing Frontiers of Kinship: A Study of Settlement in Odisha', in M.M. Cernea and S.E. Guggenheim (eds), *Anthropological Approach to Resettlement: Policy, Practice and Theory*, pp. 283–306. Boulder: Westview Press.

Bharatiya Jana Kalyan Kendra (BJKK), 1998. 'Evaluation Report on Odisha Tribal Development Project, Kashipur' (IFAD assisted project), report submitted to the Welfare Department, Government of Odisha.

Fernandes, Walter, Geeta Menon, and Philip Viegas. 1984. *Forests Environment and Forest Dweller Economy in Odisha: A Report on Deforestation, Marginalisation, and Search for Alternatives.* New Delhi: Indian Social Institute.

Government of India. 1998. *Report of OTDP Kashipur, Orissa.* Odisha: GoI, assisted by International Fund for Agriculture Development, IFAD.

———. MoTA, and UNDP. 2012. *Regional Consultations on Forest Rights Act, 2006 (FRA).* Available at http://tribal.nic.in/WriteReadData/CMS/Documents/201303010548576806640File1540.pdf (last accessed on 22 January 2016).

Government of Odisha. 1960–61. *Shifting Cultivation in Odisha.* Bhubaneswar: Agricultural Department of Social Conservation Organisation, Government of Odisha, Government Press.

———. 1971–72. *Report on the Survey on Shifting Cultivation.* Bhubaneswar: THRTI, ST and SC Development Department

———. 2000. *Conferment of Ownership Rights to Persons Cultivating Land in the Hill Slopes within 30 Degrees in Scheduled Caste.* Odisha: Revenue Department.

———. 2012. *Impact Assessment of Land and Water Management Interventions on Agriculture and Horticulture Development in Phase-I Areas of OTELP.* Bhubaneswar.

———. 2011–12. *Annual Progress Report 2011–12.* Bhubaneswar: OTELP.

GoO. 2012–13. *Annual Progress Report 2011–12*. Bhubaneswar: OTELP.

Hirvela V. 2008. *How Sterlite and Niyamgiri Mining are Non-accountable*. Finland: Forest and Bio-Diversity Campaigner, Friends of the Earth.

Industrial Management Consultants of Odisha. 1998. 'Study on Natural Resources Development Programmes of OTDP, Kashipur', report submitted to Welfare Department, Government of Odisha.

Maddox, S.L. 1897. Orissa: Final report on the Survey and settlement of the Province of Orissa (Temporarily settled areas), 1890–1900', Calcutta, IOR/V/27/314/88, 1900.

Mallik, R.M. and N. Panigrahi. 1998. 'Non-timber Forest Produce: Collection, Benefits and Management in Odisha', study report of the NKC Centre for Development Studies, Bhubaneswar, submitted to the Ford Foundation, New Delhi.

Mohapatra, L.K. 1968. 'Problems and Welfare of Odisha Tribals', in L.P. Vidyarthy (ed.), *Applied Anthropology in India: Principles, Problems and Case Studies*, pp. 396–420. Allahabad: Kitab Mahal.

———. 1998b. *Resettlement, Improvement and Reconstruction in India: Development for the Deprived*. New Delhi: Vikas Publishing House.

———. 1998a. 'Participatory Approach in Resettlement and Rehabilitation Implementation', paper presented at the seminar on Resettlement and Rehabilitation, Gopabandhu Academy of Administration, Odisha.

Office of the Principal Chief Conservation of Forests. 2009–10. Available at http://www.mahaforest.nic.in/internal.php?id=26 (last accessed on 22 January 2016).

Panda, P. and N. Panigrahi. 1989. 'The Problem of Displacement of Displaced People: A Study in the Coal Mines of Brajarajnagar, Odisha', in R.N. Pati and B. Jena (eds), *Tribal Development in India*, pp. 35–50. New Delhi: Ashish Publishing House.

Pande, B. 1998. *Depriving the Underprivileged for Development*. Bhubaneswar: Institute for Social and Economic Development.

Panigrahi, N. 1986. 'Men and Mining in Western Odisha', study report submitted to Participatory Research in Asia (PRIA), New Delhi.

Pathy, J. 1987. 'Ethnic Minorities and Processes of Their Development', report submitted to UGC, New Delhi.

Patnaik, S.M. 2000. 'Understanding Involuntary Resettlement: An Anthropological Perspective', *The Eastern Anthropologist*, 53(1–2): 141–59.

Planning Commission. 2006. *National Mineral Policy: Report of the High Level Committee*. New Delhi: Government of India.

Rao. R.S., P. Panda, and A. Mishra. 1987. 'Peoples Movement: A Study of Gandhamardan Bauxite Mining', mimeo.

Roy Burman, B.K. 1982. *Report of Committee on Forest and Tribals in India.* New Delhi: Tribal Development Division, Ministry of Home Affairs.

Saxena, N.C. 1995. *Forests, People and Profit: New Equations for Sustainability*, report produced for the Centre for Sustainable Development, Lal Bahadur Sastri National Academy of Administration, Mussorie (Dehradun: Natraj Publishers).

Swain, M. and N. Panigrahi. 1999. 'Development, Displacement, and Rehabilitation in Odisha: An Overview', *Man in Life*, 25(3–4): 163–79.

The Hindu. 8 August 2004. 'A struggle to save Niyamgiri forests'. Available online at http://www.thehindubusinessline.com/2004/08/08/stories/2004080801141600.htm (last accessed on 22 January 2016).

PART V

STATE FINANCES AND THE PLANNING STRATEGY OF THE STATE GOVERNMENT

14

The Impact of Fiscal Adjustments in Odisha*

Tapas K. Sen and *Sarit Kumar Rout*

Fiscal reforms in Odisha: The backdrop

There is usually a lack of consonance between the developmental ambitions and the available resources to follow the path for achieving the ambitions in low-income countries, or in the context of federal India, poorer states. This is mainly because the standard neoclassical process of development requires an increase in the factors of production to expand the production possibility frontier outward. In a country like India, labour is rarely the constraint, although if the skill factor is brought in, even labour could be considered a constraint. In any case, if the elasticity of substitution between factors is small, it implies that growth can be achieved only if incremental use of all factors of production is possible. Typically, it is capital (both physical

* The views expressed in this chapter are personal, and do not necessarily reflect those of the institutions to which the authors are affiliated.

and human) that proves to be a major constraint, requiring regular and large doses of investment to sustain the growth process. This is where the disconnection between the dreams and the means becomes apparent because a poor state, by definition, finds it difficult to muster the kind of resources that are needed for such investments. Moreover, low private incomes in general and the absence of profitability of the kind of investments usually needed (for example, infrastructure or other investments often in the nature of pure or impure public goods) make private investments scarce in the areas where they are most needed. The responsibility then falls on the public sector, but the public sector is equally resource constrained. The low revenue base keeps revenue collections low while the low private incomes (and often high levels of poverty, as in Odisha) translate into greater and more urgent public consumption expenditures, leaving little fiscal space for investments for growth.

The general scenario outlined here describes the situation in Odisha—one of the low-income states of India with the highest level of poverty among all the states—fairly accurately.[1] Possibly because of the mismatch between the expenditure needs and the revenue collections, the state has been showing budgetary imbalance in the form of substantial fiscal and revenue deficits throughout the 1990s as also in the next decade till 2003–04. However, all through this period, the state was being advised to contain its deficits by selectively controlling its expenditures and making better use of whatever revenue potential was available to it by independent researchers as well as multilateral and bilateral international agencies. Officially, the state government's own assessment also accepted the need to correct its fiscal imbalance in the White Paper on state finances.[2]

The fiscal problems were, of course, not confined to Odisha during that period; most of the Indian states were going through similar difficulties, but of varying degree of seriousness. The symptoms of

[1] The state's resources, projected as optimistically as possible within the bounds of feasibility, was shown to be quite inadequate to meet the projected needs of only the basic human development sectors in Sen et al. (2008).

[2] 'Prudent fiscal management is vital to providing impetus and vigour to the growth process and therefore, the State Government places significant emphasis on restoring fiscal health in the State.' (GoO 2001).

the malaise were strikingly similar across states—most of them characterized by expenditures (particularly revenue expenditure) growing faster than revenue receipts. A large part of these expenditures were accounted for by salaries, wages, and pensions, high levels of interest payments relative to expenditures, large budgetary transfers to public enterprises (biggest among them usually being the state electricity board and the state-owned public transport undertaking), indiscriminate and high levels of budgetary subsidy, inadequate tax effort, and dwindling non-tax revenues. However, in some of the cases (mostly the higher income states), the problem was not structural but relatively easily manageable, usually arising from fiscal mismanagement.[3] A common issue related to the axiomatic reliance placed exclusively on the public sector to produce and distribute every good or service that the government decided to provide. Further, there were some exogenous factors that played a role: the inability of the centre to keep inflation consistently under check, the substantial increase in salaries, wages, and pensions of the central employees that generated successful demands for similar increases at the state level, and the vicious circle of deficits causing increasing borrowings with the latter contributing to further increase in deficits through debt-servicing costs.

With the centre facing significant pressure from the states to bail them out when it was not able to contain its own deficits, the aggregate public sector deficits were large enough at the turn of the century to cause worries on the macroeconomic front, prompting it to ask the finance commission to address this issue. Given its limitations as a fiscal arbitrator, successive finance commissions could only increase the transfers to the states and incentivize them to undertake fiscal reforms that would reduce the imbalances. The Tenth Finance Commission recommended two schemes of debt relief for the states based on fiscal performance and utilization of disinvestment proceeds for retiring central loans. The Eleventh Finance Commission recommended debt relief based on improvement in receipts to expenditure ratio in the revenue account and a fiscal performance–based incentive grant. The Twelfth and the Thirteenth Finance Commissions continued debt relief based on recommended reforms, but discontinued the incentive

[3] The best example of it was (and still is) Punjab (Sawhney 2005).

grant. The Twelfth Finance Commission was successful in incentivizing all states barring two to legislate a Fiscal Responsibility and Budget Reform Act with uniform target deficit levels, although a few states had passed such legislations even earlier. The Thirteenth Finance Commission repeated this recommendation, with the two remaining states also joining the scheme. Additionally, it made all the special purpose grants conditional upon a number of fiscal reform measures.

Simultaneously, the states were also feeling the fiscal pinch with the scope for discretionary developmental expenditures narrowing down significantly. Thus, a search for ways to tackle the problem of fiscal imbalance began in earnest, with individual states coming up with various sets of reform measures on both the receipt side and the expenditure side. The centre also pitched in with measures that brought down interest costs of states, and by stepping up central expenditures on centrally sponsored schemes in priority areas like primary education, health, agriculture, power, irrigation, rural, and urban development. The tide turned around the middle of the 2000s, with most states exhibiting reduction in deficit levels.

Fiscal reforms in Odisha

Fiscal reforms in Odisha took place on at least three identifiable tracks over a long period of time, though not as a well-articulated plan of action, but instead in a haphazard manner. These three tracks consisted of a strategic withdrawal or contraction of the public interventions, measures aimed at actually increasing revenue receipts or containing expenditures immediately, and procedural and governance reforms that were needed in principle and could be fiscally useful over a longer time span.

In the first category, one could put the major privatization measures, including the much-maligned power sector reorganization (generation, transmission, and distribution activities were unbundled and separately corporatized) that privatized distribution fully and production partly. The less-noticed and less-discussed privatization of the passenger transport sector, getting rid of a number of public enterprise units, and allowing a host of private initiatives in the field of (particularly higher) education and health were all a part of this programme that was never articulated, although hinted at in many official documents. The second category included measures like shifting to a value-added tax (VAT)–like system of sales taxation, reforms in stamp duty structure and administration, and introduction of hitherto unutilized taxes like entry tax, profession tax, and forest development tax on the receipts side. Besides, some user charges were either introduced (public medical services, for example) or enhanced (for example, irrigation rates). On the expenditure side, the most significant money saver was the clampdown on fresh appointments (barring a few exceptions). A review of sanctioned posts and personnel in place was done, and posts not filled up for a certain period were abolished. All the posts vacated by retirements were not automatically filled up. Apart from this, there were deliberate departmental budget cuts, or more often, no automatic increase in their budgets, depending on utilization in previous years. Debt management to reduce interest payments was undertaken in earnest. Sectoral and public enterprise reforms were accompanied by a refusal to continue subsidies and subventions. Finally, procedural reforms included measures like computerization in many areas, building up relevant databases and information systems to aid informed decision-making, e-tendering to eliminate malpractices, monitoring and improving the flow of utilization certificates wherever required, and numerous other small changes that nevertheless added up to significant reforms. Table 14.1 shows the impact of the all the general and state-specific factors on the summary indicators of deficits in the state.

Even though the reform process started in 1999 with the signing of a Memorandum of Understanding (MoU) with the centre on a monitorable reform programme, it can be seen that the impact of the adjustments became apparent in the budget figures only after 2003–04. Although revenue deficit started declining in 2003–04, fiscal deficit started declining only from 2004–05. Taking 2004–05 as the turning point, the averages for the years 1999–2000 to 2003–04, when compared with the averages for the period 2004–05 onwards, show the changes in fiscal balances clearly (Table 14.1). The three indicators—revenue, fiscal, and primary deficits—show a large drop in the second period from the first (pre-reform). There were primary surpluses in all years starting 2004–05 to the last year of the period under consideration. In two consecutive years of this post-reform period (2006–07 and 2007–08), fiscal deficit also was changed into a fiscal surplus.

Table 14.1 Trends in fiscal imbalance of Odisha (percentage of gross state domestic product [GSDP])

Year	Revenue deficit	Gross fiscal deficit	Primary deficit
1999–2000	5.52	8.04	5.38
2000–01	4.11	7.07	2.21
2001–02	5.59	7.83	2.23
2002–03	2.92	5.22	-0.13
2003–04	2.15	5.40	1.08
Average	*4.06*	*6.71*	*2.15*
2004–05	0.67	1.76	-2.53
2005–06	-0.57	0.32	-4.02
2006–07	-2.22	-0.81	-3.94
2007–08	-3.28	-1.02	-3.47
2008–09	-2.30	0.22	-1.72
2009–10	-0.70	1.38	-0.48
2010–11	-2.00	0.34	-1.23
Average	*-1.49*	*0.31*	*-2.48*

Source: Based on Government of Odisha (various issues).
Note: (1) Minus sign (-) indicates surplus in the deficit indicators.
(2) GSDP (2004–05 base) series used to estimate various ratios.

There were two developments around 2004–05 that should have at least partly contributed to the unprecedented fiscal adjustment—a shift from a reasonable but not spectacular growth path of the Indian economy into an accelerated growth path, and the adoption of a fiscal responsibility legislation (Fiscal Responsibility and Budget Management Act [2005]) in 2005–06 as desired by the Twelfth Finance Commission. While the former provided a boost to the revenue collections (both own and transferred from the centre), the latter unambiguously targeted a reduction in deficits and indebtedness. The relative contribution of these two factors, superimposed on other reforms started earlier, to the fiscal adjustment process is however difficult to measure accurately. In what follows, an attempt is made to get a rough idea of this by examining the channels—actually elements that combine into the deficit indicators—through which the adjustment took place.

The mechanics of fiscal adjustment in Odisha

Since the change in the average fiscal deficit to GSDP ratio from the first to the second period—a reduction of 6.4 percentage points—is largely accounted for by the reduction in revenue deficits (5.55 percentage points),[4] it is the components of the latter that need an examination to ascertain the direction and extent of change in them in order to understand the change in revenue deficits fully. Table 14.2 provides data on the components of revenue receipts as also on revenue expenditures. It can be seen that each of the components of revenue receipts exhibits an increase in the latter period adding up to 2.38 percentage points (taking each of them as a ratio of GSDP). Of these, the highest increase was in own revenue (0.89 percentage points), followed by share in central taxes (0.65 percentage points), own non-tax revenue (0.54 percentage points),[5] and grants from the centre (0.31 percentage points). But a bigger adjustment can be observed in revenue expenditures amounting to 3.15 percentage points. Clearly, the relatively small increases in the components of revenue receipts could not have created any significant distress among the ordinary citizens of Odisha in general unless the benefits of economic growth were highly skewed; in fact, since the second period broadly coincides with an acceleration of economic growth (GSDP), the increases could merely reflect a higher (>1) elasticity of these with respect to the broadly defined base (that is, GSDP).

However, the contraction in revenue expenditures could possibly have caused distress if it affected the supply of major or important public services adversely. In particular, cuts in basic social services and those expenditures that largely benefit the poor would transfer a part

[4] It may be noted in passing that the rest of the adjustments (0.85 percentage points) is accounted for by the net outcome of a substantial reduction in net loans and advances given by the state government and a relatively small increase in capital expenditures.

[5] Increase in mining royalties, particularly from the middle of the previous decade, has been the main contributory factor. There has been a further surge from 2010–11 owing to the change in the system of royalty on iron ore from a specific rate to 10 per cent ad valorem.

Table 14.2 Trends in revenue receipts and expenditure (percentage of GSDP)

Year	Own tax	Own non-tax	Share in central taxes	Grants from the Centre	Revenue receipt	Revenue expenditure
1999–2000	3.66	1.54	3.75	3.68	12.62	18.15
2000–01	4.65	1.46	5.54	3.04	14.68	18.79
2001–02	4.87	1.36	5.22	2.45	13.90	19.49
2002–03	5.33	1.78	5.20	3.34	15.65	18.58
2003–04	4.99	1.65	5.03	2.59	14.27	16.42
Average	*4.70*	*1.56*	*4.95*	*3.02*	*14.23*	*18.28*
2004–05	5.37	1.73	5.12	3.02	15.25	15.92
2005–06	5.88	1.80	5.73	3.14	16.55	15.99
2006–07	5.96	2.54	6.11	3.10	17.71	15.49
2007–08	5.30	2.05	6.07	3.57	16.99	13.71
2008–09	5.38	2.14	5.58	3.47	16.57	14.27
2009–10	5.49	1.96	5.20	3.49	16.14	15.45
2010–11	5.74	2.45	5.38	3.49	17.06	15.06
Average	*5.59*	*2.10*	*5.60*	*3.33*	*16.61*	*15.13*

Source: Based on GoO (various issues).

of the burden of adjustment to those groups that are least equipped to bear them. It is a more detailed examination of this aspect that we turn to now.

Expenditure adjustments: Some details

Table 14.3 provides some details on total public expenditures in Odisha expressed as percentages of GSDP. A few important insights can be gained from an examination of these numbers. First, it is the substantial reduction in debt-servicing costs from the first to the second period that went a long way in facilitating the fiscal adjustment observed in Odisha. While interest payments were reduced by 1.76 percentage points, debt repayments came down by 0.73 percentage points, together accounting for a 2.5 percentage point decline in expenditures against a reduction of 6.4 percentage points in fiscal deficits.

Table 14.3 Pattern of public expenditure

		Share in GSDP (%)		Share in total expenditure (%)	
		Average 1999–2000 to 2003–04	Average 2004–05 to 2010–11	Average 1999–2000 to 2003–04	Average 2004–05 to 2010–11
1	*Revenue expenditure*	*18.28*	*15.13*	*78.14*	*81.01*
1.1	General services of which	8.24	6.40	35.05	34.09
1.1.1	*Interest payment@*	*4.56(24.87)*	*2.80(18.33)*	*19.31*	*14.87*
1.2	Social services	6.73	5.49	28.93	29.45
1.3	Economic services	3.06	3.01	13.09	16.20
1.4	Assignment to local bodies	0.25	0.24	1.07	1.27
2	*Expenditure on capital account*	*5.15*	*3.55*	*21.86*	*18.99*
2.1	Capital outlay	1.70	1.88	7.27	10.17
2.2	Debt repayment	2.21	1.48	9.33	7.81
2.3	Loan disbursements	1.23	0.19	5.26	1.01
3=(1+2)	*Total government expenditure@@*	*23.43*	*18.67*		

Source: Based on data taken from GoO (various issues).

Note: @ Figures in parentheses indicate share in revenue expenditure

@@ Total expenditure excludes ways and means advances

Second, the bulk of the reduction in revenue expenditures was in general services (1.84 percentage points) and social services (1.24 percentage points), with the ratios of revenue expenditure on economic services and assignments to local bodies to GSDP showing only a marginal fall each. Since there was a conscious attempt to control expenditure on salaries and wages, and these two groups of services have the largest share of such expenditures in their total expenditures, it is likely that the reduction in expenditures in these two categories of services could be largely explained by reduction in their expenditures on wages and salaries. Available information supports this conjecture. Salaries were shrunk from around 44 per cent of revenue expenditures on an average in the first period to about 33 per cent in the second, despite a salary revision pushing up the salary bill in the last three years. This represents a reduction of approximately 25 per cent. With a salary bill of above 70 per cent of the total revenue expenditures in general services and social services, a reduction of 25 per cent would amount to a reduction of about 17.5 per cent in the total revenue expenditures on general services and social services. The actual reduction was only a little larger in general services, but smaller in social services.

Third, the government clearly adopted a policy of virtually eliminating the practice of giving loans and advances (usually to public enterprises, local bodies, or its own employees). Many of these loans were effectively grants because they were never repaid, and either written off after carrying them on the books for a few years or converted into equity on which no dividend was ever paid. Obviously, these constituted a major drain of the state's resources in the past and plugging them was a step in the right direction. This reform measure also helped to a significant extent in the fiscal adjustment (to the tune of 1.04 percentage points). Altogether, adjustments in the expenditure side of the budget yielded a total reduction of 4.76 percentage points, of which the only contraction that could be of concern was that in social services, although we conjecture that this contraction could be largely explained by a fall in salaries and wages only. We now examine the reduction in social services in further detail to assess if any specific service was targeted or whether it was an across-the-board contraction of public expenditures.

Table 14.4 shows that there was a visible contraction in the public expenditure on some of the components of social services like education, health, and social welfare and nutrition as a ratio of GSDP even in the second period.[6] Prima facie, this is a cause for concern, since the contraction is understandable during a period of large deficits (as during the first period) but not during a period when fiscal space was available and for a couple of years, the government was expected to step up public expenditure as an antidote of recessionary tendencies of the economy. However, when we look at the last two columns of Table 14.4, the picture looks somewhat different. As far as education is concerned, the average annual growth was quite high at 22.5 per cent during the second period against a small negative figure during the first period. This was clearly a reversal of the trend and quite emphatic at that, but there is an apparent inconsistency between the lower ratio with respect to GSDP and the higher growth in the second period. This inconsistency is because of two reasons—the low base that the second period started with by the end of 2003–04, and the considerably higher levels of the denominator (GSDP) in the second period. It may also be pointed out that the level of public expenditure on education relative to other sectors was, and remains, high. However, the public sector has certainly refrained from investing much in higher education in particular, putting its faith in the private sector in the matter of meeting the demand. While the strategy may be broadly appropriate in a resource-constrained situation, it is a fact that that private supply of higher education is confined to only certain disciplines. Also, there are certain aspects of education (like ensuring quality) the responsibility for which the government cannot shrug off.

In comparison, the reversal of the downward trend in health expenditures was not that emphatic even though their levels have been relatively low, and the annual average growth was also not particularly

[6] The situation on the ground can be gauged somewhat with these statistics: The number of primary schools and teachers were 42,104 and 1,14,791 in 2000–01, 44,416 and 97,175 in 2003–04, and 53,814, and 1,36,407 in 2010–11. The stagnant position till 2003–04 and the addition to the capacity by 2010–11 are quite clear. In contrast, the stagnant infrastructure in health services with no change between 2000–01 and 2004–05 and only marginal improvements after that (beds per 10,000 population declined from 3.96 to 3.76 between 2005–06 and 2009–10) reflect the inadequate public expenditure on health (data taken from GoO [2012]).

Table 14.4 Expenditure on social services in Odisha (revenue + capital)

	Average share of GSDP (%)		Annual average growth rate (%)	
	1999–2000 to 2003–04	2004–05 to 2010–11	1999–2000 to 2003–04	2004–05 to 2010–11
Education, sports, art, and culture	3.55	2.87	-0.32	22.50
Medical and public health	0.89	0.65	3.87	14.36
Water supply, sanitation, housing, and urban development	0.67	0.69	2.00	25.56
Information and broadcasting	0.02	0.01	3.31	16.80
SCs, STs, OBCs	0.47	0.46	0.51	31.38
Labour and employment	0.04	0.04	-0.27	24.61
Social welfare and nutrition	1.25	1.07	5.71	23.71
Others	0.06	0.03	25.30	23.20
Total	6.96	5.82	-0.65	21.16

Source: GoO (various issues).

high during the second period. Despite numerous studies pointing out the fact of exceptionally high private (essentially out of pocket) expenditures on health for a less developed state in a low-income country and its concomitant problems, there are enough indicators to point towards continued neglect of this sector. In the case of social welfare and nutrition, the second period growth was high—and much higher than during the first period—allaying any serious concern about the government's intentions. Overall, it appears that the only broad sector that could have suffered from seriously inadequate public expenditures even during the period of relatively comfortable fiscal balances was health. This is probably a matter deserving more detailed analysis and attention of policymakers.

It may be noted that direct poverty alleviation schemes (mainly included in rural development, which is a component of economic services) are not included in this analysis although expenditures on such schemes would have obvious implications for the poor. This is wholly because our analysis is based on the budgetary data of the state government, while most of the expenditures on these schemes are outside the state budget. Thus, although the importance of such expenditures is not in doubt, the scope of the present study does not allow a systematic analysis of these public expenditures.

* * *

The reform process formally started in Odisha with the signing of an MoU between the state and the central governments in 1999 on a monitorable programme of reaching agreed fiscal goals within a specified period. The White Paper published by the state government also clearly laid out the dire fiscal scenario of the state and emphasised the urgency of fiscal reforms. However, either since the reforms were not pursued with enough seriousness or due to the lack of favourable circumstances, nothing notable happened to the bottom lines till 2003–04. It was only from 2004–05 that circumstances became favourable to reforms with the Indian economy moving on to a higher growth path that the result of the reforms became visible. This also coincided with the Twelfth Finance Commission's recommendation of incentivizing fiscal reform legislations and targeting a reduction in revenue deficits to zero and in fiscal deficits to 3 per cent of GSDP by 2008–09. The data thus clearly divides our entire reference period of 1999–2000 to 2010–11 into two sub-periods—1999–2004 and 2004–11, based not on the implementation of reforms but on their success in creating fiscal space. And the questions that we seek an answer to are: (a) did the fiscal reforms involve significant expenditure contraction in a way that would hurt the citizens and (b) whether the fiscal space created actually helped in stepping up much-needed developmental expenditures or not.

The components of fiscal adjustment in the revenue account (Figure 14.1)—which accounted for the bulk of the adjustments in fiscal deficits—show that there was indeed adjustment on all fronts before the beneficial results showed up. The positive changes are all on

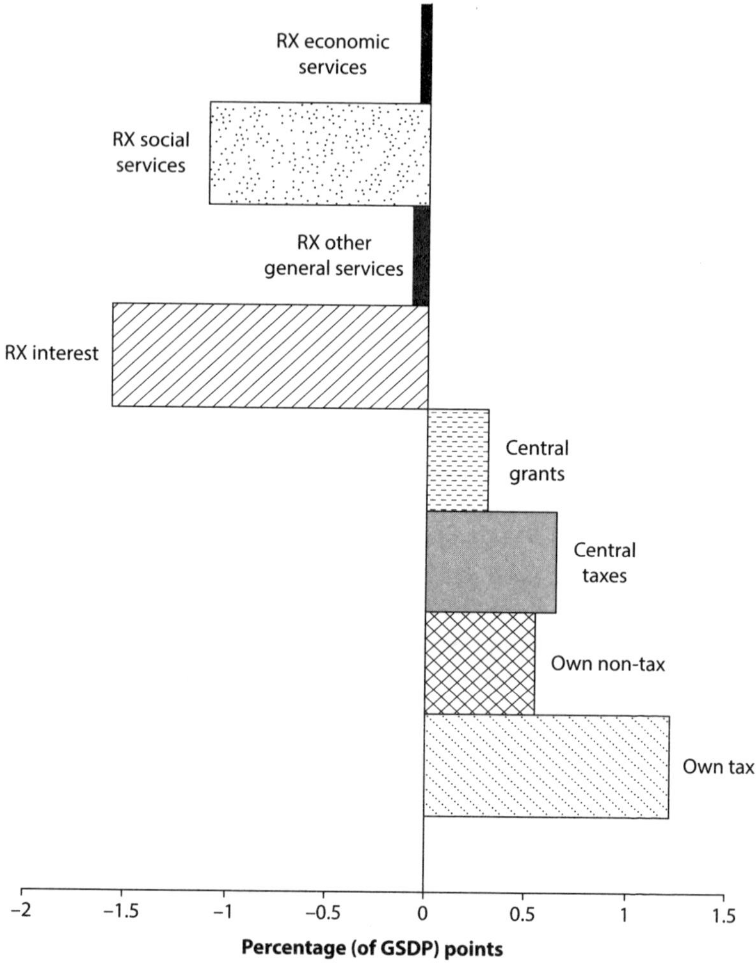

Figure 14.1 Change in average ratios from first to second period
Source: GoI (various issues).
Note: RX denotes revenue expenditure

the receipts side while the reductions are all on the expenditure side (whereby, in this figure, RX denotes revenue expenditure). The extent of adjustments are not uniform and it is easy to see that the three largest adjustments are in interest payments, own tax revenue, and social services. While the changes in interest payments and own taxes should not have caused any hardships, the fall in public expenditures on social services could have. However, a more detailed examination of the data shows that only the health sector could be said to have suffered inadequate public expenditures in the second period, though there are some indications of general expenditure contraction in the first period, in particular on education. The evidence thus points to a fiscal reform process that could be said to be broadly appropriate, with the only major blemish relating to the health sector. This is mainly because the adjustment on the expenditure side was primarily in interest payments, debt repayments, and loans advanced. The reforms even built into the process a small increase in capital expenditures, an oft-repeated prescription for higher economic growth. On balance, the fiscal adjustment process could be termed as relatively painless once fiscal space was created.[7]

The improved fiscal balances have also had a very different type of impact that ought to better serve the cause of fiscal federalism. The lack of fiscal space before the fiscal reforms had constrained the manoeuvrability of the state government with respect to choosing its own expenditure policy significantly. A large part of its total Plan Provisions were allocated for meeting the requirements of the Central Plan Schemes (CPS) and Centrally Sponsored Schemes (CSS). With the creation of greater fiscal space, the state has recovered some of the necessary autonomy. This can be gauged from the fact that in 2005–06, the share of the two types of centrally initiated schemes was more than 26 per cent in total Plan Provisions; this fell to about 14 per cent in the 2012–13 budget, despite stricter measures to ensure higher utilization of the central transfers available through these two types of schemes including making all necessary provisions for the matching requirements. This lends support to the view that for fiscal federalism to operate in an ideal manner, all levels of governmental units have to be financially sound, and overdependence of one level of government on another is not healthy. It is this general

[7] The state continues to look for greater fiscal space through additional revenue receipts. It recently set up an Expert Committee to suggest ways of enhancing tax and non-tax revenues, and the recommendations (GoO 2011) are under consideration for implementation over a period of time.

view that has a bearing on the Odisha government's futile attempts to gain a special category status, the obvious consideration being the increased central transfers and the lower matching requirements for the CPS and CSS. We believe this to be a completely uncalled-for strategy, both because of its low probability of success and its unlikely positive impact on growth. None of the special-category states that have had these benefits for a long time have exhibited a general advantage in terms of economic growth and development, though there are instances of exceptional achievements in isolated areas. A more appropriate and endogenous process would be to continue on the path of maintaining fiscal space, calibrating public expenditure policy to obtain maximum benefits in terms of growth that would help create more fiscal space, and maintain this virtuous cycle. This would no doubt be a long process since progress will be made in small increments only, but it would be far more sustainable and not suffer from the vagaries of an exogenously determined growth process.

References

Government of Odisha (GoO). 2001. *White Paper on Orissa State Finances*. Bhubaneswar: Finance Department.

———. 2011. *Report of the Expert Committee on Revenue Enhancement Measures*. Bhubaneswar: Finance Department.

———. Various issues. *Finance Accounts*. Government of Odisha, Bhubaneswar.

Sawhney, U. 2005. 'Fiscal Reforms at the Sub-national Level: The Case of Punjab', Working Paper No. 26, National Institute of Public Finance and Policy, New Delhi.

Sen, T.K., H.K. Amar Nath, M. Choudhury, and P. Kundu. 2008. 'Fiscal Reforms, Persistent Poverty and Human Development: The Case of Orissa'. New Delhi: National Institute of Public Finance and Policy.

15

A Perspective on Odisha's Recent Development Paradigm

Prabhat Patnaik

Odisha is a state where almost two-fifths of the total population (38.66 per cent according to the 2001 Census) consists of persons belonging to the scheduled castes (SCs) and scheduled tribes (STs). They also largely belong to, though they do not exclusively constitute, the population below the poverty line. Any development strategy for Odisha must therefore be focused on improving their condition. But this has scarcely been the case in the recent period. In the quest for increasing the growth rate of the gross state domestic product (GSDP), a development strategy has been adopted, which has on the contrary made the conditions of the poor, and hence, by inference, of the Dalits belonging to the SC/ST category, even worse.

True, Odisha alone is not culpable on this score; this strategy has characterized the country as a whole in the years since 'liberalization'. But that is hardly any consolation. This strategy itself is so flawed that whether we take the country as a whole, or just Odisha (which incidentally has been more successful on this strategy, having achieved a higher GSDP growth rate that the gross domestic product (GDP) growth rate for India as a whole in the last decade), high growth has been accompanied by worsening nutritional standards, and hence in poverty, which, in India, is basically defined with reference to nutritional standards even to this day. The purpose of this chapter is to examine critically some aspects of the development record of Odisha over the last decade and to make suggestions towards an alternative strategy.

Poverty and nutrition in Odisha

Odisha, according to the erstwhile Planning Commission's poverty estimates, was the poorest state in the country in 2009–10, with a rural poverty ratio of 60.8 per cent and an urban poverty ratio of 37.6 per cent, compared to 33.8 per cent and 20.9 per cent respectively for India as a whole. And yet, paradoxically, in terms of nutritional standards, which are supposed to constitute the basis for the poverty estimates, it was better off than the nation as a whole, which only underscores the vacuity of the Planning Commission's poverty estimates. The per capita daily calorie intake in rural Odisha was 2,126 compared to 2,020 for all-India'[1]; the corresponding urban figures were 2,096 and 1,946 respectively. What is interesting too is that Odisha having a better nutritional record than the country as a whole is not confined to 2009–10 alone, it is more generally valid.[2]

The key to Odisha's somewhat better nutritional record, which is often not appreciated, lies in its relatively high per capita foodgrain output. For the same year which we considered above, 2009–10

[1] All the calorie intake figures given in this paper are taken from Patnaik (2012).

[2] The only exception to the general pattern of Odisha's per capita daily calorie intake, both for rural and urban areas, being higher than the corresponding all-India figure was in 2004–05 for rural Odisha (2,023 calories compared to the all-India figure of 2,047); but this could be the lagged effect of an extraordinarily low foodgrain output in Odisha in 2002–03, a mere 3.5 million tonnes compared to close to 7 million tonnes in each subsequent year. But Odisha's nutritional status in 1993–04 again was better than for India as a whole.

(which was admittedly a drought year), the per capita foodgrain output in Odisha was 174 kg per year.[3] If we take India as a whole, including Odisha *but excluding Punjab and Haryana* (for reasons that will become clear shortly), then the figure comes to 147 kg per year.[4] Odisha, therefore, had a higher per capita foodgrain output than India as a whole, excluding Punjab and Haryana.

The proposition being advanced that the production of foodgrains in a particular region is a determinant of its nutritional status may appear strange at first sight. We are accustomed to think that a region's trade with the outside world permits a divergence between its production and consumption patterns, so that its consumption of foodgrains, which determines its nutritional status, is assumed to be independent of how much foodgrains it happens to produce. But in the context of a poor third-world economy, afflicted by substantial unemployment and underemployment, matters are quite different. A higher foodgrain output not only augments supplies, but also, since foodgrain production, especially rice, is highly labour-intensive, it increases employment and puts significant amount of purchasing power in the hands of the rural poor. This permits them to demand both larger amounts of foodgrains and also other non-food commodities, thus generating larger employment outside the foodgrain sector as well. Higher production of foodgrains in a particular region, therefore, has the effect of augmenting foodgrain consumption, and hence, improving nutritional status within it.[5]

True, one can cite obvious exceptions and counter examples. Kalahandi district, for example, which has acquired notoriety all over the country for the famine-like conditions that often prevail in it, is a 'surplus' foodgrain-producing district, which actually exports foodgrains to the outside world (Mahapatra 1994). The famine-like

[3] All figures, other than calorie-intake figures, for Odisha are taken from Government of Odisha (2012).

[4] Even this is an overestimate for India excluding Punjab and Haryana, since we have only subtracted Haryana's wheat output and Punjab's rice and wheat output from the all-India foodgrain output to get the figure for the rest of India's foodgrain output.

[5] This argument has been spelt out more precisely in the following section 'A simple illustrative model'.

condition in the district arises not from a shortage of supplies of foodgrains but from a paucity of purchasing power in the hands of the bulk of the (largely tribal) population. Kalahandi's case demonstrates that the sheer size of the foodgrain output is not enough to ensure adequate purchasing power in the hands of the rural poor to prevent even famine-like situations from arising. Likewise, there may be instances where there is a pulling away of foodgrains to the 'outside' world, creating a nutritional shortfall or even a nutritional crisis in a particular region. 'Outside' demand, being given a sudden boost, is what lay for instance behind the Great Bengal Famine of the Second World War years (Sen 1981).

While recognizing these obvious complexities, however, and conceding that a sheer increase in foodgrain output would not *necessarily* improve the nutritional status of the people in the concerned region (if it is accompanied, for instance, by a rise in the share of surplus in foodgrain production), we must, nonetheless, identify foodgrain output as one of the crucial determinants of nutritional status. This is especially so within traditional agriculture where the use of labour-economizing technology has not been carried so far as to cut the link between the output of foodgrains and the employment (and hence, the level of demand) generated by it. One reason, incidentally, why Punjab and Haryana have been excluded here from some of the calculations is precisely this: their agriculture has got greatly commercialized and moved far from being 'traditional' and, in addition, of course, their levels of per capita output are so high that in their case the link between production and consumption can be said to have been snapped long ago.

Elsewhere, however, the importance of per capita foodgrain output for the nutritional status of the population remains, and in view of this importance what is remarkable about the recent development strategy of Odisha is the decline witnessed of late in per capita foodgrain output in the state. In 2003–04, for instance, per capita foodgrain output in Odisha was 189 kg per year. By 2009–10 this figure had dropped to 183. The fact that foodgrain production could not even match the growth of population in the state is a matter of great significance. The decline in per capita daily calorie intake that we observe in Odisha between 1993–94 and 2009–10 is, in my view, directly attributable to it: in 1993–94 the per capita daily calorie intake was 2,199 on average in rural Odisha and 2,261 in urban Odisha compared to the figures quoted before here of 2,126 and 2,096 respectively in 2009–10.[6]

It may be argued that sluggish growth in foodgrain production is not specific to Odisha, but has occurred for the country as a whole. For instance, between 2003–04 and 2009–10, the same end-points as those taken for Odisha, per capita foodgrain output for all-India, including Punjab and Haryana, remained absolutely stagnant at 199 kg (and that too because of a revival in foodgrain production after a dismal performance in the earlier years). Odisha's recent development strategy, therefore, is not sui generis but one that is shared with the country as a whole.

This, no doubt, is true, but does not constitute a justification for this strategy. Even taking India as a whole, the average daily per capita calorie intake in rural areas has moved as follows: 1983: 2,221; 1993–04: 2,153; 2004–05: 2,047; 2009–10: 2,020. For urban areas the corresponding figures for all-India are 2,089, 2,071, 2,020, and 1,946 respectively.

There is a commonly held view that this decline in per capita calorie intake, far from indicating malnutrition, and hence deprivation, is a result of a deliberate diversification of consumption away from foodgrains towards more sophisticated goods. This diversification, it is argued, arises inter alia from the fact that the extent of hard manual labour which typically needs to be compensated by a large calorie intake has come down in the country. If this is so, then the decline in per capita calorie intake is indicative of people becoming better off rather than worse off. Some have even suggested that a decline in per capita foodgrain consumption actually characterizes countries as they move up the income scale, in which case again the decline in per capita foodgrain consumption, and hence, in calorie intake, is a matter to rejoice over rather than worry about. Besides, since in NSS data the decline in per capita foodgrain consumption is accompanied by a rise in expenditure on health, this decline, expressing

[6] We compare 1993–04 with 2009–10 because the 1999–2000 NSS (National Sample Survey) figures are not comparable with other years' owing to the introduction of the mixed recall period method, while 2004–05, as already mentioned in footnote 1, throws up some very odd numbers.

itself in a decline in per capita calorie intake, represents a change in tastes, reflective of more modern ways of living. Hence, no tears need be shed over it; rather, again, it should be a matter for rejoicing. The overall argument, therefore, is that the supposed decline in nutritional status, whether in Odisha or in India as a whole, is not a matter to be concerned about; if anything, it should be a cause for satisfaction.

This argument, however, is completely wrong. In fact, every single strand of this aforementioned argument is wrong. First, per capita calorie intake is positively correlated with per capita income across countries. Since nobody can claim that an average American consumer puts in harder manual labour than an average Indian consumer, this 'less manual labour argument' is not germane to the issue. There is no obvious reason why the Indian consumer should behave so differently from consumers elsewhere in the world; hence, since we observe a difference, namely a decline in calorie intake, the obvious explanation should be a growth in deprivation.

Second, while per capita direct foodgrain consumption does certainly decline with per capita real income, this is not true of per capita direct and indirect foodgrain consumption, that is if we also take into account foodgrain consumption via processed food and animal products, where they are used as feedgrains (Patnaik 2009).

If we take per capita *total* foodgrain consumption, that is, direct and indirect together, and relate it to per capita real income, then we find a strong and pronounced positive relationship.[7] Taking pooled cross section and time series data on 86 countries across the world for several years (total observations 1,548) and regressing per capita total foodgrain consumption over per capita real GDP (PPP at 2005 $)[8] by fitting four types of relationships, namely log-log, quadratic, Gompertz, and logistic, it has been found that the correlation coefficient in each case turns out to be 0.53 (0.52 for quadratic); and the independent variable turns out to be significant

[7] The results mentioned in this paragraph are taken from Krishna (2012).

[8] This can be understood as follows. If a specified bundle of commodities, which cost $1 in the U.S. in 2005, costs X rupees in India today, then India's GDP today has to be divided by X to give us our GDP at 2005 $ Purchasing Power Parity.

at 1 per cent level in each case (except for Gompertz where it is significant at 5 per cent level). So the argument that people move away from foodgrain consumption as they become better off is wrong: an average American consumes annually almost 900 kg of foodgrains, directly and indirectly, compared to around 165 kg by an average Indian at present.

Third, let us come to the change-of-tastes argument. Since we find a decline in per capita calorie intake even comparing 2009–10 with 2004–05, a span of time short enough to rule out any significant change of taste within it, that is, a span of mere five years over which people could not have suddenly become aware of the need for spending more on health (even if this has been a secular trend), it must be the case that the decline has been caused by some other factor. The obvious other factor could be a rise in healthcare costs, for which we have ample direct evidence. This rise in healthcare costs is obviously not captured adequately in the official consumer price index, which is one reason why the official 'poverty line' is kept so low and the percentage of poverty-stricken population is shown to decline. But once we reckon with the rise in healthcare costs, it is possible to argue that just as higher food prices earlier were used to explain a reduction in demand for industrial goods of mass consumption, such as textiles,[9] in a similar fashion, higher healthcare costs can be used to explain a reduction in the demand for foodgrains.

This would make the decline in nutritional status a consequence of impoverishment, a matter not to rejoice over. It would also explain the higher observed foodgrain consumption per capita in Odisha not in terms of Odisha's poverty, as is often done (on the grounds that being better off is associated with consuming less foodgrains), but in some other terms. One such explanation is the higher per capita foodgrain production in Odisha compared to the rest of India (excluding Punjab and Haryana) within a broadly traditional (that is, less mechanized) agriculture, which was suggested above.

[9] This was the conclusion of the Textile Inquiry Committee Report (Government of India 1958). A formal argument on the macroeconomic implications of the committee's finding is developed in Patnaik (1972).

The decline in per capita foodgrain output

The reason for the decline in per capita foodgrain production in Odisha lies in the fact that there has been a significant decline in the area under foodgrains whose impact has not been offset by the requisite increase in land productivity. The decline, therefore, cannot be brushed aside as some exogenous development unrelated to the government's strategy. The strategy itself was such that it permitted, at the very least by turning a blind eye towards it, the decline in area under foodgrains.

The net sown area in Odisha had declined between 1990–91 and 2010–11 by about 14 per cent from 6.3 million hectares to 5.4. Between 2003–04 and 2010–11, the decline has been of the order of 7 per cent, from 5.796 million hectares to 5.407 million hectares. What is quite striking is the fact that the while the decline in the earlier part of the period, during the 1990s, was not accompanied by any significant increase in land devoted to non-agricultural use (the increase was only about 0.15 million hectares compared to the overall decline in net sown area of about 0.5 million hectares between 1990–91 and 2003–04), in the latter part of the period the decline in net sown area has been accompanied by a significant increase in land under non-agricultural use (the increase is around 0.3 million hectares compared to a decline in net sown area of about 0.4 million hectare).

The decline in net sown area has had the effect of reducing the area under foodgrains: the gross sown area under foodgrains has declined by 0.15 million hectares from 5.457 million hectares in 2005–06 to 5.319 million hectares in 2010–11. The decline for rice—the principal foodgrain crop—is even sharper between these two periods, from a gross sown area of 4.479 million hectares in 2005–06 to 4.226 million hectares in 2010–11, which is almost 6 per cent over a five-year period. Since the yield rates of rice have increased by 5.3 per cent over this quinquennium, it is hardly surprising that the total rice output was lower in 2010–11 than in 2005–06. Even if we take the period 2003–04 to 2010–11, the increase in the average rice yield was a mere 8 per cent.

Odisha's poor performance on the foodgrain front precisely during the period of high growth (in the first four years of the Eleventh Five

Year Plan the state's average annual real growth rate is estimated to be 8.49 per cent) is a striking fall-out of the development strategy being followed in the state. The official argument is that since the land area in the state is limited, and new claims are emerging for this limited land, some amount of decline in net sown area under foodgrains is inevitable. If we put together barren and unculturable land, culturable waste, and fallow land, then Odisha had 2.227 million hectares of such land in 2010–11, which is about 23 per cent of the entire non-forested land of the state. The claims of non-agricultural use must fall on this land, rather than on net sown area. The fact that the claims of non-agricultural use have fallen instead upon net sown area suggests the complicity of the government in diverting agricultural land for non-agricultural use. This, in turn, indicates the thrust of the development strategy, which is oriented more towards the development of other sectors rather than of agriculture, and in particular, foodgrains.

This is the first serious flaw in Odisha's development strategy. Since Odisha's foodgrain yields are much lower than in several other states and lower than the average for India, considerable scope exists for increasing yields. Odisha should, in fact, be witnessing a substantial increase in foodgrain production, if the development strategy had been oriented towards increasing such production. However, the opposite has happened: the increases in yields have been minuscule while the acreage under foodgrains, especially rice, has come down, resulting in a decline in per capita foodgrain output in the recent period of high growth, and hence, for reasons we have already discussed, in nutritional standards as well.

What Odisha needs is legislation that prevents the conversion of paddy lands for other purposes, including keeping such lands fallow. In Kerala, where there has been a strong tendency for more than three decades now to convert paddy lands for commercial crops, such legislation has been enacted recently. Any paddy land that is kept fallow can be taken over by the district administration and given to some potential user for cultivation; and a rent, fixed by the administration, is made available to the owner for the use of the land. A state-wide self-help group of destitute women, supported by the government, called Kudumbasree, has been taking land on lease, bringing about not only an increase in the acreage under, and output of, foodgrains, but also an improvement in their own living standards. The area leased-in by Kudumbasree, which is cultivated through group farming, has reversed the secular decline that had taken place in Kerala's foodgrain output.

Even though the conditions in Odisha are very different from those in Kerala, new forms of government intervention can certainly be tried out in Odisha. Such intervention can take the form of both legislation to prevent any decline in foodgrain acreage and the building up of appropriate agencies, preferably group agencies, to take over land on lease, via the intermediation of some state government institution, from delinquent owners who prefer not to grow foodgrains on land traditionally used for this purpose.

Odisha, however, has been in thralldom to the development strategy that has become currently fashionable all over the country, which sees the means to development entirely in terms of enticing big-ticket investments into the state, and which sees success on the development front entirely in terms of the growth rate of GSDP. Odisha has been successful both in enticing big-ticket investment and also in achieving high GSDP growth rate. The fact that notwithstanding this success, nutritional deprivation in the state has been on the increase only points to the flawed nature of this strategy.

A simple illustrative model

The argument about the crucial role of foodgrain output in the overall development strategy of a state like Odisha can be explicated through a very simple model. Let us assume that there are two vertically integrated sectors in a region—foodgrain and non-foodgrain—each characterized by an employer–labourer relationship and a constant (not necessarily equal) wage share in output; that employers, being few and well off, have a *direct* consumption of foodgrain that is invariant with respect to their incomes and can be ignored for analytical simplicity; that non-foodgrain is not 'exported' while foodgrain has a ready 'export' market and is 'exported' to the maximal extent (because of the preference of foodgrain employers for 'imported' goods); that employers spend what they earn on investment and consumption, while workers also spend what they earn, but on consumption alone; that all wage income is spent locally within the region; and that the region's trade with the outside world is balanced.

Let us denote the total foodgrain output by O, employment per unit of foodgrain output by e, the wage rate in terms of foodgrain by w, and the proportion of it spent on foodgrain by α; let us assume that workers engaged in both foodgrain and non-foodgrain production have the same w and α.

A unit of foodgrain output in this case generates directly an employment equal to e and a wage-bill equal to $e.w$, of which $e.w.\alpha$ is spent on foodgrain and $e.w.(1-\alpha)$ is spent on non-foodgrain. Per unit of foodgrain output, therefore, $e.w.(1-\alpha)$ is the amount that is handed over to workers outside of the foodgrain sector, and this can employ $e.w.(1-\alpha)/w.\alpha$ number of workers outside the foodgrain sector. Hence, the employment generated directly and indirectly if one unit of foodgrain output is produced is $(e + e.w.(1-\alpha)/ w.\alpha)$. The total employment E in the region in any period then becomes:

$$O.e + O.e.w(1-\alpha)/w.\alpha = O.e. + O.e.(1-\alpha)/\alpha = O.e/\alpha. \qquad \text{(A)}$$

This is a multiplier like the Kahn-Keynes multiplier, but different from it in emphasizing that the total employment in the region is a multiple, greater than one, of the employment in foodgrain production.

What is striking about (A) is that the wage rate does not enter at all into the determination of employment in the region. It affects the standard of living of the workers in the region but not the total employment in the region.[10]

Denoting rates of growth of a variable by an asterisk upon it and the elasticity of employment with respect to output in foodgrain production by λ, we can say that

$$E^* = O^* + e^* - \alpha^* = -\alpha^* + \lambda.O^*,$$

so that the rate of growth of total employment in the region merely becomes a linear function of the rate of growth of its foodgrain output. Since *ex hypothesi* the unemployed in this simple universe get zero income while the employed get wage income of w (in terms of food), if E^* exceeds the rate of growth of the workforce (or of

[10] A reduction in w only means that the consumption relinquished by the workers is absorbed by the employers, with output and employment in *each of the two sectors* remaining unchanged.

population if we assume a constant work participation rate), then the people's living standards would be improving over time; if E^* is less than the rate of population growth, then there would be growing impoverishment, since the weighted average income of the employed and the unemployed would be declining over time. For a relatively short span of time we can take $\alpha^*=0$ and $\lambda=1$, in which case the rate of growth of *per capita* foodgrain output becomes the determinant of the degree of improvement of the living standard of the people, as claimed here.

This, of course, has been worked out on the basis of a number of assumptions, but they are either not too far removed from reality, for example, the assumption that the incomes of the surplus earners in the foodgrain sector represent 'leakages' from the multiplier chain, or are merely introduced, apart from one exception which is discussed as follows, for simplification, and are not critical for the argument. Even the set of assumptions which entail that there are no 'leakages' from the income of surplus earners in the non-foodgrain sector, can be dropped: all it would mean is that relative prices will now adjust to clear markets; but the dependence of total employment on foodgrain output will not be negated.[11]

It may be thought that the assumption about the organization of agriculture being on the basis of the employer–labourer relationship is so far removed from the reality of Odisha's agriculture, dominated as it is by peasant production, that any conclusions derived on this basis would be suspect. But this is not the case: even in a world of petty peasant production if peasants devote a particular fraction of their income to buying locally produced goods, foodgrains, and non-foodgrains, then the same results hold as long as the other assumptions are fulfilled. If the total foodgrain output O accrues entirely to

[11] Suppose the non-foodgrain employers, instead of spending what they earn, had an autonomous demand for this sector's output, given in real terms by D, then there will be three equations (a) $Q.\pi = D$; (b) $p.Q(1-\pi) = Q.\mathrm{l}.w$; and (c) $Q.\mathrm{l}.w.\alpha = O.e.w.(1-\alpha)$, which would determine Q, the output of non-foodgrain, π the share of surplus in this sector, and p the price of this sector's output in terms of foodgrain, where l denotes employment per unit of this sector's output. Equation (c) still determines this sector's employment as before, that is, the earlier conclusion still holds.

peasants who spend a fraction θ of it on local goods, of which, say a fraction μ on foodgrains, then, keeping the meaning of other symbols the same as before, the total employment in the region, cognizing, and hence, excluding disguised unemployment among the peasants, is given by:

$$E = O.e. + O.\theta.(1-\mu)/w.\alpha$$

where, since e, θ, μ, α, and w are given, total employment simply becomes a function of foodgrain output (even if θ is made a function of O, that is, peasants are assumed to spend more on outside goods and less on local goods if they have higher incomes, the argument still remains valid, as long as $O.\theta$ rises with O, which is a reasonable assumption).

The assumption that *does* make a difference to the results, and hence constitutes the one exception referred to above, is that there are no non-foodgrain exports from the region. Indeed the crux of the strategy which is currently favoured by almost all the states in the country is to invite big-ticket investment to undertake production located in the state for exports to the rest of the country and the world. The strategy of food production-based growth and the strategy of enticing capital into the state to undertake production for the national or international market constitute respectively 'home market–led' and 'export-led' growth strategies for the region. We have so far assumed away the latter; let us now examine this strategy, which in the case of Odisha takes primarily the form of mineral-export-led growth.

The pitfalls of a mineral-exporting strategy

Non-food export growth, including mineral-export growth, requires some diversion of land from its existing use. This in some cases requires, *necessarily*, diversion away from food production; in other cases, *even when not necessary*, it entails diversion away from food production unless the government enforces strict measures, including legislation as suggested above, to prevent such diversion. And in a situation where states are competing against one another to entice big-ticket private investment, state governments typically do not enforce any measures against such diversion.

But such a diversion entails a reduction not only in food output in the state but also in employment, as argued above; and if the new employment generated as a consequence of non-food export is smaller than the employment foregone due to the diversion of land away from foodgrains (or other agricultural uses), there is a net reduction in employment, and hence, an absolute immiserization of the people. And what is more, whether or not there is any net reduction in employment in the state, the *composition of employment* undergoes a significant change: the employment foregone because of the diversion of land away from agricultural use affects peasants, agricultural labourers, or the tribal population, while the employment generated in the 'export-oriented' mining or industrial sector is, to a considerable extent, for skilled workers, and professionals, belonging to the middle class. Apart from the possible net-employment–reduction effect, therefore, we also have an employment-composition effect of the development of 'export-oriented' sectors; and both these effects hurt the common working people.

This is no idle speculation: the very fact that the recent period of high growth in Odisha has been accompanied by a worsening of the average nutritional status of its population is suggestive of the common working people getting squeezed under this strategy.

Minerals-export strategy, however, has an additional effect of great consequence, to which Joan Robinson (1985) had drawn attention long ago. She had talked of the effect of foreign direct investment (FDI) in the minerals sector, but when we are talking not of a country but of a state, her argument remains valid for any 'outside' investment, whether FDI or from elsewhere within the country. She had argued that FDI in manufacturing, whatever its other effects, sets up at least some production units which in principle can continue operations for long. But since minerals are an exhaustible resource, FDI in the minerals sector can only give rise at best to a transient boom. Unless the investors are appropriately taxed during this boom to garner surpluses that are then used to diversify the host economy so that it can withstand the end of the boom, the exhaustion of resources leaves the host economy high and dry: it is back to square one after the end of the boom, but with the added deprivation that its mineral resources are gone forever. But taxation of the investors who come into extract minerals is in practice never particularly heavy, since they enjoy strong bargaining strength, certainly stronger than the negotiating local entity.

The case of Myanmar vindicates this apprehension. A booming economy when its oil resources had attracted companies like Royal Dutch Shell to invest in it (whence the term Burma-Shell), it got reduced to the status of a 'least developed country' in United Nations (UN) parlance when its oil resources got exhausted. Today it is one of the poorest countries in the world. And it is this prospect that has made many Latin American countries, which now have left-wing governments, adopt far stronger positions in demanding a share in the mineral resource revenue; and they have often succeeded in obtaining larger shares by holding the threat of using their own public sector companies to extract mineral resources in the event of the multinational companies' (MNCs') refusal to fall in line. Thus the left-wing government of Rafael Correa in Ecuador has succeeded in altering the 89:11 ratio in sharing oil revenue between the MNCs and the government that existed earlier, to an 11:89 ratio.[12]

Precisely because mineral resources are exhaustible, from the days of India's anti-colonial struggle the vision adopted by the country was that their extraction should be entrusted exclusively to the public sector. This was stated in the Karachi Congress resolution of 1931; and India's experience with oil multinationals in the 1950s when they had resorted to massive 'transfer pricing' (Tanzer 1969) had made it an accepted principle of public policy. But in the era of 'liberalization' not only has the monopoly of the public sector in the field of extractive industries been abandoned as the basis of policy, but even using the public sector as an instrument to control MNC aggrandizement, as Correa has done in Ecuador, is no longer favoured. This is unfortunate because aggrandizement by private companies takes the form not only of appropriating the bulk of the revenues from mineral resources for their own private use, but also of 'illegal' mining in excess of what they are entitled to do.

Odisha does have public-sector mining corporations, but their role is limited, since they only function as one set of players among

[12] This information was given to me in the course of a conversation with Ecuador officials during a visit to that country in January 2012.

the many. And their capacity to be a bulwark against private mining interests is further undermined by their imitating private corporate behaviour: there are even accusations that they too have engaged in 'illegal mining'.[13]

Under these conditions, the scenario sketched by Joan Robinson remains a disquieting prospect. In fact, the scenario may be even worse than what she had sketched: in areas where mineral extraction entails diversion of land from agricultural use, the exhaustion of the mineral resources does not even bring the economy back to square one, that is, back to the position where the economy had been before mineral development started, because the land so diverted remains unfit for cultivation, unless the mining companies have been forced to make good the damage to the land. This, however, is rarely the case.

Minerals extraction and primitive accumulation of capital

But even if the government takes a share of the revenue for diversifying the economy, that is, the Joan Robinson concern is addressed at the *macro level* for the region as a whole, there still remains the issue of addressing the problem of the *local inhabitants* who typically consist of tribal people. When a mining company enters a particular area, there are at least five different kinds of losses it inflicts upon the local population: first there is the loss of land for the local inhabitants who hand it over to the mining company (even if the land is taken from them on lease); second, there is the loss of crops that were grown on the land; third, there is the loss of mineral resources that lay underneath the land which had been occupied by the local population; fourth, there is the loss of habitat of the local population; and fifth, there is the loss of traditional employment opportunities for the local population. It may be thought that reckoning with the loss of crops already covers the loss of employment, so that taking

[13] The Government of Odisha has reportedly served notices to 103 mining leaseholders for undertaking illegal mining. Among those served notices are Odisha Mining Corporation (OMC) and Orissa Minerals Development Company (OMDC).

account of both amounts to double counting. But such is not the case: there is a loss of the dignity of self-employment; even though the compensation paid for the crop loss may include payment for the employment lost in producing the crops, nonetheless, the loss of *the dignity of self-employment* still remains uncompensated, which is why it must be separately counted.

Each one of these losses must be separately compensated, but typically this has never been the case. In large tracts of India, in other words, we have been witnessing a process of what Marx would have called 'primitive accumulation of capital', that is, the taking over of the land and the habitat of the tribal people by capitalists virtually *gratis*, 'for a song' as it were. And much the same is happening over large tracts of the country vis-à-vis the peasantry whose land is being expropriated from them by capitalists, usually through the use of state power, for the purpose of 'industrialization', or, more nebulously, for so-called 'development'. Odisha is no exception to this; on the contrary, since it is a mineral-rich state, its people have been particularly exposed to the process of 'primitive accumulation of capital', which also underlies the armed insurgency led by left extremists that one finds in some parts of the state.

This oppression of the tribal population has made many social activists demand that mineral resources should be treated entirely as the property of the local population, and that the entry of 'outsiders' to areas occupied by the tribal population should be restricted. These are extreme suggestions: making mineral resources the property of the local population would introduce enormous disparities among the people, including among the tribal people themselves, between those occupying mineral-rich land and those not occupying such land. Likewise, introducing entry restrictions for Indian citizens into particular areas within the country is fraught with serious consequences, since it would set a precedent that would strengthen those making similar demands elsewhere, for example the demand for restrictions on 'Biharis' coming to Mumbai, and boost regional chauvinist tendencies.

The principle to follow in this sphere should be that mineral development should occur, subject to the general concern raised by Joan Robinson being addressed (which is best addressed by making mineral development an exclusive prerogative of the public sector, open to parliamentary and judicial scrutiny); *but there should be no scope for any primitive accumulation of capital in the process of such mineral development.* To be sure, what constitutes primitive accumulation of capital depends crucially on how we define property relations. But if mineral resources are not defined exclusively as the property of just one entity, but rights to the surplus earned from such resources (which after all is what 'property' essentially amounts to) by a multiplicity of entities are recognized and mutually agreed upon, then primitive accumulation can be defined as a lowering of the share of the local inhabitants below their agreed share.

In some discussions it has been suggested that 25–30 per cent of the surplus from minerals should be set aside for the collective benefit of the local population to be used by elected local bodies; but the precise figure and the modus operandi need to be worked out through further discussions.

The share in the mineral resources, however, is only one of the issues. As mentioned earlier, the losses to the local population through the intrusion of mining companies occur in several different ways, and each such loss has to be separately compensated to the satisfaction of the local population. One way of ensuring this is to specify that no mining activity can occur anywhere without the approval of the elected local body of the inhabitants of the particular region; and exactly the same can be stipulated also in the case of manufacturing activity being taken up in particular areas affecting the local population.

The need for a constitutional mechanism

This too, however, is not enough. The elected local body can be cajoled or induced in several different ways to give approvals to 'development' proposals that do not adequately take cognizance of the requirements of the local people. What is more, even if an agreement is reached between all the entities involved which is to the satisfaction of the local inhabitants, there is no guarantee that it will be faithfully implemented. There have even been reports in Odisha, for instance, that many persons displaced by the Rourkela steel plant have not been compensated to this day, despite its being a public sector plant. These reports may be apocryphal, but the problem of implementation of any agreement reached between the local people and companies investing in a region, remains a serious one.[14]

What is required, perhaps, is a Constitutional body for the country as a whole, with quasi-judicial powers, overseeing all such agreements, which has the capacity to take *suo motu* note of any agreement that it believes violates the rights of the local inhabitants, and which also monitors the implementation of each agreement; needless to say, it must have the capacity to listen to grievances of the local inhabitants on the contents and the pace of implementation of any such agreement. The setting up such a body and the basic contours of what any such agreement must minimally provide for by way of compensation to the local inhabitants should be stipulated through an appropriate central legislation.

Many would complain that such restrictions on investment would damage the 'development' prospects of the country. But a 'development' that impoverishes the people through unleashing a process of primitive accumulation of capital is something whose getting impeded should be a cause for celebration rather than grief. Any talk of 'development' in Odisha, if the tribal population becomes a victim of expropriation in the course of this 'development' for the extraction of the mineral resources, is a travesty.

Two alternative strategies

The purpose of this chapter has been to draw a distinction between two different development strategies. One, which is quite pervasive these days among all the states and which has the stamp of neoliberalism, believes in attracting big-ticket private investment to the state for setting up mining and manufacturing activities. Since all states

[14] Sister Valsa John, the Jesuit nun who was involved in mobilizing the tribal population in Amrapara block in Pakur district of Jharkhand, through an organization called the Rajmahal Pahar Bachao Andolan, to secure their rights against the coal mining company PANEM, had reached an agreement that was favourable to the local people, and constituted in many ways a model for such agreements. But the agreement remains unimplemented to this day; and Sister Valsa John was murdered in November 2011. Who instigated the murder remains unclear till date.

are engaged in this competitive struggle to attract private investment, budgetary concessions are given for this purpose and facilities for the incoming investors are created even at the expense of the local population. The success of this strategy, however, whether at the level of the country as a whole or in individual states, has invariably been accompanied by an accentuation of rural distress because of the primitive accumulation of capital it unleashes. Odisha which has basically been pursuing this strategy and has been quite successful in this endeavour, as shown for instance by a higher GSDP growth rate than the GDP growth rate of the country as a whole, has also witnessed an increase in distress in the form of nutritional deprivation.

As against this strategy, however, one can think of an alternative strategy where the emphasis is on increasing foodgrain output, and in general, agricultural output, and to effect an 'industrialization from below' through the resulting expansion of the domestic market. This does not preclude the setting up of mining and manufacturing activity through the entry of big capital from outside; but there must be control over the operation of this capital to ensure that there is no primitive accumulation of capital leading to expropriation and impoverishment of the people, in particular the peasantry, the agricultural labourers, and the tribal population. Authentic development in Odisha that benefits its vast mass of the labouring poor can occur only when it abandons the first strategy in favour of the second, irrespective of what such abandonment does to the growth rate.

References

Government of India. 1958. *The Textile Enquiry Committee Report*. New Delhi.

Government of Odisha. 2012. *Economic Survey 2011–12*. Bhubaneswar: Planning and Coordination Department.

Karl Marx. 1974. *Capital*, Volume I. Moscow: Progress Publishers.

Krishna, Ram. 2012. 'Cereal Consumption as a Proxy for Real Income', mimeo.

Mahapatra, R. 1994. 'Food Crises in India: A Case-study of Kalahandi 1961–1992', MPhil dissertation, Centre for Economic Studies and Planning, JNU, New Delhi.

Patnaik, P. 1972. 'Disproportionality Crisis and Cyclical Growth', *Economic and Political Weekly*, 7(5–7, February): 329–36.

Patnaik, U. 2009. 'Origins of the Food Crisis in India and the Developing Countries', *Monthly Review*, 61(3, July–August): 85–102.

———. 2012. 'Trends in Rural and Urban Poverty in India from 1973–74 to 2009–10'.

Robinson, J. 1985. *Aspects of Development and Underdevelopment*. Cambridge: Cambridge University Press.

Sen, A. 1981. *Poverty and Famines: An Essay on Entitlement and Deprivation*. Oxford: Oxford University Press.

Tanzer, M. 1969. *The Political Economy of International Oil and the Underdeveloped Countries*. Boston: Beacon Press.

Some Political Constraints on Economic Development

Pulin B. Nayak, Santosh C. Panda, and
Prasanta K. Pattanaik

Chapters 1 through 15 have discussed in depth a wide range of issues relating to different sectors and different aspects of Odisha's economy. Instead of providing a comprehensive summary of these chapters, which have a wealth of information and insight, this chapter presents a few observations on some important aspects of the economy of Odisha.

Some indicators of the recent economic development in Odisha

It may be useful to start by considering briefly Odisha's relative economic position and the recent progress in terms of a few standard economic indicators. As noted earlier in the introductory chapter (under the section 'Growth of Odisha's per capita NSDP since 2000–01'), the per capita NSDP of Odisha at constant (2004–05) prices increased by 163.44 per cent between 2000–01 and 2011–12. This amounts to an impressive notional constant rate of growth of 9.2 per cent. The percentage of population living below the poverty line declined from 60.8 in 2004–05 to 39.2 in 2009–10 (Misra's 'Dimensions of poverty and prospects of economic change in Odisha' [Chapter 11 of this volume], Table 11.6), and, according to the data of the erstwhile Planning Commission, in 2011–12, the corresponding percentage was 32.59 per cent (Dev 2015). Inequality during this period of high growth does not seem to have increased much: Panda (2015), who considers inequality in the distribution of consumption expenditure and estimates separately the Gini coefficients for rural and urban areas of Odisha, finds that the Gini coefficient for rural areas of Odisha declined from 0.265 in 2004–05 to 0.253 in 2009–10, while the Gini coefficient for urban areas of Odisha increased from 0.340 in 2004–05 to 0.385 in 2009–10. The literacy rate for Odisha has gone up from 49.09 per cent in 1991 to 73.45 per cent in 2011 (Nayak, Dhar, and Mahakur's 'Educational outcomes in Odisha: Trends and issues' [Chapter 9 of this volume], under the section 'Trends of education in Odisha') and is almost at par with the all-India figure of 74 per cent. Thus, in general, the economy of Odisha has been far from stagnant in the recent years. But Odisha has a lot of ground to cover before the living conditions of its population get upgraded to a reasonable level and before it catches up with the more developed Indian states. In terms of per capita GSDP, Odisha had the rank of 26 among 32 states of India in 2011–12 (Dev 2015). According to Planning Commission's assessment, Odisha's rank in terms of the human development index was 21 in a listing of 35 states and union territories. Finally, at 32.59 per cent, the head-count index of poverty in Odisha in 2011–12 was much higher than the corresponding all India figure of 21.92 per cent.

There is no compelling reason why Odisha cannot make faster economic progress. With its vast reservoir of natural resources, including minerals and forests, and given its fairly stable and relatively peaceful social setting, Odisha has the potential for much more rapid all-round growth. To achieve this potential in the long run, it is necessary to promote mining and manufacturing in Odisha. It is necessary to emphasize that mining must be undertaken with the explicit concurrence of all stakeholders, especially those who may have to be displaced from their traditional habitation. Promotion of mining and manufacturing has been the avowed objective of several successive governments of the state over the last two decades or so. Unfortunately, however, the political and administrative system of Odisha has not been able to handle successfully many of the challenges that have inevitably come up in the process of industrialization. The next section comments on some of these issues, which have also been raised earlier by Mohanty (see Chapter 4 in this volume) and Das and Acharya (see Chapter 5 of this volume).

The political process and economic development

It is now fairly widely recognized that the problem of economic development has as much to do with politics as with economics; it is the complex interaction between politics and economics that determines how fast an economy can develop no matter what reasonable measure of economic development we may have in mind. Recently many proposals for large-scale mining and industrial projects in Odisha have come to a standstill because of strong resistance from local populations in project sites to the acquisition of land necessary for these projects. There are at least two distinct types of arguments which come up repeatedly in the context of such resistance. First, it is usually argued that the project under consideration will lead to the displacement of a sizable population with consequent loss of their livelihood and this is unacceptable. For instance, this has been one of the most important issues in the case of the proposed POSCO (Pohang Steel Company) steel plant in Odisha—a project which has virtually collapsed in the face of stiff local opposition. Second, it is sometimes argued that the projects will involve degradation of the environment; this is one of the major objections that were raised, for instance, against Vedanta refinery expansion project.[1]

[1] In some specific cases, it has also been claimed that the land selected for the project has religious significance for some groups and that acquisition of the land will amount to sacrilegious interference with the groups' religious beliefs; this was one of the reasons for blocking Vedanta Resources from mining bauxite in Niyamgiri. But, in the widespread resistance to mining and industrial projects in Odisha, such religious sentiments have probably played a relatively less-important role.

We believe that each of the two arguments mentioned here has some merit. But we also believe that finding a reasonable solution for many of these issues has been much more difficult than it would have been otherwise partly because of the past apathy or failures of governments and partly also because political groups have tried to exploit the situation of conflict for their own partisan interests. Consider first the issue of displacement of sizable populations with resultant loss of livelihood. In principle, the loss of livelihood should not be a major problem if a system of fair and prompt compensation could be put in place and operated effectively. But this did not happen in the past. Let us cite just two examples. While there may be disagreement about the exact extent to which compensation and rehabilitation of the displaced population was effectively carried out in the case of Hirakud Dam of Odisha, there seems to be reasonable agreement that more than 50 years after the construction of the dam, a significant number of families displaced by the dam have received either no compensation or very inadequate compensation. Similarly, as Mohanty has already noted in Chapter 4 of this volume, after more than six decades, the issue of compensation and rehabilitation of families displaced by the Rourkela steel plant of Steel Authority of India Limited is still not settled. In this respect, the experience of displaced populations in Odisha may not be very different from that of many other similarly displaced populations elsewhere in India. But the fact is that such a poor record of compensation and rehabilitation has led to massive loss of the public's trust in the promises that the state now makes to the people to be adversely affected by industrial and mining projects. If people are putting up a tough fight against the acquisition of their land for such projects, then it is in small measure due to the bitter experience which either they or people exactly like them have had in the past. The deep sense of betrayal which people have after the promised benefits failed to materialize was palpable when Banguru Jani, a tribal leader of Jhimkiguda, Odisha, said that had he and his people known what would happen to them, they would not have ceded 'even a needle-size of land'.[2] Had the problem of displacement of populations and restitution been

[2] See Khatua and Stanley (2006), who quote Banguru Jani at the beginning of their article.

handled in the past more efficiently and fairly, land acquisition for industrial and mining projects in Odisha (and, in India, in general) would not be such a crippling problem as it is today.

So far as the issue of the environment is concerned, it is fair to say that often in the past little attention has been given to environmental effects of mining and industrial projects. When serious problems have been pointed out, sometimes the initial reaction of the governments has been either to deny the existence of the problem or to cast doubts on the integrity or competence of the individuals and institutions drawing attention to the problem. Severe air and water pollution resulting from chromite mining in Sukinda, Odisha, is a case in point. Chromite mining has been going on in Sukinda for more than half a century, but for several decades little was done to mitigate the air and water pollution caused by such mining. In its 'Audit Report (Civil) Orissa for the year ended 31 March 2001', the Comptroller and Auditor General of India, Supreme Audit Institution of India (SAII), wrote (CAG 2001: 45):

> Although OPCB [Orissa Pollution Control Board] had identified the nature and magnitude of Chromium VI pollution generated at Sukinda valley and apprised Government in May 2000 for conducting an environmental study and preparation of action plan including formulation of overburden rehabilitation strategy for abatement of Chromium–VI pollution, nothing had been done so far. Government stated (April 2001) that the proposal was under examination for submission to financial institutions for funds. Thus, Sukinda valley continued witnessing Chromium–VI pollution in its environment with no respite.

When the Blacksmith Institute of New York released a report in 2007 (Blacksmith Institute 2007), claiming that Sukinda, Odisha, was one of the most polluted places in the world, the Chairman of Odisha State Pollution Control Board was reported to have said 'I see a lot of personal agenda behind the report. It is a design to stop mining activities. If there is mining, there would be some air pollution. But to say that Sukinda is one of worst polluted places in the world is ridiculous' (*The Telegraph* 2007). After the intervention of Odisha High Court, Odisha State Pollution Control Board submitted a report to the High Court, but the court was not happy with the report and asked the Central Pollution Control Board to investigate the problem again and to submit a new report. The subsequent report of the Central Pollution Control Board confirmed the presence of serious water pollution in Sukinda valley (*The Hindu* 2014b).

Air and water pollution in Sukinda is just one of many instances of severe pollution in the state caused by ineffectively regulated mining and industries. It seems fair to say that the failure of regulatory bodies has been responsible for some of the major pollution problems in the state. This, in turn, has fuelled fears that future mining and industrial projects will intensify the environmental problems which are already there. It has also generated in Odisha a fairly widespread perception that severe pollution is an inevitable consequence of industrialization and mining.

While the past shortcomings of governments are an important source of the current resistance to industrial and mining projects in Odisha, other political and social factors have also played a role. There are reasons to believe that various political groups have often exploited for partisan gains the discontent and distrust of people, especially, the tribal population. As elsewhere in India, there is also a pervasive general suspicion of the process of industrialization. Large industrial and mining companies, especially foreign corporations, are treated almost as evil by certain sections of the intelligentsia of the state and it is not unusual to find shrill and sweeping condemnations of 'globalization'. The history of the East India Company and the subsequent colonial rule in India is still invoked in popular debates over these issues. It is often taken to be axiomatic that if a foreign company makes large profits out of mining and industrial projects in Odisha, then it must be at the expense of the people of Odisha.[3] More than a 150 years ago, Marx (1853: 661) eloquently contested this view of the world in the following passage, where he pointed out that however avaricious a foreign investor's motive might be, it did not preclude the possibility of large benefits for the country receiving the investment:

> I know that the English millocracy intend to endow India with railways with the exclusive view of extracting at diminished expenses the cotton and other raw materials for their manufacturers. But when you

[3] See Basu and Pattanaik (1997), who make the same point in the context of the Indian economic reforms.

> have once introduced machinery into the locomotion of a country, which possesses iron and coal, you are unable to withhold it from its fabrication.... The railway system will ... become truly the forerunner of modern industry.

As we have already stated, we think that in the long run, Odisha will need to put to use its rich endowment of mineral resources and industrialize. This will inevitably involve some displacement of populations, but the human cost of such displacement can be minimized through extensive prior consultation and an efficiently administered system of compensation and rehabilitation. That this did not happen in the past is a tragedy, which, with the consequent loss of the public's trust in the government, is casting a long shadow on the prospect of future economic development in Odisha. As economists, we do not have any special expertise to prescribe how governments should go about this, but it is clear that acquisition of land for industrial projects will remain a huge problem in a democratic system as long as people do not have confidence in the governments' promises regarding compensation and rehabilitation.

The government also needs to ensure, and needs to convince people that it will ensure, that the regulatory bodies in charge of controlling environmental degradation will do their job more efficiently and in a more responsive fashion than they have done in the past. The position that there must not be any environmental cost of industrialization is an extreme position that can completely choke off the process of industrialization and condemn a large chunk of the population of Odisha to live in a state of perpetual deprivation, irrespective of whether we interpret deprivation as income poverty or as inadequate nutrition, housing, health, and others. At the same time, completely unregulated development of mining and industries is not acceptable either. What we need to ensure is a balance between the need to preserve the environment and the need for industrial development on a case-by-case basis. The severe air and water pollution in Sukinda valley did not have to happen. In its report, submitted to the High Court of Odisha in 2014, the Central Pollution Control Board has indicated concrete measures for reducing this pollution. Had such measures been implemented a few decades ago,[4] air and water pollution in Sukinda would probably have remained at an acceptable level. That such measures did not get implemented is not a justification for wholesale rejection of mining and industrialization. Instead, it highlights the need for making the regulatory system more efficient and more responsive to problems as they arise. As economists have long recognized, the problem of environmental degradation cannot be left to be resolved through the operation of free markets; it needs efficient and effective regulation by the state.

Some issues which need urgent attention of policymakers

While the growth of mining and manufacturing may be extremely important for generating gainful employment and the removal of poverty in Odisha, it seems unlikely that the pace of industrialization in Odisha will be much faster in the near future, given the political reasons that we have sketched in the previous section. It will take time for the democratic system to work out a reasonable solution for the conflicts and tensions, which are being generated by the process of economic development and are preventing faster industrialization. Meanwhile, can one point to issues, other than industrialization, which need urgent attention of policymakers and which are politically and financially more tractable? Inevitably, subjectivity will be involved when one seeks to identify some issues as more important than others. Despite this and without denying the importance of a host of other problems, we would like to draw the attention of policymakers in Odisha specifically to two issues, which have been discussed in earlier chapters of this volume. The first issue is that of low agricultural productivity in the state (Sarap and Sahu's 'Emerging trends in cropping pattern, crop diversification, and agricultural productivity' [Chapter 1 of this volume]). Given that 61.8 per cent of workers in Odisha are still engaged in agricultural activities (Census of India 2011, Executive Summary), increasing agricultural

[4] Recall that the Orissa State Prevention and Control of Pollution Board, which was the former name of the Odisha State Pollution Control Board, was constituted as early as 1983.

productivity and promoting diversity of agricultural production needs to be given a much higher priority than it seems to have been given in recent years. Resources need to be channelled towards building rural infrastructure by way of irrigation, roads, and power; the goal must be to increase agricultural productivity as well as to encourage cottage industries. Second, in terms of most indicators of living standards, the deprivation of the tribal people, who constitute 22.8 per cent of the total population of Odisha (Census of India 2011, Executive Summary),[5] is shockingly large. We believe that this should be one of the most urgent and immediate concerns of the state government. Not only will any strategy of economic development, which does not attach adequate importance to the living standards of this extremely deprived and vulnerable group, be inherently unjust, but it will also be self-defeating: there are already enough indications that continued neglect of the interest of the tribal people will generate much unrest,[6] which will frustrate such a strategy even if one considers it worth adopting.

References

Basu, K. and P.K. Pattanaik. 1997. 'India's Economy and the Reforms of 1990s: Genesis and Prospect', *Journal of International Trade and Economic Development*, 6(2): 123–33.

Census of India. 2011. *Executive Summary*. Available online at http://www.censusindia.gov.in/2011census/PCA/PCA_Highlights/pca_highlights_file/Odisha/Executive_Summary.pdf (last accessed on 12 January 2016).

Comptroller and Auditor General of India, Supreme Audit Institution of India. 2001. 'Audit Report (Civil) Orissa for the year ended 31 March 2001'. Available online at http://saiindia.gov.in/content/audit-report-civil-orissa-year-2000-01 (last accessed on 11 January 2016).

Dev, S. Mahendra (ed.). 2015. *India Development Report*. New Delhi: Oxford University Press.

[5] The population of scheduled tribes of Odisha is 9.59 million (Census of India 2011, Executive Summary).

[6] For an account of the tribal people's movements in Odisha to protect their livelihood and rights, see Padhi and Panigrahi's 'Tribal movements and livelihoods: Recent developments in Odisha' [Chapter 14 of this volume].

Government of Odisha. 2015. *Economic Survey 2014–15*. Bhubaneswar: Planning and Coordination Department.

Khatua, S. and W. Stanley. 2006. 'Ecological Debt: A Case Study from Orissa, India', in A.K. Peralta (ed.), *Ecological Debt: The Peoples of the South are the Creditors: Cases from Ecuador, Mozambique, Brazil and India*, pp. 125–68. Geneva: World Council of Churches. Available online at http://www.deudaecologica.org/publicaciones/Chapter5(125-168).pdf (last accessed on 11 January 2016).

Marx, K. 1853. 'The Future Results of British Rule in India', *New York Daily Tribune*, 22 July (reprinted in Karl Marx. 1936. *Selected Works*, Volume 2. New York: Interscience).

Panda, S.C. 2015. 'Economic Growth, Inequality and Poverty in Odisha, 1993–2010', in R.K. Panda and R.K. Meher (eds), *Trend, Magnitude and Dimensions of Inequality in Post-Reform India,* pp. 13–31. New Delhi: Concept Publishers.

The Hindu. 2014a. 'Court Orders CPCB to Study Pollution in Mining Belt, River', 15 May. Available online at http://www.thehindu.com/todays-paper/tp-national/tp-otherstates/court-orders-cpcb-to-study-pollution-in-mining-belt-river/article6010770.ece (last accessed on 11 January 2016).

The Hindu. 2014b. 'Consortium of Mines should Address Pollution Issue', 19 October. Available online at http://www.thehindu.com/todays-paper/tp-national/tp-otherstates/consortium-of-mines-should-address-pollution-issue/article6515688.ece (last accessed on 17 June 2015).

The Telegraph. 2007. 'Orissa Valley on World's Dirty List', 13 September 2007. Available online at http://www.telegraphindia.com/1070913/asp/nation/story_8315392.asp (last accessed on 8 July 2015).

Index

About the Editors and Contributors

Editors

Pulin B. Nayak retired as professor of Economics from the Delhi School of Economics, Delhi, India, in 2015. He is currently with the Centre for Development Economics in Delhi, India. He was a member of the Prime Minister's Economic Advisory Council during 2013–14. His areas of interest are public finance and economic development.

Santosh C. Panda is vice president and dean, Faculty of Economics at South Asian University, New Delhi, India. His main areas of interest are microeconomic theory, social choice theory, and current development issues. He was honoured with Odisha Platinum Jubilee Award in 2012.

Prasanta K. Pattanaik is professor emeritus and professor of Graduate Division at the University of California, Riverside, USA. The main areas of his current research interest are welfare economics and the theory of social choice, decision theory, and the measurement of living standards and deprivation.

Contributors

Satyananda Acharya retired as professor of Geology and vice-chancellor of Utkal University, Bhubaneswar, Odisha, India.

Currently, he is an independent director of Indian Metals & Ferro Alloys, Odisha. He is the president of Orissa Environment Society and founder secretary of the Society of Geologist and Allied Technologists, Bhubaneswar, India.

Amarendra Das teaches economics in the Postgraduate Department of Analytical and Applied Economics, Utkal University, Bhubaneswar, Odisha, India. He has served as a deputy director in the Fourteenth Finance Commission of India. His research interest lies in the areas of natural resource management and public economics.

Satya P. Das is professor at Indian Statistical Institute, New Delhi, India, and has held academic positions at the University of Wisconsin-Madison, Milwaukee, USA, and Indiana University, Bloomington, USA. His research areas include international economics, theory of the firm, growth and development, economics of terrorism, and economics of cricket.

Saudamini Das is NABARD Chair Professor at Institute of Economic Growth, New Delhi, India. She is a fellow of South Asian Network for Development and Environmental Economics, Kathmandu, Nepal. She worked as Mälar scholar at the Beijer Institute of Ecological Economics, Royal Swedish Academy of Sciences, Stockholm, during 2011–12.

Sharmita Dhar teaches economics and heads the Department of Economics at Serampore College, West Bengal, India. Her research interest lies in the area of economics of education, with special focus on transition rate.

Sarthak Gaurav teaches economics at the Indian Institute of Technology Bombay. He researches the dynamics of agricultural development, risk and uncertainty, insurance markets, and behavioural economics. He was a visiting doctoral scholar at the Wharton School, University of Pennsylvania, USA, and Young Scientist at the International Institute for Applied Systems Analysis, Austria.

Abhash Kumar Hota has received an MPhil degree from the Department of Analytical and Applied Economics, Utkal University,

Bhubaneswar, Odisha, India, in the area of efficiency measurement in health sector. He has research experience in health economics and the economics of natural resources such as water.

Pratap Kumar Mahakur is a doctoral research fellow at the Department of Humanities and Social Sciences, Indian Institute of Technology Kharagpur, India. His research interests include issues related to development economics, economics of growth, and economics of social sector development.

Padmaja Mishra is professor of economics at the Department of Analytical and Applied Economics, Utkal University, Bhubaneswar, Odisha, India, and is currently in-charge of Rama Devi Women's University, Bhubaneswar, Odisha, India, as the officer on special duty. Her special research interests are in the fields of economics of environment and economics of gender and development.

Srijit Mishra is professor at the Indira Gandhi Institute of Development Research, Mumbai, India. Some of his recent works are on farmers' suicides, a result of the larger agrarian crisis in India, on measurement of poverty, and on a refinement of the human development index.

Baidyanath Misra retired as professor of economics at Utkal University, Bhubaneswar, Odisha, India, and vice-chancellor of the Orissa University of Agriculture & Technology, Bhubaneswar, Odisha, India. The main areas of his research interest are growth, economic development, and fiscal policy. He has received honorary doctorates from Orissa University of Agriculture and Technology, Odisha, India, and KIIT University (Kalinga Institute of Industrial Technology), Odisha.

Adwait Mohanty has taught economics in various government colleges of Odisha as well as at the Gopabandhu Academy of Administration, Utkal University, and IIT Bhubaneswar, Odisha, India. His areas of specialization are international economics, monetary and financial economics, and development studies. Presently, he is involved with the preparation of 'A Manual for Decentralized Planning in Odisha' for UNICEF.

Narayan Chandra Nayak is professor of economics at the Department of Humanities and Social Sciences, Indian Institute of Technology Kharagpur, India. He has been associated with several research and consultancy projects sponsored by United Nations Development Programme, Ministry of Environment and Forests, and Indian Council of Agricultural Research, among others.

Sakti Padhi was professor of economics at Nabakrushna Choudhury Centre for Development Studies, Bhubaneswar, India. He had authored three books and a large number of research articles in the areas of poverty, health, livelihood, agriculture, and employment. He passed away in 2010.

Manoj Panda is director of the Institute of Economic Growth, New Delhi, India. His research areas include monitoring and analysis of macroeconomic trends and prospects, evaluation of alternative trade and fiscal policy options from the point of view of growth and distribution, and development and application of computable general equilibrium models, among others.

Raj Kishore Panda retired as professor of economics of Utkal University, Bhubaneswar, Odisha, India. Agricultural and rural development and rural finance constitute the main areas of his research interest. He has received Japan Foundation Fellowship and UGC Research Scientist Award for undertaking research in the field of rural credit.

Nilakantha Panigrahi teaches at the Department of Anthropology and Tribal Development, Guru Ghasidas University (a Central University), Bilaspur, Chhattisgarh, India. He has published on issues relating to tribal development, tribal livelihood, community health, disaster management, ethnicity, and impact of progressive policies like the Mahatma Gandhi National Rural Employment Guarantee Act and the Right to Information Act.

Prabhat Patnaik held the Sukhamoy Chakravarty Chair at the Centre for Economic Studies and Planning of the Jawaharlal Nehru University, New Delhi, India, at the time of his retirement. He is currently an emeritus professor at the centre. His areas of interest are macroeconomics and political economy.

Himanshu Sekhar Rout is reader in the Department of Analytical and Applied Economics, Utkal University, Bhubaneswar, Odisha, India. He is also deputy co-ordinator at Centre of Advanced Study in Economics of the University Grants Commission (Government of India) Special Assistance Programme (SAP) in the same department.

Sarit Kumar Rout is associated with the Indian Institute of Public Health, Bhubaneswar, under the aegis of Public Health Foundation of India. He teaches health economics and financing. His research interests include healthcare financing, national health accounts, economics of tobacco, economic evaluation of health care interventions, and social sector development issues.

Partha P. Sahu teaches at Institute for Studies in Industrial Development, New Delhi, India. His research interests include issues related to industry, labour, and employment. He has published papers in many peer-reviewed international and national journals and delivered lectures on quantitative and qualitative research methods.

Kailas Sarap is SR Sankaran Chair Professor (Rural Labour) at National Institute of Rural Development and Panchayati Raj, Ministry of Rural Development, Government of India, Hyderabad, Telangana, India. He has been a visiting fellow at the University of Namur, Belgium, and Commonwealth Fellow at the University of Oxford, UK.

Tapas K. Sen is professor at National Institute of Public Finance and Policy, New Delhi, India, where he has worked since 1981. He has worked on diverse topics within the broad area of public economics, but has a special interest in fiscal federalism and sub-national public finances.